# Divided Memory

# Divided

---

# Memory
## The Nazi Past in the Two Germanys

## JEFFREY HERF

**Harvard University Press**

Cambridge, Massachusetts
London, England
1997

Library of Congress Cataloging-in-Publication Data

Herf, Jeffrey, 1947–
    Divided memory : the Nazi past in the two Germanys / Jeffrey Herf.
        p.    cm.
    Includes bibliographical references and index.
    ISBN 0-674-21303-3 (alk. paper)
    1. Holocaust, Jewish (1939–1945)—Germany. 2. Antisemitism—Germany (East) 3. Anti-
semitism—Germany (West) 4. Historiography—Germany (East) 5. Historiography—Germany
(West) 6. Historiography—Germany 7. War criminals—Germany (East)—Psychology. 8. War
criminals—Germany (West)—Psychology. 9. National socialism—Moral and ethical aspects.
    I. Title.
D804.3.H474   1997
940.53′18′0943—dc21      98-11231

00 - 36 58 2098
cl

*For*
*Sonya, Nadja,*
*and Ernst*

# Contents

# Illustrations

Following Chapter 6:
Meeting of the Nationalekomitee Freies Deutschland, Moscow, 1944
Meeting of the Bewegung Freies Deutschland, Mexico City, December 31, 1943
Paul Merker in East Berlin, 1950
Demonstration for the "victims of fascism," East Berlin, September 1950
Representatives of the Jewish community lay a wreath during the Day of Remembrance, East Berlin, 1951
Former members of the French Resistance at Buchenwald during the Day of Remembrance, East Berlin, 1951
Teenagers carrying the red flag at Ravensbrück, 1952
Meeting of the VVN, November 9, 1952
Hermann Matern at the SED Party Conference, Berlin, March 30, 1954
Rosa Thälmann and Walter Ulbricht lead procession at dedication of Sachsenhausen memorial, April 23, 1961
Otto Grotewohl with Gamal Abdel Nasser, Cairo, January 4, 1959
Albert Norden denounces the "war criminal [Hans] Globke," East Berlin, March 21, 1963

Following Chapter 7:
Theodor Heuss and Nahum Goldmann at the Bergen-Belsen memorial dedication, November 30, 1952
Visit by West German Social Democratic leaders with members of the Jewish Labor Committee, April 8, 1954
Kurt Schumacher at a political rally in Frankfurt, 1947
Willy Brandt at the Warsaw memorial, December 1970
Konrad Adenauer speaking in the British occupation zone, May 12, 1946
Helmut Kohl, Johannes Steinhoff, Ronald Reagan, and Matthew Ridgeway, Bitburg, May 5, 1985
Richard von Weizsäcker speaking in the Bundestag, May 8, 1985

# Preface

History is the realm of choice and contingency. Writing history is a matter of reconstructing the openness of past moments before choices congealed into seemingly inevitable structures. In this work I return to contingencies and choices that accompanied the emergence of the political memory of Nazism and the Holocaust in the two Germanys. As in many parts of the world today, there was an abundance of voices in the early postwar years insisting that forgetfulness and amnesty were the handmaidens of future peace and stability, or that the memory of past crimes justified an avenging dictatorship. My sympathies instead are with those other voices, then and now, that expressed hope for a liberal democracy resting on clear memory and timely justice. I hope that understanding why those hopes remained unfulfilled then, and subsequently were only partially fulfilled, will contribute to their full and prompt realization in other times and places.

from World War II to the Cold War. For years the historical examination of democracy and dictatorship has been separated from that of political memory. One purpose of this work is to demonstrate the significance of political memories for the construction of democracy and dictatorship in post-1945 German history.[2]

I am interested in how past beliefs and contemporaneous political interests in domestic and international politics shaped the narratives of the Nazi past told by postwar German political leaders. Specifically, I address four questions. First, given the depth and breadth of support for Nazism among the Germans, why did German politicians after 1945 raise the issue of the Holocaust and other crimes of the Nazi era at all? Second, why did the memory of the Nazi past emerge as divided along political lines? That is, why did public memory of the Holocaust, and a sympathetic hearing for the concerns of Jewish survivors, emerge and find a home in West Germany? And why, after the early contentious months and years of the occupation era, were such views and their advocates suppressed in "antifascist" East Germany? Third, what was the relationship between memory of the crimes of the Nazi era and liberal democracy in the West and a Communist dictatorship in the East? That is, within West Germany, how did the democratic left and the democratic right approach the issues of memory and justice? Fourth, how did the Cold War affect discussion of the Jewish catastrophe in both Germanys?

From the temporal and political perspective of World War II and the early postwar years, the future of Eastern repression and Western emergence of sympathetic discussion of Jewish matters was not an obvious or foregone conclusion. On the contrary, for many contemporaries imbued with the solidarities of the war against Nazism, this subsequent history constituted an unexpected paradox. Part of the historian's task is to reconstruct the openness and contingency of past moments. In this instance that means reconstructing the hopes for a more inclusive and generous memory which emerged in emigration, in Nazi concentration camps, and in the brief Nuremberg interregnum between the end of World War II and the crystallization of the Cold War.

# 1

## Multiple Restorations and
## Divided Memory

This is a study of how anti-Nazi German political leaders interpreted the Nazi past during the Nazi era, and then remembered it as they emerged as national political leaders in the postwar occupation, in the two successor German states, and in unified Germany. It focuses on the mixture of belief and interest, ideology and the drive for power which shaped the political memory and public narratives of the Nazi era and the lessons they drew for postwar Germany. Of particular concern are the weight and place of "the Jewish question" and the Holocaust in postwar German political memory, and the multiplicity of German interpretations which contended for preeminence.[1]

The temporal core of this work lies in the formative years of the anti-Nazi emigration, postwar occupation, and founding of the two German states in the 1940s and 1950s. It was during the anti-Hitler coalition of World War II, the postwar Nuremberg interregnum, and then the Cold War that the fault lines of divided memory were established. It was then that the paradoxical and, to many contemporaries, bitterly disappointing repression of the Jewish question in East Germany and its emergence in West Germany took place. One argument of this work is that understanding how and why postwar political memory divided as it did requires placing it in the historical context of the ideologies and experiences of pre-1945 German and European history and the international context of shifting and reversing alliances

# Divided Memory

During the cataclysm of the German assault on "Jewish bolshevism" on the Eastern Front from 1941 to 1945, and in the first several years of the Nuremberg interregnum, there were some political leaders who thought that the natural home for public discussion of Jewish matters should be and would be in the Soviet rather than the Western occupation zones. Yet it was in the Western zones and then in the Federal Republic (West Germany), the land of restored capitalism and liberal democracy, rather than in the Soviet zone and the antifascist German Democratic Republic (East Germany), that the issues of anti-Semitism and the Jewish catastrophe assumed a central place in the public discourse of national political leaders. Furthermore, it was the West, not the East, German government that offered financial restitution to Jewish survivors of the Holocaust, established close relations with the state of Israel, gave the Holocaust a place—in time a rather prominent place—in the national political memory, and, after disastrous delay, even conducted more trials of suspected perpetrators of crimes committed during the Nazi era. Conversely, East German leaders kept the Jewish question on the margin of narratives of the Nazi era, refused to pay restitution to Jewish survivors or to Israel, purged those Communist leaders who sought to give it greater prominence, and even gave tangible support to Israel's armed adversaries.

To explain what appears so paradoxical from the standpoint of the cataclysm of 1941–1945, to account for both the existence and themes of public memory of the crimes of the Nazis, we need to pay attention to what I call *multiple restorations*.[3] The term refers to continuities that link German political traditions of the Weimar era and the anti-Nazi emigration to the period after 1945. In both Germanys, postwar narratives of the Nazi era rested on multiple restorations of the non- and anti-Nazi German political traditions suppressed in 1933. They were inaugurated by a founding generation of leaders who reentered political life in 1945. Because political opponents of the Nazi regime had either found political asylum abroad or survived through political withdrawal in "inner emigration" at home, the leaders of Weimar's non- and anti-Nazi parties were still alive in 1945. All of the leading political figures of early postwar political life in West and East Germany came of political age between 1900 and 1930. They experienced Nazism, World War II, and the Holocaust in their mature rather than their young and formative years. Among the West Germans, Konrad Adenauer (1876–1967), the leader of postwar Christian democracy and chancellor of the Federal Republic of Germany from 1949 to 1963, had been mayor of Cologne from 1917 to 1933. Kurt Schumacher (1895–1952), the leader of postwar social democracy, served as a member of the Reichstag in the Weimar Republic. Theodor Heuss (1884–1963), the first president of the Federal Republic, had worked as a journalist and a professor of politics, and was active in liberal politics in the Weimar years as well. Ernst Reuter (1889–1953), the mayor of West Berlin during the crucial early years of the Cold War, had been a Social Democratic politician in Weimar; after being held prisoner in a Nazi concentration camp, he went into political exile in Ankara. On the East German side, Walter Ulbricht (1893–1973), the effective head of the East German government; Otto Grotewohl (1894–1964), co-chair of the Socialist Unity Party; Wilhelm Pieck (1876–1960), first president of the German Democratic Republic; and Paul Merker (1894–1969), the key figure in the anticosmopolitan purges of 1950–1956, also represented restoration of an old German political tradition.

In the face of the apocalypse of the war and the Holocaust, the inherited traditions and ideologies these leaders carried in their hearts and minds became ever more precious sources of meaning with which to interpret the present and to shape the memory of the recent past. While the Communists and Socialists emerged more confident about their legacies than did chastened liberals and conservatives, all the founding figures interpreted Nazism through long-established interpretive frameworks. The victors' enormous impact in the occupation years did not lie only or even primarily in the importation of previously foreign ideas about liberal democracy and communism. Rather, their most important contribution to postwar German politics was to ensure that the military defeat of the Nazi regime would be followed by the end of Nazism as an organized political force after 1945, and by the reemergence of German non- and anti-Nazi traditions which had been crushed in 1933.[4] Allied military power defeated the Nazi regime. After

1945, Allied military power and occupation policy made it possible for the "other Germanys" to assume center stage. Postwar memories rested on interpretations of Nazism which its German opponents had begun to develop in the Weimar Republic. As we will see, in this longer-term perspective, the repression of Jewish matters in East Berlin and their emergence in Bonn was less surprising.

At the time, it seemed reasonable enough to argue both that Communists and Jews would find common ground and that restoration of capitalism would make the Western zones and the Federal Republic the home of unrepentent amnesia. Both capitalists and conservative politicians emerged from the German catastrophe with their reputations for political and moral judgment in tatters. Socialists and Communists, despite their differences, had fought the Nazis, and the Nazis had attacked them along with the number one enemy, the Jews. The Nazis had launched a race war against the peoples of Eastern Europe and the Soviet Union. Would not the involuntary community of victims created by Nazi barbarism continue into the postwar period, especially given that one of those victims, the Soviet Union, justly claimed the lion's share of credit for the military defeat of the Nazi regime? For every quotation from Marx or Stalin that nourished anti-Semitic sentiments, there were many wartime declarations by Communists affirming solidarity with persecuted Jewry. After 1945, reasonable people might think that the natural home for those most mercilessly targeted by "Hitler fascism" would be the "antifascist" Communist regime in East Berlin. Doing so required turning a blind eye to Soviet totalitarianism, but Russia's story of suffering and redemptive victory as well as memories of Auschwitz made that easier for many to do. The Soviet Union's early support for the new state of Israel seemed to suggest that the cataclysm of World War II and the Holocaust had indeed brought about a transformation of Communist thinking about anti-Semitism and Jewish matters.[5] For those with fresh memories of Auschwitz and Treblinka, the Communists' dictatorial rule in postwar Germany hardly seemed the worst of all possible worlds. Indeed, given the popular support in Germany for Nazism, it might almost seem the prudent thing to do. In the West as well, there were fresh memories of the breadth and depth of support for Nazism among many Germans up to the bitter end. Was not a democracy of, by, and for the Germans so soon after Auschwitz and Operation Barbarossa the height of folly? As we will see, in East Berlin, memory of the crimes of the Nazi era reinforced Marxist-Leninist inclinations to aid in legitimating the imposition of a second German dictatorship to rule over this dangerous people.

There were German Communists, especially those returning from Western emigration, who hoped that a revised and more sympathetic hearing for Jewish concerns would be the logical culmination of Communist antifascism. The rise and then bitter disappointment of these hopes occupies a central role in this volume. Because of the opening of the archives of the Communist Party and government, including the Stasi (secret police) files, it is now possible to document the remarkable story of the suppression of these wartime and early postwar hopes and their bearers in the anticosmopolitan purges throughout East Germany. The East German Communist suppression of the Jewish question, at whose center stands the case of the non-Jewish German Communist Paul Merker, constitutes one of the most significant chapters of German communism, postwar German history, Jewish history, and the history of the Cold War. It is as important for understanding these histories as the Slansky trial in Prague or the Dreyfus affair for understanding Czech or French history.[6] Owing to its intrinsic significance, the relative lack of knowledge about it, and the growth of knowledge made possible by the opening of long-inaccessible East German archives, the Communist and East German story occupies a much larger part of this history than has been customary in histories of the two Germanys or that would follow primarily from the size and political significance of the two states.

While the story of Western Germany is certainly more familiar, the relationship between memory, justice, and democracy is also complex. In 1983 the German philosopher Herman Lübbe argued that "partial silence" about the Nazi past had been a "social-psychological and political necessity for the transformation of our postwar population into the citizenry of the Federal Republic."[7] As we will see, Lübbe made explicit what was implicit in Adenauer's practice, namely, that the price for postwar integration of those Germans compromised by their beliefs and actions in the Third Reich was silence about the crimes of that period. Memory and justice might produce a right-wing revolt that would undermine a still fragile democracy. So democracy had to be built on a shaky foundation of justice delayed—hence denied—and weakened memory. If this analysis was correct, the West Germans could foster either memory and justice or democracy but not both. This inherent tension between memory and justice on the one hand and democracy on the other would appear to have been one of the central themes of postwar West German history. In the 1949 election Kurt Schumacher offered the West Germans the option of democratization with a clear commitment to memory and justice. Adenauer's victory made plain that reticence about public memory of the Nazi past was crucial, if not for the preservation of democracy in West Germany, then certainly for the electoral victories of the Christian Democratic Party. The emergence of a national electoral majority in favor of the argument that daring more democracy required more memory and more justice did not take place until the 1960s.[8]

Confronted with the combination of Adenauer's agreement to pay financial restitution to Jewish survivors and his refusal to seek justice energetically in German courts for past crimes, both the East German Communists and Adenauer's West German leftist critics sought a cynical explanation for the salience of Jewish issues in West German memory and policy. The prominence of the Jewish question in West Germany, far from representing a genuine confrontation with the past Holocaust, was seen as a clever conservative ploy to place a memory of and manipulative sympathy for Jews—"philo-Semitism"—in the service of power of the worst sort, namely, the moral rehabilitation of their former tormentors.[9] What could be more effective than to "use the Holocaust" to restore the respectability of the very establishment elites which had been compromised by their actions during the Nazi era? There are two problems with such explanations. First, they neglect the lack of enthusiasm even for restitution payments which Adenauer confronted within his own party and his own conservative electoral constituencies. Compromised elites were not rushing to pay restitution to

Jewish survivors. The second, more important and all too rarely noted aspect of the emergence of Jewish matters in West Germany was the absolutely central role played by Kurt Schumacher and his successors in leadership positions in the Social Democratic Party. Adenauer has rightly received credit for supporting restitution and initiating support for Israel. One purpose of this volume is to draw attention to the democratic left in bringing Jewish matters to the fore in West Germany.

The negative impact of the rapid shift from denazification to Cold War anticommunism on the memory of the Nazi past has long been noted among critics of Western policy. Yet in both Germanys, the rapid reversal and shifting of alliances from World War II to the Cold War made the solidarities and passions aroused by the war obsolete, at times embarrassing, and even dangerous. Cold war anticommunism hardly encouraged public recollection of German war crimes on the Eastern Front. In the Soviet bloc, favorable mention of the Soviet Union's wartime alliance with the "Western imperialists" was sufficient to arouse accusations of disloyalty. Neither binary, fascism and antifascism or communism and anticommunism, was conducive to remembering events and issues, such as the Holocaust, that did not fit these categories.[10] In the chapters that follow, I emphasize that the question of the forgetting or deficient memory of the Jewish catastrophe in the postwar years was inseparable from the forgetting of World War II and what Winston Churchill aptly called "the unnatural alliance" of the Soviet Union and the West which had made possible Nazism's defeat.

The term *Vergangenheitsbewältigung*, confronting or mastering the past, has applied to far more than the words and deeds of national political leaders. Confronting the crimes of the Nazi past constituted a, and in many distinguished cases *the*, central preoccupation of postwar German intellectual, journalistic, literary, cinematic, theological, legal, and scholarly engagement.[11] Moreover, postwar memory has at times dwelt on matters of German everyday life and survival in the Third Reich which have little or nothing to do with the main political drama of aggression and genocide. I have decided to focus on what national political leaders said and did about the Jewish catastrophe for several substantive and methodological reasons.

There were two methodological reasons that led to this approach. First, at the price of losing the full texture of societal and cultural memory at any given moment, a narrower focus on national politics facilitates reflection over a longer period of time. As a result, this book addresses continuities and breaks in German political culture before and after the caesura of 1945 from the 1930s up to the national day of memory for the victims of National Socialism in January 1996. This longer time span is important for addressing the issue of the weight and centrality of anti-Semitism and Jewish matters within German history. The impact of political standpoints on decisions about when public narratives should begin—1933? 1945?—and what should be included and excluded becomes clearer as we examine the construction of interpretation and memory over a longer period of time.

Second, it has been my firm conviction that the history of politics and the history of beliefs, ideas, ideology, discourses, narratives, and representations are inseparable from one another.[12] By writing about politicians and the discourses and memory they construct, I hope to illustrate the importance of politics for shaping the way a society thinks about its past while at the same time drawing attention to the autonomous weight that traditions and interpretive frameworks exert on political life.[13] A political history which assumes that only "interests" but not "mere" ideas matter is as remote from political reality as is cultural and intellectual history which offers descriptions of discourse and memory whose political significance is thought to be self-evident or simply ignored. In this methodological battle I continue to stake my claim in the middle, at the point where meaning and power intersect.[14]

At the level of the historical record, a focus on political leaders is needed to counter the common misperception that German politicians said next to nothing about the Nazi past until the 1960s. As we will see, German political leaders with greatly varying degrees of engagement and with contrasting interpretations shaped public memory of the Nazi era from the earliest postwar days and months. Looking at the politicians' discourse of national memory is also important for understanding what they did on a range of issues such as *Wiedergutmachung* (restitution) for the Jewish survivors, denazification, prosecution and punishment for war crimes and crimes against humanity, and Israel and the conflict with the Arabs. Most important, the political focus of this book stems from a belief I share with the founding generation of German political leaders: that both the main causes of World War II, the Holocaust, and the shame and disgrace which descended on defeated Germany as well as the most important means of preventing the renewal of aggression and genocide after 1945 were political. Politicians could not cleanse the souls of thousands who had committed murder, or completely eliminate anti-Semitism and race hatred from a society whose past traditions had been strengthened by twelve years of dictatorial fanaticism. Yet it was within their power to see that justice was done and to shape a truthful national memory about the crimes of the Nazi past. In the era that memory divided by political interest and ideological conviction, they approached those tasks with widely varying degrees of passion and conviction.

The word *memory* often evokes the influence of unconscious processes that lead to its repression or distortion.[15] By concentrating on public, consciously elaborated interpretive frameworks, I draw out a sobering insight offered by the philosopher and sociologist Theodor Adorno. In his now classic essay of 1959 on the meaning of coming to terms with the Nazi past, he wrote that "the extinction of memory is far more the accomplishment of an all too wide-awake consciousness than of its weakness in the face of the overwhelming power of unconscious processes."[16] In other words, the weakness of public memory about the crimes of the Nazi era was due to the labors of this "all too wide-awake consciousness," which remembered all too well what it would rather not see in political discussion.

The thesis of multiple restorations reminds us that not only the extinction but also the persistence and form of public memory was due to the variety of forms taken by "a wide-awake consciousness" in post-Nazi Germany. The hypothesis begins with the observations of Walter Dirks, the co-editor with Eugen Kogon of the left-liberal Catholic intellectual-political journal *Frankfurter Hefte.* In 1950 Dirks extended the notion of restoration, heretofore reserved for the persistence of the forces of capitalism or the conservative elites, to encompass the reemergence of intact traditions of communism, social democracy, and Christian democracy.[17] In fact, what Dirks observed can be understood as a chapter in the history of what the late German historian Thomas Nipperdey called the "multiple continuities" in German history. My own efforts to reconstruct the emergence of divided memory owes much to Nipperdey's stress on the need to reconstruct the openness of past moments.[18] Another German historian, Reinhart Koselleck, has elaborated on classic themes of interpretive social science to point to the endurance and continuity of political culture and political traditions, especially in periods of change and crisis, when people need sources of meaning the most.[19] World War II and the German defeat of May 8, 1945, was clearly a crisis in which the restoration of past traditions offered the Germans the possibility of making sense of the chaos and confusion around them.[20]

Alongside the multiple restorations in political culture there were breaks, most obviously involving the millions of people who had died in the most terrible war in Western history.[21] European and German Jewry had been wiped out. Four million German soldiers and civilians had died. Nazism as a major political force in German society had been destroyed. Militarism and unquestioning acceptance of authority were now discredited.[22] Prussian Junkers had lost their power and influence.[23] The fascist cult of masculine aggression had become an object of ridicule rather than a rallying point for new military aggression.[24] Fascism and Nazism had lost all intellectual and moral respectability.[25] Konrad Adenauer initiated a new tradition of West German conservatism which replaced past anti-Western resentments with an embrace of both democratic values and a Western geopolitical orientation.[26]

Change took place on the left as well. The divisive intramural battle between social democracy and communism took the form of the Cold War between West and East Germany. It also deprived the SPD (Social Democratic Party) of much of the electoral support that might very well have produced a majority government in the early postwar elections. Division, however, ended the Weimar dilemma, in which the presence of a small but still significant Communist Party drew off some potential SPD voters and scared so many more into the arms of the right that an SPD national majority became impossible.[27] In contrast to postwar Italy, where the Communist specter facilitated a half-century of conservative rule, the Communist absence in the Federal Republic made it easier for the SPD to move to the center in Bad Godesberg in 1959, and to win a national election in 1969. The prospect of Social Democratic victory increased pressures within West Germany in favor of a hard line toward the Nazi past.

The contours of postwar memory began to take shape when Nazism was triumphant and its political opponents were either in foreign exile, in the "inner" emigration of political withdrawal, or in Nazi prisons and concentration camps. Before traditions could be restored, they had to be preserved. We turn now to that labor of preservation and to the impact of foreign travel on local traditions.

# 2

# German Communism's Master Narratives of Antifascism: Berlin–Moscow–East Berlin, 1928–1945

After 1945, East German Communist official memory of the Nazi era drew on an intact "antifascist" political tradition which originated in the Weimar Republic and continued in emigration during the period of Nazi rule. In this chapter I examine the dominant strand of Communist antifascism in the Weimar Republic, which later survived in exile in Moscow. Communist antifascism fostered a bipolar discourse in which communist dictatorships became part of the democratic world fighting against fascist dictatorship. Those, the Communists argued, who criticized the Soviet Union and the Communist parties were "objectively" supporting fascism.[1] Those who sought to place the persecution of the Jews at the center of Communist antifascism were also out of step with a politics focused on class struggle and the centrality of the Soviet Union.

In 1933, following the Nazis' arrest of Ernst Thälmann (1866–1944), the leader of the German Communist Party (Kommunistische Partei Deutschland, or KPD) in the Weimar Republic, Wilhelm Pieck (1876–1960) became Thälmann's successor as party chairman. Pieck and another member of the KPD Politburo, Walter Ulbricht (1893–1973), were leading figures of the Communist emigration, first in Paris and then in Moscow.[2] While in Paris from 1935 to 1938, Ulbricht, along with Franz Dahlem and Paul Merker, led the KPD office in Paris. In Moscow from

1938 to 1945, Ulbricht demonstrated his loyalty to Stalin and consolidated his primacy over the KPD. Having emerged preeminent in Moscow, Ulbricht prevailed over potential challengers returning from concentration camps, such as Dahlem, and from emigration in the West, such as Merker. Ulbricht became the most powerful member of the German Communist Party and then the Socialist Unity Party (Sozialistisches Einheitspartei, or SED) after World War II, as well as leader of the East German government from 1949 to 1971.[3] His *Zur Geschichte der Deutschen Arbeiterbewegung* (1953) (On the History of the German Labor Movement) and *Zur Geschichte der neuesten Zeit* (1955) (History of the Recent Period) included his essays, speeches, and important party documents covering the period from Weimar to the mid-1950s.[4] Pieck, who had been a comrade of Rosa Luxemburg's, was a founding member of the KPD in 1918–19, continued as chairman of the Communist Party in exile, and ended as president of East Germany from 1949 to 1960. Collections of his essays covering the period from 1908 to 1950 appeared in 1951.[5] Together, Pieck's and Ulbricht's writings offer the canonical texts and major themes of the postwar Communist narrative of the Nazi era. Subordination of the causal autonomous significance of Nazi ideology as well as hostility to German social democracy remained enduring elements of Communist antifascism.

Several themes of Communist antifascism were particularly decisive for shaping postwar memory. First, and most obviously, was the Comintern's famous assumption that fascism was essentially a dictatorial, terrorist, and imperialist form of finance capitalism. Hence, Nazism—which the Communists always called "German fascism"—was to be understood first of all in the Marxist analysis of capitalism and class struggle; its anti-Semitic ideology was relegated to the realm of a superstructural epiphenomenon. Second, the German Communists argued that they bore no responsibility at all for the destruction of the Weimar Republic and the rise of Nazism. That, they insisted, was the fault of German Social Democrats and their refusal to make common cause with the Communists in the Weimar years.

Yet, as they privately admitted on occasion, and as historians have amply documented, the German Communist Party, and its leader Ernst

Thälmann, faced with the growth of Nazism, rejected all alliances with Social Democratic and liberal parties and denounced the Social Democrats as "social fascists."[6] Thälmann consistently blurred the distinctions between Weimar democracy and authoritarian rule.[7] In a resolution on "the struggle against fascism" of June 4, 1930, the KPD Politburo declared that "the struggle against fascism is inconceivable without the sharpest struggle against the Social Democratic Party and its leadership, a leadership which represents a decisive weapon favoring the spread of fascism in Germany."[8] In November 1931 the KPD Central Committee declared that "social democracy is our major enemy in the proletariat. In the current period of the class struggle we conduct the major blow against social democracy."[9] As late as August and September 1932, at the twelfth Plenum of the Executive Committee of the Communist International, held in Moscow, party leaders denounced cooperation between Communists and Social Democrats to resist Nazism as "right-wing opportunism."[10] During a KPD party conference in Berlin held in October 1932, Thälmann favorably quoted Stalin's view that fascism and social fascism were "twin brothers" *(Zwillinge),* not contrasting ideologies.

A third element of Communist antifascism that exerted a continuing impact on postwar interpretations was the dialectically inspired inclination to see political disasters as preludes to subsequent Communist success.[11] In a 1934 booklet titled *We Are Fighting for a Soviet Germany,* Pieck, who became chairman of the KPD after Thälmann's arrest, wrote that ten months of fascist dictatorship had "confirmed the prediction of the Communist International" that fascism would not usher in a period of reaction and that "the establishment of the Hitler dictatorship may indeed temporarily hinder but cannot put a stop to the development of revolutionary forces."[12] The Soviet victory over Nazi Germany, combined with the failure of the Germans to overthrow Nazism themselves, simultaneously confirmed his Communist faith in an optimistic, dialectical "happy ending" to the class struggle, while at the same time it shook his belief that the Germans would make a significant contribution to that outcome.

Fourth, the more the KPD sought to present itself, out of both political conviction and political opportunism, as leading an antifascist, democratic, and *national* front, the less willing the party was to emerge as a defender of the Jews. Already in the Weimar era the KPD had shown its nationalist side as it competed with the right wing in attacking the Versailles treaty.[13] A nationalism fed both by Marxism-Leninism and by traditional German hostility to "the West" would remain a key point of continuity in Communist discourse in the KPD after 1945 and in the SED regime after 1949.

Fifth, Marxist-Leninist economic reductionism and a view of ideology as primarily an instrument for other purposes also contributed to marginalization of the Jewish question. The Communists viewed anti-Semitism as above all a tool of the capitalist classes for confusing, dividing, and weakening the working class, not as an ideology with a history and an impact independent of the history of capitalism.[14] Communists who argued that Nazi anti-Semitism had an autonomous political significance were exceptional. The problem with Communist theory, however, did not consist only in sins of omission and neglect. It included active hostility to Jews. Since Marx's essay on the Jewish question, a strong undercurrent of Marxism had associated the Jews with capitalism and the bourgeoisie.[15] Although Hitler attacked "Jewish bolshevism," Communists were divided between a reflexive sympathy for a seemingly natural ally and a view of the Jews as part of the international capitalist antagonist.[16]

Sixth, basic assumptions about religion and society deeply embedded in the Marxist and Communist tradition contributed to the forgetting and marginalization of the Jewish question, including the Holocaust. Communists, after all, believed that religion was, as Marx put it, an "opiate of the people" or a "necessary illusion" linked to the existence of class society and capitalism. They reasoned that revolution, by eliminating capitalism and creating a classless, Socialist, and then Communist society, would lead to the disappearance of both religion and religious hatreds—including anti-Semitism. Hence, there was no need to devote particular attention to the Jewish question any more than to any other religious matter. The thesis of a dialectic of enlightenment which Max Horkheimer and Theodor Adorno applied to Nazism and the Holocaust fits far more plausibly as an explanation of the rage at stubborn otherness which remained a central characteristic of twentieth-century Communists who saw themselves as heirs to the tradition of Enlightenment rationalism and universalism.

Reflecting the Stalinization of the KPD in the 1920s, when German Communists thought about the oppression of nationalities, they were guided by a canonical text, Stalin's 1913 essay on the national question.[17] "A nation," he wrote, was "a historically grounded, stable community of people that emerges on the basis of a community of language, territory, economic life, and cultural characteristics rooted in the community."[18] Because the Jews lacked these prerequisites, he continued, they were not a nation.[19] Once in power, however, the Bolsheviks proved to be ideologically flexible; they recognized Jewish autonomy in local areas, and even considered giving the Jews an autonomous entity, Birobidzhan, to which they would move. The initial Soviet sympathy for Israel in 1947 and 1948 drew on such "Stalinist" recognition of Jewish claims to nationhood.[20] This labile character of Communist thinking about the Jewish question is important to keep in mind both to understand why those fighting anti-Semitism might look favorably on Communist antifascism and to grasp the interaction between contingent political events and the emergence of central and peripheral elements of Communist thinking on the issue.

Or, in simpler terms, the party line could change. At the Comintern's Seventh Congress in Moscow in July and August 1935, the Soviet-controlled Comintern replaced the ultraleftism of the Third Period with a call for a Popular Front against fascism that would bring Communists together with Social Democrats and liberals.[21] Pieck now denounced the previous Communist assault on democracy and social democracy.[22] The Communists, he said, both underestimated the fascist danger where it did exist, namely, in the "Hitler movement," and saw "fascism where it did not at all exist," namely, in some of the regional Social Democratic governments of the last years of the Weimar era.[23] At the same meeting, Walter Ulbricht made the devastating admission that the KPD had "directed its main blows against social democracy at a point at which it should have directed them against fascism."[24] Such blunt and honest assessment, however, did not then become public knowledge.

From October 3 to 15, 1935, the German Communist exile leadership in Moscow held what came to be known as "the Brussels Conference." Pieck made the case for a turn to the Popular Front in a speech soon published in France as a pamphlet titled *Der neue Weg zum gemeinsamen Kampf für den Sturz der Hitlerdiktatur* (The New Path for the Common Struggle for the Overthrow of the Hitler Dictatorship). *Der Neue Weg* became the canonical text for the KPD of the Popular Front period.[25] Pieck now publicly admitted that the Communists' "most serious error" was the failure to "bring our struggle against social democracy into a proper proportion to the struggle against fascism."[26] When they should have attacked "the fascist movement," the Communists instead attacked social democracy and "bourgeois democracy." Hence, "it was inevitable that we were unable to mobilize the working class for the struggle against fascism . . . For a long time the underestimation of the fascist danger prevented the party from taking the course of creating a unity front with Social Democratic workers."[27] The German Communists, with their attacks on social democracy, had to assume responsibility for the failure of a united front against fascism to emerge in Germany, as it had in France.[28] The result of the shift in the Comintern line and its attendant self-criticism was an abrupt reversal toward "unity of action" with all "antifascist" forces, including the previously despised Social Democrats.[29] Pieck's *Neue Weg* placed the German Communists in the causal chain of events in German history which had made the Nazi seizure of power possible. It was not only "the others" who had to bear the responsibility. In retrospect, Pieck's statement of October 1935 would remain an unusual moment of chastened and honest self-reflection.

Another aspect of the *Neue Weg* speech was less reassuring. Pieck agreed with the criticism of the Comintern leader Georgi Dimitrov that the German Communists had in effect been insufficiently nationalistic in the Weimar years. Specifically, they had "displayed great shortcomings in this struggle [against the Versailles treaty] and did not understand how to take the national feelings of the masses into account in [their] agitation."[30] They should now "stand for the complete elimination of the Versailles diktat and for the voluntary reunification into a free Germany of all those parts of the German people who had been torn away by this diktat."[31] Pieck returned to the argument that the Communists had not been nationalistic enough at a KPD conference held outside Paris in January–February 1939, known as the "Bern Conference."[32] He argued that the KPD should stress the "conflict between the policy of Hitler fascism and the interest of the German nation," and no longer avoid words such as *Nation* and *Volk:* "Saving the nation from catastrophe means saving it from traitors and destroyers, Hitler fascism, and big capital. This is the highest national deed of our era."[33] Speaking the language of nationalism appeared to contradict coming to the defense of the Jews, the great "other" in Nazi Germany.

Nevertheless, in the face of Nazi persecution, the German Communists did make common cause with German Jews. In response to the anti-Jewish pogrom of November 9, 1938, the KPD in exile published a special issue of *Die Rote Fahne,* the party's clandestine newspaper.[34] The Central Committee passionately denounced the pogrom "which has covered Germany's honor with the deepest disgrace in the eyes of the whole of humanity." All "honorable Germans" rejected the attacks on defenseless Jews.[35] The statement continues:

> The struggle against the Jewish pogrom is an inseparable part of the German struggle for freedom and peace against the National Socialist dictatorship. Hence, this struggle must be conducted with the most complete solidarity with our Jewish fellow citizens by all who have been subjected to the tyranny of the Hitler dictatorship . . . The German working class stands at the forefront of the battle against the persecution of the Jews . . . The liberation of Germany from the shame of the Jewish pogrom will coincide with the hour of the liberation of the German people from the brown tyranny.[36]

The statement was unique in the history of German communism. Never before or afterwards did the KPD, or later the SED, so emphatically proclaim its solidarity with the Jews persecuted by Nazism, or link the Jewish fate to that of the "German struggle for freedom and peace." In the postwar era, Ulbricht did not include the statement in the canon of glorious moments of Communist antifascism.[37]

Pieck, ever the revolutionary optimist, argued that the pogrom was due to Hitler's fear of popular antagonism in response to his war provocations of September 1938. The pogrom represented the Hitler regime's efforts "to intimidate the German people as a whole and thus to break their growing resistance."[38] It was, he continued, not only the Jews who were the Nazis' victims: "It is the working masses as a whole against whom these excesses are directed."[39] The working class and the Communists "feel bound in solidarity with the persecuted Jewish population, and see in their defense the preservation of their own interests."[40]

The typically Communist aspect of Pieck's argument was his rejection of the idea that the Nazi attack on German and European Jewry was made for its own sake, not in order to weaken the working class or intimidate "the people as a whole." This view of the Nazi persecution of the Jews as a functional tool for other political purposes was also evident in Ulbricht's description of the pogrom as a "weapon of fascist war policy" and a tool of Nazi domination.[41] Ulbricht asserted that the pogrom was "intended to split the mass opposition and prevent the unification of workers and peasants, intellectuals and the middle class, and of all freedom-loving people in Germany . . . The cause of the persecuted and murdered Jews is the cause of all moral men and women . . . [and] of peace, freedom, and humanity."[42] Ulbricht still viewed anti-Semitism through the prism of class struggle, as an instrument or weapon for achieving some other end. Yet underestimation or misunderstanding was not the same as hostility or indifference. He placed the cause of the "persecuted and murdered Jews" firmly within the concerns of Communist antifascism. Moreover, particularly striking in view of the subsequent hostility of the German Democratic Republic to Israel was Ulbricht's criticism of Nazi agitation against the Jews in Palestine: "Through stirring up race hatred, it [Nazi Germany] seeks to strengthen fascist influence among the Arabs and to prepare the capture of colonies by German fascism."[43] Ulbricht did not include the article in the official East German history of the German labor movement. Publication of his denunciation of Nazi imperialism in the Middle East in 1938 would have been an awkward reminder of a past moment of solidarity with the Jews, which stood in sharp contrast to the East German government's hostility to the Jewish state.[44]

The core leadership of the KPD, including Ulbricht and Pieck, spent the wartime years in Moscow, where they observed the suffering inflicted by the German armies on the Soviet Union.[45] In 1955 Ulbricht dedicated his postwar account of those years to the "fighters of the Soviet army, to whom the German people are indebted for their liberation from fascism, and also to the nameless heroes of the illegal antifascist struggle."[46] Yet the work contained very little about the German resistance to Nazism, and only 6 of the 616 pages of Volume 2 of the official history of the German labor movement, his previously published essays and speeches covering the period 1933–1946, dealt with the "antifascist opposition in Germany."[47] "Antifascist resistance" between 1933 and 1945 in Germany remained a minor episode in Ulbricht's official history.[48]

For Ulbricht, Nazism's primary victim was also the source of its defeat. While the German invasion of the Soviet Union was "the greatest crime of German history," the Red Army emerged as the main source of resistance to fascism.[49] It was only after the "blows of the Soviet army" had destroyed the legend of the German army's invincibility that "broad circles of the German people were willing to listen to arguments for reason and to face reality."[50] The Red Army's victory over the Wehrmacht at Stalingrad turned the tide in the war and demonstrated the military, political, moral, and economic superiority of the Soviet Union over Hitler's Germany, encouraged anti-Nazi opposition in Germany both among government officials and "in the ranks of working people," and made the United States and Great Britain more interested in forming a second front in Europe so that the Soviet army alone would not defeat Nazi Germany.[51] Just as he saw the German Communist Party as "the only" real antifascist force within Germany, so was the Soviet Union the leader of antifascist resistance among the warring states of World War II. Ulbricht offered a realist's assessment of the power of states, not a romance of widespread German resistance.

Ulbricht gave backhanded praise to the resistance group of Jewish Communists led by Herbert Baum in Berlin when he wrote that Baum had "taught the members to see that the essence of fascism was not only in terror against the Jews, but rather was in the oppression of the whole German people, and that therefore they must fight actively for the overthrow of fascism."[52] He was, however, openly dismissive of the conspirators of July 20, 1944. Their actions, he said, constituted "the projects and efforts of German monopolists to preserve their power beyond the lost war and to find a way out at the cost and to the detriment of the German and other peoples."[53]

The first loyalties of the German Communists in wartime Moscow lay with Stalin and the Soviet regime. Despite the emergence there of the Jewish Antifascist Committee, the Germans did not fundamentally change their views about the Jewish question during the war and Holocaust.[54] Instead they directed their appeals on Moscow radio at the invading Wehrmacht and German POWs. Pieck's wartime radio addresses document his efforts to separate the Germans from the Nazi regime, and the collapse of his hopes for an internal German revolt.[55] In April 1942 Pieck called on the Germans to restore Germany's name, which had "been disgraced before the whole world by Hitler's and his barbarians' war crimes."[56] In July 1942 he called "the Hitler clique . . . the deadly enemy of the German people."[57] The war was being waged in the interest of "a small band of robbers, of plutocrats, and Nazi big shots."[58] The "greatest national crime against the German people" was the "imperialist war of plunder against the Soviet Union." The Germans could save themselves from ruin only by overthrowing this "clique."[59] If, however, the Germans waited for Nazism to be defeated from without, they would be "burdened with a heavy guilt for having stuck with this band of criminals until the end."[60] His radio broadcasts of 1942 included extensive reports of German atrocities on the Eastern Front: "more than 900,000" Poles murdered or dead from hunger since 1939; several hundred thousand taken to concentration camps; almost 2 million shipped to forced labor in Germany.[61] Pieck stressed the particular barbarity of the ongoing war against the Jews: "The SS bandits in Poland were especially intent on annihilating the Jewish population. Seven hundred thousand Jews have already been murdered. Hundreds of thousands of Jewish families have been crammed together into concentration camps and are dying of hunger and disease."[62] He offered vivid and detailed descriptions of the "unheard-of crimes the Nazi band committed against the Russian civilian population." There was, he said, "no bestiality imaginable which the SS bloodhounds will not commit against the Russian people."[63] He repeatedly returned to the theme that the only way the Germans could regain the respect of other peoples was to overthrow the Nazis.[64] These evocations of Nazi barbarism and of the German revolt which failed to occur had enduring consequences for postwar East German politics.

Pieck's sentiments were shared by other leading German exiles in Moscow as they engaged in efforts to undermine the German armies on the Eastern Front. Toward that end, in July 1943 they founded the Nationale Komitee Freies Deutschland (National Committee for a Free Germany), or NKFD, along with the Bund Deutscher Offiziere (Association of German Officers), composed of captured German officers.[65] At the founding meeting, the NKFD issued a "Manifesto to the Wehrmacht and the German People."[66] It stated:

> If the German people continue to permit themselves to be led to ruin without will and without resistance, then with every passing day they become not only weaker and more powerless but also more laden with guilt. Then Hitler will be overthrown only by the weapons of the [Allied] coalition. Such an outcome would mean the end of our national freedom and of our state. It would bring about the dismemberment of our fatherland. And we could not bring an indictment against anyone but ourselves.
>
> If, however, the German people quickly pull themselves together and prove through their deeds that they want to be a free people, and are determined to liberate Germany from Hitler, they win the right to determine their own future destiny themselves, and the right to belong to the world.
>
> THAT IS THE ONLY WAY TO SAVE THE SURVIVAL, THE FREEDOM, AND THE HONOR OF THE GERMAN NATION.[67]

As the war continued, the anger of the Moscow exiles toward the Germans grew. Erich Weinert, a member of the KPD and the president of the NKFD, rejected the view that terror alone kept Hitler in power. It was also, he continued "your [the Germans'] obedience, your fateful bond [to Hitler] . . . your cowardly silence and hesitation which still always gives Hitler the possibility to preserve his power." The Germans, he insisted, had means—strikes, work slowdowns—to "break his power . . . You need only the will to use them.[68] The coexistence of mass crimes with the absence of revolt stretched the credibility of the view that German fascism was only the terrorist rule of a small clique of capitalists, militarists, and Nazi functionaries lacking popular support. While, on the one hand, the leaders of the NKFD spoke the wartime language of Popular Front antifascism, they were also establishing the justification for imposing a postwar dictatorship on an untrustworthy and dishonored people.

From July 19, 1943, until November 3, 1945, the NKFD published the Moscow edition of *Freies Deutschland*.[69] Reflecting the journal's Moscow location and the KPD's efforts to appeal to Germans to overthrow the Nazis, the pages of *Freies Deutschland* focused on the main battles on the Eastern Front, the impact of the war on Germany, and the contribution of the Soviet Union and the Red Army.[70] In spring and fall 1945, revelations of the full extent of Nazi war crimes occupied up to 20 percent of the paper's pages.[71] In the spring of 1945, as the Red Army was liberating the Nazi death camps, *Freies Deutschland* carried reports about the fate of the Jews in Auschwitz and Maidanek.[72]

Although they did not ignore the Jewish catastrophe, the members of the NKFD did not repeat or expand on the solidarity with the Jews which the Communists had declared in 1938. On the contrary, publicly at least they kept a certain distance. In May 1942, ten months before Soviet hopes were raised by the victory at Stalingrad, the Jewish Antifascist Committee in Moscow, composed of prominent Jewish Communists, declared that "with pride, we Jews of the Soviet Union speak to Jews of the whole world."[73] The statement specifically referred to the attack on the Jews of Europe and the Soviet Union, who "are beaten, tortured, and murdered by the bestial Hitlerites"; called the Red Army the "hope of all humanity"; and warned that in the summer of 1942, "the fate of all humanity . . . and also the fate of the Jewish people" would be decided.[74] Yet, despite the existence of the Jewish Antifascist Committee, there was no public expression of political or ideological ferment among German Communist exiles about the Jewish question in wartime Moscow. Even in the face of the Holocaust taking place on and behind the Eastern Front, German Communists' prewar assumptions about the Jewish question remained intact.

Outlines for courses in modern German history and politics prepared for German prisoners of war in the Soviet Union indicate the continuing orthodoxy of German and Soviet Communists.[75] Anti-Semitism was the "most precise expression of the cannibalistic essence of [Nazi] race theory."[76] Above all, as the lecture notes for a course taught in 1942 stress, anti-Semitism was a "tool" of reaction for diverting mass discontent "onto the tracks of a murderous war against the working Jewish masses." The fascists used this tool "to weaken the strength of the German people and break its struggle against fascism," while "the Nazi scoundrels" used the tool of anti-Semitism "to personally enrich themselves by appropriating the property of the Jewish bourgeoisie."[77] A 1944 course outline on the war and modern German history lists "Hitler fascism's campaign of annihilation against other races" as the topic of one of twenty lectures.[78] A 1944 lecture on "the Hitler fascists' campaign of extermination under the banner of race theory" still clung to the view of anti-Semitism as a "tool of the German fascists" designed to divert the anger of dissatisfied masses away from those who were "really guilty" and to mobilize "broad masses of the peoples of Europe against the so-called Jewish plutocrats in England and America as well as against 'Jewish domination' in Russia."[79]

Of course, the Communists were not alone in failing to grasp the centrality of anti-Semitism or the Holocaust at the time. Neither the United States nor Great Britain placed the Jewish catastrophe at the center of its analysis of or strategies for fighting World War II, nor understood the primacy which Hitler attributed to his war against the Jews. Nonetheless, given the proximity of Soviet military power to the scene of the crimes, this was a fateful misunderstanding indeed. So far, no evidence has come to light which indicates that the German Communist exiles in Moscow urged the Soviet government to use its army or air force to stop or delay the operations of the Nazi death camps.[80]

The poet Johannes R. Becher (1891–1958), a future member of the SED Central Committee, one of the leading East German literary intellectuals, and a future minister of culture, was also in Moscow with Ulbricht. His unpublished 1944 essay, "The Race Theory of German Fascism," intended for an internal party discussion group, indicates how one leading figure of the German exile was thinking about these issues.[81] He described Nazi racial theories as pseudoscience, as "conscious distortions and falsifications" about race and blood with catastrophic consequences. The "ideological poisoning" of the Germans, he said, had resulted in the "hatred and contempt of the whole of progressive humanity toward Germany. The fascists pseudoscholars, no less than the imperialist economic leaders and the party leaders of the NSDAP [the Nazi Party], are traitors to the German nation and criminals against humanity."[82] Despite an extensive treatment of the historical origins of modern racism, Becher gave short shrift to the specifically anti-Jewish components of Nazi racial ideology. Defense of the Soviet Union against the Nazi invaders was the Communists' first priority. Perhaps another reason for his reticence lay in the efforts of the German exiles to speak as the true representatives of the German nation in opposition to the Nazi "traitors." Explicit and frequent identification with the Jews did not help in that endeavor. On the contrary, for Germans subjected to propaganda, it might lend credence to the Nazi association of the Jews and bolshevism.[83] Despite the shortcomings and opportunism of the Moscow exiles' understanding of anti-Semitism, some Communists entertained the hope that the Communists' general revulsion against Nazi racism would extend to a postwar renewal and deepening of the solidarity expressed in November 1938 with persecuted Jewry.

The Allied victory over Nazism was bittersweet for the German Communists in Moscow. In a radio address from Moscow on May 4, 1945, Wilhelm Pieck expressed the ambivalence of anger and shame at that moment.[84] Every "honorable and true German," he said, was filled with joy at the Red Army's victory "over the forces of darkness, racist insanity, and genocide embodied in Hitlerism . . . Yet the joyful news is mixed with the bitter, tortured consciousness that the German people themselves did not free themselves from this band of murderers, but instead followed them to the end, and supported them in their war crimes."[85] Blinded by Hitler's early successes, the Germans refused to listen to the warnings of antifascists, and adopted the "Nazi poison of imperialist ideology of plunder . . . You [the Germans] became the tools of Hitler's wars and thus have taken a great shared guilt and responsibility. Now you will bear this guilt toward other people and must again clear the German name of the filth heaped on it by the Hitler band."[86]

With defeat certain, the Germans nevertheless fought to the bitter end. In late May, Georgi Dimitroff, Pieck's longtime colleague in the Comintern, told Pieck that the majority of Germans "would have been happy if Hitler had won the war."[87] In the Battle of Berlin alone, fought between April 16, 1945, and May 1, 1945, the Soviets suffered 300,000 men killed, wounded, or missing, while a half-million people were killed, injured, or wounded.[88] The German Communists in Moscow returned as realists of power politics. Pieck's lingering romanticism had been crushed when the hoped-for internal German revolts and fissures failed to materialize. If Russian soldiers raped German women, imposed harsh occupation policies, turned former Nazi concentration camps into camps for a new brand of political prisoner, then Ulbricht, Pieck, and their associates remembered that it was only the Allies, and especially the Red Army, not the Germans, which had defeated fascism.[89] While Communist romanticism about the German revolution had been crushed, the Soviet victory appeared to confirm the Marxist-Leninist conviction that history was indeed unfolding along the lines of a bloody and tragic yet triumphant dialectical logic. The returning exiles were as angry, ashamed of, and bitter toward their fellow Germans as they were filled with gratitude toward their Soviet liberators. Such deep emotions and convictions had a lasting impact.

For the Communists, World War II and the alliance with the Western powers was a kind of revival of the Popular Front era. In the early months and years after the war, the Communists spoke the language of democracy which had been the common discourse of wartime antifascism. The continuities and mixed emotions of the returning exiles were apparent in the KPD's "Aufruf" (appeal) to the German people of June 13, 1945. The statement, which was written by Anton Ackermann, editor in chief of the Moscow radio station of the NKFD, with close supervision from the Communist functionary Georgi Dimitrov and signed by the members of the KPD Central Committee, became a canonical text of East German Communism.[90] The "Aufruf" distilled the Communists' memories of war and Nazism, assigned responsibility and guilt for the German catastrophe, and drew lessons for the future. It offered a long list of those whose "policies of aggression and extermination had burdened the German people with heavy guilt and responsibility in the eyes of the whole of civilized humanity." The list included Hitler, Göring, Himmler, Goebbels, Nazi Party members, the German generals, imperialists, employers, and the large German banks.[91] The Nazis' crimes included the violent annexation of Austria; the division of Czechoslovakia; the plunder and oppression of Poland, Denmark, Norway, Belgium, Holland, France, Yugoslavia, and Greece; and the bombing of English cities.

> But the greatest and most fateful of Hitler's war crimes was the treacherous and deceptive attack on the Soviet Union . . . German workers! Could there be a greater crime than this war against the Soviet Union?
>
> The acts of cruelty which the Hitler bandits committed in foreign countries were monstrous. The Hitler Germans' [*Hitlerdeutschen*] hands are stained with the blood of millions of murdered children, women, and elderly people. Day after day in the death camps the extermination of human beings was carried out in gas chambers and ovens. Burning living bodies, burying living bodies, cutting living bodies up into pieces—this was how the Nazi bandits ravaged.
>
> Millions of prisoners of war and foreign workers seized and taken to Germany were worked to death, and died of hunger, cold, and disease.
>
> The world is shaken and simultaneously filled with the deepest hatred toward Germany in view of these unparalleled crimes, this

horrifying mass murder which was carried out by the system of Hitler Germany.

If, German people, like were to be revenged with like, what would become of you?[92]

The "Aufruf" followed the pattern of wartime agitation in its focus on the Soviet Union and a certain vagueness as to the identity of the Nazis' victims.[93] Yet its emphasis on the shame and guilt which Nazism had brought upon Germany was unmistakable. Rather than wallow in self-pity over the catastrophe that had descended on them, the "Aufruf" warned the Germans to consider themselves fortunate that the occupiers would not treat them as horribly as the Germans had treated others.

The "Aufruf" also expressed the spirit of the still intact anti-Hitler coalition. In addition to the Soviet Union, it included England and the United States as members of the United Nations which had fought for "justice, freedom, and progress. Through their sacrifices, the Red Army and the armies of its allies have saved humanity from Hitler barbarism" and thus also "brought peace and liberation from the chains of Hitler slavery to you, the productive German people."[94] Credit for the victory over Nazism was shared, not monopolized or reduced to a zero-sum game of recognition and nonrecognition between the Soviet Union and the Western democracies.

The appeal expressed deep anger at the great majority of Germans, an anger at odds with the conventional Marxist picture which limited guilt and responsibility to a small ruling class.

All the more, conscience and shame must burn in every German person because the German people bear an important part of the shared guilt [*Mitschuld*] and shared responsibility [*Mitverantwortung*] for the war and its consequences.

It is not only Hitler who is guilty of the crimes committed against humanity! The 10 million Germans who voted for Hitler in a free election in 1932 also bear a part of the guilt, although we Communists warned that "whoever votes for Hitler, votes for war!"

All those German men and women bear guilt who looked on, without will and resistance, as Hitler seized power, smashed all democratic organizations, above all workers' organizations, and imprisoned, tortured, and beheaded the best Germans. All those Germans bear guilt who saw in rearmament the "Great Germany" and glimpsed in wild militarism, in marching, and in drilling the only saving grace for the salvation of the nation.

Our misfortune was that millions and millions of Germans succumbed to Nazi demagoguery, and that the poison of beastly racial doctrine and of the "struggle for living space" could infect the organism of the people.

Our misfortune was that broad layers of the population lost the elementary feeling for decency and justice, and followed Hitler when he promised them a well-filled lunch and dinner table gained by war and thievery at the cost of other peoples.

Thus, the German people became the tools of Hitler and his imperialist employers.[95]

Mass support for Nazism was the source of German misfortune. The references to the "millions and millions" and "broad layers" who supported the Nazis coexisted uneasily with the orthodox view of "German fascism" as a tool of a small elite of Nazi leaders, militarists, and imperialists who used terror above all to govern a potentially rebellious populace.

The "Aufruf" conveyed an appeal for an antifascist democracy but also presented a rationale for imposing a nondemocratic government over the Germans. Rather than celebrating the glories of the antifascist German resistance, it recalled memories of widespread support for Nazism. During the Popular Front (1941–1945), the war on the Eastern Front (1941–1945), and the early postwar months, the Soviet Union and the European Communists presented themselves as part of the world of democracies arrayed against Nazism. The Nazi era, however, had added a new rationale for dictatorship. For Jacobins and Leninists, the answer to governing a misguided and even immoral "people" was to create an educational dictatorship. The particular German Communist distrust toward a dangerous people thus offered yet another rationale for imposing a postwar dictatorship in the name of democratic antifascism.[96] This dangerous people had refused to rally to the Communists and had fought for the Nazis to the bitter end. In the emerging postwar ideology of antifascism, assertions of the Germans' *Mitschuld* and *Mitverantwortung* for Nazi crimes could legitimize rule by the Communists and delegitimate, at least for the near future, democratic rule by the Germans.

The "Aufruf" did contain acknowledgments of past errors: "We German Communists . . . feel guilty because as a consequence of a series of our mistakes . . . we were unable to forge the antifascist unity of workers, peasants, and intellectuals in the face of all adversaries" or lead a successful revolt against the Nazi regime and thus "avoid a situation in which the German people failed in the face of history."[97] Compared to Wilhelm Pieck's statement to the Seventh Congress of the Comintern in Moscow in 1935, this reference to a "series of our mistakes" was extremely mild indeed. It said nothing about the disastrous policies of the Third Period and the attack on "social fascism." For those, such as Kurt Schumacher, who remembered these attacks, such admissions of fallibility did not go nearly far enough. Yet, as we will see, Schumacher also expressed deep disappointment in the failure of the Germans to oppose Nazism.

The "Aufruf" repeated familiar criticism of the Social Democrats. Ackermann wrote that fascism was able to spread in Germany after 1918 because those responsible for World War I were not punished, genuine democracy was not attained, reaction had a free hand, and "the anti-Soviet witch-hunt of some democratic leaders prepared the path for Hitler and paralyzed the antifascist unity front of the power of the people." Therefore, "we demand: no repetition of the mistakes of 1918!" Anticommunism was among the "mistakes of 1918" which must not be repeated. The Communists had been right about fascism from the beginning. Unfortunately, the Germans did not listen to their warnings. The German people had failed before history, but the German Communists possessed a tradition of "decisive struggle against militarism, imperialism, and imperialist war."[98]

Notwithstanding its sharp criticism of the Germans and its implicit justification for a new dictatorship over a dangerous people, the "Aufruf" promised postwar democracy. The "bourgeois-democratic revolution of 1848" should be completed by abolishing feudal residues and Prussian militarism. It would be wrong to impose the Soviet system on Germany, "for this path does not correspond to the current developmental conditions in Germany." Rather, the Germans should establish an "antifascist, democratic regime, a parliamentary-democratic republic with all democratic rights and freedoms for the people."[99] To judge from the rest of the "Aufruf," the longer the returning exiles dwelt on the crimes of the Nazi past, the more skeptical they would become regarding the wisdom of a postwar German democracy.

The Soviets and their German Communist allies did not differ from the Americans and the British in their initial determination to impose a harsh occupation policy to ensure that Nazism would be crushed. At the outset, the still United Nations agreed that the goal was a denazified and democratic Germany as well as trials of those accused of war crimes and crimes against humanity.[100] In calling for equality before the law, a purge of Nazi personnel in the educational and research institutions, education concerning "the barbaric character of the Nazi race theory," academic and artistic freedom, and "recognition of the duty for reparations and compensation ["Anerkennung der Pflicht zur Wiedergutmachung"] to other peoples for the damage done to them by the Hitler aggression," the "Aufruf" echoed Western occupation policies. Yet it also envisaged that a "block of antifascist parties" including Communists, Social Democrats, and the Center Party would be the "firm foundation" on which Nazism would be eliminated and a democratic regime established.[101]

Perhaps, given the deep bitterness felt by Social Democrats toward the Communists for their role in Weimar, twelve years of Nazi propaganda about "Jewish bolshevism," and the enormous hatreds left over from the war on the Eastern Front, there was little likelihood that even the most democratically inclined German Communist would have found willing partners in a "bloc of antifascist parties." The leaders of the democratic left such as Kurt Schumacher remained on the scene, and they held very critical and skeptical views of the Communists' renewed professions of support for democracy. Communist success in the postwar years required that the Social Democratic leaders of the Weimar era either not remember the Communist attacks of the Third Period or the Hitler-Stalin pact, or remember but be willing to forgive and forget in view of the Soviet contribution to the defeat of Nazism. Yet the policies of the Soviet occupying authorities and the returning Communist exiles further reduced what little likelihood there was of postwar cooperation among the German antifascists. Their postwar actions confirmed their critics' arguments that Communist antifascism contained a series of justifications for imposing a second totalitarian dictatorship on Germany.

For the Communists, power meant a monopoly on interpretation of the past. To judge by their numbers and the political power of their authors, interpretations of recent history became a very high priority. By December 1945 the Soviet- and KPD-controlled presses had printed 50,000 copies of Walter Ulbricht's wartime analysis of the Nazi regime, *Die Legende vom Deutschen Sozialismus* (The Legend of German Socialism).[102] Another 300,000 had been published by January 1947.[103] The book was reissued in the 1950s under the title *Der Faschistische Deutsche Imperialismus (1933–1945)* (Fascist German Imperialism, (1933–1945).[104] Its third edition alone, published in 1956, amounted to an additional 340,000 copies. *Die Legende vom Deutschen Sozialismus* was the canonical text of the East German analysis of the Nazi regime. It displayed the continuity of Communist antifascism from Weimar to the postwar era.

The original title, "The Legend of German Socialism," indicated Ulbricht's intention to refute the notion that "National Socialism" had anything to do with "socialism," and instead to assert the close links between the leading Nazis and leading German industrialists and bankers. Nazism was neither "national" or "socialist" but was instead the *Todfiend* (deadly enemy) of the German people. It was the "open terroristic rule of the most reactionary, chauvinistic, and imperialistic elements of German finance capital."[105] By using the term "fascism" in place of "National Socialism" or "Nazi," Ulbricht presented the Hitler regime as one example of a general capitalist crisis rather than as a product of specific features of German history and society. The force of the term "fascism," ubiquitous in Communist discourse since the 1920s, was not diminished by the fact that the Nazi regime had been defeated by a coalition led by the Soviet Union and the two leading capitalist democracies.

Yet, as a German Communist, Ulbricht placed Nazism back in the continuities of German history. "Hitler fascism" represented the "coalescence, development, and deepening of all that was reactionary in German history." It was the endpoint of a series of defeats for democratic forces. In the Peasant War and the Reformation, in 1848, and again in 1918–19, the forces of reaction had repeatedly enhanced their position and defeated the forces of progress.[106] Democratic forces in Germany had been unable to achieve a victorious bourgeois-democratic revolution from within. Hence, German national unity was delayed, and attained only under the direction of the reactionary Junkers. The leadership of the working class proved itself unable to assume its historic task of destroying German imperialism in 1914, while a revolutionary party was not yet in place in 1918 to lead a mass struggle for a revolutionary solution to the crisis of imperialism and the nation.[107] Yet if this Marxist variant of the German *Sonderweg* was correct, the case against capitalism in general would appear to be considerably weakened.

Ulbricht was aware of how history served as a source of both justification and legitimation. He placed the blame for the division between the Communists and the Social Democrats in Weimar completely on the SPD.[108] "Under the influence of the anticommunist witch-hunt fostered by monopoly capital," Social Democrats had turned against popular action, ruptured the unity of the working class, and thus prevented the power of monopoly capital from being broken. "The fascist dictatorship could have been prevented" if the Social Democrats had mobilized "the common power of the workers' organizations" and used their positions in government to "break the power of the reactionaries."[109] The implication for politics after 1945 was clear: to the extent to which the Social Democrats fought the Communists and made their peace with a reformed capitalism, they were repeating their Weimar errors. Those, primarily the Social Democrats, who aimed at a reform capitalism were simply repeating earlier mistakes. Ulbricht's text was a model of ideological flexibility. If the Communists had been right about everything in the past, they should govern, alone if necessary, in the future. If only a powerful few had victimized the hapless Germans, the way was clear for Communist appeals to the German nation.

*Die Legende* had another important, less rarely noted effect. The more Ulbricht focused on capitalist elites, the less heavily the burden of responsibility and guilt lay on the "millions and millions" of people mentioned in the KPD "Aufruf" of June 1945. Ulbricht placed responsibility for Nazism on "three hundred German arms industrialists and leaders of banks" who had sought a way out of Weimar's economic crisis by supporting the Nazis.[110] These "traitors to the national interest of the German people" were responsible for Hitler's seizure of power and for both World Wars.[111] The corollary to the view that the Nazis and the capitalists were traitors to the nation was that it was the Communists, not the Nazis, who represented the nation. For Ulbricht, coming to terms with the Nazi past obviously meant eliminating capitalism. Everything else was empty rhetoric. The result of that view was to acquit the "millions and millions" of Germans of the accusations of shared guilt and responsibility hurled at them in the "Aufruf" and by the Moscow émigrés. Indictment of the powerful few offered absolution to the victimized and powerless masses, who could now participate in building a socialist, antifascist democracy.

Ulbricht's analysis of anti–Semitism and the Jewish catastrophe remained within the economistic and instrumentalist conceptions of the 1930s and wartime 1940s. He wrote that after 1933, "Hitler fascism" began with the destruction of the Communist and Social Democratic parties and trade unions, as well as with pogroms against the Jews. The anti-Jewish measures spread racial hatred "as preparation for the planned annihilation of members of other peoples in war."[112] In his references to the death camps, he did not mention that their primary purpose was the destruction of European Jewry. Instead, he wrote of "mass annihilation of the civilian population and the prisoners of war in Poland and in the occupied Soviet territories" and referred to "piles of corpses, mass graves, ovens for burning human beings to which millions of innocent men, women, and children fell victim."[113] Ulbricht directed his sympathy and admiration to the Soviet Union, both the primary victim of the Nazis and the primary source of deliverance from them.[114]

In the first postwar years of what we could call the Nuremberg interregnum, Ulbricht and his colleagues did focus on mass support for Nazism and hence complicity in its crimes. On June 25, 1945, Ulbricht spoke to the first meeting of Communist functionaries of the KPD's Berlin organization. "Imperialist conquest . . . race hatred . . . wars of annihilation against other peoples" had led to catastrophe for Germany.[115] The outcome of the war "had demonstrated the superiority of the Soviet democracy over Nazi tyranny" and justified those who had supported the October Revolution of 1917.[116] Victory over Nazism could also "have been a great victory of our German people had they understood how to use the military weakness of the Hitler regime to overthrow the Nazi regime by themselves. The tragedy of the German people consists in the fact that they obeyed a band of criminals. That is the most awful and frightful thing about it all! The recognition of this guilt is the precondition for our people's definitive break with the reactionary past and for decisively taking a new path."[117] Four times in his speech Ulbricht turned to the issue of *Mitverantwortung*. The Germans' "shared responsibility" lay in permitting the Nazis to take power; indulging "propaganda of hatred against the French, Polish, Russian, and English people"; gullibly permitting themselves to be deceived; slavishly obeying "the commands of a band of war criminals"; applauding Hitler's victories; and thinking themselves "superior to other peoples."[118] Ulbricht flatly asserted that the Nazi crimes were possible because "the German working class and the productive parts of the population failed before history."[119] Only when "our people are filled with shame for having "allowed these barbaric crimes to take place" could they "summon the inner power to take a new, a democratic, a progressive path, one which alone can secure the future of the nation."[120] Certainly such a nationwide admission of shame was desirable and necessary for taking a new path.

It is important to grasp the ambivalence of Communist emotions and ideology during the Nuremberg interregnum evident in Ulbricht's statements. All of the German Communist's experience since the 1920s had made painfully clear that the overwhelming majority of the Germans despised both German and Russian communism, that "millions and millions" of Germans had in fact supported the Nazi regime, and that thousands and thousands had particpated in its crimes. Even if postwar Germans expressed their shame over Nazi crimes, why should anyone believe such belated self-serving protestations? Indeed, when the Communists spoke of German guilt and shame, they seemed to buttress their case against democratic rule by these same Germans in the near future. Protest against "antifascist" rule by postwar Germans could be and was attacked as "objectively" and often "subjectively" fascist. Those who called for popular rule by postwar Germans opposed to an antifascist regime were thus calling for rule by millions who had supported Nazism. In this way, memories of Nazism fostered distrust of popular democracy and legitimated "antifascist" dictatorship.

Ulbricht and his comrades had it both ways. On the one hand, by expropriating capitalists and large landowners, they had eliminated fascism's roots. On the other hand, the imposition of a harsh dictatorship was nevertheless necessary because, notwithstanding Marxist orthodoxy about capitalism and fascism, the German Communists were well aware how strong Nazism's mass support had been. Understandably, the Communists were reluctant to state publicly that their dictatorship rested on the fear and mistrust of the majority of Germans.[121] Vivid memories of past mass support for the Nazis, conveyed in the public language of German guilt and shame, far from deepening a willingness to "dare more democracy" deepened the Communists' willingness to establish a second German dictatorship.

The gap between the Communists' professions of democratic intent and their actual dictatorial practice became a central theme of the Cold War. Yet the problem of how to govern a people so deeply compromised by the extent of their support for a criminal regime was a, if not *the*, central political and moral dilemma of postwar politics in both Germany. During the Nuremberg interregnum, the Communists spoke the discourse of the Popular Front, Pieck's "Neue Weg" speech, and wartime antifascism, and avoided the radicalism of a rapid transition to socialism.[122] They denounced racism and supported the reeducation of German youth.[123] They did focus attention on the centrality of the Soviet contribution to the war.[124] Yet they also noted that the Western Allies had refused Nazi offers of a separate peace "because the democratic Great Powers were willing to fight together [with the Soviet Union] until Nazism was destroyed, and to work most closely together after the war as well."[125] They spoke of the "moral duty of the German people" to make restitution (*Wiedergutmachung*) for the material damage done to the Soviet Union. Restitution to the peoples harmed by the Nazis was a "matter of honor of every antifascist, a matter of honor for every German."[126] But the Communists did not talk about those things which troubled their wartime allies in the West: the attack on "social fascism" of the Third Period, the purges and terror of the Stalin regime, and the Hitler-Stalin pact.[127] Nor did they recall or emphasize in their recollections their fleeting moments of solidarity with the Jews.

Before and after 1945, the Soviet Union remained at the center of Communist narratives of antifascism. The Jews were competitors for scarce political and emotional resources. Their fate did not come close to matching the hold that the drama of the Soviet Union had on the hearts and minds of German Communists. While the Communists noted the racist character of the war on the Eastern Front—although they usually called it an "imperialist" war—they rarely if ever mentioned the Jewish catastrophe and never addressed its central role in Nazi policy. The trauma of Nazism and the redemptive Soviet victory deepened their Communist, and often Stalinist, beliefs. Beyond the importance which any coherent ideological framework has in a confusing period, the Soviet victory appeared to add the weight of history's judgment. In this regard, Walter Ulbricht was an orthodox Hegelian in his respect for those on whom the cunning of history had bestowed victory. European Jewry had been the big loser of World War II. As we will see, the Holocaust did not fit into the Communists' plans for their postwar commemorative victory parades.

We have seen that interest, ideology, and experience combined to keep the persecution of European Jewry on the margins of the dominant current of German communism. Continuity of German Communist tradition before and after 1945 was one the most striking aspects of the multiple restorations of the postwar era. Instrumentalist theoretical legacies and long-standing pejorative association of the Jews with capitalism, the primacy of the romance of Soviet suffering and victory over the tragedy of unmitigated Jewish loss, and an eagerness to emerge as the real representatives of the oft-defeated German nation had all kept the Jewish question on the margin of concern.

In the wartime German Communist emigration in Mexico City, distance from Stalin's Moscow and an intense interaction between German Communists and Jewish émigrés brought the Jewish question into the center of concern for the first and only time in German communism's twentieth-century history. It is to this brief and soon repressed moment that we now turn.

# 3

## From Periphery to Center: German Communists and the Jewish Question, Mexico City, 1942–1945

For Communists, as Marx put it in the Theses on Feuerbach, the point was to change the world. The experience of German Communist exiles in Mexico City indicated that the world could also change the Communists. Or at least exile could bring to the fore elements of Communist traditions which had remained in the background in Europe and in Moscow exile. Mexico City was the second leading center of the Communist exile during World War II. Its distance from Moscow, the experience of the Popular Front years in Paris, the beginnings of Jewish persecution in Europe, and the large number of European Jewish refugees created the preconditions for the most extensive discussions of the Jewish question in the history of German Communism.[1] Communists set out to change the world. Sometimes, in the new and unsettling context of emigration, the world changed them. The result was a new emphasis on elements of their beliefs which had remained on the margins of Communist antifascism in Europe. Paul Merker, the only member of the KPD Politburo not in Moscow or in a German prison, joined other German Communist émigrés to bring the issue of Jewish suffering from the periphery to the center of the narratives of Communist antifascism for the first—and only—time in its history.

Timing, politics, and geography made Mexico City the second major pole of the German Communist emigration in the wartime years.[2] The

Mexican government was grateful for the support that German Communists had given to the Spanish Republic during the civil war. For Communists fleeing Nazism, Mexico City was part of the western route to Moscow that led across the Pacific. After the Japanese attack on Pearl Harbor, that route was closed as well. The United States, never eager to offer haven to Communists, was even less inclined to do so after the signing of the Hitler-Stalin pact of August 1939.

At the beginning of the 1930s, there were about 20,000 overwhelmingly Eastern Europeans Jews and fewer than 100 German-speaking Jews in Mexico. By 1943, the Jewish community in Mexico had grown to 25,000, about 3,000 of whom had fled from Germany or Austria.[3] Typically, the Communists had an impact out of proportion to their small numbers. The German-speaking Communists formed two major front organizations: the Bewegung Freies Deutschland in Mexiko (BFD, or Movement for a Free Germany in Mexico), and the Lateinamerikanischen Komitee der Freien Deutschen, Sitz Mexiko (LAK, or Latin American Committee of Free Germans in Mexico). The former East German historian Wolfgang Kießling estimates that by the end of 1944, the BFD had 400 members and about 800 sympathizers and participants.[4] The West German historian Fritz Pohle estimates that there were only 200 German Communist émigrés in all of Latin America with between 2,000 and 4,000 sympathizers and supporters. He places the number of German Communists in Mexican exile at 60, over half of whom were "of Jewish origin."[5] As a result, non-Jewish "political" German refugees became a minority facing an increasingly self-conscious Jewish majority. In both Moscow and Mexico City, German Communist exiles confronted Nazism's Jewish victims. Despite a very similar ethnic mix of German Communists, Jews, and Eastern Europeans in both capitals of exile, the contrasting political context of Mexican exile and the distance from the rigid orthodoxy and terror of Stalin's wartime Moscow created the preconditions for a very different kind of Communist discussion of Jewish-related matters.

Between summer 1940 and spring 1942, an impressive collection of the literary and intellectual elite of the KPD had escaped from Vichy France via Spain, Portugal, and Casablanca in Morocco, then on to asylum in Mexico. In exile, political activity meant writing and publishing. In November 1941 the early arrivals, many of whom were Jewish, established the BFD, the journal *Freies Deutschland* (in Spanish, *Alemania Libre*), and the Heinrich Heine Club.[6] Anna Seghers was elected president of the Heine Club.[7] Beginning with the third issue of *Freies Deutschland*, Alexander Abusch (1902–1982), former editor of the KPD's underground newspaper *Die Rote Fahne*, became editor in chief.[8] *Freies Deutschland* had a circulation of between 3,500 and 4,000. It published essays and reviews by German Communist émigrés such as Ernst Bloch, Leon Feuchtwanger, André Simone, Egon Erwin Kisch, Jürgen Kuczynski, Heinrich Mann, Ludwig Renn, and Anna Seghers; statements from the Moscow-based National Committee for a Free Germany (NKFD); and essays on the Jewish question from lesser-known figures such as Rudolf Feistmann, Leo Katz, and Leo Zuckermann. The journal also had contact with German Communist émigrés in London and New York, as well as with émigrés throughout Latin America. A biweekly newspaper, the *Demokratische Post,* founded in 1943, attained a circulaton of between 2,000 and 3,000 and offered local news aimed at the German colony in Mexico City. In mid-1942 the group founded a publishing house, El Libro Libre (The Free Book).[9] In December 1942 and January 1943, with the writer Ludwig Renn as president and Paul Merker as secretary, the exile Communists formed the LAK to coordinate and lead antifascist efforts in Latin America. By 1944, the organization claimed a membership of between 2,000 and 4,000 throughout Latin America.[10]

One very public expression of Jewish identity and consciousness in Mexico was participation in Menorah, an organization of German-speaking Jewish refugees formed in 1940. Rudolf Feistmann, Erich Jungmann, and Leo Zuckermann were among the German Communists of Jewish origin who belonged.[11] Menorah sponsored evenings of chamber music, poetry reading, and political lectures and discussions; offered social welfare assistance, legal advice, and medical care to its members; and sought Mexican travel visas for Jews still trapped in concentration camps in Vichy France.[12] It was a center of expanding Jewish self-consciousness within the German-speaking Communist exile.[13] This mixture of intellectual talent and distance from Moscow, as well as the creative tension and desperation of exile and the dreadful news arriving from Europe, all contributed to the new emphasis on the Jewish question. So, however, did the boldness of Paul Merker, in most things an utterly orthodox German Communist and Comintern agent.

Paul Merker (1894–1969), the central figure in the key controversies over the Jewish question in the history of twentieth-century German communism, was himself not Jewish. He was born into a working-class Protestant family on February 2, 1894, in the town of Oberlößnitz near Dresden in the state of Saxony.[14] He left grade school (*Volksschule*) at the age of fourteen, then worked in hotels in Dresden and Hamburg until 1914. In 1911 he joined the hotel and restaurant workers' union. He fought in and was further radicalized by World War I.[15] In Dresden, Merker participated in the aborted revolution of 1918–19. He joined the German Communist Party in 1920, when it fused with the radical socialist USPD (Unabhängige Sozialistische Partei Deutschland), and worked in the Central Committee's Office of Union Affairs. In 1925 he was elected as a KPD representative to the Prussian state legislature from the district of East Düsseldorf, and held the seat until 1932. Within the KPD, Merker supported Ernst Thälmann's drive for leadership in 1925, and with it the Stalinization of the KPD. In 1926 he was elected to the Central Committee and then to the Politburo, the real center of power in the party. There he continued to focus on trade union matters.[16] In Moscow in 1926 he began his work in the Comintern. In 1927, also in Moscow, he was elected to the Central Executive of the Rote Gewerkschaftsinternationale, or RGI (Red Trade Union International) and was elected chairman in 1929. In that capacity he worked closely with and befriended the Moscow RGI functionary Solomon Lozovsky, one of the many Jewish comrades Merker would get to know through his Comintern activities.[17]

In Germany, Merker was an enthusiastic supporter of the Communists' attack on German Social Democrats, especially on the Social Democratic chief of police in Berlin, Karl Friedrich Zörgiebel, who had banned political demonstrations following the outbreak of violence between Nazis and Communists and between Communists and Social Democrats.[18] When, in March 1930, the KPD line turned toward building a "popular front from below," that is, an alliance of Communists with Social Democratic workers against the "counterrevolutionary" SPD leadership, he was made the scapegoat for the errors of the previous KPD attack on social democracy in general, and was relieved of his functions in the Politburo and the RGI.

In 1931 the KPD leadership sent Merker to Moscow. The Comintern and the Red Trade Union International sent him and his companion and future second wife, Margarete Menzel-Merker, to the United States. Under the aliases Paul and Margarete Franke, the two stayed in the United States from 1931 to 1933. Merker attended meetings of the Central Committee of the American Communist Party, met and befriended the party leader Earl Browder, and published several articles in the party's theoretical journal under the aliases Max Fischer and Siegfried Willner.[19] He helped to organize the CIO in the steel, textile, and automobile workers' unions, and "took an active part" in miners' strikes in Pennsylvania, Indiana, Ohio, and Kentucky, demonstrations of the unemployed in Pittsburgh and Chicago, and the hunger marches on Washington, D.C.[20] Merker returned to Moscow in June 1933, worked as the director of the "Anglo-American division" of the RGI, and returned to Berlin to engage in underground anti-Nazi activity in 1933 and 1934.[21] In 1935 he attended the Seventh Congress of the Comintern in Moscow and the KPD's ensuing Brussels Conference. From 1935 to 1939, along with Walter Ulbricht and Franz Dahlem (1892–1981), he directed the KPD's Auslandsekretariat (Foreign Secretariat), which briefly resided in Prague before moving to Paris from 1935 to 1939.[22] In Paris, Merker replaced his earlier attacks on social democracy with enthusiasm for the Popular Front, began an important friendship with the exiled German writer Heinrich Mann, and shared exile with the growing number of Communist as well as Jewish refugees.[23]

Merker's reaction to the news of the Hitler-Stalin pact became a subject of considerable controversy. While thousands abandoned the Communists over the pact, Merker remained loyal. Nevertheless, Anton Ackermann, then in Paris before going to Moscow, reported to the KPD and Comintern officials in Moscow that, upon hearing of the pact, Merker exploded in anger and said that "it was always the same story. What the foreign Communists build up is again destroyed by the Soviet Union's foreign policy."[24] Merker insisted that Ackermann's charge was false. Nevertheless, the Ackermann denunciation would later be used against him to support accusations of insuffcient loyalty to Moscow.

The pact included Stalin's promise to Hitler to put an end to anti-Nazi activities of the Communist parties, and thus an end to Communist denunication of the Nazi attack on the Jews.[25] For German Communist refugees in Vichy France, it also meant agreeing to enter internment camps, first in Paris, then in Vernet and Les Milles in southern France, from 1939 to 1941.[26] Merker, Franz Dahlem, and others were interned at Vernet. Merker was able to escape. He tried without success to free Dahlem and others still held there, and sought to gain travel visas for himself, Margarete Menzel-Merker, and other German Communists to get out of southern France and go to the Soviet Union via Mexico. Escape from Vichy for Merker and other German Communists cut off by the war from Moscow was made possible by the assistance of the American leftist Noel Field, a "Madame Esmiol" responsible for visas in the Marseilles city administration; officials at the Mexican consulate in Marseilles; Hizem, a Jewish refugee organization in New York; and the Antifascist Refugee Committee, also in New York.[27] In May 1942 Merker traveled from Marseilles to Oran to Casablanca, where he boarded the Portuguese ship *Guiana*. He arrived in Mexico City in June 1942. Merker's travel expenses were paid by the Antifascist Refugee Committee in New York. At the top levels of the East German government in the first years of the Cold War, these apparently unimportant details of Merker's escape from Europe became much-discussed elements in accusations of Western—and Jewish—wartime conspiracies.

Exile gave Merker time to write and reflect. Like other political exiles, he used the opportunity to continue to settle scores with his old political enemies, the German Social Democrats. He also, however, thought critically about what the Communists had and had not done regarding the persecution of European Jewry. In 1944, in *Das Dritte Reich und Sein Ende* (The Third Reich and Its End), the second volume of his major work on Nazism, *Deutschland—Sein oder Nicht Sein?* Merker addressed the shortcomings of German socialism regarding the Jewish question. He concentrated his criticism on the shortcomings of August Bebel's 1893 definition of anti-Semitism as "the socialism of fools," for anti-Semitism was "already at that time much more than that. It was an instrument of extreme reaction to educate the people into becoming fools." Merker wrote that it was necessary to focus more sharply on the issue, "to fight it in community with all liberal forces," to attack anti-Semitism "already within the imperialist-capitalist era," and to make this effort an essential component of the struggle for democracy in Germany.[28] Speaking the language of left-wing communism, Merker asserted that "the increasing opportunist degeneration of numerous leaders of German social democracy" in the era of imperialism had "prevented the masses of workers from grasping the importance of the struggle against anti-Semitism." In this way, he continued, German Socialists stood in sharp contrast to the leaders of "French liberalism" such as Émile Zola and Anatole France during the Dreyfus affair. Moreover, German social democracy had "never recognized the enormous importance of the fight against racism and anti-Semitism as had Russian social democracy under Plekhanov's and Lenin's leadership."[29] Although Merker focused his criticism on German social democracy before 1914, its applicability to the KPD of the 1920s and 1930s was easy to discern.

Much later, Merker had further occasion to reflect on the origins of his interest in the Jewish question.[30] In his "Stellungnahme zur Judenfrage" (1956) he recalled the pervasive anti-Semitism in the German officer corps in World War I, as well as the contributions of Jews such as Marx and Rosa Luxemburg to the socialist tradition.[31] The period he spent in the United States left a lasting impression. He recalled meeting "Jewish proletarians in New York and Chicago" and was aware that in New York, "about 75 percent of the members of the CPUSA [American Communist Party] were of Jewish origin," and that Jews constituted a "strong minority" in the textile unions. He recalled Jewish solidarity with blacks fighting "white chauvinism" as well as Jewish support for the American Communist Party and for striking workers.[32] He remembered Jewish families who had hidden him and other Communists, at great personal risk, in Berlin in 1933 and 1934. Both political conviction and personal experience, he wrote, had led him to become "a firm adversary of the murderous anti-Semitism of Hitler fascism." As Nazi anti-Jewish persecution expanded, he recalled, "it became ever more clear to me that the struggle of the German working class against anti-Semitism had been inadequate. It seemed to me to be the particular duty of non-Jewish individuals to decisively speak out against and actively oppose anti-Semitism."[33] These convictions became deeper still in Mexico City. He recalled the assistance of the Jewish refugees in Mexico City who had arrived before many Communists, and who had housed and fed "numerous comrades," helped them to find jobs, befriended them and their families in the Heinrich Heine Club, and through the Menorah organization contributed financially to the founding of *Freies Deutschland* and *Alemania Libre.*[34] Merker could not have been unique in receiving such gestures of support. His uniqueness among Communist leaders lay in reciprocating with an expansive and inclusive understanding of the meaning of antifascism.

Before turning to Merker's writings on Jewish issues, I want to draw attention briefly to his arguments in favor of the alliance between the Soviet Union and the West. From his first essay in *Freies Deutschland* in August 1942 to the last months of the war, Merker appealed for Allied unity against the Nazis.[35] In October 1942 he wrote that "the free Germans stand on the ground of the Atlantic Charter and the English-Russian mutual assistance treaty."[36] In January 1944 he criticized those "anti-Nazi Germans" who still failed to grasp the basic difference between the "war of the imperialist great powers of 1914–18 and the ongoing democratic war of liberation of the Allies" and again stressed the importance of "cementing the alliance" between the United States, the Soviet Union, Great Britain, and China.[37] In the last months of the war, Merker again stressed the need for Allied unity in the face of rumors of Nazi diplomatic efforts to sign a separate peace with the United States and Great Britain to establish an anti-Soviet front. They were "not enemies but allies" against the common Nazi enemy.[38] In

March 1945 Merker and the leadership of the Free Germans in Mexico sent their "greetings to all soldiers of the United Nations" whose fight for democratic freedom in the world was simultaneously a struggle to ensure that "at last Germany will be liberated from the dark legacy of a century-long [political] reaction."[39] These repeated assertions of Allied unity were both fully in line with Soviet policy and conducive to fostering the wartime illusion that the Soviet Union was in fact one of the democracies at war with Nazi Germany. After 1947, however, when the Soviet Union returned to familiar denunciations of Western imperialism, Merker's paper trail of wartime praise for the Western democracies would come back to haunt him.

Merker's praise for Roosevelt and Churchill could be written off as a dutiful expression of Soviet wartime diplomacy. But his Mexican writings on Jewish matters struck a more dissonant note. His articles in *Freies Deutschland* between 1942 and 1945, and his two-volume analysis of Nazi Germany, *Deutschland—Sein oder Nicht Sein?* published in Mexico City in 1944, were the only published works by a leading member of the KPD—and then, after 1946, of its successor, the Socialist Unity Party—in which the Jewish question occupied center stage in a Communist analysis of Nazism.[40]

Merker's first Mexican essay on the Jewish question was also his most important. "Hitler's Anti-Semitism and Us" appeared in the October 1942 issue of *Freies Deutschland*.[41] It opened:

> If all of the German rivers flowed with ink, and all the German forests were made of quill pens, they would not suffice to describe the immeasurable crimes which Hitler fascism has committed against the Jewish people. Where is there today a Jewish family from Germany which has not been robbed and deeply humiliated, whose members have not been imprisoned in concentration camps, murdered, or driven to suicide?[42]

Merker wrote, "The campaign of extermination of Hitler fascism" against German Jews had been "only the beginning." It had been "extended to all of the countries and areas conquered by Hitler." Its victims "number in the hundreds of hundreds of thousands."[43] In conventional Communist terms, he wrote that for the "most reactionary part of the ruling German monopolists and large landowners, anti-Semitism was nothing but a means to enrich themselves."[44] Yet his analysis did not end with the conventional instrumentalist framework. He understood what other leading German Communists had refused to acknowledge, namely, that Nazi racial ideology and policy had an autonomous significance beyond the demands of capitalist class interest.

Like the Moscow exiles, he spoke of the responsibility of the German people. Unlike them, however, he specified that this burden was a result of having "permitted the crimes of the ruling class against the Jewish people to take place." This responsibility extended not only to the Nazis but also to "the reactionary classes, the monopolists and the Junkers," the intellectual advocates of anti-Semitism, and the politicians of Weimar who had "capitulated to reaction." Those antifascists who had "continuously placed their freedom and their lives at risk" were "innocent of responsibility for the horrible consequences of anti-Semitism," and hence were plausible allies for Jewish refugees.[45] Merker stressed that anti-Semitism was "the darkest reaction" and could "never be progressive." The position of a "cultivated individual toward anti-Semitism" was the indicator of whether or not he was "progressive or reactionary." The "progressive forces" which fought "monopolistic, imperialist despotism" stood "on the side and among the ranks of Jewish fellow citizens. Their mortal enemy, their struggle, and their destiny were identical."[46]

Merker went on to assert that the future of the German Jews was "inseparable from the liberation struggle of the workers and the middle class." Even members of the German-Jewish bourgeoisie, from bankers of the nineteenth century to Jewish capitalists in Weimar, had became victims of anti-Semitism.[47] By contrast, he presented a bright future for Jews in the Soviet Union, which he described as a country in which anti-Semitism was actively opposed by the state. Indeed, Merker argued that the Bolshevik Revolution of 1917, by destroying tsarism and capitalism, had brought about "complete equality," religious freedom, and social advancement for Jews in the Soviet Union.[48]

Merker noted with apparent approval the "essential strengthening of Jewish national feeling." The "question of a Jewish national state," he wrote, should be handled at the peace conference following victory over Nazi Germany, "regardless of all previous principles, considerations, and prejudices, in accord with the wishes of the Jews." In addition, the civil rights of Jews in all the countries from which they had been expelled must be restored, and "the complete national equality of the Jewish people with other nationalities in the various countries" should be recognized. Though Merker did not say so explicitly, such views would require the Communists to revise explicitly the denial of Jewish nationhood enshrined in Stalin's essay on the national question. The need to subordinate everything to "the victory of the Allies over the Axis" did not preclude "clarity about what the Jewish people . . . could expect from a future regime in Germany . . . So it is our view that above all, non-Jewish antifascists, among whom I include myself, must decisively be engaged in support of the Jewish people who are in such distress as a consequence of [the Nazis'] worldwide pogrom." Such engagement was in the interests of "their Jewish fellow citizens" as well as of "their own fight for an international solution to problems created by the persecution of the Jews."[49] Here Merker was clearly moving beyond support for proposals for a Jewish state within the Soviet Union to hinting at support for a Jewish state wherever Jews would wish to found it. No other leading German Communist had so emphatically asserted a commonality of interests between the Jews and the Communists or support for founding of a Jewish state.

Merker added that the first decrees of "the coming German people's government" should include making anti-Semitism and all race hatred illegal. Special courts should handle anti-Semitic propaganda and action and punish those responsible for the persecution of European Jewry. Jewish citizenship rights should be automatically restored. Expenses for Jews who wished to return to Germany should be publicly funded, as should the emigration costs of Jewish citizens of German nationality who wished to go to another country. A new government should offer *Wiedergutmachung* (restitution) for "the economic damage done to Jewish citizens," whether or not the recipients decided to return to Germany. Returning Jewish refugees should be given apartments, and state officials should be charged with their economic security until they were able to pursue a profession or trade of their choice. The cost of educating the children who had been forced into emigration or into camps should be free. Merker sought to assure "our Jewish friends and comrades in struggle" that a new democratic regime would find ways to "destroy anti-Semitism in Germany forever."[50] These measures would both serve the interests of justice and facilitate the reconstitution of Jewish life in post-Nazi Germany.

"Hitler's Anti-Semitism and Us" evoked critical letters to *Freies Deutschland* and a response by Merker which appeared in the March 1943 issue.[51] The objections revealed the continued association of Jews with capitalism and the limits of understanding of Nazi ideology and policy in the Communist exile community. First, Merker's critics complained that he wanted to "give back millions to Jewish bankers and big capitalists." He responded that naturally "the Rothschilds" would not regain their monopolies, but the material compensation of the Jews would have to be sufficient to make possible "full, equal reintegration into the economic and social life of Germany in as short a time as possible." Second, a reader objected that compensation should take into account the class position of victims. Merker responded that "the Nazi gangsters and the Aryan plutocrats had plundered all Jews regardless of their class position." In matters of compensation, he continued, neither the class position nor the moral character of the individual could play a role. "Only the extent of material and moral damage" was decisive.[52]

Third, other readers asked why only the Jews would receive *Wiedergutmachung*. Didn't the politically persecuted—that is, the Communists, who were "fighters" against fascism—have an even greater claim? The differences and similarities between the persecution of Communists and Jews touched an especially sensitive nerve. Merker stressed the distinctions. The Jews, he responded, were persecuted because they were a "defenseless, national, religious or castelike minority" that "Hitler fascism" was using to divert attention from its own plans for world domination. Without restitution and the destruction of anti-Semitism, "the victory of freedom and the securing of democracy is impossible." The Jewish people, he said, had the same right to restitution for the damage done to them as did all the nations Hitler had invaded and oppressed. The Communists, by contrast, were persecuted because of what they did, not who they were. Those who had been punished because of their political views were not being persecuted as a "national, religious or castelike minority." They had volunteered to fight the Nazis. "Antifascist fighters" thus could not "expect material compensation for the sacrifices that result" from their voluntary commitments. Their compensation lay in "every successful battle and the final victory [over Nazism] and the erection of a democratic power." As we will see, Merker's distinctions between political and Jewish victims of Nazism would prove highly controversial in postwar discussions of the hierarchy of "fighters against" and "victims of" Nazism. Finally, in response to a reader who asked why he focused only on the German Jews and not on the Jews of countries Hitler had invaded, Merker replied that "everything" he said applied in equal measure for the Jewish population of those countries.[53]

Merker insisted that postwar economic change as well as political democratization were necessary but not sufficient conditions to attain a "moral overcoming of Nazism."[54] It was crucial to recognize, he wrote in October 1943, that because the Germans had "tolerated these crimes, they have come to share responsibility in them. Democratic transformation alone cannot compensate for or balance this shared responsibility. That can be accomplished only by the recognition of the moral obligation for restitution [*Wiedergutmachung*] of the damage caused by the Hitler armies." A future democratic German government should voluntarily assume "the moral obligation for restitution."[55] The corollary to his argument was that a postwar German government which refused to do so would not be fulfilling its moral obligations.

Like their comrades in Moscow, the German Communists in Mexico expressed their deep disappointment over the absence of an effective German resistance. Merker argued that the failures of German antifascism before 1945 made restitution after 1945 all the more necessary. Yet in contrast to the exiles in Moscow and elsewhere, Merker was more willing to include the Communist leadership publicly in the circle of those deserving criticism. An exchange of letters in May and September 1945 in *Freies Deutschland* between Merker and Wilhelm Koenen, also a member of the KPD in Weimar, and a future member of the SED Central Committee from 1946 until his death in 1964, brought these issues to the fore. The question at hand was whether there were "progressive forces" in Germany at the end of the war.[56] Koenen denounced the "reactionary role of the German people" and the "betrayal of the German proletarians" who had "closed their eyes" to the crimes taking place and instead had obeyed on command.[57] Although Merker agreed that the Germans, including the German working class, bore a "shared responsibility" for the crimes of the Hitler regime, he believed that "the guilt is also borne by those who made a timely and unified action against Nazism before 1933 impossible." In this category he included the anti-Nazi political leadership, meaning the Communist leaders as well. "We anti-Nazi emigrants" share with "the whole German people" the responsibility for the Hitler regime, he wrote, "You and I," he told Koenen, "belong to this working class and thus have to accept before the world our share of the responsibility for the fiasco of its struggle."[58]

Charging the anti-Nazi political leadership with this burden led Merker to more optimistic views of the prospects for postwar democracy. Despite the absence of a German anti-Nazi revolution, he declared that "my faith in the good and decent core of the our people [and] in the German working class remains unshaken." Having experienced the dangers of underground struggle under the Nazi dictatorship, he could "dismiss the German worker today simply as a petty bourgeois cretin and class traitor." Nor could one explain the absence of resistance with reference to "the ideological consequences of the Thirty Years' War and to the mistaken political and national mistaken development of the German people." Such an approach was "undialectical" and neglected both the "revolutionary achievements and successes for freedom" as well as the particular character of modern German capitalism and imperialism. This "one-sidedness" also amounted to

a dangerous exoneration of those who really are responsible for the tragedy of our people—traitorous leaders of former political and trade union organizations, monopoly capitalists, the Junkers, and the

Nazi gangsters. The shared responsibility of the German working people in the crimes of the Hitler regime consists above all in the fact that they allowed it to come to power, and that they offered almost no visible resistance to the Nazi attack on the Soviet Union. The guilt however, lies with those who made it impossible to take timely and united action against the Nazis before 1933.[59]

If the causes were found so far in the past, and if all of German history was merely the prehistory of Nazism, then the proximate issues of human agency and moral responsibility during the end of Weimar and in the Nazi era would be lost under the weight of retrospective historical determinism. Those who denounced German history, and the Germans in general, made it impossible to affix individual guilt and responsibility. Moreover, if the Germans were a nation of racists and murderers, then clearly a dictatorship of virtue resting on a political-moral elite—the Communist Party, for example—which had somehow broken out of these continuities was essential. Perhaps Merker meant only to repeat in veiled form his old denunciations of German Social Democrats. Yet both his protestation of continued faith in "the good and decent core of our people" and his hint that the Communists were also politically fallible undermined the case for imposing a second German dictatorship which rested on the assumption of infallible leaders and a people convicted of collective guilt.

Merker's belief that the Communist leadership did indeed share responsibility for the disasters in Germany was evident in two *Freies Deutschland* essays, "Letter to a Friend: The Movement for a Free Germany and the Future of the Jews" (April 1944) and "The Jews and the New Germany" (October 1945).[60] In "Letter to a Friend," he unequivocally supported the establishment of a Jewish state, as well as efforts to reestablish full citizenship for Jews in a new Germany, should they wish to return. He wrote that the Nazi persecution of the Jews

was possible only because our people, influenced by weak and mistaken leaders, did not recognize and rise up against the enormous danger in time. As a result, we non-Jewish though anti-Nazi Germans

do not have the moral right to express opinions in this matter . . .
The Movement for a Free Germany must, therefore, understand and
respect every expression of suffering, of anger, of hatred and mistrust
of the Jews toward the German people. It must recognize as justified
the desire of German Jews to participate in the construction of their
own national Jewish state.[61]

Presumably not every one of the "weak and mistaken leaders" he had
in mind was a Social Democrat. He appeared more willing than the
Moscow exiles to implicate German Communists in the circle of mis-
calculation and error which had made Nazism possible, and hence to
argue that a German Communist post-Nazi German government would
also carry moral burdens resulting from Nazi crimes.

Merker argued that Jews could be antifascists while also asserting
"their membership in the Jewish world."[62] Zionists could also be members of the BFD. Jewish members represented the interests of German
Jews within the BFD through their work in favor of restitution and
against anti-Semitism. "Through cooperation with non-Jewish German
anti-Nazis," they showed other Jews that "the German people are not
composed only of Nazis and anti-Semites."[63] In other words, Merker
argued that Jews, both Communists and non-Communists, should not
have to subordinate their particular identities to a universalizing logic
of class conflict. In view of Nazi crimes and German nonresistance, the
burden of proof was not on Jews to demonstrate that they were good
Communists but on Germans, including German Communists, to demonstrate to Jews that they were not all anti-Semites.

He then returned to the "fundamental difference between the fate of
antifascist politicians who fell victim to Hitler, and the destiny of the
Jewish population tormented by the Nazis."[64] The former had been
"free to participate in the struggle against the regime or to stand aside."
They joined the resistance voluntarily and "at their own risk." Victory
over Hitler, resulting in a free and democratic Germany, would be their
victory and reward. But the Nazis had not persecuted and murdered
the Jews, who had lived in and contributed so much to Germany for six
hundred years, because of their political views or actions. "Rather, they

met this fate because they were Jews. It was because they are Jews that Hitler declared them to be aliens and treated them as a hostile part of the people."[65] Because non-Jewish Germans had not prevented these crimes, they now had "the duty to recognize the Jews as a national minority" and to make restitution for "the immeasurable moral and economic destruction which the Nazi hordes inflicted on the German Jews" as they would for any other "nation subjugated by Hitler."[66] For Merker, the Jewish catastrophe was cause not only for guilt and shame but also for anger and a sense of loss at the destruction of a German-Jewish Germany he treasured. Facing the dimensions of Germany's loss, seeing that justice was done, and offering restitution were "pre-conditions for a restoration of Germany as a nation of culture" (*Kulturnation*).[67]

Merker had every reason to assume that such arguments were a plausible extension of the Popular Front mentality of the wartime anti-Hitler coalition. Nevertheless, as we have seen, they were not the common coin of wartime statements from the German exiles in Moscow. In that discourse, the proper nouns *Germans* and *Jews* gave way to the abstract, generalizing vocabulary of capitalists, fascists, imperialists, and the nameless victims of fascism. The proper nouns *Soviet Union, Stalin,* and *Red Army* were exceptions that proved the rule. The dominant German Communist antifascist discourse suggested that its exponents were "antifascists" who were only incidentally German and thus only incidentally bound up with the burdens of German history. The concrete, tangible, and specific nature of Merker's vocabulary and arguments, their embeddedness within the history of Germans and Jews, contrasted with the abstractions of orthodox Communist language.

In his last Mexican essay on Jewish matters, published in October 1945, Merker wondered if the military defeat of Nazi Germany would "also lead to a decisive blow against anti-Semitism." That outcome must coincide with the "displacement of the economic and political power of finance capital." His formulation suggested that eliminating capitalism would not necessarily bring about the end of anti-Semitism. A Communist Germany in which anti-Semitism remained was theoretically possible. Coming to terms with the Nazi past meant much more than eliminating capitalism and expropriating the Junkers.[68] Yet again he wrote about the responsibility of the Germans for Nazi crimes. Although he distinguished between the Nazis and the German people, nevertheless, "millions" had become Nazis or their accomplices and had "committed their crimes in the name of Germany." Even German "democrats" could not be absolved of responsibility for the Nazi seizure of power. "Who can dispute that there were repeated opportunities for the German anti-Nazis—if they had reacted in a unified manner—to prevent the construction of Nazi domination in Germany. But these opportunities were never used."[69] It was the Allies, not the German resistance, that had defeated Nazism. Now that the war was over, anti-Nazi leaders had to convey "the full responsibility of the German people for the crimes of the Nazi bandits and thereby as well the justified nature of the demands for restitution [*Wiedergutmachung*] and security raised by the United Nations."[70] Again, he left open the possibility that the KPD could not avoid some portion of the burdens of German responsibility.

On February 2, 1944, at a banquet to celebrate Merker's fiftieth birthday, Vicente Lombardo Toledano, a Mexican labor leader and president of the Latin American Federation of Labor (NCTAL), gave a speech in honor of "two kinds of Germans."[71] Toledano contrasted Marx's enormous positive contributions with Hitler's legacy. He called Merker a true heir of "the great Germany, a legitimate son of Karl Marx" who also represented the best of universal values and brotherhood of the proletariat across all countries. In Mexico City, the German and European refugees had formed a "common family with Mexican antifascists . . . This war had the great benefit that it has made us travel from one part of the world to another." Through personal contact "we have ever more powerfully become brothers with one another."[72] As a result, he, Toledano had come to know the kind of Germany which the Nazis were trying to crush.

In his response to Toledano and others who sang his praises, Merker expressed his gratitude to his "good friend Ernst Thälmann," to the French Gaullists, and to his comrades from the underground struggle in Vichy France; to "my numerous Jewish friends in Germany who, despite their own great danger, hid, sheltered, and helped me and many of my comrades"; to his Mexican friends; and to Margarete Menzel-Merker, "who has stood by my side in illegal struggle and, through her courage and her discretion, protected me and often made the struggle possible."[73] He interpreted his hosts' "friendly honoring" as "the expression of your conviction that the Germans are not [all] Nazi beasts," and that in Germany and in the emigration there were "German freedom fighters who have placed themselves in a front with the United Nations." Because these freedom fighters "know how large the guilt is which rests on the German people," they called for Germany's unconditional capitulation and voluntarily supported restitution for Nazi crimes. "Among German anti-Nazis, added to the pain over the crimes of the Nazis is shame over [their] deeply wounded national pride. Hence, they will all the more ruthlessly bring the Nazis to justice." Merker and his comrades saw the victories of the Soviet, American, and English armies and Tito's partisans in Yugoslavia as "decisive forces working also for the liberation of the German people." In the postwar years, he predicted, the German anti-Nazis would be "the vanguard fighters working for the destruction of anti-Semitism and to secure a genuine freedom and equality, and an unlimited self-determination for the Jewish population."[74] As subsequent events made clear, Merker would make good on this promise.

In addition to his articles in *Freies Deutschland*, Merker wrote a two-volume (over 950 pages) study of Nazi Germany, *Deutschland— Sein oder Nicht Sein?* (Germany—To Be or Not to Be?).[75] It was first published by El Libro Libre, the publishing house of the BFD in Mexico City, in 1944. Though praised by Heinrich Mann, Thomas Mann, Ernst Bloch, and other intellectual and political figures of the German emigration, it was not well known in the postwar era.[76] The SED regime prevented its publication in East Germany, and it played little or no role in West German New Leftist discussions of fascism in the 1960s.[77] Part historical justification, part detailed analysis, it remains an intriguing document of left-wing German Communism.[78] *Deutschland—Sein oder Nicht Sein?* was the most important Communist analysis of the Nazi regime to focus on anti-Semitism and Nazi racial ideology.

It offered a clear contrast to Ulbricht's *Legende des deutschen Sozialismus* in that regard. Merker's analysis of the instruments of terror and ideology had no equal among the Communist writings of the 1940s.[79]

In the first volume, *Von Weimar zu Hitler,* Merker acknowledged that "all" of the political currents of the Weimar Republic, that is, the Communists as well, "failed to recognize the danger of Nazism to its full extent and thus did not create a fighting unity opposed to Hitler."[80] Yet he placed the lion's share of the blame on the "highest leadership of the SPD" for refusing to "break with legality" and opt for armed revolt against the Nazis in 1932, a prospect he argued had a reasonable chance of success.[81] In his attack on German Social Democracy, he remained very much a left-wing Communist.

The second volume, *Das Dritte Reich und sein Ende,* offered another aspect of his left-wing communism, that is, his focus on the political importance of ideology. He began not with the economic base but with the ideological superstructure, that is, with a history of anti-Semitism from antiquity to modern Europe, modern Germany, and the Nazis, including the role of the SS, followed in order by discussions of Hitler's foreign policy, the transformation of the economy under Hitler, and the Wehrmacht and its collapse.[82] Of the volume's 498 pages of text, only 65 dealt directly with economic issues. Were not racism and anti-Semitism, he asked, "the core of all Nazi theories?" Had they not pointed the way "to the construction of total state power, to preparation of total war, and for annihilation of all adversaries who stood up against the law of the jungle?" Racism and anti-Semitism had indoctrinated "hundreds of thousands who were to joyfully carry out mass murder."[83]

He was specific regarding the signal dates of the Holocaust. In 1940 the Jews were sent to concentration camps in Poland, and "with this action, the systematic destruction of Jewish inhabitants from Germany, Poland, the Baltic Soviet Republics, White Russia, and the Ukraine began." In "winter 1940–41" the SS built the "death factory in Maidanek." He dated fall 1941 as the beginning of "factory-like mass murder." In 1943, he noted, Hitler and Himmler took the meeting of a Jewish congress in Moscow as evidence that Jewry and bolshevism were one and the same, that the Jews had inspired the alliance between

Roosevelt and Stalin, and that the annihilation of the Jews was therefore essential. This understanding of the interaction of ideology and international relations during the Holocaust was exceptional in any political camp. *Deutschland—Sein oder Nicht Sein?* was an uneven though brilliant and iconoclastic work. It was too "voluntarist" and too concerned with the Jewish catastrophe for many of Merker's comrades, too radical for Social Democrats, who would correctly see in his analysis echoes of the "social fascism" denunications of the Weimar years, and, especially after the wartime alliance collapsed, too willing to acknowledge the role of the Western Allies in the victory over Nazism. Neither the book nor its author fit into the categories of postwar East German antifascism.

In Mexico City, Merker worked with Jewish Communists such as Leo Zuckermann, Rudolf Feistmann, Leo Katz, and Otto Katz (alias André Simone), who also wrote about the Jewish catastrophe in the pages of *Freies Deutschland* and *Die Demokratische Post*.[84] In August 1943 Solomon Mikhoels and Itzak Feffer, leaders of the Moscow-based Jewish Antifascist Committee, spoke at a meeting in Mexico City at which the Soviet ambassador to Mexico, Konstantin Oumansky, who was also Jewish, also spoke. Otto Katz cultivated contact with the Jewish community in Mexico through B'nai B'rith and its representative, Adolfo Fastlicht. In fall 1944 a Spanish-language monthly, *Tribuna Israelita*, began publication. Many of the *Freies Deutschland* authors published in it.[85] Leo Katz (1892–1954), an Austrian Jewish Communist and writer in Mexican exile, also published essays in *Freies Deutschland* on the history of Jewish persecution in Europe. He argued that "the solution of the Jewish question in the Soviet Union is an instructive example of how a thousand-year-old problem was overcome by the October Revolution."[86]

In light of subsequent developments in East Berlin, Leo Zuckermann's activities in Mexico City are particularly important. Zuckermann was born on June 25, 1908, in Lublin, Poland, and joined the KPD in 1927. He had studied law at the universities of Berlin and Bonn, and worked as a lawyer. He emigrated to France in 1933, spent time in Spain in 1934, engaged in Popular Front activities in Paris in 1934–35, worked on aiding political and Jewish refugees in Paris, and was held in Vichy internment camps until he escaped via Marseilles in 1941 to Mexico City.[87] In articles in *Freies Deutschland* he made the case for "the legal claims of the German Jews for restitution."[88] The legal basis of "the coming German republic," he wrote, should be in accordance with "what President Roosevelt described as the struggle for the Four Freedoms."[89] He supported Merker's demands that a future German government make restitution to German Jews, abolish all Nazi racial laws, and return stolen property to its owners. Merker's essays in *Freies Deutschland,* according to Zuckermann, had "juridical importance as the first outlines of a new German constitution.[90] Like Merker, he viewed the restitution issue as an integral aspect of the anti-Nazi struggle, and as a key indicator of how willing postwar Germans were to accept the burdens of the Nazi past. Zuckermann also wrote that the war against the Jews had changed many Jews within or close to the Communist Party who had previously subordinated the particular Jewish claims to the universalism of the class struggle. In an essay in *Tribuna Israelita* in January 1945, he wrote that "fascism created a totally new situation for Jews all over the world. Even those Jews who for generations have been bound up with the extremely advanced process of assimilation could not escape" from the effects of demands for a Jewish state, a Jewish republic within the Soviet Union, and a Jewish brigade within the British army.[91]

Alexander Abusch, by contrast, was one of those very assimilated German-Jewish Communists in Mexico for whom the Jewish question remained subordinate to a Communist variant of Enlightenment humanism.[92] While in Mexico, Abusch both edited *Freies Deutschland* and wrote *Der Irrweg Einer Nation: Ein Beitrag zum Verständnis deutscher Geschichte* (The Nation's Mistaken Path: A Contribution to Understanding German History). The latter became a standard East German work on the origins of Nazism.[93] Abusch presented German history as a "path of error" [*Irrweg*] from the Reformation to Nazism, in which reaction repeatedly triumphed over attempts at building a more progressive and freer Germany. Among the factors contributing to Nazism, he mentioned anti-Semitism along with Prussian militarism, hatred of the Slavs and the French, the doctrine of the master race, and medieval fantasies of a European empire of the Germans.[94] His text combined vivid detail with vagueness as to the identity of the victims.[95]

> Children in underclothes, half-naked women, men in underwear—individuals paralyzed with fear—facing long graves into which they fell as the SS "Special Commandos" mowed them down with machine guns. The huge ovens and dark chimneys of the "death factories" in which millions of human beings were turned into ash. The gas chambers with their built-in peepholes, in which human beings were suffocated under exact scientific control. The piles of thin corpses of those who had starved to death stacked up like piles of wood. The camp buildings full of clothes and shoes of the victims—among which were many very small children's shoes . . . Maidanek, Auschwitz, Mauthausen, Buchenwald, Belsen-Bergen, Dachau, and the other extermination camps together form a picture that will not be erased from German history.[96]

Abusch's description contained many details of the crime yet failed to note that the victims in the death camps were overwhelmingly Jewish.

Abusch assigned primary blame to the German Social Democrats for the failure of the German left to stop Nazism.[97] Yet Abusch did not restrict responsibility to a small number of imperialists, militarists, and Nazi leaders, nor, like Merker, did he pay homage to the "good and decent core" of the German working class.[98] In view of the support for and nonresistance to Nazism among millions of members of the German middle classes, including the German educated classes, it was "historically false" to present the Germans primarily as "Hitler's victims."[99] While praising those Germans who had resisted the Nazi regime, he also noted their "isolation" from the great majority of Germans.[100] He viewed the task of German intellectuals after 1945 as one of moving Germany away from this "long path of error" and returning it to the traditions of German and European humanism. As was the case for the Moscow exiles, for Abusch these reflections on German history and on the breadth of German support for Nazism helped justify the need for an authoritative—and authoritarian—guide to lead the Germans out of the desert of past error and illusion and into the promised land of antifascism.

The foregrounding of the Jewish question in the Communist emigration in wartime Mexico City was a remarkable development in the history of twentieth-century German communism. As we have seen, it was the result of a conjuncture of elements of Communist tradition, the particular circumstances of exile, and the impact of events themselves. In the early years of the Cold War, however, Stalin and Stalinists in the postwar Communist regimes of Central and Eastern Europe acted as if wartime antifascism had had nothing at all to do with feelings of solidarity with persecuted Jews. Rather than acknowledge elements of their own traditions or of wartime exigencies that accounted for the movement of the Jewish question from the periphery to the center in Mexico City, Stalin and the postwar Communists placed Paul Merker, Leo Zuckermann, and others at the heart of an international conspiracy of American imperialists, Jewish capitalists, and Zionism. In fact, though the U.S. government and American Jewish organizations took an interest in the German Communist exile in Mexico, their interest had nothing to do with the conspiracies depicted during the "anticosmopolitan" purges in the Soviet bloc in the 1950s.

The Communist exile in Mexico, like so many episodes of political emigration, was a hothouse of intellectual creativity as well as of intense jealousies and hatreds born of insecurity and despair. When Paul Merker arrived in Mexico City in 1942, he was immediately faced with an unpleasant task. Georg and Henny Stibi, members of the KPD whom he had known in the German Communist exile in France, accused both Otto Katz and Leo Katz of being British espionage agents.[101] Merker conducted an investigation of the espionage charges against the two men and concluded that they were without foundation; he eventually removed Georg Stibi from his previously held political positions in the BFD.[102] In 1946, upon returning to East Berlin, Merker wrote a two hundred-page report on the conflict with Stibi in Mexico City. Erich Jungmann, Alexander Abusch, and Walter Janka, who was close to

Merker and later active in East German publishing, read the report and indicated their agreement by signing it.[103] They all agreed with Merker that neither Leo Katz nor Otto Katz was an espionage agent for Britain or the United States.

The SED archives in East Berlin indicate that those who returned from Mexico were asked to reconstruct in detail the intrigues, jealousies, mutual accusations, conflicts, and contacts among German exile Communists from Vichy France to Mexico City.[104] As the anti-Hitler coalition broke apart and gave way to the Cold War, those Communists in the Western emigration such as Merker, Zuckermann, and others who, in the spirit of Communist wartime antifascism, had emphasized Jewish issues and praised the American and British contribution to the war against Nazi Germany, now fell under a cloud of espionage accusations. A difference of opinion in this context was reinterpreted as evidence of treason, and, as with Merker's and Zuckermann's views on Jewish issues, evidence of participation in an anti-Communist conspiracy. One of the pillars of this conspiracy was alleged to be the American intelligence services. The archives of the FBI, the Office of Strategic Services (OSS), and American diplomatic and military intelligence make it possible to present a perhaps more mundane yet most interesting picture of how American officials did, in fact, perceive and misperceive the German Communists in wartime Mexico City.

In 1941 and 1942, when American intelligence officials thought about "subversive activities" in Mexico and Latin America, they were vastly more concerned about the activities of Nazi, Japanese, Italian, and Spanish Falange agents than with Communists. In summer or early fall 1941, Colonel William J. Donovan, the director of the Office of Strategic Services, had established a committee to examine "the possibility of German exploitation of economic and political weaknesses in Latin America" to create a "diversion" from the Battle of the Atlantic and the war in Europe.[105] From January 1941 to August 1942, J. Edgar Hoover, the director of the FBI, sent seventy-eight memos to Donovan on subversive activities in Mexico. One dealt with Communist activity. Seventy-seven dealt with espionage and fifth-column activities by German and Japanese as well as Italian Fascist and Spanish Falange agents.[106] In an effort to learn as much as possible about Nazi activities in Mexico, the FBI received information from Mexican leftists, some of whom were close to or members of the Mexican Communist Party. On January 17, 1942, Hoover forwarded a memorandum dated November 29, 1941, "reputed to have been compiled by Vincentes Lombardo Toledano, President of the Confederation of Latin American Workers at the request of, and for high Communist sources. The memorandum reveals the names and connections of persons alleged to be active in behalf of the Nazi Party in Mexico. For your information, the list was obtained here in the United States from an American Communist official."[107] Hoover also regarded Toledano's journalistic assessments in the Mexico City newspaper *El Popular* regarding "the Nazi party in Mexico" to be valuable enough to pass them on to Donovan on February 23, 1942.[108] Merker did not arrive in Mexico until June 1942, well after Toledano's reports of fall 1941 and winter 1942. By that time American concern about Nazi and fascist activities in Mexico and Latin America had begun to recede as the immediate military threat to the United States diminished. There are no further such reports from Toledano in the FBI files. American government contact with Toledano had nothing at all to do with Jewish issues.

The OSS, determined not to be taken in by antifascist slogans, viewed the Communist exiles in Mexico as Moscow's agents for whom wartime cooperation with Britain and the United States did not eliminate their fundamental antagonism toward the Western democracies.[109] On November 4, 1942, an OSS memo from the office of the Foreign Nationalities Branch ("German Political Refugees in Mexico") reported that there was "considerable evidence to suggest that the *Freies Deutschland* movement is susceptible to if not directly responsible to Comintern directions."[110] The Communists in Mexico City made no secret of their views and activities.[111] American officials worried that the Communists would make political gains as a result of their public (not clandestine) wartime antifascist agitation.

American intelligence officers kept track of Paul Merker's movements. The OSS noted his arrival in Mexico City, and dated it as June 14, 1941.[112] On October 6, 1942, the Office of Naval Intelligence noted that "MERKER was reported attempting to place the Communist inspired *Freies Deutschland* in the position of leadership of the anti–Nazi movements throughout North and Latin American and the British Empire," and that he had been in contact with various individuals in the United States, Chile, and Brazil. A December 24, 1942, memo from the same office reported that "MERKER has written an article for the monthly periodical *Freies Deutschland* in which he demands reparations for German Jews and return of German Jews to Germany at the expense of the German state." It noted that more information on Merker was "desired by the Counter-Intelligence Section."[113] This was the only time American intelligence officials commented on Merker's views on Jewish issues, and this instance was clearly in the context of concerns that he would use that issue effectively to expand (undesired) Communist influence in Mexico. Notwithstanding the wartime alliance, American intelligence regarded the Communist exiles as a threat, not as antifascist comrades in arms.[114]

J. Edgar Hoover regarded Merker within the anti-Communist framework for which he was justly famous.[115] On September 22, 1943, Hoover wrote to Assistant Secretary of State Adolf A. Berle, Jr., concerning "Paul Merker, alias Paul Merker Zeibig, Communist Activities in Mexico."[116] Drawing on Merker's published essays and public statements, mail intercepts, and twenty-four unnamed sources, Hoover presented a broadly accurate if superficial picture of Merker's political activities Germany, in the United States in the 1930s "directing infiltration of the CIO, AFL and other large trade unions," in France, and in Mexico.[117] Hoover stressed the Soviet connection. He noted that at a conference on Nazi terror in Mexico City in October 1942, Merker had asserted the Free Germans' opposition to Hitler and anti–Semitism and their support for a second front. At a meeting to celebrate the twenty–fifth anniversary of the Soviet Union, Merker praised the "Soviet Revolution." One of Hoover's sources wrote that Merker's *Was Wird aus Deutschland* made clear that "while MERKER pretends to set forth a democratic future for Germany, his basic ideology follows the Communist Party line."[118] Hoover also reported that Merker was "active in the HEINRICH HEINE CLUB," which he described as "a Communist front organization established for the benefit of 'innocents' among the German emigration and allegedly a literary society, although actually highly political."[119] The last paragraph of a January 1943 "radio appeal in German, ostensibly against the Nazi persecution of the Jews issued jointly with LUDWIG RENN," Hoover describes as containing an argument and ideology "identical with similar appeals from German Communists and Comintern sources in the United States."[120] Far from seizing on the persecution of European Jewry to infiltrate agents into the Communist movements, Hoover clearly viewed Merker as a clever Comintern operative who was using the Jewish issue to win over political "innocents."

The last American intelligence report concerning Paul Merker in Mexico City was filed by the military attaché at the American embassy in Mexico City on January 9, 1946. It reported that Merker and Ludwig Renn had left for Russia in late December 1945 to participate in "a new German government which will be set up by the Russians and which will be headed by Marshal von Paulus. Traveling expenses of subject [Renn] and MERKER are reportedly being paid by the Russian Embassy in Mexico City."[121] From beginning to end, American intelligence was intent on proving both that Merker was a Communist and that, as such, he was an instrument of Soviet foreign policy. That Merker and other leaders of the BFD were Communists who often had complimentary things to say about Stalin, the Red Army, and the Soviet Union was obvious to every reader of *Freies Deutschland*. To the limited extent to which American intelligence took note of Merker's interest in the Jewish question, it was in the context of suspicion that a veteran Comintern agent might use the issue to advance Communist and Soviet purposes. The attitude of American intelligence agencies toward Paul Merker and his associates in Mexico City ranged from wariness to hostility.

If the American government did not use the Jewish issue to penetrate the Communist movement, what about private Jewish organizations in the United States? American Jewish organizations such as the World Jewish Congress were trying to save Jewish lives in Europe and fight Nazism. In so doing, they contacted many exiles, including Merker and Zuckermann and the German Communists in Mexico.[122] Merker's and

Zuckermann's efforts regarding the Jewish issue did come to the attention of the New York office of the congress in a November 1943 report by a Dr. Gerhard Jacoby.[123] Jacoby wrote that at the First Congress of the Movement for a Free Germany, "the Jewish question was profoundly discussed." He pointed out that the movement "is considered politically radical" and that the leading personalities of the congress, "Ludwig Renn, Anna Seghers, and Paul Merker[,] are former German Communists."[124] Jacoby also noted the BFD's stated intention to nationalize German big industry and landed property after the war. If there was a meeting of hearts and minds, it was not, as postwar legend would have it, over saving Jewish property but over saving Jewish lives and defeating Nazism. Neither the image of shrewd Communists manipulating naive Jewish innocents nor the reverse image of wealthy and powerful Jews corrupting desperate exiled Communists accurately captured the realities of the interaction of German Communist exiles and Jews in wartime Mexico. As we have seen, the Communist exiles in Mexico developed their views on Jewish matters on the basis of their own long-held beliefs.

In wartime Mexico City a conjuncture of geography, timing, and political conviction had brought the Jewish question from the periphery to the center of Communist thinking. Merker and Zuckermann returned from exile hoping that this shift of focus would survive in postwar East Berlin. For these loyal Communists, who regarded their views on the Jewish question to be a logical outcome of Communist wartime antifascism, this hope did not seem illusory during the open and labile period of the Nuremberg interregnum following World War II and preceeding the Cold War.

# 4

# The Nuremberg Interregnum: Struggles for Recognition in East Berlin, 1945–1949

In East Berlin during the brief Nuremberg interregnum between the end of the war and the crystallization of the Cold War, the Communists debated how to construct the political memory of the Nazi era. To be sure, the Moscow-oriented narrative which placed the Jewish catastrophe on the margins of discussion was both ideologically and politically dominant. Yet in these early days, exiles returning from the West, from Mexico, and from the concentration camps who wanted Jewish matters to play a larger role in East German memory and policy were able to make their voices heard at the top levels of the Communist Party and the emergent governing structures. For the Jews among them, the loss of relatives and friends added personal urgency to their determination to emphasize the mass murder of European Jewry in Communist postwar memory.[1] And indeed, in the relative openness of the first several postwar year, veteran Communists could find plausible political grounds to buttress hopes that the Jewish question might shift from the periphery to the center of Communist antifascist thinking.

The most important of these grounds was the impact of the war and the solidarities it had fostered. While the Jewish catastrophe was not foremost in the minds of Soviet Communists, neither was it completely absent. The Jewish Antifascist Committee did exist. Stalin had entered an alliance with Roosevelt and Churchill. The Red Army had liberated the Nazi death camps in Poland. To be sure, the memory of Jewish suffering competed with the memory of the sufferings of others. As a result of the Nazi race war against "Jewish bolshevism" in the East, about 25 million soldiers and citizens had died in the Soviet Union, almost 6 million (including 3 million non-Jews) in Poland, and millions more elsewhere in Central and Eastern Europe.[2] Yet was it not possible that the experience of shared suffering and common wartime solidarities would indeed make self-described antifascist regimes the natural home of the memory of the Holocaust? Who could be faulted for thinking that victory in a war of unprecedented proportions against a regime which drove anti-Semitism to its most evil conclusion might alter how Communists thought about Jews?

Of course, rather than expanding human compassion for all, including the most persecuted, memories of war on the Eastern Front could also generate a struggle for the scarce resources of recognition among mourners. Memory could become a zero-sum game of mutual exclusivity in which remembering some came at the expense of others. Moroever, if the numbers of survivors and their share of political power alone determined the shape of postwar narratives, then the destruction of European Jewry would itself become a powerful—perhaps the most significant—cause of the continued marginalization of the Holocaust. In 1945 there were only about 4,500 Jewish survivors in the Soviet zone of occupation.[3] Obviously, in the Soviet as well as in the Western occupation zones, the memory of the Jewish catastrophe would not assume a prominent place in postwar German political memory without support from non-Jewish German political leaders.

Yet it was also possible that Stalin's denial of Jewish nationhood could again dominate Communist thinking. The Soviet wartime alliance with the West might collapse after 1945. The anti-Jewish currents within Communist thinking might revive. Soviet victory, far from fostering a rearrangement of past ideological traditions, could reinforce their most orthodox variants. The terror of the purges of the 1930s might again be unleashed, with anti-Semitic consequences. The romance of Soviet and Communist suffering and redemption through victory could displace the unmitigated character of the Jewish tragedy. Yet in the openness and uncertainty of the early postwar months, the place of the Holocaust in postwar Communist memory was not yet firmly established and codified. Between 1945 and 1948, the issues of *Wiedergutmachung,* modes of official memory, definitions of heroes and victims of the antifascist struggle, and the implications of the Nazi era for postwar democracy and dictatorship were debated both in public and behind the scenes in intraparty and intragovernmental forums in the Soviet occupation zone.

In the first postwar months, the German public was presented with the horrible details of the Nazi death camps. The *Deutsche Volkszeitung,* the KPD's official daily newspaper during the occupation years, prominently featured stories on Nazi war crimes and crimes against humanity, German guilt and responsibility, the coming war crimes tribunals, the charges raised against German industry, the "duty for restitution" to peoples conquered by the Nazis, and details about Auschwitz and other "factories of death."[4] The most important public discussion of the crimes of the Nazi era came about as a result of reports of the Nuremberg Trial. For a whole year, from October 1945 until October 1946, the Soviet-run press published full and prominent accounts of the indictments, testimony, evidence, and verdicts in the trial of Nazi leaders.[5] The evidence brought forth at Nuremberg and the successor trials, combined with the Allied destruction of Nazi organizations in all occupation zones, further eliminated any doubts about the factual existence of Nazi war crimes and the crime against humanity of a continent-wide genocide. In the postwar era, no major national politician in either of the two German states raised doubts about the actual occurrence of Nazi crimes. Silence or marginalization, not denial, became the dominant mode of avoiding an uncomfortable past. Communists and non-Communists argued about who could best explain how Nazism and its crimes had been possible, not about whether they had happened.[6] By establishing causal links and chronological sequences that led from "Nazi aggression" to the outcome of May 1945, the Nuremberg prosecutors reminded postwar Germans that the roots of their troubles lay in the policies of the Nazi regime.[7]

Although the category of "war crimes" assumed greater prominence in Nuremberg than that of "crimes against humanity," the trials dealt far more extensively with the specifics of the Jewish catastrophe than has often been assumed.[8] That said, newspaper reports of the trial in the Western occupation zones gave more attention to the persecution of the Jews than did the press in the Soviet zone, which emphasized those aspects of the trial that concerned Nazi crimes in the Soviet Union. On June 22, 1945, the *Deutsche Volkszeitung* described June 22, 1941, as "the darkest day in German history" and quoted from the KPD appeal ("Aufruf") of June 11, 1945, to describe it as "the greatest and most fateful of Hitler's war crimes."[9] The first article in the *Deutsche Volkszeitung* devoted exclusively to the Holocaust, "Six Millions Jews Murdered," did not appear until December 15, 1945.[10] Yet while the Jewish catastrophe received less attention in the Soviet than in the Western, and especially the American, occupation press, it clearly figured in the general Communist indictment of "fascism."

The public language of memory was related to occupation-era policies of denazification and judicial procedure. In the Potsdam accord of August 1945, the Allies agreed to implement a policy of thoroughgoing denazification in their respective zones. In the first postwar year alone, the Soviets fired 390,478 former members of the Nazi Party (NSDAP) from their jobs. By April 1947, 850,000 former members had been examined by 262 denazification commissions composed primarily of members of the newly formed successor to the KPD, the Sozialistisches Einheitspartei (Socialist Unity Party, or SED), and 65,000 persons received punishment of some kind or another. By February 1948, the Soviet Military Administration in Germany, known as SMAD), declared denazification in the Soviet zone to have been successfully completed. By April 1948, 520,000 former members of the Nazi Party in the Soviet zone had been fired from their jobs, a figure that amounted to about 2.7 percent of the population. Though in a purge of these dimensions the temptation to use the "Nazi" or "fascist" accusation to destroy political enemies who had displeased the Communists for other reasons was significant, so too was the displacement of old and compromised elites.[11]

By 1950, in procedures that have yet to be exposed to scholarly scrutiny, special German courts had convicted more than 12,500 persons of war crimes. Between 200 and 300 received life sentences, and 100 more were executed. With the declaration of Article 3 of Control Council Directive 38 on October 12, 1946, a powerful tool was placed in the hands of Soviet and East German prosecutors. It stipulated punishment for anyone who, after May 8, 1945, "endangered or possibly endangered the peace of the German people or the peace of the world through propaganda for National Socialism or militarism or by the invention and diffusion of tendentious rumors."[12] The law became a potent weapon for use against critics of the East German regime and was applied in internal party purges as well. According to Soviet documents released by the Brandenburg Ministry of the Interior just before the collapse of the German Democratic Republic (GDR), of about 122,671 Germans who were interned in camps in the Soviet zone between 1945 and 1950, 42,889 died "as a result of sickness." Recent works by Norman Naimark and Karl Wilhelm Fricke indicate that the actual figures are closer to 240,000 internees, of whom between 78,500 and 95,643 died.[13]

A great deal more study needs to be done regarding political justice in the Soviet zone. According to the Soviet figures, the Soviets handed over 14,202 persons to the East German Interior Ministry in 1950. They sent 12,770 prisoners to the Soviet Union and 6,680 to POW camps. More than a third died in the camps.[14] In 1964 the East Germans noted that of a total of 12,807 convictions related to the Nazi era, 11,274 took place between 1948 and 1950. In 1950 alone the Waldheim trials led to 4,092 convictions, including 49 executions, 160 life sentences, and 2,914 sentences longer than ten years.[15] The Waldheim trials took place from April to June 1950. Trumpeted as an example of East German determination to confront the Nazi past, the trials instead did more to undermine East German claims to upholding the rule of law. Many cases were decided on the basis of past membership in organizations such as the Nazi Party, the SS, or the Wehrmacht, rather than demonstration of individual responsibility for crimes. The Waldheim verdicts became infamous as examples of arbitrary, secret injustice in which the label "Nazi criminal" became a blanket accusation covering some persons who were actually guilty of such crimes as well as others who had simply displeased the East German authorities for a multitude of reasons.[16]

While in the Western zones issues of individual responsibility were foremost, judicial antifascism in the Soviet zone operated with categories of social class. The aristocracy, officer corps, and middle classes were assumed to be followers of National Socialism, while the working class was, a priori, assumed to be antifascist.[17] In the judiciary, schools, and civil service, Soviet denazification led to the installation of new, upwardly mobile, and politically correct elites. By the end of 1950, for example, 89 percent of all prosecutors and 63 percent of all judges belonged to the SED.[18] Afterwards, the Communists would point with pride to the purge as evidence of a commitment to overcoming the Nazi past which contrasted favorably with the greater continuity of elites in the Western zones.

Among the Communists returning to East Berlin, those who had been political prisoners in German concentration camps attempted, with some success, to shape the form and content of political memory. In so doing, they displayed a generosity and compassion which became rare following the codification of East German antifascism. Franz Dahlem (1892–1981), who survived Gestapo interrogation as well as the Mauthausen concentration camp, was the leading figure within the KPD and then the SED among the concentration camp inmates who returned to East Berlin after 1945. Immediately following the liberation of the camp by American troops in May 1945, Dahlem delivered a speech on the Nazi era and "problems of our future work in Germany."[19] It was a passionate denunciation of Nazism's crimes and of German capitalism, an assertion of the "collective guilt" of the German people, and a demand for a radical break with the fascist past. Dahlem's speech was remarkable because it was both a political statement and a detailed eyewitness account. In contrast to the zero-sum games to come, his memory of Nazism's victims was inclusive and comprehensive:

> For years, we ourselves [German Communist interness at Mauthausen] were powerless witnesses as every Jew in the Mauthausen concentration camp was beaten to death, driven into the electrified wires, driven through a cordon, and as week by week Russian officers among the prisoners of war, and especially the political commissars, were shot by a firing squad or in the back of the

neck. We saw the intentionally planned extermination of Poland's and Czechoslovakia's intellectuals, of the Communist cadres of different countries, and of captured partisans and men of the resistance movements of Yugoslavia, Greece, France, Belgium, Italy, who were hanged, killed with lethal injections, poisoned, and simply starved or frozen to death. We had to watch with clenched teeth in the last two weeks of the war as 3,000 individuals who had been starved to the point of skeletons and could barely stand were driven into the gas chambers, and as in the last moments before the collapse 40 more of our best Austrian party comrades were killed. In view of the intended destruction of the camp, we ourselves escaped death thanks only to the rapid strikes of the United Nations.[20]

The detail with which Dahlem described the methods of murder and the identity of the victims set his account apart from standard political denunciations of Nazism. As we have seen and will see again, personal experiences decisively influenced the memories of political leaders in both postwar Germanys. For Dahlem, an antifascist worthy of the title would have to understand that "hatred against everything German" had "real foundations. It would require powerful evidence of a renewal of the German people before Germany will gain the trust of humanity again."[21] The "ideological poisoning of the German people," including "the great mass of the German youth," with "chauvinist, imperialist ideology" meant that antifascists faced an enormous task in the years to come.[22] For Dahlem after Mauthausen, personal experience reinforced his Communist convictions. Once they had witnessed their fellow Germans committing mass murder, it is hardly surprising that Dahlem and other Communist survivors of the camps would regard democracy—meaning rule by this same people—as rather low on the list of postwar requirements for bringing about a turn away from the Nazi past.

Even more explicitly than Merker in Mexico, Dahlem cast a critical gaze at the past policies of the Communist Party. Why, he asked, had the KPD, a political party with 5 million votes in March 1933 and an active underground organization, been unable to mobilize the German working class into an effective resistance movement? This failure "of the party and the working class" was "the most depressing chapter . . . the great minus which burdens us" at the outset of building a new Germany.[23] Hence, political renewal in post-Nazi Germany should come from the resistance veterans, "whose hatred for fascism is deep in their flesh and blood and for whom there can be no compromise with any sort of fascist remnants." It was they who had had the courage to tell the "German people the whole truth about their shared guilt in the crimes of the Nazi regime" and who were willing "to assume responsibility to expiate Germany's collective guilt and to make good, so far as it is humanly possible, the injustice and damage [inflicted by the Nazis]." He argued that acknowledging shared guilt and accepting responsibility for "expiating this guilt" and for making restitution for harm done was "the fundamental precondition for any sort of reconstruction of Germany."[24]

Dahlem was serious when he used the term "collective guilt." He denounced "SS bandits" but also Wehrmacht soldiers and the German workers who had continued to produce weapons throughout the war. "The great part of the German people [had] watched" the enslavement and exploitation of "many millions of foreign men, women, and children with silent toleration . . . Many German citizens, male and female, [had] profited" from this imported enslaved labor. "Anti-Bolshevik hysteria" had led to a horrendous mistreatment of prisoners of war. "The fact is that the German people silently tolerated the extermination of millions of Jews from all over Europe by the Gestapo and the SS. Yes, the poison of anti-Semitism penetrated so deeply into the Germans' blood that broad layers viewed Jewish fellow human beings as inferior and accepted their destruction with great indifference."[25]

"As a German," Dahlem noted these facts "with shame and rage." Yet political renewal demanded that the German people face these truths and recognize the extent to which "broad layers" had succumbed to imperialist and fascist ideology and racist illusions of their own superiority and the inferiority of others, and therefore had "actively or passively supported Hitler's policies."[26] So much "simply could never be made good again . . . The German people will not escape this guilt." A different Germany could emerge "only on the basis of self-knowledge of their [the Germans'] own sinking into Nazism's ideological swamp, of their own shared guilt in its crimes, and of a genuine will for restitution."[27] Himself a victim, Dahlem placed himself also within the broad circle of German history and guilt. The converse of his assertions of collective guilt was the need for some other, less guilt-ridden group of Germans to play a leading role in building a new Germany.

Several months later, on September 9, 1945, Dahlem spoke in East Berlin at the first "day of memory [Gedenktag] for victims of fascism" organized by the Communist-dominated Main Committee for the Victims of Fascism (Hauptausschuß für die Opfer des Faschismus, or OdF).[28] He argued that those who had led the anti-Nazi resistance should also be leaders in postwar politics. He was grateful to "the victorious Red Army and the armies of the United Nations. Thanks to them, and them alone, the liberation of the German people from the Hitler yoke and the beginning of a new democratic life have taken place." He recalled the death of Ernst Thälmann, members of the KPD, and members of the International Brigades in Spain. "These sacrifices must not be in vain," he said.[29] The memory of shared sacrifice and solidarity among Communists and non-Communists, Germans and prisoners from other European countries, offered the basis for political unity at home and the beginnings of contact with Germany's European neighbors. Like most exiles returning from East and West, Dahlem conveyed indebtedness to the Allies and anger at the Germans.

In view of the these oft-repeated antifascist declarations, it seems plausible to expect that the Communists would have included the story of Jewish suffering in their postwar narratives. In fact, in the Soviet occupation it was the OdF which delivered the news that, as a page one headline in the September 26, 1945, Deutsche Volkszeitung put it, "Jews are also victims of fascism" and therefore should also receive the honors and benefits due to those so classified.[30] Ottomar Geschke (1882–1957), a veteran of the KPD and the International Brigades in Spain, a former prisoner in Buchenwald and Sachsenhausen, and now chair of the OdF, supported inclusion of the Jewish catastrophe in antifascist memory of the war. Julius Meyer, also a KPD member and a leader of Jews who had survived in or returned to East Berlin, was named to the executive committee of the OdF. The OdF established a committee to focus on "those persecuted on the grounds of race" *(rassisch Verfolgten)*, that is, Jews.[31] The establishment of September 9 as a day of memory for victims of fascism in the Soviet zone, as well as the inclusion of Meyer in the leadership of the OdF, suggested that the destruction of European Jewry might find an appropriate place in Communist rituals of remembrance.

Another sign of apparent inclusiveness came from Johannes R. Becher. His essay "Germany Accuses!" ("Deutschland Klagt An!") was first published in January 1946 in the inaugural issue of *Aufbau,* the SED's leading cultural-political journal.[32] He departed from the vagueness about anti-Semitism apparent in his wartime Moscow writing. Now his anger and shame over the Nuremberg revelations, as well as his solidarity with the Jews, was unambiguous:

> What was done to the Jews, was done to us. The persecution of the Jews, the systematic extermination of our Jewish fellow citizens, has placed such a burden of shame and disgrace upon us that we will have to bear it long after the wind has blown away the dust of the Nazi criminals. In the name of the martyrdom of our Jewish fellow citizens, we raise an accusation, just as we express our brotherhood with all of those who were persecuted and died a martyr's death because of their religious faith.[33]

The Nazi war criminals in Nuremberg, he continued, would "only first become part of the past when we have cleaned out from inside ourselves and in our German people that which made it possible for the Nazi war criminals to vault to power and to be able to commit their crimes."[34] The stain was deep and wide, not small and shallow. It affected the many, not a few. In Mexico, Merker and Zuckermann had written that facing the Jewish question was essential for building a postwar democracy. Yet reflection on the extent of German support for Nazism could lead to just the opposite conclusion, that is, that a people so implicated in Nazism's crimes could not and should not be trusted with democracy. In this way, memory of the dark past could bolster the inclination to impose a new dictatorship of antifascist enlightenment and offer a sense of purpose and justification to those seeking to cleanse and reeducate a people gone astray.

In their comments on German history in the fall of 1945, Walter Ulbricht and Wilhelm Pieck focused on lessons of the past with other contemporaneous implications. Both spoke to a large demonstration in East Berlin on November 9, 1945, not in order to recall the Nazi pogrom of November 9, 1938, but to draw the same lesson for the present from the failed November revolution of 1918.[35] Division within the German working-class movement must now be replaced by unity, they urged. After 1918 a divided left had made fascist victory possible. After 1945 a unified political party of both Communists and Social Democrats was essential if the missed opportunities of 1918–19 were to be regained in a second era of restoration. Just as the division of the German left had made Nazism's seizure of power possible, so division of the German left after 1945 would make possible a second 1918, that is, a second postwar era in which the promise of fundamental social, political, and economic change would be frustrated.

The Communists claimed to lead a "unity front of antifascist democratic forces" whose aim was restoration of democracy and prevention of a fascist restoration.[36] In drawing these lessons of November 9, 1918, the Communists placed the anti-Communist Social Democrats in Berlin on notice that refusal to join in a "unity" party, this time one clearly dominated by the Communists, would lead Ulbricht and Pieck to hold the Social Democrats responsible for splitting the left and again opening the door to conservative restoration. To disagree with the Communists' appeal for unity was to split both the working class and the nation. Just as anti-Communism had led to an imperialist restoration after 1918, so would it now at best impede denazification and at worst aid a Nazi restoration. Since the Communists were antifascists, then those who opposed them "objectively" gave aid and support to fascism.[37]

As we will see, there were aspects of wartime antifascism that would become embarassing for the postwar Communist regimes. Nevertheless, the association of the Soviet Union and the Communists with the "democratic antifascist struggle" had the great emotional advantage of placing the Communists in the ranks of the democrats while tarring their opponents "objectively" with the hint of fascism.[38] Memory of the Nazi past alone did not necessarily lead to liberal democratic intentions. Neither Ulbricht's partisan account of Weimar politics nor Dahlem's vivid memories of Mauthausen's horrors legitimated construction of what they called an antifascist democratic order. For them, memory of past crimes implied justification for a second German dictatorship.

As we have seen, *Wiedergutmachung* means literally "to make good again." The more modest English word "restitution" more accurately describes what contemporaries knew to be the case, namely, that decency demanded that the survivors of Nazi crimes be helped, although nothing could "make good" the losses caused by Nazi criminality. The restitution issue merged the symbolic politics of memory with the practical politics of distributing welfare benefits and offering financial compensation to "victims of fascism." The KPD "Aufruf" had spoken obliquely of a "duty of restitution for the damage done to other peoples by the Hitler aggressors." But a number of questions became the the subject of intense debate and conflict within the Communist administration between 1945 and 1948. Who were these "other peoples"? Did they include the Jews? Among the officially designated "victims of fascism," would Communist "heroes" of the political opposition to the Nazi regime be given preferential treatment over "those persecuted on grounds of race"? Moreover, historic Marxist associations of the Jews with capitalism entered into the debate about who was a victim, a hero, or even an enemy of the working class.[39]

One result was the creation of a clear moral hierarchy among those who had survived Nazi persecution. Communist "fighters" outranked Jewish "victims." Jews, those recognized as having been "racially persecuted," received pensions higher on average than those for other DDR citizens but lower than those for "fighters against fascism." They could retire five years earlier than non-Jews, could use public transportation without cost, and were permitted additional vacation days. But though East Germany recognized Jews as "victims of fascism," it did not offer restitution payments to individuals or to the state of Israel as reparations for past suffering.[40]

Jewish members of the OdF and their non-Jewish allies argued that the Communists' support for restitution articulated in the "Aufruf" should apply to Jews as well.[41] The Communists' initial impulse was to limit the numbers of those honored as "victims of fascism" mostly to Communists but also to some non-Communists—Protestant ministers, Catholic priests, and Social Democrats—who had actively engaged in political resistance. They were not willing to include the majority of Jews, Gypsies, Jehovah's Witnesses, and homosexuals as "victims of fascism." In the fall of 1945, the OdF did recognize 2,352 persons in Berlin as victims of political persecution, and over 6,000 persons, mostly Jews, as *rassisch Verfolgte*, "victims of racial persecutions."[42]

In a 1947 speech to the OdF, Alfred Kantorowicz, a veteran Jewish German Communist, explained the distinction between "victims of" and "fighters against" fascism.[43] Although it was true, he said, that "we" had "fallen victim to" fascism, "many of us were not, in this sense, passive victims. Rather, we were essentially fighters."[44] Fascism was not "a destiny" which came over "us." It was "our deadly enemy" whose "horror we recognized and against which we consciously fought." The veterans of the antifascist resistance thus had a "duty" to see that the martyrdom and death of their comrades had not been in vain. This "past filled with honor" was a basis for postwar political legitimacy.[45] His remarks clearly implied a pejorative contrast between supposed Jewish passivity and active "antifascist resistance." The latter would be a source of far greater honor and prestige.

Nevertheless, the OdF was the primary institution in which Jews were able to raise their concerns with East German Communists. Already in the summer of 1945 Probst Heinrich Grüber (1891–1975), a Protestant theologian and church leader, as well as Julius Meyer and Heinz Galinski, who later became the leader of the organized Jewish community in postwar West Germany, fought to recognize Jews as victims of fascism, or, in the language of the time, "to include the racially persecuted in the circle of those victims of fascism."[46] Meyer, a member of the Volkskammer, became a member of the executive committee of the OdF and director of its office dealing with the "racially persecuted" in Berlin.[47] As a result of the efforts of Meyer, Grüber, and Ottomar

Geschke, the OdF was the first political institution in the Soviet zone to stress that an antifascist and a democratic Germany should understand that "Jews are also victims of fascism."[48] The OdF announced that "those persecuted on grounds of race" would now be included in the antifascist canon of officially recognized "victims of fascism."[49]

At a conference of the OdF in Leipzig on October 26, 1945, Karl Raddatz (1904–1970), the organizational secretary, spoke to two hundred functionaries from throughout the Soviet zone.[50] Raddatz defined two categories of members in the OdF, *Kämpfer gegen den Faschismus* (fighters against fascism) and *Opfer des Faschismus* (victims of fascism).[51] He regretted that the overall organization referred to "victims of fascism," thereby obscuring the difference between the "active side," present in the "conscious political struggle" among the "fighters against fascism," and those who, "despite their passivity[,] became victims."[52] "Fighters acting on the basis of political conviction" (*politischen Ueberzeugungskämpfer*) constituted the moral and political elite of the organization. They included Communists as well as Catholic and Protestant opponents, all of the participants in the attempted coup of July 20, 1944, the relatives and survivors of antifascists murdered by the Nazis, political émigrés, veterans of the International Brigades in Spain, and soldiers who deserted from the Wehrmacht out of political conviction.[53] "Victims of fascism" included, among others, Jewish survivors, Gypsies, and family members punished for the actions of relatives.[54] Both "fighters" and "victims" would receive social welfare provisions. Raddatz took note of Western support for restitution to the Jews. He argued that "the antifascist fighters" also had "a claim to restitution for all the years during which they suffered."[55]

For all of Raddatz's empathy for Jewish suffering, the invidious moral and prestige distinctions built into the fighter/victim, active/passive dichotomy were apparent. The former pole of these binaries was clearly winning the battle for primacy of place in the hierarchy of Communist memory. Yet the battle was not over. Within the OdF a debate was talking place in which dissonant voices could be heard. At the same meeting Heinz Brandt (1909–1986), a Jewish member of the KPD, a survivor of Brandenburg, Auschwitz, Buchenwald, and Sachsenhausen prisons, and the director of the cultural division of the OdF from 1945 to 1953, spoke in favor of recognizing Jews as victims of fascism, as did Julius Meyer and Leon Löwenkopf, a leader of the Jewish community of Dresden.[56] Löwenkopf angrily asked those delegates who were reluctant to afford equal treatment to Jewish victims if they had not seen "what had taken place in Germany" and in the concentration camps.[57] Jenny Matern, a KPD member whose husband, Hermann, was one of the most powerful members of the party, also spoke at the Leipzig conference. In responding to Meyer and Löwenkopf, she said that "in these [Jewish] circles, the question of financial support—I would like to say this openly and frankly—plays a special role that often is not very fortunate."[58] The old anti-Semitic stereotypes of the Jew as capitalist and as passive weakling would continue to lurk within the muscular Communist discourse of East German antifascism.

As the former East German historian Olaf Groehler has noted, most of the Communists in Leipzig in October 1945 "scarcely comprehended" the dimensions of the Holocaust and Nazi anti-Semitism, and offered forthcoming policies on the issue only out of tactical considerations. Yet these shortcomings did not distinguish them from many non-Communists.[59] The point to keep in mind is that to the extent to which Jewish concerns were voiced and Communist solidarity with Jews persisted in the Soviet zone, they did in the OdF as well. This was so partly because "the racially persecuted," that is, Jews, represented the majority of its membership, and partly because the shared experience of persecution made some Communists more, not less, understanding of the history of Jewish suffering.[60] These early debates shaped the first Soviet zone guidelines on restitution, issued on June 18, 1946, which applied to 15,536 "fighters against fascism" and 42,287 "victims of fascism."[61] In the immediate postwar months and years, antifascism required taking a morally respectable position regarding the Jewish question. Jews within the Soviet zone of occupation still made the argument that genuine antifascists should do at least as much to help Jewish victims of fascism as the authorities in the Western, especially American, zones of occupation.[62] Arguments of the interregnum era about the need to emulate the exemplary conduct in the West obviously did not survive the collapse of the wartime alliance and the emergence of the Cold War. On the contrary, the leading East German Communists came to view the prominence of Jewish matters in the Western occupation zones and in the Federal Republic as evidence of a much-regretted "second 1918," that is, of the restoration of the discredited old order.

Tensions over the memory of "political" as opposed to "Jewish" victims of Nazism were evident at the founding conference of the Vereinigung des Verfolgten des Naziregimes (Association of Those Persecuted by the Nazi Regime, or VVN) in February 1947. Franz Dahlem did denounce "the plague of anti-Semitism."[63] In his remarks at the same meeting, Karl Raddatz supported the "much-disputed issue" of restitution but rejected what he called any "capitalistic type of restitution." He stressed that there was a "duty" to resolve the restitution problem "as a matter of social justice."[64] But the focus of Dahlem's address was on the legacy of the "political" resistance. He noted with pride that most of the 215 delegates held leading positions in the government, administration, and economic and cultural life in the Soviet zone of occupation. The veterans of the resistance, he continued, formed the core of the "other" and better Germany, around which a new Germany could be built. They had a special responsibility to convey the history of the antifascist resistance.[65] For Dahlem, memory of the camps held another lesson for postwar politics: the unity between Communists and Social Democrats which had emerged in the camps should continue.[66] Hence, he criticized Social Democratic leaders of the postwar period such as Franz Neumann, Louise Schröder, Otto Suhr, and Kurt Schumacher for their "policy of splitting," for in so doing, they were "denying the solidarity of common experience" and the unity of the antifascist struggle. "Perhaps it would make sense if one would remind these comrades where and how Hitler united us in the concentration camps," Dahlem remarked.[67] The history of the camps and the underground struggle would reveal, he believed, the "prefigurative solidarity of Communists and Social Democrats" when another and a better Germany took shape.[68] But these memories of brief wartime solidarity came up against the mutual suspicions and antagonisms between Communists and Social Democrats that had dominated the history of the German left since it first split during World War I.

Paul Merker returned to East Berlin in July 1946 as one of the leading figures, if not the leading figure, of the German Communist emigration in the West. In his absence he had been elected to the SED Politburo. In East Berlin he worked on land reform, expropriation of Prussian large landowners, and refugee problems. At the Department of Labor and Social Welfare, he plunged into the debate about restitution policy. As he had done in Mexico, he continued to argue that the claims of Jewish memory should be equal to those of the Communist resistance. In East Berlin, even more so than in exile, his views regarding the priority of restitution to Jews conflicted with the prestige hierarchy of fighters and victims which had emerged before his return.

In the fall of 1946, Merker asked his friend the Jewish Communist historian Helmut Eschwege for advice regarding postwar Communist policy toward the Jewish question. In his response of February 1946, Eschwege suggested that a postwar German government make the following statement:

> The German people hope that they will regain the trust of the Jews in the future. They hope to bring this about as a result of their future leadership and its actions. The German people recognize their guilt toward the Jews, which stems from their active or passive participation by an overwhelming majority in the Hitler system. Through the most far-reaching restitution of the economic and physical damage to the few surviving Jews and Jewish communities, it seeks to remove a part of its guilt.[69]

Property lost by Jews after January 30, 1933, Eschwege said, should be transferred to central Jewish organizations, while those Jews entitled to property who were living abroad, or who wished to do so, should be supported by the government in receiving it. Furthermore, the government should state that "the German people do not regard these measures as a replacement for the extermination of Jewish life but rather as an important act of justice."[70]

Eschwege's statement further urged that the government announce its intention to purge Nazis and anti-Semites from German public life and bring to justice those responsible for Jewish suffering. The government would fight anti-Semitism, and grant full citizenship to Jews within and outside Germany. Moreover, Eschwege argued that the war and the Holocaust called for a change in Stalin's views on the national question. The government should declare that the Jews were "free to claim the rights of a national minority. In his fundamental essay on the national question (1913), Stalin rejected the recognition of this right. In view of the developments since 1933, however, new points of view place this problem in another light."[71] Eschwege's memo captures the hopes of some veteran Communists, both Jews and non-Jews, who hoped that even Stalin would change his views on the national question in light of "the developments since 1933," and that a postwar German Communist government would unambiguously accept obligations created by Nazi anti-Jewish persecution. In February 1946 both Eschwege and Merker hoped that its guidelines would shape postwar Communist policy. Within the government, Merker unsuccessfully urged first the OdF and then the VVN to support a restitution law for Jewish survivors. The fine sentiments of speeches and essays written in exile now became part of the postwar debates on government policy.

From 1946 to 1950 Merker argued in favor of restitution as a member of the SED Central Committee. He prodded his colleagues to do more to combat anti-Semitism in the Soviet zone of occupation, and to look after the welfare of the approximately 1,500 Jews there.[72] During this time he worked in the Abteilung Arbeit und Sozialfürsorge of the Zentralsekretariat (Department of Labor and Social Welfare of the Central Secretariat) of the SED.[73] Together with the secretary of the department, Helmut Lehmann, and assisted by Leo Zuckermann, who returned to East Berlin in 1947, Merker fought for adoption of Jewish restitution provisions, and argued that more must be done to fight postwar anti-Semitism in the Soviet zone and to aid Jewish survivors in their efforts to recover stolen property.[74]

In January 1947 a memo at the Department of Labor and Social Welfare from Jenny Matern ("Guidelines for the Recognition and Issuing of Identity Cards for 'Fighters against Fascism' and 'Victims of Fascism' in the Soviet Zone of Occupation") codified the distinction between "fighters against" and "victims of" fascism which the OdF and the VVN had first articulated.[75] In many cases, the fighter/victim distinction overlapped that between "political" opponents, above all Communists, and those persecuted on "racial" grounds, such as the Jews.[76] The memo included no provisions for restitution to compensate Jewish individuals or community institutions for property and goods stolen or destroyed by the Nazis, or which had been expropriated by the new Soviet-controlled administration for its postwar purposes. The guidelines also became a tool of political control. Benefits could be withdrawn if individuals damaged the reputation of a "fighter against fascism" or a "victim of fascism," or "did not respond with sufficient grounds to requests to work for the construction of an antifascist, democratic Germany."[77] Jews were the last "victims" of fascism to be named, and their mention was shrouded in vague references to "victims of the Nuremburg racial laws" and "those who wore the Yellow Star."[78]

In 1946 and 1947 laws stipulating restitution payments for Jewish survivors were passed in the Western occupation zones. In May 1947 Leo Löwenkopf, leader of the organized Jewish community in Dresden, wrote to Merker to urge the SED to adopt a similar law, especially in view of the move by the Liberal Democratic Party (LDP) in Dresden to support a comprehensive restitution to Jews for property the Nazis had stolen.[79] On June 4, 1947, Merker sent a memo to Ulbricht and Central Committee member Max Fechner to express his exasperation over delays in addressing the Jewish question within the SED government and party. "For a long time" he had "tried to convince the comrades in the OdF" to develop a plan for restitution for the "Jewish victims of fascism . . . Unfortunately, the comrades have taken no action to develop such a proposal." Meanwhile, he continued, "the LDP has taken the initiative in a question which has complicated international significance . . . [W]e must work out an acceptable position . . . I will be very glad to participate in working on this question."[80] Merker argued that the SED's lack of support for restitution to the Jews had become a political liability in view of contrasting policies in the Western zones, as well as in one of the non-Communist parties in the Soviet zone.

In 1947 and 1948 Julius Meyer, Leo Löwenkopf, Heinz Galinski, and Heinrich Grüber continued to press for an East German restitution law. Merker and Zuckermann continued to challenge the distinctions between active, heroic Communist fighters and passive, presumably unheroic Jewish victims expressed in the Jenny Matern memo of January 1947. Instead it was decided, as one memo from Lehmann's office of August 8, 1947, put it, that "the same principles should apply for restitution" for all those persecuted, whether on "political, racial, or religious grounds. General rules favoring one or another of the OdF groups should be rejected."[81]

In January 1948 Merker and Lehmann completed their draft of a restitution law.[82] They pointed to the restitution laws which had already been passed in the Western occupation zones and urged that their proposal be quickly brought before the state parliaments in the Soviet zone for approval. In contrast to the Matern guidelines of the year before, Merker and Lehmann's proposed legislation did not draw a sharp distinction between "fighters" and "victims." The proposal placed "political" and the "racial" victims on an equal plane and in the same sentence. "Individuals persecuted by the Nazi regime" were defined as "those persons who, on the basis of democratic conviction, participated in resistance against the National Socialist state and were thereby subjected to persecution by the Nazi regime, as well as those persons who were persecuted because of their religious views or as a result of Nazi racial laws."[83] Merker and Lehmann argued for equal treatment, not special preferences. Those designated as falling within the specified category became members of the VVN and thus would receive a broad range of social welfare, education, and pension benefits designed to assist them in restoring shattered lives, families, and careers.[84]

Many apartments and homes previously occupied by Jews or political émigrés had new occupants who had benefited from the persecution of others. Merker and Lehmann stipulated that former inhabitants had the right to return to their previous house or apartment. If an apartment was occupied by people who knew "or had to know" that it had belonged to a member of the VVN, the "apartment would be considered empty" and placed at the disposal of the member of the VVN. If a VVN member could not get his or her apartment back, the government would make a one-time grant to provide an apartment "appropriate to the social standing" of the VVN member.[85]

Furthermore, Merker and Lehmann advocated establishment of a government commission staffed partly by members of the VVN to implement a restitution policy. It would return property which had not been transferred to public ownership after 1945 back to the persons from whom it had been stolen "in the period from January 30, 1933, to May 8, 1945, for reasons of race, religion, [political] belief, or political opposition to National Socialism." This task was to be accomplished rapidly and in "particular cases through appropriate measures which would make good the damage done by National Socialism at the cost of those who had benefited" from the Nazi thefts.[86] If the victim was dead, restitution would be made to close relatives. If the victim now lived abroad, relatives living in Germany could receive the claims. Restitution was to be carried out "quickly and completely," without procedural delays. Where eyewitnesses to crimes were dead or not available, the claimant's sworn statements would be sufficient, even in cases where the author of the written statement was dead. Finally, and very important, Clause 56, written by Leo Zuckermann, recognized the rights of those persecuted by the Nazis who were living outside Germany after 1945.[87] Nonetheless, the Merker-Lehmann draft, with its inclusive conception of antifascism, did not become law.[88]

In April 1948 Leo Zuckermann made public the arguments he and Merker had made in Mexico City and were still making within the occupation apparatus in East Berlin. He did so in "Restitution und Wiedergutmachung," an essay published in *Die Weltühne,* a political-cultural monthly written by leading Communist politicians and intellectuals.[89] Zuckermann repeated arguments Merker had made in the

pages of *Freies Deutschland* in Mexico. Although the Nazis had persecuted political opponents as well as the Jews, he wrote, the grounds for
persecution differed. Political opposition to the Nazi regime was the
result of a free decision which carried the risk of persecution and loss
of freedom, health, and life. The "wages" of the struggle could not be
translated into money. For "antifascists," restitution meant helping to
build and being a part of a new, democratic state. It was a "matter of
honor" for the German people to take measures to heal the physical and
psychological wounds suffered by those who had risked so much to
defeat fascism.[90]

That said, Zuckermann continued, the persecution of the Jews was
different. The Jews had been attacked "because they were Jews, not
because they had conspired against the Third Reich," that is, because
of who they were, not what they had done. The Nazis had declared war
on the Jewish people "not in order to defeat an internal political opponent, but to annihilate a national minority."[91] To deny restitution to the
Jews after 1945 was to identify oneself with the barbarities of National
Socialism and its ideology, something an antifascist state obviously must
not and could not do. The issue of restitution for individual Jews living
abroad and for a collective claim of the Jewish people could best be
settled when the Jewish state envisioned by the UN partition resolution
of 1947 was established.[92]

Zuckermann distinguished his views from American proposals to
return factories and stores expropriated by the Nazis to their Jewish
owners living abroad. Would not such a proposal, he asked, place
restitution "in the service of foreign economic interests?" He continued:

> The restitution claims, which rest on the loss of almost 6 million
> people, and which embody unspeakable suffering and rivers of tears,
> should exclusively serve the purpose of reconstruction of the Jewish
> people. It is not the instrument of a particular minority to expand its
> egoistic economic power position. The Jewish people reject the notion
> that their legitimate claims for restitution should be misused for
> imperialist purposes, whether it be to the advantage of Jewish or

non-Jewish groups. Such a misuse would endanger the moral basis of the whole effort of restitution as well as the political and educational purposes it should serve.[93]

By contrast, Jews residing in Germany, including returning émigrés, remained part of the German economy. Hence, property stolen from them by the Nazis should be returned to them. Zuckermann's arguments regarding restitution and its misuse by "foreign" and "imperialist" interests were a response to his intraparty opponents who pejoratively associated Jewish restitution demands with capitalism and as yet unspecified "international" powers. In these early years, memory of the Nazi past had already become intertwined with political battles over money.

The Merker-Lehmann draft challenged the emerging Communist orthodoxy on restitution. It aroused intense debate and opposition within the party, the government, and regional parliaments. On April 30, 1948, Zuckermann, then an official in the SED office dealing with regional governments, wrote to Merker to report that a "political campaign" had recently been launched against the "political conception of restitution as such." The opponents came from the Justice Division of the SED Central Committee and the Central Administration of Justice (the future Ministry of Justice). The objections they raised were:

1. The émigrés no longer have any claims [on Germany]. Why should we throw something at them?
2. When we recognize [a right] to have damage replaced, we only strengthen the Jewish capitalists.
3. The [German] refugees don't receive anything. Why should the Jews get anything? That isn't just. The Jews must also share in the general impoverishment brought about by the war.
4. The Jewish immigrants don't belong to the working class. In the Eastern zone we are taking the path to socialism. As a result, we have no interest in shifting new burdens onto the working class.
5. If we recognize the collective claims of a Jewish state, then we are also recognizing the claims of the leaders of trusts and monopolies.

6. Today the Soviet Union rejects the idea that the German people were responsible for Hitler's war. It acts on the basis of other principles.[94]

Four days later, on May 4, 1948, Merker wrote to Wilhelm Pieck to urge support for a restitution policy which addressed the Jewish issue. Restitution, he wrote, was an issue in which the "national question" played a certain role.

> The Jewish population was plundered and almost exterminated owing to so-called racial-political grounds. This was a matter of the destruction of a national as well as religious minority, a destruction which was tolerated by the German people. In this case, in our zone as well, certain measures for restitution for damage done, which is in part material in nature, cannot be avoided. Such restitution is not a matter of giving back to Jewish big capitalists their previously owned property, factories, or banks. The property of the Jewish communities, the movable and immobile property of Jewish private individuals living in the [Soviet] zone, excluding all those objects which have been transferred into the hands of the state, must be returned. Furthermore, it is necessary to register Jewish property which today still remains in the possession of Nazis or other reactionary elements and to place it in trust by [public] administration.[95]

Pieck did not respond.

Within the SED, Zuckermann's and Merker's noble view that victory was its own reward, and that beyond care for physical and psychological health no restitution was due to political opponents of the regime, also aroused deep antagonism. From the perspective of his adversaries, Zuckermann's arguments, whatever their historical merits, had the disadvantage of placing Jewish suffering on the same level as that of the Communists. For those Communists who associated Jews with capitalism, restitution for property stolen by the Nazis amounted to payments to the class enemy, and one whose "international" character placed it outside the emerging German socialist nation.

On May 13, 1948, supporters and critics of the Merker-Lehmann draft met in the Department of Labor and Social Work in Berlin. The following day Götz Berger, an official in the SED's Justice Division dealing with the restitution issue, sent a report of the meeting to Fechner and Ulbricht. Berger expressed relief that Zuckermann's "extremely dubious" clause providing for claims to "persons now living abroad has fortunately been withdrawn."[96] Instead only persons living in Germany would have the right to make claims for restitution. Berger noted that he and Ernst Melsheimer, the future chief prosecutor in many political trials in the East German Supreme Court, opposed the proposal. The danger of such conceptions, he wrote, was evident in "the proposals of the representatives of Jewish property interests, Comrades [Leo] Löwenkopf and Julius Mayer." These leaders of the Jewish communities of Dresden and Berlin, respectively, had proposed that property which had been transferred to state ownership by the Nazis or in the Soviet zone after 1945 be either returned or fully compensated. Such proposals, Berger continued, were dangerous. "Not only do they pose an extraordinary burden to our state. They are also insupportable from a socialist standpoint . . . This would be the case because these new rules would mean nothing other than that socialization would come to a halt before Jewish capital, and that Jewish capitalists alone would be granted special privileges in contrast to all other capitalists."[97] The use of terms such as "Jewish capital" and "Jewish capitalists" represented a startling persistence of anti-Semitic discourse. No less jarring was Berger's argument that bearing the burden of the Nazi anti-Jewish persecution conflicted with socialist construction after 1945 in Germany.

On June 16, 1948, Zuckermann wrote to Ulbricht to reject the "gross falsehoods" in the Berger memo.[98] He insisted that his position in the *Weltbühne* essay was in agreement with the Soviet position in the peace accords with Italy, Austria, Romania, and Hungary, as well as with declarations of foreign Communist parties. Berger was attacking not only restitution for the Jewish population but also the idea of "the duty for restitution of the German people as such." Furthermore, Berger's memo stood "in direct contrast to the Marxist position on the national problem, so extensively developed by Lenin and Stalin."[99] Zuckermann's defense of his Communist credentials was successful for the time being. Nevertheless, the link between Jews, capitalism, and foreigners raised in the restitution controversy of 1947 and 1948 by critics of Merker and Zuckermann would soon reemerge in more public and more devastating forms when the intraoffice critics of 1947 and 1948 became the prosecutors, accusers, and hostile witnesses of the 1950s.

On May 15, 1948, the draft of a "law concerning the legal position of those persecuted under the Nazi regime" (Gesetz zur Rechtstellung der Verfolgten des Naziregimes, or VdN-Gesetz) was published in the VVN press, as well as in West Germany. It was discussed and amended in all of the parliaments in the Soviet zone, and then sent to the Soviet authorities. In November 1948 the SED and the VVN approved it and sent it for approval to the Soviet occupation authorities, where it languished without a decision. On February 18, 1949, Ottomar Geschke, now chairman of the VVN for the Soviet zone, wrote to Merker to urge him to persuade the Politburo to push "with all energy" to have the Soviet occupation authorities accept the law.[100] He reminded Merker that the Soviet zone had the dubious distinction of being the only zone of occupation which had not yet passed a law on restitution, and that the SED was now paying a political price in the form of anger among VVN members: "No local conference of the VVN [takes place] without the passing of unanimous resolutions against the delay and foot-dragging [in the Soviet zone] and for an immediate acceptance of the law. No meeting of the [national] council of the VVN in Germany takes place without comment on the nonexistence of a law in the Soviet zone regarding those persecuted under the Nazis. The major conference of the VVN threatens to become a political catastrophe."[101]

Although Merker was troubled by the anomaly of the absence of such a law in the "antifascist" zone of occupation, he was the odd man out.[102] By contrast, rather than seeking to emulate Western policy by paying restitution to "Jewish capitalists," Ulbricht viewed the very prominence of the Jewish issue as evidence of capitalist restoration. The international contacts of the resistance organizations in the Soviet zone, whether with Germans in the Western zones of occupation, Jews from the United States, or Israeli officials, far from recalling the inclusive solidarities of wartime antifascism, instead aroused suspicions at the highest levels of the SED about subversive Western influences.[103]

It was only on October 5, 1949, two days before the German Democratic Republic was founded, and almost four years after debate on the issue began, that the Soviet occupation government adopted a "Regulation for Securing the Legal Position of Those Recognized as Persecuted by the Nazi Regime."[104] It included the distinction between mostly Communist "fighters" and mostly Jewish "victims." The two categories had clearly unequal status and prestige. The law concentrated on welfare provisions for health, housing, and employment for those recognized as persons persecuted by the Nazis. It precluded restitution for property taken by the Nazis, and made no provisions for returning stolen property to the Jewish communities. As in the Matern guidelines of 1947, the restitution law of 1949 made political conformity to policies in the Soviet zone and in the German Democratic Republic an explicit condition for receiving benefits. Many recipients would lose their benefits in the coming years as a result. On February 10, 1950, the East German government issued the orders for implementing the regulations. The law numbered Jews among those persecuted by the Nazi regime, but included no restitution clauses comparable to those which had been passed in the Western zones.[105] The outcome of the restitution debates between 1946 and 1950 was victory for those who believed that there was "no particular German responsibility toward the Jews," and that restitution was a term which applied first of all to German obligations to the Soviet Union.[106] Merker, Zuckermann, and their allies in the VVN had been defeated. While the public rhetoric of antifascist unity in East Berlin continued, the policy outcome of the restitution battles made clear that the wartime solidarity between Communists and Jews proclaimed in Mexico City and elsewhere was diminishing. The struggle also represented a historical chapter in the history of the dialectic of enlightenment in the history of modern communism, that is, the ascendancy of a universalizing and monopolistic rationality over the particularism, in this instance, of stubborn Jewish otherness.

Symbolism and memorial ceremonies were also a source of contention. Here, too, the VVN played a significant role in defining symbolic politics of remembrance at "liberation days" held at former Nazi concentration camps. On April 9–11, 1948, three thousand people attended ceremonies at Buchenwald under the slogan "Fighters against Fascism, Fighters for Peace."[107] It was one of the first of the postwar ceremonies at which the Communists placed memory of the Nazi past in the service of a propaganda offensive against Western policy. Stefan Heymann, a VVN official, offered a grim welcome:

> We greet the 55,000 victims of Buchenwald concentration camp . . . the 4 million Jews and Poles murdered in Auschwitz . . . the millions murdered in other concentration camps . . . the 10,000 who courageously ended their lives on the scaffold . . . the many thousands of victims, brave resistance fighters in Spain, France, Yugoslavia, Poland, and the other countries of Europe. Our very special greetings, however, go to the undying heroes of the Allied armies, above all of the Soviet army, through whose blows German fascism came crashing down.[108]

Heymann expressed solidarity with those who were persecuted by and who fought against Nazism, and included the Jews within this circle of remembrance, victimization, and martyrdom.[109] The key link between past and present, though, was that "as fighters against fascism we were always fighters for peace."[110] He placed the political and moral prestige of anti-Nazi resistance and "above all of the Soviet army" in the service of current Soviet and East German foreign policy.[111] The corollary to his argument was that those who took issue with the Communists were abandoning and betraying the legacy of the antifascist resistance as well.

In accordance with the relatively open nature of the interregnum period, Julius Meyer and Heinz Galinski also spoke. Galinski stressed that "the concept of anti-Semitism must also be discussed in this circle [i.e., the VVN]." Anti-Semitism, he noted, still existed in postwar Germany. He welcomed the decision of authorities in the Soviet zone to make anti-Semitism a criminal offense, and urged the VVN to recall the central role anti-Semitism had played in "reaction." He appealed for solidarity between the "racially" and the "politically" persecuted, that is, between Jews and Communists. "Just as we [Jews] have the greatest respect for the political fighter, precisely because he undertook the fight against Hitler on the basis of conviction, so for the same reason we call for a recognition of all of those who, on racial or religious grounds, entered the concentration camps. The indissoluble bond between all those persecuted on racial grounds and all those persecuted on political grounds is perhaps the brightest chapter in German history."[112] Meyer also stressed the shared bonds between the "politically" and "racially" persecuted. Germans and Jews were fighting similar battles. The Jews in Palestine were fighting for their homeland and government, while the Germans were fighting for a just peace and their own government. This common struggle for justice "must bind us together," he said, recalling Jewish resistance at Auschwitz, the "Aryan wives" of Jewish men who had protested the arrest of their husbands by the Gestapo, and the support of the Soviet Union for the Jews. He warned that he wanted "no empty promises like [the ones] we [Jews] were given in the past."[113]

Walter Bartel (1904–1992), chairman of the International Buchenwald Committee, an assistant to Wilhelm Pieck, and later a historian of the anti-Nazi resistance, also linked the memory of antifascism to the contemporary "fight for peace."[114] He "completely accepted" the criticism from "Comrade Galinski and Julius Meyer . . . Every appearance of anti-Semitism contradicts democratic development" in Germany. Those persecuted on racial or political grounds should "fight against every form and expression of anti-Semitism with all of their might . . . Whoever attacks one of our Jewish comrades attacks us all and should not be surprised if the answer is political, proletarian, and very drastic."[115] So long as Jewish Communists and their allies in the SED had the ability to speak at such occasions, Communist memories of antifascist resistance would include the subsequently unfashionable memory of Jewish persecution.

The emerging East German stance toward the Jewish question in domestic affairs was inseparable from the issue of Israel. In 1947 and

1948 future GDR president Otto Grotewohl secretly met with Julius Meyer and Israeli representatives and hinted vaguely at the possibility of establishing relations with the new Jewish state.[116] Paul Merker's public views of the matter were clear. In a speech delivered to the VVN in 1948, he said that postwar German democracy would be judged by how Germany treated survivors of the political resistance as well as those persecuted as a result of "criminal Nazi racial theories." It should extend toward the Jews' "national efforts [for a Jewish state in Palestine] the dignity and respect they deserve."[117] In February 1948 in the SED's official daily paper, *Neues Deutschland,* and in a more extended essay on "the war in Palestine" in *Die Weltbühne,* Merker supported "the new state of the Jewish people."[118] He interpreted opposition to the UN agreement to partition Palestine between the Jews and the Arabs in light of the interests of "American-English oil companies" in the Middle East. English imperialism during the Nazi era had suffered setbacks as "Hitler's agents" sought the support of Arab princes and feudal lords for German imperialism: "The Nazi agents found support from the side of the anti-English and anti-Semitic Grand Mufti of Jerusalem, Haj Amin el Husseini." Yet with the German defeat in Stalingrad, Ribbentrop's dream of suppressing the peoples of the Middle East ended.

Merker told a story of British imperialist manipulations, opposition to Jewish emigration, and "hundreds of thousands" of Jews who "fell victim to the Nazi murderers" because of British restrictions on Jewish emigration to Palestine.[119] Even though the British had refused to change their emigration policy during the war, Merker noted that 45,000 Jews had fought in the British army and air force in Syria and in Lebanon, against the Rommel Corps, and against Mussolini's forces in Egypt, Libya, and Greece. He criticized the British Labour government for opposing the formation of a Jewish national state. British policy, he said, was "at one with the reactionary group interests of the Arab princes and feudal lords who saw a danger to their absolute domination in the creation of a modern, progressive, democratic state of the Jews in the territory of Palestine."[120] The UN resolution of November 1947 to partition Palestine between Arabs and Jews was the result of the "determined struggle of the masses of the Jewish people for a national homeland. It can help, if only in marginal way, to make up for the immeasurable injustice done to the Jewish people since 1800, and especially in the recent era of Nazism and fascism, if the Jewish people themselves make the most of this chance."[121] Merker spoke of the joy the creation of Israel had brought to Jews and described it as a turning point in the history of the Jewish people.

Merker also said that Israel faced opposition from the British government, American oil interests, and the Arab League, which planned to attack the new Jewish state with an army including "Nazi and fascist elements." The Jewish state would be best served by a policy of independence, good relations with the Arabs, and avoidance of dependence on "the imperialist powers," combined with "close friendship" with the Soviet Union, "the new democracies" of Eastern Europe, and "progressive forces" around the world.[122] He depicted as most natural an affinity between the Communist left and the new state of Israel: support for Israel was the logical conclusion of Communist opposition to racism and anti-Semitism, and to coming to terms with the Nazi past.[123]

On June 12, 1948, the press office of the SED Central Secretariat issue a statement concerning Israel. Merker wrote the introduction, which placed Israel in the vortex of a struggle against imperialism.

Powerful interests of Anglo-American imperialism are involved in the battle for Palestine . . . The Jewish working people are fighting for their homeland. Their national consciousness has been greatly strengthened as a result of the frightful terror of Nazism and fascism against the Jewish people. This heightened consciousness has made them capable of extraordinary accomplishments in battle . . . The struggle of the Jewish workers in Palestine is a progressive struggle. It is directed not against the Arab working masses, but instead against their oppressors. It is supported by the Soviet Union and by all of progressive humanity.[124]

Unfortunately for Paul Merker, and for the Jews living in the Soviet zone of occupation, within a year the meaning of who was and who was not a member of "progressive humanity" would undergo a drastic transformation.

The division of memory along the fault lines of the Cold War was evident in controversies that broke out in 1948 in the VVN between non-Communist and Communist inheritors of the resistance mantle. One of the most important defections from the VVN was that of Eugen Kogon in May 1949. Kogon, who had been imprisoned in Buchenwald from 1938 to 1945, was co-founder and co-editor, with Walter Dirks, of the left-liberal journal *Frankfurter Hefte,* and he played a prominent political role in West German intellectual life in the 1950s and 1960s. His book *Der SS Staat,* published in German in 1946 and in 1950 in English as *The Theory and Practice of Hell,* became a classic description of the horror of the Nazi concentration camps.[125] Stefan Heymann had been one of Kogon's research collaborators.[126] The concluding chapter of the second German, and first English, edition was titled "The German People and the Concentration Camps—after 1945."[127] Kogon now wrote about both the anti-Nazi resistance and resistance to "the shadows of Soviet dictatorship," including Communist concentration camps and the political prisons which had emerged in the Soviet zone in Germany by 1949.[128] He thus turned the legacy of the anti-Nazi resistance against postwar Communist practices in Eastern Germany. Those who had been persecuted by the Nazi regime for their race, religion, or political convictions, he wrote, now "must raise their voices against the new and glaring injustices throughout the world and in Germany, particularly against Soviet Russia and the eastern zone!" Their protests would be more effective than those "from any other source" and certainly from those Germans whose protests would "be suspect because of their own prior guilt or weakness"[129] For Kogon, the old antifascism had lost its moral force because it was failing "to oppose the new injustices." He hoped for a "wholesome revulsion against any form of concentration camp" among the Germans.[130]

In an article in the May 1949 issue of the *Frankfurter Hefte,* "The Political Collapse of the European Resistance," Kogon examined the breaking of bonds between Communist and non-Communist antifascists.[131] The wartime hopes that anti-Nazis would remain united in a postwar Germany had proved excessively optimistic. The European anti-Nazi resistance as a political factor was now only a memory. The organizations that cultivated that memory now played a "dangerous and sad" role. In the East "antifascism" directed its aim at Western capitalism, while those who criticized "totalitarian dictatorship" in the West generally focused on the postwar Communist regimes. Contemporary enemies had replaced the shared enemy of the past.[132] While non-Communists in the resistance supported individual liberty against Hitler, and later Stalin, the Communists remained "soldiers of the class struggle" and now dominated the postwar resistance organizations. They used their control to turn the resistance organizations into tools of international politics to divert attention from dictatorial developments in the Communist states.[133] As they degenerated into vehicles of Soviet policy, and refrained from criticizing violations of human rights in the Soviet occupation zone, the VVN and other resistance organizations lost their moral authority.[134]

Several weeks later Heymann, now director of the Office of Culture and Education in the SED Central Committee, angrily responded to Kogon's arguments in a page one article in the VVN journal *Die Tat*.[135] Kogon's claims about concentration camps and a Communist terror were "lies" which "only benefited the warmongers and neofascists." He went on, "Today, to divide or weaken the antifascist front in Europe means to open the door to a return of fascism. This may not ring so pleasantly in Dr. Kogon's ears, for he was unquestionably a confirmed fighter against German fascism. However, he appears not to have seen that with his article, he opened the path to a new anti-Semitism and a new racism, in short, a new neofascist movement."[136] Because the Communists were by definition antifascists, any criticism of the Communists "opened the path" to a new era of fascism. The political utility of antifascism in immunizing the Communists from criticism had outlived Nazism. For Heymann, those such as Kogon who voiced such criticism were now beyond the pale of legitimate antifascism.

It was one thing for a German Catholic leftist intellectual such as Kogon to break with the "myth" of antifascist resistance. It was quite another for a German Jewish Communist such as Leo Zuckermann to give up his hopes for a renewal of solidarity between Communists and Jews. In March 1949 an article appeared in Moscow which attacked "cosmopolitans without a fatherland." The Western press interpreted it as the beginning of a new anti-Semitic campaign in the Soviet Union. In view of his experiences since returning to East Berlin, Zuckermann might have taken the article as a sign that the days for Communists with views such as his were numbered. Instead, he attacked the messenger. In June 1949 he wrote a remarkable article in *Die Tat* titled "We Will Never Fight against the Liberators of Maidanek and Auschwitz." In it, he stated, "The reactionary press has started a new anti-Soviet smear campaign concerning a supposed 'anti-Semitic campaign' in the Soviet Union. Who can fail to grasp the purpose of these lies? The working people of Jewish origin are bound up in the deepest manner with the Soviet Union and with the social order that is taking place there."[137] While the Soviet Union had opened its borders to hundreds of thousands of Polish Jews fleeing the Nazi invasion, the United States had "reduced the right of exile to nothing for all practical purposes." It was the Red Army which had defeated "the Nazi cannibals" and "saved those Jews still alive from the gas chambers of Maidanek, Auschwitz, Mauthausen, and many other death factories." Furthermore, the Soviet Union was the first state to recognize the new state of Israel and was instrumental in bringing about its recognition by other states in the United Nations. Since the end of the war, Zuckermann continued, anti-Semitism and race hatred had steadily increased in the United States, England, and France. "The experience of fascism" had led "Jewish working people" to see that anti-Semitism and nationalist hatred were an "inherent feature of capitalist society."[138]

In the socialist states, by contrast, "the Jew is a new man, an equal among equals, who as a Soviet man is most deeply rooted in the socialist fatherland." The government fights against racism and anti-Semitism. The Jewish working people, Zuckermann wrote, understood that the creation of Israel alone would not solve "the Jewish question as a whole." That required socialism and the "international solidarity of the workers against nationalism, fascism, and racism." It was this deep bond of the Jewish workers in the capitalist countries with the socialist Soviet Union and its army that the reactionaries of all nationalities, including Jewish reactionaries, are trying to undermine. That is why they publish false news reports at regular intervals about anti-Semitic measures in the Soviet Union and in the people's democracies. Reactionary Jewish organizations, whose leadership is personally and financially linked to the ruling circles of the United States, rejected any participation in the [Communist-controlled] World Peace Conference in Paris. They are ensnared with preparations for war against the progressive sector of humanity. With their false reports they want to create anti-Soviet sentiment, disorient the Jewish working people, and bring them into the imperialist camp. Jewish working people know only one answer to these maneuvers: We will never fight against the liberators of Maidenek and Auschwitz!"[139]

The "liberators of Maidanek and Auschwitz" who had defeated Nazism could not possibly be anti-Semites. Yet the reports were true. These "liberators" were indeed purging, arresting, and in some cases even murdering prominent members of the wartime Jewish Antifascist Committee.[140] They were the same persons who had appealed to Jews around the world to aid the Soviet Union in its most desperate hours, and who had visited Mexico City in August 1943 in that effort.

Paul Merker remained a member of the SED Politburo until spring 1950. On December 21, 1949, on the occasion of Stalin's seventieth birthday, Merker published birthday greetings to the "the best friend and helper of the German people." He thanked Stalin for "the liberation from the Nazi yoke" and for the "trust" Stalin had shown the Germans. "In the spirit of Stalin, we are conducting the struggle against American imperialism, for German unity, and securing peace," Merker wrote. "With Stalinist energy, we will attain a peace treaty in 1950."[141] With the exception of his views on Jewish matters, Merker was fully at home with the spirit of the emerging Cold War. He could again give vent to his long-standing hostility to German Social Democrats. In 1949 he published *Sozialdemokratismus: Stampfer, Schumacher und Andere Gestrige* (Social Democracy: Stampfer, Schumacher, and Other Relics of the Past).[142] It was an attack on Social Democratic leaders that recalled his infamous attacks on social democracy in the Weimar Republic's last years. His animus against the Social Democrats and the Western powers was evident in a speech he delivered at the Soviet cultural center in East Berlin on February 3, 1950, titled "Was geht im Westen vor?" (What's Going on in the West?).[143] The Adenauer government was "a Quisling regime of the most evil sort" composed of "marionettes" seeking to place the Germans on the side of "Anglo-American imperialism and their German monopolist clients."[144] This was not, he continued, "the first time that immediately after a lost war these German gentlemen have sold themselves to the former enemy in order to move against their own people and against progressive humanity. I recall 1919 and 1920 all too well." Moreover—as in 1919 and 1920—the Social Democrats, "the Schumacher clique," were supporting the same powers, that is, "Anglo-American imperialism" and the leaders of German industry responsible for "the Nazi war."[145] The Communists, with help from the Soviet Union, were fighting against "the enslavement of Germany" and for peace and "national liberation."[146]

Merker was a loyal though left-wing Communist. In a sense, for him the Cold War represented a turn away from the relative moderation of the Popular Front to his radicalism of the 1920s, including the Comintern's Third Period attacks on Weimar social democracy. Yet Merker's orthodoxy in matters regarding acceptance of dictatorial power in the Soviet zone, the assault on the democratic left in the West, and the international politics of the Cold War would not prove sufficient to overcome his by now well established public and intragovernmental record on the Jewish question. While his views on Jewish matters were tolerable during the wartime emigration and the immediate postwar era, they became intolerable heresies as the wartime alliance collapsed and was replaced by the new fault lines of the Cold War. Institutions of repression created while he was a member of the Politburo and whose repressive measures he had not protested would now be turned against him. The long paper trail of his interoffice memos of the occupation years and published works of the Mexican emigration would come back to haunt him. In the struggle for power and influence in the Politburo, his sympathies for the Jews would now be held against him. The interregnum was ending, and with it hope for the solidarity between Communists and Jews evoked by Merker and Zuckermann. The year 1950 was not to be a good one for Paul Merker. In East Berlin the purge of the "cosmopolitans" began.

# 5

## Purging "Cosmopolitanism": The Jewish Question in East Germany, 1949–1956

---

By 1948 the wartime alliance had collapsed and been replaced by the new, and reversed, fronts of the Cold War. In both East and West, present politics was projected back into the past with the result that wartime solidarities became at best a political embarrassment and at worst grounds for suspicion of disloyalty. In the Soviet bloc the anti-fascist allies of 1941 to 1945 once again became Western imperialists. Stalin's own wartime "Western alliance" was now an embarrassing and fleeting chapter, at best a cynical alliance of convenience, and at worst a source of subversive ideas about democracy and human freedom. Those Communists who had spent the war years in Western emigration fell under a cloud of suspicion. The German Communists returning from Stalin's wartime Moscow had little difficulty mobilizing their version of wartime antifascism in the service of the Cold War. Those returning from the West, Jews, or simply anyone who could not or would not make such a dramatic and sudden shift of allegiance and memory were in an especially precarious position. The marginalization of the Jewish catastrophe was inseparable from the forgetting of the Soviet Union's wartime alliance with the West.

Postwar Communist antagonism to the West overlapped with and reinforced both older and more recent anti-Western and illiberal currents of German nationalism.[1] The conjuncture of Cold War antago-

nisms with older nationalist resentments reinforced the existing marginalization of the Holocaust in official Communist memory, fueled a
purge of those within the Communist world who supported postwar
solidarity between Communists and Jews, and sustained four decades of
anti-Jewish policies at home and abroad.[2] Since the mid-nineteenth
century, German liberals and socialists had argued that the struggle
against anti-Semitism was inseparable from the struggle for democracy.
The purging of "cosmopolitans" and a wave of government-initiated
anti-Semitism were important steps in the consolidation of the "antifascist" dictatorship in East Berlin. These were also among the most
grotesque ironies of German history since 1945.

In 1948–49 the crystallization of the Cold War brought with it a
re-Stalinization of the SED into what the Communists called "a party
of a new type" modeled on the Communist Party of the Soviet Union.[3]
World War II and the occupation era had blurred distinctions between
Communists and non-Communists. In 1948 a third of the 2 million
members of the SED had been Social Democrats. Re-Stalinization
meant the end of any pretense that there would be parity between
Communists and Social Democrats and brought repression of the hints
of fresh air that had entered the Communist parties during the period
of the Popular Front and the war. It also meant the formation of the
Zentralparteikontrollkommission (Central Party Control Commission).
Led by Herman Matern, the ZPKK, as it was known, enforced ideological conformity and uncovered ideological deviations. The SED's first
party conference in January 1949 represented a high point of the
Stalinization campaign. At its sixteenth meeting, on January 24, 1949,
the party leadership elected a Politburo that would lead the party in
the direction of Marx, Lenin, and Stalin. This new leadership included
the veteran Communists Wilhelm Pieck, Franz Dahlem, Paul Merker,
Walter Ulbricht, and the former Social Democrats Otto Grotewohl,
Friedrich Ebert (1894–1979), and Helmut Lehmann.[4]

From 1949 to 1953 the essential instruments of Stalinist dictatorship
were put in place in the German Democratic Republic. Article 6 of the
East German constitution stipulated that incitement to racial and nationalist hatred, fostering a "witch-hunt [*Boykotthetze*] against demo-

cratic institutions and organizations," and opposing efforts at equality were crimes.[5] Such vague and general formulas could be and were used to criminalize and then repress political dissenters. In December 1949 the Oberste Gericht, the East German Supreme Court, was established. In 1950 alone it convicted over 78,000 persons of political crimes, and carried out fifteen death sentences.[6] On February 8, 1950, the Ministerium für Staatssicherheitsdienst (MfS) was established. Although other parties had seats in the East German parliament, or Volkskammer, the SED in fact had a monopoly of power.[7] At the SED Third Party Conference of July 20–24 in East Berlin, the leadership demanded a sharpened struggle against the "Tito-clique," Trotskyists, and the "remains of Social Democratism" within the SED. It called on party members to increase their "revolutionary vigilance" and to "expose and destroy the bourgeois-nationalist elements and all other enemies of the working class and agents of imperialism, no matter what flag they flew."[8] In the year that followed, as a result of investigations by the Central and by local party control commissions, 150,000 people, most of them Social Democrats, were expelled from the SED. The vast preponderance of Communist repression was directed at non-Communists.

Yet the revolution devoured its own as well. Paul Merker was the most prominent Communist Party victim of the Stalinist apparatus which was constructed when he was at the pinnacle of power. I have noted that Merker combined Communist orthodoxy with continuing solidarity with Jewish survivors. With the shift of alliances to the Cold War, his sympathies for the Jews became a political liability, what the Germans call *ungleichzeitig*, or "out of phase." At the Third Party Conference he was not reelected to his position in the Politburo. Stalin and the Stalinists of the Soviet bloc such as Ulbricht threw overboard the excess baggage of the dissonant memories of World War II and the Holocaust as they turned their ship of state around to fight the Western imperialists.

The anticosmopolitan campaign drew on mutually reinforcing associations of Jews with the West, as well as Stalin's personal blend of paranoia and anti-Semitism.[9] While World War II had expanded contact with the West and with Jews in the West, the Cold War would now immunize the Soviet bloc from their subversive impact. The campaign began with the murder of Solomon Mikhoels on January 12, 1948.[10] In November 1948 the Soviet government abolished the Jewish Antifascist Committee and arrested its leaders.[11] In March 1949 an article on "the uncovering of bourgeois cosmopolitanism" was published in Moscow in the German-language paper *Neue Zeit*. It described cosmpolitanism as a key element of reactionary bourgeois ideology and American imperialism.[12] In the Middle East, Soviet policy turned from its initial support to enduring hostility to the new Jewish state. The anticosmopolitan campaign had clearly been initiated and inspired by Stalin. The East German Communists, however, far from protesting against the campaign, made their own distinctive contribution to it.

In Moscow in 1943 Walter Ulbricht's answer to his question "Who is the enemy of the German nation?" was the Nazis and German big industrialists.[13] Conversely, the Communists were the genuine representatives of the nation. In East Berlin in 1949, he again presented the Communists as defenders of the nation against new threats. Ulbricht and Pieck placed the entire blame for the division of Germany on the United States and Great Britain, and on those within Germany, especially the Social Democrats around Kurt Schumacher, who had refused to ally with the Communists.[14] In a speech delivered to a party conference in Berlin in May 1949, Ulbricht argued that it was the SED that was leading the "struggle against the division and for the unity of Germany."[15] Dispensing with the now obsolete rhetoric of wartime cooperation, he projected Cold War antagonisms into the past. The American and British war aim had not been the democratization and demilitarization of Germany but "the destruction of Germany as an independent state."[16] In the face of the "division and colonization of West Germany" at the hands of the United States, he called for "struggle against the forces which sought to colonize Germany and enslave the German people, above all, the working class."[17] Indeed, "in its essentials," he continued, Western propaganda resembled Hitler's "fascist propaganda" about the "community of the European peoples." Cosmopolitanism was "nothing other than the ideology of the Western military bloc, of the Atlantic bloc, and of preparation for military aggression." In contrast to this cosmopolitan betrayal of the nation, the Communists took "the standpoint of preservation of the national interest of every people, respect for their particular national characteristics, and friendly relations between the individual peoples and between their states."[18] In July 1949 Pieck argued that the Communists were defending the German people against "the acute danger" of loss of national independence and colonization which would follow from the Marshall Plan and the linking of West Germany to a Western alliance.[19]

Throwing off the burdens of a dark past, Ulbricht and Pieck spoke confidently as leaders of a future-oriented German anticolonial revolt against Western domination. Remarkably, within only three years the Communists had removed the Germans from the ranks of those "millions and millions" who had been complicitous with the perpetrators of mass crimes and transformed them into a nation of innocent victims of American imperialism. Communist nationalism went hand in hand with the task of unburdening the Germans of their difficult past.

Moreover, and very significantly, Ulbricht made clear that in the Soviet zone today's political attitudes were more important than yesterday's actions.

> Today, the measure of who is a peace-loving individual and who seeks German unity is not what party membership book they had earlier, and whether or not they belonged to the Hitler party. Rather, the only measure is: Are you for a peace treaty? Are you against the Atlantic Pact, as a result of which West Germany would be made into a base for war? Are you for the unity of Germany? Are you for the withdrawal of occupation troops following the conclusion of a peace treaty, or are you for a forty-year occupation and colonization of West Germany? Today, under these conditions, anyone who raises the question "Is this person a former member of the Nazi party or not" works against the formation of the National Front.[20]

Not only did such comments open the door to employment of former members of the Nazi Party and government in the emergent Communist government. Ulbricht went much farther. Demonstration of politically correct views in the present were sufficient to erase the past, while those—perhaps misled by the spirit of antifascism—who raised questions about the Nazi past of others were now threats to national unity! The new outsiders were old Communists unable or unwilling to change their hearts and minds to adapt to the reversal of alliances—and, of course, those permanent cosmopolitans, the Jews.

The meaning of coming to terms with the Nazi past was simple and straightforward: smash capitalism. The Communists had always claimed that capitalism contained the roots of Nazism. Because these roots had been ripped up in the Soviet zone of occupation but were being replanted in the Western zones, the possibility of a renewed fascism now lay outside, and only outside, East German borders in Western Germany. Antifascism was now directed against the West German present. It no longer referred exclusively or even primarily to the Nazi past. Antifascism and Nazism, signifier and signified, were split apart in both place and time.[21]

The most thorough East German explanation of the meaning of cosmopolitanism appeared between October and July 1949 in the theoretical and cultural monthly *Einheit* in a four-part series of articles written by SED Central Committee member Ernst Hoffmann (1909–?).[22] Hoffmann was a member of the Volkskammer who worked in the East German Ministry of Culture.[23] First, his article distinguished between proletarian internationalism, which was good, and bourgeois cosmopolitanism, which was bad.[24] Marxists understood that proletarian class consciousness, as in Germany, "could be temporarily buried" yet, as was happening in postwar East Germany, could also renew itself with "powers of regeneration and ascension to socialist, internationalist class consciousness."[25] Cosmopolitans and cosmopolitanism, however, posed a threat to this reviving proletarian consciousness and to the nation. "Cosmopolitanism is the ideal of the 'money man,'" he wrote, a "man without a country." The worldview of the cosmopolitan bourgeois consisted of "complete indifference" to the destiny of his own country and his people, "cynical contempt" for all moral bonds and national duties, and "beating and betrayal of his own

people." It represented "the most complete image of capitalist exploitation" which dissolves all human and national bonds, leaving only
"naked, brutal capitalist exploitation on a world level." Hoffmann descended to remarkable degrees of abuse. "The cosmopolitan" was, in
so many words, a murderer who was "out to kill the working men of
all peoples and transform them into abstract, schematic objects of
exploitation, tear them out of the connection with their own people and
class, and rob them of their national characteristics."[26] The home and
"global center" of cosmopolitanism was the United States, and its
agents were in place in West Germany.[27] Although Hoffmann did not
specifically refer to the Jews, his readers, politically experienced and
educated Communist intellectuals, knew that this description was a
rather complete catalogue of traditional anti-Semitic stereotypes. Some
may also have recalled that the Nazis attacked the United States in
similar terms, or noticed that when Hoffmann referred to the racist
implications of cosmopolitanism, he mentioned hatred directed against
Poles and Slavs but left out any mention of anti-Semitism.

For German Communist eyes and ears in 1949, there was no doubt
that these cosmopolitans were Jews, and that it was West German
politicians such as Konrad Adenauer and Kurt Schumacher who had
"betrayed" and "split" the nation by opposing the Communists.[28] In the
early days of the Cold War, the anti-Western resentments of German
nationalism, the *Sonderweg* in new clothes, emerged with renewed vigor
in the form of the attack on cosmopolitanism. Stalin launched the
anticosmopolitan purges, but the national Communist leaderships provided the detailed narratives of the vast conspiracy. So far, no evidence
has emerged that points to East German opposition to or criticism of
the anticosmopolitan campaign. After all, the initiatives from Moscow
struck familiar ideological chords in East Berlin, and constituted a
powerful weapon with which the exiles returning from Moscow could
destroy potential rivals returning from the West.[29]

Within the SED, the key institution charged with purging the party
of "spies and saboteurs" and "corrupt elements" was the Central Party
Control Commission, or ZPKK.[30] The ZPKK was created in September
16, 1948.[31] Its chair was Hermann Matern (1893–1971), a member of

the KPD since its founding, and part of the Ulbricht group in Moscow. Matern spent the wartime years in Moscow and had been a member of the Nationale Komitee Freies Deutschland. He was a member of the SED Central Committee, and chair of the ZPKK without interruption from 1946 until he died in 1971.[32] He was the SED's grand inquisitor and primary enforcer of political conformity.[33] With the creation of the Ministerium für Staatssicherheit (Ministry for State Security, or MfS), better known as the Stasi, on February 8, 1950, and its close coordination with political courts, the SED had constructed the key elements of a new totalitarian regime.[34]

Because in the Communist parties yesterday's correct line could and did become today's deviation, the guardians of orthodoxy of the moment had a special interest in the past. The Communists returning from Mexican exile, sometimes called "die Mexikaner" (the Mexicans), and their views on Jewish matters posed a challenge to the SED's conception of antifascism. Paul Merker and Leo Zuckermann both had long track records of expressing views that could now be denounced as "cosmopolitanism." During the emigration they had fled west, not east. They had publicly praised the wartime Atlantic Alliance. After the war they had supported restitution for the Jews and good relations with Israel.[35] Merker's speeches and publications in Mexico City from 1942 to 1946 and his bureaucratic politicking in the restitution debates in postwar East Berlin represented the most, indeed the only, extended confrontation with the Jewish catastrophe by a member of the KPD Politburo or the SED Central Committee in the history of German and East German communism. When first expressed, these views were part of a current—though, to be sure, a minority current—of German and European Communist thinking. From the perspective of the Cold War and the anticosmopolitan campaign, they fell under a cloud of suspicion. Why, the inquisitors asked, would a *Communist* pay attention to *these* issues? As a result of the opening of the SED and Stasi archives, it is now possible to write the history of the internal purges and secret political trials in which "cosmopolitans" within and outside the Communist Party were expelled, denounced, and imprisoned.[36] The evidence indicates that the silences of East German antifascism concerning the

Jewish question rested on the repression of a minority tradition among Communists as well as of non-Communist voices.[37]

In September 1949 the Rajk trial in Budapest initiated a series of spectacular show trials of leading members of the Communist parties in Hungary, Bulgaria, Czechoslovakia, and East Germany. Most were Jewish. During World War II in wartime France, all had had contact with one Noel Field, an American leftist and perhaps a member of some Communist party. He helped many leftists fleeing Nazism, including German Communists escaping from Vichy France on their way to Mexico City.[38] In the espionage hysteria of 1950, the leftist Field became transformed in Communist accusations into an "American agent." Even heroes of the antifascist resistance were not above suspicion. In October 1949 Franz Dahlem was relieved of responsibilities for "cadre questions" in the SED and fell under suspicion as a result of his activities in France. In the first week of June 1950, the ZPKK interrogated Rudolf Feistmann, a friend of Merker, Zuckermann, and Otto Katz, who had written often on Jewish matters in Mexico in the pages of the *Demokratische Post*. On June 9, 1950 he was reported to have died of food poisoning, though it is more likely that he committed suicide rather than face further interrogations.[39] Others who had been in Mexico or who knew Field lost their jobs or endured demotions.

On August 24, 1950, in a resolution concerning "the connections between former German political emigrants and the director of the Unitarian Service Committee, Noel H. Field," the SED Central Committee and the ZPKK formally began the East German purge in connection with the Field affair.[40] According to the resolution, the Rajk trial in Budapest and other investigations had revealed that Paul Merker was an agent of Anglo-American imperialism. As a result of their contact with the supposed American agent Field, and their alleged help for "the class enemy" Merker, Leo Bauer, Bruno Goldhammer, Willy Kreikemeyer, Lex Ende, and Maria Weiterer were fired from their government positions and expelled from the SED.[41] Merker was given a job as a waiter in a restaurant.

According to the Central Committee and Control Commission denunciation, the purpose of Field's assistance was to infiltrate the Communist parties and undermine the antifascist resistance in Europe. The fact that Merker and the other members of the resistance had fled to Mexico rather than remain in France was said to confirm this hypothesis.[42] Their political sins included showing "no trust in the Soviet Union" following the Hitler-Stalin pact, failing to understand that agreement or "to grasp the character of American imperialism," being lulled into complacency "by Roosevelt's progressive stance," and regarding "every American as an antifascist and officials of the USA State Department as allies of the working class." They had been so foolish as to imagine "that the goal of American, English, and French imperialism consisted in the liberation of Europe from fascism." Merker, Lex Ende, Willy Kreikemeyer, Paul Bertz, and Leo Bauer, allegedly under orders from American imperialists, had "sabotaged the development of an antifascist resistance movement." They had done so supposedly to prevent Hitler's overthrow by an indigenous German resistance in order to create a divided postwar Germany whose Western half would become an "anti-Soviet bulwark."[43]

There was method in the madness of this paranoid construct, one which sheds light on the official memory of the Nazi past in East Germany. First, and most obviously, with the exception of Merker, all of the accused were Jewish, thus stressing the link between cosmopolitanism, disloyalty, espionage, and the Jews. The ZPKK officials also interrogated suspects at length about their wartime contact with Jews.[44] Second, the Field denunciations attacked the suspects for taking seriously the spirit of the anti-Hitler coalition, that is, for regarding the alliance with the West as anything more than a marriage of convenience with the class enemy. Third, in asserting that Churchill's Britain and Roosevelt's America aimed not at the "liberation of Europe from fascism" but rather at establishing an anti-Soviet bulwark in Europe, the denunciations projected the antagonisms of the Cold War back into the war years. Not only were the Western democracies enemies in 1950 but also, according to the Field denunciations, they had not even been "antifascists" when they were fighting the Nazis! By implication, among the great powers only the Soviet Union had been genuinely interested in the "liberation of Europe from fascism." Fourth, the denunciations assumed amnesia about the Soviet Union's own four-year "Western alliance" with the United States and Great Britain. They also generated a climate of fear in which even family members sought to distance themselves from the accused.[45]

The Jewish issue was an undercurrent of the Field affair but not the main theme. As a public event, it was the Communist counterpart to the famous Cold War spy trials taking place in the United States. If the Merker case, and the anticosmopolitan campaign, had ended with the Field denunciations, it would have remained, like the Hiss and Rosenberg cases, only an espionage case linked to the rapid reversal of alliances and loyalties entailed in the shift from the anti-Hitler coalition of World War II to the Cold War, a chapter in the history of discipline and punishment that followed the multitude of contacts between Communists and non-Communists during World War II. Or, given Merker's two years in the United States, six years in France, and four years in Mexico, it would have been another example of the suspicion and paranoia which greeted so many Communists who had fled to the West during the Nazi era. The Field affair, however, was only the beginning of Merker's difficulties, and of the difficulties of many other, less prominent "cosmopolitans" returning from Western emigration. As the Control Commission files indicate, as early as the fall of 1950, Merker's contacts with Jews, along with his public arguments concerning Jewish matters, were playing a large role in accusations that he was an agent of American imperialism and Zionism.[46] Anti-Semitic prejudices had become part of the consolidation of power by the Moscow émigrés over potential rivals among "the Mexikaner."

Even in a purge, even among Jewish Communists in East Berlin, even in the early 1950s, some "Communists of Jewish origin" managed to save their necks—and careers. Between 1949 and 1961, when the Berlin Wall was built, 2.6 million people fled East Germany, most to West Germany.[47] Rather than flee the purge, some party members, such as Alexander Abusch, successfully fought to regain status and power within the SED. Upon returning to East Berlin in 1946, Abusch became active in the SED's Cultural Association for the Democratic Renewal of Germany (Kulturbund zur demokratischen Erneuerung Deutsch-lands) and was on the way to a successful career as a high-ranking cultural functionary when, in July 1950, as a result of his wartime contact with Noel Field, the ZPKK relieved him of all of his party functions. Yet by summer 1951, he was back in the party's good graces and again working in the Kulturbund. From 1954 to 1956 he was deputy minister to Minister of Culture Johannes R. Becher, and from 1956 to 1958 he was a state secretary in the Ministry of Culture. From 1956 until his retirement in 1975, he was a member of the Central Committee of the SED. Abusch was at the pinnacle of his career in Communist cultural politics from 1958 to 1961, when he served as the East German minister of culture and oversaw the construction of the memorials to victims of fascism at Buchenwald and Sachsenhausen. He was a mem-ber of the SED Central Committee from 1956 until his death in 1982.[48]

To understand the suppression of the Jewish question in East Ger-many, it is as important to trace Abusch's path from disgrace to redemp-tion as it is to document Merker's fall. On July 18, 1950, a month before the Field denunciations were made public, the Control Commission expelled Abusch from the Central Committee Secretariat and denied him further permission to hold any positions in the party.[49] Soon after receiving the news, Abusch wrote directly to Walter Ulbricht. "Today, in the most difficult situation of my life," he asked for a "rapid con-frontation with those who have made false assertions about me. Other-wise I am politically destroyed before things are even explained."[50] Abusch's problem was guilt by association. After all, he had been editor of *Freies Deutschland* in Mexico City. In November 1950 the ZPKK interrogated him and probed into his involvement with Jewish organi-zations in Mexico. Abusch insisted that, though born into a Jewish family, he had no interest at all in Jewish matters, and did not agree with Merker's views on the Jewish question which he had published in *Freies Deutschland*.[51] The ZPKK and the SED Central Committee were not convinced. They decided to uphold the decision to relieve him of all his party functions, in part because "he published Merker's false views on the question of Jewish emigration in the nationalities question and on restitution without limits."[52]

On March 19, 1951, Merker wrote to Abusch to request a meeting. "You can imagine that I'm very alone, and probably things are not much better for you," he wrote. Merker wanted to talk about "presentation of our work in Mexico with the fewest possible gaps."[53] The letter, probably intercepted by the Stasi, did not arrive at the Abusch home until April 12. Abusch, fearful of having anything to do with the now disgraced Merker, immediately brought the note to Ulbricht's attention. On May 15, 1951, Merker called the Abusch home. Abusch's wife, Hilde, answered while Alexander was in the room. Upon hearing that Merker wished to speak to Abusch, she said, "We have nothing to say to one another" and immediately hung up. Abusch wrote to Ulbricht right away to inform him of Merker's call. Ulbricht sent the letters, notes, and envelopes from Merker to Abusch, and from Abusch to Ulbricht, to Central Committee member Erich Mielke, who was also the state secretary and, after 1953, minister of the Stasi.[54] By going directly to Ulbricht, Abusch hoped to demonstrate that he wanted nothing to do with Merker, and to show Ulbricht and Mielke how badly he sought rehabilitation.

Determined to demonstrate his loyalty to the party and to escape guilt by association with his former Mexican comrades, on May 30, 1951, Abusch wrote to officials at the Ministry of State Security to express his readiness to be of assistance: "In the interest of the party and the working class, and for socialism, I undertake the obligation to the best of my abilities to be helpful, in cooperation with the organs of State Security in uncovering enemies of the party and other enemies of the working class. At the same time, I solemnly swear to keep silent about these obligations and about everything that I learn in connection with them toward everyone, including my wife."[55] From May 30, 1951, until October 26, 1956, Abusch worked as a "secret informer" for the Stasi.[56] Abusch knew all of the prominent intellectuals in East Germany and offered Ulbricht and Mielke a splendid window into the cultural elite. During the summer of 1951, Abusch began a journey to redemption and rehabilitation. He regained his party positions and was again at work in the Kulturbund zur demokratischen Erneuerung.

Redemption did not come easily, however. On April 18, 1953, Stasi officers summarized their case against Abusch.[57] His crimes constituted a list of associations with the wrong people and expression of wrong ideas. In Vichy France he had had contact with Willy Kreikemeyer, who had been denounced in 1950 for her contact with Noel Field. Field was said to have helped Abusch get to Mexico. Merker pointed to the support Abusch had given him when he found Otto Katz innocent of Georg Stibi's accusations of espionage. In building their case, the ZPKK and the Stasi cleverly exploited the political and personal conflicts and jealousies of the Mexican emigration for their own purposes.[58]

On December 31, 1952, Stasi officers interrogated Götz Berger, the Justice Department official who had opposed Merker and Zuckermann's restitution policies in East Berlin. His testimony damaged Merker, Zuckermann, and Abusch. Berger revealed that Abusch, as editor of the *Weltbühne,* had prevented publication of a critical response by Berger to Zuckermann's article on restitution to the Jews and support for creation of a Jewish state.[59] Indeed, Berger recalled that Abusch had told him that "Zuckermann should be the adviser to the Central Committee for Jewish issues."[60] Erich Jungmann, another former member of the Mexican emigration, further damaged Abusch when he told Stasi interrogators that Abusch had had close contact with and defended Otto Katz, had helped to popularize Katz's "false politics," and had expressed "Zionist views."[61] If Berger and Jungmann were telling the truth, the Stasi and the ZPKK officials had to conclude that Abusch was being less than completely truthful when he insisted that he had no interest in Jewish matters.

In fact, the Stasi officers did complain about Abusch's reports, which began on October 12, 1951.[62] He wrote most extensively about people, such as Otto Katz and Merker, "who were already officially known" [to be agents] or who were dead, such as Rudolf Feistmann. They concluded that "he wants to keep still unexplained cases hidden, and protect the persons involved," and was doing little to explain "enemy activity in the Western emigration." His "whole effort," they judged, was devoted "to whitewashing" his own activity, and to "minimiz[ing] his own possible incrimination by claiming lack of knowledge on the basis of Merker's dictatorial behavior in Mexico." He had submitted "self-critical statements of his loyalty to the party without, however, offering the party any help worth mentioning in the investigation" of the Mexican emigration. They recommended that Abusch be subjected to "sharper interrogation," with the use of "methods of pressure" to make him "write something concrete and specific about the questions that are of interest to us."[63]

Abusch was walking a fine line, cooperating enough to gain rehabilitation and political survival while harming as few people as possible in the process. He knew that the espionage charges against Merker were absurd. His own defense rested on the assertion that Merker, acting every bit the Politburo member he was, had created a mini-dictatorship in Mexico City, which had led to the publication of his views on Jewish matters against Abusch's wishes. If this were true, the appearance of the essays in *Freies Deutschland* would be less incriminating for Abusch. As implausible as the "mini-dictatorship" hypothesis was, it did grease the wheels of Abusch's rehabilitation. Abusch's case illustrates the harsh terms of assimilation under which "Communists of Jewish origin" were able to remain at the top levels of the East German party and government. Those terms unequivocally precluded a prominent place for remembering the Jewish catastrophe or supporting Israel in the present.

Leo Zuckermann could not take Abusch's path. His paper trail was too long. On November 10, 1950, Herte Geffke of the ZPKK interrogated Zuckermann, who was at the time state secretary and chief of staff the office of President Wilhelm Pieck, a position he occupied from October 1949 to May 1951.[64] "We especially want to know," Geffke told him, "something about the political line [of the German Communists in Mexico City] regarding the Jewish question," and about Menorah, the organization of German-speaking Jews in Mexico City.[65] She asked Zuckermann about the decision of the German Communists in Mexico to participate in activities of the exile Jewish community. When his questioners asked if he too had joined these activities, Zuckermann said, "Yes. We joined. It was the time of the persecution of the Jews. We joined to show a certain solidarity." Geffke replied that "this is a peculiar stance." He assured her that their intent was to organize Jews into the Freies Deutschland organization. But didn't he know, she asked, that "members of the Jewish community had been called to the American intelligence agencies?"[66] She also asked him about Merker, André Simone (Otto Katz), and their support for restitution in Mexico City and in postwar East Berlin.[67]

Three days later Zuckermann wrote to Geffke to underscore his orthodox credentials. In 1948 he had publicly opposed the laws in the American zone of occupation which called for restitution to Jews who had emigrated and had no established residence in Germany. These proposals were "an additional attempt at penetration of foreign capital and at the foreign control of the German economy," he declared. Furthermore, his arguments had elicited "catcalls from the well-known American commissioner for property in Bavaria, Dr. Auerbach." Also, at a meeting of VVN members from all of the occupation zones, held in 1948 or 1949, he had publicly stated that restitution in the Soviet occupation zone would mean "the creation of political and social relations which would make a repetition of fascism impossible. The return of property would be a bad joke if leaders of the SS and the [Nazi] war economy would again, as in West Germany, be appearing in key positions in the administration and economy." In addition, the restitution law he had developed with the VVN and the Office of Labor and Social Welfare (which he and Merker had helped to shape) "ha[d] nothing in common with the laws in the West." State and public property were left intact. The law applied only to persons with established residence in Germany and to "property which has been proven to be in certain private hands owing to Nazi expropriations." It did not propose a "general replacement of damage" and had been "arranged with agreement of the friends." ("Friends" was the term the Communists used to refer to the Soviet occupation authorities.) Zuckermann's draft restitution law had "unleashed vigorous protests among many Jewish members of the VVN. I myself had many sharp discussions in the process of commenting on and defending the draft."[68]

Zuckermann's defense illustrates the dramatic change in the politics of the Jewish question brought about by the Cold War and the purge.

In 1948 VVN officials had argued that the East Germans should not be outdone by Western zone restitution proposals. By fall 1950, Zuckermann's *defense* rested on rejecting assertions that his views were similar to those same proposals or differed from Soviet restitution plans. After all, had he not been criticized by an official in the American zone, and even by "many Jewish members of the VVN"? The Zuckermann letter to Geffke captures the fear of being accused of treason and disloyalty which surrounded those Communists in the Soviet zone, Jews and non-Jews alike, who had spoken out on behalf of the Jewish survivors. Political survival demanded that one *not* be identified with Jews, with arguments for restitution to Holocaust survivors living abroad, or for return of buildings which had since been seized for public purposes. In 1948 it had still been possible to argue that the East Germans should emulate Western policy on restitution. By the summer of 1950, those same arguments could be taken as evidence of treasonous Western sympathies.

Evidently Zuckermann's deviations on Jewish matters outweighed the protestations in his letter to Geffke. He was able to retain his position in Pieck's office until May 1, 1951, although on November 27, 1950, several weeks after the ZPKK interrogation, he had written to Walter Ulbricht to "request that the Politburo relieve me of my function as state secretary" in Pieck's office. "Under the deep impact of the Nazi persecution of the Jews," he confessed, "I have made mistakes—such as remaining in close proximity to the party chairman [Ulbricht] and the president of the state [Pieck], which the government cannot permit. Should the party entrust me with another task, I will seek to fulfill it with all of my ability."[69] The source of his errors was now clear to him: the "deep impact" of the destruction of European Jewry had led him to make mistakes such as supporting the new state of Israel and arguing in favor of restitution to the Jewish survivors.

The first memo in the Stasi file on Zuckermann, is dated June 14, 1951. It conveys the spirit of the anti-Jewish purge. Unlike earlier SED documents, this one records Zuckermann's citizenship as "German citizenship (Jew)." The memo notes Zuckermann's "bourgeois background," and records that in Mexico he had worked with Merker,

Abusch, and Leo Bauer, some of whom "work at the present time for American and English secret services." He had promised the "German emigrants (Jews) who remained in Mexico" that he would represent their interests "inside Germany as a lawyer regarding the return of their property." The memo concludes by noting his "close connections to German Jews who were in England, America, and France during the Nazi period."[70] On June 27, 1951, Erich Mielke signed the order which formally placed Zuckermann under suspicion of being a foreign agent. According to the MfS document, Zuckermann was serving as a lawyer aiding German Jewish refugees still in Mexico who were seeking restitution of stolen property. "He has received money from a series of emigrants. He is still in contact with these people and received money and packages from them."[71] It is clear that these international contacts became a source of suspicion.

On July 18, 1951, presumably in response to increasing pressure, Zuckermann wrote a second, far more extensive letter of resignation to the SED Central Committee.[72] It is one of the most shattering documents of unsuccessful self-abasement and recantation in the history of the purge of cosmopolitans in East Berlin. First, he accepts as fact the accusations "that the imperialist espionage agents succeeded in planting agents and spies inside the Communist emigration in the capitalist countries." He continues, "In this period of sharpened and increased struggle against imperialism," it was best that "the function of chief of the Chancellery of the Presidency be assumed by a comrade who could not be subjected to doubts as a result of his whereabouts during the emigration. Therefore, I ask the party to free me from this function." Yet most of his resignation statement was devoted to explaining why,

> after I returned to Berlin [in 1947], I joined the Jewish community in Berlin and the office of those racially persecuted by the Nazi regime. Naturally, I had not become religious or anything like that. However, the Nazi massacre of the Jews, in addition to the other cruelties, and the annihilation of many of my relatives and friends, haunted and moved me very deeply. When I returned to Berlin I encountered not only the population's widespread lack of interest in

this mass extermination but open anti-Semitic sentiments as well, and this despite everything that had happened. On the other hand, I met those who had returned from the [Nazi death and concentration] camps. I took this step [of joining the Jewish community] because I wouldn't think of denying my Jewish descent. Since membership in the Jewish community was not associated with affirmation of a religious confession, in that situation I viewed this decision as an act of solidarity with persecuted Jews.

Looking back on this now, I see that this decision was a false and sentimental reaction. I will not excuse or justify it in any way, but I do want to try to make it understandable. I come from an East European Jewish family in which Yiddish and Russian were spoken, and in which certain Jewish traditions and national residues were much more present than they were among Jews in Germany. The social development which has taken place in the GDR since that time [1947] has also solved this problem [of postwar anti-Semitism and the place of the Jewish community in Germany].[73]

This remarkable statement offers further evidence of the terms of assimilation on which "Communists of Jewish origin" sought to remain at the highest levels of power. Wartime emigration in the West was clearly a postwar obstacle, but, as Abusch and others had shown, it was not an insurmountable one. The key to Zuckermann's problems lay with his active participation in Jewish affairs in both Mexico City and postwar East Berlin. Ironically, the fact that he was Jewish and that many of his relatives had perished in the Holocaust made it possible for Zuckermann to offer a plausible explanation for his actions other than that he was an American or British spy. The East German Communist leadership was so uncomprehending of or insensitive to the Jewish catastrophe that it was not intuitively obvious to them why a Jew in Germany would want to express solidarity with the Jewish victims of Nazism. Zuckermann's description of widespread anti-Semitism in East Germany did not accord with the image of the antifascist state conveyed by the top leadership. The result was that Zuckermann believed that he could save his political career, and perhaps more than that, only by describing his perfectly human and humane responses to the Holocaust as "false and sentimental."

The SED Central Committee and the Stasi officials were neither convinced nor sympathetic. On August 5, 1951, the Stasi officer handling his case ordered that all letters sent to Zuckermann be immediately given to the MfS.[74] On September 26, 1951, several months after leaving his position in Pieck's office under pressure, Zuckermann was appointed professor, dean of the Faculty of International Law and Foreign Policy, and director of the Institute for International Law at the Forst Zinna Deutschen Verwaltungs-Akademie Walter Ulbricht in Potsdam, the elite educational institution preparing students for government service, especially diplomatic service.[75] By fall 1952, however, the Stasi was keeping a closer watch on Zuckermann.[76] As had been the case since the French, and especially the Mexican, emigration, Leo Zuckermann's fate would be inseparable from that of his friend and comrade Paul Merker. He had not fallen so far nor so fast as Merker, but he knew his situation was precarious. The farther Merker fell, the worse things would get for his friends.

Paul Merker's fate was sealed by the outcome of the show trial of Rudolf Slansky, the second most powerful figure in the Czech Communist Party, and other high-ranking Communist defendants in Prague in November 1952.[77] The fourteen defendants, eleven of whom were Jewish, were convicted of being agents of American imperialism and Zionism. Three were sentenced to life in prison. The remaining eleven, including Slansky and Otto Fischl, the former Czech ambassador to East Berlin, were executed by hanging on November 30. During the trial, confessions of extremely dubious origin had included accusations that Paul Merker was conspiratorially linked to Slansky and Fischl. On November 26, 1952, *Neues Deutschland,* in its commentary on the Slansky trial, began the search for a "German Slansky" by linking Merker with Fischl and Katz.[78]

On the same day Slansky and the others were executed in Prague, the MfS in Berlin opened an "investigative procedure" against Merker on the grounds that "Merker is an agent of imperialist intelligence services and has been active in their service and their purposes before and after 1945." In so doing, the memo asserted, he had committed crimes against Article 6 of the GDR constitution and Directive 38 of the Allied Control Council, that is, against the law originally written as part of Allied denazification efforts.[79] Article 6 made it a crime to express "religious, racial, and national hatred [or] militaristic propaganda." Directive 38 defined an "activist" who could be punished as one who "after 8.5.1945 has endangered or is likely to endanger the peace of the German people or the peace of the world, through propaganda for National Socialism or militarism or through the invention or circulation of tendentious rumors."[80] The Communists frequently used these denazification measures against dissidents and opponents such as Merker. On December 3, 1952, near his home in Luckenwalde near Potsdam, Stasi agents arrested Paul Merker and took him to Brandenburg Prison in Berlin, where he was held in "investigative detention."[81] Two weeks later, on December 19, Stasi agents concluded that Leo Zuckermann and his family were no longer in Berlin. Indeed, following the Slansky convictions and executions, Zuckermann had decided it was time to get out. On December 14 he fled to West Berlin with his wife and children. He spent some months in West Germany before returning for a second and permanent emigration to Mexico City, where he resumed the private practice of law. Zuckermann was one of the highest-ranking Communists ever to flee East Germany. His escape was a news item in the Western press.[82]

On December 20, with the publication of "Lessons of the Trial against the Slansky Conspiracy Center," the Party Control Commission and the SED Central Committee struck the decisive blow against Merker, crushed what faint hope remained that Jewish concerns would find their proper place in the policy-making councils of the East German government, and raised the prospect of a show trial in East Berlin of a "German Slansky."[83] "Lessons" is one of the key documents concerning the Jewish question in East German history. Hermann Matern, its author, thundered against "the criminal activity of Zionist organizations" in league with "American agents" who were said to be engaged in efforts to destroy the "people's democracies" of Eastern Europe.[84] Anticipating charges of anti-Semitism, Matern said that the Slansky trial showed that "a method of these criminals included efforts to discredit vigilant, progressive comrades by charging them with anti-

Semitism." Yet, he continued, "the Zionist movement has nothing in common with the goals of humanity. It is dominated, directed, and organized by USA imperialism, [and] exclusively serves its interests and the interests of Jewish capitalists."[85] Matern linked Merker to the Slansky conspiracy through Merker's friendship with Otto Katz.[86] Although the defendants expressed loyalty to the Soviet Union, Matern denounced their efforts to use "the poison of chauvinism and cosmopolitanism . . . to contaminate the workers with the most reactionary bourgeois ideology."[87] Matern's "Lessons" made the connections between cosmopolitanism, Jews, and Zionism clear for all to see.

The vocabulary of "poison" and "contamination" had a long history in German and European anti-Semitism. Once again, German political leaders were publicly identifying the Jews as international cosmopolitans rather than true citizens of the nation. Once again, only seven years after the Nazi visions of a world Jewish conspiracy had ended in genocide, Matern was describing the current conspiracy as small in numbers but extremely powerful and a major threat to the Communist states and parties. And once again German nationalism, this time of a Communist variant, was defining itself in opposition to a Western, capitalist, rootless, international, liberal Jewish conspiracy.[88]

As proof of the indictment, Matern pointed to Merker's published work in Mexico City; assistance with travel funds and visas he had received from the Joint Antifascist Refugee Committee in New York to travel to Mexico from France in 1941; his meetings with representatives of that committee and representatives of the World Jewish Congress while in Mexico City; his public efforts on behalf of financial restitution for the Jews in postwar Berlin; his support for Israel; and his friendship with and defense of Otto Katz.

Matern denounced the Mexico City edition of *Freies Deutschland,* saying that, under Merker's influence it had defended "the interests of Zionist monopoly capitalists."[89] There was "no further doubt that Merker is a subject of the USA financial oligarchy who called for indemnification of Jewish property only to facilitate the penetration of USA finance capital into Germany. This is the true origin of his Zionism."[90] Matern suggested that Merker's interest in restitution had grown in part from his links to J. P. Warburg, a member of the famous German Jewish banking family, who, according to Matern, was director of the U.S. Information Service in Mexico City during the war. That is, Matern argued that Merker cared about the Jews because the American imperialists and the Jews paid him to do so. Here was the origin of Merker's support for "financing the emigration of Jewish capitalists to Israel" and transporting "Jewish citizens of German nationality" to a land of their choice after the war. Matern retrospectively recast the wartime cooperation and solidarity between German Communists in Western emigration, on the one hand, and American Jewish organizations, American Communists, leftists, and liberals, on the other, as an espionage plot of "imperialists" and "Jewish capitalists."[91]

The statement on the lessons of the Slansky trial reached a peak of anger over Merker's plea for restitution for Jews whether they had returned to Germany after 1945 or remained abroad. According to Matern, Merker had "dishonestly transformed the maximum profits of the monopoly capitalists which had been squeezed out of the German and foreign workers into a supposed property of the Jewish people. In reality, the Aryanization of this capital [the expropriation of Jewish businesses, banks, and so on by the Nazis] amounted only to placing the profits of 'Jewish' monopoly capitalists into the hands of 'Aryan' monopoly capitalists." Not only did Matern use a verb—"Aryanization"—rooted in Nazi racial discourse to describe the theft of the property of German Jews. But by inaccurately describing Merker's arguments on behalf of the Jewish survivors as serving the interests of "Jewish monopoly capitalists," Matern also reasserted the link in public discourse between Jews and capitalism, and dismissed the idea that the Jews had been singled out as victims by the Nazis. Matern noted Stalin's assertion that the Jews were not a nation. By assuming otherwise, Merker had abandoned the "platform of Lenin and Stalin."[92]

Matern then turned to Merker's involvement in the restitution debates in postwar East Berlin and the competition for money and prestige among victims of fascism. He charged that Merker did not care about working-class Jews or the Nazis' victims in Eastern Europe and the Soviet Union, but rather and "above all" was concerned for "the wealthy Jews, so-called economic emigrants with whom Merker, André Simone, and other German emigrants in Mexico were in closest touch." These close contacts with wealthy Jews in Mexico City were the reasons for Merker's support for facilitating Jewish travel to Palestine.[93] Matern was especially angered by Merker's wartime arguments that Nazism's political opponents, unlike the Jews, were free to participate or not in the fight against Nazism.[94] He distorted Merker's praise of the courage of Communist antifascists to suggest that this was a contemptuous effort to imply that the Communists' "sacrifice and suffering counts for nothing compared to the sacrifices and the suffering of the Jewish people."[95] It was Matern, however, not Merker who turned the memory of the past into a zero-sum game in which recognition of Jewish suffering had to come at the price of nonrecognition of the suffering of others, including that of the Communist anti-Nazi resistance fighters. Stalin and Stalinists represented a jealous god. Matern would not extend recognition of suffering beyond the Soviet Union and German Communists to European Jews. He misconstrued Merker's praise for the Communists' voluntary decision to join the struggle against the Nazis as an expression of disdain and contempt for their suffering, sentiments Merker never expressed.

The purge affected even those Jews who were completely orthodox Communists. On December 29, 1952, the information office directed by Gerhart Eisler was dissolved, and Albert Norden had to leave his position as government spokesman.[96] With Merker in disgrace, his old adversaries seized the opportunity to contribute evidence of his treasonous past. On December 31, 1952, Götz Berger wrote to Hermann Matern about Merker's role in the restitution discussions in 1948.[97] He recalled that Merker and his followers had supported full restitution to the Jews for the damages they had suffered. Berger cited three reasons for his opposition to Merker. First, such restitution would "benefit to a large extent Jewish and now American or American-oriented capitalists" as had happened during the Weimar era, when, according to Berger, "a large proportion of Berlin's houses" had fallen into the hand of foreign, often Jewish owners. Second, it would benefit fascists as well as opponents of fascism who had lost property. And third, restitution should amount to offering victims of fascism a secure existence and preventing a return of race hatred. Merker and his supporters had tried to counter Berger's arguments by saying that "avoiding a 100 percent restitution would amount to sanctioning the Nazi persecution and to yet another expropriation of the Jews."[98] Merker and his supporters had made "Zionist" arguments in favor of dual Israeli and German citizenship, and, along with Leo Zuckermann, had spoken of a "Jewish people" and a "'Jewish national minority' in Germany and similar things which more or less come from the conceptual arsenal of Zionism."[99] Berger named names, adding that Leo Zuckermann, Kurt Nettball, Julius Meyer, and Leon Löwenkopf had supported Merker, but he also spoke vaguely of "obligations which Merker accumulated in Mexico toward Jewish circles."[100]

In a manner that was now common in the midst of the purge, Berger's letter turned political disagreement into a crime. By connecting Merker's arguments in Mexico to the restitution discussions in postwar East Berlin, he provided another explanation for Merker's postwar actions, namely, that he was a paid agent of Jewish capitalists in Mexico and Jews in New York who had helped him and his wife escape from France in 1941. Merker's engagement with Jewish issues, according to the Control Commission and the Central Committee, far from being an expression of deep moral and political conviction, was simply a tawdry payback to wealthy Jews who wanted their money and property returned.

On March 23, 1953, Otto Winzer (1902–1975) wrote to Hermann Matern at the Control Commission. Winzer was Zuckermann's successor as chief of Pieck's office, a future high-ranking official in the East German Foreign Ministry (1956–1965), and then East German foreign minister from 1965 to 1975, when East German "anti-Zionist" policy in the Middle East deepened. Winzer informed Matern that he had discovered among Zuckermann's papers an essay which "should be published because of its special political significance." To Winzer's evident astonishment, Zuckermann had found "all Jews, lock, stock, and barrel, including Jewish bankers and big capitalists, to be totally innocent of any guilt for the emergence of fascism."[101] Zuckermann's apparently unpublished essay of 1947 to which Winzer took exception was titled "Knowledge Not Shared Guilt." In it Zuckermann rejected arguments, which he presumably was hearing or reading in East Berlin at the time, concerning the collective guilt of the Jews in the coming to power of Nazism! He pointed out the obvious: Jews had constituted 0.97 percent of the German population in 1933. While the German Jews did underestimate the unprecedented degree of Nazi murderousness, "it helps no one to construct guilt retrospectively from that."[102]

Perhaps what angered Winzer most was Zuckermann's belief that the well-being of the Jewish people was inseparable from the existence of democracy, and that the Jewish people were determined to survive as Jews.[103] Zuckermann wrote that although "Hitler fascism" had intended to exterminate "the Jews in the whole world" and did succeed in murdering 6 million, "it did not succeed in realizing its program" of global extermination. "The Jewish people live," he wrote, "reduced by one-third, but more determined than ever to survive and to rebuild Jewish life." There could, however, be "no living development of the Jewish people outside" a framework of justice and democracy. Without more democracy, "the danger grows of a renewed threat for those who survived Hitler fascism." One of "the most important insights of the years of persecution" was that "the fate of the Jewish people is inseparable from the democratization of the world."[104] Here Zuckermann was found to have deviated on two counts. First, Communist orthodoxy held that Jews and Judaism would wither away in a classless society. Second, Zuckermann's retrospectively established deviations regarding Jewish matters suggested that he had succumbed to "bourgeois" conceptions of democracy.

That a high-ranking official of an "antifascist" German government, rather than discussing the issue of the possible collective guilt of the German people, responded to this essay by referring to a supposed guilt of the Jews for the rise of Nazism indicates how bizarre the internal discourse in the highest ranks of the SED had become. Few statements capture the anti-Semitic tone of the period in East Berlin as well as Winzer's. That such a heartless and bigoted man could become an influential foreign policy official underscores the deeply anti-Jewish hatred, not merely anti-Zionist politics, that contributed to subsequent East German pronouncements on the Middle East.

On January 6, 1953, officials of the ZPKK interrogated Julius Meyer in East Berlin about a trip to Israel, the restitution debates in postwar East Berlin, and his contacts with Israelis.[105] Meyer was then head of the Federation of Jewish Communities in East Germany, a member of the executive committee of the Jewish community in East Berlin, of the SED and the Volkskammer (since 1949), and a leading member of the VVN. Meyer mentioned the support which both Merker and Zuckermann had given in 1948 for the idea that "all property which had been stolen from the Jews should be returned to them."[106] He also recalled a 1948 meeting concerning restitution in Otto Grotewohl's office in East Berlin at which Grotewohl, Meyer, Zuckermann, and representatives of the state of Israel were present. Meyer said that he "remembered very well that comrade Grotewohl said: 'We are inclined to conduct negotiations [about restitution], but first we must establish diplomatic relations between the two countries [Germany and Israel].'"[107] The Control Commission file on Meyer noted his two trips to Israel in February 1949, his travels to West Germany, and his interest in the issue of restitution for Jews living in Israel.[108]

A week after the interrogation, on January 13 Meyer, along with his family, fled to West Germany and then to the United States. Also fleeing with them were three of the eight leaders of organized Jewish communities in East Germany: Helmuth Lohser (Leipzig), Leon Löwenkopf (Dresden), and Guenther Singer (Erfurt).[109] On the same day in Moscow, the Soviet news agency TASS announced its discovery of a "doctors' plot" of Jewish doctors responsible for the deaths of leading government officials.[110] On January 16 Georg Dertinger, the non-Communist East German foreign minister, was arrested in East Berlin.[111] On January 19 the *New York Times* reported that "flying squads of Communist police hunting 'Zionist spies' swooped down on the houses and offices of Jews in East Germany today, seized papers and identity cards, and ordered Jews to stay close to home." Hans Jendretsky (1897–1992), then a candidate for membership in the Politburo and a member of the SED Central Committee, demanded the exclusion of Jews from public life and called them "enemies of the state."[112] On January 21 the *New York Times* reported that 355 Jews, a quarter of the remaining Jewish population, had fled. It was primarily the old and the ill who had stayed behind. On the same day the East German government announced that the four Jewish leaders who had fled had been expelled from the VVN since their flight "proved" they were guilty of being Zionist agents.[113] On February 23 the East German government dissolved the VVN, the organization which had made it possible for Jews to express their views and interests and replaced it with a reconstituted and politically reliable Committee of Antifascist Resistance.[114]

The flight of the Jewish leaders was big news in some of the Western press. On January 24 in an interview with the widely read newspaper of the American occupation authorities, *Die Neue Zeitung,* Julius Meyer and the other former East German Jewish leaders said that they had fled out of fear of becoming defendants in a show trial in East Berlin modeled on the Slansky trial.[115] According to Meyer, "there was no anti-Semitism among the German people. There was only an anti-Semitism in the SED which was directed from Moscow for political reasons . . . All of the Jews in the Soviet zone fear a repetition of the pogrom of 1938." Meyer contrasted Hitler's racially motivated persecution with the political motives behind the SED's anti-Jewish measures. He stressed four political reasons for the purge: to gain sympathy among the Arab countries, to break the links between Jews in the Soviet zone and their friends and relatives in the West, to use the Jews as a scapegoat for economic problems, and to eliminate potential critics of Ulbricht's policies.[116] The Jewish leaders had decided to flee when, following the Slansky trial, the SED Central Committee demanded that they denounce the restitution agreement between West Germany and Israel of fall 1952 and agree to state publicly that the Joint Distribution Committee, which had been assisting Jewish survivors in postwar Europe, was a tool of American espionage; that Zionism was the same as fascism, and Israeli president David Ben-Gurion was an agent of American imperialism; that American justice was criminal because it had condemned the Rosenbergs to death; and that restitution for the injustice done to the Jews amounted to exploitation of the German people.[117]

On February 8, 1953, a headline at the center top of page one of the *New York Times* read: "Jewish Fugitives Reveal Pressures by East Germans: Eight Leaders Say They Were Asked to Back Slansky Case and Denounce Zionism." The *Times's* reported that "Communist terror by interrogation and pressure to support the current purges and the campaign against Zionism prompted the decision by leading Jews of Eastern Germany to flee to the West."[118] Meyer and the others had decided to flee "when party officials tried to make them issue a statement supporting the trial of Rudolf Slansky and others in Czechoslovakia and denouncing Zionism." They referred to secret police inquiries into their own activities and family ties in Israel and the West. Meyer had been under heavy pressure from the SED to persuade other Jewish leaders in East Germany to support the resolution "Lessons from the Trial of the Slansky Conspirators," and to denounce the Joint Distribution Committee.[119]

Soon after he arrived in West Berlin, on December 14, 1952, Leo Zuckermann contacted American authorities, presumably to gain protection against East German efforts to find him and return him to East Berlin. In February 1953 officers of the Counter Intelligence Corps (CIC) of the U.S. Army in Munich interrogated him.[120] Zuckermann told the American officials that he had been subject to SED investigations "beginning with the Rajk trial in 1950" and increasingly so after the denunciations of Merker, Lex Ende, Maria Weiterer, and Leo Bauer in the Field affair. The investigations led to his resignation from the chancellery of the president in April 1951, and the Slansky trials brought matters to a head. He started to plan his escape because he knew that he would "presently be subject to accusations of treason" as a result of his former association with the recently executed Otto Katz.[121]

Although the winter purge of December and January 1952–53 made the front page of the *New York Times* and some West German papers, it has remained in the back pages of postwar history. Yet it was the defining moment of political contention over Jewish matters in East

German history. With Merker's arrest and the flight of Zuckermann, Meyer, and other leaders of Jewish communities in East Germany, the participation in East German politics of Communists, both Jews and non-Jews, who would speak out on behalf of Jewish interests came to a definitive and enduring end, as did the already weak remnants of Jewish-Communist solidarity.

On December 31, 1952, Alexander Abusch, seeking to avoid guilt by association, reported to the Stasi that in Mexico, Leo Katz, Leo Zuckermann, and his wife, Lydia Zuckermann, had all advocated "the Jewish chauvinist line which condemned the whole German people without any distinction." Their "false line," he said, had led to "sharp conflicts." The sharpest criticisms came from Lydia Zuckermann "owing to her completely chauvinist anti-German stance."[122] In the midst of this purge, however, naming names and delivering the dirt on others was not enough. Between January and March 1953, Abusch wrote an extended self-criticism which was placed in his Stasi file. "My Errors in Mexico and Their Lessons for the Present" dramatically illustrated what this Jewish Communist was required to do to remain in the SED leadership.[123] "The decision of the Central Committee," he wrote in reference to "Lessons of the Slansky Trial," "shows that we comrades of the German group in Mexico did not practice enough revolutionary vigilance" in the face of "refined methods of imperialist subversion and infiltration."[124]

Abusch confessed that he had permitted Merker to publish in *Freies Deutschland* the "absurd anti-Leninist theory" that "the Jews in Germany were a national minority." Furthermore, he had failed to criticize Merker's 1944 article "Deutsche Aussenpolitik in Vergangenheit und Zukunft," "in which Merker openly supported cosmopolitanism and thereby the imperialist plunder of a future democratic Germany." He had waged an "inadequate struggle against these false theories" and failed to recognize that they were "hostile to the revolutionary principles of Marx, Engels, Lenin, and Stalin." It was his "duty" as a party member of long standing "to quickly recognize and to decisively fight against the enemy nature of Merker's theories on the Jewish question." He should also have applied "the Lenin–Stalin theory of imperialism."

His neglecting to do so, he said, "constituted my serious ideological error in Mexico."[125] Having seen the errors of his ways, he supported "without reservation the decisions of our Central Committee of August 24, 1950, and of January 4, 1953," that is, the decisions concerning the Field affair and the "Lessons of the Slansky Trial."[126]

Abusch wrote that he had made these grave errors in Mexico because he had been unaware of Merker's "cooperation in Marseilles with the American espionage director, [Noel] Field," and of Merker's "Trotskyist position concerning the signing of the German-Soviet Nonaggression Pact in 1939."[127] Merker's "Anti-Semitism and Us" had been published "suddenly and without any previous discussion in the group." Now Abusch called it an attempt to "falsify the line of the journal in the direction of Zionism." Merker had furthermore established a "personal regime" in Mexico in which there was "no party democracy" or criticism and self-criticism. It was Merker's authoritarian rule in Mexico City which had prevented discussion of the Jewish question according to Marxist-Leninist principles and concealed the "criminal activity [of] the spy André Simone [Otto Katz]."[128] Abusch insisted that unlike Merker, he had always tried to stress the "leading role" of the Soviet Union, the "unforgettable" accomplishments of the Red Army, demands for a second front, the "great national struggle of the illegal German antifascists and the heroic cadres of the KPD under the leadership of Ernst Thälmann and Wilhelm Pieck."[129] Nevertheless, Abusch admitted, because of his own neglect of Marxist-Leninism, he had contributed to the errors of the Mexican group.[130]

In Mexico, Abusch admmitted, he had opposed "advocates of Jewish chauvinist views such as [Leo] Zuckermann" and been "sharply attacked by Zionists because of my unambiguous engagement for the German people."[131] Nevertheless, by permitting the publication of articles by Merker, Simone, Zuckermann, and Erich Jungmann in *Freies Deutschland,* he had "allowed concessions to Jewish chauvinism." The only way to avoid such a "deviation and to clearly distinguish friend from enemy" was by "continuous deep and self-critical reevaluation of our whole politics based on Marxist-Leninist fundamentals." The "decisive lesson from our mistakes in the German group and from my personal mistakes in Mexico" was that the "penetration of enemy ideologies and imperialist agents into our party" could be prevented only if all comrades exercised greater "vigilance" *(Wachsamkeit),* avoided "ideological carelessness," and made "the revolutionary science of Marxism-Leninism . . . the living foundation of our daily politics. Our party must be the highest value for every comrade." His own self-criticism should serve to "mobilize every comrade" to greater vigilance and struggle against "imperialist agents and all enemies of the working class." Above all, Abusch would undertake the "serious obligation to prove in my work for socialism that I have genuinely and seriously drawn the lessons from my own past mistakes."[132]

Abusch concluded his self-criticism by asserting that anti-Zionism was not identical with anti-Semitism. "Working and progressive Jews of the whole world understood very well that every person of Jewish origin, who loyally devotes his efforts to productive and creative labor, has the same right as every German to full equality and to the great free possibilities of socialist life."[133] Furthermore, while the East German constitution made racial hatred a crime in West Germany, monopoly capitalists and their American employers had restored "the mass murderers of Maidanek, Treblinka, and Auschwitz to official positions and honor" because they wanted "proven commanders" to prepare "an American war on German soil."[134] He continued, "The fundamental purging of our republic of all imperialist espionage nests" was part of "our patriotic struggle against the American policy of division [of Germany] and preparation for war, for the unity of our German fatherland, and for peace."[135] Lest there be any doubt that Abusch placed loyalty to the party above loyalty to "Jewish chauvinists" such as Zuckermann, he disclosed that "Leo Zuckermann's house near Paris is in Eaubonne (Departement Seine et Oise)."[136]

Outside the Communist parties, however, it was doubtful that "progressive Jews," or at least Jewish liberals around the world, agreed with Abusch. By early January, the SED's espionage accusations and arrest of Merker, Leo Zuckermann's flight, and a general purge of the few remaining Jews in East German public life had been prominently reported in the major German and American newspapers.[137] In the *New*

*York Times* of January 6, 1953, James P. Warburg denied that he had ever been in Mexico during the war.[138] On January 7 the *Times* reported that Leo Zuckermann had told American officials that he foresaw a "mass flight of Soviet zone officials to escape arrest and trial."[139] On January 8 the same newspaper reported that Jews in West Berlin were speaking of a widening purge directed at the 2,700 Jews remaining in East Germany, and especially at pushing Jews out of public life.[140] Western officials doubted that anti–Semitism was the driving force of the purge. Rather, they thought that the greater concern of the Communist leadership was "the degree to which party members had been tainted with Western ideas during the years of exile," as if the two issues were not related.[141]

Jews in West Germany were not at all sanguine about anti–Semitism in East Germany. On January 9, 1953, the lead story on the front page of the *Allgemeine Wochenzeitung der Juden in Deutschland,* the only newspaper published by and for Jews still living in Germany, dealt with the East German purge and Matern's statement on the "Lessons of the Slansky Trial," and drew comparisons between current events and the Nazi past.[142] Given "the clear anti–Semitic turn of the Communist regimes," the article began, it was "logical that the next blow would be directed against restitution [*Wiedergutmachung*] for the injustice done to the Jews" by the Nazis.[143] In referring to *Wiedergutmachung* as a "shift of the property of the German people," however, the SED Central Committee had "exceeded all expectations."[144] The article continued:

> The Jews should be set up as "the enemy of the German people." It was not so long ago that this formula was used by a regime which collapsed in disgrace. No one would have thought it possible that it would ever again be taken up and used, least of all only seven years after the collapse of the Nazi regime, and by a party whose members were no less mercilessly persecuted than the Jews.
>
> The Jews, who between 1933 and 1939 were driven across German borders in complete poverty, are today denounced by the SED as "monopoly capitalists." The seizure of their property [by the Nazis] is deceitfully described as "the transfer of the profits of Jewish

monopoly capitalists into the hands of Aryan monopoly capitalists."
When, in addition, it is claimed [by the SED] that the Jews still living
in Germany cannot be declared innocent of guilt for fascism's victory
in 1933, one may ask if those who say such things are in full possession of their mental faculties. The memory of the 6 million Jews
murdered by the Nazis has probably never been desecrated in such
an outrageous manner as has happened in this instance.[145]

The *Wochenzeitung* noted that the Joint Distribution Committee, which
the SED denounced as a tool of American imperialism, had cared for
and nurtured the Jewish survivors of the camps. What purpose could
be served by such distortions of history? Did the SED seek to "give
support to the neo-Nazi elements which had recently again made a
strong appearance? Is a new alliance between National Socialism and
Communism being prepared" similar to the Hitler-Stalin pact of
1939?[146]

While the answers to these questions remained in the future, the
article said, "today it is clear that the Jews in the countries of the
Eastern bloc face new and extraordinarily dangerous enemies." The
image of the Jews conveyed there compared to that in Tsarist Russia
and Nazi Germany and "calls forth the most base instincts."[147] The SED
had unleashed a "witch-hunt" against the Jews who had been driven
from Germany by the Nazis, and who were now said to be committing
a crime for seeking restitution. "Everything that has happened in the
last twenty years appears to have been extinguished from the memory
of those who composed the statement ['Lessons of the Slansky Trial']
of the SED Central Committee." All that remained for the SED was
"cold reason of state." In the future, anyone engaged in "the restoration
of law and justice in West Germany must assume that they will be
denounced in East Germany as a traitor of the people. We are certain
that there will be many who will know how to bear this reproach with
dignity."[148]

The *Wochenzeitung* did not equate the SED regime with that of Nazi
Germany, but it did assert that the East German regime, abroad and at
home, was willing to use German nationalism and anti-Semitism as a

"secret weapon of the Cold War."[149] Whether in Europe, including Germany, or in Asia, Africa, and the Middle East, the Communists were turning to the ideas of their past enemy, "fascist nationalism," to mobilize the masses against the West in the Cold War. But the significance of the events of the winter purge of 1952–53, so apparent to Jewish observers and to some Western journalists, remained peripheral to the main narratives of the early history of the Cold War. The popular rebellion of June 17, 1953, understandably received much more attention than the persecution of some Communists by other Communists behind the scenes of a secretive dicatatorship. Meanwhile, the deepening of dictatorial rule in this period did appear, as Merker and Zuckermann had argued, to demonstrate a close connection between anti-Semitism and dictatorship in modern German history.

Ulbricht and the SED Politburo decided to keep Paul Merker in "investigative detention" in East Berlin from December 1952 to March 1955.[150] During that time, and with particular intensity from early December 1952 through the end of March 1953, Stasi and NKVD agents interrogated him, twice a day, often late at night. In 1953 and 1954, in preparation for the possible spectacular show trial of the "German Slansky" in East Berlin, they also interrogated all of the leading figures of the French and Mexican Communist emigration.[151] Merker's Stasi file of over a thousand typed and handwritten pages illustrates that the theory behind the case, suspects, lines of investigation, witnesses, and testimony closely followed the outline established by the initial Control Commission investigation of 1950–1952. It includes the fifteen-page guilty verdict of the East German Supreme Court following Merker's secret political trial on March 29–30, 1955, and the equally secret decision in 1956 to drop the espionage charges and release him.[152] Also included are the official transcripts of those interrogations, notes of his conversations with his cellmate (who was a Stasi agent), records of pretrial interrogations of Merker and witnesses, the theory of the case developed by the general prosecutor's office, witness lists, and the court verdicts.[153] The Merker case and the Merker file document the key events in the suppression of the Jewish question in the highest ranks of the East German government. Although the Merker case never received enough public attention to make him either the German Slansky or the German Dreyfus, it was as important for the history of anti-Semitism and Jewish-related matters in East Germany as those two more famous episodes were for the modern history of Czechoslovakia and France.

If Merker was to be the "German Slansky," this meant a public show trial in East Berlin with Merker as the chief defendant. That, in turn, called for a public confession, which Merker refused to give. During two and a half years of investigative detention, with the exception of the interrogation session of December 12, 1952, thirteen days after his arrest, Merker rejected all of the charges against him. On that day, in the face of threats against his wife, who he believed was also in prison, and his family, he signed a transcript of his interrogation which clearly had been written by his interrogators. He confessed to having had an "enemy connection to the member of the American secret service Noel Field." He had become "an imperialist stooge because in the era of emigration" he had "deviated from Marxism, made a false assessment of imperialism, and was blind and unaware" of imperialist methods used against the labor movement. An "absence of normal party life in this period in capitalist foreign countries" had led to a decline of ideological awareness, which in turn had facilitated the infiltration of antiparty elements. "Moreover," he confessed, "I had also fallen for the illusion that Roosevelt's policy and the declarations about help for the political emigration were progressive in character and could be in the interest of anti-imperialist movements." Field, he said, took advantage of these vulnerabilities.[154] Perhaps a product of the shock of his arrest, these admissions had nothing to do with the core of the charges against him since the Field affair, namely, those which had emerged from the Slansky trial and concerned the Jewish question. In any case, from then on Merker insisted on his innocence and viewed the accusations against him as an absurd and grotesque violation of what he termed Marxist-Leninist legality.

After interrogations such as that of January 16, 1953, Merker understood the centrality of the Jewish question to the purge. A week after the Control Commission interrogated Julius Meyer, and the same day Meyer fled to the West, the interrogation proceeded.

Q: Did you have any connections to the representatives of the state of Israel in the GDR?

A: I don't know any of these representatives.

Q: Did you have any connections to Jewish organizations in the GDR?

A. No. I had no connections to Jewish organizations in the GDR.

Q: Are there Jewish organizations in the GDR?

A: I don't know if there are Jewish organizations in the GDR.

Q: Are you familiar with the Jewish organization "Jüdische Gemeinde" [Jewish Community] in the GDR?

A: I know that the organization "Jewish Community" exists in the Soviet sector of Berlin.

Q: Did you have connections to this organization?

A: No. I had no connections to this organization.

Q: Do you know the chairman of the of the Jewish Community?

A: No. I know Julius Meier [Meyer], who has actively worked for the Jews in Berlin.

Q: Were you in touch with Meier [Meyer]?

A: Yes. I was in touch with him in 1946 and 1947.

Q: What was the nature of this connection?

A: In the spring of 1947, I formed a commission to prepare a law for restitution to the victims of fascism. As a part of the law concerned the Jews, it was supposed to deal with that. Meier also belonged to this commission.

Q: Who authorized you to form such a commission?

A: The Central Secretariat of the SED, of which I was then a member, passed a resolution to that effect.

Q: Who made the suggestion to do so?

A: I did.

Q: What was your position concerning Jewish affairs?

A: I took the view that the former property of those Jews which had been expropriated [by the Nazis], their apartments, homes, stores, or workshops, should be given back to them.

Q: Did you demand the return of the capitalist property of the Jews?

A: No.[155]

The interrogation of March 3, 1953 (which began at 10:30 P.M.) offers an eerie mirror image of the question "Are you now or have you ever been a member of the Communist Party" of the McCarthy era in the United States. It also dealt with Merker's connections to Jewish organizations.

Q: Are you a member of Jewish-Zionist organizations?

A: I do not belong to any Jewish-Zionist organizations, and I have never belonged to such organizations.

Q: Were you in contact with Jewish-Zionist organizations?

A: No, I had no contacts with Jewish-Zionist organizations.

Q: Isn't "HICEM," with which, according to your earlier statements, you were in contact, a Jewish-Zionist organization?

A: The "HICEM" is a Jewish organization that organized circles of Jewish and other emigrants. In 1941 and 1942, at the request of the Antifascist Refugee Committee in New York, "HICEM" provided me with boat tickets to travel from France.

Q: With what other Jewish organizations were you in contact?

A: None. In 1944 Fastlichter [Adolfo Fostlicht], the chairman of a Jewish organization in Mexico whose name I cannot remember, congratulated me on the occasion of my fiftieth birthday, as did another representative of this or another Jewish organization. In addition, in

Mexico I took part in two press conferences of the Jewish organizations in Mexico as a representative of the journal *Freies Deutschland*. A representative of the World Jewish Congress spoke at these press conferences.[156]

As we have seen, there was indeed contact between the German Communists in Mexico and the World Jewish Congress (WJC). The Antifascist Refugee Committee in New York did help Communists flee from Vichy France. But just as WJC officials understood that the first priority of German Communist refugees was not saving the property of foreign Jewish capitalists, so Merker and Zuckermann reached out to the WJC in the context of a shared struggle against the Nazi regime. It was the most natural of connections in a period when lines between Communists and non-Communists blurred. None of this is apparent from the interrogation transcript.

Despite an investigative detention that lasted until March 1955, Merker refused to offer a public confession.[157] A January 15, 1954, request to extend his detention noted that after a year of interrogations, "the accused has not in any way admitted to engaging in his criminal activity . . . His stubborn, dogged, and impenitent denials have impeded the course of the investigation."[158] The interrogations proceeded as if there had not been a Nazi regime, persecution of the Jews, or for that matter an "antifascist resistance." As the Jacoby memo to the World Jewish Congress had made clear, Jews in the World Jewish Congress were in contact with Communists in Mexico not to recover lost property but to save Jewish lives. Comparisons of Western anticommunism and Soviet bloc anticosmopolitanism can be overdone, but in one respect they did parallel each other. Both McCarthyites and those who purged "cosmopolitans" acted as if the alliance between the Soviet Union, Britain, and the United States had not and should not have existed, and should be erased from memory.

Merker's Stasi file includes extensive handwritten notes from Merker's cellmate, a Stasi agent placed in Merker's cell to encourage him to confess.[159] Merker was interrogated twice daily, was threatened with death, and was told that his whole family would be "annihilated" if he did not cooperate.[160] The Stasi agent in Merker's cell described him as "a clever old fox" who "did not reveal either his name or the names of others." The informant recorded Merker's anguished reflections over the choice of saving his family "by naming names of friends and acquaintances," thereby ensuring the arrest of "a very large circle of people," or remaining "steadfast and firm until death," not naming names, and thereby, he feared, bringing "danger for my family." The latter option, Merker said, meant that "my conscience would remain clear," and that he would retain the respect and affection of the "many comrades in Germany and abroad" who admired him. The informant wrote that "Merker will tell everything if his family is in danger."[161] Merker had told him that the interrogators wanted him to confess that he was a Zionist who wished to sell out East Germany to Israel or to Jewish capitalists. They had told him that they were going to organize a "second Slanksy trial" in East Berlin, and had pointed out that it was Jews who had been convicted in Prague—the same Jews who had had connections to England and France and had "made millions." Merker had told his interrogators he had no such connections and was not an agent.[162]

By early February 1953, Merker had undergone eighty-five interrogation sessions. The cellmate–agent asked him if his friends outside could help him.[163] Merker responded that no one "dared to give anything to my wife" or be seen spending the evening at the Merker home. If they did so, they "would be exposed as enemies of the party and also arrested."[164] Yet why, the agent asked, hadn't the members of the Communist parties in France, Mexico, and the United States come to his defense? Merker responded that "the friends abroad cannot help either because they can do so only by writing via their own Central Committees," and if they were to do that they would be treated as "enemies of the party." The only thing to do was to maintain his innocence and hope that the interrogators would give up trying to break his resistance.[165]

His Stasi inquisitors told him that his 1942 article "Antisemitism and Us" showed that he was a *Judenknecht,* or "servant of the Jews." They mocked him as "the king of the Jews," as one who "had been bought by the Jews" and whose intention was to "sell the DDR off to the

Jews."[166] They viewed his contact with and assistance from Jews, both Communists and non-Communists, during the French and Mexican emigration as further evidence of his participation in an espionage conspiracy. The Joint Antifascist Refugee Committee in New York, which had raised funds to help Jews and leftists escape from Europe; his friendship with Jews in Mexico who gave financial support to *Freies Deutschland;* his defense of Otto Katz in Mexico City and their continuing friendship in postwar Europe; his alleged angry outburst in Paris in 1939 upon hearing the news of the Hitler–Stalin pact; and published essays and books from the Mexico City days all confirmed their conviction that Merker was an agent in a conspiracy of foreign Jewish capitalists and American imperialists.

From 1950 through 1954 the ZPKK and the Stasi interrogated all of those who had been in exile in France or Mexico, including over twenty people who had known Merker.[167] The pressures of interrogation combined with principles of loyalty to the party and individual survival led comrades willingly to name names, testify against a disgraced former friend, and destroy friendships or, conversely, seize a marvelous opportunity to settle scores with the now powerless Merker. In May 1953 Matern again called for vigilance against "spies and agents." The purge claimed another prominent victim. Franz Dahlem, the great antifascist hero, was expelled from the Central Committee and deprived of all his party functions as a consequence of "blindness toward imperialist espionage activity," that is, his contact with Noel Field in Vichy France.[168]

Following the purge of the cosmopolitans in winter 1952–53, inadequacies and silences concerning Jewish issues were no longer a result only of the inadequacies of Communist theories of fascism and antifascism. The arrest of Paul Merker in December 1952, and the associated purge of his like-minded comrades, was a decisive demonstration of how state power was being used to enforce political conformity. Matern's "lesson" to SED members was that approaching the Jewish question as Merker had tried to do was now not only "incorrect" but also dangerous. Everyone in the party, with the exception of some stubborn "old Communists" such as Merker, got the message.

On May 14, 1953, the same day that Matern announced Dahlem's fall, Anton Ackermann delivered a confidential speech to the Central Committee in which he accounted for Merker's alleged response to the news of the Hitler-Stalin pact in August 1939.[169] Before World War II, Ackermann said, "a dangerous ideology spread among even the ranks of the Communist emigrants in the Western capitalist countries." Merker was "a leading exponent" of the ideology, which "consisted in seeing the Western countries and their governments as allies against Hitler." From the fact of "contradictions among the imperialist powers in many questions," Merker and others "drew the false and dangerous conclusion of either underestimating or completely denying the imperialist character of these governments." Such views represented "the abandonment of the principal standpoint of Marxism-Leninism and sinking to the position of social democracy."[170] It was one thing to note that the alliance between the Soviet Union and the West between 1941 and 1945 was the exception that proved the rule of hostility since 1917. Ackermann went further by placing the template of current conflicts over the patterns of the past and projecting Cold War antagonisms back into the period of World War II. Such displacement was an enduring element in the obliteration of memories of the anti-Hitler coalition. Indeed, to remember wartime solidarities with the West was now part of a "dangerous ideology." Merker was guilty as charged of supporting the anti-Hitler coalition with the West. Ackermann neglected to point out that during the war, even Stalin and the Comintern had taken the same position. While American wartime intelligence viewed Merker as a shrewd Comintern operative seeking to expand Soviet influence behind the fog of deceptive wartime antifascism, Ackermann and the Politburo in East Berlin presented him as a prisoner of the illusion that the United States and Britain were genuine allies in a war against Nazi Germany![171] In postwar East Berlin a good memory of wartime antifascism had become dangerous. Equally important, the attack on Merker and those Communists who dared to criticize the Hitler-Stalin pact served to repress the embarrassing fact that from 1939 to 1941, the Soviet Union had abandoned "antifascism" in word and deed in the nonaggression pact with Hitler.

After concluding hundreds of hours of testimony from anyone who had had any contact with Merker in France, Mexico, East Berlin, or Prague, Stasi officials settled on Erich Jungmann, Alexander Abusch, Henny Stibi, and Leo Katz as the most important witnesses who could testify to Merker's connections to "agents of imperialist secret services."[172] The purge files are a depressing account of how a totalitarian regime destroyed human solidarity as individuals tried to save themselves.[173] Abusch, for example, denied that he had ever heard of a long report on the Mexican years which Merker insisted he had read and signed, and which gave a detailed account of the Stibi and Otto Katz disputes.[174] Erich Jungmann, a friend of Merker's, referred to Merker's "dictatorial regime" in Mexico City, which he said had greatly damaged the party organization. He admitted to having agreed with Merker's views in Mexico. In March 1953, a month after his interrogation, Jungmann was fired from his position as a newspaper editor because of "Zionist deviations."[175]

The logic of the purge and espionage fears also transformed differences of opinions into matters of loyalty and betrayal. Merker had defended the Austrian Jewish Communist Leo Katz against Henny Stibi's espionage accusations. In articles in *Freies Deutschland* in Mexico, Katz had offered an orthodox Marxist analysis of European anti-Semitism and supported a territorial solution within the borders of the Soviet Union. He did not agree with Merker's support for a Jewish state in Palestine or his position on restitution.[176] But in his report on Merker's activities in Mexico to the SED Control Commission of March 13, 1953, Katz did not reciprocate Merker's goodwill in Mexico. Instead, he said that Leo Zuckermann, Zuckermann's Mexican law partner Carmen Otero, and Otto Katz formed the "lines of connection between Paul Merker and the wealthy Jews of America."[177] Leo Katz was interrogated by the Stasi on May 12, 1954. He repeated the essentials of his testimony to the ZPKK of March 1953 but added that Merker's Zionist line "was, as everybody knows, brought into being by the State Department of the USA."[178] Soon after returning to Vienna, Katz suffered a fatal heart attack.[179]

Johann Schmidt, Anna Seghers's husband, also testified against Merker. In his Stasi interrogation of May 4, 1954, he repeated the already public accusation that the basis of Merker's politics was "blind faith in the imperialist states of the USA, England, and France" and his belief that they had been sincere in their desire to work together with the Soviet Union during the war.[180] Schmidt noted that Merker had especially close ties to "Jewish industrialists and big retailers . . . Merker regarded these wealthy Jews not as capitalists, that is, as class enemies, but only as victims of fascism, and he used them as sources of money."[181] Repeatedly, witnesses transformed the World Jewish Congress, B'nai B'rith in Mexico, and the Antifascist Refugee Committee in New York into organizations of stereotypically wealthy Jews. All searched their memories to uncover a nonexistent international conspiracy. The alternative of recalling the truth about the past was much more dangerous.

Margarete Menzel–Merker rejected the SED's attack on her husband from the very beginning. On May 18, 1953, several members of the local party organization near Potsdam reported that she was "very embittered, does not understand her husband's arrest, and repeatedly insisted that he was innocent." She "did not see the whole question from the standpoint of the party and the working class but only from her own personal standpoint."[182] Four days later they concluded that "it would not be appropriate for Comrade [Margarete] Merker to continue to remain a [SED] party member." They suggested that she be brought before the local District Party Control Commission and asked "if she is prepared to declare in writing that she dissociates herself from her husband's actions. With her current views and attitudes toward her husband's Trotskyist actions, she cannot remain in the party any longer."[183] Margarete Merker refused to dissociate herself from her husband and was expelled from the SED.

In addition to, and in some ways much more important than the hours of testimony purporting to point to an espionage conspiracy were Merker's own published words, as interpreted and misinterpreted by the Stasi's literary critics. One Stasi official devoted the eleven months from January to December 1953 examining Merker's published work in Mexico.[184] Following standard procedure, the reviewer projected the fronts of the Cold War onto the very different grid of World War II.

The critic found grave sins: illusions about imperialism; lack of discussion of the Soviet Union; praise for Allied victories over the Nazis in North Africa, Sicily, Corsica, and Italy; glorification of American democracy; celebration of the accomplishments of "the American armies and their goals without mentioning the glorious victories of the Soviet Union"; and a tendency to quote Churchill more frequently than Stalin.[185] When Merker stressed the shared responsibility of the German people for Nazi crimes but also pointed to Germans who had fought against the Nazis, his Stasi agent concluded that Merker "demanded from the international labor movement that it should not criticize the failure of the German working class."[186] This despite the fact that the ZPKK and Stasi had previously denounced Merker for "Jewish chauvinism" and a lack of faith in the German working class.

The reviewer then attacked Merker's support for Israel. Zionism served American imperialism and conducted espionage against the Communist states. Zionists betrayed the "national interests of the countries and the states to which they belong." Their claim to be a nation was "completely un–Marxist." Stalin had pointed out that the Jews were not a nation and would eventually assimilate.[187] Merker's published arguments for restitution were really efforts to give property back to Jewish capitalists.[188] But "Jewish capitalists plundered the workers just as much as Nazi capitalists. One cannot talk about a progressive stance [among Jewish capitalists] any more than among Nazi capitalists."[189] Merker's support for state aid to Jews who wished to return to Germany or for restitution was support for "theft of German property by foreign powers with the help of Jewish and capitalist elements."[190] Merker's plea that a post-Nazi Germany should be devoted to Europe-wide economic recovery indicated that Merker took the "standpoint of cosmopolitanism, the American doctrine of the plunder of foreign countries, and wishe[d] to play German industry and German raw materials into the hands of American monopolists."[191] Merker furthermore disagreed with Stalin's views on nationalism and the Jewish question. As Stalin was obviously correct, and the Soviet policies of the anti–Hitler coalition were now erased from official memory, it was inconceivable that any real Communist could have the views Merker expressed in Mexico City.

Hence, those views must have been the result of external influence and interests, such as American imperialism, Zionism, and the Jews. While the author may have been aware of the existence of Jews who were not "wealthy capitalists" or "Zionist agents," he did not mention them. This review of Merker's writings is striking for its lack of sympathy, use of stereotypes, and open hatred for and mistrust of the Jewish victims of Nazism.

In 1954 in Budapest, all of the espionage charges against Noel Field and his wife, Herta, were dropped. The Field affair was over. But Paul Merker was not released. As we have seen, by the winter and spring of 1953, the focus of the Stasi interrogations had shifted to the Slansky conspiracy and the Jewish question. Perhaps Ulbricht realized how incomprehensible it would appear to the outside world if the supposedly antifascist East German government were to try a veteran Communist on charges of participating in an international imperialist Jewish-Zionist espionage conspiracy. Or perhaps, following Stalin's death, he was uncertain about the future course of the anticosmopolitan campaign in the Soviet bloc. In any case, Paul Merker was finally brought to trial in the East German Supreme Court in March 1955, though his was a secret trial *(Geheimprozess)* rather than a show trial. It remained a secret until the collapse of the DDR in 1989 and the opening of access to the Stasi archives.[192] Neither Paul nor Margarete Merker tried to flee to the West or to publicize the case within or outside East Germany. The documents of the case were held in the archives of the East German Ministry of Justice and then transferred to the Stasi archives.

The court convicted Merker of violating Article 6 of the East German constitution, and Allied Control Council Law 10 of December 20, 1945, in connection with Allied Control Council Directive 38 of October 12, 1946.[193] Hence, this lifelong German Communist and prominent leader of the antifascist emigration was indicted under a law designed to thwart a revival of Nazism in postwar Germany. Coming to terms with the Nazi past now included sending veteran Communists to prison. On March 30, 1955, the judges of East Germany's highest court sentenced Merker to eight years in prison.

The fifteen-page Supreme Court verdict is another of the major documents of the history of the Jewish question in twentieth-century German Communism.[194] It closely followed the lines of Matern's denunciations of 1952–53 and of the Stasi interrogations and transformed Merker's political judgments during his years in France (1936–1942) and Mexico (1942–1946) into criminal acts. The verdict also displayed the overcoming of the "bourgeois" separation of political and legal institutions and concepts.[195] It stated that as a result of the success and spread of socialism after World War II, the imperialists needed to find new ways to destroy socialism "from within."[196] Their solution was to corrupt leading members of the Communist parties, put them under pressure, and then use them to advance the interests of capitalism. These methods had been revealed at the Kostoff trial in Bulgaria, the Rajk trial in Hungary, and especially the Slansky trial in Prague, which had shown that the "renegades" had sought to replace the Communist parties, destroy the Soviet Union, and once again establish capitalism "as the only ruling economic system in the whole world." Merker, the court claimed, had pursued this policy "in close contact" with the Slansky group in Prague.[197]

It further noted that "the Jewish aid organization 'Hicem'" (the Antifascist Refugee Committee in New York) had helped Merker to escape from France. Furthermore, since Gaullists in the French intelligence service working in the resistance had helped Merker get out of France, he had returned the favor by himself becoming an agent in their service.[198] Guilt by association was an important theme of the verdict. The court took Merker's friendship with Otto Katz, who had been denounced in the Slansky trial as an "international spy, Zionist, and Trotskyist," as further evidence of his participation in espionage. It also took him to task for his contact with the American Communist leader Earl Browder, someone who, the court declared, had "decisively weakened the struggle of peoples against fascism."[199]

Merker's writings and actions concerning the Jewish question played a decisive role in the indictment. The court painted a picture of a veteran Communist seduced and corrupted into becoming an "agent of American imperialism." The court declared that "the leading role [of the Mexican political emigration] went to the so-called Latin American Committee of Free Germans, which came under the strong influence of capitalist Jewish emigrants." Here Merker "played a dominant role" in proposing a postwar policy for Germany which "did not correspond to the interests of the German people but rather to the those of American imperialism."[200]

The evidence to support these charges were Merker's essays in *Freies Deutschland,* in which he "argued for the compensation of all Jewish capitalists based on the extent of their losses, regardless of whether they wanted to return to Germany or wanted to remain abroad"; supported recognition of Jewish emigrants returning to Germany as a national minority; rejected payment of restitution for antifascist resistance fighters because they did not represent a "national, religious, or castelike minority" but rather had conducted their struggle against fascism out of conviction; and urged that Germany's mineral resources be made available for the reconstruction of the European economy. This program for postwar Germany, the judges asserted, was "inspired by American monopoly capital." The court explained Merker's engagement on behalf of the Jewish people as a result of his reliance in Mexico on a "circle of emigrant Jewish capitalists" and his "continuous contact with Zionist circles, especially with the organization of the 'World Jewish Congress.'"[201]

From reading the verdict, one would not know that there had been a time when Communists had expressed solidarity with Europe's and Germany's Jews, or that during the Holocaust the primary goal of the World Jewish Congress had been to save Jewish lives and defeat the Nazis. Rather, the court assumed that loyalties to Jews and Communists were mutually exclusive. Hence, it asserted that Merker had sought his political base in Mexico not "in the political but rather in the racial emigration" and had sought support from "emigrant capitalistic Jewish circles."[202] With these arguments the justices of the Supreme Court explained—and discredited—Merker's efforts to place the Jewish catastrophe at the center of Communist antifascist politics as the result of his corruption by Jewish capitalists and clever intelligence services in whose debt he stood. Because of the linkage between Jews, capitalism, and financial corruption at its core, the verdict stands as a significant document in the history of German and European anti-Semitism.

Ten months later, on January 27, 1956, shortly before Khrushchev's "secret speech" and the period of de-Stalinization, Merker was released from the Brandenburg-Görden Prison.[203] On April 14 he wrote to Wilhelm Pieck to press his case for full political rehabilitation.[204] He blamed his mistreatment on Lavrentii Beria and the Soviets, insisted that he was innocent of all charges, and called his persecution a "criminal aberration of Marxism-Leninism."[205] In prison he had fought to prevent the representatives in Berlin from "arranging a trial which in the last analysis would severely damage the party."[206] He would never abandon his Communist convictions, he said, but would not rest until he understood why, after the revelations about and the "clarification of the Field matter," he had been tried on the foundation of obviously baseless charges. "In the trial against me, I did without a defense lawyer in order to contribute to keeping the proceedings absolutely secret," Merker argued. He had taken steps to prevent "enemies of the GDR" from using his case. In the future, he and his wife would remain silent about the matter.[207]

In April and May 1956 the ZPKK concluded that espionage accusations against Merker stemming from the Slansky trial "were insufficiently proven," that the guilty verdict was to be rescinded, and that Merker was to be declared innocent and thus "rehabilitated."[208] On July 29, 1956, the whole Central Committee adopted the decision of the Control Commission, and on July 31 Ulbricht wrote to Merker of the decision: "The reexamination undertaken under new points of view led to the conclusion that the accusations made against you in the most important matters were of a political nature and do not justify judicial prosecution."[209] Merker wrote back to Ulbricht, angered by the absence of a full political rehabilitation. He noted the "unclear formulation" of the decision and asked what the political objections were and when a full political rehabilitation would take place.[210] His request for a full political rehabilitation and return to a leading position in the party and government was unsuccessful.[211]

On July 13, 1956, the same judges and prosecutor in the Supreme

Court, again meeting in secret session, followed the Central Committee directives and decided that "the judgment of the Supreme Court of March 30, 1955, is rescinded. The accused is innocent. The cost of the proceedings will be borne by the state."[212] The court agreed with the state prosecutor that after the publication of the materials of the Twentieth Party Congress in the Soviet Union—Khrushchev's "secret speech"—and of the reexamination of the Slansky trial, "the evidence of the protocols and verdicts from this proceeding no longer suffices to support a condemnation of Merker."[213] The court found that his actions from 1936 to 1946 were no longer "judicially significant." Yet Ulbricht's letter made clear that Merker's views of that period remained politically unacceptable.[214]

The SED archives reveal further evidence of the connection between Merker's views on Jewish matters and his political downfall. Upon his release, and in response to his efforts at gaining full political rehabilitation, the Control Commission asked Merker to respond to the accusations made against him by Matern and the Central Committee in December 1952. On June 1, 1956, Merker submitted a remarkable thirty-eight-page statement of his "position on the Jewish question."[215] He wrote that his Soviet and German interrogators were convinced that he must have been an agent for the United States, Israel, or "Zionist organizations" because he had taken such a strong position on the Jewish question during World War II. They found no evidence that he was Jewish. Why, they wondered, would any non-Jewish German Communist pay so much attention to the Jewish question *unless* he was an agent of American imperialism or Zionists and Jewish capitalists?[216] To such charges Merker responded:

I am neither Jewish nor a Zionist, though it would be no crime to be either. I have never had the intent to flee to Palestine. I have not supported the efforts of Zionism. I have . . . occasionally said that, after having been plundered by Hitler fascism, most deeply humiliated, driven from their homelands, and millions of them murdered only because they were Jews, the feeling of a deepest bond and the desire for their own Jewish country emerged among Jews of different countries. This feeling was the expression of those most deeply harmed and outraged. Moreover, Hitler fascism emerged among us [Germans]. We did not succeed, through the actions of the working masses, in preventing the establishment of its rule and hence the commission of its crimes. Therefore, we Germans especially must not and ought not ignore or fight against what I call this strengthening of Jewish national feeling.[217]

He recalled Soviet support for a two-state solution in Palestine in 1947 and Soviet foreign minister Andrei Gromyko's criticism of the influence of American oil interests on American Middle East policy, and pointed to the role played by the Israeli Communists in the Hagannah in the fighting against the Arab Legion during World War II. Although he was not an active supporter of a Jewish state, he believed that "it would be wrong to actively oppose these efforts."[218] He took issue with the SED's 1953 denunciation for assuming that Zionism was an agency of American imperialism rather than being a movement of the Jews. Such characterizations were "historically inaccurate." Zionist efforts to form a Jewish state in Palestine had met with "strong resistance from English as well as from American imperialists" in contrast to support from "the masses of Jews" in many countries, as well as from the government of the Soviet Union. "No one," Merker boldly told his former colleagues on the SED Central Committee, "will want to claim that the Soviet government was an 'agent of American imperialism.'"[219] He argued that the logical result of Communist resistance to Nazism was support for the Jewish state, a view that was by then utterly out of line with Soviet and East German policy toward Israel.

What made Paul Merker such a difficult man for the Central Committee to handle was his insistence that his views on the Jewish question had nothing to do with his alleged corruption by Jewish capitalists. Rather, they had everything to do with his self-understanding as a German Communist. He noted the contributions of Jews, including Marx and Rosa Luxemburg, to German communism. He recalled the American Jewish Communists in New York and Chicago who had fought for racial equality in the United States, and the German Jews in

Berlin who had hidden him in their apartments when he was in the Communist underground in 1934. He rejected the assertion that his first concern was for Jewish capitalists, and he repeated his view that German socialists had done too little to connect anti-Semitism to the struggle for democracy in Germany.[220] In short, his statement made clear to Ulbricht, Matern, and the other members of the Control Commission and the Central Committee that, despite arrest and imprisonment, he had not changed his long-held, oft-stated, and yet now supposedly incorrect views concerning the Jewish question.

In July 1956 the Central Committee reviewed the wreckage of the purges that followed the Field and Slansky affairs. Margarete Merker was among those whose expulsion from the party was rescinded. "She was," the report laconically states, "expelled in 1953 because she refused to label her husband, Paul Merker, an imperialist agent."[221] Although Paul Merker was also readmitted to the SED, he never held an important political office again. He made no public effort to seek redress for the injustice he had endured, and never spoke publicly again about Jewish-related issues. The SED issued no public admission of regret for his denunciation, arrest, and imprisonment on the basis of accusations which Ulbricht had known all along were false.

Paul Merker died on May 13, 1969. An obituary was published in *Neues Deutschland*. Kurt Seibt, a member of the Central Committee, delivered a eulogy at Merker's funeral, praising his contribution to the class struggle. Neither statement contained a word about the years of his persecution or his public efforts concerning the Jewish question in Mexico City and East Berlin.[222] In the same year, Merker was allowed to publish his recollections of the Movement for a Free Germany. But he said little about the Jewish question, and nothing about the postwar purge.[223]

The marginalization and forgetting of the Jewish catastrophe in postwar East Germany was due to a combination of long-dominant traditions of Marxism-Leninism, the interaction of German nationalism and German communism, and Stalin's and the East German Stalinists' use of the Jewish question to tar opponents with the brush of disloyalty in the early years of the Cold War. The result was repression of those German Communists, both Jews and non-Jews, who had kept faith with promises of solidarity and who envisioned a postwar Germany with a revived Jewish community. While Moscow coordinated the general outlines of the prosecutions, the evidence of the SED and Stasi archives depicts a Central Committee unified in its determination to bring about Merker's downfall. It was left to the ingenuity and industriousness of the ZPKK and the Stasi officials in East Berlin to provide the details of the German branch of the alleged conspiracy in the Western emigration. Ulbricht and Matern used Merker's wartime and immediate postwar expressions of solidarity with the Jews as a powerful weapon in his successful efforts to consolidate dictatorial power. Wilhelm Pieck, the archetypical old Communist who knew both Merker and Zuckermann well, and who must have grasped the absurdity of the accusations against them, did not use his power and prestige to stop the anticosmopolitan purge. True, unlike Slansky, Merker was not given a show trial and executed. Nevertheless, there is no evidence of any division or debate at the top or of efforts to moderate or resist Merker's persecution. Stalinism in the GDR was not just a Soviet import.

In the next four decades, de-Stalinization did little to soften the impact of Merker's downfall, imprisonment, and partial rehabilitation. There were Jews in leading roles in the SED regime. Yet, as Alexander Abusch insisted in his 1950s exchanges with the Control Commission, out of conviction as well as an instinct for political survival they displayed a distinct lack of interest in the Jewish question. To have done otherwise would have meant political failure, public disgrace, imprisonment, or emigration. For Jewish Communists, terms of assimilation and reentry were as strict as, if not more strict than, in pre-Hitler Germany. The purge of the cosmopolitans and the suppression of the Jewish question was one of the first consequences of the consolidation of the East German dictatorship.

The links between Jews, capitalism, American imperialism, France, and Israel all evoked deep-seated, long-standing anti-Semitic traditions of anti-Western German nationalism. These traditions had, of course, been at the core of the ideological origins of National Socialism.[224] The

Merker case made clear that, as the East German Communists formed a government resting on a *German* antifascism, they distanced themselves from any identification with the Jews and the familiar catalogue of despised "others" and "outsiders" of modern German history. The *Sonderweg,* the definition of the German nation as the opposite of the West, survived the destruction of Nazi Germany and lived on in different discourses in East Berlin.[225] Paul Merker's political blunder was to continue to express solidarity with the Jews at the moment when the Communists were seeking to establish their credentials as leaders of the unified German nation.

Yet the anti-Jewish and at times anti-Semitic themes of East German policy and political culture were not only, or even primarily, a residue of the old anti-Western German *Sonderweg* in its Communist incarnation. As the cases of Abusch and Norden, among others, indicate, these policies and sentiments also had roots in the Marxist and Communist conviction that all religious traditions, including Judaism, were embarrassing relics of an unenlightened past. While some Communists attacked the Jews because they were associated with Western imperialism, others such as Abusch and Norden viewed their commitments to modern, enlightened, progressive Communism as irreconcilable with continued defense of Jewish traditions and interests. Their desire to suppress and marginalize Jewish issues, including the Holocaust, was based less on attacks on Western rationality than on a dialectic of enlightenment in the history of modern communism. They incorporated a secularizing, rationalist tradition going back to Voltaire, the German Enlightenment, and Marx which expressed growing rage at the stubborn refusal of the Jewish "other" to subordinate its claims to those of communist Reason.

Multiple continuities existed not only among German political traditions but within them as well. The SED regime's official memories of the Nazi era rested as much on the repression of the minority traditions within German communism as on repression of non- and anti-Communist views. It was not only the destruction of European Jewry which was marginalized and erased from official Communist memory. The anticosmopolitan purge also rested on repressing the memory of the Soviet Union's own "Western alliance" during World War II. Official postwar Communist antifascism rested on the forgetting of the "real existing" antifascism of the "United Nations" in the Second World War. Forgetting "Auschwitz" also entailed forgetting "Mexico City," that is, those moments when German Communists had reached out to assert their solidarity and friendship with the great "other" of modern German history. Such moments were a standing rebuke to the immorality and forgetfulness of what antifascism in East Berlin had become. Hence, they were expelled from the history of German communism and inserted into another narrative, that of Western espionage and Jewish conspiracy.

The suppression of the Jewish question in East Germany points to a general issue regarding Communist politics and memory, namely, that the ability to forget past positions and adopt new, often diametrically opposed views was an indispensable requirement for political survival. Those who could not forget or would not abandon past orthodoxy were in danger. The history of the Communist parties and governments is littered with the political corpses of persons who were unable or unwilling to change political colors at all, or to do so with sufficient speed and conviction. When yesterday's correct line became today's heresy, those who had made public statements or who had committed their views to paper were particularly vulnerable. As it became clear that bold expression of any views could be dangerous if and when the party line changed, purges rewarded the timid and the slavishly obedient. In this sense, Communist purges made amnesia, timidity, and opportunism into elements of political success. Those with long institutional memories, unchanging convictions, and strong minds sooner or later had to fall victim to a system that rewarded the capacity either to forget past positions or to denounce them as politically incorrect errors.

The winter purge of 1952–53 constituted the decisive and irrevocable turning point in the history of the regime regarding Jewish matters and the politics of memory in East Germany. With some minor modifications in the 1980s, none of the basic choices of these months and years were fundamentally revised. While some East German novelists and filmmakers addressed anti-Semitism and the Holocaust, these issues remained on the margins of East Germany's official anti-fascist political culture. The purges and trials of these years left wounds that never healed and forms of memory and politics which over time deepened the gap between Communists and the vast majority of Jews inside and outside Germany. The purges engaged vast amounts of time and energy of large numbers of high-ranking East German officials. In these crucial years, time and energy which should have been devoted to examining the Nazi past were instead squandered in grotesque searches for conspiracies supposedly hatched by Nazism's victims. The purge of the cosmopolitans set the framework within which the codification of East German political memory of the Nazi past occurred.

# 6

## Memory and Policy in East Germany
## from Ulbricht to Honecker

The anticosmopolitan campaign left a wound that never healed and an official memory of Nazism that remained intact until the collapse of the East German regime in 1989. The anticosmopolitan purges were succeeded by the codification, institutionalization, and diffusion of their prejudices and hatreds, and also by their translation into policy. Merker's and Zuckermann's assertions concerning the link between the fight against anti-Semitism and the fate of German democracy were soon spectacularly borne out by events. On June 17, 1953, just six months after the publication of "Lessons of the Trial against the Slansky Conspiracy Center," widespread protests and strikes against political repression and economic hardship spread throughout East Germany. The revolution which had devoured its privileged children in the Politburo now crushed a dangerous people with Soviet tanks.[1] In the months preceding the revolt, Wilhelm Zaisser (1893–1958), a member of the SED Central Committee and the minister of state security, along with Rudolf Herrnstadt (1903–1966), the editor in chief of *Neues Deutschland* since 1949, advocated a relaxation of the regime's Stalinist course.[2] Zaisser had directed the Stasi during the anticosmopolitan campaign. Herrnstadt, who was Jewish, had been editor of *Neues Deutschland* when it published the denunciation of Merker and other "Zionist spies" on its front pages. In July 1953 they too were expelled from the Central Committee and from the SED for "factional activity."[3]

Those who had willingly participated in the purges now fell victim to them. The repression of the Jewish question had become a constitutive element in the consolidation of the second twentieth-century German dictatorship.

East German dissent was partly diverted by the safety valve of flight to West Germany. During the 1950s, before the Berlin Wall was built, over 10 percent of the population voted with their feet. Yet for those leftist and liberal intellectuals whose counterparts led dissent elsewhere in Eastern Europe, the political culture of antifascism was also decisive in blunting criticism of the "antifascist" regime. As Sigrid Meuschel notes, they too "experienced the trauma of National Socialism and felt more solidarity with a party [the SED] whose antifascism they shared . . . than with a society they did not trust."[4] The sentiments of May 1945 expressed in the "Aufruf" concerning the "millions and millions" of Germans who had followed Hitler did not disappear. Potential intellectual dissenters feared that open criticism of Stalinism in East Germany would lead the East Germans to relativize or diminish the burden of the Nazi crimes and give aid and comfort to "fascists" and "imperialists" abroad. In this way, official memory of the Nazi era immunized the "antifascist" East German regime from criticism. The enemies of the antifascist regime must "objectively" be fascists. Within the bipolar Manichaeanism of fascism and antifascism, it made perfect sense to use denazification laws to indict veteran Communists such as Merker, and to describe the workers' revolt of 1953 as a "fascist provocation" and the Berlin Wall as an "antifascist protection wall." Meuschel trenchantly observes that antifascism "merged into a dreadful syndrome which placed narrow limits on the critique of Stalinism."[5] Those who, in Albert Hirschmann's terms, had not taken the option of "exit" now found that the requirements of "loyalty" set limits on the possibility of "voice."[6] Official memories of the Nazi dictatorship became crucial to consolidating the Communist dictatorship, immunizing it from criticism, and placing its critics on the defensive.

As we have seen, the East German struggle against fascism had increasingly less to do with the Nazi past and ever more to do with the Cold

War. The Communists kept memory alive and put it in the service of current policy. They put the annual September International Day of Remembrance for the Victims of Fascist Terror, a practice that began during the Nuremberg interregnum in the fall of 1945, into the service of the contemporary "struggle for peace." In September 1950 the day of remembrance was marked by a huge peace rally in Berlin.[7] By 1951, the VVN was describing the annual day of remembrance for the victims of Nazi persecution, as a "day of struggle [*Kampftag*] against war and fascism."[8] The ceremonies, the VVN proclamation read, should both stress the "legacy of the millions brutally murdered in the fight against Hitler fascism" and ensure that it "live on in the present unwavering, decisive struggle for peace."[9] It continued, "Eleven million men and women of all European nations fighting against Hitler fascism went to painful and tortured deaths," Yet they died "confident that they were doing so for the cause of peace and humanity . . . All who opposed fascism . . . were in the first place fighters for peace."[10]

In fact, the vast majority of those who were murdered were not in any political or military sense "fighting fascism," and they certainly were not "fighting for peace," whatever that might mean. They were "fighting" to survive, and were simply human beings whom the Nazis had chosen to murder. These modified days of remembrance were essentially Hegelian moments. They redefined unredeemable and sense-less tragedy into a redemptive martyrdom that contributed to the victorious end of History. They thus lent past heroism a specific ideological purpose that reinforced the current "struggle for peace" of Soviet diplomacy. Remembrance did not imply mourning and melancholia but evoked instead the uplifting legacy of the "heroes of the antifascist resistance struggle." Ernst Thälmann, above all, became a model whom "succeeding generations should follow in the battle for peace."[11] The spirit "of all the fighters killed by the fascists" would teach the Germans to do all they could to fight for peace.[12] Equality for women in these days of remembrance meant that they too were included in the pantheon of redemptive martyrs of the German resistance. By 1951, the Communists were comparing American policy in Europe and in the Korean War to Hitler's aggression. U.S. policy was fostering the "reemergence of German imperialism and militarism" and the restoration of war criminals to positions of responsibility.[13] Thus we see that a seamless web linked the past "struggle against fascism" to the contemporary assault on the Bonn government. The presentist meaning of coming to terms with the Nazi past was obvious: it meant fighting against the "fascism" emerging in Bonn. Among the most important charges which the East Germans were hurling at the Federal Republic was that, in contrast to the antifascist regime in East Berlin, the Bonn leadership had refused to confront the burden of the past.

Photographs in the SED archives taken at the day of remembrance in 1951 show large pictures of Thälmann, banners proclaiming "Resistance against Fascism," red flags, and large crowds listening to anti-imperialist speeches. The scenes exude an atmosphere of militant contemporaneity and triumph.[14] A photograph of a massive demonstration for the victims of fascism in Berlin in September 1950 shows a banner reading "Long Live Peace" in French, German, and Russian.[15] A striking shot of a demonstration by women at Ravensbrück concentration camp in September 1952 shows Thälmann's daughter Irma leading a march of women, many of whom are carrying flags.[16] Another startling image shows girls and boys carrying red flags past what appears to be one of the crematoria in Ravensbrück.[17] Only four months before Merker's arrest and the publication of "Lessons of the Trial against the Slansky Conspiracy Center," the VVN ceremonies in Ravensbruck indicated the tendency toward inclusiveness of the memory of the victims of fascism. A photograph taken that day shows VVN leader Walter Bartel speaking in front of a sign which states "1933–1945: The Following Were Murdered." At the head of the list of victims is written "6,000,000 Jews," followed in order by "4,000,000 Members of Various Countries"—which are then listed—and "7,000,000 Germans."[18] The picture is unusual because the Jewish victims of Nazism are first on the list, yet it also is indicative of a certain confusion. In fact, about 4 million Germans died in World War II, the vast majority of whom were soldiers killed in battle rather than defenseless civilians "murdered" in the same sense as civilians on the Eastern Front or inmates of concentration camps.[19]

Although many tears must have been shed at these days of remembrance, the photo archive of the SED in Berlin contains only two pictures recording simple human grief and mourning. Both were taken on September 9, 1951. The first shows representatives of Berlin's Jewish community, their faces taut and somber, laying a wreath covered with the Star of David.[20] The second is of a delegation of "former resistance fighters" honoring the memory of members of the French resistance who died in Buchenwald. As the usual flags of victory and militancy fly, two women are seen wiping away tears, while the men appear to be reflecting on their lost comrades more than on the bright socialist future.[21]

Such displays of individual grief and loss, however, are unusual. More typical are photos of determined men and women, militant children and teenagers, marching through the former concentration camps, carrying red flags in the "struggle for peace." These Hegelian moments combined mourning for fallen martyrs with the heroic spirit of redemption through the victory of communism and the Red Army.[22] The "days for women" evoked the female heroes of the resistance who did not break under torture and were brave beyond the point of endurance.[23] The incorporation of women and teenagers into the heroic mode of recollection is captured in two striking pictures taken in September 1952 at the "women's peace demonstration" at the former Nazi concentration camp in Ravensbrück. In a remarkable and disturbing image teenagers, presumably in the uniform of the Freie Deutsche Jugend, the Communist youth organization, are carrying flags past one of the ovens at the camp.[24] Another photo taken at the same event shows Irma Thälmann and four other women leading a group of flag-carrying women as they march inside the Ravensbrück camp.[25] Whatever their private grief may have been, the women in this photo display a determined look of progressive faith in History and in ultimate victory. The heroic, presentist dimension of the memorial days is also apparent in a photo taken at a meeting of the VVN on November 9, 1952, to commemorate the fourteenth anniversary of "Kristallnacht." Two banners are visible behind the podium, where leading VVN and SED functionaries sit: "Long

Live the Firm, Unbreakable German-Soviet friendship!" and "Against Racial and National Hatred—Against Fratricide and War—For Peace and Understanding between Peoples!"[26]

These ceremonies displayed a relentlessly "progressive" (that is, forward-looking) redemptive spirit. Occasioned by losses in the past, they were devoted to victory in the present and future. Like the ubiquitous socialist realist statues of Ernst Thälmann, this discourse and these ceremonies combined public mourning with a pervasive sense of historical muscularity, optimism, and confidence in the future.[27] They fostered identification with History's winners, with the victors and heroes of the antifascist resistance, not with lost causes such as the Jews. The deaths of Jewish victims did not fit into Hegelian narratives in which the cunning of History crowns suffering with success.[28]

The Jews of pre-Nazi Germany have been much criticized for their failure to assimilate into German society by demonstrating their patriotic allegiance to the Kaiser Reich. In view of that failure, it is particularly remarkable that it was in the self-described antifascist Germany that Communists of Jewish origin contributed to defining even more stringent terms of assimilation. Let us now turn our focus to the small number of highly assimilated Jews who remained in the SED after the purge of the cosmopolitans. They were heirs to the Karl Marx who wrote the essay of 1843 on the Jewish question. If, as Liah Greenfeld has argued, German nationalism is a component of Marx's thought, then in this sense as well they were his genuine and legitimate heirs.[29] Those Jewish Communists who remained in the East German government thought of themselves as German patriots and advocates of a progressive, antifascist, but decidedly German nation. They defended this socialist, humanist Germany against the home of cosmopolitanism, the United States. To have done so *after* Auschwitz amounted to what could be called hyperassimilation, an assimilation more radical and complete than its Enlightenment predecessors. By 1953 there were few Jews left in prominent positions in East Germany, and, to put it mildly, they did not cultivate their Jewish identity. They were a tough bunch, having survived first Nazism and then the anticosmopolitan purges. We will look more closely at two of them: Albert Norden and Alexander Abusch.[30]

We recall Abusch's spectacular comeback from the recantations and Stasi testimony during the Merker affair, including his membership in the powerful Kulturbund (1951) and the prestigious German Writers' Association (1952); appointment as deputy minister of culture (1954–1956) then minister of culture (1958–1961); and membership in the SED Central Committee from 1956 until his death in 1982.[31] In order to have a voice, Abusch had to demonstrate his loyalty. In 1949, before the Noel Field affair but after the Cold War had begun, Abusch published *Stalin und die Schicksalsfragen der Deutschen Nation* (Stalin and the Fateful Questions Facing the German Nation).[32] The book supported Soviet foreign policy from Weimar through "the rescue of European civilization" in World War II.[33] The text is strewn with quotations from Stalin. Abusch, the author of *Der Irrweg der Nation*, now argued that Stalin and the Soviet Union had rescued the Germans and all of Europe from the consequences of Germany's dismal historical trajectory. It is hard to say what mixture of conviction, fear, and opportunism animated this unfortunate text, but it clearly shows Abusch's unwavering determination to return to the ranks of the Communist elite. Part of the payoff was the opportunity to play a key role in the codification of East German memories of Nazism. In a 1954 collection of essays, *Restauration oder Renaissance* (Restoration or Renaissance), Abusch contrasted the "restoration" of reaction in West Germany to the "renaissance" of humanism in the East.[34] The imperialists in the West, he wrote in 1948, counted on the "forgetfulness of individuals."[35] The association of the GDR with memory and the Federal Republic with forgetfulness remained an enduring theme of East German cultural politics.

Abusch also offered a defense of censorship based on both a mistrust of liberal democracy and the memory of German fascism. East Germany, he wrote, fostered freedom of artistic production, though not "freedom for works which present war as inevitable and foster hatred toward other peoples." The latter could be left to the West Germans, whose "entire book market is overflowing, barbarized, and militarized with the so-called literature of the soldiers."[36] Abusch stressed that "the experience of our generation teaches us that the freedom [to publish] militaristic and warmongering literature" led to the absence of freedom for "humanistic literature . . . We know from the history of our own people, from its not yet forgotten bloody reality," that once fascists seize power, they suppress cultural humanism.[37] Hence, censorship of "militaristic literature" was a small price to pay to spread "the spirit of humanity and peace among our people and to defeat the evil spirit of militarism, the SS, and war."[38] Taken to its logical conclusion, here was an argument that an educational dictatorship was necessary to prevent the return of a fascist dictatorship.

Abusch was not impressed with West German democracy. "Exactly as it was under Hitler," he wrote, the "still surviving mass murderers from Auschwitz and Maidanek [under the name of] 'the West'" express themselves in the "official American, cosmopolitan ideology as 'Europeans.'"[39] The "war treaty between Bonn and Paris," West German rearmament, and admission into the NATO alliance were, in Abusch's terms, "the direct continuation of the so-called Europe policy of the SS." A Europe dominated by the SS, he said, "ideologically merges with the 'cosmopolitan European' policy with an American color."[40] Konrad Adenauer viewed the integration of West Germany into Atlantic and European structures as a check on the revival of German nationalism and an end to Germany's anti-Western, antidemocratic conservatism. Looking at the same processes, Abusch saw a repetition of the era after World War I, when the forces of the old order were reconstructed with assistance from international, or "cosmopolitan," forces. For Abusch, if Germany's path of error was going to be brought to an end, the impetus would come from Moscow, not from Washington, Paris, and London.

In the same work Abusch pointed with pride to the very close links between intellectuals and political power manifested in the creation of a Ministry of Culture. In response to West German critics who asserted that Minister of Culture Johannes R. Becher was placing art in the service of politics, Abusch argued that the apolitical tradition of German intellectuals had proved disastrous for the survival of German humanism in politics. In "our republic, however, real humanism came to power, and the great thoughts and dreams of the genius of German poetry have assumed reality."[41] Following the repression of the rebellion of June 17, 1953, he and Becher encouraged artistic realism and approved aesthetic guidelines "to protect German culture against decadence and cosmopolitan loss of roots."[42] Abusch thus gained the dubious distinction of becoming one of the few Jewish intellectuals in modern German history to have attacked cosmopolitan rootlessness.

Albert Norden (1894–1982) was one of the most influential of the Communists of Jewish origin in the upper echelons of the East German government. The son of a rabbi, he became a dedicated Communist. He was a member of the founding generation of the KPD, and he edited party newspapers before and after 1933. In 1933 he fled into exile, first in Paris and Prague, then from 1941 to 1946 in New York. In 1949 he became the press spokesman for the East German government, and from October 1949 to December 1952 he served under Gerhart Eisler as press chief of a division within the East German Office of Information.[43] In the purge of December 1952 he lost this position, though he landed on his feet with a professorship in history at Humboldt University. In 1954 he returned to an official political position as director of the Nationale Rat der Nationale Front des Demokratischen Deutschland (National Council of the National Front of a Democratic Germany). In 1955 he was elected to the Central Committee of the SED and became Secretary for Agitation in April 1955. By 1958 he was a member of the SED Politburo and remained in the position until 1981.[44] He was best known in both Germanys for his leading role in the National Front for a Democratic Germany and the Ausschuss für Deutsche Einheit (Committee for German Unity). From those positions he directed the East German government's propaganda offensive against West Germany.[45]

After four years in wartime Manhattan, Norden, along with another German Communist exile, Gerhart Eisler, and Albert Schreiner published *The Lesson of Germany: A Guide to Her History*.[46] Norden, Eisler, and Schreiner concluded that the German capitalists and imperialists could not be "reeducated." Their existence as powerful social classes had to be ended. What hope there was for Germany's future lay in the reeducation of its working classes. But, like German Communists everywhere in 1945, Norden, Eisler, and Schreiner took a dim view of the German working class. They blamed the Social Democrats for contributing to the disorganization, demoralization, and corruption of the German workers. For whatever reason, the working class had failed to bring Nazism down. Instead, they wrote, saving the world from Nazism had been "the work of people outside Germany."[47] Unlike workers in other countries, who had presumably led the struggle against Nazism, "under Nazi rule the German labor movement plunged to its lowest level." Its deeds "stood in complete antithesis to its historical role and many positive traditions." Thus, until the German working class "can find a way to cleanse itself by deeds of the consequences of its passivity and its subservience to Nazism," it could not raise "itself and its nation" to a higher level and "regain the trust of the peoples and labor movements of other countries."[48] Although the authors acknowledged that the Nazis "in three Polish 'extermination camps' alone—Maidanek, Sobibur [sic], and Osviecim-Birkenau . . . slaughtered over 5 million prisoners of war and civilians, all unarmed, from all European countries which were under the control of the Gestapo," their text remained vague as to the identities of these victims.[49]

Despite their anger over Nazi crimes and their pessimism about the German working class, Eisler, Norden, and Schreiner ended with a striking link between the tasks facing the German nation and the eradication of Nazism: "The extirpation of German Nazism and militarism is the decisive national task of the Germans, without which they cannot take a single step forward." They hoped that a "new German nation" would be born so that Germany would then "cease to be identical with bestiality" and would no longer "represent a horrible nightmare to the peoples of the world."[50]

One can plausibly interpret Albert Norden's political career in the East German government as an effort to bring about a rebirth of a new German nation. He published over thirty essays during the emigration period. Most dealt with fascism and antifascism.[51] He discussed appeasement and the efforts of the Soviet Union to oppose Nazism in 1933. He stressed the role of German capitalism in bringing Nazism to power and benefiting from it.[52] When he did examine anti–Semitism, he viewed it as tool the Nazis used to divert middle-class anger over "capitalist anarchy" onto the Jews.[53] He discussed *Mein Kampf,* including Hitler's views of expansion to the East, without mentioning either the role of anti–Semitism in Hitler's ideology and policy or the links between anti–Semitism and anticommunism in Nazi ideology in general.[54] His essays of the postwar decade were equally lacking in any discussion of the Jewish catastrophe.[55]

In the darkest days of the anti–Jewish purge in 1952 and 1953, Norden's Jewish origins and his wartime emigration to New York placed him under suspicion of infection by the cosmopolitan virus. His 1952 essay collection, *Um die Nation,* accomplished two tasks necessary for his reentry into the upper echelons of the East German government.[56] First, he displayed his anti-American credentials, thus dispelling suspicions that four years in wartime New York had left him with "illusions" about such things as the antifascist character of the United States in World War II. Second, as a Jewish-born Communist who was also a German nationalist, he offered the regime a unique and valuable asset, for by joining in the chorus of anticosmopolitanism, he demonstrated his loyalty and seemed to refute those who said that the purge was anti-Semitic at its roots.

The essays in *Um die Nation* present German history since the Thirty Years' War as a series of lost opportunities in which unity and progress are repeatedly defeated by division and reaction.[57] The division of Germany after 1945 and the emergence of "the second West German separate state"—that is, West Germany—was part of this long continuum of division sponsored by the forces of reaction.[58] Norden argued that the Western alliance against the Soviet Union recalled the offers of the defeated remnants of the Hitler regime to form a common anti-Soviet front.[59] Far from signifying a break with the anti-Western elements of Nazi ideology, he wrote, the decision of the German upper classes after 1945 to join a Western alliance was in accord with their class interests narrowly understood, and in conflict with "the unity of the nation." The "crime" of dividing Germany again had been perpetrated by "foreign accomplices"—the United States, Great Britain, and France—who wanted to use part of Germany for their "reactionary and aggressive foreign policy." The "same finance capitalists" who had tried to divide Germany after World War I had again placed "Mammon" ahead of national unity and gone along with Anglo-American plans to keep postwar Germany divided. "The imperialists of 1933 and 1939 to 1945 are the imperialists of today," he continued.[60] The enemies of unions and supporters of "the unadorned fascist dictatorship now call for Western orientation. Yesterday's Hitler imperialists are the cosmopolitans of today," for they supported "bending Germany to the yoke of the USA." The same elements who had supported Nazism "were sacrificing Germany" to the plans of the Western powers.[61] Although American and German "monopoly capital" had parallel interests, both "run strictly counter to Germany's national interest" and would end with "Germany's total annihilation" in "a Third World War on German soil. Finance capital *or* the nation—that is the question to which only the proletariat and its allies can offer a saving answer."[62] Norden clearly stood with the nation and against capital.

With such slogans Norden reversed the customary relationship of right and left to the nation. It was the Communists who were the genuine nationalists, while Adenauer and Schumacher were sacrificing the nation to American interests. Norden called Adenauer's 1951 agreements with the occupying powers "a thousand times worse than the Versailles peace diktat." At least the Versailles treaty had preserved the unity of Germany, whereas the post-1945 settlements codified division.[63] A "foreign tyranny" was now being established over West Germany which amounted to the "abdication of the nation . . . For the first time since the Napoleonic era, German troops are subordinate to foreign tyrants." Because of American policies, West Germany had become a "permanently occupied country" which was losing its national independence.[64] Conversely, German communism, far from being a Soviet imposition, had deep roots in German history, from Marx and Engels to the youthful political activities of Pieck, Grotewohl, and Ulbricht.[65] Hence it was Marxism and communism, not international capitalism, which were most deeply rooted in the German nation.[66] "National treason was the law of declining finance capital," Norden wrote, while the proletariat remained rooted within intact, national traditions.[67]

The Westernization of West German political culture and the delegitimation of the radical conservative attack on "the West" is one of the central themes of postwar West German intellectual and political history.[68] In Marxist-Leninist language, Norden and other East German political and intellectual leaders articulated traditional German anti-Western resentments in the context of a strikingly unashamed pathos of German national liberation. For Abusch, Norden, and other leading East German political and intellectual figures, there was one and only one continuity or restoration, in German history after 1945, and it took place in West, not East, Germany.[69] The regrettable restoration of post-1945 German history recalled in important respects the era immediately after World War I. Just as in 1918, so again in 1945 had hopes for a Socialist and Communist Germany been crushed by an alliance of Anglo-American intervention, domestic reaction, and "betrayal" by German Social Democrats. The difference was that after 1945, Soviet power had prevented the extension of this reactionary restoration to East Germany.

Most remarkably, in a 1952 essay titled "Cosmopolitanism—the Ideology of the Trans-Atlantic Thieves," Norden adopted the discourse of anticosmopolitanism yet diverted it away from its original targets.[70] When he wrote that "yesterday's Hitler imperialists are today's cosmopolitans," he diverted the charge of "cosmopolitanism" away from the Jews and back to "capitalism . . . the father of cosmopolitanism," especially American capitalism.[71] Furthermore, he stressed what he saw as a "cultural-intellectual affinity" between U.S. policy and Nazism. The difference between Hitler's desire for a world state and the Truman-Dulles policy was that between a "global imperium" under the auspices of either a German or an American imperialism: "In both cases, the driving forces [are] identical, namely, the drive of finance capital to dominate the world."[72] Minimizing or denying uniqueness to the Nazi dictatorship compared to other capitalist states had been and would remain an important feature of Communist interpretation of the Nazi past.

Norden's attack on cosmopolitanism, though shorn of Matern's anti-Semitism, echoed the anti-Western resentments and "German anticapitalism" of pre-1945, predominantly right-wing German nationalism.

Then too, German nationalists had juxtaposed American commercialism to the ways of the cultured Old World. After Auschwitz it was remarkable, to say the least, to see a leading Communist of Jewish origin contrast a presumably benign German national identity to an allegedly corrosive American cosmopolitanism. Norden had nothing to say about the role of the United States in defeating Nazism, and seemed either oblivious to or unconcerned about parallels between the anti-Western resentments which had nourished Nazism and his own assault on cosmopolitanism during the Cold War.[73]

Norden's determination to defend the German nation stood in marked contrast to his indifference to the eventual disappearance of the Jews. Norden shared Marx's vision of a German revolution which would lead to the "emancipation" of the world from the Jews. As he argued in a letter of May 19, 1959 to the prominent East German Jewish author Arnold Zweig, the construction of a classless society in East Germany would eventually mean the complete assimilation of the remaining few thousand German Jews. As anti-Semitism was a product of imperialism, it would disappear only with the attainment of socialism.[74] Presumably the German nation which Norden wished to preserve was less anachronistic than the Jews, whose disappearance through assimilation he viewed with equanimity.

Both Abusch and Norden were survivors, and as such were fully aware of the limits of tolerable discourse about Nazism and the Jewish catastrophe within the SED—and of the price for transgressing those boundaries. Hence, the presence of Jews in the East German government on terms of assimilation more restrictive than those in pre-Nazi Germany did not lead to the inclusion of the Jewish question in East German memory of the Nazi past.

In 1958 and 1961 the East German government dedicated its two major memorials to the victims of fascism at the sites of the former Nazi concentration camps in Buchenwald and Sachsenhausen. The memorials set in stone the ideas that survived the purge of 1949–1956. Both Otto Grotewohl at Buchenwald in 1958 and Walter Ulbricht at Sachsenhausen in 1961 delivered speeches that drew political significance from past suffering. Both came to praise fallen soldiers more than to mourn innocent victims.[75] The texts were major statements of official antifascist memory in East Germany.

Planning for the memorials began in 1954 with a committee chaired by President Otto Grotewohl. The actual planning was directed by Minister of Culture Johannes R. Becher and his deputy Alexander Abusch. Other members included Rosa Thälmann, widow of Ernst Thälmann, Walter Bartel, Propst Heinrich Grüber, Stefan Heymann, Jenny Matern, Anna Seghers, Hans Seigewisser, and Arnold Zweig.[76] In a 1954 memo Grotewohl wrote that the memorials' most important goal was "to place the shame and disgrace of the past before the young generation so that they can draw lessons from it." Yet, he continued, they must also "indicate the path toward the future [and] give expression to the will for life and struggle which developed among the prisoners" in their "resistance to Nazi barbarism." They should combine remembrance of the past with warnings for the present and future, while demonstrating that the resistance legacy was alive in the policies of East German antifascism.[77] Although the memorials would recall the suffering of the victims, "above all they bear witness to the indefatigable strength of the antifascist resistance fighter" and should be seen as "towering signs of victory over fascism."[78] The memorials were Hegelian moments set in stone, intended to encourage optimism about the future based on memory of past heroism, rather than reflections of an unredeemable tragedy.

A planning committee statement for the ceremony conveys Grotewohl's intended meaning. For the "honor of the dead" and for the "sake of the living," memory admonished "all of us" to action. "German militarism," it said, was "again a major danger for peace in Europe," threatening the "security and independence of peoples. Again the militaristic and fascist gang in West Germany presents new aggression against peace-loving peoples."[79] The statement denounced West German plans to introduce atomic weapons and missiles into the hands of "fascist murderers" and "old Nazi generals." The statement demanded an immediate halt to nuclear weapons tests, the creation of a nuclear weapons–free zone in Central Europe, negotiations for disarmament and détente, and peace.[80] If East German foreign policy continued the legacy of the victims of Buchenwald, dissent from that policy was not merely a political error. It was a desecration of the sacred memory of fascism's victims. The clear message of the Buchenwald and Sachsenhausen memorials was that East Germany was the successor to the antifascist resistance fighters, while West Germany was the successor to the fascists and Nazis.

In his speech at the dedication of the Buchenwald memorial on September 14, 1958, Grotewohl praised the courage and "heroism of the European resistance fighters."[81] The East German government, he said, carried on their antifascist legacy. The Buchenwald memorial would inform future generations of the "immortal glory" of their struggle against tyranny and for freedom, peace, and human dignity.[82] From Buchenwald, Grotewohl called "the living to action; we urge you not to be paralyzed in the struggle against fascism" and for peace. Apparently the "millions and millions" of Germans who had followed Hitler had either disappeared or been forgiven. Gone were the days of accusing the German people of having failed to overthrow Nazism. These accusations were replaced by militant identification with the German and European resistance. But gone as well were the public affirmations of solidarity between the "political" and "racial" victims of Nazism which had been voiced by veterans of the Communist resistance at ceremonies of remembrance between 1945 and 1948. "Resistance" to war and fascism now meant opposition to West German rearmament, while fighting the Cold War was equated with *Vergangenheitsbewältigung*. "Fascism" referred no less to 1950s West Germany than it did to the Nazi past.

The Buchenwald ceremony, according to Grotewohl, was a "manifestation of the struggle against preparation for an imperialist atomic war, which today, especially from West Germany, threatens the German people and humanity."[83] Although "Hitler fascism" had been defeated militarily in 1945, its roots had been eliminated only in the DDR, where the "ideas of the antifascist fighters were realized and a state of peace" prevailed. The two German states, he continued, had had totally contrasting responses to the Nazi past. The East had "learned from the errors of German history" and "drawn the good and correct lessons." The West German government, however, was "a bulwark of reaction, in which militarists and fascists have again gained power, and whose aggressive character expresses itself in reactionary deeds."[84] With reference to the Suez crisis of 1956, Grotewohl attacked the "acts of aggression" of the United States and England "in the Middle East against the Arab peoples" and called for opposition to the Bonn government's support for this aggression.[85] Grotewohl did not mention the Jewish catastrophe. On the contrary, he used the occasion of the dedication of the first major East German memorial to the victims of fascism to signal East German support for the Arabs in the Middle East conflict. The special responsibility of the German people lay in forming "a unified, all-German people's movement against preparations for atomic war," which would bring about an atomic weapons–free zone in Europe and build "friendship and understanding between all peoples."[86] In other words, facing the Nazi past meant, first and foremost, supporting Soviet foreign and military policy.

On April 24, 1961, only four months before he ordered the construction of the Berlin Wall, Walter Ulbricht came to Sachsenhausen to dedicate the new antifascist memorial, praise past heroes, and claim their legacy. The dedication ceremony was front-page news in *Neues Deutschland*. A crowd estimated at 200,000 had gathered. Representatives from twenty-three foreign countries, including officials from the Warsaw Pact countries, and Western Communist parties, spoke. Banners held aloft in the crowd bore slogans such as: "Our Struggle against War and Fascism Continues," "Peace Will Always Come from East Germany," "The German Democratic Republic—Bulwark against the Spirit of Nazism in West Germany," "Sachsenhausen Demands the Triumph of Peace and Humanity," "In the Spirit of Antifascist Resistance Fighters," and "Down with the War Criminals in Bonn."[87]

Ulbricht delivered a classic political funeral oration intended to link the national past to its present and future and to make a fundamental statement of East Germany's memory of the Nazi era.

With deepest respect we turn to our precious dead, the fighters against war, fascism, and militarism, and to the victims of Nazi terror.

This place is dedicated to memory and warning: to the memory of countless martyrs and heroes of the antifascist resistance struggle and to warning coming generations never again to allow fascist barbarism to break out among our own people, or among other peoples.

Every foot of this earth is soaked with the blood and sweat of ten thousand martyrs from many countries, and of many different world-views. They were driven and tortured to death, and murdered only because they loved their people, because they loved freedom, peace, and democracy more than their own life, because they were socialists, because they rejected hatred among peoples and rejected genocide, and because they dedicated their lives to humanism and to friendship among peoples.[88]

Neither torture nor terror, he said, was able to break the fighter's spirit. The history of the resistance "under inhuman conditions of a factory for the extermination of human beings in Sachsenhausen [was] a painful but honorable chapter of the heroic history" of antifascist struggle by German Communists and other antifascists. Inside and outside the concentration camps and torture chambers, "people of diverse beliefs fought together with unheard-of sacrifices against the blood-soaked Hitler regime. *In so doing, they saved the future of the German nation.*"[89] He then recalled the thousands of Communists, Social Democrats, Soviet prisoners of war, and citizens of Poland, Luxembourg, Yugoslavia, Holland, Belgium, Denmark, Austria, Hungary, Czechoslovakia, and France, as well as British prisoners of war, who had been murdered in Sachsenhausen. Ulbricht did not mention that Jews had been killed in Sachsenhausen or anywhere else.

To be sure, there was some truth in what Ulbricht had to say. There were "martyrs and heroes" who had been murdered "only" because of their political convictions and activities. Many did die heroic deaths in the struggle against fascism. But the falsehood of Ulbricht's text outweighed its truth. In Sachsenhausen and other concentration camps the Jews were murdered not because of their political actions or beliefs but simply because they were Jews. Yet Ulbricht clearly privileged that small minority of Nazism's victims that consisted of German political opponents. Solidarity with the Jews had no part in these ceremonies of remembrance.[90] There was something heartless and arrogantly presentist about the pride with which he turned past suffering to his own purposes. As was now common practice, the Jewish catastrophe found no place at all in this narrative of past martyrdom that saved the German nation. Nevertheless, Ulbricht insisted that in contrast to the West Germans, the East Germans had grasped the true lessons of the World Wars: "We have offered restitution, as far as this was at all possible. By destroying Nazism and militarism at their roots, we have overcome the militarist and reactionary evil traditions which so deeply influence the German past."[91] Ulbricht may have been referring to reparations to the Soviet Union or pension benefits paid to officially designated "victims of fascism," for the East German government had consistently refused to make any financial restitution to the Jewish survivors of the Holocaust.

Ulbricht drew a straight line connecting the anti-Nazi resistance in the Sachsenhausen concentration camp with the East German propaganda offensive against West Germany. He juxtaposed the spirit of the anti-Hitler coalition and the Potsdam agreement, presumably alive and well in East Berlin, to the "remilitarization and reemergence of fascism [*Refaschisierung*] in West Germany" and to the delivery of atomic weapons to "Hitler's generals" now serving in Bonn. It was in East Germany that "the other Germany" had sunk its roots. "Comrades and friends died together in Sachsenhausen," he said, "so that we, together, could complete their work and secure freedom, democracy, and peace for humanity."[92] Ulbricht's speech made clear that memory of past martyrs had become an integral aspect of contemporary East German policy. Those whose deaths could not serve current political purposes were ignored. Talk of the "millions and millions" of Germans who had supported Nazism had given way to diffusion of the aura of antifascist martyrdom to the whole of "antifascist" East Germany.

After the speeches at Sachsenhausen, political dignitaries led a march out of the memorial. The photograph of that march is the defining image of the East German memory of the Nazi era. It shows Walter Ulbricht leading the SED leadership in their march. Behind him, visible above a crowd of people, is the smokestack of the concentration camp.

Otto Grotewohl, Rosa Thälmann, and other members of the Politburo are among those walking alongside Ulbricht. On either side East German soldiers stand at attention. Ulbricht is giving the politician's wave of victory. The photo could be entitled "Communism Rises Like a Phoenix from the Ashes of Defeat." It was a supremely Hegelian moment, a moment of historical triumph and identification with history's heroes and victors rather than with its tragic and unredeemed victims. Within four months the regime would begin building the Berlin Wall to stem the flow of refugees to the West.

Following the infamous Waldheim prosecutions, the anticosmopolitan purge and Jewish exodus of winter 1952–53, and repression of the June 17, 1953, revolt, the East German regime was in a very weak position. In the face of a continuing mass exodus of between 150,000 and 200,000 people a year, the East German government launched a propaganda offensive aimed at the "Nazis in Bonn."[93] Mass emigration, economic failure, unsuccessful efforts to gain diplomatic recognition, and the acceptance of West German integration into NATO by the West German Social Democrats left the East German government isolated abroad and lacking support at home. An ideological offensive against West Germany had the advantage of diverting attention from domestic difficulties and from East Germany's own abysmal human rights record.[94] East Berlin's antifascist ideology provided the core element of its attack on the West German government. The East Germans claimed that former members of the Nazi Party and government remained in important positions in the West German establishment, and that they were continuing Hitler's anticommunist and "revanchist" policies. One key assumption of this offensive against the Federal Republic was that the issue of who was and who was not a Nazi was entirely a matter of *past* actions and affiliations rather than of *present* attitudes— or once a Nazi, always a Nazi. The idea of political "sins of youth" followed by introspection or "deradicalization" did not enter into the equation.[95] Yet the East Germans did not invent the problem. West German politicians, journalists, and intellectuals with impeccable anticommunist credentials had been criticizing Konrad Adenauer's restoration of old elites since

1949. Whatever measure of hypocrisy and self-interest fed the assault, Adenauer's refusal to carry out a deeper purge of the West German establishment offered East Berlin one of its most effective propaganda themes of the Cold War.[96] Nonetheless, East Germany's own human rights violations, including episodes such as the anticosmopolitan campaign, weakened the force of its criticism and made its accusations relatively easy for the West Germans to dismiss.

Undaunted by the task, Albert Norden led the assault as director of the Ausschuss fur Deutsche Einheit (Committee for German Unity). From 1957 to 1963, in numerous press conferences, speeches, and essays he waged a relentless campaign alleging that ex-Nazis and Nazi war criminals were in place in the Adenauer administration and active in West German judicial, military, economic, diplomatic, and intellectual elites. At a press conference in May 1957, he released a statement, "Yesterday Hitler's Blood Judges, Today's Judicial Elite in Bonn," which listed 118 Nazi-era judges and prosecutors who still served in the West German judiciary.[97] On October 14, 1957, a statement titled "Hitler's Special Judges—Pillars of the Adenauer Government" named currently serving West German judges who had "sent to the execution block Communists, Social Democrats, those involved in the conspiracy of July 20, 1944, bourgeois pacifists, pastors, workers, intellectuals and peasants, because they offered resistance to fascism, listened to foreign radio broadcasts, expressed their hatred of war, or criticized the Nazi system."[98] In 1959 the Committee for German Unity published *We Accuse: Eight Hundred bloodstained Nazi Judges Uphold the Adenauer Regime.* The report claimed that these judges "were guilty of terrible crimes during the Nazi period," had been "willing tools of German imperialism and militarism," and had "sent thousands of Germans and non-Germans to the scaffold."[99] It accused the West German government of covering up their past crimes, and by retaining such figures in positions of responsibility "intentionally and systematically" breaking international agreements on the democratization of Germany and thus turning "West Germany into the center of a new war danger."[100] By contrast, according to Norden, all of the leading political figures of the East German government had participated in the anti-Nazi resistance.[101]

In short, the difference between East and West Germany was the difference between *Vergangenheitsbewältigung* and its absence.

Norden's accusations did not remain at the level of general indictments of capitalism and imperialism. Rather, he pointed to specific "murderers in West Germany" whom the Committee for German Unity, as "the conscience of the nation," had a duty to expose.[102] Almost six hundred judges who had served in the Nazi regime now occupied influential positions in the West German judiciary, said Norden: "Hitler's victims are Adenauer's victims, and Hitler's murderous judges are today Adenauer's judges."[103] Not only had the West Germans failed to bring to justice those guilty for Nazi crimes, but also in "Adenauer's state . . . the mass murderers are again in office and treated with honor." From the bench "Hitler fascists" were once again imprisoning antifascists, that is, members of the West German Communist Party.[104] When West German officials agreed to the deployment of American nuclear weapons, said Norden, it was the Nazis in Bonn who were "the trailblazers of a new policy of terror against the German people and the people of Europe."[105]

Two of the best-publicized of Norden's assaults were the staged "trials" in the East German Supreme Court of Theodor Oberlander in April 1960 and Hans Globke in July 1963.[106] Oberlander was the West German government official responsible for dealing with Germans expelled from the Eastern territories at the end of World War II.[107] Following a nine-day show trial, the East Germans predictably found Oberlander guilty of having participated in war crimes in World War II.[108] Norden charged that Adenauer had known about Oberlander's alleged criminal past since 1953 but refused to fire him.[109] A government that would have such an individual in office was one that "wants to leave the fascist past unmastered because it is planning new wars of revanchism and aggression" and needed for this purpose "the old forces" which had led Germany to disaster twice before.[110]

Hans Globke was the central target of SED criticism. As an official in Nazi Germany he had written commentaries on the anti-Semitic Nuremberg race laws. Nevertheless, Adenauer had chosen him to be the director of the chancellor's office. In the 1950s the Globke affair became an open sore in West German politics. The East German campaign only raised the profile of the issue. Critics accused Globke of direct involvement in the mass murder of Jews. The mere mention of his name became shorthand for the failures of denazification in the Federal Republic.[111] In 1963 Norden organized a public "Globke trial" intended to mirror the Eichmann trial in Jerusalem. One historian has called it "the most extravagant propaganda action since the foundation of the GDR."[112]

Had Norden tried to create a figure to suit his purposes, or had Adenauer been seeking ways to give the Communists a tempting target, neither could have done much better than Globke. As one of Adenauer's closest advisers, Globke wielded enormous influence over sensitive personnel decisions in the West German government. Norden called Globke "the Eichmann of Bonn" and said he had been "Himmler's right-hand man" who had engaged in a "natural cooperation" with Adolf Eichmann.[113] Norden did not support these accusations. Yet it was true that Globke had served the Nazi regime. Adenauer's West German critics wondered if there really was no one else in the Federal Republic who could administer the chancellor's office who did not have questions hanging over him from the Nazi past. What, after all, was anyone who had had the remotest connection to the Nuremberg race laws doing in the West German government? Norden had no doubts on the matter. He declared, "Adenauer's solidarity with Globke proves that this is not an isolated example or minor blemish. Rather it embodies the identity of Adenauer's policies with Hitler's."[114] In July 1963 the East Germans staged another nine-day show trial of Globke.[115] The trial, he claimed, would show that it was the directors of murder in Nazi Germany who "set the tone in West Germany's administration, police, secret service, army, and judiciary."[116] At the trial's end, the "good Germany, the Germany which had confronted, mastered, and overcome the past . . . the conscience of the nation which had become a state" found Globke guilty of involvement in the destruction of European Jewry and "sentenced" Konrad Adenauer's chief of staff to life in prison for crimes against humanity.[117]

These were absurd but powerful exaggerations. As grotesque as it was to have the East German dictatorship throwing stones at West German democrats, especially after the anticosmopolitan purges, a great deal of German and foreign opinion was not impressed by Globke's rationalizations about the subtleties of survival within the Nazi regime. It was one thing to leave a man such as Hans Globke in peace in private life but quite another for the chancellor to make him a top aide. Adenauer, notwithstanding his claims of Christian-inspired moral renewal, never understood the difference. One of the more bitter ironies of postwar German history lay in the fact that Leo Zuckermann was forced to resign from Pieck's office owing to his outspokenness in favor of Jewish concerns, while in Bonn Globke's job security was unaffected despite his connection with Nazi anti-Semitic legislation.

In July 1965 Norden and the National Front published the *Brown Book: War and Nazi Criminals in the Federal Republic: State, Economy, Army, Administration, Justice, and Scholarship.*[118] It was the definitive East German torrent of mud regarding the presence of former Nazis in the West German establishment. The *Brown Book* contained the names of "over 1,900 heavily incriminated former leading nazi officials and war criminals who today either hold key positions in the West German government or economic apparatus or else receive high pensions for their 'valuable services' in the 'Third Reich.'"[119] Norden argued that these former Nazis stood in the way of punishment for those accused of war crimes, remained the dominant political force in West Germany, and used their positions to pass on the "same evil spirit" to succeeding generations.[120] For those who had grown skeptical of the apologias of the generations who had lived under Nazism, especially those coming of age in the 1960s West German New Left, the *Brown Book* was not so easily dismissed as Communist propaganda and thus false. Some of the mud stuck.

I have noted that in May 1949, Walter Ulbricht stated that current views were more important than past actions in defining who was and who was not for peace and German unity. By the late 1950s, the West Germans were hurling accusations about "ex-Nazis" in *his* government. Beginning in 1952, a group of lawyers in West Berlin, the Untersuchungsausschuss Freiheitlicher Juristen (Investigating Committee of Free Jurists), in conjunction with Bonn's Ministry of Inner-German Affairs, began to publish reports on political repression and human rights violations in East Germany.[121] In 1958 the Investigating Committee published the first of five editions of *Ehemalige Nationalsozialisten in Pankows Diensten* (Former National Socialists in Pankow's Services).[122] The first edition contained the names, political affiliations, and positions of seventy-five former members of the Nazi Party who occupied important posts in East German politics, administration, journalism, and scholarship. The Investigating Committee avoided the issue of the validity of the East German assault on ex-Nazis in Bonn, responding only that "the Communists do not have the slightest grounds for their assaults against the Federal Republic because they themselves have placed former National Socialists in important, key positions in their own state."[123] The Investigating Committee reported that at least twenty-nine members of the East German parliament had been members of the NSDAP, and that former Nazis occupied high-ranking posts dealing with technical matters such as health, water supply, and machine construction. Yet success for ex-Nazis was not limited to those with scientific or technical expertise; it encompassed more politically sensitive areas such as law, journalism, and the universities.[124]

The East Germans took special pride in contrasting their purge of the judiciary with West German continuities. Yet, according to the Investigating Committee, the GDR also had skeletons in its closet. Kurt Schumann, who from 1949 to 1960 was the president of the East German Supreme Court in the period of numerous show trials and secret political trials, had joined the Nazi Party in 1937 at the age of twenty-nine. He was captured on the Eastern Front, and presumably repented the sins of his youth while in Soviet captivity.[125] Former Nazis worked on the editorial board of *Neues Deutschland*, in Communist Party publishing houses, and on East German textbooks.[126] The East Germans repeatedly attacked the continuing presence of ex-Nazis in West German universities. The Investigating Committee reported that the presidents (*Rektors*) of the universities of Greifswald and Jena, of technical universities in Dresden and Freiburg, of the Akademie fur Staats- und

Rechtswissenschaften (Academy for State and Legal Scholarship) in Potsdam-Babelsberg, and even the rector of East Germany's elite flagship Humboldt University had all been members of the Nazi Party.[127] The case of Herbert Kröger, rector (1955–1964) of the Walter Ulbricht Akademie für Staats- und Rechtswissenschaft, was typical of many who joined the Nazi Party at a relatively young age but then allied with the Communists following captivity in the Soviet Union. Kröger joined the Nazi Party at the age of twenty in 1933 and the SS in 1938 after completing his legal studies in 1937. During the war he was captured in the Soviet Union and worked with the Nationale Komittee Freies Deutschland. Upon returning to the Soviet zone, he began a steady rise from a professorship at the Potsdam Academy to membership in the Volkskammer, followed by nine years as rector of the elite institute for law and administration.[128]

In January 1965 Josef Streit, Ernst Melsheimer's successor as East Germany's chief general prosecutor, publicly asserted that "there was not one single colleague who was burdened [with a Nazi past] in the areas of justice, the army, education, or in any other branch of the GDR state apparatus or any other part of the state."[129] The 1965 edition of *Ehemalige Nationalsozialisten in Pankows Diensten* reported that former members of the Nazi Party were members of the Volkskammer, twelve ex-Nazis were members or candidates for membership in the Central Committee of the SED, and five were government ministers. Former Nazis served as editors in chief of *Neues Deutschland* and the journal *Deutsche Aussenpolitik*.[130] One Franz Gold who had joined the Nazi Party in 1938 worked with the Nationale Komitee Freies Deutschland in Moscow during the war, worked on building the Stasi, and was now director of the office charged with protecting its leading officials.[131]

The case of Ernst Grossman illustrated that even membership in the SS did not stand in the way of success, albeit temporary success. He joined the Nazi Party in 1938 at the age of twenty-seven, joined the SS in 1940, and in 1944 was promoted to the rank of *Unterscharführer*. From 1940 on, he was a member of the SS Death Head Division in Oranienburg/Sachsenhausen and was also an SS guard in the Sachsenhausen concentration camp. After the war he quickly changed uniforms and joined the SED, participated in organizing agricultural production, and was a candidate for membership in the Central Committee of the SED from 1952 to 1954. From 1954 to 1959 Grossmann served as a member of the SED Central Committee. In 1959, following the revelation of his SS past and activities in Sachsenhausen in the second edition of *Ehemaligen Nationalsozialisten in Pankows Diensten,* Grossmann was expelled from the Central Committee for offering "false information about his past." He was, however, allowed to remain a member of the SED.[132]

The case of Ernst Melsheimer (1897–1960), the state prosecutor in the East German Supreme Court, was as bizarre as it was troubling.[133] Though a member of the SPD from 1928 to 1932, from 1933 to 1937 he was the director of the third district court in Berlin, and from 1937 until the conquest of the city by the Red Army, he was a judge on the Berlin district court. In 1936 Melsheimer joined a Nazi organization of judges.[134] In 1945 and 1946 he joined the KPD and then the SED, and from 1946 to 1949 was the vice president of the Central Administration (Zentralverwaltung) of Justice in the Soviet occupation zone. From December 1949 until his death in 1960, Melsheimer was the chief public prosecutor (*Generalstaatsanwalt*) of the German Democratic Republic. In that capacity he worked very closely with Hilde Benjamin when she was vice president of the East German Supreme Court (1949–1953) and East German minister of justice (1953–1967) to conduct both open and secret political trials against, among others, dissident Communists such as Paul Merker, Max Fechner, Wolfgang Harich, and Walter Janka.[135] A photograph taken on April 9, 1947, his fiftieth birthday, shows a smiling Melsheimer sitting at a table with Walter Ulbricht and Hilde Benjamin.[136] The riddle of his rapid transformation from "Nazi judge" to colleague of Ulbricht and Benjamin remains unsolved.

East German journalism had its own share of embarrassing episodes. Following the 1967 Six Day War in the Middle East, Simon Wiesenthal, known for his efforts to find Nazi war criminals and bring them to justice, was struck by similarities between the discourse of Nazism and the vocabulary of East German denunciations of Israel. In a 1968 report titled "The Same Language: First for Hitler—Now for Ulbricht," Wiesenthal reported that among former members of the Nazi Party were the East German government's press chief Kurt Blecha; the editor-in-chief of the authoritative *Deutsche Aussenpolitik* (German Foreign Policy) Hans Walter Aust; as well as members of the editorial board of the main party newspaper, *Neues Deutschland.*[137] He compiled a list of "39 persons who belonged to the Nazi Party and had influential posts during the Nazi era, but who today have at least the same influence in the press, the radio, and the propaganda organs of the GDR."[138] These former members of the Nazi Party active in the East German press "provide a natural and . . . a very simple explanation for the terminology used in the GDR newspapers."[139] That is, the reason why East German propaganda sounded like Nazi propaganda, with the substitution of a few words such as "Israeli" for "Jew" and "progressive forces" for "National Socialism," was that it was written by former Nazi propagandists![140] In fact, as I have argued, East Germany's antagonism toward Israel had its roots in the Soviet and East German Communist traditions. Yet these anti-Western, "anticosmopolitan," and at times anti-Semitic currents overlapped with an anti-Semitism connected to right-wing nationalist conspiracy theories.

There were many more former officials of the Nazi regime in West Germany than in the East. But the image of a pristine antifascist government cleansed of all ex-Nazis was more antifascist mythology than East German reality. Just as the Cold War against the Soviet Union could evoke familiar memories for anticommunists in West Germany, so could official antifascism and anticosmopolitanism tinged with anti-Semitism make other veterans of the Third Reich feel at home in the East. If ex-Nazis felt comfortable with rearmament and a Western alliance against godless communism, then ex-Nazis could also feel at home with an antifascism which defended the German nation against cosmopolitans and Zionists. If the definition of a "peace-loving individual" depended more on current attitudes than past actions, then Ulbricht's approach to the Nazi past of East German government officials was not so very different from that of his nemesis Adenauer. In East Germany as well as in West Germany, there was a Cold War to fight and new institutions to staff, and there were many ex-Nazis with valuable skills. Toward those in their respective camps who had seen the error of their youthful ways and were of current usefulness, both German governments were capable of displaying an understanding of the complexities of political involvement under the "totalitarian" or "fascist" regime. Nonetheless, no such understanding of historical nuance and political subtlety was applied to ex-Nazis in the other Germany who had committed similar sins of youth. During the Cold War it was reasons of state more than a passion for justice which shaped this dimension of the public memory of the Nazi past.

The same ideology and discourse, and the same dependence on Soviet power, which shaped East German domestic politics also established the framework for East German foreign policy, including four decades of hostility to Israel. But in one crucial respect, active hostility was a qualitative step beyond silence about or avoidance of the past. In coming to the aid of states and movements at war with the Jewish state, the government which defined itself as the heir to the mantle of anti-Nazi resistance would be helping to attack Jews in Israel.[141] Certainly the Soviet Union's policy toward Israel and the West in general set the framework for East German policy. Yet in the 1950s and even 1960s, East German policy still came as a shock for many German Communists with memories of Communist professions of solidarity with persecuted Jews. These old Communists rejected the idea that an "antifascist" German government could become a partisan in the Arab-Israeli wars on the Arab side. That hostility was due not to repression of the Nazi past but to the repression of one set of interpretations of that era in favor of a now dominant, no less "old" and no less Communist interpretation that led to opposite conclusions. East Germany supported Israel's enemies not in spite of but because of what had become its official antifascist ideology.

Of course, East German foreign policy toward Israel was, in large measure, Soviet foreign policy. When that policy shifted from initial support to enduring hostility, the East Germans dutifully and often enthusiastically went along. The foundation of a Jewish state was difficult, often impossible, to reconcile with the assimilationist, secular assumptions of Marxism. So the shift in East German policy from mere indifference and coldness to active hostility toward Israel resulted from a conjuncture of Communist ideology, Soviet power politics, and competition between the two German states. The East Germans looked to Israel's Arab adversaries to assist them in gaining the diplomatic recognition which the West Germans were seeking to deny them. Good relations with Israel would only earn East Germany the enmity of the Arab states. Conversely, if only one Arab state were to establish diplomatic relations with East Berlin, others might follow, and then a broader international recognition might ensue. Thus, as Bonn's relations with Jerusalem deepened, so too did East Berlin's ties to the Arabs. Ironically, East Germany's fight against alleged Nazis in Bonn fostered rapprochement with Israel's adversaries.

East German efforts to woo the Arab states began as early as 1953 with the signing of a trade agreement with Egypt.[142] In 1955 the West German government articulated what became known as the Hallstein Doctrine, which rested on Bonn's "claim to be the sole representative" (*Alleinsvertretungsanspruch*) of the German people. The corollary to the doctrine was that formal recognition of the East German government by other states would be regarded by West Germany as "an unfriendly act."[143] East Berlin appealed to Arab and other "nonaligned" states with the goal of breaking out of isolation. Toward this end, further trade agreements between East Germany and Lebanon, Syria, and Yemen were signed in 1955 and 1956. These were accompanied by East German denunciations of Israeli aggression and of Israel's West German supporters.[144]

Otto Grotewohl, whose speech in Buchenwald in 1958 was so instrumental in placing the memory of Nazism in the service of the Cold War, also played an important role in connecting East Germany's antifascist self-legitimations to its foreign policy in the Middle East. On June 24, 1957, in a letter to Gamal Abdel Nasser, the president of Egypt, Grotewohl wrote of the dangers of a Germany unified under West German auspices and within the "bloc of imperialist states."[145] Increasingly, he continued, the political life of the Federal Republic was "determined by those forces which served criminal Hitler fascism or even were among its initiators . . . Humanity still remembers [the murderous deeds of] Hitler fascism . . . The forces of fascism and militarism [must] never again have the opportunity to seize power and threaten peace." Unification under West German auspices would result in a nuclear-armed Germany along with the "restoration of those social forces in all of Germany from which fascism was born, which unleashed the Second World War, and which are preparing the Third World War." The GDR could not permit this to happen.[146] Therefore, in the interests of peace and of preventing the emergence of a unified, nuclear-armed fascist Germany, it was crucial that East Germany and Egypt develop warm and friendly relations.[147] Fulfilling the legacy of antifascism thus translated into establishing close relations with Israel's primary adversary.

Grotewohl gave public support to Egypt in the Suez crisis.[148] He traveled to Egypt and Iraq in January 1959, after which general consulates were established in Berlin and Cairo.[149] The East Germans eagerly seized on West German restitution payments to Israel as a splendid opportunity to drive a wedge between Bonn and the Arab states. On November 2, 1956, Grotewohl described these payments as "so-called reparations which Israel uses in its struggle against the national independence movements of the people of the Middle East," and urged that the West Germans cease the payments forthwith.[150] At a press conference held by an East German trade delegation in Baghdad in 1958, Gerhard Weiss, then a leading official in the Ministry for Foreign and Inner-German Trade, stressed that while the German Democratic Republic had "no relations of any kind with Israel," the Federal Republic's "so-called reparations payments" were making "an essential contribution to Israel's material and moral strength" which had been repeatedly felt "in the imperialist policy of hostility against the Arabs.[151] Attacking this West German means of coming to terms with the Nazi past remained a central component of East German diplomacy. In 1958 and 1959 East Germany publicly supported the Arabs in their "struggle against imperialism" and denounced American, Western, and Israeli "aggression" in the Middle East.[152]

From February 24 to March 2, 1965, Walter Ulbricht culminated a decade of increasingly close East German–Egyptian ties by visiting Nasser in Cairo. On March 7 the Federal Republic announced its decision to offer formal diplomatic recognition to Israel, and on March 14 the Israelis accepted the offer to negotiate the initiation of formal relations. That day and the next, a majority of the thirteen states of the Arab League voted to break diplomatic relations with Bonn, and six— Egypt, Iraq, Yemen, Algeria, Sudan, and Kuwait—indicated a readiness to offer formal recognition to and initiate diplomatic relations with East Germany.[153] The combination of the establishment of formal diplomatic ties between the Federal Republic and Israel along with East German efforts to woo the Arabs brought about the most important diplomatic achievement in GDR history up to that point: recognition by states not formally members of the Communist bloc, and thus defeat of West Germany's Hallstein Doctrine and Bonn's *Alleinvertretungsanspruch*. At the same time, Bonn paid a high diplomatic price among the Arab states for its pro-Israeli policies.

During and just following his trip to Cairo, Ulbricht explained what a German head of state was doing in the capital of Israel's enemy. He spoke of "common struggle" against shared enemies. He denounced "all efforts of monopoly capital to construct Israel as an imperialist outpost in Arab space" and to use the Palestine question to heighten tensions in the area. He attacked the military cooperation between West Germany and Israel.[154] He revealed that the "solidarity of the German people, and especially the people of the German Democratic Republic," had been ignited by Egypt's "heroic struggle" against "imperialist aggression" during the Suez crisis. The East Germans and the Egyptians, he said, met on the common terrain of anti-imperialism and socialism.[155] Ulbricht signed a joint declaration with Nasser recognizing "all rights of the Arab peoples of Palestine, including their inalienable right of self-determination," and condemned "the aggressive plans of imperialism" to make Israel the spearhead of a campaign against the Arabs.[156] The two governments signed an agreement for dramatically expanded exchanges at the level of universities, communications, cultural centers, and sports.[157]

Upon returning to East Berlin from Cairo, Ulbricht in a radio interview accused West Germany and NATO of using "the imperialist military basis of Israel" to implement a "forward strategy" against the Arabs just as they had implemented a "forward strategy" against East Germany.

> We have never confused the problem of the state of Israel with the problem of atonement and restitution for the suffering and injustice inflicted by the criminal Hitler regime on the Jewish citizens of Germany and other European states.
>
> In any case, it is mockery of atonement and restitution when in West Germany, Nazi criminals, who are responsible for the murder of millions of Jewish men, women, and children are free to walk about and occupy influential positions. And on the other hand, for the purpose of camouflaging and concealing the perpetrators, the government of the West German state delivers gifts of heavy weapons and other war materials to the imperialist outpost Israel.[158]

Far from expressing defensiveness over the absence of East German restitution payments, Ulbricht cast aspersions on the motives behind the West German payments and offered an explanation for the prominence of the Jewish dimension of the Nazi past in the Federal Republic. As he saw it, the West Germans were not making a genuine effort to face the Nazi past; the "real" purpose of making restitution to Jewish surivivors and of close relations with Israel was "camouflaging and concealing the [Nazi] perpetrators." For Ulbricht, the very prominence of Jewish matters in the Federal Republic was part of a *failure* to come to terms with the Nazi past. West Germany would gain credibility as a peaceful government only by breaking with its past imperialist and aggressive traditions. "The dangerous conservation of Nazi war criminals and their ideas in the state apparatus in Bonn" had to lead to mistrust in other places.[159] Other peoples, he said, "rightly demand that the West Germans finally and once and for all come to terms with and overcome the Nazi past, which is also part of the West German present."[160] Ulbricht's interviewer, Gerhart Eisler, chairman of the government-run radio, commented that Ulbricht and the East Germans had won acceptance in Egypt because of their fifty-year record of anti-imperialism and anticolonialism. Moreover, Eisler added, in the GDR the imperialist and Nazi past "was mastered and overcome long ago." Ulbricht agreed.[161]

Five days later, in a report to high-level officials about his Cairo trip, Ulbricht elaborated on these arguments. He said that West German efforts to establish diplomatic relations with Israel were "nothing other than an encouragement of the most aggressive goals of Israel's ruling circles."[162] The West Germans were "shamelessly misusing the argument for restitution for the crimes of the Hitler regime against Jewish citizens. Restitution means first of all overcoming the causes of the crimes of German fascism through depriving of power the forces which brought German fascism to power. [Second, it means] that the war criminals who carried out the shameful deeds of German imperialism should receive their just punishment."[163] According to his argument, support for the enemies of the Jewish state had nothing to do with anti-Semitism and failure to confront the Nazi past. West German restitution was simply a good investment which drew attention away from a continuity of personnel and a paucity of trials for war crimes. Although his government had not spent one pfennig in restitution payments to Jewish survivors, Ulbricht argued that it was his government, not Adenauer's, which had truly learned the lessons of the Nazi past.

The East Germans were blazing a trail of *Vergangenheitsbewältigung* on the cheap. Even assuming for the sake of argument that West German restitution payments were nothing but a clever and cynical diversion, the East German refusal to respond positively to Jewish appeals for restitution did not at all follow logically. As we have seen, in East Berlin official antifascism never gave priority to the memory of the Jewish catastrophe. Nor did it follow, morally or logically, that Ulbricht's criticism of the West Germans required East German hostility to Israel. Certainly, as Moscow's loyal ally and satellite, East Berlin could not openly oppose Soviet policy in the Middle East. As we have seen, however, the anticosmopolitan purges eliminated those few East German Communists who would, at the very least, have argued for a low profile in the Middle East conflict. The evidence now available suggests that the East German leadership under Ulbricht and his successor, Erich Honecker, never tried to moderate Soviet or radical Arab hostility to the Jewish state. On the contrary, they saw the "struggle against Zionism" as a grand chapter in the history of East German antifascism.

Speaking several weeks after Ulbricht's trip to Egypt, Lothar Bolz, the East German foreign minister from 1953 to 1965, addressed the connection between policy toward Israel and the Jewish question.[164] "In the eyes of every Arab," he said, it was clear that the Federal Republic and the German Democratic Republic were distinguished from each other regarding "their position on the question of Israel and the Jewish question." Yet Bolz insisted that the two issues were "fundamentally different" and "in a certain sense . . . opposed to each other. Confusing and meshing one with another only serves the purpose of hiding the real content of the question of Israel behind the Jewish question."[165] Bolz then offered a remarkable version of East German history.

> Who had ruthlessly brought the murderers of the Jews on its territory to account for their deeds? Who had destroyed anti-Semitism on its territory at all of its roots? The German Democratic Republic! Who had always struggled against the disgrace of anti-Semitism and the persecution of the Jews? The German labor movement, the Communists, and all antifascists, the people who today stand in the leading positions of the German Democratic Republic. Where was restitution implemented and honor bestowed to all victims of fascism without distinction to so-called race? In the German Democratic Republic. Where, however, was the effort made to use money to buy one's way out of destroying the roots of racism and to avoid punishing the guilty? In West Germany. And where are such efforts viewed with contempt? In our Republic.[166]

In the absence of political freedom, there was no one who could publicly recall the counterhistory of the postwar restitution debates, the anticosmopolitan purges, and the marginalization of and silence about the Holocaust at official memorial ceremonies. Hence, Bolz could deny with impunity that taking sides against Israel in the Middle East conflict had anything at all to do with anti-Semitism. Indeed, West German partisanship for Israel was evidence that the Federal Republic had avoided facing the Nazi past! The radical right had denounced the Weimar Republic as a republic of the Jews. Now East German diplomats were denouncing the Federal Republic with classic anti-Semitic associations of Jews and money. In place of "so-called race," everything was expressed as a matter of imperialists and anti-imperialists. Unfortunately, Israel was on the side of the former and therefore had ceased to remain in the charmed circle of victims of fascism. Once again, as in the fascism debates of the 1920s and 1930s, so in the discourse of anti-imperialism in the Cold War era, Marxism-Leninism had the great advantage of lifting issues out of German history into transhistorical abstractions of imperialism versus struggles for national liberation. The vocabulary of antifascism and anti-imperialism relieved its users of the burdens of German history, in part through political and psychological solidarity between East Germans and the Arabs against the "Zionist aggressors."

This East German sleight of hand seemed to perplex even some Egyptian journalists. In August 1965 a journalist for the Egyptian newspaper *Akhbar el Yom* in an interview with Ulbricht noted that the West German government had said that one of the grounds for its assistance to Israel was "a feeling of guilt which leads it to seek atonement for the suffering of the Jews during the Nazi regime." Ulbricht responded that West German restitution payments had "nothing to do with repentance for crimes committed against the millions of Jewish citizens of Poland, the Soviet Union, France, Belgium, Austria, Hungary, and many other countries." Furthermore, "nothing" justified Israel's claim to be the heir to the Jewish citizens of Europe who had been murdered by Hitler. The presence of "the intellectual and actual participants in the mass murder of Jewish people during Hitler fascism with high offices in the state apparatus" in West Germany made a mockery of West German restitution efforts. Why didn't West Germany pay restitution for suffering inflicted on other peoples in Eastern Europe and the Soviet Union?[167]

In fact, Ulbricht continued, the origins of West German policy in the Middle East lay in "the interests of West German imperialism and neocolonialism." Making genuine restitution, expiating guilt, and honoring the victims of fascism meant eliminating the roots of fascism, of imperialism, and of racial and national hatred. These measures had been taken "only by the German Democratic Republic . . . All of the victims of the Hitler terror, all those persecuted by the Nazi regime—whether Jews or non-Jews—are treated equally," he said, and "[are] highly respected and receive special pensions. Many of them occupy leading positions in the state and economy. Toward the state of Israel, the GDR has a feeling neither of guilt nor of obligation."[168] Ulbricht's glowing picture of East Germany would have come as news to those who had struggled unsuccessfully to have "fighters against" and "victims of" fascism treated equally, or to "cosmpolitans" purged from party and government positions. His response did clearly articulate the contours of divided memory: memory of the Jewish catastrophe was a proper matter only for the West—the same West which ignored the suffering of Nazism's other victims.

The Six Day War of 1967 brought long-standing East German views to the attention of a broader global audience. In a famous speech delivered on June 15, 1967, in Leipzig, Ulbricht denounced the United States, West Germany, and "Israeli aggression" in the Middle East.[169] The East Germans repeatedly denounced "Zionist aggression," described Israel as the "spearhead" of a powerful "anti-Arab conspiracy between Bonn and Tel Aviv," and expressed their solidarity with the Arabs.[170] The regime's policies elicited neither public enthusiasm nor protest.[171] Conversely, Albert Norden published a "Statement of Citizens of the GDR of Jewish Origin" on June 7, 1967, which denounced Israel's military aggression. On June 9 Norden wrote a memo on how the war should be treated in the East German media. It should "be stressed that the Israelis are acting as Hitler did on June 22, 1941, when he attacked the Soviet Union in night and fog . . . When the West

German imperialist press, radio, and television defame Nasser as an Egyptian Hitler, it can and must be pointed out, in view of the facts of June 5 how the Israeli imperialists exactly imitated Hitler's illegal tactics and methods of invasion."[172] Who could be better placed to make the scandalous comparison of Israelis with their Nazi murderers than a Communist of Jewish origin? Norden's efforts to enlist other prominent Jewish writers and public figures as signers of anti-Israeli manifestos met with limited success. Most of the Jewish Communists who would have protested East German policy had long since fled or been driven from political life.

In 1969 East Germany established diplomatic relations with Egypt, Iraq, Sudan, Syria, and South Yemen. In 1971 Yasser Arafat made his first visit to East Berlin, and in August 1973 the Palestine Liberation Organization opened a consular office there, the first in the Soviet bloc, and signed agreements with East Germany for delivery of arms, supplies, support for students, and medical treatment of PLO wounded and orphans. In the 1970s there were frequent visits by Arafat and high-level PLO functionaries to East Berlin, accompanied by declarations of solidarity between East Germany and the PLO and statements of gratitude for assistance.[173]

Erich Honecker (1912–1994), who replaced Ulbricht as head of the party and state in 1971 and governed until the collapse of the regime in 1989, continued to deepen East German relations with the Arab states, the PLO, and Arafat.[174] In 1975 the East German delegation at the United Nations was elected to membership in the Committee for the Realization of the Inalienable Rights of the Palestinian People.[175] At the UN and at numerous international conferences, the East Germans joined in resolutions that denounced Israeli aggression and expressed solidarity with the Arabs, the PLO, and other "third world national liberation movements." They voted for the 1975 resolution equating Zionism with racism.[176] In 1980 the PLO consulate in East Berlin was elevated to the status of an embassy. In the same year the East Germans denounced the Camp David accords as an "imperialist separate peace."[177] While the details of East German support for training and equipping Arab and Palestinian terrorists remained secret, the fact of military cooperation between East Berlin and the PLO was clearly implied in articles in *Neues Deutschland* describing meetings of "military delegations" of the PLO with Erich Honecker.[178]

Nor did the East Germans refrain from any rhetorical excess when discussing Israeli policy. On September 24, 1982, the East German representative in the United Nations responded to the massacre in Sabra and Shatilla in Lebanon by declaring before the General Assembly that "state terrorism and criminal genocide were firm components of Israeli policy" and that "genocide of the Palestinian people" was the method which Israel's "ruling circles" had chosen to solve the Palestinian problem.[179] East Germany was the only Communist government in the Soviet bloc which up to 1989 did not have diplomatic relations with the state of Israel. Its support for Israel's adversaries never wavered.[180]

Thomas Mann, in his famous speech on Germany and the Germans delivered at the Library of Congress in 1945, said that there were not two Germanys, one good and one bad, but only one which had placed some of its virtues in the service of evil. One could not, he said, deny membership in the "evil Germany burdened with guilt and declare: 'I am the good, the noble, the just Germany in white clothes. I leave the evil for you to destroy."[181] Yet that is precisely what the East German Communists did. They were the good Germany which was free from the burdens of the evil Germany. Instead they were part of a global struggle against imperialism and racism. The East German argument that antifascism should logically lead to helping the armed adversaries of the Jewish state indicated how a totalitarian ideology had substituted fantasy for common sense and theories of universal liberation for the burdens of local knowledge and memory.

Meeting of the Nationalekomitee Freies Deutschland (National Committee for a Free Germany), Moscow, 1944: Wilhelm Pieck (far right), Erich Weinert (second from right), and Walter Ulbricht (fifth from right) with German officers working with the NKFD. (Source: SAPMO-BA, Berlin, Photoarchiv 777/69N)

Meeting of the Bewegung Freies Deutschland (Movement for a Free Germany), Mexico City, December 31, 1943, on the occasion of the twenty-fifth anniversary of the founding of the German Communist Party: a representative of the American Communist Party (left), Erich Jungmann (fourth from left), a representative of the Spanish Communist Party (fifth from left), Paul Merker (fourth from right), Alexander Abusch (standing, second from right). (Source: SAPMO-BA, Berlin, Photoarchiv 1683/66 N)

Paul Merker in East Berlin, 1950. (Source: SAPMO-BA,
Berlin, Photoarchiv 35/93 N)

Demonstration for the "victims of fascism" in front of the Alten Museum, East Berlin,
September 1950. In French, German, and Russian, the banner behind the speakers declares,
"Long Live Peace." (Source: SAPMO-BA, Berlin, Photoarchiv 73/71 N)

Representatives of the Jewish community in East Berlin lay a wreath bearing the Star of David during ceremonies held on the Day of Remembrance for the Victims of Fascism, September 9, 1951, East Berlin. (Source: SAPMO-BA, Berlin, Photoarchiv 1274/79 N)

A delegation of former members of the French Resistance paying their respects at the former Nazi concentration camp in Buchenwald during ceremonies held on the Day of Remembrance for the Victims of Fascism, September 9, 1951, East Berlin. (Source: SAPMO-BA, Berlin, Photoarchiv 399/71 N)

Teenagers carrying the red flag past the ovens in the former Nazi concentration camp in Ravensbrück during the Women's Peace Demonstration of September 13, 1952. (Source: SAPMO-BA, Berlin, Photoarchiv 1269/80 N)

Meeting of the VVN on November 9, 1952, the fourteenth anniversary of "Kristallnacht" in Berlin. The slogans above and behind the speakers declare, "Long Live the Firm, Unbreakable German-Soviet Friendship!" and "Against Racial and National Hatred— Against Fratricide and War—For Peace and Understanding between Peoples!" (Source: SAPMO-BA, Berlin, Photoarchiv 1331/79 N)

Hermann Matern, chairman of the Central Party Control Commission (ZPKK), and author of the denunciations in the anticosmopolitan campaign, delivers a report of the ZPKK to the SED Party Conference, March 30, 1954, Berlin. (Source: SAPMO-BA, Berlin, Photoarchiv 23556 N)

Rosa Thälmann (front row, fourth from left) and Walter Ulbricht (front row, fifth from left) waving, lead procession at conclusion of dedication of Sachsenhausen memorial, April 24, 1961. (Source: SAPMO-BA, Berlin, Photoarchiv 566/80 N)

Otto Grotewohl with Gamal Abdel Nasser in Cairo, January 4, 1959.
(Source: SAPMO-BA, Berlin, Photoarchiv 36/93 N)

Albert Norden denounces the "war criminal [Hans] Globke" at a press conference, East Berlin, March 21, 1963. (Source: SAPMO-BA, Berlin, Photoarchiv 214/87 N)

# 7

## The Nuremberg Interregnum: Divided Memory in the Western Zones, 1945–1949

The German political leaders who emerged in the Western occupation zones during the Nuremberg interregnum differed from their Communist counterparts in one fundamental way: they all believed in liberal democracy and in the absolute necessity of preventing another German dictatorship. Their option for democracy posed a fundamental and enduring dilemma for the attainment of justice and the establishment of public memory of the Nazi era. Both ideology and the experience of the Nazi era had deepened the Communists' suspicion of a democracy of Germans. For the democrats in the West, their own ideology and experience of the Nazi era were at cross-purposes as they sought to establish rule by and for a people who had fought for Nazism to the bitter end.

During the occupation years, these tensions were held somewhat at bay as the Western victors imposed denazification and extensive trials on the defeated nation. Multiple restorations defined the political culture of the Western occupation zones no less than they did that of the Soviet zone. The leading political figures of the postwar era—Konrad Adenauer (1876–1967), Kurt Schumacher (1895–1953), and Theodor Heuss (1884–1963)—had all come of political age before 1933. They had all been opposed to the Nazi regime, though only Schumacher could be said to have actively opposed it. In this chapter we turn to their first interpretations and memories of the Nazi era. The power of the victors in both East and West lay in arresting thousands of members of the Nazi Party and government, and in encouraging and supporting those German politicians who had been defeated in 1933 and driven into exile or internal emigration. The resulting choice was not between "antifascists" in Berlin and "Nazis" in Bonn, but between differing kinds of non-Nazi and anti-Nazi politicians, different varieties of "the other Germany." The political culture of the two Germanys was the result less of the importation of heretofore unknown traditions than of a radical shift in the balance of power among preexisting German traditions. The Nuremberg interregnum in both West and East rested on a combination of imposition, repression, and selection.

From 1945 to 1947, JCS 1067, a directive signed by President Truman on April 26, 1945, guided American occupation policies in Germany and placed their focus on denazification. It stated that "Germany will not be occupied for the purpose of liberation but as a defeated nation."[1] The occupation was meant to ensure that Germany would not threaten world peace again. Democracy would be the eventual result of denazification. The policy was not intended to be popular. In a speech delivered in Stuttgart in February 1946, U.S. Secretary of State James F. Byrnes changed the focus of American policy. "It never was the intention of the American government," he said, "to deny to the German people the right to manage their internal affairs as soon as they were able to do so in a democratic way with genuine respect for human rights and fundamental freedoms." The United States did not intend to impose a "prolonged foreign dictatorship"; instead, the intention was that "the German people throughout Germany, under proper safeguards, should now be given the primary responsibility for running their own affairs."[2]

Byrnes's unfortunate choice of words in juxtaposing the notion of a "prolonged foreign dictatorship" to the hope for German democratic renewal nevertheless pointed to the tension between democracy and memory. Denazification was profoundly unpopular with significant sections of the German people. On May 8, 1945, 8 million Germans were members of the Nazi Party.[3] They and their friends and families would constitute a formidable voting bloc opposed to any serious efforts at postwar judicial reckoning or frank public memory. Implicitly the Western Allies grasped this tension between democracy on the one hand and memory and justice on the other. One could have either democracy or justice but, certainly in these early days, not both. In the first postwar years, in the form of the Nuremberg war crimes trials, extensive denazification procedures, and indictments of thousands of Germans for suspicion of war crimes and crimes against humanity, the Allies clearly opted in favor of justice and memory. In May 1945 neither the Western Allies nor the Soviet Union regarded a democracy by and for Germans as necessary or desirable in the very near future. The work of justice would have to come first, and that labor would have to be carried out by the victors.[4] The Byrnes speech was the first sign that the breakdown of the wartime alliance and the emergence of Cold War would shift the balance of Allied policy closer to support for an early establishment of democratic rule in Western Germany even if it meant, as it eventually did, less memory of and justice for past crimes.

The Allies could and did exclude politicians advocating Nazi or neo-Nazi ideas from engaging in politics in the Western zones. Yet German political leaders learned that support for denazification and speaking out clearly and extensively about the crimes of the Nazi era antagonized a significant bloc of voters, who could and did make the difference in close national elections. The lesson was that one could speak openly about the Nazi past or win national elections, but not both. The Communists did not suffer such agonies. They imposed a dictatorship of a supposedly enlightened elite. Democratic politicians willing to bring up the Nazi past faced an enduring dilemma: doing so was unpopular with a majority of the electorate. Democratic politicians reluctant to do so faced an enduring temptation: silence won votes.

These were also years of popular disillusionment and elite "deradicalization" among the Germans. Hitler was not only evil. He was a failure, and with his failure the myths of German racial invincibility and superiority collapsed. In sharp contrast to 1918–19, military defeat was now unambiguous. There was no second *Dolchstoßlegende* ("stab-in-the-back legend") with which the military could shift responsibility for national disaster onto civilian democrats. The country was occupied, and no German government remained.[5] Although the Nazis had extolled their own heroism for twelve years, when faced with defeat they aroused popular contempt as Nazi leaders and thousands of less prominent party and government officials engaged in what one historian has called "self-denazification" by suicide.[6]

Disillusionment, however, rarely expressed itself in a passion for justice for the crimes of the Nazi era. The initiatives of the victors in these crucial early years were indispensable.[7] The Nuremberg interregnum of 1945–1947 was the golden era of judicial confrontation with the Nazi past. Through their own measures, the Allies ensured that the Nazi Party and movement were definitively crushed. From 1945 to 1949, the Western Allies interned 200,000 former Nazi officials, 100,000 in the American zone alone.[8] In the first half of 1946, in the three Western zones 150,000 German officials lost their positions in government and civil service, while an additional 73,000 in industry and commerce were fired from their jobs.[9] Between 1946 and 1948, 13,180,300 German citizens in the American zone, 669,000 in the French zone, and over 2 million in the British zone were compelled to fill out questionnaires (*Fragebogen*) concerning their activities during the Nazi era.[10] Less than 1 percent of those questioned were labeled "guilty of" or "burdened by" the Nazi past. One German historian has bitterly described these denazification proceedings as "fellow traveler factories" which did more to rehabilitate than to punish ex-Nazis.[11] Despite the shortcomings, some of them severe, Allied denazification of the occupation era crushed the Nazi Party and contributed to keeping it and its would-be successors on the margins of German politics and society after 1945.

Nevertheless, officials working for OMGUS (Office of the Military Government, United States) found abundant evidence of anti-Semitic and antidemocratic sentiment.[12] In 1946 one of these officers, Moses Moskowitz, wrote that the very presence of Jewish survivors in displaced persons camps and of returning refugees aroused hostility. These Jews, he said, were "the accusers who haunt the Germans and will continue to haunt them until the thousands or millions of individual Germans who had a personal part in the extermination of the Jews are brought to justice."[13] Weekly OMGUS political reports from Bavaria in 1945 and 1946 spoke of persistent and even "rising" anti-Semitism.[14] An OMGUS study of March 1947 based on surveys taken over the preceding two years concluded that "four in ten Germans are so strongly imbued with anti-Semitism that it is very doubtful that they would object to overt actions against Jews . . . [L]ess than two in ten could probably be counted on to resist such overt behavior."[15] Richard and Anna Merritt, in their analysis of the OMGUS survey results for the whole four-year occupation period, conclude that roughly 15 to 18 percent of the adult population remained unreconstructed Nazis.[16] In 1945–1947, between 47 percent and 55 percent of Germans thought that National Socialism had been a good idea badly carried out. The number of those who viewed it as a bad idea actually declined from 41 percent to 30 percent! An American survey report of March 1948 indicated that in 1946–1948, between 55 percent and 65 percent of Germans subscribed to the view that "some races of people are more fit to rule than others."[17] Commenting on an OMGUS survey result of 1947, the Merritts wrote that "it is not difficult to demonstrate the persistence in postwar Germany of perspectives closely associated with National Socialist ideology." Fifteen percent of Germans in the American occupation zones, including West Berlin, were willing to suppress left-wing parties; 18 percent agreed that a dictator was important for creating a strong nation; 29 percent were amenable to censorship of publications critical of the government; and 33 percent felt that Jews should not have the same rights as others. The Merritts concluded, "Perhaps one in six could be said to have held explicitly Nazi orientations." In December 1946 the OMGUS Opinion Survey Section classified 21 percent of its American zone respondents as anti-Semites and another 18 percent as intense anti-Semites, a potential voting bloc of 39 percent.[18] The main finding of the 1947 survey was that although "most Germans had perspectives that were by and large democratic," a significant minority was "by and large" undemocratic and still deeply infused with anti-Semitic and authoritarian views. With the emergence of democratic institutions, this minority became citizens willing and able to barter votes for politicians' promises to leave the past behind.

Before the Allies would permit the Germans to govern themselves, they had to make sure that a record of the crimes of the Nazi era was presented to the Germans and to world opinion. The International Military Tribunal that met in Nuremberg from November 20, 1945, to October 1, 1946, and the successor trials from 1946 to 1949, were at the center of this endeavor. Reports of the trial were carried on radio and in the occupation press. The main trial and the twelve successor trials held from 1946 to 1949 established that Hitler and the Nazi regime had launched World War II as a war of aggression and racism, had ordered and implemented the mass murder of European Jewry and millions of others in the concentration camps and death camps, and in so doing had drawn upon the cooperation of tens of thousands of officials in the Nazi government and army. At the conclusion of the trial of the major defendants in October 1946, OMGUS surveys indicated that 55 percent of the German population found the guilty verdicts to be just, 21 percent thought them too mild, and only 9 percent found them too harsh. Overall, 78 percent regarded the proceedings as fair.[19]

The successor trials also established the complicity of SS "intellectuals," doctors, judges, diplomats, civil servants, industrialists, and the leadership of the Wehrmacht.[20] Between November 1945 and October 1947, American, British, and French military courts also conducted trials against lower-level personnel of the concentration camps at Buchenwald, Dachau, Flossenberg, Mauthausen, and Dora-Mittelbau, participants in the euthanasia campaign, and those who had murdered over 1,200 downed American pilots.[21] Of 1,517 persons who were convicted, 324 received the death penalty and 247 life sentences. British military courts convicted 1,085 persons, 240 of whom received death sentences. French courts convicted 2,107 people, of whom 104 received a death sentence. In 1946–47 alone, the United States delivered 3,914 persons being sought for trial to sixteen European countries, two-thirds of them to France and Poland. In the three Western zones, 5,025 persons were convicted of war crimes or crimes against humanity by the occupying powers; 806 were condemned to death, and 486 of the death sentences were carried out.[22]

The Nuremberg and other Allied trials left an enduring mark on the memory of Nazism in both Germanys. They established beyond doubt that war crimes and crimes against humanity had occurred and that they were the direct result of decisions taken by the Nazi leaders. In so doing, Nuremberg helped to discredit Nazism and fascism in Germany and Europe for decades, kept "Holocaust denial" on the fringes of postwar politics in both Germanys, and presented a detailed picture of the crimes of the Nazi regime to the postwar public. In view of the evidence presented in Nuremberg, no major national political figure in East or West Germany publicly raised doubts about whether or not the Nazi regime had actually carried out a genocide of European Jewry and waged a race war on the Eastern Front. After Nuremberg, expressions of such historical revisionism were immediately understood to be efforts to revive Nazism by declaring it innocent of war crimes and crimes against humanity. For major mainstream political leaders in both Germanys, the issue was not *if* but *how* and *why* such events had occurred and *what* must be done to ensure that the Germans would never do anything like that again.

Although the concept of "war crimes" played a far greater role than "crimes against humanity," a great deal of testimony regarding the persecution of European Jewry was presented in Nuremberg.[23] At the national level, political debate about the Nazi past in both Germanys centered on the weight to be accorded different acts of persecution, not whether persecution had actually taken place. As we will see, the Nuremberg judgments, the policies of the Western occupiers, the political beliefs of national German political leaders, and the ability of Jewish survivors to make their voices heard all meant that the Nazi persecution of the Jews assumed a more central place in Western than in Eastern public discussion and government policy.[24]

The Nuremberg trials also constituted a very public expression of political *history* within which individual memory could be placed. If the Germans focused on postwar suffering but conveniently forgot its antecedents, the Nuremberg judgments accentuated the causal connection between the aggression and crimes of the Nazis and postwar German misery. Before and after 1945, in the form of expulsion from the Eastern territories and rape in the postwar Soviet zone, the Germans reaped the whirlwind which their race war on the Eastern Front had unleashed.[25] Given the enormity of the crimes of the Nazi regime, the barbarity of the Nazi invasion of Eastern Europe and the Soviet Union, and the presence of the Soviets as one of the occupying powers, the Allies showed little enthusiasm for drawing attention to the suffering of the Germans after 1945. The Nuremberg Trials repeatedly turned causal historical narratives back to the consequences of 1933 and to what the Germans had done to others before 1945. As the Cold War refocused Western attention on what the Soviet Union had done after May 8, 1945, the Nuremberg narratives became an increasingly dissonant and uncomfortable but never extinguished counterpoint.

Nuremberg also represented rejection of the collective guilt of the entire German people and reaffirmation of the principle of individual political and moral responsibility. The Nuremberg Trials replaced a language of destiny and fate which had figured so prominently in the apologetic discourse of German cultural conservatism with a analysis of political causality and moral responsibility.[26] The message of the Nuremberg Trials was that human beings and their political decisions had made Auschwitz possible—not being, fate, destiny, instrumental reason, the Enlightenment, modernity, or the West.[27] As the German scholar Herbert Jäger wrote, the trials "peopled the empty, anonymous image of the totalitarian past with [human] forms which would never again be banished from that image."[28] Assertions of the incomprehensibilty of the awful past could become a convenient rationale for failing to punish the guilty. The message to postwar Germans was that political outcomes had comprehensible political causes. Memory and understanding of the Nazis' crimes should lead to political engagement rather than political withdrawal. The denazification measures of the occupation era and the Nuremberg and other Allied war crimes trials, despite their shortcomings, were thus indispensable preconditions for public memory of Nazi crimes against humanity and war crimes in the two Germanys.

The Cold War with its shifting alliances and emphases ended the Nuremberg interregnum. Although anticommunism began to assume priority over denazification, the impact of the Cold War on the willingness to confront the Nazi past can be exaggerated. For even if the Cold War had never taken place, or had not taken place so soon, any movement toward democracy in postwar Germany would have given voice to those German voters opposed to further trials for crimes of the Nazi era. Hence, daring more democracy at this early point would have meant less public memory and less justice. We have seen that the tension between antifascism and popular rule reinforced the long-standing Communist mistrust of both democracy and the Germans, and fit very well with the imposition of a second German dictatorship. By contrast, the German political leaders in the Western zones believed that the only antidote to the Nazi regime was democracy, not another dictatorship. Yet the practices and inclinations of liberal democrats did not align well with the occupation and its tough denazification policies. Popular will, whether representing a majority or powerful but crucial minorities, could block a thorough confrontation with the past. There were political leaders who argued that reticence about past crimes was important for the emergence of a democracy, which was essential to prevent a repetition of such evils.

Beginning as early as the spring of 1946, Konrad Adenauer, the dominant figure of West German politics from the time he emerged as leader of the Christian Democratic Union in the occupation years to his exit from the chancellor's office in 1963, clearly articulated his views on politics and memory: in order to avoid a renewal of German nationalism and Nazism, economic recovery and political democratization must take priority over a judicial confrontation with the crimes of the Nazi past. Adenauer strongly supported measures that were far less threatening to the voters, namely, restitution for Jewish survivors and good relations with the state of Israel. In opposing both a thoroughgoing purge of the West German establishment and further trials and punishment of those accused of war crimes and crimes against humanity, he effectively represented the wishes of at least some of his electoral constituents.

Adenauer came of political age before 1914. In 1933, when he was fifty-nine, his political career appeared to be over. He did not participate in the anti–Nazi resistance, nor did he flee into exile. The Gestapo arrested him several times, the most serious episode occurring in August 1944 following the failed July 20 coup. He was held in prison near Cologne for two and a half months, and his wife was jailed for ten days. In 1945 he emerged from inner emigration in a Benedictine monastery with his past convictions not only intact but reinforced by a deepening of his Catholicism. He was now sixty-five years old. The Nazi era had not been a formative experience for him. The lessons he drew from it rested on long-held beliefs. Kurt Schumacher called him the "chancellor of the Allies." Walter Ulbricht labeled him a puppet of American imperialism and a traitor to the nation. Yet Adenauer's views of the Nazi past and postwar politics owed nothing to American, British, or French "reeducation."

As the mayor of Cologne from 1917 to 1933, Adenauer established a reputation as a moderate conservative with impressive accomplishments in public works. As leader of the Catholic Center (Zentrum) Party and president of the Prussian *Staatsrates,* he was also involved in national politics. At the national level, he supported the presidential regime of Franz von Papen and advocated the participation of the Nazis in the Prussian government. He did not do so out of sympathy for the Nazis, however. Rather, like the conservative political establishment in general, he underestimated Hitler and believed that the Nazis' participation in government would make their incompetence apparent to all.[29] He placed his faith in von Papen's presidential regime and hoped that the Nazi Party could be tamed by participating in government.[30] His dislike for Hitler and the Nazis was genuine. Although Adenauer was not a hero of the anti-Nazi resistance, he did suffer politically as a consequence of the Nazi seizure of power. In March 1933, as mayor of Cologne, he ordered Nazi flags removed from the bridges over the Rhine, where they had been hung in preparation for a visit by Hitler. Soon afterwards the Nazis forcibly removed him from the mayor's office. He was briefly arrested in connection with the Röhm affair in June 1934 and released a few days later. In 1937 he concluded an agreement with the city of Cologne for 153,000 Reichmarks, with which he was able to build a beautiful house in Rhöndorf, an affluent suburb on the west side of the

Rhine about ten miles north of Bonn. He lived there quietly and undisturbed until the Gestapo arrested him and detained him again in 1944.

In this period Adenauer's lifelong friend, the Belgian-born American Jewish businessman and electrical utilities executive Dannie Heinemann, regularly sent him money.[31] The banker Robert Pferdemenges and Adenauer's brother August, a successful lawyer, also lent financial assistance. Adenauer was certainly not cast adrift. These gifts, combined with regular payments from the city of Cologne, left him reasonably well off. He was not so well off as before 1933, but he did not suffer the insecurity and poverty of German émigrés and opponents of the Nazis. He never had to emigrate or spend time in a concentration camp. In the Third Reich he lived the life of a comfortable retired pensioner who avoided political activity.[32]

As a supporter of Franz von Papen and of the participation of the Nazis in the government, he had little reason to fear the Nazis at the outset. Although members of Christian trade unions in the Rhineland and former fellow leaders of the Zentrum such as Jakob Kaiser did participate in the resistance, Adenauer either criticized it as a product of the Prussian aristocracy or simply did not believe it had realistic prospects of success.[33] Fearing a new "stab-in-the-back legend" should it succeed, he did not participate in the July 1944, conspiracy. Although after 1945 he indicated that he had been better informed than most Germans about Nazi criminality, he did not risk his life to stop the war in the East and the Final Solution to the Jewish question.

Following the failed coup of July 20, 1944, the Gestapo arrested Adenauer on August 25 and placed him in a camp near Cologne. He was released after two weeks owing to illness and went into hiding. His wife, Gussie, was then arrested. When threatened by the Gestapo, she told the police where they could find her husband. Desperate with guilt at having revealed his whereabouts, and alone in prison, she made two unsuccessful attempts at suicide.[34] The Gestapo again arrested Adenauer and put him in prison near Cologne, but released him on November 26, 1944. He returned to Rhöndorf, where the Nazis kept him under constant surveillance. Although many suffered far more than he, his life during the Third Reich was difficult. Gussie, his wife of fifty-four years, died in March 1948 from what he described as "an illness which probably had to do with her presence in a Gestapo prison."[35] The shock of his own arrest and his wife's death stemming from her suicide attempts certainly deepened his hatred for the Nazis. Despite this mixed history of political misjudgments and a survivor's unheroic realism, as well as antipathy to the Nazis, his political career, which seemed to have come to an end in 1933, experienced an amazing revival after 1945.

Adenauer was sixty-nine when the war ended and seventy-three when he was elected first chancellor of the Federal Republic in 1949.[36] He entered the historical and popular consciousness as the best symbol of the restorative character of the epoch. Yet this oldest and most conservative of the leading political figures of the postwar era implemented a decisive break in German political culture. His prominence signaled the Westernization of German conservatism, that is, the displacment of anti-Western resentments that had dominated it before 1945.[37] He was able to be an agent of change because the world around him had been transformed while his views remained intact. His political Catholicism and the associated mistrust of Prussian authoritarianism had been shaped by persecution of German Catholics in the Kaiser Reich. With the destruction of Nazism, which the Protestant churches had generally supported, Adenauer moved from the margins of prewar German conservatism to the center of a new West German conservatism.[38]

Adenauer's first public postwar statement addressed the subject of German suffering. He delivered the speech as mayor of Cologne on October 1, 1945, to the city council and the British occupying authorities.[39] He focused on the devastation in Cologne and placed the responsiblity for this "indescribable suffering" on those "escapists" who had come to power in 1933 and who had covered "the German name" with "shame" before the whole civilized world, "destroyed our country," and brought upon it the "deepest suffering." He continued: "We, you and I, are not the ones [who are] guilty for this suffering. We, you and I, are condemned and impelled, impelled by love of our people, whom we do not want to see completely destroyed, to take upon ourselves this heavy and frightful burden so that at least the worst emergency conditions can be overcome."[40] Adenauer's concentration on the suffering of the people of Cologne, and his decision to emphasize that neither he nor his audience was guilty of bringing this disaster upon themselves, did not make a favorable impression on the British occupation officials. On October 6, 1945, they removed him from office and forbade him to participate in political activity. They also criticized the rehiring of former Nazis and the underrepresentation of "antifascist parties" in the city administration. In December 1945, however, he was permitted to return to political work, and in January 1946 Adenauer was elected to the leadership of the newly founded Christian Democratic Union (CDU) in the British zone of occupation.[41]

In fact, Adenauer had thought more about the lessons of German history than this first speech indicated.[42] On March 26, 1946, now back in office as mayor, he delivered his first major statement about the German past and present in a speech at the University of Cologne.[43] "How was it possible," he asked, that the Weimar Republic collapsed, that National Socialism came to power, that the Nazis started World War II, that "great crimes" were committed, and that the Germans came to be despised all over the world?[44] How would the Germans bear their "frightful fate" after 1945? Since 1933, he said, he had "often been ashamed to be German, ashamed deep in my soul." He had known perhaps "more than others about the shameful deeds which Germans perpetrated on other Germans, and of the crimes which were planned against humanity. But now," he declared, "I am again proud to be German. I am proud of it as never before, more than before 1933 or 1914." The source of his pride was the courage with which the Germans were bearing their postwar "fate."[45] Given that in March 1946 the occupation press was filled with daily reports from the ongoing Nuremberg war crimes trials, it was an odd moment to speak of rediscovered national pride. Yet, he continued, the Germans could find their way toward a better future only by trying to understood the past. Although he did not demand a "confession of guilt of the whole German people," he believed that "an examination of our conscience" was in the Germans' best interest and was necessary for their renewal.[46]

Adenauer then offered a devastating account of what he regarded as the unfortunate legacies of modern German history. Like the Communists and the Social Democrats, Adenauer focused on the breadth and depth of support for Nazism in Germany.

> National Socialism could not have come to power if it had not found in broad layers of the population soil well prepared for its poison. I stress—in broad layers of the population. It is not correct to say that the bigshots, senior military, or big industrialists bear the only guilt. Certainly they bear a large measure of guilt, and their personal guilt, on account of which they must be brought to account by the German people before German courts, is all the greater, the greater their power and influence were. But broad layers of the people, the farmers, middle classes, workers, intellectuals, did not have the right mentality. If they had had a different outlook, the victory of National Socialism in 1933 and afterwards among the German people would not have been possible.
>
> The German people suffered for decades in all of their strata from a false conception of the state, of power, [and] of the position of the individual person. They made the state into an idol and raised it on an altar. They sacrificed the individual and his or her worth and dignity to this idol. The belief in the omnipotence of the state, of the primacy of the state, and of the powers concentrated in the state before all other enduring, eternal goods of humanity assumed dominance in Germany in two stages. First, this conviction spread from Prussia following the wars of liberation. Then it conquered the whole of Germany after the victorious war of 1870–71.[47]

Adenauer further argued that the counterpart to the Prussian celebration of the authoritarian state was neglect of the value of the individual. The intellectuals of the German Idealist tradition, such as Herder and Hegel, had celebrated the "spirit of the people" and seen in it the embodiment of reason and morality. The Germans had made the state into "an almost godly being." This diminution of the value of the individual had reinforced militarism, which "became the dominant factor in the thinking and feeling of broad layers of the people."[48] In

Adenauer's view, this militarist and authoritarian mentality had prepared the soil for Nazism.

Adenauer further argued that materialism, especially the "materialist worldview of Marxism," was yet another German tradition which had made National Socialism possible. It favored the centralization of political and economic power in the state and supported a doctrine of class struggle that threatened individual freedom and paved a path to dictatorship.[49] He went so far as to describe National Socialism as "nothing other than the consequence driven to the point of criminality of the idolization of power and dismissal of—yes, contempt for—the value of the individual person of the materialist worldview." Materialism, when combined with the Prussian celebration of the authoritarian state and economic crises, had fostered a doctrine of "the total state and a mass without will. It viewed one's own race as the master race, one's own people as the master nation, other peoples as inferior, in part worthy of annihilation, and justified the annihilation of the political enemy in one's own race and in one's own people at any price."[50]

For Adenauer, overcoming National Socialism meant breaking with certain central aspects of Germany's past national identity and political traditions. Although he was more reluctant to focus on the Nazi past than Ulbricht and Schumacher, his interest in the history of ideas and of cultural traditions was not encumbered by theories which interpreted such ideas primarily as tools for class interests. Hence, he was more willing than most of his leftist contemporaries to focus on the autonomous force of racist and anti-Semitic ideology.

In contrast both to the generalizing discourses of Communist antifascism and conservative *Kulturkritik* which in different ways explained Germany's history by reference to transhistorical forces, Adenauer focused on what had gone wrong in German history.[51] He offered pointed and specific criticism of German Idealism and romanticism, Prussian statism and militarism, as well as of the anti-individualist, anti-Western currents of German conservatism which had found their radical endpoint in the Nazi *Volksgemeinschaft*. The ascendancy of Adenauer to the center of Christian Democracy after 1945 reflected an ideological shift in German politics. The previously peripheral Francophile, Western-oriented, Catholic-influenced Rhineland conservatism had become central while Prussian conservatism had become peripheral. These political shifts mirrored geographical shifts toward the West.[52] Up to a point, then, Adenauer offered a deeply critical view of central traditions of modern German history and of their contributions to the rise of National Socialism. Although he was too quick to deflect guilt away from an undefined "we," he clearly stated his belief that Nazism had broad support in German society. Yet he did not address the place of anti-Semitism in European and German history or its role in the prehistory of National Socialism.

Although he had been mayor of a major cosmopolitan center, Adenauer liked to juxtapose a virtuous, small-town Rhineland to Berlin's rootless modernity. In his view, Westernization meant a deepening of Christian religious convictions rather than the growing secularization of what had becom a nihilist society. Restoration of "Christian natural right" was key.[53] It was the antidote to Prussian statism and Marxist materialism, and would lead "to a conception of the state, economics, and culture which is novel in contrast to what has been customary in Germany. According to it, neither the state, the economy, nor culture are ends in themselves."[54] Christian natural right offered the foundation of a liberal and individualist view of the relationship of the state to the individual in contrast to the collectivist and statist tradition of German conservatism. The purpose of education, he said, was not to foster a "readiness to let oneself be controlled and led" but instead to develop "the will and ability to incorporate oneself as a free individual aware of one's responsibility into the whole."[55] Adenauer's Cologne speech of March 1946 signaled the beginning of what could be called an "anti-authoritarian right" or, alternatively, the new prominence in modern German conservatism of a long-standing German Catholic skepticism about the celebration of state power.

Adenauer viewed Nazism as pagan and atheistic. After 1945, he saw Christian Democracy as a necessary alternative to the secular left. He considered the West and Christianity unambiguously positive traditions. Yet just as he had ignored the issue of anti-Semitism in his otherwise highly critical view of modern German history, he also had nothing to say about centuries-old tradition of Christian anti-Semitism and the contribution it had made to German and National Socialist anti-Semitism. On the contrary, he argued that Germany suffered from too little, not too much, Christianity. The Nazis, he said, had tried to de-Christianize Germany, which was "one of the least religious and most un-Christian" of Europe's nations.[56] Adenauer believed that democratization should coincide with re-Christianization. His reluctance to examine critically the anti-Semitic components of the Christian tradition or the role of the Catholic Church during the Third Reich remained significant blind spots of postwar West German conservatism.

Adenauer did want to stamp out Nazism and militarism in Germany. Active Nazis, military leaders, and certain economic leaders had to be called to account and dismissed from their current positions. At first he demanded trials, in German courts, of those accused of committing crimes. Yet already in March 1946 he was saying that "we finally [*endlich*] should leave the followers in peace, those who did not oppress others, who did not enrich themselves, and who broke no laws." Soldiers and lower-ranking ex-Nazis, he believed, could enter the Christian Democratic Union (CDU), "though at first they cannot assume any functions in it." But to punish "harmless followers and soldiers who believed that they were doing their duty" would "foster a growing and extreme nationalism."[57] In view of the daily revelations from the Nuremberg war crimes trial, then in its sixth month, it was remarkable that Adenauer, only ten months after the German surrender, had already adopted a tone of exasperation, evident in the use of the term "finally," in referring to hopes for an end to questioning of former members of the Nazi Party.

In fact, the questioning had barely begun. In March 1946 Adenauer could not possibly have known the identities and numbers of Germans who had engaged in war crimes and genocide or who had and who had not been a "harmless" follower. In view of the Nuremberg revelations alone, his use of the phrase "in an honorable manner" [*in anständiger Weise*] to refer to German soldiers who had done their duty in the Wehrmacht betrayed a failure to grasp the character of the war on the Eastern Front or the complicity of the Wehrmacht in the race war in the East and the Holocaust. The Nuremberg Trial was demonstrating that the leadership of the German army was well aware of the racist character of the Eastern war as well as of the Final Solution. His fears of a renewed nationalism in the event of a massive and indiscriminate purge were also peculiar because, at least in the Western zones, no such indiscriminate purge was in progress. Both the Nuremberg Trial and the denazification measures in the American and British zones focused on individual guilt, even for those proven to be members of organizations determined "criminal" such as the SS.[58] When Adenauer said that the general principle concerning dealings with former Nazis should be "punishment for the guilty, but instruction and enlightenment for the broad circles of our people who, without being guilty themselves, were intentionally misled," he seemed to contradict his own asertions regarding the extent of authoritarian nationalism and racism in the German past. Instead, he turned the very depth of those traditions into an argument against arousing the slumbering but pervasive ghosts of the past.[59]

Adenauer vehemently rejected Schumacher's accusations that former Nazis and antidemocratic conservatives were streaming into the Christian Democratic Union, and that the CDU had become a party devoted to protecting the interests of the propertied classes. He also rejected the claim that big capital had brought National Socialism to power.

> Big capital did not create National Socialism. National Socialism was not its invention. This can be clearly demonstrated. From the beginning, National Socialism was sharply directed against the Jews. However, Jews were important in [the circles of] big capital. Does anyone believe that these influential Jewish gentlemen would help their deadly enemies, the National Socialists, to attain political power? No, that powerfully underestimates the cleverness and intelligence of these men.[60]

Rather than big capital, he contended, it was the German military at the highest levels which had been the "inventor" of National Socialism.

The military had recognized the power of the two words "national" and "socialism" among the Germans, combined them into one, "and created a new kind of socialism, National Socialism." Adenauer thus "sharply condemned" the economic and military circles which had financed the NSDAP, but he rejected the view that socialism meant "salvation for the German people" or that capitalism and the bourgeoisie were responsible for Nazism.[61]

The issue of what terms should be used to refer to the recent German past preoccupied all of the postwar leaders. The choice of "Nazi," "fascist," "Third Reich," "National Socialism," or very rarely simply "Germans" told much about one's political orientation. Adenauer never used the word "Nazism" or "Nazi." Instead he referred to "National Socialism," a term Ulbricht and Schumacher never or very rarely used. Both Ulbricht and Schumacher had gone to some lengths to separate the term "socialism" from its misuse by the Nazis, while Adenauer insisted on using the term "National Socialism" to stress his conviction that nationalism and socialism were two dominant German traditions which the National Socialists had cleverly combined. In his view socialism, however democratic, was not a break with the language and statist practice of National Socialism. While Schumacher asserted that the Social Democratic Party (SPD) had been the only party of the past eighty years to support democracy consistently in Germany, Adenauer associated the SPD with "the old Prussian spirit, the ruthless, undemocratic striving for exclusive power with which the Prussian Junkers had once been obsessed."[62] He argued that materialism and class struggle had both enhanced the dubious traditions of statism and anti-individualism which had contributed to the rise of National Socialism. Hence, the question for Germany's future was whether "the Christian or the Marxist and materialist conception would rule."[63] He concluded that "in spite of the atrocities of National Socialism, the Germans have a right not to be judged only by this epoch of their history."[64] He hoped for a decentralized, Western- and European-oriented Germany. This Germany would be reconciled with France and would break from its militarist, authoritarian, de-Christianizing traditions.[65] For Adenauer, this decentralized Germany, which the Communists and Social Democrats denounced as the home of reaction, was a necessary barrier to a renewed authoritarian state.

The primary historical and practical lesson which Adenauer drew from reflecting on Nazism was the need for a moral, political, strategic, and economic Western integration of a new German state, and the need for the new German state to accept the burden of the Nazi persecution of the Jews. The two were not always mutually reinforcing policies. As we have seen, Christian Democracy broke with anti-Western German nationalism and replaced justifications for an authoritarian state with focus on individual freedoms. Yet West German membership in an alliance intended to contain the Soviet Union so soon after Hitler had attacked "Jewish bolshevism" was bound to evoke associations between past and present anticommunism. Adenauer was not one to reflect on such ambiguities of Westernization. In his view, Westernization of Germany was an unqualified and indispensable good.[66]

Adenauer wanted to do the best with the material he had been given, namely, the German people as they were, not as he wished them to be. He had no desire to play the role of the avenging angel or national moralist. He did want postwar Germany to be firmly embedded in a set of Western supranational institutions. He believed that Germany's wandering between East and West during the Kaiser Reich and the Nazi era had twice led to wars. Now Germany had to end this wandering and become firmly planted in the West. This was the single most important practical policy implication which he drew from the Nazi era. For Adenauer, facing the Nazi past meant above all moral and strategic integration into the West. Integration of the Germans into a Western alliance and of Germans who had gone astray into a postwar democracy within Germany was his central preoccupation, taking precedence over memory and justice.[67] He drew this conclusion as a geostrategist and as a politician who understood that Nazism had popular support among the Germans and had left residues that would not vanish overnight. Embedding West Germany into a Western alliance, for Adenauer no less than for the Allies, was a defense against the Soviet present as well as a possible return of the Nazi past.

As chairman of the CDU, Adenauer campaigned in the first elections held in Germany since 1933. His speeches of spring and summer 1946 were variations of the speech he had delivered at the University of Cologne in March. He called for justice in German courts for those who had committed crimes. Adenauer always received applause when he said that the *Mitläufer*, those who "had not oppressed others, had not enriched themselves, had not committed any punishable offenses, should now at last be left in peace."[68] On May 5 in Wuppertal at the conclusion of his stock speech, he turned to the issue of denazification.[69] "Finally," he said, "leave the Nazi fellow travelers in peace!" He then made a striking comparison of the Nazi and occupation periods.

It is intolerable that the German people should [now] be divided, just as in the past twelve years, into a better and a worse part. Where is the unity of the German people supposed to come from as a result? (Strong applause.) For twelve years under the National Socialists, I myself belonged to the worse part. I was not permitted to move. I was not permitted to work. I was arrested three times. I was in prison twice. For a while I was in a concentration camp. I know what that is all about. But injustice plus injustice will never equal justice. And today we do not want to imitate what was done then. (Very strong applause.) Punish the guilty, forgiveness and reintegration for the misled or the fellow travelers who did not do anything evil . . . We unconditionally capitulated, but, ladies and gentlemen, right and justice and mercy have not disappeared from the world as a result of this unconditional capitulation. That cannot be the case. According to human law and God's law, the victors have duties and the defeated have rights. (Strong applause.) The duty of the victors and the right of the defeated rest on divine mercy and divine justice, and no one who breaks the commandment of divine justice will go unpunished.[70]

The injustices to which Adenauer was referring were the denazification procedures in the British and American zones. Here he seems to have equated them with the repression of the Nazi regime, clearly to the pleasure of his audience. He evoked religious themes to stress the importance of forgiveness and mercy rather than justice. Thus, long before he could have any idea who had and who had not committed war crimes or crimes against humanity in the Nazi era, he claimed that the American and British occupiers were breaking the commandments of divine justice. It was a peculiar notion of moral renewal. Adenauer did not seek to convince his listeners that justice was being done in Nuremberg. Nor did he explain how former members of the Nazi Party would be prevented from occupying influential positions in a government he would form. One could infer from his remarks that employment possibilities existed for all but the most blatantly compromised. Adenauer warned the Allies that denazification would foster nationalist resentments. As the Wuppertal speech indicates, at times he too could play on the resentments of a defeated nation.

A week later, on May 12, 1946, Adenauer returned to the issue of denazification at a CDU rally in Düsseldorf. He said that majority of the Germans had been shocked by the extent of Nazi criminality. They knew that the future held a heavy burden of guilt, but they trusted in the Allies that it would not be one without hope and that the truly guilty would be punished in German courts. Yet, he asked, "where are our prisoners of war?"[71] What plans had been made for educating the Germans for democracy and for political and economic reconstruction? When would a peace conference take place? He approvingly cited an editorial in the British newspaper *The Observer* which warned that an absence of recovery measures in postwar Germany was aiding a revival of Nazi sentiment. Without plans for economic recovery, the old Nazi argument that "British plutocracy and Russian bolshevism" would destroy not only the Nazi regime but also the German nation was gaining adherents. The anti-Nazi parties, such as the CDU, were suffering as a result of a lack of political responsibility and economic recovery. The "only effective form of denazification," he said, would be to give real leadership and responsibility to the anti-Nazi German parties and hasten the pace of the transfer of power from the occupiers to democratically elected leaders.[72]

In an address the following day in Cologne, Adenauer returned to the issue of German prisoners of war. Assuming that at least two relatives were concerned about each of the 6 million German POWs, that meant that "18 million Germans" were bearing the burden of the Nazi past. To the accompaniment of "very loud applause," he urged the Russians to "give us back our prisoners of war!"[73] He suggested that the Communists use their influence to send home German prisoners of war in the Soviet Union as soon as possible. (In the postwar decade the issue of German POWs in the Soviet Union kept the Nazi era and World War II very much alive for millions of Germans, though obviously not in a way that led to reflection on what Germany had done to the Soviet Union during the war.) As for the Nuremberg Trial, Adenauer said that it "has already lasted much too long." Those who committed crimes should be punished. But the party members who did not commit crimes "should finally be left alone in peace and quiet to get on with their work."[74] The Allies had been in Germany long enough to know that "not all Germans, yes, not even half of the Germans, were National Socialist criminals. It is not true. They [the Allies] should finally have trust in us, just as we must show trust toward the Allies." The Germans wanted nothing more than to live in peace, to work, and to "again enter as an equal member in the circle of nations."[75] Yet it would not be easy for a country which, in Adenauer's words, had many "National Socialist criminals" in its midst to regain that trust.

In a speech to a CDU gathering in Cologne on July 24, 1946, Adenauer said that denazification was "last[ing] much too long." "Leading Nazis" were being left untouched while other "poor devils were being hanged."[76] On August 11, in a major speech to the CDU Party Congress, he repeated his plea to "now at last leave the followers in peace."[77] To illustrate his point he related an anecdote about an official who had lost his job because he had been "a simple card-carrying member" of the Nazi Party. The man was now starving, and his children were ill with tuberculosis. Adenauer described this as "an intolerable situation" which was "not acceptable."[78] In his view, democracy in post-Nazi Germany required that such former Nazi Party members be reintegrated rather than treated like "second-class persons."[79] On June 2 in München-Gladbach he expressed doubt that the past could be overcome "when we see how the Allies have fostered nationalism and militarism in the German people in ways Hitler and his consorts never were able to do. For this he received "strong applause."[80] In other words, denazification was the cause of postwar nationalism. Forcing the Germans to face the Nazi past would only make things worse.

On July 24, speaking to the state committee of the CDU in Cologne, Adenauer commented on proposals supported by the KPD and the SPD for a memorial day for victims of National Socialism. He viewed such a proposal as "justified" but only if it also included "a special day for the victims of war, that is, those who lost their lives as victims of National Socialism on the field [of battle] or at home."[81] Yet, he warned, there were too many Germans who, rather than seeking "the cause of present and future difficulties where they must be sought, namely, among those who started the war," were looking instead "toward those who are now trying their best to make up for the damage."[82] On these grounds, and in order to enhance the prospects for peace, he supported the proposals for a memorial day. From the early postwar days Adenauer had included Germans soldiers among the victims of Nazism. On these early campaign trails he pointed to the suffering of German POWs and expellees, yet said little about what these Germans had done to others. His constituency was preoccupied with its own problems, more than with the hell which the Wehrmacht had inflicted on Europe, especially Eastern Europe. On April 13, 1947, in a speech in the main lecture hall of the University of Cologne, Adenauer appealed for understanding for those who had been misled into following the Nazis. After all, the fact that the Allies themselves had signed treaties with Hitler or that other countries had sent young athletes to the Berlin Olympics might appear to party members as a "certain excuse."[83] Memories of appeasement in the 1930s diminished the exclusive focus on German error and recalled the illusions shared by the democracies.

Adenauer's age and his emphatically nonmilitary bearing stood in sharp contrast to the Nazi ideal of masculine aggression. Adenauer, the ultimate bourgeois, viewed the fascist cult of the body with unconcealed contempt. The *Realpolitiker* concluded a speech to a CDU party congress on August 11, 1946, with a comment on "the politics of men" (*Männerpolitik*). A woman had remarked to him that the male pursuit of "power and force" had left behind "nothing but rubble and debris."

There was "a lot of truth," he confessed, to what the woman had said. Women were more inclined to settlement and discussion, while men were "much more inclined to violence." Germany and Europe did not need force. "We need settlements and discussion." Cheers and applause greeted this statement.[84] Although Adenauer would carry out West German rearmament, he did so without the cultural baggage of masculine assertion which had been discredited by the lost war. Adenauer in 1946 was worlds removed from the bluster of the young and middle-aged fascist and Nazi men of the 1930s and 1940s. A European patriarch of the old school, he viewed women as a remnant of decency and humanity in a world destroyed by young thugs. The memory of fallen soldiers recalled grief-stricken families rather than heroes eager for yet another war, or the fierce militance of "antifascist resistance fighters" in East Berlin. Adenauer's image as the firm but gentle patriarch thus broke with past images linking leadership with masculine aggression.[85]

Adenauer's early postwar speeches offer a mixture of insight and defensiveness, honesty and apologetics. The deeper he found the roots of Nazism in German history and society to be, the more he feared that a harsh occupation policy would revive the old ghosts of nationalism and even National Socialism. Hence, he believed that the best way to overcome Nazism was to avoid a direct confrontation with it while transferring ever more authority to German political leaders. Economic recovery and political legitimacy, not additional purges, were the proper medicine. Democratic renewal went hand in hand with silence and the forgetting of a dark past. Too much memory would undermine a still fragile popular psyche.

The Cold War and anti-Soviet politics, which focused attention on Soviet actions after 1945 rather than Nazi warmaking between 1941 and 1945, reinforced this line of thinking. It did not create it, however. Like his antagonist Ulbricht, Adenauer had a keen memory of how popular Nazism had been among the Germans, and after 1945 he worried about how to prevent a revival of Nazism. Yet whereas Ulbricht concluded that the answer was to impose a dictatorship over a dangerous people, Adenauer argued that democracy was possible, provided it was inaugurated by a period of silence about the crimes of the Nazi past. A democracy of and by the Germans, as Adenauer put it in the spring and summer of 1946, meant that "finally" and "at last" postwar Germans would be spared the pain of excessive reflection on the Nazi past. More democracy in this situation, could entail less denazification, less purging, fewer trials for perpetrators of the Holocaust and war crimes, and less reflection on that history from the political leadership. Adenauer led the Germans out of the desert of dictatorship to the promised land of democracy with Old World tact rather than Old Testament indignation. He was the representative figure of the era, in part because he understood the conflict between popular will and a sharp confrontation with the crimes of Nazi past.

Many years later Herbert Blankenhorn, Adenauer's chief foreign policy adviser, in a interview with the journalist Inge Deutsckron, came straight to the point: "For years, Dr. Adenauer did not say anything about the Jewish issue because he wanted to win the German people in their entirety for democracy. If Adenauer, as early as 1949, had said what we did in the past was wrong, then certainly the German people would have been against him."[86] Actually, not all the people but, at the very least a bloc of voters essential to a CDU electoral majority would have been against Adenauer had he said more about "the Jewish issue" in those early years. In a democracy, of course, that was decisive, for it meant that recalling the crimes of the past would be harmful to his electoral prospects. There were other politicians after the war who were more willing to speak about Nazi crimes. Partly as a result, they lost elections or remained the leaders of small parties. We turn now to Theodor Heuss, who raised "the Jewish issue" within the confines of the Adenauer administration, and to Kurt Schumacher and Ernst Reuter, who made the politically damaging argument that democracy should and could be based on more rather than less memory of the dark chapters of the Nazi past. Although they did not speak for the majority in 1945–1949, all three left a valuable legacy which eventually found broader acceptance. Their minority status underscored the connection between democratization and a reluctance to discuss Nazi crimes during the Adenauer era.

Theodor Heuss (1884–1963), one of the major figures of political liberalism in West Germany, was the first president of the Federal Republic, serving from 1949 to 1959. He grew up in Würtemberg in a family attached to the liberal democratic traditions of 1848. He studied the history of art and literature as well as social policy, politics, and economics at the universities of Berlin and Munich from 1902 to 1905, then from 1905 to 1912 he co-edited the weekly magazine *Die Hilfe* with Friedrich Naumann. In 1912 he returned to Heilbronn, where he became the editor in chief of the *Neckarzeitung*. From 1913 to 1918 he edited the biweekly journal *Der Marz*, then returned to Berlin in 1918 to work on the journal *Deutsche Politik* and in the office of the Deutsche Werkbunde. From 1924 to 1928 and from 1930 to 1933, he served in the Reichstag as a member of the Deutsche Staatspartei, with a special interest in cultural and constitutional questions. He also taught at the Deutsche Hochschule für Politik in Berlin, where he lectured on the history of German political parties and constitutions, German history in the nineteenth century, and Germany's political development during and after World War I. In 1933 the Nazis brought Heuss's political career to an end and dissolved the Hochschule, thus eliminating both of his sources of employment.

In 1932 Heuss published *Hitlers Weg: Eine historisch-politische Studie über den Nationalsozialismus* (Hitler's Path: A Historical-Political Study of National Socialism).[87] After 1933 the Nazis publicly burned the book. In it Heuss examined Hitler's *Mein Kampf* and Alfred Rosenberg's *Mythos des zwanzigsten Jahrhundert*, the writings of Gottfried Feder, and the Nazi Party program in order to analyze the "background of the history of ideas" as it applied to Nazism.[88] Heuss understood how Hitler sought to use "legality" and the instruments of democratic institutions to destroy democracy. He wrote that National Socialist scientific pretensions played a similar role for the "consolidation of political emotions as the scientific side of Marxism" had.[89] In place of class and class struggle, the Nazis substituted "blood and race." But in both instances, he wrote, "the psychological schema of simplification and the moralizing formation of typological elements is the same."[90] The race politicians, he wrote, live with "similar fictions of the Nordic race and its monopoly on 'creative qualities.'" In place of Marx's historical materialism, the Nazis had introduced "biological naturalism."[91]

In attacking Nazi racial ideology and its scientific pretensions, he wrote that the race theorist's "ideal types extend beyond the threshold of empirical research" and become instead "moral and cultural evaluations."[92] He rejected the notion of a unitary, undiluted German race: "Germany, yes, the people of all of Europe represent a mixed product [*Mischprodukt*] which stirs together types and elements through families and landscapes." To speculate if "my brother [or] my mother" has other racial characteristics "is indeed a childish exercise."[93] In view of the interweaving of European peoples through centuries of migration, travel, and interchange, "the nonsensical nature of the whole undertaking [of Nazi race theory] is obvious." He scornfully dismissed the combination of naturalist thinking in racial theory with political celebration of the Nordic race "as nothing other than cheap romanticism, which frequently serves to overcome feelings of inferiority."[94]

Heuss called Hitler's chapter on the Jews in *Mein Kampf* a "distorted and ignorant" description of their economic impact. The whole "controversy over the Jews" he described as an "occasion for shame for the rest of us." It was a matter of "a shared German concern [which] dirties us all" when the Nazis attacked the honor of Jewish war veterans or when Jewish cemeteries were desecrated.[95] Heuss assailed the nation's alleged "need for cleansing" (*Reinigungsbedürfnis*) which had led to Nazi attacks on Jewish-owned newspapers, and he criticized "the endless catalogue of one's own virtues and the burdens of others."[96] The historical picture that emerged from Hitler's juxtaposition of Aryans and Jews was "false because it is built on concepts that are too crude and simple and consist of wishes and feelings of hatred, and because its fundamental thesis of the 'most fateful possession' of blood is not appropriate to politically constitutive forces."[97] He asked his readers if they were "ready to think this path to the end." What would happen to the ethnic Germans living throughout Eastern Europe, he asked, if "national chauvinism" were to apply Hitler's race theories and thereby "rob the German minorities there of their public rights? . . . The history of settlement of the German people in all of Europe means that the 'blood-oriented' National Socialist theory of the state would be more dangerous and more destructive for the German people than it must be for the Jews."[98]

Heuss wrote that "the birthplace of the National Socialist movement is Versailles, not Munich." He stressed the centrality of the *Dolchstoßlegende* and the attack on the "November criminals" for the emergence of Nazism among ex-soldiers. These legends and myths had been a "tragedy" because they encouraged the Germans to look for scapegoats rather than to understand their problems. "Wounded national pride needs an Other against which it can be compared. It is not able to rest silently and confidently within itself."[99] Hitler had turned those who disagreed with him into "enemies of the people," thus making "discussion so hopeless and fruitless."[100] *Hitlers Weg* was one of the most important liberal anti-Nazi works of the period. Heuss correctly understood both that Nazi race politics would set in motion a sequence of terrible events which would come to haunt the Germans themselves, and that the *Dolchstoßlegende* had been central to Hitler's success. This realism, opposition to anti-Semitism, and clarity about how the second postwar era differed from the first became enduring features of Heuss's political interventions after 1945 as well.

In 1932 in the Reichstag, Heuss warned again that Nazi policies, if adopted by other countries in Europe, especially Eastern and Southeastern Europe, would place the millions of Germans living outside Germany's borders in danger because the Germans themselves were legitimating persecution and expulsion on racial and ethnic grounds.[101] He dismissed Nazi economics of autarky as "theoretical nonsense."[102] He called the SA "an instrument of intimidation, simple terrorization, a continuing appeal to anxious petty bourgeois citizens" and called for the government to ban it.[103]

Heuss's anti-Nazi credentials were profoundly compromised, however, when on March 1, 1933, along with the four other members of the parliamentary fraction of the Demokratische Volkspartei, he voted in favor of the so-called Enabling Law which bestowed dictatorial powers on Adolf Hitler. He thus was part of the German political establishment which underestimated Hitler and Nazism.[104] He edited the newspaper *Die Hilfe* from 1933 to 1936, when the Gestapo forced him to resign. Thereafter he avoided political controversy. In 1941 he began to write under a pseudonym for the *Frankfurter Zeitung.* From 1942 to 1944 Heuss was in close contact with Carl Goerdeler, a leader of the German resistance, and would have been the press secretary of a new government had the coup been successful.[105] By August 1945, American occupation authorities were negotiating with Heuss about a license to publish one of the first newspapers to appear after the end of the war.[106]

In the first postwar elections in Baden-Würtemburg, opponents attacked Heuss and other Weimar politicians who had voted in favor of the Enabling Law. An investigative commission was established to examine the issue. Heuss's testimony of February 12, 1947, was not a statement of contrition. Instead he pointed to the uncertainty of the moment and the advantages of hindsight, and stressed that the small size of the Liberal Party had made its yes or no on the vote politically insignificant.[107] In 1963, however, as he was composing his memoirs shortly before his death, he admitted that "stupidity" was far too weak a term to describe his vote for the Enabling Law. He had known even then, in March 1933, that he would "not ever be able to expunge this 'yes' from my biography."[108] Yet, as he had in 1947, Heuss still insisted that the passage of the Enabling Law in 1933 had had "no importance for the practical subsequent course of National Socialist politics."[109] In view of the significance which the Nazis attached to the strategy of using legal appearances to destroy democratic institutions, Heuss's claim was a dubious one. To his critics, Heuss was the typical proponent of West German "philo-Semitism," a politically inconsequential focus on the Jewish question meant to help restore West German sovereignty and the "good name" of the Germans and integrate them into the Western Alliance. To his admirers, he was a voice of conscience who discussed issues that his pragmatic contemporary Adenauer would not raise.[110]

Immediately following the end of the war, in May 1945, Heuss wrote that this defeat was totally different from the defeat of 1918.[111] The "only honorable" feature of this surrender was the fact that Generals Jodl and Keitel had signed their own names on the documents of capitulation rather than, as their predecessors had done in 1918, pushing the unpleasant task off onto the politicians. Both the German military and the Nazi Party had clearly been defeated. The Nazi Party "had already intellectually and spiritually prepared the collapse of the Wehrmacht." Military catastrophe had been preceded "by a moral catastrophe" that had been introduced by Hitler and Himmler.[112] Yet there was a silver lining to the totality of the German defeat. "We must be almost grateful," he wrote, "to the enemy army leadership because in their harshness they made sure that this time—and for the foreseeable future—a stab-in-the-back legend [*Dolchstoßlegende*] cannot bloom again . . . The shared guilt and shared responsibility of the leading generals cannot be either denied or glossed over."[113] Moreover, the nazification of the German military leadership, and their slavish obedience to Hitler even after it had become apparent that military victory was no longer possible, had undermined the prestige and legitimacy of the generals. The situation stood in stark contrast to 1918, when the end of the war seemed ambiguous to the German public and the military leadership emerged with its prestige intact while the civilian leadership was tainted with the responsibility for defeat. Now there would be no illusions or legends either about the end of this war or about its having been lost on the home front.[114]

At the end of May 1945, Heuss returned to this theme.[115] He wrote:

As painful as the complete military capitulation may be for German historical consciousness, it has been necessary for German spiritual-political development. Because the first military authorities themselves had to and did bring it about, the German future has been freed from the possibility of a false domestic propaganda, such as that of the *Dolchstoßlegende* which poisoned the period after 1918. In the midst of misfortune, that is a gain. National Socialism went down to defeat in large part because it lacked the courage to face the truth. The Germans must again regain this kind of courage.[116]

Heuss's point, which he repeated in the years to come was crucial: after 1945, democratic political leaders would not be burdened with blame for the lost war. It was clear to all that the sole responsibility for having started and having lost the war lay with Hitler and the Nazi leadership. The very finality of the war's end contributed to clarity of memory about the history of the Nazi era, in part because the Nazis were no longer in a position to obscure the truth. Heuss defined courage not as the willingness to engage in unthinking sacrifice but as the ability to face unpleasant truths. Recasting the language and meaning of patriotism was one of Heuss's most important contributions to the renewal of democratic political culture in Germany.

Heuss also urged his fellow Germans to engage in an intellectual and moral confrontation with the consequences of National Socialist domination. Although, he wrote, Nazism had "soiled the German name," the Germans, who "have experienced countless tragedies," did not need to be instructed about the sins bound up with the Hitler regime.[117] He recalled that concentration camps and torture had first been used against Germans. "Only later was this form of annihilation of the Germans and then the foreign Jews and the members of foreign nations developed to infernal degrees."[118] Even though the majority of the Nazis' political victims were Socialists and Communists, the resistance did not have "only Communist martyrs." It had also included members of the churches and nonsocialist parties, the conspirators of July 1944, members of the military, trade unionists, conservatives and Social Democrats, academics, property owners, and workers. Indeed, Heuss was concerned that the breadth of the resistance was not appreciated either by the German people or abroad.[119]

Heuss was also concerned about the future of Nazism after 1945. In contrast to Adenauer's appeals to leave the rank-and-file Nazi Party members in peace, Heuss called for "drastic and prompt punishment of those middle-level party functionaries who terrorized the people" in addition to punishment for well-known leaders. Like Adenauer, he warned that punishing everyone who had joined the Hitler Youth would unjustly create new sources of radicalization.[120] Yet he also stressed that the Germans had a special responsibility to document and remember Nazi crimes, especially while memories were still fresh.

> The decisive confrontation with National Socialism as the evil inter-lude [*Zwischenstück*] of German history remains a German task . . . [W]e Germans also have to think about the coming generations. Now we must prepare the battle against any kind of emergent Hitler legend. How much material has already been destroyed which could document to the German world after Nazism the wickedness and criminal stupidity of the National Socialist leadership and their offices. One almost wishes that the foreign radio would call on the Germans, now that their memory is still fresh, to write down the facts of this time [and thus create] documents for future German histori-ans, not denunciations for the Allies, who have already received enough of those. This would make a most necessary contribution toward reestablishing the tasks and special position of the Germans in the geographic and spiritual space of Europe."[121]

Throughout his subsequent political career Heuss held firmly to the core conviction that facing the evil of National Socialism remained a German task, and that truthfulness about the Nazi past was essential if postwar Germany was to recover its moral and political standing in Europe.

At a time when millions of Germans associated the German resis-tance with treason, Heuss praised the actions of those who had actively opposed the Nazi regime. In Stuttgart, in November 1945, in a memo-rial speech for the "victims of the internal struggle of the past twelve years," he praised the martyrs of the German anti-Nazi resistance and warned against forgetting the horrors of the recent past.[122] The German people, he continued, had made it easy to put on the chains of National Socialism. But "it must not be made easy to throw off evil things like a bad dream."[123] He rejected the description of the conspirators as opportunists who had acted only at the last moment. The "most im-portant historical motive," he said, was the "meeting of young, activist

Social Democrats . . . with the, if I may used the pathos of Luther's terms, 'Christian nobility of the German nation.'"[124]

Contrary to their intentions, Heuss remarked, the Nazis had fostered solidarity among those they had persecuted together in the concentration camps. There Communists and religious prisoners, pacifists and military officers, free-thinkers and Catholics, Social Democrats and landowning nobles had all learned to respect one another as human beings despite their differences. Many had died horrible deaths. But "with their deaths they may have accomplished a political purpose that extended beyond Germany, by making visible the other Germany [*das andere Deutschland*] with the evidence of their own blood."[125] Heuss then linked the claims of memory to the task of clearing the now dishonored name of Germany.

> The inner German political victims, and on their side the hundreds of thousands, yes, millions of foreigners who were tortured to death, speak to the heaviest and costliest sacrifice of National Socialism: the honor of the German name, which has sunk in filth. As we say this, angered, depressed, and ashamed to have been defenseless contemporaries of this darkest period of German history, we feel the duty once again to clear our name and the name of the German people. The memory of those who suffered yet were innocent, and who died bravely, will be a quiet, calm light illuminating our path in the dark years through which we are going.[126]

Heuss ennobled National Socialism's victims, drew inspiration from their struggles and those of the resistance, and linked recovery of Germany's good name to a promise of solidarity with those whom Nazism had sought to condemn to oblivion. He also expressed a sense of a permanent loss that could not be made up. While the leaders of the big political blocs of the early postwar years preferred to look forward to a brighter future, Heuss was more inclined to look back in sorrow and mourning. Because he remained active in liberal politics, and eventually became president of the Federal Republic, this disenchanted liberalism, this sense of tragic loss, this knowledge that some part of Germany had been destroyed and could not be re-created, this refrain from uplifting speeches about the future of the class struggle, of socialism and democracy, or of a Christian religious revival, this mournful sobriety, also became part of West German political culture.

On September 5, 1945, Theodor Heuss, along with Klaus Knorr, a Social Democrat, and Rudolf Agricola, a Communist, received one of the first newspaper licenses issued by the American occupation authorities to publish the *Rhein Neckar Zeitung* in Heidelberg.[127] From 1945 to 1949, Heuss's views on postwar politics and on the Nazi past appeared in the form of editorials in the paper. In the first issue the editors called on readers to reflect on the moral and ethical collapse that had made possible Nazism's rise to power and its crimes. Such reflection was necessary before "atonement and overcoming of this rubbish" could occur.[128] Political "education" and "reeducation" would be difficult in Germany, with its legacy of defeated freedom movements and the absence of even a word for "fairness." Yet Heuss wrote that democracy was not an utterly foreign import. Education for democracy meant *"again* to learn to see and respect human dignity."[129] After twelve years of Nazi-enforced provincialism, it was time for Germans to engage in self-reflection and to reconnect with the outside world and its values.[130] Although foreigners had destroyed Nazism, "the debate and discussion about it and its heritage [was] a German task" which could be accomplished only through reconnection with Germany's suppressed and now revived democratic traditions.[131]

"The German military was defeated by allied armies. The German army was destroyed by the NSDAP."[132] So Heuss began his page one commentary "The End of the German Army" on September 12, 1945. He again noted that the "stab-in-the-back legend" which had arisen after the German defeat in 1918 was absent in 1945. Now, he said, "the catastrophe is too clear."[133] There was now no doubt that World War II had been lost on the battlefield. General Keitel, one of the German generals who signed the statement of surrender, was typical, Heuss wrote, of those careerists and opportunists in the Wehrmacht who had subordinated military judgment to Nazi ideology and policy. The German military tradition of Gneisenau, Moltke, and Schlieffen had died, and the Germans now had to come to terms with the consequences of these developments.[134]

Like all of the licensed newspapers of the occupation period, the *Rhein-Neckar Zeitung* contained extensive coverage of the Nuremberg trials. Heuss called the trials important for fostering an "inner emotional and political debate" by the Germans.[135] His greatest disappointment, he wrote, was that they were not being conducted by Germans, an outcome which itself was due to "the deprivation of power toward which we have been led by the National Socialists." The Germans, no less than the rest of the world, had an interest in seeing that justice was done: "We must be the accusers. We must provide the judges!" Whereas the Italians had settled scores with Mussolini, the Germans had "less of an inclination for that kind of thing. At any rate, they missed the opportunity and can no longer do so."[136] On the first anniversary of the "capitulation" of May 8, 1945, Heuss wrote that the Nuremberg Trial had "confirmed very bitter truths" about the Nazi regime. The Germans would have to come to terms with them. The "moral-political balance" could not be paid off cheaply: "The accounts are written, and their settlement will be hard and heavy. There are no illusions about that."[137]

Heuss's efforts to restore links to past moral traditions were evident in a January 1946 essay titled "Bonds and Freedom."[138] It was an appeal for autonomous scholarship, individual moral responsibility, and a renewal of connections to the West and to Christianity. For Heuss, "the West" meant "the unity of the Germanic-Roman cultural sphere," antiquity and Christianity, the Ten Commandments and the Sermon on the Mount, all of which amounted to "duties for the individual, the group, the nation, and for nations."[139] Like Adenauer, Heuss saw a connection between materialism and Nazi pseudoscientific racism. He criticized Communist and Socialist materialism as well, and he rejected the Marxist argument that Nazism was the product of capitalism. Instead he stressed the peculiarities of German history. "If Hitler had only been a function of private monopolistic capitalism," he contended, "why couldn't he appear in England or America? England had an older capitalism than Germany. America had a younger but more compact capitalism. Yet both had neither a Marxist movement nor any tendency to plebiscitarian dictatorship. Why not? Because they had in their past what we lack, a history of freedom."[140] Germany's history of struggles for freedom was "a history of defeats. We suffer from those defeats."[141]

In March 1946 Heuss repeated these themes when he spoke in Berlin at the first meeting of the Communist-dominated Kulturbunde zur demokratischen Erneuerung Deutschlands at the invitation of its chairman, Johannes R. Becher.[142] Nazism had been possible because in Germany "the history of struggles for freedom . . . was and remains a history of defeats."[143] The Russians, French, English, and Americans had their revolutions, but the Germans repeatedly lost the battle for freedom, first in the Peasants' War, then in the struggles of 1815, 1830, 1848 and the socialist conflicts of the late nineteenth and early twentieth centuries. The Germans lacked the experience of "elementary liberalism," a spirit of tolerance and freedom.[144] They now must turn to humanism, to Western traditions, and purge and denazify their own language. Allied victory had made possible a return to the defeated "other Germanys" of their own past.

In 1947, at a meeting of the Liberal Party in the American occupation zone, Heuss returned to this theme.[145] "The tragedy of German history" he said, "is that the history of freedom struggles in Germany is a history of defeats." Other nations had victorious revolutions, but the Germans' heritage was a fear of freedom. Now Germans had to give liberal values and freedom a home in Germany.[146] Heuss did not offer his listeners tales of antifascist heroism. His postwar liberalism did not include an optimistic historical teleology. He did stress that there had been multiple currents within the German past, and that postwar memory had to recall not only the Nazi abyss but also the other, better, if oft-defeated, Germanys. In the words of the German poet Hölderlin, he found the appropriate stance to past and present one of "sacred sobriety" (*heilige Nüchternheit*).[147] The Germans had become a people "without illusions" who had gone through "the school of skepticism."[148] The absence of illusions and continuing skepticism would provide an essential antidote to the mass fanaticism and engagement of the Nazi era.

For the Communist and Social Democratic left, the date May 8, 1945, was one of unequivocal liberation from Nazism. Yet, as was evident in an essay written for the fourth anniversary of the end of the war, Heuss regarded the date as marking both liberation and a political catastrophe. He criticized Soviet policy in Germany, yet he was quick to add that it was Hitler who, "by gambling away Germany's life destiny," had brought Russian power to Germany. Hitler bore responsibility for the fact that much of Germany "today lies in the Russian sphere of influence!"[149] But the chain of events had not begun on May 8, 1945. The catastrophe of Nazism was part of German history, and Heuss admitted that despite his opposition to Nazism, he was implicated in those historical continuities. By 1945 Konrad Adenauer had publicly expressed "pride" in the German people. By 1948 Walter Ulbricht was speaking of leading them in heroic struggle against American colonizers. By contrast, Heuss's public statements from these early years displayed none of what he probably regarded as premature and unseemly expressions of national enthusiasm.

In September 1949, in one of his last signed editorials in the *Rhein-Neckar Zeitung* before he became *Bundespräsident*, Heuss reflected on the theme of remembering and forgetting the Nazi past.

Human nature possesses the ability to be able to forget. How could an individual, how could a people live if they were constantly accompanied by the consciousness of the pain they had suffered and the disappointments they had experienced? They could disappear into a grave of forgetting. But mercy can also be misused. Many Germans, faced with the suffering of the present, which will remain a present full of need for a long time, gladly place the memory of the source of suffering behind them. This is a much too comfortable procedure. If a view of a historical date is meaningful, then it is so only if it renews knowledge of the connections and relationships which surround that date. The May day of 1945 when we were "both redeemed and destroyed at the same time" was prefigured in the beginning of September 1939. In the end we got out of the war that had long since been robbed of any sense in order to seek a peace which again and again disappeared from our hands.[150]

History, in this case understanding of the temporal sequence of events which begain with German aggression in 1939, could not be separated from memory of the particular date of the German defeat of May 1945. Appeals for mercy and forgiveness could easily become forms of apologia. If the Germans wanted to build a better future, they had to remember the past and resist the temptation to forget "the connections and relationships" which had led to May 8, 1945. Memory alone without an understanding of political history and its attendent focus on temporal causal sequences could itself become a form of apologetics.[151]

In his inaugural address as president of the Federal Republic on September 12, 1949, Heuss noted that there were times when individuals had to be able to forget past suffering and disappointments and get on with their lives.

> For peoples as well, the ability to forget is also a mercy. But my concern is that many people in Germany misuse this act of mercy and want to forget too quickly. We must preserve a feeling for the traces of what led us to where we find ourselves today. This is not an emotion of revenge or hatred. I hope that we will get to the point of creating a unity following on the confusion in the souls in our people. But we must not and cannot make it so easy now to forget what the Hitler era brought us.[152]

With this statement, and his subsequent speeches and statements, Heuss affirmed that he, as the first *Bundespräsident*, would remember what many postwar Germans would rather forget. In the coming decade, those who wanted to remember the dark past turned to him. His office became the place from which a number of dissonant notes were sounded during the 1950s.

The Social Democratic leaders expected to ride a wave of revulsion against Nazism and capitalism to a national electoral majority. For Kurt Schumacher, frank discussion of the Nazi past was a moral and political necessity. More than any other of the founding figures of postwar German politics in East or West Germany, Schumacher offered the

Germans the opportunity to come to terms with the Nazi past, including the Jewish catastrophe, in consequential, not only symbolic, ways. Ernst Reuter came to international attention as the Social Democratic mayor of West Berlin who rallied the city during the Berlin airlift and the early Cold War. During these years Reuter stressed the common basis on which he had fought the Nazis and was now opposing the Communists. Yet, given the choice in free elections, postwar Germans preferred Adenauer's Christian Democracts to "the other Germany" of Schumacher and Reuter. The democratic left, though defeated at the national level in the early postwar years, would continue to exert a powerful and growing impact on the politics of memory in the Federal Republic.

Schumacher was born on October 13, 1895, in the West Prussian city of Kreisstadt, which before that time and again since 1920 was called Chelmno and was part of Poland. He served in the German army in World War I, was severely wounded in December 1914 on the Eastern Front, and had to have his right arm amputated at the shoulder. During the rest of the war he worked as a civil servant in Berlin. He also wrote a doctoral dissertation at the University of Berlin on the idea of the state in German social democracy in which he expressed lifelong Marxist and democratic convictions. From 1920 to 1930 he was the political editor of the *Schwäbischen Tagwacht,* a Social Democratic Party newspaper published in Stuttgart.[153] From May 1924 to January 1931, Schumacher was a member of the Social Democratic fraction in the Würtemberg state parliament. In this period, though he regarded both the Nazis and the Communists as threats to the Weimar Republic, he stressed that the main threat came from the radical right.

Schumacher was elected to the Reichstag in 1928 and remained there until 1932. His only speech in the parliament was delivered on February 23, 1932, in response to Joseph Goebbels's denunciation of the Social Democrats as a "party of deserters." Schumacher responded scathingly that it would take the German people "decades" to recover from the moral and intellectual wounds inflicted by the Nazis' political discourse.

> The whole of National Socialist agitation is a continuous appeal to the inner swine in human beings . . . If there is something specific to

recognize about National Socialism, it is the fact that for the first time in German politics it has succeeded in bringing about the ceaseless mobilization of human stupidity . . . Finally I say to the National Socialists: You can say what you want [about the Social Democrats], but you will never match the level of contempt which we have for you.[154]

As a result of this denunciation, Schumacher became a national political figure and earned the Nazis' hatred. Despite his deep skepticism about the Communists, Schumacher did not rule out a political coalition with them to stop the Nazis. In Stuttgart on February 1, 1933, the day after Hitler became German chancellor, Schumacher appealed for a common front with the Communists against the Nazis. "In the hour of danger," he said, "we turn to the Communist workers because now class struggle, not fratricide, is essential. Today, even the most embittered members of the KPD must have understood that the much scoffed at freedom, democracy, and social measures must be defended. The new era of the struggle against fascism should also introduce a new relationship between us and the Communists."[155]

After January 30, 1933, Schumacher briefly hoped that Nazi repression would lead to popular revolt. Instead the KPD was banned, and by late March, Schumacher himself was living a quasi-underground existence. Because he felt that he could not abandon his party comrades, he decided not to flee abroad. In the short period in the spring of 1933 before he was arrested, Schumacher contributed to SPD anti-Nazi pamphlets published by the party leadership active in Prague. In "Revolution against Hitler" he wrote that because "fascism must lead to national disaster for Germany and would lead its people and country to catastrophe, overthrowing the regime was the highest duty for the sake of saving the people and their country."[156] The national interests of the Germans were in conflict with the Nazi regime, he declared, while social democracy and an antifascist revolution were in accord with the interests of the nation. Even in this moment of revolutionary appeal, Schumacher took the Communists to task for preventing the unity of the working class and thus weakening the battle against Hitler. He warned of their dictatorial inclinations: "It cannot be the goal of the great struggle for freedom against the fascist state to replace a fascist labor prison with a bolshevik one."[157] Opposition to a dictatorship, whether of a Nazi or Communist variety, remained an enduring political conviction. Schumacher came to define what postwar Germans called a "militant democrat" of the democratic left, that is, someone who advocated an "antitotalitarian consensus" against both the antidemocratic right and the antidemocratic left.

Schumacher suffered greatly as a result of his outspoken attacks on the Nazis. He was arrested in Stuttgart on July 6, 1933, and imprisoned in the Nazi concentration camps in Heuberg and Kuhberg before being sent to Dachau in July 1935. He was held there until March 1943, when, as a result of his declining health and appeals from abroad, he was released.[158] Going to live with his sister in Hannover, he recovered his health and refrained from political activity. Although he did not participate in planning the July 20, 1944, conspiracy, the Nazis arrested him again and placed him in the concentration camp in Neuengamme near Hamburg. After he was released in April 1945, he kept a low profile, and with the help of the American military, which liberated Hannover on April 10, he survived the remaining weeks before the final defeat of Nazi Germany.[159]

On May 6, two days before the Nazi surrender, Schumacher delivered a speech to the members of the Hannover Social Democratic Party. "We Do Not Despair!" was the first document of the political culture of postwar Germany.[160] Schumacher dealt extensively with the place of Nazism in German history and the prospects for a renewal of German society, politics, and culture. He focused on the history of "German imperialism" in the 1870s, when the idea of right and humanity gave way to "blind faith in the exclusive determining role of violence." He made invidious comparisons between imperial Germany on the one hand and the colonial powers of France and England on the other. In its inclination to war, "German practice . . . was more brutal . . . than that of the propertied fanatics of any other country."[161] Although democratic socialists could not "befriend any kind of imperialism," and Germany had not been the only imperialist state before 1914, he placed primary blame for World War I on Germany, and exclusive blame for "the war of annihilation that is now coming to an end" on "the Nazis and the economic powers standing behind them." German imperialism, he said, was distinguished "from all other parallel phenomena in the world" in that "from the beginning it proceeded with the most brutal threats and with an aggressive stance toward everyone."[162] He linked aggression in foreign affairs with the domestic alliance of iron and rye, that is, heavy industry and "the forces of Prussian-German militarism" rooted in the agrarian landowners. From this domestic alliance there had emerged a "threatening and malicious cultural and intellectual outlook" consisting of intense nationalism and anti-Semitism. The Nazis continued and deepened these trends until they led to catastrophe.[163] Nazism was thus one possible outcome of his version of a German *Sonderweg*, a special path that distinguished Germany from the other major Western capitalist nations.

Schumacher also said that the German people were more "intellectually and culturally defenseless" in the debate over a militarist foreign policy than were other peoples. Whereas these others—that is, the Americans, the British, and the French—had conducted "successful struggles" for political freedom, German history had remained "a history of princes, the military, and governments." He recalled the defeat of liberalism in 1848 and of Social Democracy in the years preceding World War I, the diffusion of nationalism to the middle and lower classes, and the link between foreign expansion and opposition to democratization at home. While capitalism and democracy had coexisted in the "Anglo-Saxon democracies and in Western Europe," democracy in Germany had a different "class and political significance."[164] Yet imperialism had found a mass basis of support among farmers and the peasantry, the old and new middle classes, small factory owners, white-collar workers in trade and industry, and the civil service, all of whom opposed the aspirations of the German working class.

Although Nazism had succeeded in gaining broad support among the Germans, Schumacher rejected its revolutionary and socialist claims.[165] He viewed Hitler and the Nazis with moral and intellectual contempt. Servants of the propertied classes, they had "no independent ideas" of their own or any coherent program. Because of their ignorance and "illogic," it was impossible to conduct any kind of "intellectual debate" or argument with them.[166] Schumacher also underestimated the impact of Nazi ideology. Inclined to debunk Nazi ideology as a mask for economic interests, he declared that "unlimited greed" was the real reason behind talk about a new "natural law of the blood." Nonetheless, while he noted the persecution of the Jews, he did not place racial ideology at the center of his analysis, nor did he fully understand its significance for the Nazi leadership.[167]

Schumacher held heavy industry, armaments makers, militarists, feudal remnants, and the upper classes in general responsible for Nazism and its crimes. The role of German capitalists in the Nazis' rise to power was indicative for him of their moral failure and miserable political judgment. This past rendered them unfit for future political leadership.[168] Although "we socialists," he said, had warned the German people "before 1933 in all clarity and urgency . . . out of short-sightedness and lack of political imagination, the people did not take these warnings seriously enough."[169] Yet foreign countries, too, had failed to heed the German Social Democrats' early warnings about Hitler.[170] The old German elites were, in his view, discredited by their support for Nazism. Hence, the Social Democrats should be the rightful postwar leaders of Germany because their judgments about the Nazis had been politically and morally correct from the outset.

Schumacher rejected the idea of a collective guilt of the German people. In the chorus of voices speaking of "the guilt of the German people," he discerned previous supporters of German militarism. Their admissions of guilt were welcome, he said, assuming that they spoke "for themselves and their circles" and did not "extend guilt to people and currents which had always been deadly enemies of the Nazis. When these militarists speak of the guilt of the whole German people, then we are beginning with the big lie and are dishonorably hiding behind a broad skirt."[171] For Schumacher, rejecting the idea of collective guilt and apportioning individual responsibility were requirements of both justice and future democratization.

Schumacher, however, did not inflate the extent of anti-Nazi resistance. The Nazi dictatorship had brought about moral decline among many Germans. The assertions of Nazi followers or supporters who, when confronted with the full horror of the regime's crimes, said that they had not known about such things had "no moral and political value," argued Schumacher. "It may be that they didn't know everything, but they knew enough . . . Above all, they saw with their own eyes with what common bestiality the Nazis tortured, robbed, and hunted the Jews. Not only did they remain silent, but they would have preferred that Germany had won the Second World War, thus guaranteeing them peace and quiet and also a small profit."[172] This "comfortable egoism" would have been guilt enough. But the Germans' "real guilt" was above all political.

> *The shared guilt of large parts of the people in the Nazis' bloody rule lay in their belief in dictatorship and violence.* This guilt cannot be expunged. It must be diminished through an honest insight that an uncontrolled and uncontrollable regime in Germany must never again be permitted. *Because the Germans allowed themselves to lose control over their own government, now others control us today. This political insight is the precondition for a spiritual-intellectual and moral repentance and change.*[173]

For Schumacher, coming to terms with the Nazi past meant, first of all, preventing any new German dictatorship from emerging. Whereas the Communists returned willing to impose a dictatorship on a dangerous people, and Adenauer sought democracy with limited discussion of the painful past, Schumacher argued that postwar democracy should emerge from extended discussion of that difficult past. His hope lay in the revival of German social democracy. Certainly compared to their predecessors of 1918, the victors had lost faith in "the indigenous abilities of the German people for political renewal." Yet in spite of this dire situation, "we cannot and we do not want to succumb to despair. We will put all our energy toward a new life with a new content."[174] He thus offered an interpretation of the past, a guide to the future, and a moral claim to leadership of a new democracy. As he put it in 1945, "Facts and actions group themselves around the great political ideas.

These ideas and their bearers are there!"[175] In his view, the restoration and renewal of intact traditions such as social democracy offered a basis for a democratic future.

Schumacher's criticism of the Communists did not signal an end to his criticism of capitalism. "The last seventy years of German history" had made clear that it was the "class struggle of German large propertied interests which had brought disaster to the world . . . *The fundamental transformation of the political mentality in Germany is possible only on the basis of the transformation of the economic relations of power.*"[176] "Bitter experience" had demonstrated that in Germany, democracy was possible only after "certain socialist preconditions had been fulfilled." A democratic Germany should also be a socialist Germany. Although he called for deep changes in German society and economics, Kurt Schumacher was also an agent of restoration, that is, of the continuity of the Social Democratic tradition after 1945 with its antecedents from Weimar and the anti-Nazi resistance.

In the summer of 1945, Schumacher offered guidelines for Social Democrats in dealing with other political parties. He placed the "class character of Nazism" at the center of his confrontation with the past. Hence, coming to terms with the Nazi past meant creating a Germany that combined socialism and democracy.[177] In his view, both dictatorship and capitalism had been discredited by the Nazi era. In July he criticized the "dangerous reactionary thesis of the guilt of the whole German people for fascism and war." Memories of the dictatorship just ended led him to urge the Western powers to pay close attention to developments in the Soviet zone of occupation. He appealed to the victors of 1945 to avoid "the cardinal error of 1918" and not to treat German democrats as "a guilty enemy."[178] Even in the face of Nazi crimes, the Germans should not be asked to give up their "right to national self-determination" or to accept the division of the country.

Change in the economy was a necessary but not sufficient basis for democracy. The state bureaucracy also had to be transformed. Its historic claim of "objectivity" beyond class conflicts was a "more or less conscious deception of those without judgment." Claims of expertise must not be permitted to rescue elites either in the economy or in the civil service, for in both there remained "a large part of the forces which helped put Nazism in the saddle and thus in the deepest sense of the word are guiltier than their instruments."[179] The bitterness of the Nazi years were evident in Schumacher's low opinion of the bourgeois parties and the churches. The former were all "burdened with a more or less strong entanglement with Nazism." Although the churches had had their martyrs in the struggle against Nazism, their protests had primarily arisen from Nazi attacks against them rather than political attacks against others. He viewed German liberalism as nothing but a combination of opportunism and economic interest, and he regarded German farmers as hostile to democracy. As Schumacher put it, democracy in postwar Germany was no stronger than the Social Democratic Party itself.

Nor was Nazism simply a thing of the past. Great political danger lay in the millions from among the lower middle classes and unemployed workers who had come of age during the Nazi era, joined the NSDAP, and were now without work, as well as from the possessing classes and the military of the Nazi era. For Schumacher, the belated opposition to Hitler among some in the military, industry, and landed classes could not make up for the crimes which these same circles had committed or helped to bring about. Far too much was being made of their participation in the July 1944 revolt. The tensions within the officer corps had erupted only when the Nazi Party tried to take over the military.

> Before then, the officers of July 20, 1944, did not protest against Hitler's policies, against the concentration camps, the pogrom against the Jews, the demoralization and bestialization of the German nation, or against the barbaric conduct of the war. It was only the fear of being pushed into the background in their own military sector that mobilized them.
>
> Fundamentally, the revolt of July 20 did not emerge among its reactionary participants from any feeling of responsibility toward the German people or the world. It was concern over the fate of their own class and its property which drove these people to make the effort to intervene and thus to save their property and their social position.
>
> It was the same concern that drove the generals to come together

in the Bund Freies Deutschland at the end of 1942 in Moscow. All the talk about democracy and freedom is empty opportunism.[180]

Schumacher remembered those who had fought Nazism from the outset, even when it was at the height of success, as opposed to those who had turned against it only when it was no longer the wave of the future.

Schumacher's memories of the end of Weimar deeply influenced his decision to reject a postwar popular front with the Communists. In objecting to the scale of Russian reparation demands he said, "We want to deliver reparations . . . but we do not want to commit suicide . . . One cannot excuse the injustice of today by pointing to past injustice . . . The Nazi policy of plunder must not be a model for the policy of the United Nations."[181] He did not believe that the Communists had become democrats, nor did he accept their analysis of the Nazi era as presented in the "Aufruf" of June 1945. The Communists were "the only party in Germany which confesses the guilt of the whole German people for Nazism and thus for the war. This thesis, which declares every Nazi and every capitalist guilty in order offer them an excuse . . . is a thoroughly reactionary formula which hinders the political emergence of a new, purged German people."[182] It was the result, he continued of a "naive propaganda of contrition," the primary purpose of which was justification of Russian reparation demands. He was not impressed with the Communists' admission of guilt in the public appeal of spring 1945. Their only real regret, he believed, was that their methods before 1933 had not been more successful. He argued that the "Aufruf"

> does not contain a genuine admission of guilt, one which would encourage all of the other enemies of Nazism to examine their own policies in a self-critical manner. A genuine admission of guilt on the part of the Communists could only consist in admitting to the German public their own great guilt in the coming to power of fascism. This guilt lay in their struggle against democracy, in their talk of "social fascists," in their declaration that social democracy was the primary enemy, in their doctrine that in Germany it was only through

fascist rule that an "objective revolutionary situation" could emerge. But [the "Aufruf"] does not contain a syllable about any of this.[183]

Schumacher said publicly what Wilhelm Pieck and Georgi Dimitrov had admitted behind closed doors in Comintern meetings in Moscow in 1935. Perhaps if the Communists in East Berlin in the months following the end of the war had spoken as honestly to others in public as they had to one another in private, Schumacher would have been more willing to accept the seriousness of their admissions of past error. Their refusal to do so and his memory of Communist antifascism in Weimar had an enduring impact on postwar politics. His knowledge of Communist policies in the past nourished skepticism about postwar Communist united front tactics. As he put it in February 1946, "The idea and practice of every dictatorship collapsed with the [collapse of] the Nazi dictatorship."[184] For Schumacher, memories of one dictatorship, far from justifying a new one, should act as an antidote to it.

In his speeches at the First National Party Congress of the SPD held near Hannover May 9–11, 1946, Schumacher repeatedly drew the attention of the delegates to the Nazi past.

Our first thoughts concern the dead. The victims of fascism among our own people. The dead from the freedom struggles of oppressed peoples. The army of millions of victims of the war of all nations. The women and children who were swept away by bombs, hunger, and illness. The Jews, who fell victim to the bestial racial madness of the Hitler dictatorship. All who, without regard to nation or race, who lost their life in struggle against dictatorship, oppression, and the mad illusion of domination.[185]

Schumacher recalled the Social Democrats killed in fighting the Nazis.

The victims are not forgotten. We will erect a memorial to those who died in the German freedom struggle, those who gave their blood for the existence of an "other" and better Germany. They will live on in our hearts, in our thoughts, and in our work.

Every one of our comrades who, in these dark and difficult years, fell on our side lives on in us. Whether hanged "for high treason," tortured to death as a "dangerous Marxist," shot while fleeing as a "weakling," or beaten down from behind as a "traitor," every one stands before our spiritual eyes and our conscience as an individual and fighter, as warning and appeal to the living.[186]

When, he continued, the history of this period is written, "the names of our dead will be mentioned" and the "great moral idea" of the movement, namely, that "personality not rank matters," will be recalled. The legacy of those who gave their lives to defeat Nazism was "struggle and work" to make "the idea of freedom, human dignity, justice, and peace become reality."[187]

For Schumacher, the postwar SPD bore not only the burden but also the opportunity to ensure that the fallen heroes of the anti-Nazi resistance had not died in vain. In these early days Schumacher's view of better days ahead was driven more by the memory of the dead than by visions of a happy future. Social democracy had emerged from the war's ruins intact but shorn of the Marxist-inspired evolutionary optimism with which its proponents had entered World War I in 1914. For the first time in its history, a tragic sensibility and memories of past disasters now became driving forces of Social Democratic engagement.

In his major speech to the First Party Congress, Schumacher remembered who had first opposed Nazism, and who had jumped on the anti-Nazi bandwagon only after the tide had turned against the regime. Aware of opportunism and cynicism in Germany, he warned that the German people "have not yet reached the stage of self-reflection"; they "regret more that they lost the war than that the war was possible and [had] begun" in the first place.[188] He continued, "Today in Germany democracy is no stronger than the Social Democratic Party. All of the others needed the war potential and supremacy of the Anglo-Saxon powers for their hearts to discover democracy. We did not need them for that. We would be democrats if the English and Americans had been fascists."[189] He attacked the "new nationalism" of the SED and said that its blend of socialism and nationalism appeared to be "a dangerous model of Nazism." Whether one called the result "National Socialism or national communism, the end result was the same." For "twenty-

eight years" the German Communists had been making mistaken political judgments, and they remained "true to this beautiful tradition"
of doing everything wrong.[190] Faced with possessing classes compromised by their involvement during the Nazi era and a Communist
movement still hostile to democracy, Schumacher argued that "the
Social Democratic Party will be the decisive factor in Germany, or
Germany will be an abyss and Europe will become a herd of decay and
unrest."[191] Schumacher concluded the SPD congress by recalling that
"in all the years of the transformation of the German people into evil
and in the period of the Hitler dictatorship, there was always an "other"
Germany composed of men and women who made every sacrifice to
bring the Third Reich to an end.[192] In his view, this "other Germany"
was synonymous with the Social Democratic Party.

Although his Marxism led him to deemphasize the causal significance
of Nazi ideology, Schumacher was the first of the postwar German
leaders to stress the issue of the destruction of European Jewry. In an
internal statement to the SPD's party executive on January 11, 1947, he
regretted that many Germans "still lived in [a] world of illusions" and
tried to "repress their share of the historical guilt."[193] Guilt and atonement were "realities . . . [F]inally [*endlich*] the fundamental inner reflection and change of heart must be made apparent." He spoke of the
"basic stupidity" of those who "would like to ignore the whole Jewish
complex." But the blame for avoiding a "fuller discussion was not the
Germans' alone." He criticized the Allies as well, for they had made "a
great debate and discussion" of the entire Jewish issue] "impossible."[194]
While Adenauer was saying that it was "finally" time to leave in peace
Nazi Party members who had committed no crimes, Schumacher
stressed that postwar Germans must "finally" address the issue of the
Jewish catastrophe. In this early period Schumacher alone among the
leading political figures in the Western zones raised the issue that many
Germans wished would go away. Speaking to German youth in a spirit
of friendship and comradeship, he declared, "must not mean that from
the beginning they must receive the absolution of forgetting. To be
young in this instance does not mean complete absence of guilt but also
[includes] the possibility of a better understanding and pardon." Those

young people who wished to avoid such a debate "are a danger for the future."[195]

Schumacher's public statements regarding the persecution of the Jews were all the more remarkable because that persecution had eliminated any tactical necessity to raise the issue: there were practically no Jewish voters anymore. He was nonetheless the first national politician in postwar Germany to address specifically the concerns of Jewish survivors. In a February 1947 interview with Karl Marx, editor of the *Judisches Gemeindeblatt* for the British zone, a journal that would become the *Wochenzeitung der Juden in Deutschland* (Weekly Newspaper of the Jews in Germany), Schumacher admitted that the Germans had not yet faced the full dimensions of the Jewish catastrophe.[196] The postwar process of "moral purification" had been delayed and diverted by the hunger, cold, suffering, and concerns for sheer survival afflicting the Germans. All of these problems were compounded by the expulsion of millions of Germans from their previous homes in Central and Eastern Europe after the war. Although the "suffering of one's own people" took precedence for many postwar Germans over the suffering which the Third Reich had inflicted on others, Schumacher insisted that many Germans "seriously regretted the [Nazis'] crimes against the Jews and against humanity."[197]

He promised that the SPD would fight against anti-Semitism in postwar Germany, and would offer full support for Jewish claims for restitution. He said, "Those persecuted on political and racial grounds can count on the support of the SPD in the question of a just restitution," which should be a consistent policy in all of the occupation zones.[198] He believed that it was in the best interest of Jews who had emigrated as well as the Germans that a "common life together in all areas" should develop, and that through this "symbiosis" the perception that postwar Germany was synonymous with Nazi Germany would be eroded. Jews and Germans before the rise of Hitler had formed a "unity." Freedom and justice for every German citizen, regardless of race and religious convictions, was "an indispensable precondition for Germany's revival, and for its integration into the world."[199] Marx observed that Schumacher, "like us, had suffered for twelve years . . . [W]e know that we can trust him and his politics."[200]

Solidarity between Jewish survivors and the Social Democratic Party would remain an enduring feature of West German politics over the next several decades. In a speech to the Second Party Congress of the SPD in Nuremberg on June 29, 1947, Schumacher became the first of Germany's postwar political leaders publicly to support German restitution *(Wiedergutmachung)* payments to Jewish survivors.

> Comrades, we are astounded to see that today the part of humanity which was most persecuted by the Third Reich receives so little help and understanding from the world outside. I don't want to talk about us, the political fighters against the Third Reich. Rather let's talk for once about the part of humanity which as a result of the frightfulness of the blows which it actually received had to become the symbol of all of the suffering. Let us talk for once about the Jews in Germany and the world.[201]

Schumacher regretted that the Allies had not yet agreed on a uniform policy regarding restitution to Jewish survivors. Hence it was "the task of the Social Democratic Party in Germany to speak out and to state that the Third Reich made the attempt to exterminate Jewish life in Europe. *The German people are obligated to make restitution and compensation.*" The SPD supported punishing those who had participated in the persecution, banning all anti-Semitic propaganda, and guaranteeing human rights in Germany. The SPD had been "the most active fighter against racial madness" in Germany. Now it ought to be even more decisive in that effort. The party, he said, "stands and falls with the idea of the equality" of all human beings.[202] The logical extension of this principle was to support restitution for those who had suffered most from its violation. Regrettably, largely owing to Adenauer's central decision-making role in the restitution issue in the early 1950s, the early and enduring postwar solidarity with the Jews offered by Schumacher and the Social Democrats faded from the public awareness.[203]

In the same speech, Schumacher attacked "Communist totalitarianism." His opposition to the Communists shattered their hopes of monopolizing the postwar terrain of anti-fascism. Adenauer's conservative anticommunism was easy for the Communists to dismiss. Schumacher's challenge from the democratic left was far more serious precisely because he was intent on facing up to the Nazi past and because he was critical of postwar capitalism. For Schumacher, anticommunism had nothing to do with avoiding or forgetting Nazi crimes. On the contrary, while the Communists claimed to be Nazism's polar opposite, Schumacher stressed their shared dictatorial bent. Totalitarianism, he said, had made the Germans "weaker and poorer in spirit and ethics but not so weak that they were unable to recognize that what is going on today [is] the same thing that went on for twelve years [of the Nazi regime]."[204] He did not criticize Ulbricht in order to forget Hitler. Rather, principled opposition to the Nazi regime implied rejection of any other form of dictatorship. Finally, he attacked the blend of nationalism and communism that reigned in East Berlin. The Communists, he said, were "speaking the same language as the Third Reich, the Kaiser Reich, and Bismarck's Reich." The Social Democrats, by contrast, rejected nationalism, whether the "neonationalism of the Communists or the old nationalism of the propertied classes."[205]

Schumacher's speech in Nuremberg was one of the formative statements of the "anti-totalitarian consensus" in West Germany. In the same text he recalled the Jewish catastrophe, supported restitution, proudly reasserted his socialist convictions, and denounced totalitarianism in both the Nazi past and the Communist present. His criticism of the emerging dictatorship in East Berlin drew on remembering, not forgetting, the Nazi regime.

After the war Schumacher was eager to overcome the hatred and mistrust of the Germans left by the Nazi era, and to restore Social Democratic links to political allies elsewhere. In September 1947 he became the first nationally prominent postwar German political leader to visit the United States. He did so at the invitation of the Jewish Labor Committee and the American Federation of Labor.[206] This early visit gave evidence of the unbroken solidarity between émigré Social Democrats and American Jewish labor leaders which had emerged during World War II. For the Social Democrats, no less than the Communists, the Nazi seizure of power had led to repression, arrest, death, escape, and political emigration. As political émigrés, the German Social Democrats fled first to Paris and Prague, then to Stockholm, Ankara, London, and New York.[207]

The Jewish Labor Committee (JLC) had been formed in 1934 in New York as an umbrella anti-Nazi organization of mostly East European Jewish trade unionists. In 1940–41 the JLC, by lobbying officials in the State Department and appealing directly to President Roosevelt, was able to gain emergency visas for German and Austrian Social Democrats then living in France.[208] As a result of these efforts, the State Department issued over 800 visas that led to the rescue of over 1,500 people, including prominent Socialist and labor leaders from Germany, Austria, France, Belgium, Russia, and Eastern Europe.[209] Those Germans whom the JLC helped to escape included Hans Vogel, chairman of the party executive in exile; Erich Ollenhauer, later chairman of the SPD in West Germany; Friedrich Stampfer, a former SPD member of the Reichstag; and Fritz Heine, who went on to become a founding member of the postwar SPD.[210] The JLC also lent financial support to Social Democratic émigrés. In contrast to the story of broken solidarity that would unfold in East Berlin, these acts of wartime assistance were reciprocated with continued postwar cooperation between West German Social Democrats and American labor leaders, including Jewish labor leaders.

Schumacher's first trips abroad were to the sites of the Social Democratic emigration, London and Stockholm. His third was to the United States. Schumacher's American trip took place between September 21 and October 30, 1947. Rudolf Katz (1895–1961) had been a leading Social Democratic exile in wartime New York, where he edited *Die Neue Volkszeitung,* the Social Democratic paper aimed at the German émigré community. In the 1950s he became a member of the Supreme Court of West Germany. In December 1946, following a meeting with Schumacher and other members of the SPD executive committee in Hannover, he wrote to Jay Lovestone, director of the international department of the American Federation of Labor, about the possibility of a trip by Schumacher to the United States. Now that Schumacher had visited England and Sweden, Katz wrote, it seemed "very appropriate that he should also and as soon as possible visit friends of the German Social Democratic movement in the U.S.A. In my opinion, the *Jewish Labor Committee* should invite him openly and procure the necessary travel permits." Katz suggested that perhaps the AFL or the International Ladies Garment Workers Union (ILGWU) might also participate and asked Lovestone to "take this matter up with Brothers [Adolph] Held and [David] Dubinsky." If and when a new German government was formed, Schumacher was sure to be "a very important government member. Special problems regarding German labor, the Jewish problems, the Jewish refugees and the Jewish reparations question could be openly discussed with him in the U.S.A. As a good Socialdemocrat he is, in his convictions, an outspoken internationally-minded man and has a very pro-Jewish mind."[211] Katz understood both that the JLC was well placed to initiate contact between the postwar leader of German social democracy and the American labor movement, and that Schumacher's "pro-Jewish mind" was crucial in renewing such contacts. Schumacher also understood that his views on matters of concern to Jews were essential to breaking through what he described as "a wall of silence" which surrounded the SPD's party program and stood in the way of its broader understanding and recognition of these issues.[212]

Schumacher's trip demonstrated that the wartime solidarity forged between American Jews and émigré German Social Democrats was continuing into the postwar era. For the Social Democrats, New York played a role similar to Mexico City's for the exile Communists. It was there that the fullest debate and interaction between German political émigrés, Jewish émigrés, and American Jews took place.[213] In a letter of July 17, 1947, to Adolph Held, a leading figure in the Jewish Labor Committee, Schumacher expressed his appreciation for the understanding which the JLC had shown toward German Social Democrats. "We know today," he wrote, how in "word and deed" the Jewish Labor Committee had stood by the German anti-Nazi underground and German Social Democratic exiles. He praised the "great rescue action which was primarily guided by the Jewish Labor Committee" following the German invasion of France in the 1940s, and noted that leading figures of the SPD executive committee owed their survival to this action. Schumacher asked Held to "give my best greetings to David Dubinsky as well as all of the friends and colleagues in the Jewish Labor Committee and in the American trade union movement."[214] In contrast to the suppression of Merker and Zuckermann in postwar East Berlin, the bonds of solidarity which had deepened in New York in the 1930s and 1940s persisted in the ideas and policies of the West German Social Democrats after 1945.

In a report to Erich Ollenhauer on the first week of his American trip in late September 1947, Schumacher recounted his meetings with American trade unionists and German émigrés and spoke of the "great importance" of his meeting in New York with members of the JLC, including Held and Abraham Cahan, the editor of the *Jewish Daily Forward.* "The critical discussion and questioning went to the heart of the matter, and in both a human and political sense were conducted in a very noble and insightful spirit."[215] Leaders of the Jewish Labor Committee had told him bluntly that "6 million dead stand between a Jewish and a German socialist." Thousands of Germans had directly participated in mass murder. Hundreds of thousands had known about Auschwitz and other death camps. Millions of Germans had marched through Poland as it was "turned into a German national slaughter-house." Yet "nothing from a half-century of Social Democratic rebellion was to be seen." There had been resistance in occupied countries but not in Germany. The Jews had rebelled. But "where were the Social Democrats?" the JLC wanted to know. Furthermore, since the end of the war they had seen no evidence of a German change of heart. Anti-Semitism was again apparent. "Didn't this mean that Hitler's spirit was still dominant in Germany?" they had asked. Schumacher replied that the German Social Democrats felt a burden of guilt for the German people. They were demanding the harshest punishment for those who were guilty of crimes against the Jews, favored making anti-Semitism a serious crime, and had distributed much literature denouncing anti-Semitism.[216] The JLC leaders responded favorably to Schumacher. Cahan said that he "represents for us the best type of humanity."[217]

In speaking to the JLC leaders, Schumacher stressed the deep bonds between democratic socialists in Germany and in the United States. He pointed to their shared opposition to both the Nazis and the Communists, and warned of the dangers of postwar anti-Semitism in Germany and Europe. He proposed that reparations should be allocated "according to the extent and depth of the misery which the Third Reich inflicted. I believe that if anyone in the world has a claim to reparations, then it would be as a result of the tragic evil which was inflicted on the Jewish people. The whole German people, those who are innocent and those who are guilty, have an obligation [to make] reparations to the Jews."[218] He warned of the revival of a new anti-Semitism in any form of postwar German nationalism. He stressed that a democratic and socialist movement in Germany must be animated by the spirit of equality of all people, and he appealed to the Americans to support those goals in Germany. In an interview with the German-Jewish newspaper *Aufbau* in New York, Schumacher discussed what the Germans had known about the persecution of the Jews ("certainly a lot but by no means everything"), the conflict between democracy and anti-Semitism, the far harsher treatment given to Jewish as opposed to political prisoners which he had witnessed as a concentration camp prisoner, and the nature and depth of anti-Semitism in post-1945 Germany.[219] Schumacher's meetings with the Jewish trade unionists in New York City left behind a legacy of lasting solidarity, respect, and support.

On October 14 in San Francisco, Schumacher addressed the national convention of the American Federation of Labor. He received what a report in *Justice,* the ILGWU's newspaper, called a "stormy ovation." He spoke in German, then waited as George Meany, the secretary of the AFL, followed him section by section with an English translation.[220] Schumacher appealed to an audience that shared his opposition to the Communists. He said, "The great question of our time, whether we in Europe will reach an era of freedom or sink into a system of slave labor, remains unanswered."[221] He gratefully recalled the support the German

Social Democrats had received from the AFL in the postwar years, especially in view of the "enormous means" of the Communist apparatus and "their unlimited use." Support for the "freedom-oriented forces within the German labor movement" was a precondition for "success in the battle against Communist *Gleichschaltung* [dictatorial coordination] of Germany and Europe." After describing the material suffering and deprivation in postwar Germany, he noted that there still was no German state capable of uttering a

> clarifying word about the disgraceful and barbaric excesses of the Third Reich. Therefore, the German Social Democratic Party declares that *the German people have the duty of making reparations to and compensating the Jewish people*. The Social Democrats demand the punishment of all those who participated in the persecutions of the Jewish people or acquired wealth as a result of those persecutions. The Social Democrats are for the prohibition of all anti-Semitic propaganda and activities, for the establishment of all rights which had been denied, for the preservation of human rights, and for an international guarantee for the Jews. Social democracy opposes racist anti-Semitism with the same determination and relentlessness with which it rejects totalitarianism. With the same seriousness with which we want to ensure that the Germans should not become a second-class people with fewer rights, we fight for equality for the Jews with all of the other peoples of the earth. In this sense, the cause of Jews in a new Germany is also a German cause and a cause for equal treatment of all people.[222]

He denounced "Bolshevik totalitarianism . . . For the Germans, communism is a foreign system that serves foreign interests. We do not want a dictatorship. We have experienced totalitarianism on our own soil."[223] According to the report in the *Justice,* both Schumacher and Meany "were awarded a tumultuous applause at the finish."[224]

Schumacher's speech in San Francisco was a vintage expression of the antitotalitarian consensus of postwar social democracy. He made a principled defense of a labor movement committed to democracy in opposition to both the Nazi dictatorship of the past and the Communist dictatorship he believed was emerging in East Berlin. Schumacher's opposition to the Communists, however, did not signal a repression of the Nazi past. On the contrary, Schumacher and the Social Democrats were the most steadfast supporters in either West or East Germany of confronting Nazi crimes and accepting German responsibilities toward Jewish survivors. The Communists at the time, and subsequently leftist critics in West Germany as well, disparaged West German restitution policy as a cynical ploy of the conservative restoration. In fact, it was leaders of the democratic left, not devious capitalists, image-conscious diplomats, or unrepentant ex-Nazis, who were the first and most emphatic supporters of restitution to the Jews.

The efforts of the American labor movement and the Jewish Labor Committee to save the lives of German Social Democrats left behind an enduring bond born of both political agreement and memories of solidarity during the Nazi era. On December 5, 1946, two weeks after he was elected mayor of Hamburg, Max Brauer, one of those German Social Democrats who had escaped from Nazi-dominated Europe to New York with the help of the JLC, wrote a warm letter to Adolph Held to express

> personally and to the entire Jewish Labor Committee my special gratitude. I want to thank you for the assistance which the Jewish Labor Committee, during all the time of the Nazi dictatorship, has given to the democratic German Labor Movement in Germany and in exile, and to the German Labor Delegation in U.S.A. and to me personally likewise.
>
> I hope and trust that out of that collaboration during the times of dictatorship and war, a close and friendly cooperation will arise during the coming period of peace and reconstruction. . . .[225]

The bonds between the founding generation of Social Democrats especially but not only those who had been in exile in New York, and Jews inside and outside Germany remained a deep, enduring, and still too little appreciated feature of West German political life. In this instance, memories of past solidarity between Germans and Jews during the struggle against Nazism remained intact in postwar political culture.

Whereas Adenauer thought it best not to disturb the ghosts of the Nazi past, Schumacher opted for direct confrontation. They were both anticommunists, and if anything, Schumacher was even more emphatically so because he knew the Communists much better than Adenauer did. They were both Westernizers, though in different ways. While Adenauer was supporting the re-Christianization of German politics, Schumacher appealed to the secular legacies of the French Revolution, to British parliamentary traditions, and to an indigenous "Western" tradition of Marxism. Schumacher became famous for his geopolitical neutralism and opposition to a Western alliance. Yet if Westernization included support for liberal democracy in Germany, he was no less a "Westernizer" than Adenauer.[226] They had serious differences about how to confront the Nazi past while building a postwar democracy. A series of free elections in the Western zones ended with Adenauer's election as chancellor of the new Federal Republic in 1949. The West German electorate opted for Adenauer's emphatic support for social market capitalism, a Western alliance to contain the Soviet Union, and his tactful silence about the Nazi past rather than Schumacher's discomforting, outraged memories.

Like the rapid shift of alliances in the East, the Cold War in the West also turned attention away from the crimes of the Nazi regime. At the level of ideology, opposition to communism and the Soviet Union, for utterly different reasons, equaled opposition to an enemy which millions of Germans had grown to hate during the Nazi war against "Jewish bolshevism." Moroever, the decision to turn the Germans from enemy to ally at a time when the vast majority of participants in genocide and war crimes had yet to be brought to justice was bound to conflict with the memory of the Holocaust borne above all by Jewish survivors.[227] As the rapid establishment of a West German state called for use of expertise of some with a compromised past, the Cold War offered postwar West Germans an opportunity to drape amnesia about Nazi crimes in the cloak of an eerily familiar-sounding struggle against communism.[228] Yet these arguments capture only part of the nature of postwar anticommunism in Western Germany and leave out one of its strongest sources, namely, the anticommunist Social Democratic left. Kurt Schumacher was not the only politician of the left whose memories of the crimes of the Nazi era reinforced his opposition to postwar Communist dictatorship. Ernst Reuter (1885–1953) was in the midst of the fight with the Communists in postwar Berlin. He too drew on dark memories of the Nazi regime.

Reuter began his political career in the KPD but soon turned toward social democracy. From 1926 to 1931 he was a member of the Berlin city council, and was mayor of Magdeburg from 1931 to 1933. The Nazis arrested him, placed him a concentration camp in Magdeburg in 1933–34, and released him following pleas from Reuter's friends and supporters in England.[229] He spent the Nazi years in exile in Ankara, then returned after the war to become one of the founders of the SPD.[230] He was mayor of West Berlin from 1948 until his death in 1953. Especially because so many of Reuter's public statements focused on the East-West struggle over the city, it is important to examine what this Cold War anticommunist had to say about the lessons of the Nazi past. For, like Schumacher's, his opposition to Soviet policy was a logical progression, not a contradiction, of his opposition to the Nazi regime.

For Reuter, memory of the Nazi era and World War II included memory of the diplomatic appeasement of Nazism in the 1930s. In a speech to SPD functionaries in Berlin in 1947, Reuter rejected postwar German complaints about the Allied occupation. He recalled that in the 1930s, the Nazis had also complained about foreign interference, although the prehistory of World War II "clearly showed that because countries surrounding Germany wanted peace at any price, they anxiously avoided shaping war plans to be used against it."[231] In the first years of the Hitler regime, he continued, there was an opportunity whereby "a determined common leadership of foreign policy by the victor powers of World War I could have brought about the collapse of Hitlerism like a house of cards." The price for a military intervention in 1936, after Hitler had occupied the Rhineland, would have been small compared to the catastrophe that would have been avoided. Contrary to

Nazi propaganda of the time, there was no "devilish plan to encircle Germany. There were no plutocratic powers infused with the desire to destroy Germany. There was only the German war machine itself which had fallen into the hands of a madman," and drivers of the machinery, the German generals "who willingly placed themselves at his disposal and recognized too late where the train was going."[232] Just as there had been no international anti-German plot in the 1930s, so there was none after 1945. On the contrary, because the world had "destroyed the [Nazi] beast," said Reuter, "we must pay for what Hitler brought to us and our people." He continued:

> We owe thanks to the "Führer" for the fact that we are hungry and freezing in the ruins of this horrible city of ruins. We cannot bring the millions who fell victim to [the Nazis'] murderous madness back to life. We cannot make up for the horrors which they inflicted on all countries. But we must, whether we want to or not, atone for them. The difficult days which stand before us for some time to come are the inevitable consequence of the undeniable fact that the great majority of our people, in a case of unparalleled political shortsightedness, did not want to be aware of or know about the way the powers in the world were truly divided. Even worse, that they were unable to distinguish justice and injustice from each other. For a decade, mind-numbing propaganda gave this blood regiment the possibility of sticking it out to the bitter end. Sometimes, I don't deny it, even I think that perhaps the bitter end was necessary so that finally and once and for all it would become clear to the great mass of our people, and especially the petty bourgeoisie on which Hitlerism rested, both inflamed with chauvinism and without comprehension of the real forces in the world, what happens to a people which ceases to distinguish between right and wrong, justice and injustice, which thinks only of itself, and which never understands that it constitutes only a part of the world.[233]

It was often said, Reuter continued, that the Germans lacked a grasp of the realities of the world, found recourse in wishful thinking, were inclined to self-pity and to making unreasonable demands on others. "I cannot deny that there is a justified core to these criticisms," he said. He often thought that the Germans had still "not yet understood the dimensions of the catastrophe into which Germany has fallen."[234]

Although he understood how various victims of Nazism could be filled with hatred toward the Germans, "I do not feel justified in giving sermons about Christian love of one's fellow man to a Jewish refugee whose whole family has been killed in Hitler's gas chambers."[235] Rather, the Germans should focus on "the first precondition of our political renewal," that is, "inner moral and political renewal. No sentence is more dangerous than: 'Eating comes first, then morality.' We are hungry and freezing because we followed the erroneous doctrine which this sentence expresses."[236] The Germans must now be willing to offer reparations and restitution for the damage they had done. They must recognize that they had lost World War II and had to pay dearly for its consequences. "The more soberly we grasp this fact, the better will things be for us. The less we complain about [these burdens and responsibilities], the more will people respect us."[237] Rather than appease nationalist resentments, postwar Germans had to understand that they had no one to blame but themselves for their dire postwar circumstances. Forgetting the roots of present circumstances in the Nazi regime or trying to shift blame to the Allied victors would serve no constructive purpose. Present politics was best served by recalling that the causal sequence leading to postwar problems had begun not as nationalist demagogues suggested in 1945 but in 1933. For Reuter, memory of the Nazi past was an antidote to nationalist self-pity and a precondition for moral, political, and economic recovery.

As the mayor of Berlin, Reuter was at the center of Social Democratic opposition to the Communists. Like Schumacher's, Reuter's memories of Nazism reinforced his opposition to the Communists. As he noted in an April 1947 essay, "The totalitarian state that lies behind us can be replaced only by a free democratic regime."[238] He warned against "the adventure of a new totalitarian attempt" under Communist auspices. He was determined that, despite Soviet pressure in Berlin, the Germans would not "bend in the face of an external effort to import in new colors the old methods . . . The will for freedom and independence, not a totalitarian one-party state with its drumbeat of propaganda . . . will prevail."[239] While the Communists insisted that as "antifascists" they were the opposite of the Nazis, Reuter stressed their common dictatorial bent. Speaking to the National Conference of Mayors in Washington, D.C., in 1948, he commented on the Berlin blockade and the Allied airlift of 1948 and again linked opposition to the Nazi dictatorship to the postwar events. "Once again," he said, the Germans were faced with "a dictatorship that wants to oppress our people and is trying to break our moral and political will to resist . . . This time we must stand up for our freedom."[240] He appealed to his American counterparts to regard him as "a man who always opposed every dictatorship and who with his people will always again rise up against every dictatorship" until the goal of real freedom and peace is attained.[241] He rejected a double standard. For Reuter, failure to oppose Communist policy in postwar Berlin meant failing to remember and learn the lessons of the first German dictatorship.

At one point during the Berlin airlift, Reuter went so far as to suggest that in the course of opposition to Soviet pressure on the city, "this blemish on the German people"—that is, the burden of guilt from the Nazi past—"will be washed away." For the Berliners' opposition to Soviet policies during the blockade and airlift had indicated that "this German people had learned something" and were "beginning to become a free, truly courageous, politically mature people."[242]

When Reuter asserted that courage in the face of Soviet pressure could wash away guilt over the Nazi past, he misconstrued the effects of unrelated policies. In fact, the Cold War did give priority to anticommunism over denazification.[243] The breakdown of Allied unity, the emergence of the Cold War, and the perceived need for a loyal West German ally shifted Western, especially American, policy away from denazification to Cold War anticommunism. Social Democratic leaders such as Schumacher and Reuter combined opposition to the Communists with a desire to confront the Nazi legacy. Yet for many West German anticommunists to their right, the move toward the Cold War reinforced the political leverage of those in West Germany who preferred to forget about the Nazi past and focus on the Soviet threat.

Yet the Cold War, anticommunism, and the shift of alliances was not the primary source of repression of the memory of the Nazi past in the Western zones. The deeper dilemma lay in the expresion of popular will as manifested in democratic processes and fair and free elections whose outcome was defeat of those politicians who advocated a harder line on denazification. Daring more democracy gave voting power to citizens who vehemently opposed a public discussion of the Nazi past. Hostility toward Communism and the Soviet Union in postwar West Germany could draw on past indigenous German sentiment as well as on anger at Soviet occupation policy. The leading figures of the democratic left, Schumacher and Reuter, combined opposition to Soviet and SED policies with a continued desire for denazification. But they were exceptional in so doing. In 1949, in an extremely close election, West German voters turned instead to Adenauer, who had clearly expressed his distaste for extensive trials for crimes of the Nazi era. Along with the new president of the Federal Republic, Theodor Heuss, Adenauer now had the opportunity to define how a democratically elected German government would face the Nazi past. We next examine what they did with that opportunity, and how they grappled with the tension between memory and democracy that became apparent in the occupation era.

Theodor Heuss (right) and Nahum Goldmann (left) during the dedication ceremonies of the Bergen-Belsen memorial, November 30, 1952.
(Source: Spiegel Bilddokumentation, Hamburg)

Visit by West German Social Democratic leaders with members of the Jewish Labor Committee, April 8, 1954. Front row, left to right: Adolph Held, chairman of the Jewish Labor Committee (JLC); Carlo Schmid, leader of the Social Democrats in the Bundestag; David Dubinsky, president of the International Ladies Garment Workers Union and treasurer of the JLC. Standing, left to right: Charles Kreindler, vice president of the ILGWU; Charles S. Zimmerman, vice president of the ILGWU; Fritz Erler, SPD member of the Bundestag; Gunther Klein, SPD member of the Bundestag; Benjamin Tabachinsky, National Campaign Director, JLC. (Source: Robert F. Wagner Labor Archives, New York, Jewish Labor Committee Collection NP 48, file: International Socialists)

Kurt Schumacher addressing a political rally, Frankfurt, 1947. (Source: Archiv der sozialen Demokratie der Friedrich-Ebert-Stiftung, Bonn)

Willy Brandt at the Warsaw memorial, December 1970. (Source: Bundesbildstelle)

Konrad Adenauer speaking at a political rally of the Christian Democratic Union at the Dusseldorf tramway depot in the British occupation zone, May 12, 1946. (Source: Stiftung Bundeskanzler-Adenaueur-Haus, Rhondorf. Copyright © Carl August Stachelscheid, Dusseldorf.)

Helmut Kohl, Johannes Steinhoff, Ronald Reagan, and Matthew Ridgeway at the Bitburg ceremonies, May 5, 1985. (Source: Bundesbildstelle, Bonn)

Richard von Weizsäcker speaking in the Bundestag on May 8, 1985, on the fortieth anniversary of the end of World War II. (Source: Bundesbildstelle, Bonn)

# 8

## Atonement, Restitution, and Justice Delayed: West Germany, 1949–1963

During the founding years of the Federal Republic, the democratic left and democratic right held contrasting views of the relationship between democracy and memory. Konrad Adenauer's implicit argument was that the establishment of a functioning democracy required less memory and justice for the crimes of the Nazi era and more "integration" of those who had gone astray. Kurt Schumacher, on the whole, took the opposite view, namely, that a new democracy must be accompanied by a settling of accounts and bringing the guilty to justice in German courts. Both Adenauer and Schumacher had a bleak view of the German past. Yet Adenauer sought support from conservative voters who were, in fact, likely to be more compromised by past association with Nazism than was the case with Schumacher's electoral base. Not surprisingly, "integration" was the key word for Christian Democrats, while "justice" was just as important for leaders of the democratic left.

The democratic right and democratic left also held contrasting views of the connection between Westernization and memory. Adenauer's assessment of German history was even more bleak than Schumacher's, which was one reason why Adenauer wanted the Federal Republic firmly embedded in a Western alliance. Such an alliance would end the anti-Western *Sonderweg* and help to prevent a Nazi or nationalist revival, whereas a unified but "neutral" Germany again wandering between East and West was a sure recipe for another catastrophe for Germany and all of Europe. Schumacher, by constrast, believed that in social democracy, Germany already possessed a strong and indigenous set of Western traditions. Moreover, while Adenauer looked to a religious, Christian West to fight "atheistic communism," Schumacher's West was one of secular modernity willing to subject religious traditions, including the Christian tradition, to public criticism. Schumacher argued that the way in which Western integration was taking place under Adenauer made it possible for compromised elites of the Nazi era to regain power and respectability in the Federal Republic. The fear that Western integration came at the price of clear memory of and timely justice for Nazi crimes contributed to an enduring fissure between right and left in West German politics. By opting for Adenauer's way, West German politicians attained far less than justice and morality demanded but more than a simple electoral majority wanted, and a great deal more than their counterparts in East Berlin achieved. Even in the classic era of silence and of democratization through integration, the crimes of the Nazis found a place in early West German political narratives, though not a prominent or ubiquitous one. That place nonetheless became larger and more prominent until eventually in the 1960s the connection between memory and democracy was reversed: daring more democracy eventually came to entail more, not less, national political discussion of the Holocaust and other crimes of the Nazi era.

Although Adenauer did not frequently mention the persecution of the Jews, a focus on this aspect of Nazi persecution went hand in hand with his overall view of the need for Westernization of Germany after 1945. Whereas the antidemocratic right, including the Nazis, had associated the Jews with a despised Western modernity, Adenauer's West German conservatism embraced political as well as economic modernity and praised the contributions which the Jews had made to it. For him, the Jews were an inseparable part of "the West," of bourgeois Europe and Germany, while Nazism and "atheistic communism" represented nihilist revolts against it. One piece of evidence attesting to Adenauer's view of the Jew's self-evidently Western character lies in his postwar correspondence with the Belgian and American businessman Dannie

Heinemann, one of his oldest friends, and his closest Jewish friend. Their friendship began before World War I and continued as they cooperated on various public works projects in Cologne.

The two friends exchanged several letters beginning in July 1945 and had their first postwar reunion in the spring of 1949.[1] Heinemann had valuable contacts in American political and business circles. On May 13, 1949, in an assessment of Adenauer and other German business and political leaders, Heinemann described Adenauer as "a type who, although bitterly anti-Nazi (and who was a victim of the regime), is intensely German, and is profoundly saddened not only from his years of suffering but also by the present plight of the German people."[2] In their correspondence neither Adenauer nor Heinemann raised the issue of the present plight of the Jewish people. In a long letter of November 15, 1950, Chancellor Adenauer wrote to Heinemann to express his "serious worry" over the Soviet threat in Europe and the absence of a "will to resistance" or "insight into the danger" in Western Europe.[3] On December 14 Heinemann translated the letter and gave copies to American officials, including General Eisenhower, "who was very much impressed and asked for additional copies."[4]

Adenauer made the remarkable argument that the Western Allies' treatment of the German military and people after "the collapse" had "largely destroyed" the Germans' respect for anything having to do with the military. To counter the "defeatist mood" that followed the North Korean attack on South Korea, an Atlantic treaty must be signed, and American troops should be brought to Germany "as quickly as possible."[5] The Germans would make the sacrifices needed to defend their freedom only if they were convinced that they were free. The Allies must also display "visible and convincing" proof that "in the shortest possible time freedom will be given back to the German people." Delivery of Germans suspected of war crimes to the French for trial and punishment, justified by the primacy of the occupation authorities over German law, had created "much bad blood." The Social Democrats were having some success with their efforts to use the antimilitary mood for their own electoral purposes. "The war, National Socialism, and the treatment of all military questions since 1945 by the Western Allies in

Germany have created a very unfavorable atmosphere" for Western resistance to Soviet pressure, Adenauer told his friend.[6]

Earlier Adenauer had argued that Western occupation policies would undermine efforts at democratization. In effect he now added that memories of what the Germans had done in World War II, and Allied postwar efforts to keep those memories alive, were fostering an "unfavorable atmosphere" in Germany toward rearmament. His reference to French war crimes trials suggested that for Adenauer in 1950, freedom for Germany meant the freedom to put an end to further denazification. Dannie Heinemann did not take his old friend to task. But in a letter of March 27, 1951, to John J. McCloy, U.S. High Commissioner for Germany, he wrote that "Adenauer's intense Germanism is coupled with a limited experience of foreign countries. It may perhaps be somewhat difficult for him to realize that the people West of the Rhine are not too quickly impressed by Germany's good intentions, whatever government may be in office."[7] As Adenauer emerged from the enforced provincialism of Nazi Germany, he was forced to understand that integration into the Western alliance could not take place only or primarily on the basis of forgetting the crimes of the Nazi era. Part of the price for moral and diplomatic reintegration with the West was public acknowledgment of memories which Adenauer had earlier criticized as sources of Cold War defeatism.

The primary issues in the first national elections in the summer of 1949 were whether or not the Federal Republic would pursue a socialist or a social market economic policy, and how closely it would be tied to American policy in the Cold War. Adenauer's Christian Democrats, together with the Bavarian Christian Social Union (CSU), gained 139 seats in the Bundestag. The Free Democratic Party (FDP), led by Heuss and Thomas Dehler, gained 52 seats. The SPD, led by Schumacher, gained 131 seats, and the Communists were represented with 15 seats.[8] Although Adenauer's own anti-Nazi credentials were unassailable, a vote for him was also a vote to end denazification, trials of former Nazi officials, and purges of former members of the Nazi Party from industry and the civil service. Moreover, his coalition partner, the self-described liberal FDP, represented a judiciary and civil service determined to avoid any more denazification proceedings or trials for war crimes. As a result, the 1949 elections produced a Bundestag with a solid majority in favor of launching democracy in post-Nazi Germany without careful scrutiny of Nazi-era crimes.

On September 20, 1949, Adenauer delivered his first *Regierungserklärung,* the parliamentary equivalent of a State of the Union address.[9] Adenauer regretted that though "great progress" had been made in Germany since 1945, "Germany and the German people are not yet free" or equal to others, and were now divided.[10] He stressed his support for the career civil service. To the accompaniment of shouts of approval from the parties of the center and right, he said that denazification had brought about "much unhappiness and much harm." As he had since the spring and summer of 1946, he maintained that "those who were really guilty of crimes committed during the National Socialist period and in the war should be punished with all severity," but that the Germans should not be divided into "two classes . . . those without political blemishes and those with such blemishes [*die politisch Einwandfrei und die Nichteinwandfreien*]. This distinction must be overcome as soon as possible."[11]

He did not announce that his Justice Ministry would vigorously pursue the issue of Nazi crimes. Rather, he elicited applause from Christian Democrats and many Free Democrats by saying that his government would examine "the question of an amnesty," including amnesty for those who were awaiting punishment as a result of convictions in the Allied military courts of the occupation era.[12] He continued: "The government of the Federal Republic, in the belief that many have subjectively atoned for a guilt that was not heavy, is determined where it appears acceptable to do so to put the past behind us [*Vergangenes vergangen zu lassen*]. On the other hand, it is absolutely determined to draw the necessary lessons from the past regarding all of those who challenge the existence of our state whether they come now from right-wing radicalism or left-wing radicalism." This last statement was greeted with shouts of "Bravo!" and "Very good!"[13] Adenauer did not explain how he knew that "many" had atoned for past acts, what the practical meaning of such atonement was, or how he had determined that this guilt was "not heavy." After all, if criminals could gain amnesty merely by expressing remorse for their past acts, no one would be in prison. Like Ulbricht, Adenauer placed emphasis on *current attitudes* toward the new government rather than on *past actions*. From the collapse of Weimar, Adenauer drew the lesson that the new democracy must be on guard against radicalism of the right as well as the left, even though "left-wing radicalism"—that is, the Communist Party in West Germany—posed no serious threat to the new democracy. His warning sent a disappointing signal, especially in the context of his lack of enthusiasm for a vigorous judicial punishment of the "right-wing radicals" of the past. The primacy of "integration" over "justice" was apparent.

One of Adenauer's main themes of this and subsequent speeches was that Nazism was not returning to postwar West Germany. He "condemned anti-Semitic efforts most sharply. After all that happened in the National Socialist period, we view it as unworthy and unbelievable that there are still people in Germany who would persecute or despise the Jews because they are Jews."[14] That was all he had to say about the subject. It is odd that someone who, in 1946, had said that the roots of Nazism in Germany were deep and broad found it hard to imagine only three years later that anti-Semitism still existed in Germany. He devoted far more attention in his speech to German prisoners of war in the Soviet Union, and to the *Vertriebenen*, Germans who had been expelled from their homes in Central and Eastern Europe after 1945. He concluded with statements of determination to overcome the French-German conflicts of the past century, and with thanks for American support and assistance since the end of the war. Finally, he repeated that "our whole work will be supported with the spirit of Christian-Western culture" and the respect for individuals on which it was based.[15]

On the following day, Kurt Schumacher, now leader of the Social Democratic fraction in the Bundestag, gave the opposition's response.[16] He warned, on the one hand, of the formation of a new "authoritarian state devoted to the defense of property" in West Germany and criticized Adenauer for the paucity of his comments about workers and the equality of women. On the other hand, he attacked the Communists and promised to confront the danger to national unity that stemmed from the "national revolutionary discourse of the East."[17] Schumacher noted that Adenauer had uttered "not one word" about the anti-Nazi resistance or the victims of fascism. One could not be against Nazism "without thinking about its victims" and by establishing a hierarchy among them.[18] Specifically, one ought not, as Adenauer had done, focus on German prisoners of war, widows, and the expellees while giving short shrift to the persecution of the Jews and political opponents of the Nazi regime. Schumacher redressed this inbalance.

What was said yesterday in [Adenauer's] government statement about the Jews and the frightful tragedy of the Jews in the Third Reich was too feeble and too weak. Resigned comments and a tone of regret in this matter don't help at all. It is not only the duty of international socialists to place the fate of the German and European Jews in the forefront of attention and to offer help where it is needed. It is also the duty of every German patriot to do so. [He was interrupted at this point by applause from the SPD.] By the extermination of 6 million Jewish human beings, Hitler barbarism disgraced the German people. We will have to bear the consequences of this disgrace for the unforeseeable future. Of the 600,000 German Jews [in pre-Nazi Germany], today in the four occupation zones only 30,000, mostly old and ill, remain. And even they repeatedly experience shameful and degrading episodes. In Germany, no political current should forget that every form of nationalism has anti-Semitic effects, and that every form of anti-Semitism fosters nationalism. Such trends would bring about Germany's voluntary isolation from the world. [More agreement from the SPD.] Anti-Semitism rests on ignorance of the great contributions of German Jews to the German economy, German intellectual life, to German culture, and to the fight for German freedom and German democracy. Today the German people would be better off if these strengths of Jewish intellect and economic potential were included in the construction of a new Germany.[19]

Even at this very early point, the leader of the democratic left had spoken far more clearly than Adenauer did about the Holocaust and the moral obligations, including restitution, which it placed on postwar Germans.[20]

In light of polling data gathered by the office of the American High Commissioner of Germany (HICOG), blunt talk about the crimes of Nazism was not popular in the new Federal Republic. In November 1949 HICOG surveys found that only 30 percent of respondents rejected National Socialism outright, and 59 percent thought it had been "a good idea badly carried out." In eight nationwide surveys conducted between May 1951 and December 1952, an average of 41 percent of respondents saw more good than evil in Nazi ideas, and only 36 percent saw more evil than good. Only 4 percent thought that all Germans "bore a certain guilt for Germany's actions during the Third Reich," and only 21 percent felt "some responsibility for rectifying these wrongs."[21] In this climate, which did not point to a public suffering from an excessive burden of guilt, Schumacher's statement displayed his courage and depth of conviction.

The HICOG surveys also indicate that Adenauer expressed majority sentiment when he urged amnesty rather than trials and punishment. From 1946 to 1949, the mood in West Germany had turned against denazification, the Nuremberg Trials, and new West German trials of those accused of crimes against humanity. Betweeen 1946 and 1949, the proportion of respondents who thought the Nuremberg Trials had been unfair climbed from 6 percent to 30 percent. Furthermore, there was growing support for terminating all trials based on wartime actions. In mid-1952, only 10 percent of a national sample approved and 59 percent disapproved of the way the Western powers were handling the issue of war criminals. These respondents thought the punishments unfair or too harsh. When asked what should be done with the remaining prisoners, about half called for outright release, and the rest for legal review by Allied or German courts. Respondents viewed Nuremberg as "political," that is, as victor's justice, and were less worried that placing former Nazis in positions of power would be a threat to a new democratic state. A HICOG survey of November 1952 found that 58 percent approved unrestricted opportunities for former members of the Nazi Party. An August 1952 survey found that 42 percent even felt that

German generals whom the Allies had convicted of war crimes had experience and abilities that entitled them to hold positions in a new German army. However disillusioned with Nazism these Germans were, their primary impulse was to leave the Nazi past in the past rather than to seek justice for Nazi crimes.[22]

Several months after the Adenauer-Schumacher exchange, Karl Marx, editor of the *Allgemeine Wochenzeitung der Juden in Deutschland*, expressed a pessimistic view of the German political scene.[23] It was an illusion, he said, to believe that the Germans had become good democrats within only five years after the war. Neither hunger, currency reform, nor military occupation had brought that change about. He feared that the Western democracies after 1945 would again pursue the same "line of least resistance" they had adopted in the 1930s. A "democratic minority" in Germany was struggling against

the reviving forces of Nazism and a politically indifferent mass which has not yet arrived at a belief in democracy. The magnetism of power exerts a great influence on the mass. Every weakness or every stance of the occupying powers which is seen as weakness related to filling key positions with former National Socialists is a direct setback. One cannot and must not forget that the great majority of high-level civil servants and the overwhelming majority of judges and prosecutors are composed of former National Socialists. Therefore, a rational peace treaty concerning Germany is inconceivable without guarantees [banning] discrimination against democrats, those who fought National Socialism, and the victims of the system of violence.[24]

Marx viewed the occupying powers as crucial for "protection of the proven fighters against National Socialism in Germany." In response to the "already oft-repeated suggestions such as an amnesty for Nazi criminals," Marx asked if leaders in Washington, London, and Paris understood that implementation of such proposals would represent "abandonment of the people within Germany who truly tried to fight for democracy" and who supported the Allies' denazification measures after 1945. Amnesty would "destroy the foundations of the Nuremberg judgment" and erode the possibility of democratic renewal. It would represent a "return to the position of peace in Munich . . . to the political conceptions of 1938," that is, to the era of appeasement.[25]

Adenauer had often applied the Munich analogy to support the policy of Western integration and containment of the Soviet Union. Marx was unique, however, in applying it to Western Allied toleration of Adenauer's reluctance to carry out a purge of his own establishment. For Marx, not only had liberation come from the Allies in 1945, but also guarantees for the safety and political rights of Jews and opponents of Nazism in West Germany after 1949 depended on continued Allied occupation for an extended period of time. Outside pressure was essential if denazification was to proceed. Ironically, anticommunism and containment of the Soviet Union created a politically popular legitimation for a continued Western presence. Yet Marx's hope for a West Germany that would implement a deep purge as part of the process of Western integration remained unfulfilled.[26]

Schumacher's views on the obligations created by the Holocaust contrasted with those of the Communists as well. Whereas wartime solidarity between the Communists and the Jews was broken in the early 1950s in East Germany, it continued under West German social democracy. In November 1950 the *Jewish Daily Forward* of New York interviewed Schumacher.[27] Asked if the founding of a German army was a threat to democracy, Schumacher expressed concerns that the "current government" had neither the knowledge nor the will to oppose "interests from the circles of the former general officers and old career soldiers." In addition, his opinion of the officials of the Adenauer government was "not exactly high." The "average member of the cabinet does not think much about the Jewish question," he said, "and is generally cool and passive about it." Among these officials, practical concerns pushed a "living feeling for the dimensions of the injustice into the background." Schumacher nonetheless said that he was sure that the "necessary moral and practical engagement concerning the injustice done to the Jews was alive in Bundespräsident Heuss."[28]

Asked if the Germans were filled with remorse and a sense of atonement, Schumacher replied that the majority were aware of the dimensions of the persecution of the Jews. Postwar Germans, however, were preoccupied with daily survival, the expulsion of 13 million Germans from the East, and repression in the Soviet zone. Some were fully aware of the dimensions of the Jewish catastrophe. Others fled from such knowledge "because they feel implicated in the sins of Nazism" and hence sought to minimize the extent of the horrors. A third, small group, rejected by the overwhelming majority of Germans, remained true to old Nazi beliefs.

Schumacher was asked if it would ever be possible to overcome the deep gap between Germans and Jews. That would depend in the last analysis, he said, on the Jews to whom the injustice had been done.

> One can only and with justice point out to the Jewish people that segments of the German people fought against the Hitler regime and themselves suffered the greatest injustices, including loss of life and freedom. The precondition for appeasing and placating Jewish sensitivities is that this part of the German people has in its hands the political leadership, education, and formation of the German nation. When, however, the Jewish people see that those circles who went along with everything [in Nazi Germany] and tolerated it without inner revolt and indignation [*die alles mitgemacht und ohne innere Empörung geduldet haben*] or even circles who were more or less active in [committing] the injustice inflicted on the Jewish people have influence in Germany, then the future is very bleak and dark. The strongest of all factors in historical development is time. It is uncertain to what extent [the wounds that have been inflicted] it can heal. In any case, through their political and moral position the German people must strive to attain a slow rapprochement and meeting of hearts and minds [with Jews].[29]

Improved German-Jewish relations and hopes for genuine confrontation with the crimes of the past required that "those segments of the German people" who had fought and suffered in the fight against Nazism attain political primacy in the Federal Republic. Schumacher had often said that democracy in postwar Germany was no stronger than the Social Democratic Party. The same was true of his view of

*Vergangenheitsbewältigung:* its fate lay with the political fortunes of postwar social democracy and an uprooting of the old elites who had participated in or tolerated past crimes.

It was, he stressed, the Social Democratic Party which first and most consistently had supported "moral and material restitution" to the Jews. He also stressed how much he had appreciated the warm reception he had received from Jewish labor leaders in the United States during his visit in 1947. The deepening of ties between Germans and Jews "will always be dependent on the strength and the importance of a humane and democratic left, that is, the Social Democratic Party and the unions."[30] In Schumacher's view, the SPD, not the Communist or Christian Democratic Party, was the natural and historic home of and enduring partner for the Jews.

The issue of what to do about contacts with persons compromised by the Nazi past, though it primarily affected the right, also concerned the Social Democrats. Even Schumacher made the case for integration in the interests of stabilizing the new democracy when, in October 1951, he addressed the issue of whether SPD officials could or should have contact with former members of the Waffen-SS.[31] The SPD, he wrote, rejected any notion of collective guilt, though he had no intention of "replacing collective guilt with an equally impossible collective innocence [*Kollektivunschuld*]."[32] The 900,000 men in the Waffen-SS were not identical with the SS. The former was "intended for the war," in contrast to the SS with its special extermination units, and many young men had been forced to join against their will. By 1951, the majority of these 900,000 former SS members had acquired a pariah status and had been made collectively responsible for the crimes of the SS. It was crucial, he continued, "to open the way to life chances and citizenship to former members of the Waffen-SS . . . A compact complex of about 900,000 men without social and human prospects together with their relatives is not a good thing for a young democracy torn by tensions of class and ideas." Those without criminal guilt, he said, should be reintegrated. "The overwhelming majority" had abandoned National Socialist ideology. Yet Schumacher worried that without citizenship and employment, these young men could become a reservoir of right-wing antidemocratic sentiment. Of particular concern were organizations of 320,000 to 350,000 former members of the Waffen-SS.[33] The whole matter, he continued, was especially "depressing when one sees how the worst, intentionally cold and calculating beneficiaries of the twelve-year dictatorship today were everywhere in the state and economy, and how people want to burn the mark of Cain for all time on the young men who succumbed to such a widespread political psychosis or were forced into the Waffen-SS."[34]

Furthermore, "many Allied forces were playing an inglorious and irresponsible role" when, "without any reservations," they sought to use former members of the Waffen-SS, whether guilty of past crimes or not, for current military purposes. In a period in which "the democratic relations in Germany are still not yet clear," reducing the threat posed by embittered veterans of the Waffen-SS impelled democratic politicians to speak to them and ease their reentry into civilian society. "Fairness" thus came to mean amnesty for former members of the Waffen-SS rather than greater efforts to purge tainted elites.

Kurt Schumacher's health had been seriously damaged during his imprisonment in Dachau. He died at the age fifty-seven on August 20, 1952, depriving German democracy and the small postwar German-Jewish community of the most prominent and passionate West German advocate of a sharp political confrontation with the Nazi past. Hendrik van Dam, a leading official of the Central Council of Jews in Germany (Zentralrat der Juden in Deutschland), wrote, in a front-page article in the *Allgemeine Wochenzeitung der Juden in Deutschland,* that "with the death of Kurt Schumacher, we have lost a true friend," one who "took up the issue of the victims of National Socialism as his own. He understood their wishes and disappointments because he was a hero of the resistance and a martyr for justice."[35] Van Dam then quoted in full the passage I have quoted from Schumacher's first speech in the Bundestag and noted that such sentiments were not popular. Schumacher, he continued, had been "a man of the people, but not a slave to popularity." He was "a German statesman who was free from any guilt [yet] recognized the historical responsibility which came from the mass crimes of the Third Reich. Schumacher certainly loved his people, but out of this love he wanted to place them under a moral law before which a people of culture in history must stand."[36]

Since his trip to the United States in 1947, Schumacher had remained in touch with American labor leaders, including David Dubinsky. On August 21, 1952, Dubinsky sent a telegram to Erich Ollenhauer in Bonn stating that he was "deeply grieved at [the] death of Kurt Schumacher," and joined in "mourning this irreparable loss to human freedom and to the cause of democracy and social justice in Germany for which he fought so valiantly in his courageous struggle against Nazi terror, Communism, antisemitism and all reaction."[37]

The Communists hated Schumacher because he defeated their popular front tactics after 1945. Conservatives distrusted him because he was intent on breaking the continuity of elites after 1945. The Americans were suspicious because of his geopolitical "neutralism" in foreign policy. The German electorate did not want him, in part because he would remind them of a past which Adenauer was willing to help them forget. Yet, as Dubinsky understood, Schumacher stood out among the leading German national political figures of the postwar era in combining rejection of the Communist dictatorship with a determination to join democratization with a clear memory of Nazi crimes. By that standard, Kurt Schumacher was the preeminent moral figure among the founders of the Federal Republic. His death was indeed an irreparable loss.

The prominence of the restitution issue in the early years after the war reflected the urgent human needs of the survivors of the Holocaust as well as the narrow political limits set on facing the Nazi past in Germany. In the absence of trials and a housecleaning of compromised elites, it bore more of the weight of *Vergangenheitsbewältigung* than it could bear. It was easier for politicians to offer financial restitution than to dispense justice or purge compromised elites. Yet resistance to doing even this much was considerable. Restitution had been a prominent topic in the noncommunist emigration during the war. In the Western occupation zones after 1945, the Allies, especially the United States, supported the restitution claims of Jewish groups and of political opponents of the Nazi regime.[38] This was taking place as the division between Communists and noncommunists split the resistance organizations in the Western zones. By May 1948 the SPD no longer permitted its members to belong to the Communist-dominated VVN, a decision which deepened that domination still further. In 1950 former VVN members formed the noncommunist Bund der Verfolgten des Naziregimes (Association of Those Persecuted by the Nazi Regime), or BVN. In the same year the Adenauer government declared that members of the VVN were precluded from employment in the civil service. In East Germany, persecution of "antifascists" (i.e., the Communists) took center stage while Jewish persecution was becoming marginalized. In West Germany the restitution issue focused on persecution of the Jews and on noncommunist political opponents of the Nazi regime.[39]

It was the restitution issue that brought Adenauer to make his first public statement about the Holocaust and other crimes of the Nazi era. Those who hoped that he would use the occasion of a speech in the Bundestag on the National Day of Reflection of the German People (September 7, 1950) to address this aspect of the national story were surely disappointed. Beyond noting that "we all"—that is, the political leadership, including the opposition—were striving to lead Germany "from the deep abyss into which it fell," Adenauer said nothing at all about the Nazi era. His focus was on postwar reconstruction.[40] On March 12, 1951, the government of the state of Israel sent a note to the four occupying powers concerning the moral imperative for restitution payments from the Federal Republic and the German Democratic Republic.[41] The approximately three thousand–word statement recalled succinctly but in graphic detail the genocide of European Jewry. The Israelis wrote that though the dead could not be brought back to life or their suffering extinguished, the German people must return stolen Jewish property and give assistance to the survivors. The Israeli government called for reparations of $1.5 billion, a figure based on the cost of resettling 500,000 European emigrants in Israel.[42] A morally and legally acceptable settlement required at least this sum. "The establishment of equal status for Germany in the community of nations is unthinkable," the Israelis wrote, "as long as this fundamental measure of restitution has not been met."[43]

Neither the Soviet Union nor the government of the German Democratic Republic ever responded to the Israeli request. Adenauer's historic reply came in the Bundestag on September 27, 1951.[44] Its key passage reads:

> The government of the Federal Republic of Germany, and with it the great majority of the German people, are aware of the immeasurable suffering brought to the Jews in Germany and in the occupied territories in the era of National Socialism. In an overwhelming majority, the German people abhorred the crimes committed against the Jews and did not participate in them. During the period of National Socialism there were many Germans, acting on the basis of religious belief, the call of conscience, and shame at the disgrace of Germany's name, who at their own risk were willing to assist their Jewish fellow citizens. In the name of the German people, however, unspeakable crimes were committed which require moral and material restitution [*Wiedergutmachung*]. These crimes concern damage to individuals as well as to Jewish property whose owners are no longer alive. The first steps have been taken on this level. A great deal remains to be done. The government of the Federal Republic will support the rapid conclusion of a law regarding restitution and its just implementation. A portion of identifiable Jewish property is to be returned. Further restitution will follow.[45]

Adenauer committed the Federal Republic to discussions with Jewish representatives and the state of Israel to resolve the issue and "to ease the way to an inner purification of endless suffering," for doing so was part of the "most noble duty of the German people" in helping to revive the "spirit of true humanity."[46] Adenauer never wavered from this frank acknowledgment of the burdens and obligations of the Nazi past. The contrast with the East German and Soviet denial of any such obligation was glaring and obvious.

Yet in his remarkable early acceptance of the burdens of Nazi criminality for the successor government in West Germany, Adenauer also resorted to troubling circumlocutions. He spent more time exculpating the majority of Germans than enumerating the specifics of the crimes of the Nazi regime.[47] His use of the passive voice in referring to "suffering brought to the Jewish people" did not identify the perpetrators. The phrase "in the name of the German people" had the effect, and perhaps the intent as well, of distancing these acts from the Germans of the Nazi era. Both his acknowledgment of the burdens and obligations of the past and his effort to soften the blow to the national psyche remained enduring features of Adenauer's public discourse regarding the Nazi past.

The Social Democratic parliamentary response to Adenauer's statement was presented by Paul Löbe. Germany, he said, had "the moral obligation to place its entire energy into reconciliation with the state of Israel and with Jews in all of the world."[48] The Social Democrats supported Adenauer's statement, he said, "and would have welcomed it if it had been offered sooner, and with more decisiveness."[49] Where Adenauer had been vague about criminal responsibility, Löbe was specific: "The criminal power holders of the National Socialist rule of terror inhumanely persecuted the Jewish Germans and the Jews in Europe and murdered 6 million human beings—men, women, children, the elderly—only because of their Jewish background."[50] Whereas Adenauer had spoken of easing the path toward "inner purification," Löbe said, "We will never forget this immeasurable suffering." In addition, Löbe spoke of the Jews who, "like us, were born as Germans" and to whom "we are inseparably linked." The contributions to German history of Felix Mendelsohn, Heinrich Heine, Walter Rathenau, and numerous Nobel Prize winners were not be forgotten. "Every German," he stressed, was obligated to offer restitution for these crimes and to fight racism past and present. "Sacrifice" was required. Restitution was "the measure for the renewal of law and justice in Germany."[51] For Löbe, as for Schumacher, restitution was only part of a more comprehensive effort to address the Nazi past.

Given Adenauer's reluctance to encourage judicial activism regarding war crimes trials, restitution played a central role in defining *Vergangenheitsbewältigung.* He could reassure conservative voters that it was not the first step toward a more extensive judicial, political, and social confrontation with crimes of the Nazi era. Nevertheless, Adenauer faced considerable resistance from within his own cabinet and party. His finance minister, Fritz Schäfer, doubted the Federal Republic's ability to pay. His own CDU expanded the definition of "victims" of Nazism to include Germans who had suffered in the war. His "liberal" coalition partners in the FDP, led by Thomas Dehler, were less than enthusiastic. His minister of transportation, Hans-Christoph Seebohm, went so far as to place the moral claims of Germans forced to flee after the war on the same plane as those of the Jews.[52] Adenauer's strongest support in the restitution debates of 1951–52 came from Schumacher and other Social Democratic leaders such as Erich Ollenhauer, Carlo Schmid, and Jakob Altmeier, some moderate members of the CDU such as Franz Böhm and Eugen Gerstenmaier, and Bundespräsident Theodor Heuss.[53]

When Israeli-German negotiations over restitution began, the SPD executive expressed the hope that the talks would "prove that the entire German people recognize the right of the Jews to reparations and restitution, and that this will result in effective aid for the state of Israel as well as for the Jews who, fleeing the Nazi terror, established new homes elsewhere. We also hope that the negotiations will show the way for reconciliation between Jews and Germans."[54] The statement declared that although it was "impossible to offer compensation for the horrible misdeeds of the Hitler regime against the Jews of Germany and other countries" or to compensate fully for material damages, it was "all the more important that we give proof of our good will to the extent that our resources allow." This was "not only a material committment but a moral one as well. The SPD has always affirmed the responsibility of the Germans for the Jewish victims of the Nazi atrocities." Schumacher had stressed that "the recognition of the right of the Jews to material and moral reparations" occupied an important place in the SPD program. Hence, "every effort must be made in Germany to wipe out all signs and acts of anti-Semitism," to prevent anti-Semitic demonstrations, and to ensure that "all people whose names appear on the blacklist of those guilty of reprehensible acts under the National-Socialist regime shall be barred from public employment."[55] Without this strong support from the SPD, Adenauer would not have been able to push the restitution agreement through the Bundestag.

In May 1952 anger over Adenauer's delays in coming to an adequate restitution agreement with Israel led Franz Böhm and Otto Kuster, Adenauer's own negotiators, both members of the CDU, to resign from the German delegation. Adenauer urged Böhm to withdraw his resignation and decided to accept Böhm's terms as a basis for resuming negotiations. They were the terms that formed the basis for the Luxembourg agreement of September 10, 1952.[56] In the Bundestag and in the press, Böhm was a harsh critic of delays and denial. Later, in January 1955, he sarcastically described the West German atmosphere in which the restitution agreement was being debated.

> No one will admit his guilt for National Socialism, for the Nazi rise to power, or for the terror of the Third Reich. The German people stand by, without comprehension, unable to understand how such events could all have happened.
>
> The position is similar in restitution matters. No persons were guilty of any persecution, and where is it written that persons not guilty of a wrong should make restitution? Such a conception is not in keeping with German sentiments of right and wrong.[57]

Böhm criticized German judges for resorting to the narrowest possible interpretations to deny restitution claims, and for denying any link between past injustices and subsequent suffering. He attacked "the jurisprudence of the desiccated brain and the shriveled heart, of bad will and mendacity," and of the "evasiveness" of the Federal government, which was encouraging the German states "to behave in a heartless and stingy fashion."[58]

In such a climate, Adenauer understood that moral arguments alone were not going to be decisive with the CDU leadership. In September 1952 he addressed members of the CDU in Bonn in the hope of gaining support for a restitution agreement.[59] To his "great regret" he acknowledged both that there were anti-Semitic tendencies still at work in German society and that "certain inclinations" of an anti-Semitic character were also at work within the CDU. He stressed, however, that the Federal Republic had legal as well as "moral obligations" toward the state of Israel. He said that although "we, I mean our circle" (in the

CDU), did not participate in Nazi cruelties against the Jews, "a considerable portion of the German people" not only participated but also "enriched themselves as a result. We cannot overlook these facts." He added that it was one of the "noblest moral obligations of the German people" to demonstrate clearly that "they do not agree with what was done to the Jews in the years of National Socialism."[60] The Bundestag, he continued, had made clear its regret over the Nazi crimes, but "words are cheap" and had to be followed by actions. If the West Germans refused to support restitution, then doubts would be intensified as to whether they did or did not "agree" with "what was done to the Jews." Restitution would therefore be a signal to an outside world which did not know the answer to this question.

Adenauer went on to make the case for restitution on the basis of West German national interest on the one hand and the power of the Jews to affect West Germany on the other. If his own cabinet turned against him on this issue, he said, a "foreign policy catastrophe of the first order" would result which would severely impair West German efforts to receive foreign credits. "Now as before, the power of the Jews in the economic sphere is extraordinarily strong." Hence "this reconciliation . . . with the Jews from the moral and political as well as the economic standpoint is an essential requirement for the Federal Republic."[61]

Here, having just moments earlier expressed his regrets about the existence of anti-Semitism in the Federal Republic and in the CDU, Adenauer resorted to a standard myth—the power of the Jews. In fact, in 1952 the power of the Jews in the United States was minor and in Germany was essentially nil. The survival, far less the power, of the state of Israel was far from assured. Nonetheless, Adenauer hinted that he was concerned about the "power of the Jews" to the extent to which it influenced the United States, in particular its High Commissioner, John J. McCloy. Adenauer quoted an unnamed "very influential American" official who had told him that a West German agreement with Israel and with Jewish organizations would be a "political event that can be placed in the same league with" the treaties establishing West Germany's sovereignty, and making possible its entry into the European

Defense Community.[62] It was thus essential, he declared, to overcome "the resistance in our own ranks," for "agreement with the Jews is an absolute moral, political, and economic necessity."[63] On this occasion Adenauer stressed self-interest more than moral obligation. Restitution was part of the price of West German entry into the Western alliance. In any event, from 1954 to 1991 the Federal Republic of Germany made restitution payments to Jewish survivors of roughly 110 billion German marks.[64]

McCloy, having offered amnesty to some convicted Nazi war criminals in 1951, was intent, in Thomas Schwartz's words, on "press[ing] the Germans even harder" to implement a generous restitution policy toward the Jews and the state of Israel. He believed that a generous policy was essential to convince liberal and Jewish opinion in the United States that a new Germany was emerging, one intent on making amends for Nazi crimes. McCloy told Adenauer that without a restitution agreement, "Germany's integration into the West would be either endangered or made impossible."[65] Yet, as McCloy knew, American pressure could also backfire by encouraging a nationalist response in West Germany. Given the balance of power considerations demanded by containment of the Soviet Union, the United States needed West Germany as an ally more than it needed West Germany to pay restitution to the Jews. A West German refusal to make restitution would have offended liberal and Jewish opinion in the United States, though it is hard to imagine that it would have led the architects of the Cold War to refuse to integrate the Federal Republic into the Western alliance. West German self-interest as well as a sense of moral obligation certainly played a role in the restitution decisions. Yet in 1951 Jewish sensibilities and liberal opinion in the United States were far less significant in the calculations of American policy makers than were the balance of power considerations that called for West German integration into the alliance. Had Jews in these years had the power so often attributed to them by their enemies, the Adenauer government would have had to do far more than agree to make financial restitution.

Adenauer stressed, and David Ben-Gurion and Nahum Goldmann agreed, that his religious and moral convictions played a decisive role in the adoption and implementation of the restitution agreement. When, on March 18, 1953, the Bundestag ratified the Luxembourg restitution agreement, it was the democratic left, not Adenauer's own coalition, which offered the strongest support. Of the 360 members of parliament present, 239 voted for the agreement. Thirty-five voted against it, including all 13 members of the Communist Party. Of the governing CDU-CSU-FDP coalition, 106 members voted yes, but 86 members from the ranks of the Bavarian Christian Social Union, the FDP, and the Deutsche Partei abstained. Only the SPD fraction was unanimous in its support of the Luxembourg agreement. From 1953 to 1965, as a result of the agreement the Federal Republic delivered to the state of Israel goods such as ships, machine tools, trains, autos, medical equipment, and telephone technology that were crucial for the construction of infrastructure. The West German deliveries amounted to between 10 and 15 percent of annual Israeli imports. According to reports of the Federal Republic, restitution payments to individual survivors of Nazi political, racial, and religious persecution, most of whom were Jewish survivors, amounted to 40.4 billion marks by 1971, 77 billion marks by 1986, about 96 billion marks by 1995, and would total about 124 billion marks in all.[66]

This impressive record in the area of restitution was not matched by an equally impressive performance in matters of justice. On the contrary, delay and thus denial of justice was the greatest single failing of Adenauer's approach to building a democracy after Nazism. By giving primacy to the integration of millions of former Nazis and others compromised by actions during the Nazi era rather than to justice for those who had committed war crimes and crimes against humanity, Adenauer's approach had the ironic consequence of lending credence to accusations of collective guilt which the Allies had never made. If the Germans were not collectively guilty, and if Nazi Party membership in the past was not a crime, why should the millions who did not commit crimes refrain from public discussion about the thousands who did, or permit former officials of the Nazi era to remain in positions of responsibility? Were the skills of those who had served the Third Reich so indispensable and irreplaceable that a democratic state and a market economy could not be built without them?

In some sense Adenauer agreed with Ulbricht that, except in the most obvious and already exposed cases, current political views counted for more than past actions. On May 11, 1951, the Bundestag passed Article 131. It stipulated that 150,000 persons who had been members of the civil service and armed forces at the end of World War II and who had lost their positions since then were legally entitled to pensions and to possible reemployment in their former positions.[67] The West German parliament ceased investigation of government bureaucracies and supported the reemployment of those who had been excluded from jobs in the public sector as a result of negative decisions by denazification proceedings during the occupation years.[68] What the Germans called the "right to political error" was extended to former officials of the Nazi regime, whether disillusioned or simply opportunistic. The same generosity, however was not extended to those who had deserted from the German army during the war, even though the army leadership had been found guilty in Nuremberg of condoning and ordering commission of war crimes. The political price of "131" was a continuing series of scandals about the Nazi past of West German officials, especially in the judiciary and the diplomatic corps, and attendant political disaffection among the young. The less former officials of the Third Reich were willing to discuss openly their actions during the Nazi era, the more their critics suspected them of hiding something worse than youthful errors in judgment.

More than any other personnel decision of his tenure as chancellor, Adenauer's appointment and retention of Hans Globke (1898–1973) as chief of staff in 1949 and as *Staatssekretär* in the chancellor's office after Adenauer's election victory in 1953 signaled his policy of democratization via integration.[69] No other personnel decision aroused so much criticism and controversy, and none damaged Adenauer's moral standing so severely. Globke had been a member of Weimar's Catholic Center Party since 1922 and had been an official in the Prussian Interior Ministry since 1929. After 1933 he served as an official in the Nazi regime and in the Prussian Ministry of the Interior. In 1936 he began work on commentaries on what became the Nuremberg race laws. Globke and his defenders claimed that in some cases his commentary had helped to protect children of marriages between Jews and non-Jews and had facilitated the emigration of many Jews from Nazi Germany. His critics pointed out that his commentaries had also contributed to racist and anti-Semitic legislation. To be sure, in 1936 Globke did not know that the persecution of the Jews would end in mass murder.[70] Yet the claim that he had only contributed to commenting on racist legislation but had not been an advocate of genocide set a remarkably low standard, especially for one of Adenauer's very closest advisers. Some former members of the anti-Nazi resistance claimed that Globke had been an opponent of the Nazi regime, while Globke argued that he had remained in his post to try to prevent worse things from happening. Adenauer's critics asked if he really could find no one who was not burdened with Globke's compromised past. His stubborn insistence on holding on to Globke implied that indeed the entire German civil service and judicial elites were in fact deeply compromised by their actions in the Nazi era.

The Globke appointment was controversial in West Germany from the start. Given that Adenauer wanted to convince a skeptical world that a new Germany was emerging, why did he choose Globke to begin with and stand by him in the face of public criticism of his involvement in the Nazi regime? Adenauer's biographers Henning Kohler and Hans-Peter Schwarz both suggest that the very things which enraged Globke's critics, namely, his involvement in and familiarity with the policies and personnel of the Nazi regime, made him invaluable for Adenauer as he staffed his new government and dealt with the government ministries. That is, Adenauer chose him because of, not in spite of, his involvement in and familiarity with the old regime. Globke was a "walking lexicon" of Nazi officialdom with a massive institutional memory of the personal histories of current and former government officials.[71] His knowledge of the actions of German officials during the Nazi years would prove invaluable as Adenauer was staffing the domestic side of his government ministries. Adenauer argued that he now could find persons with expertise who were not guilty of war crimes and crimes against humanity.

Critics argued that because Globke himself was a compromised figure, he would be inclined to make excuses for other officials who had stayed in their positions during the Nazi era. Furthermore, his presence sent a strong signal that Adenauer—like Ulbricht—gave greater priority to current behavior and expertise than to the claims of justice and memory. If Globke could serve alongside Adenauer, what rationale could there be for a purge of compromised officials in less important positions?

In June 1951 both the *Allgemeine Wochenzeitung der Juden in Deutschland* in a front page editorial and the Central Council of Jews in Germany rejected the argument that Globke's efforts had saved any Jewish lives.[72] The Central Council statement read as follows:

> 1. It was and remains the view of the Jewish community that every functionary of the Hitler regime, of whatever rank, who actively cooperated in the creation, interpretation, and implementation of National Socialist race laws and in the measures of persecution which resulted from them broke the moral law and disgraced the moral foundations of the human community. A jurist who lowers himself to offer pseudoscholarly justification for barbaric, unjust laws and norms has forfeited the claim to be active in high-level service of the law.
> 2. We know of no cases in which any Jewish lives were saved as a result of any kind of commentary on the Nurenberg racial laws. On the other hand, we know very well that these laws led to the criminal murder of 6 million men, women, and children whose single and only offense, in the eyes of the National Socialist leadership, was that they were born Jews.[73]

Adenauer ignored such protests and continued to pursue democratization via integration of officials compromised by their actions during the Nazi era. He paid a political price for his appointment of Globke in the form of criticism in Israel, among liberal and Jewish organizations in the United States, and in vulnerability to the East German propaganda campaign against Bonn. But his most important constituency, the West German voters, accepted Globke's presence without protest. In September 1950 the *Wochenzeitung* bitterly editorialized that denazification had given way to a "renazification."[74] The paper urged that "at last, for once a serious effort be made to purge the civil service of the National Socialist fossils and all of the elements who were responsible" for World War II and mass murder. The "scandal of de-democratization" (*der Entdemokratisierungsskandal*) which had permitted "opportunistic and antidemocratic" elements to regain positions of responsibility had to be brought to an end.[75] Yet Adenauer's majority was large enough to rebuff easily the combined forces of Jews, liberals, Social Democrats, trade unions, critical journalists, and dissenting intellectuals seeking a continuation of denazification. Jewish weakness, not Jewish power, was a defining feature of the period.

Given the need for the Federal Republic to present a face of renewal to the outside world, the presence of former officials of the Nazi regime serving in the Foreign Office of the Federal Republic proved a more sensitive issue. The first major scandal about "ex-Nazis" in the Bonn government took place from spring to fall 1951 as Adenauer and his main foreign policy aide, Herbert Blankenhorn, built a new Foreign Office and diplomatic corps. In September 1951 the French High Commissioner reported that 62 of 100 members of the West German diplomatic corps had received ratings of complicity from denazification courts, 43 were former members of the SS, and 17 were former officials of the SD or Gestapo.[76] Adenauer argued for understanding the differing degrees of involvement in Nazi crimes, and for the need to employ those with diplomatic expertise. In October 1951 the SPD in the Bundestag initiated a parliamentary investigation. The committee, which met for a year, investigated twenty-one officials and urged that four be fired and seven be given limited assignments.[77] In the Bundestag, the SPD leader Fritz Erler argued that the presence of so many former officials of the Nazi regime and members of the NSDAP in "such a politically exposed place is not healthy for our state" and undermined efforts to create trust and confidence in the Federal Republic.[78] Adenauer responded by stressing that a Foreign Office required people who knew something of its history, understood foreign languages, and knew how diplomacy was conducted. Exasperated, he responded to his opposition critics that "we should finally put an end to this sniffing after

Nazis [*Naziriecherei*] . . . If we begin this kind of thing, no one knows where it will stop." He urged not continuing along these lines "in the interest of the reputation of the Federal Republic abroad."[79] The SPD argued that far more damage was being done to West Germany's reputation by Adenauer's reluctance to rid his diplomatic corps of those compromised by service in the Nazi regime.

Adenauer's and Theodor Heuss's hostility to Prussian militarism, as well as deep Allied involvement in rearmament, helped to avoid the kinds of scandals in the staffing of the upper levels of the Bundeswehr that were afflicting the Foreign Office.[80] That said, in April 1951 Adenauer again demonstrated his blindness toward the role of the Wehrmacht in the Nazi era when he stated in the Bundestag that the number of German soldiers who had committed crimes was "so extraordinarily minor and so extraordinarily small" that the honor of the German military had not been injured.[81] Later he extended this declaration to include members of the Waffen-SS, but only those "who had fought for Germany with honor."[82] In doing so Adenauer reflected and reinforced a popular view that the German military was not responsible for the criminal excesses of World War II.[83] He did staff leading positions in the emerging Bundeswehr with officers identified with the July 20, 1944, conspiracy. Nevertheless, in 1955 and 1956 there was considerable public controversy in West Germany and the United States over West German plans to permit former members of the Waffen-SS, and even former members of the SS who met certain criteria of age, rank, voluntary or forced recruitment, and democratic outlook, to enter the West German armed forces. Although the numbers involved were small, the presence of any former SS or Waffen-SS members in a new West German army aroused protests within and outside West Germany. The creation of institutions of a new state in the context of open political discussion repeatedly drew attention to continuities and discontinuities with the old regime.

After 1949 the West Germans had the opportunity to continue and broaden the work done by the Allies in Nuremberg. In the occupation era Heuss and others had spoken of the need for German courts to bring the Nazis to justice. Yet neither Adenauer nor Heuss used his newly gained sovereignty to realize this aspiration of the German anti-Nazi resistance. Instead they joined in a widely supported appeal for amnesty for those placed under suspicion and in some cases convicted by Allied denazification procedures and courts during the occupation years and did not initiate any new investigations and trials. Criticism and repression of the unreconstructed Nazis, who briefly flared into prominence in the Sozialistische Reichspartei (SRP) in 1951, went hand in hand with reintegration of former Nazis willing to accept the new democracy, and an absence of prosecution for crimes of the past.[84] The absence of vigorous prosecution in the early years in both Germanys was a severe blow to hopes that justice would be done. By 1951, the *Allgemeine Wochenzeitung der Juden in Deutschland* and Social Democratic leaders such as Carlo Schmid were speaking bitterly of the replacement of the idea of collective guilt with a new myth of collective innocence and collective nonresponsibility.[85]

The new government faced the problem of what to do about approximately five thousand persons whom the Allies had convicted of war crimes and crimes against humanity. Some of the most prominent defendants were in Landsberg Prison facing death sentences. Pressures from within German society for leniency and amnesty grew while American resistance to such pressures weakened as the Cold War shifted U.S. attention from the Nazi past to the Soviet present.[86] By 1949, the Allies had executed more than four hundred war criminals. The drafters of the new constitution of the Federal Republic, pointing to the executions carried out by the Nazi regime, abolished the death penalty. When and if the Allies carried out executions in Germany after 1949, such actions would be seen as an affront to German sovereignty. Protestant and Catholic religious leaders, far from demanding that evil be punished, actually led campaigns against war crimes trials.

John J. McCloy, criticized at the time for excessive leniency toward the already convicted defendants, reminded Adenauer that the defendants were guilty of heineous crimes and that any amnesty "would . . . be taken as an abandonment of the principles established in the [Nuremberg] trials" and might convey the idea that "those crimes have been sufficiently atoned for [and] that the German people should now be allowed to forget them."[87] Nevertheless, in a November 16, 1950, meeting with the Allied High Commissioner, Adenauer renewed his request for an end to all war crimes trials and commutation of all death sentences.[88] German officers threatened that support for rearmament in a Western alliance would be undermined if the Landsberg defendants were punished. Even Schumacher said that executions would violate German sovereignty, while Inge Scholl, whose sister and brothers, members of the White Rose anti-Nazi resistance, had been killed by the Nazis, urged McCloy to show mercy in view of the fact that the United States was calling on Germany to serve as a barrier against bolshevism.

On January 31, 1951, McCloy extended commutations, paroles, and reduction of sentences to seventy-nine of eighty-nine war criminals still imprisoned in Landsberg Prison. He affirmed five death sentences and commuted four others to life imprisonment. By 1958, all of the war criminals in American custody had been released.[89] Liberal opinion in the United States, France, and Great Britain was incensed over what was viewed as McCloy's unseemly haste to rehabilitate and rearm Germany before the work of justice, memory, and punishment had been carried out.[90] Yet at no time during this matter did Adenauer, Heuss, or Schumacher make the case to their fellow Germans in favor of the convictions, nor did they insist on the prompt and urgent need for German trials. McCloy was angered that the West German leaders had failed to support his decisions and did not understand that "we face a situation where the sympathy should be not so much for the perpetrators of the deeds as for their victims."[91] Indeed, as Thomas Schwartz argues, the stubborn opposition on the part of Adenauer and most of the West German political establishment in the Landsberg matter "may well have reinforced" McCloy's view of the need to bind Germany to the West and to "oppose any solution that would give it the freedom to revert to its old nationalism and authoritarianism."[92] McCloy's Landsberg decisions represented a concession to an already well entrenched West German inclination to "leave the past in the past" regarding issues of war crimes and crimes against humanity.[93] They did not create such sentiments.

The political leaders were responding in turn to an "amnesty lobby" which was calling on the West German government to urge McCloy to commute the sentences of the already convicted Landsberg inmates.[94] As a former American prosecutor in Nuremberg, Robert M. Kempner, noted, amnesty had both short-term and long-term consequences. First, "several dozen notorious murderers" received an amnesty in the early 1950s. Second, these decisions had a profoundly negative impact on subsequent trials in German courts because higher-ranking officials who had been amnestied in 1951 offered testimony in trials in the 1960s against lower-ranking officials who bore less guilt. As a result, it became more difficult to gain convictions in these later cases.[95] This climate discouraged the initiation of any new trials for those accused of war crimes or crimes against humanity. In these years when memories were fresh and trials should have been taking place, the primacy of Western integration and leaving the past behind meant that justice was delayed—and in far too many cases denied.

In 1958 in a trial of an *Einsatzgruppe* in Ulm, the West German public first faced the cost of the integration and amnesty policies of the early 1950s. A former police director who had been reinstated in accordance with Article 131 was implicated in the murder of four thousand Jews. He was convicted and sentenced to a long prison term. Journalists, liberal politicians, lawyers, and intellectuals now called for a systematic examination and judicial prosecution of Nazi war crimes and crimes against humanity.[96] The era of democratization based on silence and integration was coming to an end, and a more intensified period of West German judicial confrontation with Nazi crimes was beginning.

On October 5, 1958, the justice ministers of the West German states, led by the Justice Ministry in Baden-Würtemberg, established the Central Office of the State Justice Ministries for the Investigation of National Socialist Crimes of Violence (Zentrale Stelle der Landesjustiz-verwaltungen zur Aufklärungen nationalsozialistischer Gewaltverbrechen).[97] West German prosecutors shifted the focus from "war crimes" to "crimes against humanity" and genocide, that is, to the actions of the SS and *Einsatzkommandos* behind the lines and in the extermination camps. In the early 1960s, documents in the National Archives in

Washington and the Berlin Document Center were made accessible to German authorities. The investigations of the Central Office in Ludwigsberg and the resulting trials made a decisive contribution to the growth of knowledge about Nazi crimes of violence.[98] By 1958, one government office was focused on seeking justice for crimes committed during the Nazi era. It was an important development, yet nine years had been lost, during which time memories had become vaguer, witnesses had moved or died, and perpetrators had fled, covered their tracks, changed identities, and enjoyed a life outside prison.

Adenauer's Westernization efforts were to be his most lasting and important contributions. He believed that integration into a Western alliance was a key element in avoiding a return to German nationalism and Nazism. His critics argued that his anticommunism and Cold War rhetoric had the additional effect of deflecting attention from the Nazi past to the Soviet threat in the present. Yet Adenauer justified his Cold War policies with reference to critical lessons from the Nazi era. Just as Nazism had been nihilist and anti-Christian, so the Cold War juxtaposed a Christian West to the "anti-Christian spirit" of the Soviet Union.[99] Just as the Nazi regime had been a form of totalitarian rule, so the Soviet regime posed a contemporary totalitarian threat. On November 8, 1950, in his second *Regierungserklärung* to the Bundestag, Adenauer focused on the nature of "totalitarian states."[100] Such states, unlike democratic states, he declared, do not respond to law and freedom. "They know only one determining factor: power." The association between the Nazi threat in the 1930s and the Soviet threat to Europe after World War II remained an enduring theme in Adenauer's public statements and became a permanent element of the political culture of West German conservatism. In a speech in Goslar in October 1950, Adenauer said, "It has taken several years" for the Western Allies to recognize the dimensions of the Soviet and Communist threat, and to "remember the lessons they received in the negotiations with the totalitarian Hitler regime in the years before the outbreak of World War II." At that time the democracies had also tried to bring the dictator "to the path of normal peaceful cooperation between peoples." Austria and Czechoslovakia had paid with the loss of their freedom for this "false estimation of a totalitarian regime, and a frightful war was finally the end of this whole kind of negotiation with Hitler . . . Now, finally, the Western Allies faced with the Soviet Union have recognized that a totalitarian state knows only one language, the language of power, and that in negotiations with a totalitarian state, one comes to a reasonable result only if one is at least as strong as it is."[101]

While the left was drawing antimilitarist and often pacifist lessons from the two world wars, Adenauer focused on the need to avoid repeating the mistakes the democracies had made in the 1930s. For Adenauer and West German conservatives, the lessons of the Nazi era centered on the dangers of appeasement. Whereas "antifascists" agreed that in the 1930s and 1940s, appeasement and lack of will had opened the door to Hitler's aggression, the post-1945 West German left generally was uncomfortable with applying these lessons to the West's confrontation with the Soviet Union. For Adenauer, a foreign policy of Western integration and rearmament, denounced by his critics as a revival of German militarism, was the result of his interpretation of the "lessons of Munich."[102] The difference between left and right in the Federal Republic was not only between those who remembered and those who wanted to forget the Nazi era. It was also between contrasting interpretations and memories of the same events from that period.

That said, Adenauer rarely connected his discussion of appeasement of the 1930s to the Nazi crimes of the 1940s. Indeed, as in a speech to a CDU party congress in 1950, his chronology could be conveniently vague and filled with gaps.[103] He described the previous four decades of international politics as having been marked by "storms, with a breathtaking pace of development . . . Enormous forces had been unleashed by both [world] wars." Europe had been "decisive for the destiny of the world. And now? Germany [was] violently divided in two parts, politically and economically damaged, a vacuum in foreign policy."[104] France, Italy, and England were diminished. Two superpowers remained. The Soviet Union, with its "massification," totalitarianism, "slavery, concentration camps, persecution of Christianity," stood face to face with the "freedom, the dignity and worth of the individual" of the United

States.[105] The stunning feature of this narrative was the disappearance of Germany from international history between 1914 and 1945. It was simply that a "storm," impelled by "enormous forces," had descended on Europe.

One of the most remarkable of Adenauer's postwar reflections on Nazism took place on June 30, 1952, when he spoke on "understanding, peace, and freedom" at the University of Frankfurt am Main.[106] At the time, the rector of the university was Max Horkheimer, famous in Europe and the United States as the leader of the Frankfurt school of critical theory.[107] Adenauer told his listeners that the Germans were a "dynamic people." Dynamism at the level of economic and political reconstruction had its place, but it also "carries great dangers with it." Dynamic individuals "forget too easily" and too gladly, he said, "especially when the past is not exactly the past which they would like it to be. In so doing there is a great danger, for the past is a reality. It cannot be eliminated from the world. It continues to have an impact, even if one closes one's eyes in order to forget it." Working for a better future should not mean "simply extinguish[ing] reflections on the past. Rather, one should try to learn from the past for the sake of the future."[108]

With the exception of his statements regarding restitution in the fall of 1951, this was as specific as Adenauer ever became about the Nazi past while chancellor of West Germany. He stressed how important it was to ask "how was [Nazism] possible" and then devote all of one's efforts to preventing its recurrence. "Dynamism which is not bound to a view toward the past and with a view toward the world around it is very dangerous," he remarked.[109] The Germans must endeavor to recognize and overcome the mistrust of others. This they could do only by pursuing a steady and consistent foreign policy that would offer no new sources for mistrust. Words were not enough. "Only deeds" could set aside the suspicion of others. Nothing, he continued, would cause mistrust more than "lack of clarity" in policy.[110] The Federal Republic could reassure the world by being a good ally of the West. The burden of reassurance lay on foreign policy.

At the university associated with Horkheimer and the Frankfurt school's criticism of mass culture, Adenauer warned of the dangers of massification, conformity, and leveling of individuals. Neither Italian Fascism nor National Socialism in Germany would have been possible, he declared, "without a certain vulnerability of broad layers of the population to abandoning one's own personality."[111] To counter the trend toward materialism and a mass society, Germany once again needed a "stratum of a cultured elite" [*Gebildeten*], not mere experts and specialists.

A year earlier Adenauer, in contrast to his first postwar speeches, had said that the "overwhelming majority of the German people" had been opponents of Nazism, while the military catastrophe and postwar suffering had "opened [their] eyes about National Socialism and its consequences."[112] Nevertheless, the cautiousness of his public statements suggests the degree of his concern about lingering support for Nazism among sections of postwar mass society. Adenauer's actions implied that preventing a return of Nazism—or anything like it—called for saying as little about it as possible. When, in 1959, Theodor Adorno, the other leading representative of the Frankfurt school in the Federal Republic, said that "in the house of the hangman, one ought not talk about the rope," he voiced an anxiety which occasionally came through in Adenauer's speeches. Blunt talk about the crimes of the past could bring passions from that dangerous past to the surface. In any case, the primary lessons which Adenauer drew from the Nazi past concerned power politics and the similarities between totaltiarian rule in Germany and the Soviet Union. The Holocaust and associated crimes remained on the margins of his narratives of the Nazi era.

In the early years of the Federal Republic, memorial ceremonies were held for victims of Nazi terror. Adenauer was notable for his absence. He did not deliver a major speech on any such occasion. Compared to the East German ceremonies, these memorials were small. Dozens or hundreds rather than thousands of survivors were joined by small numbers of politicians, intellectuals, theologians, and journalists. The most important national political figures who spoke were Theodor Heuss, Ernst Reuter, and the leader of the Social Democrats in the Bundestag, Carlo Schmid. Yet from these ceremonies emerged an alternative narrative about the Nazi era which brought its crimes to the forefront of political retrospection.

On September 10, 1950, in Plötzensee in Berlin, Reuter spoke about the Nazi past on the site where the Nazis had executed their political opponents.[113] He said:

> In this place we come together to honor the victims who fell here, victims of all nations. We do not forget that the victims were not only of our own nation . . . Only those who have themselves experienced it can know what such pain and such torture means. Only those who have experienced this horror know what horror is, but they alone also can find the power to say: Until the end of our lives, so long as we are still breathing, we will fight to see that such horror is no longer possible.[114]

Memory of past horrors and injustice fueled Reuter's determination to prevent their repetition. With the Soviet pressure on West Berlin in mind, he expressed regret that the Germans "confronted the same dangers"—the lust for power, the "bestial desire for oppression"—no matter under what "banners and flags" they might arrive.[115]

Reuter spoke as one of those who "had looked death in the face" and who felt "inwardly bound" to the victims of Nazism. The "happiest hours of my life," he said, were those spent with other prisoners in the concentration camp, when,

> left alone with our tormentors, we thought of the future, and could think back with a clear conscience on what we had done in the past. Perhaps we did not do enough, perhaps we were too weak, but our hands and conscience always remained clean and we had nothing to regret, and we knew that someday the time would come when we would offer people a better future. And in the memory of those hours I repeat again today the warning of the dead. May they remain alive in all of us.[116]

His Plötzensee speech was striking for the freshness and detail of his memory of particular dark hours when he had glimpsed that his time would come. Now that it had come, he recalled those moments as a source of ongoing inspiration. Reuter's postwar Social Democratic convictions were shorn of the faith in an optimistic historical dialectic for which German social democracy had become famous. He too was driven by the "warnings of the dead" to ensure that such horrors would not be repeated.[117]

While Reuter was determined to speak publicly about the crimes of the past, he refrained from referring specifically to the Jewish identity of the victims in his speech of November 9, 1951, on RIAS (Radio in the American Sector of Berlin) on the thirteenth anniversary of "Kristallnacht."[118] "We must" remember this day, he said, even if "the years which followed it were so full of enormous and horrible events that it is almost beyond the human ability of recollection to keep it all in perspective." This "day of shame for Germany" began a "new chapter of injustice" that led to war, murder, and annihilation. These horrors "must never be forgotten. They must repeatedly be recalled to memory so that the certainty and unconditionality of our pledge 'Never again!' does not fade."[119] "This night" he said, "was the beginning of the rage of destruction and annihilation that grew year by year, set peoples and parts of the globe in flames, and finally made Germany and the German people sink into an almost hopeless abyss."[120]

Reuter reminded the Germans, especially those inclined to indulge in self-pity or to view themselves as innocent victims, that their current situation should be understood as a link in a causal chain that led back to dates such as November 9, 1938.

Then the organized terror of the Nazi bands was aimed at defenseless German men and women, whose only crime consisted in the fact that their religious faith made them into an easy target for limitless lies of propaganda and witch-hunts directed at them by the power holders of the "Third Reich." For us today, it is still a shameful warning and reminder that this crime was committed here in Germany and here in our Berlin and in other German cities. We want to and we must overcome the awful past, not only in an external sense, but above all we must do so within ourselves. But we cannot and must not forget what happened because we must devote all of our power and energies to ensure that something like this cannot and must not ever happen again.[121]

It was possible, he continued, to clean up the rubble, build new houses and streets, and make the cities beautiful. But "the hundreds of thousands and millions of human beings" whom the Nazis murdered could not be replaced. "This mad system" had committed an enormous "sin against the spirit . . . against the idea of law and humanity." Its traces were ingrained "more deeply in the hearts and minds of people than we ourselves believe and know." Reflection on November 9, 1938, "this day of shame and disgrace," demanded a "pledge and vow" to "completely eliminate the poison" which had made it possible.[122] Eradicating Nazi ideology and its remnants and recalling the causal chain of events that had led the Germans to their postwar predicament were crucial for the new German democracy, Reuter said. Yet even in this appeal to the powers of memory, he made no reference to anti-Semitism or to the Jewish identity of the victims, whom he described with the uninformative generalization "defenseless German men and women."

Reuter often criticized the postwar West German inclination to self-pity and resentment, expressing this theme most clearly in an essay titled "Flight into Self-Deception" in the intellectual monthly *Der Monat* in November 1952.[123] He denounced the German and European inclination to blame the United States for problems which "we Europeans" had caused. Instead, he wrote, Europeans should reflect on "what mistakes we made and what intellectual-cultural climate led us into these catastrophes" so that past errors could be overcome. "Unfortunately," he remarked, "one cannot say that the European peoples have made serious progress in this regard. The ghost of resentment is still walking about."[124] The advocates of old resentments who juxtaposed European *Kultur* to new and superficial American *Zivilisation* were still at work. Yet they offered "nothing other than a whining self-deception concerning their own inadequacy . . . The inclination always to find the guilt and blame in others" rather than to manifest responsibility for one's own actions was "our heaviest burden."[125]

Even though Reuter was not always as forthright about anti-Semitism and the genocide against the Jews as Schumacher had been, there were occasions when he faced the issue directly. On April 19, 1943, at a memorial on the tenth anniversary of the destruction of the Warsaw Ghetto, Reuter delivered his most impassioned statement regarding the genocide of European Jewry.[126] It remains one of the most moving and powerful statements of its kind in postwar German political culture.

> Ten years ago today, on April 19, 1943, following Hitler's orders, the attack on the Warsaw Ghetto began. Its goal was, as totalitarian discourse put it, liquidation of the ghetto. And then something began in the history of these awful years that indeed are behind us but still today burden our souls like a nightmare. It was something which the world had not seen before: Hitler's victims rebelled. They stood together. They fought to their last breath. They defended their lives. But by sacrificing their lives to the last person, they defended more than a short span of their lives. They defended their honor. They defended their rights. They defended everything that is sacred to every one of us in this room: the right of every human being to be free, free to live and free to raise his head to the heavens . . .
>
> We live in a time that is inclined to forget all too quickly. But in this hour we want to say that there are things which we are not permitted to forget, and which we do not want to forget: as Germans—I speak to you here as well as to my Jewish fellow countrymen as a German—we must not and we cannot forget the disgrace and shame that took place in our German name.[127]

Reuter expressed assurances that his listeners, including "our Jewish friends," rejected the concept of collective guilt. Yet there existed "a responsibility of all Germans" to try to "make up for and overcome" what "took place in their name" not only in the twelve years of the Nazi regime but in a "long historical past" as well.[128] While the Germans living in Germany did not know what was taking place in Warsaw, "we Germans" who had to or were able to live abroad "knew all these things." In Ankara in 1943, Reuter was aware that the attack on the Warsaw Ghetto was "only a small link in a great chain of a horrible campaign of annihilation which the National Socialist regime undertook and pursued with a scientific-technical precision against the Jews in Germany, against the Jews in all the European countries it could dominate up to the awful end." "Day after day," he heard the frightful reports on the radio and "more than once" was tormented by the questions "when will our German people ever again be able to wash away this shame and disgrace?" and would those to whom this was done not forget but forgive?[129] Memory of the past was indispensable, but it alone did not ensure a better future.[130] "Until the end of my life," he said, "I will never forget the scream in the night, the scream of my comrade who had been beaten to death. And because I will never forget it, I, along with all of the others who experienced these things, swore the following: We must dedicate our whole life to the task of making this impossible for all time. We cannot again allow individuals and peoples, races and religious confessions, to attack one another."[131] These very personal memories drove him to future political action. But again, this postwar Social Democratic leader was impelled less by the confident theories of future happiness for which social democracy had become famous than by his recollection of past injustice and cruelty.

In his Warsaw Ghetto memorial speech Reuter also raised questions about the "tendency to rationalization" and the spread of technology. They fostered "grand illusions" (*Größenwahnsinn*) which had "crashed the world into the most horrible disaster." Humanity had to "turn away" from the "madness of the lust for power, the hunger for power, the need for prestige, and the madness of domination," and learn that freedom required an "inner redemption" (*innere Erlösung*). The Germans needed an "inner rebirth of the intellectual, political, and moral foundations of our whole economic, public, and political life."[132]

He welcomed the *Wiedergutmachung* agreement and the accord with Israel. Yet the "genuine restitution and the one "which alone matters for our Jewish colleagues" is the "inner restitution and the inner rebirth of our people" and their turn away from racism.[133] True restitution meant creating a free Germany in which all were treated with respect. To engage in "genuine restitution," Germany must become "a peaceful member of the community of free peoples." It would not do to say that "the others" had also done wrong. "If the others made mistakes . . . we can heal these errors only by addressing our own mistakes." Grasping the "tragic history" of Germany and the "roots of evil in the past" were parts of the process of an inward transformation necessary for becoming a free people.[134] Memory and critical reflection would strengthen a new democracy.

He then recalled his German-Jewish professor of philosophy, Hermann Cohen, who, other than Reuter's parents, had "left the deepest traces in [Reuter's] intellectual development." Reuter knew "what the Jewish component in our people meant" and that Jewish and German traditions had been more intensely intertwined "than in any other country."[135] Postwar German youth knew nothing of this past. They must be taught German history, not only about its music and literature but also about the role the Jews had played in the "whole intellectual structure of our people" and the intersection of the German and Jewish peoples and traditions. The dead could not be brought back to life and the past could not be undone, but the Germans must seek to eliminate "everything evil which remains from [the Nazi] regime." It would take more than one generation to accomplish this task, but it should be accomplished "with the help of our Jewish compatriots" and be accompanied by time set aside for "an hour of reflection [*Stunde der Besinning*]."[136]

Reuter concluded with an argument about the link between the obligations of memory and duties toward the present and future. We Germans, he said, must not forget the "exact picture of the frightful events" of the destruction of the Warsaw Ghetto, but "we must overcome it by taking a new path, carefully, slowly, and with great patience . . . Precisely because we do not want to forget what happened, we must gather the strength to overcome the past and build a new future." Reuter hoped that this future Germany would produce new voices of tolerance and cooperation. A German intellectual and moral renewal was essential in order to assert that those who had died in the Warsaw Ghetto "did not die in vain. For they moved our conscience, and our conscience has not and will not let us sleep until we have reached this great and beautiful goal."[137]

Reuter was one of the first, if not the first, of the West Germany political leaders to evoke Jewish martyrdom and heroism as an inspiration for a democratic renewal in the Federal Republic. His view of the relationship between public memory of past crimes and construction of a postwar democracy stood in sharp contrast to Adenauer's practice. For Reuter, memory of the Nazis' victims and of the struggle against Nazism reinforced democratic renewal. He articulated a contrasting and minority view of the relation between democracy and memory which was dominant in the Adenauer era. With the institutionalization in West Germany of a national day of mourning (*Volkstrauertag*) in 1952, distinctions between perpetrators, bystanders, and victims were often thoroughly obscured. Indeed, at this early stage some West German politicians included among the "victims of fascism" those German soldiers who had died at the front, victims of Allied bombing of German cities, and the *Vertriebenen*. Reuter kept the focus on the victims of Nazi persecution and terror.[138]

On July 20, 1953, shortly before his death, on the occasion of the unveiling of a memorial to those who had died in the failed coup of July 20, 1944, Reuter delivered his last speech addressing the Nazi past.[139] He praised the coup attempt as the first sign that the will to freedom in Germany had not completely collapsed. Those who had risked and lost their lives out of a sense of duty had come from all political camps. Had they succeeded, millions of Germans and non-Germans would still be alive. He spoke "with deep respect" before the surviving relatives of those whose names would certainly be incorporated in "the proud history of our fatherland."[140] He addressed the sons and daughters of the conspirators as "the bearers of proud names, because these names are bound up with a heroic, courageous, and true act of patriotism." Their fathers' actions were a source of pride. The "only honor" which postwar Germans could bestow on the legacy of the resistance was "to try with all of our strength to complete the work that still stands uncompleted before us."[141] In the West Germany of 1953, many conservatives still regarded the conspirators of 1944 as traitors, while the Communists, and even Schumacher to some extent, dismissed them as the last gasp of German conservatism. Reuter praised their courage and sacrifice as a decisive moment in the German postwar turn away from Nazism. He then associated July 20, 1944, with the "great days of June 17, 1953," the workers' revolt against the Communist regime in East Berlin. In both instances the Germans had shown the world "the firm determination that we Germans want to be free . . . We know that this June 17 was just as much a beginning as was July 20 . . . The connection between the two events is the firm will not to disappear as a people, the firm will to be free."[142] In comparing the German resistance against the Nazi dictatorship with the German workers' revolt against the Communist dictatorship, Reuter articulated a common theme of the "antitotalitarian consensus" of a shared opposition to dictatorship whether of the right or the left. In place of a zero-sum game of divided memory in which criticism of Communist dictatorship obliterated memories of the Nazi era, he saw the two as mutually reinforcing reflections. For Reuter, the fact of opposition to dictatorship, be it Communist or Nazi, was decisive.[143]

Social democracy was intact and restored after 1945, but it was also changed. Reuter and Schumacher found in moments of past suffering and resistance sources for renewal and a rebirth in the future. It was screams in the night, not a confident dialectic, that inspired their visions of democracy and political freedom. These "militant democrats" were exceptional figures in their efforts to avoid the blind spots and double standards of divided memory. They opposed the Communist and Nazi dictatorships but did not equate one with the other or denounce one in order to excuse or minimize the crimes of the other.

From the earliest moments, postwar political memory included efforts to balance and weigh the relative suffering and victimization of different groups, including the Germans themselves. Carlo Schmid, the leader of the Social Democratic parliamentary fraction in Bonn, was one of the politicians who criticized efforts to place Germans as victims on the same plane as the Jews and other victims of the Nazis. Schmid was a leading voice in favor of restitution payments to Jewish survivors.[144] In the Federal Republic, no less than in the GDR, the issue of restitution required determining who was, and who was not a victim of National Socialism, and who among these victims had a moral claim to restitution. The *Wiedergutmachung* debates forced participants to make distinctions among the kinds and extents of suffering during the Nazi era. In the February 1951 Bundestag restitution debates, Schmid declared:

Certainly, there are many victims of the Third Reich. One could say that almost all of those who survived the period are victims. But one shouldn't make this all too easy and forget that there are distinctions among them. People are beginning to forget. Indeed, things are getting to the point at which even former SS and SD men are beginning to regard themselves as victims of National Socialism . . . and those who were given a negative classification by the denazification counsels are already beginning to consider themselves victims of National Socialism![145]

Schmid warned against forgetting just who "the really special victims of National Socialism" had been.[146] Generalizing the victim category went hand in hand with obscuring the particular extermination of the Jewish people.[147] He continued:

Among all that the Nazi regime brought about, the crimes committed against Jewish fellow human beings were the most awful, not only because of the extent of murder, not only because it was a matter of millions of victims, not only because of the methodical mercilessness of the gassing in Auschwitz and Maidenek, not only because these acts of butchery also fell on women and children, but also because the whole Third Reich at its basis, at its core, was set up to exterminate the Jews! [Here he received vigorous applause.] The Third Reich was integrated very much more around anti-Semitism than around, one is ashamed to use the term, "pro-German" sentiment.[148]

Though many Germans had risked their lives to help the Jews, millions more were Nazi Party members. Though only a few knew the specifics about Auschwitz, the guilt of the greater number lay in not having stopped the Nazis and the Jewish persecution at the outset. Because of these sins of omission and commission, the Germans had a moral obligation to make restitution to the Jews. They had no right to expect "reconciliation" from its recipients. Restitution should be paid "without asking how the creditor wishes to relate to us as people."[149]

Schmid rejected an apolitical remorse which made no distinction between perpetrators and victims. Such a stance was not a sign of higher morality. Rather it represented an enduring failure to think clearly about politics and morality or about the nature of the Nazi regime. In contrast to those who wished to place the Holocaust on the fringes of the Nazi era, Schmid insisted that it was at the core of what the Nazi regime was about, and that the Germans had understood this to be so at the time. Hence, to equate all victims was both morally unacceptable and historically inaccurate. It rested on a distorted and apologetic understanding of the Nazi regime.

In a speech in the Paulskirche in Frankfurt on March 6, 1955, to the Society for Christian-Jewish Cooperation, Schmid returned to the issue of memory and victimization in postwar discussion.[150] Did not each of us, he asked, hear the biblical question, "Cain, where is your brother? . . . Don't the shadows who once lived here in this city until they were taken to the gas chambers in Auschwitz direct these words to us from every street and every square? And don't they direct these words to us also on behalf of those millions of other Jews and non-Jews who were murdered as they were?"[151] There were many, he continued, who thought that the meaning of a week of brotherhood was to "finally forget" the past and again take up a "friendship of forgiveness." After all, they would say,

life goes on—and furthermore there are certainly also other massive episodes of evil in the world! Wasn't the bombardment of our cities also a horrible thing? A sin against the commandment of humanity and brotherhood? Thus, aren't the "others" just as bad as us? In one of these demolished cities, in whose ruins thousands [were killed]— not only soldierly men but also peaceful women, innocent children—

in this city I want to say: It is different if wounds are caused and life is destroyed in the course of . . . military actions which, like falling bombs, touch one and not the other, or if one consciously seeks to make a group of people disappear from the face of the earth and is devoted to their annihilation, as was done to the Jews.[152]

The Jews were not the victims of "unfortunate developments of war," said Schmid. Their status as human beings had been denied. They were declared to be subhuman. The Nazis decreed "they should be exterminated like vermin. That is the particular and most inhuman aspect of this crime—and none of the crimes of the others can cleanse us of it."[153]

While *Wiedergutmachung* was necessary, Schmid believed that it too could not cleanse the Germans of these crimes. The Germans had "many grounds for shame" in light of the legalistic, heartless, and "more fetishistic than Shylock" approach of "many of our officials" regarding restitution. He rejected the idea of collective guilt.

> But I just as vehemently reject the legend of collective innocence [*Kollektivunschuld*]. And I object to the view that we should not be held responsible for that which was done in our name because the great mass among our people did not participate, and were not even aware of the details . . . At the very least, we did not try to prevent what was done in our name! Among our people there were far too few who stood up to prevent the horrible things that were done so that we could be relieved of our responsibility.
>
> Whoever belongs to a people may not only enjoy the good wine. They must also want to drink from the bitter parts of the cup of fate! . . . Where was the outcry that would have torn down the walls of terror?[154]

Returning to the biblical question, Schmid insisted that the Germans must not view themselves as without guilt because they personally did not commit crimes. They should not respond as Cain did, "Am I my brother's keeper?" The first command of brotherhood was "again and again to ask about your brother! Whoever asks learns and also knows where the Buchenwald, Auschwitz, and Waldheim of the time is."[155] Like Reuter, Schmid also asserted that public memory of past crimes was necessary to foster a sense of moral and civic responsibility and political engagement crucial to building a new democracy.

Theodor Heuss's singular accomplishment as *Bundespräsident* was to make the memory of the crimes of the Nazi era a constitutive element of national political memory. Freed from electoral considerations, he made the office of *Bundespräsident* into a political center of national memory and liberal conscience. To his critics he was the cultured veneer obscuring the failures of denazification in the Adenauer era. Yet in speeches about German history and extensive private correspondence with Jewish survivors, resistance veterans, and West German and foreign intellectuals, Heuss planted the seeds within the West German political and intellectual elites for subsequent broader public discussion and action. He evoked German liberal aspirations and honored those who had stood for democracy and human rights throughout German history. He could have done much more. Others in his position would have done, and later did do, much less.

In December 1949 he delivered a speech, "Courage to Love" ("Mut zur Liebe") to the Society for Christian-Jewish Cooperation (Gesellschaft für christlich-jüdische Zusammenarbeit). This remained one of his best-known speeches, as his focus on "love" as opposed to justice set the tone for the next decade. In the presence of religious leaders, politicians, and High Commissioner McCloy, Heuss addressed the issue of German guilt for Nazi crimes. The speech was broadcast on radio, published in the German and foreign press, and presented in weekly film newsreels.[156] Heuss rejected the notion of collective guilt as a mirror of the Nazis' perception of the Jews. Just as "the mere fact of being Jewish already decided the issue of guilt" for the Nazis, so the idea of collective guilt (*Kollektivschuld*) treated all Germans as a group. In its place he proposed the idea of "collective shame" (*Kollektivscham*). "The worst thing Hitler did to us," he said, "was . . . that he forced us into the shame of having to bear along with him and his crew the same German name."[157] Heuss continued:

We must not, we may not simply forget the things which people would gladly like to forget because it is so unpleasant. We must not and may not forget the Nuremberg laws, the burning of the synagogues, the transport of the Jews abroad to misfortune and to death. This is a set of facts which we should not and cannot forget because it makes us uncomfortable. The awful thing in these events, about which we must speak openly, is this: It was not a matter of the raging fanaticism of pogroms in Russia, Rumania, or wherever, which we read about previously in the newspapers. Rather it was the *cold brutality of rational pedantry.* This was the peculiar German contribution to these events. And the most terrible aspect of all this is that this process was not carried out with great emotion, which would have been bad enough. Rather it made use of [legal] paragraphs and was supposed to [draw on] a worldview for a long time. What, then, was this "worldview?" It was *biological materialism,* one which recognized no moral categories but which wanted to represent them. It had no idea that there are individual values established between individuals.[158]

While the "cold brutality of rational pedantry" and "biological materialism" certainly were in evidence, Heuss's story of the persecution of the Jews was remarkable for the absence of any mention of anti-Semitism in Germany.

Heuss discussed relations between Germans and Jews by referring to his own experience. "Two or three" of the "five closest friends" in his life were Jewish. He was friendly with them not because they were Jewish but "because the spark of human love passed between us." We must, he continued, "move away from global assessments of people." Rather than refer to a human being as a German, a Frenchman, or a Jew, "we must regain a free evaluation of human character in the relations of one person to another."[159] Nazism treated individuals primarily as members of groups. Alluding to the "Jewish problem" of the past and present, Heuss said that the Nazis "knew nothing about the broad color and the tensions and strains within Jewish life itself." For Heuss, the antidote to Nazi racism was not a philo-Semitic hagiography of Jewish group accomplishment. Rather, it was to restore regard for individuals and to cease viewing them as manifestations of group qualities.

On this as on other occasions before and after, Heuss stressed "Germany's infinite loss due to this [Nazi] madness."[160] He referred to letters that German-Jewish refugees had sent to him from all over the globe in which their links to Germany came to the fore, as did their pain and anguish over the desecration of the "graves of their parents . . . In Germany's fight for its place among the nations, every such cemetery desecration is a battle lost."[161] Those who sought to forget the Nazi past, to look the other way when Jewish cemeteries were desecrated, or even to engage in such acts were themselves undermining the Federal Republic. Yet he did not combine his call to remember the past with a repetition of his plea of the summer of 1945 that German courts take up the work of justice which the Allies had begun.

Heuss, a former professor of politics, spoke often at German universities in the early years to urge students to face the past honestly. On one such occasion on November 1, 1949, Heuss fondly recalled the intellectual atmosphere of Berlin in his student days at the turn of the century.[162] He said that during the Third Reich, the regime had appealed to young people to show courage (*Tapferkeit*) and comradeship (*Kameradschaft*). Now he again asked courage of them, but "that kind of courage which grasps reality and does not collapse in the face of . . . harsh reality." Comradeship now meant forming bonds and friendships regardless of social origins and career goals.[163] His plea that scholarship must be more than career training but must serve the search for truth met with "strong applause." The most difficult task facing Germany, he said, was to build "a new national feeling." It could emerge only on the basis of "unconditional truthfulness toward our own history . . . Self-criticism is not self-destruction. Rather it is the path to reformation."[164]

One of Heuss's most important accomplishments was to associate the language of patriotism and terms such as courage, honor, and friendship with memory of the Nazi era. On December 16, 1949, in an address to faculty and students at the University of Heidelberg, he contrasted the illusions of the returning generation of 1919 with the disillusioned

German students of 1949.[165] While warning against cynicism and paralysis owing to lack of vision, he welcomed the absence of the post–World War I "romanticism of substitute heroism." "Long applause" accompanied his expressions of relief that there were no student parades in the midst of the ruins. Students and scholars had the task of reshaping and recovering past German traditions. The universities, he stressed, must nourish respect for truth and for a "free humanity."[166] Scholars had an important role to play in building a free society and polity, provided they put their disillusionment to productive use.

Speaking in the Bundestag on the Day of National Reflection of the German People on September 7, 1950, Heuss urged his fellow Germans to keep the "total catastrophe" in mind, for "the grace [*Gnade*] of being able to forget, without which the individual and people could not live, will be misused by the desire of wishing to forget, one that is so comfortable and which shoves aside the measure of judgment."[167] Heuss did not combine this oblique reference to the importance of memory with an explanation of the catastrophe to which he referred, nor did he specify what judgment he thought was being pushed aside. On this day of reflection, Heuss focused on the dilemmas of and prospects for the German present.

His public reticence did not mean lack of interest. Heuss carried on an extensive correspondence with leading figures of German and German-Jewish intellectual life, both those living in the Federal Republic and refugees living abroad, including Theodor Adorno, Leo Baeck, Martin Buber, Max Horkheimer, Thomas Mann, and Karl Marx, the editor of the *Allgemeine Wochenzeitung der Juden in Deutschland*.[168] Much of the correspondence concerned his efforts to help restore traditions of Jewish culture in Germany. Beginning in September 1949, and continuing every year of his presidency, Heuss published a message on Rosh Hashanah, the Jewish New Year, addressed to the Jewish community in Germany.[169] He lent a sympathetic ear to the urgings of those inside and outside the Federal Republic who urged that attention be paid to the burdens of the Nazi past. When Adenauer issued the 1951 statement on the willingness of the Federal Republic to offer restitution to the Jews, Jacob Blaustein, president of the American Jewish Committee in New York, wrote to Heuss that Adenauer's statement "recalls your own courageous lifelong service to the principles underlying this action."[170]

There were limits, however, to Heuss's willingness to face the Nazi past. Even he pleaded for leniency for industrialists, soldiers, and former officials who had been convicted by Allied courts in the occupation era. On January 16, 1951, Heuss wrote to High Commissioner McCloy, and in February 1951 to General Thomas T. Handy, commander in chief of the European Command of American forces, to request leniency in several of the Landsberg cases. While many of the convicted deserved severe punishment, he wrote to McCloy, there were several cases in which he believed the establishment of guilt "remained thoroughly questionable" and new arguments should be heard. "My concern is great," he wrote, that executions of the Landsberg prisoners "would disturb our sensitive discussions about the incorporation of the Federal Republic into a European and Atlantic community."[171]

In a firm, at times sharp response the following week, McCloy dismissed warnings—or threats—that German integration into a Western alliance would be threatened by punishment of convicted war criminals.[172] As he had with Adenauer, he reminded Heuss that the Landsberg decisions were the result of long and careful study by himself and "very distinguished" American advisers. There had been "no subject on which I have spent so much time and thought since I have been in Germany," McCloy wrote. He was "very glad" to have been able to find "a basis for very extensive grants of clemency." But there were "some crimes the extent and enormity of which belie the concept of clemency." These involved the "murder of helpless women and children by the tens of thousands under circumstances which we would not credit were it not for the contemporaneous reports of the perpetrators themselves and their own admissions." The German people, McCloy continued, could not "possibly associate the interests of such criminals with their own." He had also considered and rejected various "heat of battle" arguments about extenuating circumstances. Furthermore, he reminded Heuss that he, McCloy, had international obligations regarding crimes committed against non-Germans and crimes committed outside Germany. He had to maintain "the prestige and authority of the international tribunals," specifically judgments of the Nuremberg court. McCloy wished that the German government and people "had a wider concept of the crimes which are represented by many of those at Landsberg," for the letters he had received from Germans pleading for clemency displayed "the most abysmal ignorance of both the offenses and the character of the proof of the guilt which prevails in respect of them."[173]

Despite this very sharp response from McCloy, Heuss never once spoke out forcefully in his next eight years as *Bundespräsident* in favor of a more vigorous program of "German justice." He did, however, place the destruction of European Jewry at the center of the meaning of memory of the Nazi past. Heuss delivered his most important speech on the subject at memorial ceremonies in Bergen-Belsen on November 29–30, 1952. Officials of the Federal Republic and many other governments, as well as representatives of Jewish organizations, gathered to dedicate a memorial to those persecuted at the Nazi concentration camp at Bergen-Belsen. It was the same week in which the Slansky defendants were executed in Prague and Paul Merker was arrested in East Berlin. The Bergen-Belsen ceremonies reflected the realities of divided memory. It was a very Western event. Attending were government representatives from Britain, the United States, Denmark, Belgium, the Netherlands, Switzerland, Sweden, France, Yugoslavia, Israel, and the Jewish communities in Germany, Europe, and the United States. None of the Communist states were represented. M. S. Henderson, speaking for the British High Commissioner for Germany, stressed the centrality of the rule of law.[174] Nahum Goldmann spoke on behalf of the World Jewish Congress. The speeches were broadcast over national radio.[175]

Sixty-five Jews in attendance represented themselves and Jewish organizations.[176] They included the Israeli government, the World Jewish Congress, the Jewish Agency for Palestine, the American Joint Distribution Committee, and leaders of organized Jewish communities in Germany. Their participation offered a striking contrast to the East German anticosmopolitan purge. Jewish presence and Communist and Soviet bloc absence manifested the divided, partial, and politically influenced nature of postwar German memory. The Jewish catastrophe, which had been marginalized in official East German antifascist narratives, came to the fore in the West German contributions at the Bergen-Belsen ceremonies. By contrast, the centerpiece of Eastern memory, namely, the narrative of tragedy and triumph on the Eastern Front and the martyrdom of the Communist anti-Nazi resistance, received scant mention. Memorials in stone, however, were written in Czech, Polish, and Russian, as well as in English, Dutch, Flemish, French, Danish, Yiddish, Hebrew, German, and Latin for those whose nationality was not known.[177]

Jewish survivors had been gathering at the former concentration camps for memorial services since 1945. The 1952 ceremony in Bergen-Belsen was the first time they were joined by the head of state of the Federal Republic. In the presence of Heuss and the assembled officials, Nahum Goldmann delivered a powerful narrative of Jewish suffering.[178] Goldmann spoke of the

> deep pain and anguish and mourning for the millions who suffered and died as victims of National Socialist terror. No one had to pay so frightfully for the Hitler period as did we Jews. A third of our people were exterminated with devilish refinement and scientific thoroughness. World history knows other cases of extermination and annihilation of whole groups. What characterizes the destruction of European Jewry by the Hitler regime, and what makes it into a unique, awful event, is the cold calculation, the systematic thoroughness, the organized planning of this process of extermination. This gives to it its unique, awful character, and makes it into a unique tragedy, even in the history of our people, a history so rich in tragedy. In this decade we lost a third of our community, a loss that can never be made good again. It is understandable that in this hour our thoughts and feelings go first of all to the 6 million Jews who perished. They suffered as human beings have seldom suffered in history. They endured tortures that one can scarcely imagine. And in the gas chambers and the institutions of extermination of the Nazi regime, they found an end for which there are no analogies in history. Speaking in the name of Jews around the world, I repeat in this hour our

pledge never to forget these dead. For all time we will carry the memory of these martyrs, who died only because they were Jews, in our hearts and in the hearts of our children and our children's children. With the inextinguishable memory that is the characteristic of our people, we will forever keep reflection on the Jewish victims of Nazi terror in our history. The ten thousand who are buried here symbolize for us all the millions who found their tragic end in Auschwitz, Treblinka, Dachau, and in Warsaw and Vilna and Bialystok and in countless other places.[179]

Goldmann brought the memory of the extermination of European Jewry into a postwar national German commemorative ceremony with unprecedented forthrightness. Furthermore, the negotiator of the restitution agreements with Adenauer stressed that the loss of European Jewry could never be made "made good." Whatever the Germans did or did not remember about the Nazi past, "world Jewry" would keep the memory of the Holocaust alive, then and in the future, "in the hearts of our children and our children's children." While the Germans might want to forget, the Jews would not and could not do so.

Goldmann's speech in Bergen-Belsen was the fullest account of the Holocaust presented at a political memorial ceremony in the first postwar decade in West Germany. Had he delivered it in East Berlin, it could have landed him in prison. Yet Goldmann, who fit the image of the Jewish cosmopolitan denounced by the Communists, drew attention to the Eastern geography of the Jewish catastrophe. His memory of the Holocaust did not fit within the constraints of divided memory. In Bergen-Belsen, Goldmann broke through the barriers of Cold War thinking to recall the millions who were murdered in places now "behind the iron curtain," at Auschwitz, Treblinka, Warsaw, and "countless other places." At the same time that Stalinists such as Hermann Matern were denouncing the Jews as a source of Western influence, Goldmann pointed out that the geography of memory did not fit easily within the fault lines of the Cold War in the West. Now, in the very weeks and months of the Slansky trial, and at the outset of the winter purge in East Berlin, Goldmann's speech inevitably recalled Nazi barbarism on the Eastern Front in World War II. Such memories were not at all common in the anticommunist narratives of the time. The Holocaust remained an uncomfortable, troubling, often inconvenient accompaniment to the West German elite's recollection of the war. Although most of the Holocaust took place in Eastern Europe and the Nazi-occupied Soviet Union, it was here in the West in the bitterest days of the Cold War where the memory of the Holocaust first found adequate public expression. Yet even in his narrative Goldmann did not make explicit the implicit connection between the Nazi assault on the Jews and the general war on the Eastern Front.

Goldmann's speech was also important because he recalled Jewish heroism and martyrdom as an inspiration to survivors.[180] Despite the Nazis' best efforts, Jewish history had not ended in 1945. Nazism was dead but the Jews remained. Goldmann stressed that the history of the Jewish people and of the Holocaust had a "general significance for humanity," and for the Germans specifically. It constituted an "everlasting warning" about the dangers of exaggerated nationalism and racism. What Hitler did to the Jews, he did to a lesser extent to others as well. Had his regime prevailed, other peoples would have followed the path of the Jews. "I know," Goldmann said, "that there are many Germans, symbolized by the president of the Federal Republic [Heuss], who are with us, who fully understand this warning, and who want to do everything to spare their people a second experience like the Hitler period."[181] But there were others among the Germans who did not want to hear these warnings, who closed their eyes in the face of the "awful facts of the extermination of the Jews." In all nations there were people who were ready to adopt extreme nationalism and racism. The Bergen-Belsen memorial, Goldmann continued, should sound an "eternal" warning. "Hitler did not only exterminate 6 million Jews. He destroyed 6 million human beings, and many millions of non-Jewish people as well . . . The idea of the connectedness and bonds of all the peoples of humanity is a hundred times more legitimate, greater, and more fruitful" than that of extreme nationalism.[182]

By combining the particular features of the Jewish catastrophe with an appeal to the universalism of Western humanism, Goldmann's

Bergen-Belsen speech was also a distinctively German-Jewish statement. He stressed those common elements of life which unite all peoples. The Jews had suffered more than all others and would never forget that suffering. Yet from that memory Goldmann urged rejection of "the sins and passions of racial darkness," and support for peace, the belief in one humanity, and in the possibility of overcoming the past and building a better world.[183]

Heuss's speech in Bergen-Belsen became known by its famous refrain, "No one will lift this shame from us" ("Diese Scham nimmt uns niemand ab!"). It was the most extensive public reflection to come from a leading official of the West German government regarding the crimes of the Nazi era. It was broadcast on radio and was the subject of reports in the West German press, especially the liberal press. The West German government press office reprinted the text.[184] Manfred George, the editor of *Aufbau*, the German-Jewish newspaper in New York, published it on page one. George wrote to Heuss to say that "your words moved me personally very much" and to express his "firm conviction that your words will contribute to advancing, strengthening, and forming the bridge building that we all take so seriously and think is so important."[185] Roger Baldwin, the American liberal long active in civil rights affairs, wrote to Heuss to express his "admiration for one of the great utterances of a philosopher and statesman, touched with warm humanity." It was a source of "great satisfaction to all liberals everywhere to have you in a position where such words carry weight."[186]

It would have been an act of cowardice, Heuss began, to refuse the request to speak at the Bergen-Belsen memorial. The Germans needed to face the truth, especially on soil which had been devastated by human cowardice. For it was "always cowardice to strut around with bare violence" in the face of defenseless poverty, illness, and hunger. "Whoever speaks here as a German," he said, "must have the inner freedom to face the full horror of the crimes which Germans committed here. Whoever would seek to gloss over, make little of, or diminish the depth of these crimes, or even to justify them with reference to any sort of use of so-called "reason of state," would only be insolent and impudent."[187] He told his listeners that he had first heard the name Belsen on the BBC in 1945. Earlier he had heard of Dachau, Buchenwald, Oranienburg, and Theresienstadt. He had heard of Mauthausen, "where my old friend Otto Hirsch, the noble and important director of the national organization of German Jews [*Reichsvertretung*] was 'liquidated,'" from the mouth of Hirsch's widow, "whom I tried to support and console." Yet this comment "should not be a crutch for those who gladly say: 'We didn't know anything about all that.' We knew about these things." The Germans knew from the reports of Protestant and Catholic bishops. "Our imaginations and fantasy, nourished by bourgeois and Christian traditions, did not encompass the quantity of this cold and sorrowful destruction."[188]

Heuss rejected the arguments of postwar Germans concerning what "the others" had done in the Allied internment camps of 1945–46, or the camps in the Soviet zone and the show trials in Waldheim. He rejected all such efforts at exculpation. Such balancing of accounts, he said, "endangers the clear, honorable feeling for the fatherland of everyone who consciously knows our history" and faces up to it. Violence and injustice were not to "be used for mutual compensation."[189] In Bergen-Belsen there had been many victims from other countries, and many Germans as well. But this place, he said, had a "deep meaning, which Nahum Goldman expressed for everyone." Economic competition and religious fanaticism had made their contribution to the Nazi crimes. Those who had been murdered were not abstract groups but "human beings, like you and me. They had fathers, children, husbands, wives."[190] In the end, he said, everything came down to the individual. "It depends on you, that you understand the particular language of the others, for your own sake, and for all of our sakes."[191]

There were many, Heuss said, who asked if it would not be better "to have the plough's furrows run here and to allow the mercy of the earth's ever youthful fruitfulness to offer forgiveness for what happened here." Some argued that the "obelisk [of the Bergen-Belsen memorial] could become a thorn in wounds which should heal over the course of time, and thus not allow the goal of healing to be attained."[192] He continued:

We want to talk about this in all candor. The peoples who know those who lie here in mass graves think about them, none more so than the Jews, whom Hitler forced into a consciousness of their peoplehood. The Jews will never forget, they cannot ever forget, what was done to them. The Germans must not and cannot ever forget what human beings from among their own people did in these years so rich in shame.

Now I hear the objection: And the others? Don't you know about the internment camps of 1945–46 and their brutality and injustice? Don't you know about the victims in foreign custody, and about the suffering of the formalistic, cruel justice to which Germans are today subjected? Don't you know about the continuation of mistreatment in camps, about death in the Soviet zone, about Waldheim, Torgau, Bautzen? Only the emblems and flags have changed.

I know about all this, and I have never hesitated to talk about it. But to search for excuses by referring to the injustice and brutality of the others is the method of those who lack a demanding moral code.[193]

Whatever the Germans might or might not remember, Heuss understood that the Jews would not and could not forget. Hence, all German efforts to forget were both morally debased and doomed to failure. While aware that Germans had suffered during the war, Heuss criticized what Theodor Adorno would later describe as the neurotic quality of postwar German memory evident in efforts to change the subject or point to German suffering when the issue of Nazi crimes was raised.[194] Heuss eloquently made the moral case for the demands of memory and against avoidance.

It seems to me that the tariffs of virtue [*Tugendtarif*] with which the peoples rig themselves out is a corrupting and banal affair. It endangers a clear, honorable feeling for one's country which everyone who consciously places himself or herself in its history carries. It is a feeling for the great things which may offer pride and security but does not permit a descent into the dullness of a philistine self-certainty. Violence and injustice are not things to which one should or may resort for reciprocal compensation. For they carry within themselves the evil danger that they will accumulate in the soul of consciousness. Their weight becomes the worst burden in individual destiny, but even worse in the destinies of peoples and nations. Every people has in reserve its poets of revenge or, when they get tired, its calculated publicists.[195]

Heuss spoke up for a patriotism self-confident enough to face the dark past honestly. "Honorable feeling for one's country" was not composed of comforting myths and resentment of others. Heuss sought to place the language of patriotism in the service of memory rather than avoidance and resentment.

There was, he continued, a deep meaning in Belsen. It was here that the Jews had died. Goldmann had spoken of the catastrophes of Jewish history, but "certainly what took place between 1933 and 1945 was the most frightful thing ever which happened to the Jewish diaspora. Something new had occurred." The Jews had known persecution due to religious fanaticism and social-economic resentments. But it was the "breakthrough of biological naturalism of the half-educated which led to the pedantry of murder as a sheer automatic process . . . This is the deepest corruption of our time. No one, no one will lift this shame from us. And this is our shame, that something like this took place in the history of the people from whom Lessing and Kant, Goethe and Schiller, entered world consciousness. No one, no one will lift this shame from us."[196]

To those who saw German history as a direct path "from Luther to Hitler," Heuss responded with a moral and a historical argument. Precisely because Germany possessed the moral resources and the multiple historical continuities to have prevented genocide yet failed to draw on them, "no one will lift this shame from us." The shame would never be lifted, above all, because the Germans themselves, and not only or primarily censorious foreigners, understood that Nazism represented a departure from the civilized morality which was also a part of German history. For Heuss, the moral imperative to recall the crimes of the Nazi era was not a burden imposed by the occupiers and victors but an imperative demanded by the better traditions of a still existing "other Germany."

Heuss also spoke personally about the Nazi era. He recalled one Nazi official in his hometown who scratched out the Jewish names on the town memorial to soldiers who had died in World War I and replaced them with the names of various battles. Some of Heuss's boyhood friends were among those erased names. He mentioned the episode to remind his listeners that "respect for the dead" had declined as the Nazis were thinking of starting a new war. A "cynical guy" would say that it was "only" Poles, Russians, French, Belgians, Norwegians, Greeks, and others who died in Bergen-Belsen. Heuss rejected such racist callousness. The dead were not members of an abstract "other." "They were human beings, like you and me. They had fathers, children, husbands, wives."[197] And indeed, many had been his friends. Mourning their loss was not a favor owed to the Jews or an act of clever public relations. For Heuss, mourning the destruction of the German-Jewish Germany in which he had come of age was both a moral imperative and an expression of a sense of his and his nation's loss.

Heuss avoided happy endings. Yes, there had been German doctors and nurses who, driven by shame, morality, and duty, had cared for the survivors of Bergen-Belsen in spring and early summer 1945, often at the risk of their own health. This manifestation of goodness and justice was "indeed a consolation." Yet that was hardly sufficient reason to end on an uplifting note. Contrary to Rousseau's assumptions about the goodness of human nature, "we have learned that the world is more complicated than the theses of moralizing literati" suggest. The noun "humanity" (*Menscheit*) was an abstraction. The fact of being humane, of humanity (*Menschlichkeit*) in this sense, was a matter of how individuals acted toward one another. In the end, he said, "it depends on you, that you understand the particular language of the others, for your own sake, and for all of our sakes."[198]

In his "No one will lift this shame from us" speech, Heuss placed the discourse of fatherland, patriotism, honor, courage, and morality in the service of remembering the Nazi past. Although he stopped considerably short of examining the weight and significance of anti-Semitism, he made memory of the "pedantry of murder as a sheer automatic process," that is, the death camps, an element of the narrative of the Nazi past as told by the political leaders in Bonn. Heuss put the conservative forces in the Federal Republic on notice that he would oppose those who sought to equate amnesia with the national interest or national honor, or again to misuse the discourse of patriotism for their own purposes. For him it was memory of a difficult past, not avoidance of it, that was a matter of national honor. He initiated an often unpopular but never completely extinguished component of the Federal Republic's identity.

The second of Heuss's major speeches of the 1950s on the Nazi past concerned the legacy of the German resistance, and specifically the legacy of the conspirators of July 20, 1944. The divisions of the Cold War expressed themselves in the divided memory of the German resistance. The Communist cult of "antifascist resistance fighters" largely excluded the July 20 conspirators. Yet in the early years, memory of the men who had tried and failed to kill Hitler was not wildly popular in West Germany either. For many West Germans, a hint of treason clung even to the actions of even the conservative elements of the anti-Nazi resistance.[199] In this climate Heuss permitted publication in the press of his letter of July 19, 1952, to the widow of one of the conspirators.[200] In it he praised their sense of responsibility "before God and [their] people" and acknowledged that he had "lost many friends and relatives" in the revolt. He wrote not as *Bundespräsident*, he said, but as a "survivor." In making clear that "the other Germany" was visible and willing to sacrifice for its principles, the conspirators' deaths had "performed a political service" for Germany. Recalling their actions should lead Germans to foster "above all . . . reflection, decency, [and] moral and ethical self-consciousness."[201]

On July 20, 1954, the tenth anniversary of the plot to kill Hitler, Heuss delivered a speech to students at the Free University in West Berlin in praise of the resistance. As was his custom, Heuss consulted in advance a wide range of intellectuals and scholars. On July 9 Hans Bott, director of Heuss's office, wrote to Max Horkheimer for suggestions on how best to commemorate the anniversary. On July 12 Horkheimer sent a remarkable reply. In view of assertions that praise for the conspirators served to legitimate a conservative restoration in the Federal Republic, the arguments of one of the most prominent of Germany's left-liberal intellectuals about their legacy for a new democracy were particularly significant.[202] "In Germany," Horkheimer wrote, "there is much too little thought given to those who, during the years of horror, saved the name of humanity." The too often forgotten members of the German resistance "deserve . . . greater love." Even if one did not share the conspirators' political views, "nevertheless their act expressed the yearning for the whole." Horkheimer continued:

> A great deal would be gained if, in the new Germany, events such as those of July 20 would serve to educate its citizens. This would accomplish far more than expressions of abstract respect for democracy as such. Democracy is a vague concept, which has no automatic link to freedom and justice. It demands the spontaneity of the individual, which cannot be exhausted in formal principles. One of the few survivors of the July 20 plot was once asked how he could participate in the enterprise when he must have known that should it fail, he would face a fate worse than death. He responded that the existing state of affairs was so unbearable that everything, every torture and every ordeal, was preferable [to tolerating the status quo]. It is this spirit of the determinate negation [*das bestimmten Nein*] which needs to play such a decisive role in not fully articulated goals and programs. Practitioners of realpolitik all too gladly dismiss it as hazy and remote from reality. Yet in this spirit there lies that concrete connection to the possibility of something better. Its realization depends on it.[203]

Horkheimer believed that memory of the German resistance should play a part in the revival of democratic values in the Federal Republic. Heuss and Horkheimer found common ground in their shared commitment to restoration of the autonomous individual, able and willing to resist the pressures of the times in the name of morality, liberal democracy, and political justice.[204] As rektor of the University of Frankfurt,

Horkheimer sought to encourage such values in the student generation coming of age after the war.[205]

Heuss delivered "The Right of Resistance: Gratitude and Confession of Principles" in the main lecture hall of the Free University of Berlin on the tenth anniversary of the attempted coup.[206] He placed the resistance of July 20, 1944, in a longer tradition of lost causes in German history, including the liberal revolt of 1848, Weimar democracy, and the intellectual accomplishments of the German-Jewish synthesis. But failure did not detract from the dignity of these actions. At a time when cowardice, brutality, and the absence of honor had disgraced the German name, the individuals of July 20, 1944, "in full knowledge of the danger to their own lives, broke with the state of murderous evil" and sought to "save the fatherland from destruction."[207] In doing so the anti-Nazi resistance had written a chapter in the history of German patriotism. Fundamental morality had bound the conspirators together. Making an explicit reference to Luther's address of 1520, Heuss described them as the "Christian nobility of the German nation," who had joined with leaders of the workers' movement, socialists, trade unionists, state officials, and soldiers. While many found it uncomfortable to discuss such matters, said Heuss, "I am not in favor of that kind of comfort. Rather I consider it to be a gain when historians, theologians, jurists, and soldiers engage in serious discussions about these events and exhaust the issues in their spiritual and moral depth."[208]

Heuss described the Nazi regime as one of injustice and brutality, features which were in plain view of the political and military establishment by 1934, when Generals von Schleicher and von Bredow were murdered. He criticized the military leaders of the Wehrmacht for failing to protest. He rejected the notion of "unconditional obedience" within the military, stressed the importance of following individual conscience, and thanked the participants of July 20, 1944, for the legacy they left to the nation. "Their blood," he concluded, "washed away from the bespattered German name the shame that Hitler forced upon the Germans."[209] Military obedience did not mean abandoning law and morality.

The friends and relatives of the participants in the attempted coup had welcomed Heuss's election as *Bundespräsident* in 1949. Emmi Bonhoeffer, the widow of Dietrich Bonhoeffer, wrote to Heuss following his inaugural address that she was "indescribably happy . . . that you have become a father of the country [*Landesvater*]. I listened to your speech with tears in my eyes. Ah, what a relief it is, after years of ordinary bickering, to again hear the voice of a noble individual, a voice full of monarchical calm and dignity. Now, dear fatherland, rest . . . God, how well I will sleep tonight."[210] Following his 1954 speech, she wrote to him again to say that "your truly classical speech on July 20 in Berlin meant a great deal to all of us."[211]

Heuss defined the office of president as one that should lead and prod the West Germans rather than reflect or echo the popular mood. His contributions to the public discourse about the Nazi past marked the limits of official recognition of the burden of that past. He was the house critic, gently yet persistently reminding the West Germans of episodes many would rather forget, as well as of their own democratic traditions which many had abandoned. He stood for sobriety, modesty, reflection, and a rejection of nationalist demagoguery. In 1955 he declared the term "German wonder" or "miracle" to be "dumb, yes hateful. Its repetition is most alarming." The forces behind the German "wonder" were, in fact, "a few very simple, very natural, and not at all miraculous facts" of hard work and the return of "healthy sobriety after years of becoming drunk on speeches."[212] Heuss remembered and understood the language of reification and mysticism which Nazism had fostered. He urged his fellow citizens to keep their feet firmly planted in the mundane causal nexus of political and economic realities.

On September 12, 1959, Heuss delivered his farewell address.[213] He noted with pleasure that his departure from office was in accord with the constitution and with the principle of democracy understood as "governance for a limited time." Among the accomplishmens of the Federal Republic's first decade, he stressed reconstruction, recovery, and "restitution for the shameful injustice which so many, especially the Jewish people, had to suffer in the whole Hiltlerite power sphere." Again he rejected the term "wonder" or "miracle" to describe German economic recovery in the 1950s. Rather, he said, "simple and completely sober things took place." The "most visible legacy of Hitler's policy" was the division of the country and the imposition of a dictatorship in the Eastern zone.[214] He mentioned only one major political figure of West German politics, Ernst Reuter, who had reminded the free world of the importance of self-determination in the political battle over Berlin. Heuss was leaving office, he said, with his sense of "inner freedom" intact, something that was "the most precious possession that God had given to human beings as a possibility. To grasp it as a task determines our worth and dignity."[215]

Heuss's legacy was one of both content and form. As we have seen, he urged his fellow citizens to accept the burden of "collective shame" for the Nazi past while reminding them as well of the multiple, more humane continuities of German history. By recalling them he helped to restore a sense of pride and self-worth in a society short of both. Aware of his own misjudgments at the end of Weimar, he conveyed the humility and wisdom that come from awareness of one's own fallibility. Heuss's style was the polar opposite of the militant certainty of Ulbricht and Grotewohl. Where they presented themselves as inheritors of a morally pristine heroic antifascism, and therefore free from the debts accumulated by the actions of other Germans, Heuss stressed the enduring collective shame of Nazism for postwar Germans. He offered a muted alternative to Adenauer's reticence regarding public memory of the Nazi era. When unrepentant nationalists in the Federal Republic denounced the supposedly paralyzing effect of reflecting on the Nazi past, Heuss defined strength, integrity, and individual conscience as the ability to face a difficult past directly. In contrast to the reifying and mystifying discourse of the apolitical German tradition, Heuss urged the young generation of intellectuals and scholars to connect memory to history and to elaborate the causal political narratives which had led to moral catastrophe. However sharp his moral vision was in some areas, Heuss stopped short of using the pulpit of the presidency to criticize the delay and denial of justice which characterized the Federal Republic's first decade.

Just before he left office in 1959, he wrote to Nahum Goldmann to send his greetings to an upcoming meeting of the World Jewish Congress. It was "not morally permissible," he said, to minimize or forget what had happened to the Jews, but it was essential to increase the interaction between Germans and Jews. He recalled that in 1949 he had spoken not only of collective shame but also of the "courage to love" which had to be regained between Germans and Jews, and of "the fruitful accomplishments for the consciousness of the world that had emerged from the Jewish-German symbiosis of the last century and a half . . . You know," he continued, how very much he wished that after he left office, "the dark shadows of an insane past will not prevent the illumination of a better and a good future."[216]

Heuss's letter underscores an important point which distinguished the memory of the Nazi past among Heuss and Goldmann's generation from that of their successors. The founders came of age in a pre-Nazi, German-Jewish Germany and experienced Nazism firsthand. With the passage of time, public discussion of the past would inevitably be based less on personal memory and more on mediated history. In one sense, Heuss's dual stance—to remember the worst but also the best of German, Jewish, and Jewish-German history—was very much in accord with Goldmann's view: both men recalled the German-Jewish world that had been destroyed as well as the act of destruction. Unlike succeeding generations, they were able to summon these memories on the basis of personal experience.[217] Yet Heuss's arguments did influence his successors in the office of *Bundespräsident*. He had defined the job in part as keeper of the nation's terrible memories. The respect and affection with which he was held in the Federal Republic made it difficult for his successors to regress into silence and apologetics about the Nazi past. That said, not until the presidency of Richard von Weizsäcker in the 1980s did another *Bundespräsident* confront the crimes of the Nazi era as Heuss had done.

Heuss's immediate successor, Heinrich Lübke (1894–1972), was in office from 1959 to 1969. In an early speech to the Society for Christian-Jewish Cooperation, he said that any reconciliation between Germans and Jews must presuppose that the Germans directly face the full extent of the Jewish catastrophe and do all they could to make restitution for it. Lübke recalled Hitler's racist anti-Semitism and the "insanity of the destruction of the Jews." Yet a different tone entered into Lübke's speech. He said that "only a few ringleaders" had "consciously organized and wanted" to exterminate the Jews, a deed carried out with the "misuse of the name of the whole German people." Unfortunately, Lübke continued, outside Germany the impression that all of the Germans were involved was widespread.[218] Whereas Schumacher had rejected the accusation of collective guilt in order to focus on those who had been responsible, Lübke now fostered a new myth of a supposedly extremely small number of perpetrators. In so doing, he minimized the sense of collective shame and responsibility which Heuss had stressed.

Lübke pointed out that while the East German government regularly denounced the Federal Republic as a "new edition of the Third Reich," it refused to pay restitution to the Jews. Yet Lübke then followed with a most un-Heussian expression of impatience with Jewish survivors. "We Germans cannot forget what happened. We hope that the Jews will not leave the goodwill present in our contribution to restitution unanswered. It would be unfruitful, and over time would be paralyzing, if we did not feel that trust grows on the other side as well." The Germans, according to Lübke, wanted "recognition, encouragement, and response" for their efforts.[219] By contrast, Heuss as well as Adenauer had viewed the restitution agreements as atonement for past injustices, not an effort to purchase goodwill. Lübke went further when he warned that the Society for Christian-Jewish Cooperation would lose its effectiveness if it remained "only an association opposed to the revival of National Socialism" but did not see "defense against communism as lying within its circle of tasks." Were it to do so, it would "run the danger of becoming an association of veterans of the persecuted." He stressed the "double role" of the Germans as supporters but also victims of Nazism. Only a "small minority" of Germans, he said, were involved in perpetrating crimes.[220]

Lübke articulated the impatience of those in West Germany who had heard enough talk about the Nazi past, who did not want to be burdened by the actions of a "small minority," and who wanted the West German president to focus less on what the Nazis had done to others and more on the victimization of Germans by the Nazis and by the Allies. In view of the full coverage of the anti-Jewish purge in East Berlin in the *Allgemeine Wochenzeitung der Juden in Deutschland* and the *Frankfurter Rundschau* and in the leading West German liberal newspapers of the time, it was presumptuous for Lübke to urge Jews to furbish their anti-Communist credentials. In fact, West German liberals of the 1950s had not been shy about criticizing communism.

There was a great discrepancy between the West German discourse of repentance and acceptance of restitution obligations on the one hand and the paucity of justice on the other. It was thus not surprising that not only the leaders in East Berlin but also Western critics angered by judicial delay would dismiss the West German restitution agreements as "the political and financial price for the definitive Western integration of the Federal Republic."[221] Certainly restitution was a path of less resistance than justice. Certainly Adenauer knew that restitution would enhance the image of the Federal Republic in Israel and the United States. Yet it is also important to remember that in this fundamentally conservative era dominated by the Cold War between the Soviet Union and the West, the Jews past and present were a footnote to the main drama. The United States was not about to reject West German membership in NATO if it rejected restitution agreements. If paying restitution and making moving speeches about the Holocaust seemed the least a decent West German government could do, there were many West German voters who would have supported a far more forgetful and coldhearted policy. Adenauer deserves the credit he has received. Yet far more so than has heretofore been appreciated, so too do Schumacher and his colleagues on the postwar democratic left. Without their prodding and initiative, a West German democracy would have emerged with far less memory, far less justice, and far less compassion for survivors. Just as the democratic left had pushed hardest to address the Nazi past in the early years, so at the end of the 1950s politicians in the Social Democratic Party warned their fellow West Germans that the postponement of justice during the Adenauer era could become a moral and judicial scandal of enormous proportions. We turn now to the resulting change in the relationship between memory and democracy evident in West German politics since the 1960s.

# 9

## Politics and Memory since the 1960s

---

The purpose of this chapter and the next is to offer an overview, not a complete history, of the politics of memory in the Federal Republic and then in a unified Germany since the 1960s, and to place the ferment of the decades since then in the historical context of the founding traditions of the two Germanys. Both 1968 and the leftist dissent of the 1960s were a caesura in the history of West German reflection on the Nazi past. But, as the preceding chapters have indicated, the familiar dichotomies employed to distinguish the Adenauer era from West Germany since the 1960s, such as silence and speech or repression and recollection, capture only part of the postwar politics of memory. They neither do justice to the significance of the elite political and intellectual discourse of the immediate postwar years nor confront the ambiguous legacy left by claims of the sixties generation to confront the past which their elders had avoided. But they do touch on an essential truth: since the 1960s, discussion of the Nazi past did expand in West German politics and society, and the relationship between democracy and memory in the Adenauer era was challenged and reversed. Social Democrats and the New Left both argued that more democracy required more memory and more justice. While both factions turned away from Schumacher's vehement anticommunism, they deepened West German democracy in ways he had urged in the spring and summer of 1945.

Evidence of ferment within West Germany's national political institutions included three major parliamentary debates on extending the statute of limitations on prosecution of crimes of the Nazi era; trials in West German courts of those accused of being death camp personnel; Willy Brandt's initiation and implementation of *Ostpolitik* and Helmut Schmidt's blunt speeches about Auschwitz and Nazi persecution of the Jews; Helmut Kohl's renewal and modification of Adenauer's approach in the Bitburg ceremonies; and Bundespräsident Richard von Weizsäcker's reassertion of the Heussian tradition of recollection in his speech to the Bundestag of May 8, 1985. During the 1960s the New Left challenged the views on Jewish matters of Schumacher's generation of Social Democrats. During the 1980s, in the *Historikerstreit* [historian's dispute], conservatives attempted to reduce the presence which the crimes of the past had attained in West German official discourse since the 1960s.

In 1958 the Central Office for the Investigation of National Socialist Crimes was established in Ludwigsburg in the state of Baden-Würtemberg. Its investigations, as well as the publicity generated by the Adolf Eichmann trial in Jerusalem in 1961, raised troubling issues. Unless West Germany's fifteen-year statute of limitations on the crime of murder was extended, many tens of thousands of persons suspected of participation in war crimes and the Holocaust would escape indictment, trial, and punishment merely by virtue of the passage of time.[1] In 1960, 1965, 1969, and 1979, the Bundestag held extensive debates over extending the statute of limitations. These *Verjährungsdebatten* brought the crimes of the Nazi past as well as the magnitude of judicial failure of the 1950s to center stage in West German politics.

The number of suspects yet to be brought to trial was large. By the late 1950s, West German prosecutors and scholars estimated that about 100,000 persons had participated in some way in the destruction of European Jewry.[2] From May 8, 1945, to the mid-1980s, Allied and then West German courts accused 90,921 persons of participating in war crimes or crimes against humanity. Of this number 6,479 persons were convicted. Twelve were executed, 160 were sentenced to life in prison, 6,192 received extended prison terms, 114 paid fines, and one youth received a warning; 83,140 cases were closed without convictions owing to findings of innocence, nonopening of the proceedings by the court, or the death of the accused.[3] Of these 6,479 convictions, over 80 percent (5,487) were handed down by Western occupying powers between 1945 and 1951. The 1,819 convictions in 1948 constituted the high point of the postwar judicial proceedings.[4] At the time of the 1965 West German debate over extending the statute of limitations, 13,892 persons were still the subject of judicial proceedings, while proceedings against 542 persons had been stopped because the accused were abroad or in unknown locations. Cases against 41,212 persons had been closed without convictions.[5] By 1986, the number had risen to 83,140.[6] Despite the efforts of some West German prosecutors, it was obvious that thousands of murder suspects were successfully avoiding justice.

After the formation of the Federal Republic in 1949, trials were held in West German courts for crimes including the consolidation of the Nazi regime in the 1930s, the November pogrom of 1938, euthanasia experiments, the *Einsatzgruppen,* and the mass murder of Jews in ghettos and camps. The number of West German convictions dropped from 800 in 1950 to slightly over 200 in 1951, slightly under 200 in 1952, and about 125 in 1953. For the decade from 1954 to 1964, the number of convictions by courts in the Federal Republic hovered between 25 and 50 a year.[7] Between 1958 and 1986, the Central Office in Ludwigsburg opened 4,954 cases. By the end of 1985, 4,853 of those cases had been settled, and 101 were still pending.[8] In total, during the period from 1951 to 1986, West German courts handed down 992 convictions. The trials presented the facts of Nazi criminality to that part of the public which took an interest in them and delivered justice to some of the perpetrators. Yet thousands of persons whose cases should have been brought to trial never confronted the full force of the law.

Between 1945 and 1949, the Soviet occupation authorities convicted 12,500 persons of war crimes during the Nazi era. Given the propensity of the Soviet occupation authorities to use the Nazi label against political opponents, however, these figures must be treated with great caution. The convictions delivered in the 1950 war crimes trial in Waldheim also had very dubious legal foundations.[9] After 1950, East German authorities claimed that justice had largely been done and that most of the

Nazis were among the hundreds of thousands annually fleeing to the West. Whether for lack of Nazis to convict or, more likely, lack of prosecutorial zeal, convictions in the German Democratic Republic dropped dramatically to 331 in 1951, 140 in 1952, 85 in 1953, 35 in 1954, and 23 in 1955. In any given year between 1955 and 1964 in East Germany, there were at most ten convictions and as few as one. From 1951 to 1964 in the GDR, there were a total of 329 convictions for crimes committed during the Nazi era, of which 286 took place before 1956 and 46 occurred between 1956 and 1964.[10] The three-to-one ratio of convictions between West and East Germany was roughly the same as the population ratio. While more work remains to be done on justice in the two Germanys, these figures indicate that despite its antifascist legitimations, the German Democratic Republic was, if anything, even less aggressive in prosecuting crimes of the Nazi era than was the Federal Republic. That said, in the two Germanys many thousands of persons who should have been brought to trial for participation in the crime of murder were never indicted, and only a small minority were punished.

In each of the four *Verjährungsdebatten* the Social Democratic Party led the fight to continue prosecuting crimes of the Nazi era. The first of the West German parliamentary debates began on March 23, 1960, when SPD leaders in the Bundestag proposed that the statute of limitations on crimes which led to a sentence of ten years to life in prison be based on a starting date of September 15, 1949, rather than May 8, 1945.[11] On May 24, 1960, the full Bundestag debated the issue.[12] The minister of justice in the Adenauer government, Fritz Schäfer, asserted that all of the major episodes of mass murder had been researched. He disputed the assertion that there were individuals who were yet to be found and tried. The SPD initiative was rejected. Nevertheless, the SPD members of the Bundestag succeeded in making the failures of West German justice in the 1950s a political issue.[13]

In 1965 the Bundestag engaged in a second, far more extensive *Verjährungsdebatte*.[14] The Auschwitz trial conducted in Frankfurt-am-Main in 1964, as well as trials of those who had participated in murders in the *Einsatzgruppen* and at the extermination camps in Belzec, Treblinka, Sobibor, Chelmno, and Maidanek, offered further details to the West German public about the Holocaust and the death camps in Poland.[15] Support in the Bundestag for extending the statute of limitations, though strongest in the SPD, now came from moderates in the CDU and Ludwig Erhard's Justice Ministry. Research in American, German, Polish, and Soviet archives now led the minister of justice to conclude in his report to the Bundestag of February 24, 1965, that the possibility "could not be ruled out" that as yet undiscovered acts and perpetrators might become known after May 8, 1965, that is, twenty years after the war.[16]

Ernst Benda, a CDU member, a past president of the German-Israel Society, and a future president of the West German Supreme Court, disputed members of his own party who argued that further trials would damage the honor of the nation. National honor, he said, included the idea that "this German people is not a nation of murderers."[17] Those, including much of the Free Democratic Party (FDP) and most of the CDU, who opposed extending the statute argued that doing so amounted to creation of an ex post facto law, that the memories of witnesses and the accused were becoming weaker with time, and that some witnesses had died or were no longer willing to testify.[18] The Social Democrats made the case for extension. Their speakers argued that in the face of a crime of such magnitude and historical uniqueness, political and moral rather than legal-juridical considerations must be primary. The issue at hand was not political error but murder.[19] The Free Democrats, the nominal liberal party argued, were also a party defending the interests of professionals and civil servants who had served in the ministries of Nazi Germany. Thomas Dehler, an FDP parliamentary leader, opposed extension of the statute of limitations on the grounds that it would create a special law for particular crimes, and thus undermine efforts to place law on a firm foundation following the arbitrariness of the Nazi era.[20]

The SPD's Adolf Arndt (1904–1972) was the most effective and passionate advocate in favor of extending the statute. A lawyer from Berlin, Arndt had helped Jews and others to escape from Nazi Germany in the 1930s. He recalled in bloody and graphic detail the crimes at issue.[21] He stressed that these were not war crimes committed in the excesses of battle. They "had nothing to do with war. It was an ice-cold, planned, considered act of murder carried out by the whole machinery of the state."[22] In other words, the crime was genocide, a crime against humanity. In the 1965 *Verjährungsdebatte* genocide and crimes against humanity assumed greater prominence than the "war crimes" of conspiracy to commit aggression which had dominated the Nuremberg Trials.[23] Arndt also spoke of the Germans' "historical and moral guilt" for their indifference to and failure to protest Nazi anti-Jewish measures.[24] In response to those German young people who denied responsibility because they had been children at the time or not yet born, Arndt said: "A people does not live in the present. It lives in the succession of generations, and one cannot say: I was not yet born. This legacy doesn't concern me at all." For the victims, for the honor of all of those who lay in "unknown mass graves," it was necessary to bear the heavy and "today unfortunately still most unpopular burden" rather than to run away from the "mountain of guilt and havoc."[25]

Fritz Erler, another leader of the Social Democratic Party in the Bundestag, raised the issue of the moral responsibility of individuals living under dictatorship.[26] He stressed that the need for individual conscience in the face of dictatorship applied to the East German present as well as to the Nazi past.[27] "We all belong to all of German history," he said, and thus bear a responsibility to see that such horrors are not repeated, and that a new unjust regime not emerge in Germany. Therefore, the responsibility to face the Nazi past included "a merciless confrontation and debate with the Ulbricht regime . . . because in this regime a chapter of the German past in the form of totalitarian rule by force is again staring us straight in the face."[28] In the social liberal era of the 1970s, left-of-center efforts like Erler's to connect criticism of the Nazi dictatorship to criticism of the East German regime would become relics of increasingly unfashionable Cold War anticommunism.

On March 25, 1965, the Bundestag overwhelmingly voted in favor of changing the date on which the statute of limitations on crimes of murder would be based from May 8, 1945, to the beginning of West German sovereignty in fall 1949. In so doing, it made possible further prosecutions at least until December 31, 1969. In all, 344 members of parliament voted in favor, 96 voted no, and 4 abstained. The majority was composed of 184 members of the CDU/CSU, 180 members of the SPD, and 3 members of the FDP. Voting against extension and thus for an effective end to investigations and trials were 37 members of the CDU/CSU and 60 of the 63-member parliamentary representation of the FDP.[29] Support for extension in the SPD was almost unanimous (except for one abstention) but was also very widespread within the CDU/CSU. The core of opposition lay among right-wing representatives in the CDU/CSU, especially the Bavarian Christian Social Union, but even more so in the FDP.

The third of the *Verjährungsdebatten* took place in spring 1969. A "grand coalition" of Christian Democrats and Social Democrats now governed in Bonn. The justice minister, Social Democrat Horst Ehmke, proposed that the statute of limitations for crimes of murder and genocide be eliminated. In the June 11 Bundestag session he argued that refutation of the "false reproach of collective guilt can succeed only if we find the murderers among this people and make them accept their responsibility . . . If we were, intentionally or not, to express solidarity with the National Socialist crimes and for this reason . . . call for an end also to their judicial prosecution, we would retrospectively justify the thesis of collective guilt."[30] The majority of the Bundestag rejected Ehmke's proposal to eliminate the statute of limitations completely for crimes of murder. Instead it extended the statute to thirty years, thereby making possible further investigations and prosecutions in West German courts until December 31, 1979.[31]

The fourth and last debate took place in 1979. This time the great majority of conservative members opposed abolition of the statute. Alois Mertes, one of the leaders of the CDU in the Bundestag, spoke of a conflict between the two "equal moral values and goals" of justice and law. Anticipating objections, he insisted that his opposition to abolition had nothing to do with "amnesty, pardon, excuse, rendering [past crimes] harmless, or wanting to forget" the crimes of the Nazi era. Instead he defended statute of limitations by pointing to the difficulty of obtaining reliable evidence and testimony as time passed.[32] He contrasted the West German judicial record to that of the "self-righteous" and "hypocritical" regime in East Berlin, "which slanders Bonn's policy of friendship toward Israel as fascist and which cannot place anything comparable alongside Konrad Adenauer's policy of restitution."[33] Mertes, who was outspoken in his opposition to anti–Semitism and in his support for close West German–Israeli relations, repeated Adenauer's earlier warnings that "one-sided demands for atonement," in this instance extension of the statute, would "harden" German sentiments and presumably encourage a right-wing nationalist revival.[34]

SPD representative Herta Däubler-Gmelin said that in 1979, as in 1965 and 1969, expiration of the statute of limitations would mean that those "Nazi murderers" who had managed to escape from the law would be freed from fear of prosecution. That, she added, would be an "intolerable situation."[35] In 1979, she said, it was apparent that the hopes expressed in 1965 and 1969 that justice would be done in a timely fashion had not been fulfilled. Many cases remained to be pursued.[36] In response to concerns about protecting the rights of the accused after the passage of so much time, Däubler-Gmelin said that legal norms would be far more seriously damaged "if due to the statute of limitations a murderer can no longer be held accountable even if his deed is obvious and even if verification of his participation in the crime posed no problem." She added that the "call from the victims must not go unheard."[37] In making such arguments in 1979, Däubler-Gmelin and the Social Democratic leadership repeated what had become since Schumacher firm Social Democratic tradition. Hildegaard Hamm-Brucher, a Heuss protégée and a leader of the minority liberal wing of the Free Democrats, also spoke in favor of abolishing the statute of limitations. She regretted that in the early postwar period the West Germans did not "decisively enough eliminate the root of the evil . . . and that the rapid process of material reconstruction unjustifiably abbreviated, yes, repressed the slow and painful process of catharsis."[38] She regretted, too, that in the 1950s there had been an absence of public discussion aside from "a few politicians, theologians, and writers," but welcomed the broader public discussion of the Nazi past that had begun in the 1960s.[39]

On July 3, 1979, the Bundestag voted 253 to 228 to abolish the statute of limitations on crimes of murder and genocide. Voting in favor of the extension were 38 members of the CDU/CSU faction, 219 SPD representatives, and 15 members of the FDP. Voting against were 2 members of the SPD, 24 members of the FDP (including Foreign Minister Hans-Dietrich Genscher), and 207 members of the CDU/CSU (including Helmut Kohl).[40] Compared to the votes of 1965 and 1969, this one indicated that conservative opposition to extending the statute had greatly increased while support had grown within the FDP. The SPD continued to be the strongest supporter of further investigations and trials. In sum, the *Verjährungsdebatten* were important because they led to continued prosecutions and drew public attention to the crimes of the Nazi era and to the judicial fiasco of 1950s West Germany.

Adenauer's successor, Ludwig Erhard, served as West German chancellor from 1963 to 1966. Erhard had been Adenauer's economics minister.[41] He followed Adenauer's approach to the crimes of the Nazi past. He rarely spoke about them but instead focused his efforts on relations with Israel.[42] On ceremonial occasions, such as the dedication of the rebuilt synagogue in Worms which had been destroyed in the pogrom of 1938, he denounced anti-Semitism and expressed his "grief and shame about the evil deeds" of the Nazis.[43] Erhard was like other members of the founding generation in that his personal memory included the German-Jewish Germany which Nazism had destroyed. On April 30, 1964 at the Free University in West Berlin at a ceremony marking the one hundredth anniversary of the birth of the German-Jewish economist and sociologist Franz Oppenheimer (1864–1943), Erhard fondly recalled his doctoral adviser at the University of Frankfurt. Oppenheimer, he said, had been his "honored, admired, beloved teacher . . . who was at the same time a fatherly friend."[44] Erhard said that "for a long time there has been only one photograph in my study. It is the picture of my teacher Franz Oppenheimer," who "embodied German spirit and culture in their purest and most noble sense."[45] Erhard, like other members of the founding generation, expressed not only shame and guilt over Nazi crimes but also a sense of personal loss over the German-Jewish world the Nazis had destroyed.

In the spring of 1965, Erhard made the decision to establish diplomatic relations with Israel.[46] During a visit to Jerusalem in November 1967 after he was out of office, Erhard stressed that the decision had grown from "human convictions and political morality . . . [A]mong those of us in the older generation the deep shock about the shameful deeds and endless suffering remains alive."[47] The discrepancy between support for Israel and the paucity of justice for Nazi crimes at home led critics, then and since, to interpret West German policy toward Israel as an effort to gain the moral respectability which Bonn refused to acquire through vigorous judicial confrontation with the Nazi past.[48] West German diplomatic recognition of Israel was certainly accelerated by Cold War competition with East Germany following Ulbricht's March 1965 visit to Cairo and Egypt's implicit recognition of the GDR.[49] Opposition from West German industry with interests in the Arab world, on the one hand, and early and strong Social Democratic support for warm relations with Israel, on the other, complicate the picture painted by those who view West German policy toward Israel as *Vergangenheitsbewältigung* on the cheap.

From 1966 to 1969, in a "grand coalition" with Social Democrats and Free Democrats, Kurt Georg Kiesinger (1904–1988) became the first and only former member of the Nazi Party to be elected West German chancellor.[50] He had joined the Nazi Party in 1933 and worked in the Reich Broadcasting Company during the war. After 1945 he became a member of the moderate wing of the Christian Democratic Union in southwestern Germany, and was one of the few members of the CDU to call for recognizing the status quo in Eastern Europe. Kiesinger enjoyed good relations with his foreign minister, Willy Brandt, and the minister of federal affairs, Carlo Schmid. Brandt gained long-sought access to power. Kiesinger gained a kind of tacit absolution. The "grand coalition" presided over the beginnings of *Ostpolitik* toward Eastern Europe and the Soviet Union, reform at home, and radical extraparliamentary leftist protest.[51]

With the ascendancy of Willy Brandt (1913–1992) in West German politics, the "other Germany" at last came to power intent upon daring more democracy at home and initiating a new *Ostpolitik* in foreign policy. Both initiatives rested on very different views about democracy policy and memory from those of the Adenauer era. Brandt served as chancellor of the Federal Republic from 1969 to 1974. He was the first active participant in the anti-Nazi resistance and the first returned political exile to occupy that office.[52] He had been the Social Democratic Party's candidate for chancellor in 1960, party chairman from 1964 to 1984, foreign minister from 1966 to 1969, and chancellor from 1969 to 1974.[53] The views of Gustav Heinemann in the office of *Bundespräsident* during Brandt's term reinforced Brandt's views on the politics of memory.[54] Whereas Adenauer had linked democratization to minimal discussion of Nazi crimes, Brandt argued that their public memory should be part of a program of daring more democracy. Whereas conservatives had either focused on West German reconciliation with the West or argued that memory of Nazi aggression and genocide damaged the national image, Brandt and his foreign policy adviser Egon Bahr argued that public reflection on the German war on the Eastern Front in World War II was necessary to rebuild trust and normalize West German relations with Eastern Europe and the Soviet Union.[55] Conservative silence about the Nazi era bred mistrust. Memory was essential for allaying that mistrust and for any hope of securing Soviet agreement to end or moderate the division of Germany.[56]

Brandt's *Ostpolitik* marked a change in both policy and political culture.[57] Remembering the crimes of the Nazi past required a much sharper break with that past than had taken place during the Adenauer era. As Brandt put it in 1962, "in official Bonn" there had "not always been a deft hand" in "establishing distance to people who are now seen abroad as representatives of a past epoch of German history and not as representatives of the democratic present."[58] When Adenauer spoke about suffering in Eastern Europe, he was referring first of all to suffering inflicted by the Soviet Union since 1945. Brandt, by contrast, wrote in his 1968 book *Peace Policy in Europe*, "I do not ever forget that it was Hitler's 'Greater Germany' above all that brought so much unspeakable suffering to Eastern Europe."[59] Brandt's *Ostpolitik* pushed West German political memory back from the early Cold War period to the Nazi seizure of power in 1933, and the German invasions of Poland in 1939 and the Soviet Union in June 1941. Such memory would, he hoped, overcome the "underbalance of trust" that was the legacy of "criminal activities for which there is no parallel in modern history" and which had "disgraced the German name in all of the world."[60]

The West had a powerful case against Soviet policy in Eastern Europe after 1945, a case that Social Democrats, including Brandt, had made. Now Brandt and the supporters of *Ostpolitik* argued, in effect, that Cold War anticommunism and its memories were both geographically provincial and chronologically self-serving. It was provincial because of the ease with which it overlooked the fact that without the German invasion of the Soviet Union in 1941 the Red Army would not have been in the center of Europe in May 1945, and self-serving in focusing on Soviet actions after 1945 without giving equal attention to the chronology of German aggression. In the heated left-right divide of West German politics, Brandt and Egon Bahr found it difficult to combine memory of the Nazi past with criticism of existing Communist regimes. The erosion of the tradition of Social Democratic anticommunism was one result of these shifts in the politics of memory.[61] That said, Brandt's bent knee at the memorial for Jews killed in the Warsaw Ghetto marked the first time that a West German chancellor had so publicly acknowledged and expressed remorse and atonement for what the Germans had done to the peoples of Eastern Europe and the Soviet Union during World War II.[62] Just as Adenauer's acknowledgment in 1951 of German responsibility for shouldering obligations created by the genocide of the Jews was a step in West German reintegration into the Western alliance, so Brandt's acknowledgment of the Nazi past was essential for diplomatic success in Eastern Europe and in Moscow. Just as Adenauer had sought to reassure the French, the Americans, the Israelis, and Jews worldwide, so Brandt now tried to reassure the states and peoples of Eastern Europe and the Soviet Union that West Germany was not the fascist regime bent on regaining lost territories which Communist propaganda had depicted for twenty years.[63] In both instances memory of a terrible past was indispensable for serving West German policy in the present.

Although Helmut Schmidt, West German chancellor from 1974 to 1981, brought a realist's skepticism to some of Brandt's views about the Soviet Union, he continued the policy of *Ostpolitik* and also made important contributions to West German political memory.[64] On November 23, 1977, Schmidt became the first West German chancellor to deliver a speech at Auschwitz-Birkenau. He said that "the crime of Nazi fascism and the guilt of the German Reich under Hitler's leadership are at the basis of our responsibility. We Germans of today are not guilty as individual persons, but we must bear the political legacy of those who were guilty. That is our responsibility."[65] The focus of his remarks was on relations between Germans and Poles. He hoped that the Poles, "because they [had] suffered the most," would understand that Hitler's first victims were Germans, and recall that anti-Nazi resistance, albeit in "tragic futility," was carried out by Germans "to bring an end to the murderous tyranny over Europe." It was "not up to us Germans to say that Auschwitz is a memorial whose message is one of reconciliation. That can be said only by those whose fellow citizens suffered here. We know one thing, however: the path to reconciliation cannot avoid Auschwitz, but the path to mutual understanding must not and cannot end here in Auschwitz."[66] Schmidt's speech was an eloquent expression of West German atonement and remorse. Yet, given its purpose of normalizing German-Polish relations, it was strangely silent about the fact that Auschwitz-Birkenau was above all a death camp in which the Nazis had murdered 1.5 to 2 million Jews.

On November 9, 1978, on the fortieth anniversary of the anti-Jewish pogrom, Schmidt did focus on the Nazi persecution of Jews. Indeed, his speech was the most forthright yet made by a West German chancellor about the Nazi attack on German Jewry and about the failure of the German population to protest that persecution.[67] November 9, 1938, he said, "remains a cause of bitterness and shame."[68] After describing in detail the violence, arson, and arrests of that day, Schmidt recalled that though "all of this came to pass before the very eyes of a large number of German citizens . . . most people, faint of heart, kept their silence. The truth is that the churches, also faint of heart, kept their silence even though Synagogue and Church serve the same God and remain rooted in the spirit of the same testament."[69] He focused on the weakness of democratic convictions in the German middle classes, as well as "the striking antithesis between the technico-economic modernity of the old imperial Germany on the one hand and its politico-reactionary spirit on the other."[70] Hatred for democracy found in the Jews its primary scapegoat. Although Hitler and his henchmen had launched the war and carried out the Holocaust, Schmidt stressed that they had been able to do so because in Germany support for democracy and respect for the dignity and freedom of the individual "had been inadequate for generations." It was important to reflect on these events "to learn how people ought to behave toward one another and how they ought not to behave." Even though most Germans living in 1978 were "individually free from blame" and ought not to be cast "into the debtors' prison of history," German young people "can become guilty, too, if they fail to recognize the responsibility for what happens today and tomorrow deriving from what happened then."[71] That meant support for independent thinking, respect for the other, rejection of scapegoating, extremism, and violence, and acceptance of responsibility for one's actions. Like the West German founders, Schmidt sought political explanations for the Nazi persecution of the Jews in order to prevent its recurrence and to foster a peaceful, liberal, democratic Germany and Europe.

Following Theodor Heuss's speech of July 20, 1954, praise for the German resistance became a standard theme for his successors in the office of the presidency.[72] In 1964 Heinrich Lübke praised the 1944 revolt as a "symbol of the self-respect of our people and the beginning of its rehabilitation in the family of nations."[73] This conservative *Bundespräsident* added that "we should not remain silent" about the fact that many "undoctrinaire Communists" as well as advocates of authoritarian politics "which we no longer share" were victims of political persecution.[74] Gustav W. Heinemann viewed the resistance as a warning against the dangers of uncritical obedience and an inspiration for the spirit of protest and dissent of the 1960s.[75] Walter Scheel, *Bundespräsident* from 1974 to 1979, also stressed the role the Communists had played in the German resistance.[76] In 1979 the CDU majority in the Bundestag prevailed over SPD and FDP objections to elect Bundestag speaker and CDU member Karl Carstens *Bundespräsident*. The objections stemmed from Carstens's youthful membership in the Nazi Party. Even this former Nazi now praised July 20, 1944, as "an outstanding day in German history. It is the day on which Germans tried to kill Hitler and thereby free Germany and Europe from the tyranny of National Socialism." That date not only recalled the crimes of Nazism but also linked the present to traditions of freedom, human dignity, and morality in German history.[77] Even in West German conservative public discourse, praise for the resistance had became part of a search for precursors of a "good Germany" in the German past.

Although this study concentrates on national political leaders, a brief comment on the West German New Left and the Jewish question is in order. The debates of the 1960s and 1970s offer interesting parallels and contrasts to the controversy over the Jewish question in the early years in East Germany as well as in the early years of West German social democracy.[78] The revival of Marxism in the 1960s, just as it had in the 1930s, focused debate on the connection or lack thereof between capitalism and fascism. It either completely diverted attention from issues such as anti-Semitism, Nazi ideology, and the Holocaust or made them marginal to analyses of economic and social conflicts. Even those variants of Marxism, notably the Frankfurt school's critical theory, which did examine anti-Semitism tended to shift attention away from the specifics of German history onto more general themes of modernity, the dialectic of enlightenment, and instrumental reason.[79] This Marxist presence and Jewish near-absence, and the Israeli victory in the Six Day War in 1967, brought about a turn among some on the left away from the SPD's early strong empathy for Israel and Jewish concerns of the 1950s and early 1960s.[80]

The clash of generations within the left that took place in response to the Six Day War initiated more than a decade of intraleftist public debate about the Jewish question.[81] When the West German conservative publisher and antagonist of the New Left, Axel Springer, lavished great praise on Israel for its military accomplishments of 1967, the political reflex of the young left was to oppose the friends of their local enemy. Through victory in 1967 and guilt by association with the United States, Israel appeared to some in the young left as another link in the chain of American imperialism. In response, a now "older" generation of leftist intellectuals, including the novelist Günter Grass and philosopher Ernst Bloch, warned that an ahistorical and abstract anti-imperialism threatened to become a vehicle for "anti-Judaism." Nevertheless, parts of the West German New Left, like the East German Communists since the 1950s, concluded that facing the "fascist" past implied opposition to Zionism and the state of Israel.[82] The nadir of this current of thought and action took place in the summer of 1976, when West German and Palestinian terrorists together hijacked an Air France flight from Paris to Tel Aviv and brought it to Entebbe in Uganda. One of the West German radicals separated Jewish from non-Jewish, not Israeli from non-Israeli, passengers at the point of a gun.[83]

These actions and ideas ignited an intense intraleftist and German and Jewish dispute about politics, history, and memory. Some young West German Jewish intellectuals angrily announced that they were emigrating to Israel because of their disgust with what they viewed as leftist anti-Semitism.[84] Others stayed, however, and in the pages of newspapers such as *Die Zeit* and journals such as *Tribune, Links,* and *Pflasterstrand* criticized anti-Israeli and anti-Semitic sentiment within the West German left. In contrast to East Germany after the winter of 1952–53, the issues of anti-Semitism and the causes of the Holocaust became an enduring if beleaguered element of the leftist debate in the Federal Republic in the 1970s and 1980s.

As we have seen, in the early years in both Germanys a struggle for recognition, sometimes of a zero-sum nature, took place among the various victims of the Nazi regime. Following the broadcast of the American television docudrama *Holocaust* in the Federal Republic and the *Verjährungsdebatte* of 1979, discussion of the Holocaust became more frequent in West German political discourse. It was not long before the emotive power of the term "Holocaust" was put to use in contemporary politics. During the bitter debates about nuclear weapons in West Germany, opponents of the deployment of American missiles in West Germany used the term "Europe's Holocaust" and "nuclear Auschwitz" to refer to a nuclear war supposedly being prepared by "both superpowers" whose primary victims would be Europe, and especially the two Germanys.[85] The implicit denial of the uniqueness of the Holocaust contained in these accusations from the nationalist left during the Euromissiles dispute would become explicit in the writings of conservative historians during the *Historikerstreit* of 1985–86.

Like his admired predecessor Adenauer, Helmut Kohl wanted to integrate those who had gone astray into West German democracy, and integrate the nation which had gone astray into the Western alliance.[86] Yet if Kohl wished to make the CDU/CSU a governing party again, generational change and the shift to the left since the 1960s precluded a repetition of Adenauer's public reticence about the Nazi past. When Kohl did talk about the terrible past, he also tried to soften the blow. In a speech to the CDU youth organization in April 1976, Kohl, chairman of the CDU since 1973, noted that recent German history included "the horrors of Auschwitz, Maidanek, and Treblinka but also Graf von Stauffenberg and the men and women of the July 20 revolt against Hitler barbarism."[87] He added that it was necessary to fight not only against fascism but also against "Communist totalitarianism which in the middle of Germany in the GDR every day oppresses people."[88] It was one thing for a former inmate of Dachau such as Schumacher to denounce Communist totalitarianism. But by the 1970s, Social Democrats willing to take up Schumacher's vehement criticism of Communist regimes were often outflanked by others who regarded the application of the term "totalitarianism" to these regimes as a threat to *Ostpolitik* and peace itself. Although Kohl criticized the left for its double standards on human rights questions, his criticism of Communist governments would have been more powerful had he and his party supported extension or abolition of the statute of limitations on murder in 1979.

In January 1984 Kohl became only the second West German chancellor to visit Israel.[89] He uttered the now traditional Adenauerian sentiments of remorse regarding Nazi crimes against the Jews, but he added a startling new accent. Noting that he had been fifteen years old at the end of the war, he spoke of a generational change taking place in Germany and Israel. A young German generation did "not understand German history as a burden but as a task for the future. It is prepared to assume responsibility. But it refuses to admit collective guilt for the deeds of its fathers. We should welcome this development."[90] Neither the Israelis nor any of West Germany's allies had ever accused the West Germans, either those who were adults during the Nazi era or succeeding generations, of collective guilt. Did Kohl mean that those Germans alive during the Nazi era were in fact collectively guilty for the Nazi crimes but the accident of belated birth exonerated subsequent generations? Did his rejection of accusations never made express the old desire "finally" to leave the past behind?[91]

The Bitburg incident, of course, suggested that this was exactly what Kohl intended. His desire to honor the memory of German soldiers who fought in World War II was partly vintage Adenauer. In 1951 Adenauer had spoken of their honor. By asking the American president in 1985 to lay a wreath in honor of German war veterans buried at the military cemetery at Bitburg, Kohl sought to put an American imprimatur on West German conservative sentiment. He hoped to use the close ties created by the Western alliance in general, and the recent Euromissile dispute in particular, to stage a ceremony of reconciliation between the victors and vanquished of World War II. In Ronald Reagan he found an American president no less willing to place a distorted and divided memory of World War II in the service of the Cold War. Reagan agreed that on his visit to West Germany in 1985, he would not go to a concentration camp in order to avoid reawakening old memories and imposing "unnecessary" feelings of guilt on Germans, "none" of whom had been adults or "participated in any way in World War II" and "very few" of whom "even remember the war."[92] Instead he would attend the ceremony at Bitburg.

In April 1985 the announcement of Reagan's plans set off a storm of protest in the United States extending from Jewish and veterans' groups to fifty-three members of the Senate, who urged Reagan to cancel the Bitburg visit and instead to attend "an event commemorating the Holocaust." That protest in turn outraged West German conservatives.[93] Kohl wrote to Reagan that cancellation of the Bitburg visit "would have a serious psychological effect on the friendly sentiments of the German people for the United States of America and for the Reagan administration."[94] Reagan stood by the original plans, especially after Kohl phoned to tell him that he had a choice between going to Bitburg or canceling the visit and seeing the Kohl government fall.[95] In the Bundestag, the CDU/CSU/FDP majority defeated by a vote of 262 to 155 an SPD resolution which "regretted" the organization of Reagan's visit. A resolution from the Greens which called for cancellation of the visit to the Bitburg cemetery because its purpose was "to honor a criminal organization—the Waffen SS" failed by a vote of 398 to 24.[96]

Whether through calculation or incompetence, Kohl at Bitburg created yet another of the zero-sum games of nonrecognition in the history of divided memory which pitted "Jewish" against "German" suffering and again used the excuse of Western alliance solidarity to manipulate interpretation of the Nazi past. Unfortunately, in contrast to John J. McCloy in the early 1950s, Reagan failed to remind Kohl that American–West German relations did not and ought not rest on forgetting the crimes of the Nazi past or on offering sentimental fictions about the victim status of the Wehrmacht and the SS. As a result, Reagan placed himself in the absurd position of honoring soldiers who had fought for Nazi Germany supposedly in order to help an ally in the Atlantic alliance, an alliance which had its origins in the war against Nazism. In the decade preceding Bitburg, Kohl had been a persistent critic of the tendency to obscure the moral and political differences between the Soviet Union and the West. The Bitburg symbolism also was a projection of the doctrine of moral equivalence back into the past. If members of the Waffen SS were innocents, then what meaningful distinction could be made between perpetrators of crimes and victims in the Nazi era? As we have seen, projection of present Cold War politics onto the era of Nazism and World War II had taken place in both postwar Germanys.

On April 21, 1985, Kohl undid some of the damage wrought by plans for the Bitburg ceremony in an address to representatives of the Central Council of Jews in Germany at a ceremony marking the fortieth anniversary of the liberation of the Bergen-Belsen concentration camp.[97] He spoke eloquently and with passion about the need to keep alive the memory of the "systematic inhumanity of the Nazi dictatorship," this "darkest chapter of our history," which "must always serve as a reminder to us. The decisive question is why . . . so many people remained apathetic, did not listen properly, closed their eyes to the realities when the despots-to-be solicited support for their inhumane program, first in back rooms and then openly out in the streets."[98] He spoke of the persecution of Gypsies and the mentally handicapped, the 3 million Russian prisoners of war who died in German captivity, the suffering inflicted on Central and Eastern Europe, the 20 million people in the Soviet Union who died during the war, as well as those Germans who suffered retribution for Nazi injustices at the end of the war. "Germany bears historical responsibility for the crimes of the Nazi tyranny. This responsibility is reflected not least in never-ending shame."[99] He praised Adenauer, David Ben-Gurion, and Nahum Goldmann and the restitution agreements. He recalled Goldmann's reference to the "creative mutual influences of Jews and Germans" and announced plans to promote the study of Jewish history in Germany.[100] Kohl's speech in Bergen-Belsen, though a fine example of the established tradition of West German retrospection, was largely lost in the tumult over Bitburg.

The supposed power of the American Jewish lobby counted for naught.[101] On May 5, 1985, President Reagan laid wreaths first at Bergen-Belsen and then at Bitburg. Kohl described the event as "a reaffirmation and a widely visible and widely felt gesture of reconciliation between our peoples."[102] It was hard to conceive how honoring the memory of members of the SS could foster reconciliation between the United States and postwar Germans, unless one viewed reconciliation as inseparable from forgetting what World War II had been about. Bitburg opened such deep wounds in part because it offered a wholly untenable choice: recollection of the Holocaust and the race war waged by the Wehrmacht, the SS, and the Waffen SS versus celebration of the Western alliance and displacing the realities of the Nazi era in a fog of manipulative sentimentalism. If going to Bitburg was an expression of friendship, was remembering the distinction between perpetrators and victims an expression of anti-German sentiment? Kohl's policy and the popular support he received in West Germany seemed to offer symbolic confirmation of an unbroken continuity between the Wehrmacht's war against the Soviet Union and the Cold War which followed. Was this not what Communist propaganda about "Nazis in Bonn" had been saying for decades?

Reagan's Bitburg comments were noteworthy for their ignorance, sentimentality, and cynicism. He said nothing about what not only the Waffen SS but also the SS and the German army had actually done in Europe during World War II.[103] He said, "We who were enemies are now friends; we who were bitter adversaries are now the strongest of allies." This dangerous half-truth ignored the links between the United States and those Germans such as Adenauer, Brandt, Reuter, Heuss, and Schumacher who had been "bitter adversaries" of the Nazis, not of the Allies. Furthermore, it presented as a great accomplishment one of the most regrettable aspects of the formation of the Western alliance, namely, the failure to purge the West German establishment more deeply in the postwar decade.[104] Reagan appeared to echo the Communist claim that after 1945 the Western Allies actually did join with ex-Nazis in order to form a new anti-Soviet alliance, and that therefore the Western alliance rested on a shaky moral foundation of amnesia and denial of justice. In the history of the Cold War, no American president had so badly misunderstood the links between memory and politics as did Ronald Reagan at Bitburg.

In the Adenauer era Theodor Heuss used the pulpit of the *Bundespräsident* to counter the pressures to put a distorted image of the past in the service of present politics. In the Kohl era Richard von Weizsäcker used the same pulpit to reinvigorate the beleaguered traditions of West German national political retrospection.

In the decade following Bitburg, one current of West German conservatism, flushed first with electoral success at home and then with victory in the Cold War and peaceful German unification, sought to displace, relativize, and reduce the subject of the Holocaust and the crimes of the Nazi era in West German and then German public discourse. Each time, contemporary exponents of the traditions imitated by Heuss and Schumacher rebuffed those challenges. Moreover, the collapse of the East German government ended four decades of self-righteous and misleading "antifascism" and unleashed new energies of reflection on the Nazi past. German unification meant that memories of Nazism ceased to be a weapon in the political competition between the two Germanys. Memory remained divided, but along political lines within one polity. Contrary to initial fears, the Holocaust and the crimes of the Nazi era assumed an even greater place in the national political discourse of a unified Germany.

The reassertion of the Heussian tradition in the office of the presidency began with Richard von Weizsäcker's soon world-famous speech in the Bundestag on May 8, 1985, in ceremonies marking the fortieth anniversary of the end of World War II. It was the most important speech about the crimes of the Nazi era delivered in the national political arena since Heuss's address in Bergen-Belsen in November 1952. Delivered only three days after the Bitburg ceremony, it dispensed with sentimentalism and manipulative public relations.[105] In some ways Weizsäcker (1920–) was an unlikely figure to urge Germans to face the truth about the crimes of the Nazi past. He had been a soldier in the German army from 1938 to 1945. At one of the successor trials in Nuremberg, he served as defense counsel for his father, Ernst von Weizsäcker, who was on trial for his actions as state secretary in the Foreign Office of the Third Reich. Richard von Weizsäcker joined the CDU in 1954 and was a representative of its moderate wing in the Bundestag from 1969 to 1981. He served as mayor of West Berlin from 1981 to 1984, when he was elected to the office of *Bundespräsident*. He had also been a leader of West German Protestantism. From 1964 to 1970, and again in 1977, he was president of the annual Protestant "Church Days" (Kirchentäge).[106]

The central theme of Weizäcker's speech was the need for Germans to "look truth straight in the eye—without embellishment or distortion."[107] Whatever the Germans had believed before May 8, 1945, he said, after that date it was clear that they "had served the inhuman goals of a criminal regime." Hence, that date represented the defeat of Nazi Germany, but it also "was a day of liberation" from "the inhumanity and tyranny of the National Socialist regime." In response to his countrymen who regarded May 8, 1945, as the beginning of flight, expulsion, and dictatorship in the East, von Weizäcker insisted that the cause of Germany's postwar problems "goes back to the start of the tyranny that brought about war. We must not separate May 8, 1945, from January 30, 1933."[108]

Rather than remember the sufferings of one group at the expense of another, he urged Germans to mourn for "all the dead of the war and the tyranny."[109] He listed the victims in the following order: 6 million Jews; "countless citizens of the Soviet Union and Poland"; German soldiers and German citizens killed in air raids, in captivity, or during expulsion; the Sinti and the Gypsies; homosexuals and the mentally ill; those killed for their religious or political beliefs; hostages; members of resistance movements "in all countries occupied by us"; and "the victims of the German resistance—among the public, the military, the churches, the workers and trade unions, and the Communists."[110] This was the most comprehensive list yet made by a West German chancellor or *Bundespräsident* of the victims of Nazism, and it was one that crossed the Cold War fault lines which had distorted memory in Bitburg.

The narrative structure of the speech dispensed with a happy ending, whether Ulbricht's victorious socialism in Sachsenhausen in 1961 or the reconciliation of former enemies offered by Reagan and Kohl in Bitburg. Memory meant the ability to mourn and to grieve for "the endless army of the dead" and the suffering of those who survived.[111] Like Heuss, Weizsäcker presented a most un-Hegelian narrative of unredeemed suffering and tragedy. Where the experience of women had been either absent or incorporated into heroic archetypes in most postwar political reflection on the Nazi past, Weizsäcker spoke of "their suffering, renunciation, and silent strength [which] are all too easily forgotten by history. In the years of darkness, they ensured that the light of humanity was not extinguished."[112]

He then dealt with the Jewish catastrophe and with what the Germans had known and not known about it. "At the root of the tyranny was Hitler's immeasurable hatred against our Jewish compatriots."[113] While hardly any country was free of violence in its history, he remarked, "the genocide of the Jews is . . . unparalleled in history."[114] Although "the perpetuation of this crime was in the hands of a few people" and was concealed from the public, "every German was able to experience what his Jewish compatriots had to suffer, ranging from plain apathy and hidden intolerance to outright hatred. Who could remain unsuspecting" after the persecutions of the Jews in the 1930s? Anyone who "opened his eyes and ears and sought information could not fail to notice that the Jews were being deported." He continued:

> The nature and scope of the destruction may have exceeded human imagination, but in reality there was, apart from the crime itself, the attempt by too many people, including those of my generation, who were young and were not involved in planning the events and carrying them out, not to take note of what was happening. There were many ways of not burdening one's conscience, of shunning responsibility, looking away, keeping mum. When the unspeakable truth of the Holocaust became known at the end of the war, all too many of us claimed that we had not known anything about it or even suspected anything.[115]

Weizsäcker's rejection of claims of ignorance contrasted with the symbolism of Bitburg, which presented Germans, even members of the SS, as victims of the Nazi regime. In place of the distancing reference to crimes committed "in the name of Germany," Weiszäcker's used the first-person plural—"we" and "us." Despite this forthrightness, his narrative remained one without subjects, a story of crimes without specified perpetrators.

His acknowledgment of collective responsibility did not mean acceptance of collective guilt. "There is," he said, "no such thing as the guilt or innocence of an entire nation. Guilt is, like innocence, not collective, but personal."[116] The young could not profess guilt "for crimes that they did not commit. No discerning person can expect them to wear a penitential robe simply because they are Germans." But they did have a responsibility to "keep alive the memories . . . [A]nyone who closes his eyes to the past is blind to the present. Whoever refuses to remember the inhumanity is prone to new risks of infection."[117] Remembering the past was both a moral obligation and a political necessity. Furthermore, no matter what the Germans remembered, "the Jewish nation remembers and will always remember. We seek reconciliation . . . [T]here can be no reconciliation without remembrance." Reconciliation with "the Jewish nation" had to pass through memory of the Holocaust.[118]

As the dispute over the Euromissiles had recently demonstrated, in West German political culture, with few exceptions, the lessons of genocide at Auschwitz and appeasement in Munich had been neatly apportioned between left and right. Weizsäcker brought together the memories of appeasement in the 1930s with those of genocide and war in the 1940s. Although he stressed that Hitler had been "the driving force" on the road to disaster, he recalled the failure of the Western powers to stop Hitler, as well as the nonaggression pact with the Soviet Union in 1939. Yet, while some West German politicians had referred to these episodes to point the finger of blame at others, Weizsäcker emphasized that the failures of the other powers "does not mitigate Germany's responsibility for the outbreak of the Second World War." Moreover, he traced the postwar division of Germany to the policies of Nazi Germany. Although events after 1945 had cemented the division of Europe and Germany, "without the war started by Hitler it [the division] would not have happened at all."[119]

Weizsäcker's speech showed the impact of Brandt's challenge to the political culture of the Adenauer era. By insisting that May 8, 1945, must not be separated from January 30, 1933, Weizäcker, placed postwar history into a longer chronological causal sequence. Given the extent to which he generally broke with the limits of divided memory of West German conservatism, his speech included an odd lapse. He saw a parallel between "the arbitrariness of destruction" during the war and the arbitrary distribution of burdens" afterwards.[120] Yet neither the Nazi attack on European Jewry and the racially driven assault on the "subhumans" of Eastern Europe and the Soviet Union nor the hatred and revenge directed at ethnic Germans in the last months of the war and the postwar months and years was arbitrary. Both, as Theodor Heuss foresaw in 1932 in *Hitlers Weg,* were the products of the anti-Semitic and racist policies of the Nazi regime. That said, the speech constituted a remarkable effort to "look truth straight in the eye."[121]

Weizsäcker challenged those who would interpret the Nazi era primarily through the prism of the Cold War or the resentments of a new German nationalism. He named the Nazis' victims, and included the Communists in the anti-Nazi resistance. He asserted that many Germans had known that genocide was taking place and that too many members of his own generation had either remained silent or refused to learn more about what was taking place. He stressed that the postwar division of Europe and Germany had its roots in the Nazi seizure of power and World War II, and he called May 8, 1945, a day of liberation. These assertions angered and provoked some West German conservatives.[122] Yet, especially because it came only days after Bitburg, the response to Weizsäcker's speech both in West Germany and abroad was overwhelmingly favorable.

The *Historikerstreit* of 1986–87, already the subject of voluminous commentary, grew out of efforts on the intellectual right to reduce the burdens of the Holocaust in West German national political discourse by questioning its uniqueness.[123] In October 1988 Weizsäcker criticized those who compared or equated Auschwitz with the Gulag and other cases of ruthless extermination. Just as he had reasserted the major themes of the Heussian legacy of recollection after Bitburg, Weizsäcker now stressed that "Auschwitz remains unique. It was perpetrated by Germans in the name of Germany. This truth is immutable and will not be forgotten."[124] As he had on May 8, 1985, Weizsäcker defended the presidency's Heussian legacy against conservative efforts to displace it.

On November 9, 1988, the fortieth anniversary of "Kristallnacht," the Nazi pogrom against German Jews, Chancellor Kohl spoke to members of the Jewish community of Frankfurt am Main. November 1938 was, he said, "the latest point at which everyone must have become aware that anti-Semitism was the core of National Socialist ideology, and that it was not a mere instrument of domination among others—and certainly not an accidental, peripheral manifestation of dictatorship."[125] It remained a "source of deep shame" that the majority of the population had remained silent owing to a lack of civil courage, fear, or indifference. He stressed the centrality of Jewish culture in Western history and tradition and the shared Jewish and Christian opposition to totalitarianism, and described the presence of Jews in the Federal Republic as a "precious" but also a "fragile, easily broken gift. I am aware that your trust is easily shattered: by the presence of the eternal yesterday, and sometimes also by the thoughtlessness of the well-meaning."[126] Perhaps this last phrase was a reference to his own efforts in Bitburg. Although he was interrupted by protesters who criticized the Bitburg ceremony, his audience was generally receptive.

The difficulties of public memory of the Nazi past were again dramatically demonstrated on November 10, 1988, when Phillip Jenninger, president of the Bundestag and a member of the moderate wing of the CDU, delivered a speech about the pogrom of 1938 to a special session of the Bundestag. The speech was a blunt account of the Nazi persecution of the Jews and a public relations and political disaster for Jenninger.[127] He offered a detailed historical narrative of the pogrom, the event, he said, which marked the beginning of the "destruction of the Jews in Germany and in large parts of Europe." He recalled German passivity and indifference. "Everyone saw what happened, but most everyone looked away and remained silent. The churches remained silent, too."[128] Then he referred to the "fascination" of the years of Hitler's popularity in the 1930s. His intent was to explain how an evil man could have gained popular support, but his political adversaries misconstrued his efforts at historical explanation as an apologia or justification. As he completed the part of his speech which reconstructed the anti–Jewish and pro–Nazi popular mentality of 1938—views which he obviously found repellent—about fifty members of the Green and Social Democratic parties walked out in protest.

Thus, they did not hear his well-informed discussion of the history of German anti-Semitism, Hitler's radicalization of that tradition, and its implementation in the Holocaust, or his criticism of an overly eager and hypocritical postwar West German identification with the victors. Nor did they hear this moderate conservative politician agree with those who argued that "the planning of the war in the East and the destruction of the Jews were inseparable from each other, that one without the other would not have been possible."[129] Jenninger's speech marked one of the first times, if not the first, that a major West German national political figure publicly connected the Nazi attack on the Soviet Union and the war on the Eastern Front to the Holocaust. In so doing, he broke with one of the most enduring elements of divided memory of the Cold War era, namely, the separation of the Holocaust from the racist nature of the Nazi attack on "Jewish bolshevism." For Jenninger, opposition to Soviet pressures in the 1980s did not preclude clear public recognition of the connections between anti-communism and anti-Semitism and racism which had been central to Nazi ideology and policy.

Jenninger also eschewed comforting tales about German resistance. In the end, Jenninger said, "the Jews stood alone. Their fate met blindness and cold hearts." He rejected efforts to place the historical truth in question, to play with numbers or deny facts. Such efforts were "senseless," he said, for "until the end of time, people will remember that Auschwitz was part of our, of German, history." No less senseless was the effort to "finally put an end" to talk about the past. "Keeping memory fresh and alive and accepting the past as part of our identity as Germans—only this promises that we of the older generation as well as the young liberation will learn from the burden of history."[130]

The negative reaction to Jenninger's speech was so intense that he was forced to resign as president of the Bundestag. His leftist critics charged him with insensitivity and with failing to distinguish between the historical reconstruction of attitudes he did not share and offering an apology for them. It was a peculiar reaction because Jenninger's depiction of a nazified Germany and an abandoned Jewry restated what critical historical scholarship had already demonstrated. By linking the Holocaust to the war on the Eastern Front, he undermined apologetic attempts to salvage the reputation of the Wehrmacht. While his assertions regarding popular support for Nazism in the 1930s offended leftist visions of popular antifascist resistance, his arguments regarding the links between the Wehrmacht and the Holocaust may have contributed to a conservative reluctance to rally to his side. He had, after all, said many things which, as Adenauer and Kohl had understood, Christian Democratic voters did not want to hear.

The cumulative impact of the *Verjährungsdebatten*, trials for crimes against humanity, the New Left's challenge to the avoidance and judicial delays of the Adenauer era, controversies over the New Left and the Middle East, *Ostpolitik*, the broadcast of the American docudrama *Holocaust*, Bitburg, the speeches by Weizsäcker and Jenninger, and the *Historikersstreit* made the Holocaust and the crimes of the Nazi era more frequent topics of public discussion within and beyond West German political institutions. A conservative government comfortable with Adenauer's approach confronted a society which had increasingly adopted the contrasting arguments about democracy and memory inaugurated by Heuss and Schumacher. West Germany as a society and polity had changed in this regard.

In this same period the winds of change had not blown through the German Democratic Republic with the same intensity. In East Berlin the place of the Holocaust in official narratives of anti-fascism remained where it had been put during the anticosmopolitan purges of the 1950s. Just as the repression of the significance of the Holocaust constituted a chapter in the history of the consolidation of dictatorship, so its reemergence in the 1980s was inseparable from the dissident challenge to the East German dictatorship and to its antifascist legitimating formulas.

Erich Honecker (1912–1993) succeeded Ulbricht as head of the SED in 1971. By 1976 he had accumulated the combined power of head of state and general secretary of the ruling Socialist Unity Party (SED). He governed East Germany until the regime collapsed in the face of a peaceful revolution in the fall of 1989. As I noted earlier, in the Honecker era East Germany sustained a warm relationship with the Arab states, and especially with the Palestine Liberation Organization. With a few beleaguered exceptions, East German historians kept the

Jewish catastrophe on the margins of their work.[131] In 1987, perhaps hoping to improve relations with the United States, East Berlin initiated negotiations with representatives of the World Jewish Congress about the possibility of East German restitution for Jews of German descent residing in other countries, and permitted the installation of a new rabbi in East Berlin.[132] Yet the fundamentals of East German antifascism remained intact. Until its demise, the German Democratic Republic had no diplomatic relations with the state of Israel, paid no restitution to Jews or to Israel, remained a loyal ally of the PLO and Arab states, and kept the Holocaust on the periphery of its national political culture. As the Marxist-Leninism of the postwar years wore thin, the regime tried to situate itself in older, noncommunist continuities in German history, including those of Luther and Bismarck. These efforts reinforced nationalist sentiments which had earlier been expressed in Marxist-Leninist terminology.[133]

The first East German breaks with official antifascism came during the 1980s from political dissidents.[134] On May 8, 1985, the same day Weizsäcker spoke in Bonn, Markus Meckel and Martin Gutzeit, two leaders of the East German Protestant peace movement, published an important challenge to official antifascist orthodoxy.[135] Rather than displace guilt or responsibility for the crimes of the Nazi era exclusively onto the West Germans, they wrote that "the guilt of the others, even of the fathers, is not alien to us." They argued that, despite official antifascism, the GDR had failed to reflect on its own guilt. To be sure, many of its leaders had fought in the anti-Nazi resistance. Yet "the great majority of the people who then became citizens of the GDR" had helped to support the Nazi regime with "their passivity and silence." Despite the antifascist nature of the government, "National Socialist ideas also remained intact and unworked through" among East Germans. Denazification had been "external" and "defined by a change of political relations" which had not brought about "a genuine confrontation with one's own guilt-ridden past."[136]

The really explosive implication of their essay lay in its arguments about memory and democratization. "Coming to terms with the past includes the obligation to actively oppose the system of fear and threat and injustice and misuse of power within our own society." It meant demanding "civil courage," assumption of "political responsibility," and respect for "the rights and dignity of all human beings" regardless of "their worldview, race, and gender."[137] In short, coming to terms with the Nazi past did not justify the imposition of a second dictatorship over a dangerous people. Rather it called for the rejection of dictatorship and the attainment of individual rights and political democracy. In the hands of Meckel and Gutzeit, German Protestantism, which had contributed so much to authoritarian rule in German history, now fostered democratic lessons that subverted official Communist antifascism. Meckel and Gutzeit turned the discourses of *Vergangenheitsbewältigung* and antifascism against their official advocates. Between 1933 and 1945, support for Nazism had been stronger among German Protestants than among Catholics. In the 1980s in both Germanys, Protestant voices from Weizsäcker in the West to dissidents in the East spoke in favor of frank confrontation with the Nazi past.

The marginalization of the Jewish question was a chapter in the consolidation of the East German dictatorship. Appropriately, its return to prominence in East German politics was another important chapter in the regime's collapse. Indeed, the first act of East Germany's first democratically elected government was to end forty years of Communist denial and evasion regarding the Holocaust and its consequences. On April 12, 1990, the Volkskammer voted 379 to 0 with 21 abstentions to approve a resolution which accepted joint responsibility for Nazi crimes and expressed a willingness to pay reparations and to seek diplomatic ties with Israel.[138] On April 14, 1990, the headline of the left-liberal *Frankfurter Rundschau,* the West German daily which had most carefully reported on the anti–Jewish purges of the 1950s, firmly established the link between democratization and discussion of the Holocaust. Its front-page headline read "Volkskammer Recognizes Guilt for the Holocaust: First Freely Elected GDR Government in Office."[139] The Volkskammer statement read in part as follows:

> We, the first freely elected parliamentarians of East Germany, admit our responsibility as Germans in East Germany for our history and our future and declare unanimously before the world:

Immeasurable suffering was inflicted on the peoples of the world by Germans during the time of National Socialism. Nationalism and racial madness led to genocide, particularly of the Jews in all of the European countries, of the people of the Soviet Union, the Polish people, and the Gypsy people.

Parliament admits joint responsibility on behalf of the people for the humiliation, expulsion, and murder of Jewish women, men, and children. We feel sad and ashamed and acknowledge this burden of German history.

We ask the Jews of the world to forgive us for the hypocrisy and hostility of official East German policies toward Israel and also for the persecution and degradation of Jewish citizens after 1945 in our country.

We declare our willingness to contribute as much as possible to the healing of mental and physical sufferings of survivors and to provide just compensation for material losses.[140]

The Volkskammer statement broke completely with the view that West Germans alone should bear the burden of the crimes of the Nazi era or that it was a marginal event in the history of Nazism and World War II. Gone was the arrogance and lack of historical self-consciousness with which East German political leaders had aided Israel's armed adversaries. Gone was a forty-year legacy of anti-Semitic code words clothed in Marxist-Leninist slogans and denials that anti-Semitism could exist in an officially antifascist regime.[141]

During its short life from January through October 1990, the democratically elected government in East Germany made good on these promises. In January and March, Markus Meckel, now the East German foreign minister, met with Israeli diplomats in Copenhagen. As conditions for establishing diplomatic ties, the Israelis insisted that the East German government assume responsibility for Nazi crimes against the Jews. This would include changing relevant portions of school curricula, entering into negotiations over restitution, and ending East Germany's one-sided policy of favoring Arab states, beginning with an end to "training terrorists for warfare against Israel." East German Prime Minister Hans Modrow, in a letter to Israeli Prime Minister Yitzhak Shamir, agreed to meet many of these conditions.[142]

Yet this East German democracy was short-lived. In the fall of 1990, German political unification arrived and the era of divided memory ended. While the collapse of Communist antifascism brought down one powerful barrier to a forthright recollection of the Nazi past, unification on West German terms raised the possibility of a new bout of amnesia under conservative auspices. Among intellectuals a young right had emerged. Styling itself the "generation of 1989," it attacked Adenauer's option for Westernization and the leftist "generation of 1968," and hoped to end the "rituals of atonement" of the Bonn Republic.[143] In the streets, neo-Nazi and skinhead violence against foreigners as well as Jews aroused fears that a unified Germany would unleash the racist ghosts of the past. Indeed, from the beginning of 1991 to the fall of 1993, German government officials listed 4,500 acts of violence attributed to right-wing extremist groups directed at immigrants and Jews. These attacks resulted in 26 murders and 1,800 injuries. Several synagogues were the targets of radical right violence.[144] Thousands of Germans marched in the streets to protest the wave of violence. Yet fears about the new Germany were reinforced when the activist left, in response to Saddam Hussein's threats to attack Israel and his invasion of Kuwait, marched under the banner "No Blood for Oil."[145]

In this climate Rita Süssmuth, the president of the Bundestag, delivered one of the first major national political statements about the Nazi past following German unification. The occasion was the fifty-fifth anniversary of the pogrom of November 9, 1938. She connected memory of the Nazi past with defense of human rights in the present.[146] As many West German leaders had previously done, Süssmuth recalled the details of the pogrom, anti-Semitism and antidemocratic traditions in Germany, and the absence of resistance to the persecution of the Jews. She called Auschwitz "the cold-blooded, organized, and systematic genocide of the Jews . . . [the] deepest break in our history," which had permanently changed how people looked at humanity and how Germans would look at their own history.[147]

Noting that November 9, 1989, was the day when the Berlin Wall was opened, Süssmuth said that the end of the German division "was also the beginning of a common memory," not, as many had feared, the first chapter of a new era of forgetfulness and nationalism. Common memory, she continued, would help to guard against intolerance and violence. She expressed shame and anger over the recent attacks on foreigners, immigrants, Jewish citizens, and cemeteries, praised the thousands of German citizens who had protested against antiforeign hatred and violence, and urged everyone to fight against anti-Semitism, hatred of foreigners, and a "falsifying engagement with history."[148] Just as the citizens of the GDR had courageously won their battle for freedom, so courage was essential in the unified Germany of 1993 to defend "human dignity and democracy in all of Germany." She continued: "Memory of the negatives of our own past does not weaken us, as we once feared. Rather it frees us from its burdens, transforms weaknesses into strengths, leads us toward one another rather than against one another. Vigilant and alert memory [*Wachsames Erinnern*] is the protector of freedom. If we forget unfreedom, persecution, and annihilation, we endanger our own freedom . . . Memory does not stop when the Germans regained freedom and unity."[149] While memory would remain subjected to political dispute, Süssmuth's speech marked the beginning of a "vigilant" and "common" memory in unified Germany. She drew on both traditions of official memory from West Germany and the dissenters in East Germany to fashion this common memory of the Nazi past and the Holocaust, and to apply its lessons to the defense of human rights and democracy in the present.

At ceremonies marking the fiftieth anniversary of the end of World War II in the spring of 1995, German political leaders, along with thousands of participants, traveled to former Nazi concentration camps to recall the crimes of the Nazi era and to speak out for human rights in the present.[150] On April 27 in Bergen-Belsen, Ignatz Bubis and other leaders of the Central Council of Jews in Germany, former Israeli president Chaim Herzog, the new *Bundespräsident* Roman Herzog, Chancellor Kohl, Rita Süssmuth, the chairmen of the political factions in the Bundestag, and four thousand guests including five hundred former camp inmates, assembled.[151] Herzog, who had begun his presidency with the assertion that the Germans should be less "uptight" (*unverkrampft*) about the Nazi past, returned to Heussian orthodoxy on this occasion. Everything that reminded the young of their responsibility for democracy, freedom, and human dignity was good. "Everything that ended in alibis . . . was false."[152]

The irritation of the intellectual and political hard right in the face of the outpouring of spring 1995 was apparent in several political newspaper ads which denounced the liberal media and politicians for forgetting that May 8, 1945, was not only a day of liberation but "also . . . the beginning of the terror of expulsion [*Vertreibungsterror*] and new oppression in the East and the beginning of the division of our country."[153] On April 8, 1995, Bubis responded that it was a "scandal" to suggest that the division of Germany and the expulsion of Germans from their homes in Central and Eastern Europe had had their beginnings on May 8, 1945. Rather they were the "logical consequence" of the Nazi seizure of power on January 30, 1933.[154] In another ad on April 27, 1995, the conservatives complained that stressing May 8, 1945, only as a day of liberation was a sign of the "opinion terror of 'political correctness'" in unified Germany.[155]

Chancellor Kohl kept a relatively low profile and did not set off another Bitburg explosion. "Multiple memories are awake," he said. "There is no common denominator for all of these memories and emotions."[156] He stuck to making general statements about the need to remember the suffering among Germans and others. "The decisive lesson" of the experiences of the twentieth century was the need to work for peace based on the "unlimited respect for personal human rights and the rights of peoples."[157] Much to the consternation of his nationalist-right, even the combined effect of thirteen years of the Helmut Kohl era, Western victory in the Cold War in 1989, and German unification in 1990 was not sufficient to consign memory of the Holocaust and other crimes of the Nazi era to long-desired oblivion. Instead the collapse of Communist antifascism, and perhaps also the liberation of "antifascist" impulses from their official Communist interpretations and the continued presence of the reinvigorated West German tradition of *Vergangenheitsbewältigung*, had given these difficult memories a continuing, if not even more prominent, place in the national political discourse.

If one can judge by speeches, attendance at memorial ceremonies, and press accounts, it did appear that the Germans' focus on the crimes of the Nazi past in the spring of 1995 was greater than at any time since World War II.[158] Thousands attended observances at former Nazi concentration camps and viewed exhibitions about Nazism in museums in Berlin, Hamburg, Cologne, Kiel, Hannover, and other cities. A new museum on the "topography of terror" opened on the site of the former headquarters of the SS in Berlin. A few of Germany's largest companies, including Daimler-Benz, Volkswagen, and the Deutsche Bank, hired leading historians to offer a full and frank account of the use of slave labor and profits from stolen Jewish property.[159] Even in conservative Bavaria, Minister-President Edmund Stoiber of the Christian Social Union told a gathering of five thousand people, including two thousand former prisoners of the Dachau concentration camp, that there "is no way a line can be drawn under this darkest chapter of German history."[160] At one such memorial service a former leader of the Protestant Church in East Germany said that "in contrast to the usual practice in the GDR, we cannot steal away from shared responsibility" for the Nazi past and special guilt toward the Jewish people by "distinguishing between the National Socialists and the German people."[161]

Bundespräsident Herzog delivered the central political statement of the fiftieth anniversary commemorations in a speech in the Reichstag in Berlin in the presence of representatives of Britain, France, the United States, and Russia.[162] Herzog stated that Germany had unleashed "the most horrible war there had ever been" and had suffered grievously as a consequence. He warned against dwelling on German suffering as a way to "allow the guilt of German political leaders to disappear behind a picture of general ruin . . . The Germans carried out a Holocaust against the innocents of many peoples." Yet, he continued, "today we do not need to discuss that again." Today the Germans knew very well that the Nazi regime was responsible for the Holocaust and Europe's suffering. In West Germany after 1945, he continued, there was no shortage of efforts to minimize or deny the worst, but "the basic feeling of collective shame, as Theodor Heuss put it so well, was there and became clearer with time."[163]

In previous weeks Herzog had indeed spoken about the war and the Holocaust in Warsaw, Jerusalem, and Bergen-Belsen. On May 8, 1995, his focus was on the postwar era as a history of success leading to the consolidation of German democracy. He extolled the Marshall Plan, Western integration, the "strong hand of the occupying powers," and the gradual emergence of a tradition of respect for human rights. In 1995 German democracy rested on lessons the West Germans had learned since 1948 as well as on the East German revolution of 1989. For Herzog, May 8, 1945, represented above all "a day on which a door was opened to the future," in part through a return to "the better traditions of Europe and, as the work of Kant indicates, to those of Germany as well."[164] Yet even in his Whiggish rendition of the postwar success story, Herzog placed German aggression and the Holocaust at the center of his narrative. Democracy's success in Germany rested on reflection on dictatorial pasts.

On May 9, 1995, Bubis proposed that either January 20, the date of the Wannsee Conference, or January 27, the anniversary of the liberation of Auschwitz-Birkenau, become a German national day of remembrance for the victims of Nazi persecution and genocide.[165] On June 1 a majority in the Bundestag approved the January 27 date.[166] On January 20, 1996, Bundespräsident Herzog spoke in the Bundestag to mark the Day of Commemoration for Victims of National Socialism. In so doing, he gave further evidence that an ever sharper and more detailed memory of the crimes of the Nazi era was now part of the national political recollection of a unified Germany.[167] Like Heuss, Weizsäcker, Süssmuth, and others before him, he took issue with those who wanted to forget the past. Memory, rather than serving to weaken the nation by recalling the shameful past, "is in our own interest," he said, because it makes learning possible. "Remembrance gives us strength, since it helps to keep us from going astray."[168] In contrast to past efforts to minimize the extent of general participation in Nazi murders, Herzog now spoke of the "many Germans" who had "accumulated guilt." The suffering of the Jews and other victims "was reported on the radio and in the newspapers. It was something anyone could have known about who had eyes to see with and ears to hear with." Terror had not been restricted to the first months of the regime or to the concentration and extermination camps. "The gradual escalation of cruelty took place publicly and was published in the law gazettes." He recalled the expulsion of Jews from public service; boycotts of Jewish lawyers, doctors, and businesses; the Nuremberg race laws; and the requirement that Jews wear the Star of David, marking them as "'subhumans' and exposing them in everyday life to every form of cruelty and attack by the rabble." He also recalled the "snide remarks and humiliations . . . the progressive restriction of living space and freedom of movement, the exclusion of children from schools, a ban on frequenting theaters and cinemas, a ban on using public transport and communications media, even the use of park benches, the seizure of typewriters, radios, jewelry, furs, even pets."[169]

The *Bundespräsident*, who had entered office advocating a more "laidback" approach, surprised his critics with the detail and passion of his denunciation of Nazi racial ideology and mass murder. Moreover, he asserted that Nazi racial ideology "gradually became part of public opinion," which thus became inured and looked away and did not want to know what was happening. His focus on the importance of Nazi ideology implied that perhaps the crimes of the Nazi era were not so incomprehensible after all. If so, memory was inseparable from prevention of future crimes. January 27 was intended as a day of remembrance specifically to draw attention to the victims of an ideology "that propagated a [doctrine of] 'Nordic master race' and 'subhumans' and denied the right of the latter to exist." Its purpose was also to encourage Germans, especially young Germans, to recognize the dangers of totalitarianism and racism and to resist them at the earliest possible moment. It was their "collective responsibility," said Herzog, to keep memory alive in order to overcome evil and to understand the precious nature of democracy, the rule of law, human rights, and human dignity. Every "older democracy" is faced with the problem that its citizens "take freedom and the rule of law for granted" and display "an insufficient awareness of the dangers of arbitrary rule and tyranny." In Germany the problem of memory was more sensitive because "it was here and from here that the atrocities which we are remembering today were committed." The "generation of witnesses to those times" which "drew their conclusions from those experiences" was now stepping down from the political stage.[170] With the passage of time and of the founding generation, public memory of the crimes of the Nazi era became more, not less, important for German society and democracy. As Heuss and Schumacher had first argued, memory of past crimes was not synonymous with accusations of collective guilt. On the contrary, it was essential to preserving norms of the rule of law, justice, and individual moral accountability which were necessary for the preservation of postwar liberal democracy. These convictions had now become firmly entrenched in the official calendar and national memory of the German political establishment.

The resurgence of German nationalism, neo-Nazism in the streets, antiforeign violence, and a desire to leave the Nazi past behind remained aspects of the German political scene in the 1990s. Yet efforts to expunge from the national political memory or minimize the weight of the Holocaust and other crimes of the Nazi era had failed. These difficult memories remained a constitutive and powerful element of the nation's central political narrative of its past.

# Conclusion

Why did any political memory of the Holocaust and crimes of the Nazi era emerge at all in either German state after 1945? Why did memory divide along political lines, and why was "the Jewish question" suppressed in East Germany while a sympathetic hearing for some postwar Jewish concerns emerged in West Germany? What was the relationship between memory of the Nazi past and postwar dictatorship and democracy? How did indigenous traditions interact with international and external factors to influence political memory of the Nazi past in the two Germanys?

Three factors account for the emergence and the division of postwar memory: Allied victory and postwar occupation, multiple restorations of "other Germanys," and the personal experience of shared solidarity and persecution among the founding generation. Allied victory followed by occupation-era destruction of the Nazi Party, revelations of Nazi war crimes and crimes against humanity at the Nuremberg and other trials, and imprisonment and in some cases execution of perpetrators of those crimes did not eliminate anti-Semitic and antidemocratic thinking, but these measures did destroy Nazism as a central political force in postwar Germany. The Nuremberg interregnum was the golden age of postwar justice. Afterward, no major national political figure in either of the two Germanys questioned the factual occurrence of such crimes. Instead they argued about what caused the mass murder, where commonly accepted facts should fit into public narratives, which of Nazism's victims should receive primacy in public memory, and how such horrors could be prevented in the future.

Allied victory made possible multiple restorations of political traditions of the "other Germanys" which Nazism had suppressed from 1933 to 1945. Even where the victor's control over the vanquished in both East and West was total, this power was manifested less in the imposition of previously foreign interpretations than in the repression of Nazism and the encouragement of other previously *local* German political traditions. As representatives of those traditions, German political leaders played a central role in bringing the memory of the crimes of the Nazi era, including the Holocaust, to the attention of their fellow Germans. As we have seen, they varied greatly in their willingness to discuss these issues or the extent to which they placed the genocide of European Jewry at the center of their concerns. Yet from Ulbricht to Adenauer, all of the postwar founders shared a deep and enduring hatred of Nazism.

Personal experiences of persecution during the Nazi era were also decisive. With greatly varying degrees of severity, all of the members of the founding political generation had suffered as a result of their political opposition to the Nazis. The Nazis had driven them all out of public life, political office, and employment. For Adenauer and Heuss, this was followed by "inner emigration," a relatively mild fate, though one that did not spare Adenauer from arrest or his wife from Gestapo interrogation. For thousands of Communists and Social Democrats, Nazism meant imprisonment, torture, even death, or escape through exile abroad. As the postwar testimonies of Franz Dahlem, Paul Merker, Ernst Reuter, and Kurt Schumacher made apparent, political persecution gave these non-Jewish German politicians a sharp awareness of crimes being committed against German and European Jews.

There was no doubt that the German political opponents of Nazism would devote their efforts to creating postwar memories of the injustice and persecution which they had endured and witnessed. Exile decisively shaped postwar memory in two ways. First, it made possible the survival of leaders of the "other Germanys," who were then able to tell their fellow Germans what had happened to them and their comrades. Second, exile placed the German political émigrés in proximity to the Jewish and non-German victims of National Socialism, be they the peoples of Eastern Europe and the Soviet Union or Jewish refugees in New York and Mexico City. Communists and Social Democrats found asylum abroad first in Paris and Prague, then in Moscow, New York, and Mexico City, as well as in Ankara, Stockholm, and London. The experience of exile made their postwar memory less provincial, self-centered, and self-pitying, and made them more aware of what the Germans under the Nazi regime had inflicted on others. Communists returning from Moscow had the suffering and victory of the Soviet Union foremost in their hearts and minds. Above all, the circumstances of exile in New York and Mexico City forced German political exiles to think more deeply about the persecution of European Jewry. As opponents of Nazism, the German exiles clearly intended to talk about its crimes upon their return to power. After 1945 the issue was less whether these crimes would be recalled than which among Nazism's many victims would be remembered, and whether the Jewish catastrophe would find an appropriate place in the national memory. Understanding the experience of German exiles in Moscow, New York, and Mexico City is indispensable for explaining the subsequent history of memory of the Nazi era in the two Germanys.

Foreign travel broadened horizons, but many of the political opponents of Nazism had a deep personal affection for the German-Jewish Germany which had preceded the Nazi era. The personal was indeed political. German Jews had been their friends, relatives, teachers, comrades, and colleagues. Such memories of German-Jewish contact were evident in Paul Merker's recollection of the Weimar Republic and the anti-Nazi underground in Berlin; Franz Dahlem's eyewitness accounts of mass murder in Sachsenhausen; Ernst Reuter's memories of screams in the night in a Nazi prison; Konrad Adenauer's lifelong friendship with Dannie Heinemann; Theodor Heuss's angry and bitter memory of his Jewish friends whom the Nazis had murdered or driven into exile; Kurt Schumacher's witness of shared persecution in Dachau; the exiled Social Democrats' gratitude to the Jewish Labor Committee and the American Federation of Labor for rescuing them from Vichy France in

1940 and 1941; and Ludwig Erhard's recollections of his doctoral adviser, Franz Oppenheimer. For these German political leaders of the founding generation, the crimes of the Nazi era and the destruction of European Jewry were causes of guilt and shame as well as anger at the injustice which they themselves and others had had to endure. Participation in or knowledge of Nazi crimes led thousands of their compatriots to postwar silence. But the experience of shared persecution and witness to the persecution of others was a common denominator for the founders of both Germanys. After the war these shared experiences led them to express solidarity with Nazism's victims. The *nature* of that solidarity—whom it *included* and whom it *excluded*—varied greatly according to their differing political beliefs. For Schumacher and Merker, memories of persecution led to postwar memory marked by inclusion, recognition, and solidarity with the Jews. For Ulbricht and the East German leadership, the Soviet Union remained both primary victim and source of deliverance.

The multiple restorations of past traditions also help to explain memory's postwar division. The suppression and marginalization of the memory of the Holocaust in East Germany reproduced the subordinate position of the Jewish question in Communist ideology before 1933, and certainly in the German Communist emigration in Moscow. From Marx's early essay on the Jewish question, to Stalin's pamphlet on the national question, through the Comintern's instrumentalist dismissal of anti-Semitism as a capitalist tool, Marxist and Communist theory had consistently placed Jewish matters on the margins of the class struggle. Communists inside and outside Germany believed that both the Jewish question and Judaism as a religion would disappear with the overcoming of their supposed roots in class society and capitalism. These—in their view—secondary matters did not call for special attention. It is striking how little the cataclysms of World War II and the Holocaust changed these long-held views. Walter Ulbricht and his colleagues and successors believed that their opposition to and persecution by Nazism exonerated them from shouldering obligations stemming from Nazi-era crimes.

Before 1933 the Social Democratic Party was the fiercest defender of German democracy and of the Jewish minority in Germany. During the Nazi era and after 1945, Schumacher and the SPD constituted the major political force favoring West German confrontation with the Holocaust and the crimes of the Nazi era. From August Bebel through Schumacher, leaders of German social democracy had argued that a commitment to equality and democratic rights for all citizens required principled opposition to anti-Semitism. In the German Social Democratic political emigration in Stockholm, London, and especially New York, this already existing solidarity between German Social Democrats and German Jews was deepened by shared political views and by moral and practical solidarity in dark times. In sharp contrast to events in East Germany, these wartime bonds between Germans and Jews persisted into the postwar era. In the 1950s, German Social Democrats were the strongest supporters of a sharper judicial confrontation with the Nazi past, restitution to Jewish survivors, and close relations with Israel. Adenauer's prominence has diverted our gaze from the central role played by Social Democrats in putting the memory of the Holocaust on the national agenda of West German politics and policy. Furthermore, as Schumacher's postwar speeches in Germany as well as on his American tour of 1947 indicated, and as David Dubinsky noted when Schumacher died, his opposition to the Communists did not leave him any less ready to denounce Nazism and anti-Semitism. On the contrary, for Schumacher democratization in Germany was inseparable from the demands of memory and justice.

In this era of restoration, one of the most noticeable changes in the Social Democratic tradition after 1945 was the replacement of its world-famous and much criticized dialectically inspired historical optimism with a deep and enduring tragic consciousness. Ernst Reuter and other Social Democratic leaders had experienced too many defeats and seen too many catastrophes to repeat the optimistic secular theodicy that consoled democratic Marxists before 1914. It was Reuter's memories of screams in the night more than a socialist optimism about an inevitable happy future that drove him towards postwar political engagement. In May 1945, when Schumacher urged his comrades not to despair, he too evoked the memories of past suffering and heroism to animate aspirations for a better future. While the Communists brought the anti-Jewish and nationalist resentments within the Marxist tradition to the fore, the Social Democrats argued that a democratic and socialist Germany must decisively confront and defeat anti-Semitism and place the memory of persecution of the Jews at the center of German memory of the Nazi past.

Konrad Adenauer and postwar Christian democracy left behind a decidedly mixed legacy regarding memory of the Nazi past. Adenauer's view of modern German history was deeply critical and pessimistic; he was haunted by memories of the breadth and depth of mass support for Hitler. He deserves the major credit for displacing the anti-Western currents of German conservatism with Westernizing themes of individual dignity, natural rights, and criticism of the authoritarian state. Westernization for him meant anchoring the Federal Republic in a Western alliance, reaching reconciliation with France, and ending the uncertain German wavering between West and East. His acceptance in September 1951 of West Germany's obligation to offer financial restitution to Jewish survivors and to Israel and his support for the Jewish state in the face of opposition from his own right wing were among what he called his "noblest" accomplishments. That a conservative chancellor made such commitments gave them broader support than if they had been only a cause of the left. The connection between Adenauer's opting for the West and his views on Jewish issues was both powerful and decisive for the emergence of divided memory. Whereas the reactionary modernists of Weimar and the Third Reich had associated the Jews with a despised modernity, Adenauer's West German conservatism embraced political as well as economic modernity. For him, the Jews were an inseparable part of "the West," while Nazism, like "atheistic communism," represented a nihilist revolt against it. A focus on the persecution of the Jews went hand in hand with his understanding of a Christian Democratic reintegration of Germany into Western Europe.

Although Adenauer's opposition to anti-Semitism was a matter of deep conviction, this Christian Democratic leader did not critically interrogate the Christian sources of European and German anti-Semitism. Although his democratic credentials were impeccable, he did not dwell on the German war on the Eastern Front in World War II. While he denounced the totalitarianism of the Nazi past and the Communist present, he could have done far more to explain publicly how the anticommunism of the Cold War differed from the Nazi war on "Jewish bolshevism." His early willingness to recognize the "honor" of German soldiers hardly contributed to West German public reflection on that score. Adenauer's very somber view of German history and his awareness of the degree of popular support for the Nazi regime, combined with short-term electoral calculations, led him to stress "integration" of former Nazi supporters rather than memory of and justice for Nazi crimes. His decision to do so preceded the crystallization of the Cold War. As early as spring 1946, before he could possibly have known who had or had not committed crimes against humanity, he urged that ordinary members of the Nazi Party "finally" be left in peace. Despite continuous criticism by the press and the opposition Social Democrats, Adenauer insisted on keeping a figure as compromised as Hans Globke as one of his closest and most powerful assistants. The ambiguity of his legacy is unmistakable. He did not want to dwell on the crimes of the Nazi past, and when he did, he separated the issue of memory from the imperatives of justice. His acceptance of moral obligations regarding restitution coincided with a general policy of silence about the crimes of the Nazi era. Adenauer's decision to seek amnesty and leniency rather than justice at a time when memories were still fresh and thousands of cases remained to be investigated or even opened was a primary cause of the judicial fiasco of the 1950s. This was his greatest moral and political failure.

Theodor Heuss shared Adenauer's conviction that Germany after 1945 must definitively break with past antagonism to the West, especially to liberalism. Heuss's liberalism, more than Adenauer's political Catholicism, formed the starting point of West Germany's official political memory of the crimes of the Nazi past. Like Adenauer he was a Westernizer, but in a secular, very political sense. He criticized the disdain for politics and political history of the German educated middle class. Echoing the spirit of the Anglo-American narratives of the Nuremberg Trial, Heuss criticized German inclinations to substitute philosophical profundity for political narratives which sought to fix moral and political responsibility. In his reflections on the Nazi past, he urged a disillusioned public to think more about causality, facts, and history than about destiny, fate, and being. Politics had led to crime and disaster. Only different politics, not withdrawal or cynicism, would lead to a decent future.

From 1949 to 1959, when so many Germans put the Nazi past out of mind, Heuss used the platform of the office of *Bundespräsident* to bring memory of the crimes of the Nazi era into West German national political retrospection. Freed from electoral pressures, he spoke about the "collective shame" of the Nazi era, the treasure of the legacy of the German resistance, and the murder of German and European Jewry. He wrested the discourse of patriotism, courage, honor, and duty away from the nationalist right to place it in the service of a liberal, postnationalist, reflective, democratic Germany. He defined acceptance of the burden of the Nazi past as a sign of courage, responsibility, and patriotism, while its avoidance was an expression of cowardice and a betrayal of the best of Germany's albeit oft-defeated political traditions. At a time when many Germans regarded the conspirators of July 20, 1944, as traitors to the nation, Heuss praised their heroism as a founding moment of a new, different, and far better Germany. Condemning nationalist self-pity, he urged the West Germans to extend the causal chain of their memories of wartime and postwar German suffering back to the Nazi policies beginning in 1933. It was all the more disappointing that this apostle of West German political memory failed to use the pulpit of the presidency to protest against the delay and denial of justice in the Adenauer era.

On May 8, 1945, neither the emergence of memory of the Holocaust in West Germany nor its suppression in East Germany was a foregone conclusion. The contingencies and possibilities of the early postwar period suggested the possibility of the opposite outcome. After all, whatever faults the Communists had, they were antifascists. The Nazis had attacked "Jewish bolshevism." Who could be faulted for hoping that the experience of shared persecution and struggle from 1941 to 1945 would encourage the "Bolsheviks" to continue to express solidarity with the Jews and to consign anti-Semitic components of Marxist and Soviet traditions to the past? The fact that the Communists spoke less frequently about the murder of 6 million European Jews than about the deaths of over 20 million Soviet soldiers and civilians was hardly a sign of anti-Semitism or anti-Jewish hostility. Given the Soviet Union's own wartime "Western alliance," Communist veterans returning from Western emigration, such as Paul Merker and Leo Zuckermann, had grounds for hoping that the solidarity with the Jews that had come to the fore in wartime Mexico City would persist in postwar Communist ideology and policy while others returned from Nazi concentration camps as eyewitnesses to the Holocaust. The existence of the Jewish Antifascist Committee in Moscow and the Soviet Union's early support for a Jewish state in Palestine suggested that such hopes were not misplaced.

It was during the Nuremberg interregnum, that contingent period after World War II and before the Cold War, that the postwar Communist debate about the memory of the Jewish catastrophe took place. The German Communists and the Soviet occupation authorities regarded Soviet suffering and triumph and the narrative of Communist martyrdom as the core of postwar memory. For many of them, memory of the Holocaust was an irritating competitor for the scarce resource of postwar recognition. Preference for Communist "fighters" over Jewish "victims," a focus on Soviet suffering and redemptive victory at the expense of the Holocaust, and official delay followed by rejection of requests for restitution payments to Jewish survivors were hardly encouraging signs for Jewish Communists and their non-Jewish comrades. Before the anticosmopolitan purges, some veterans of the Communist resistance did seek to give a prominent place to the Jews within the circle of those honored at memorial ceremonies. Publicly, at least, the Communists returned to the rhetoric of the Popular Front and even admitted to having made some errors in the past. Paul Merker and Leo Zuckermann did have positions of power and influence in the emerging Communist apparatus. As late as spring 1948, Merker could publish an article in *Neues Deutschland* praising the struggle for a Jewish state in Palestine. Leo Zuckermann's assertion that he and other Jewish Communists would "never fight against the liberators of Auschwitz and Maidanek" expressed the hope that commemoration would not be divided, and that memory of the Holocaust should and would be compatible with recognition of the suffering of the peoples of Eastern Europe and the Soviet Union, and of the sacrifice and heroism of the Red Army.

Although the thesis of multiple restorations primarily addresses the importance of indigenous traditions, it also clarifies our understanding of how external influences shaped the national narratives, and how shifting international alliances influenced memory of the Nazi past. In the early years in particular, the power of the victors lay less in writing on blank slates than in repressing Nazism and strengthening other elements of prior German traditions. The forgetting of the Holocaust and the suppression of sympathetic treatment of Jewish matters in East Germany were inseparable from the forgetting of the Soviet Union's Western alliance in World War II, the Marxist-Leninist philosophy of history and Soviet triumphalism, and the emergence of the Cold War. In the East, incorporation into an alliance against "Western imperialism" meant that memory of the wartime alliance crossed the new and reversed Cold War fault lines. At best it was an embarrassment and at worst the cause of charges of disloyalty. In the East as well as the West, World War II brought the subversive danger of blurring the lines between Communist and anti-Communist in the common struggle against the Nazis. Stalin and fellow Stalinists wanted to expel dangerous ideas about democracy from the West. As memories of wartime solidarity with the West became taboo, the Communists focused ever more on the primary role of the Red Army in defeating Nazism. May 8, 1945, became the supremely Hegelian moment of modern history, one that vindicated Communist dogma with victory. The Holocaust, a story of unmitigated disaster, did not fit into the story of victory and redemption of official antifascism. While the Jewish catastrophe had entered the center of Communist discourse in distant Mexico City, it was the narrative of Soviet suffering and redemption that dominated Communist memory after 1945. The East German marginalization of the Jewish question in the Nuremberg interregnum and its suppression during the anticosmopolitan purges of 1950–1956 crushed the public sympathy for the Jews which, though peripheral, had been a dissonant current within German communism before 1945.

In Russia, Eastern Europe, and East Germany, Marxist-Leninist assaults on Western imperialism overlapped with and reinforced indigenous anti-Western nationalist resentments. Both traditions associated the Jews with the despised "cosmopolitan," capitalist West, this despite the fact that the vast majority of the Jews who perished in the Holocaust lived in Eastern Europe and Russia. No wonder that the Communists returning from Western emigration, Jewish and non-Jewish alike, fell under a cloud of suspicion. Political disagreement escalated into accusations of treason and disloyalty. They were accused of having wrongly believed in the sincerity of American and British anti-Nazi convictions, and of having been infected with the virus of bourgeois democracy. During the war American intelligence agencies either ignored Paul Merker's Mexican efforts on the Jewish question or regarded them suspiciously as an example of deceptive Communist Popular Front tactics designed, as J. Edgar Hoover put it, to lure "political innocents" into the Communist camp. Yet in the first days of the Cold War, Merker's comrades in the Politburo accused him of actually believing the praise of Western democracy which had been a staple of Communist wartime antifascist discourse. The anti-Semitic component of the purges became more apparent when the Politburo explained and discredited Merker's support for Jewish concerns in Mexico by referring to the influence of Jewish wealth and power. The Cold War did not create Communist hostility to the Jews. Rather, by emphatically granting a monopoly of power to the dominant current of Communist thinking on the subject, it ended lingering ambiguities about the treatment of Jewish matters within the Communist tradition. The projection of Cold War tensions backward onto the history of World War II led either to silence about the fate of the Jews or to their excommunication from the ranks of progressive and suffering humanity, and their placement in the higher circles of humanity's exploiters and imperialists.

In East no less than in West Germany, the end of the Nuremberg interregnum and the beginning of the Cold War reinforced provincial and divided memories of the war and the Holocaust. Once the two

German states were established, pursuit of their respective national interests in foreign policy also influenced national memory, though in very different ways. The East German struggle for diplomatic recognition and status, as both a loyal member of the Warsaw Pact and a friend of "national liberation struggles" in the Third World, reinforced the predominant claims of German communism. Neither solidarity with the Soviets in Europe nor anti-imperialism in the Third World required painful reflection on the Holocaust or German anti-Semitism. On the contrary, both seemed magically to lift East Berlin's leaders out from under the burdens of German history and even added a moral halo to older anti-Western and anti-Jewish resentments. Paul Merker and Leo Zuckermann had shown Walter Ulbricht and Otto Grotewohl that there was more than one way for a Communist government to establish its antifascist credentials in foreign policy. But Ulbricht, Grotewohl, and Honecker chose another, grotesquely ironic path. They made antifascism compatible with repression of the memory of the Holocaust at home and antagonism to the Jewish state in foreign policy. Although East Berlin remained Moscow's loyal and dependent ally, these options also had strong local roots. There is much more archival research to be done on the diplomacy of the Warsaw Pact, but East German support for the Soviet bloc attack on Zionism, including support for states and movements engaged in armed conflict with Israel, is a matter of public record. As is generally the case, national identity and political memory shaped the definition of the national interest. For the East Germans, engagement in international politics built on and reinforced the outcome of the anticosmopolitan purges.

The East German government was not an anti-Semitic regime in the sense that the Nazi regime was. Hatred for the Jewish people was not one of its core principles. But then neither did it display the kind of warmth or empathy that might be expected from any German government after the Holocaust. This conflict between antifascist legitimation and anti-Jewish policy constitutes a major, if too rarely noted, theme of East German history. The East Germans were willing to adopt the language of traditional European anti-Semitism. That cold-hearted willingness was apparent in the conspiracy accusations during the anticosmopolitan purges, and in the refusal to give adequate recognition to the memory of the Holocaust, to pay financial restitution to Jewish survivors, to conduct an adequate program of trials for crimes of the Nazi era in the 1950s, or to refrain from active partisanship on behalf of Israel's armed adversaries in the Middle East. The anticosmopolitan purge of winter 1952–53, the arrest and imprisonment of Paul Merker, the purging of those Jews and their sympathizers who supported restitution or opposed East Germany's active antagonism toward Israel, the flight of Leo Zuckermann and of the leadership of the tiny Jewish community all irrevocably broke those bonds of solidarity which had emerged between some Communists and some Jews during the war. Those Jews who remained in the East German regime did so on terms of assimilation far more self-effacing than those accepted by German Jews before 1933. These events are central episodes in the history of postwar East German efforts to face the Nazi past.

Compared to government policy and the Jewish experience in East Germany, the oft-criticized era of Jewish assimilation in the nineteenth and early twentieth centuries of German history appears as a golden era of Jewish particularism and resilient identity. The Enlightenment rage at stubborn otherness, no longer moderated by the existence of any democratic institutions and political pluralism, made an important contribution to the suppression of the memory of the Holocaust and other anti-Jewish components of East German policy. The dialectic enlightenment did not lead to Nazism and the Holocaust. Yet the famous though problematic thesis of Horkheimer and Adorno does contribute to explaining anti-Jewish ideology and practice among the self-proclaimed heirs of the radical enlightenment in the Communist parties and governments of the twentieth century. As the anticosmopolitan purge and the subsequent developments in East Germany made apparent, there was no room for Jewish otherness within the Communist dream of total rationality.

Why, then, did sympathy for the Jews emerge in West Germany? In striking contrast to that of East Germany, West Germany's policy included restitution payments for Jewish survivors, close ties to Israel, numerous parliamentary debates regarding judicial confrontation with the Nazi past, an elite and then a popular discussion of the Holocaust and anti-Semitism, and, inadequate and delayed as it was, much more vigorous prosecution of the crimes of the Nazi era than that pursued by its antifascist neighbor to the east. Yet those who focused on the gap between the fine words of official memory and the paucity of justice in the 1950s had a different answer for West German engagement with Jewish issues. The East Germans put it most bluntly: the prominence of the Holocaust in West German memory and Adenauer's willingness to accept its burdens was due to a combination of seemingly indestructible Jewish power and the influence of West German politicians who used sympathy for the Jews to purchase their country's moral rehabilitation and integration into the Western alliance. For such critics, this "philo-Semitism" was simply a conservative ploy which substituted lofty sentiments for justice and used the discourse of atonement to foster undeserved absolution to postwar capitalism and compromised elites. It was a bitter and ironic component of the failure to break with the Nazi past and, during the Cold War, the refusal to acknowledge what the Nazis had done to the non-Jewish victims of Eastern Europe and the Soviet Union.

Such explanations confuse effect with cause. More important, the evidence presented in this study points to other, and in my view more compelling, explanations for the significance of the Jewish dimension in West German memory and policy. The experiences and beliefs of the founding generation of West German politicians offer the most important part of the answer. Schumacher above all, but also Heuss and Adenauer, believed that it was the responsibility of postwar Germans to accept the moral obligations and burdens left by the genocide of European Jewry. Because Adenauer rather than Schumacher was the founding chancellor, the role played by West German Social Democrats in the issues of restitution and relations with Israel has too often been obscured from view. The same democratic left that was calling for timely justice and a deeper purge of the West German establishment was also the strongest supporter of restitution and close relations with Israel. During the occupation and the early years of the Federal Republic, Western—especially American—officials, the state of Israel, Western liberals, and private Jewish organizations also encouraged German politicians to adopt this position. Yet such pleas could easily have fallen on deaf ears and hard hearts; there was no shortage of either in postwar Germany. In the 1950s, memory of the Holocaust, restitution to Jewish survivors, and timely justice were peripheral issues in an era dominated by the Cold War and by the moral compromises that flowed from American and Western desires to integrate the West Germans into a new Western alliance. The beliefs of the founding democratic leaders were indispensable for realization of even the minimal program of restitution and public memory which took place in the early years. They simply thought it was the morally right thing to do. West Germans such as Schumacher and Heuss who most strongly articulated the memory of the Holocaust in the Adenauer era did so more from a sense of moral responsibility than from political calculation. While Adenauer gave priority to reintegration of compromised elites over vivid reminders and timely justice for past crimes, Heuss and Schumacher inaugurated a tradition of public recollection in which the Holocaust eventually found an enduring place in the dominant West German public narratives of the Nazi era.

In West no less than in East Germany, international politics and the pursuit of the national interest had a major impact on memory of the Nazi past. We have seen that the shift from the Nuremberg interregnum to Cold War anticommunism often countered efforts to obtain justice and remember the crimes of the Nazi era. Just as the Communists wanted to forget wartime alliances with the West, so the Cold War made it easier for West German conservatives to neglect the crimes committed by the Nazi regime in Eastern Europe and the Soviet Union. The argument that "too much" memory of the Nazi past would weaken or paralyze West Germany's will to resist Soviet pressures played a part in West German conservatism from Adenauer through Kohl, and even more so among politicians to their right. Although Cold War anticommunism offered a convenient pretext for public silence about the Nazi past, it was not its source. We have seen that there was no electoral majority in the 1950s for political leaders who spoke bluntly about and sought timely justice for crimes of the Nazi era.

While the baneful impact of Cold War anticommunism on West German memory of the Nazi past has been much discussed, historians have less frequently noted that the policy of containment meant opposing governments which were pursuing policies harmful to Jewish survivors. Adenauer had complained that memory of Nazism and the war contributed to an atmosphere unfavorable to containment. The corollary appeared to be that integration into the Western alliance would bring with it freedom from *Vergangenheitsbewältigung*. Indeed, it did coincide with the era of public reticence and delayed justice. Yet in striking contrast to the situation in East Germany, the West German quest for postwar international recognition included increasing public memory of the crimes of the Nazi past. Schumacher first of all, then Heuss, and eventually even Adenauer understood that public acknowledgment of the truth about those crimes was a moral but also a practical precondition for international acceptance. Bonn's engagement in international politics had a double-edged impact on national memory evident in the contrasting ceremonies in Bergen-Belsen in 1952 and in Bitburg in 1985: it both encouraged a tradition of public memory and gave rise to pressures "finally" to leave the past behind.

The option for dictatorship or democracy in the two Germanys decisively influenced political memory. In East Berlin, memories of the anticommunism of German voters before 1933 and awareness of enduring German support for Nazism up to 1945 reinforced Leninist traditions and Stalin's determination to impose a second German dictatorship in order to keep watch over a dangerous people. The suppression of the memory of the Holocaust and of the Jewish question was only one episode, though an important one, in the history of the consolidation of the East German dictatorship. Although Marxist-Leninist theory asserted that a tiny capitalist-Nazi-military clique had oppressed the mass of suffering Germans, the Communists acted as if they had never really given up the bitterness and mistrust they had expressed in the early wartime years regarding the complicity of "millions and millions" of Germans. Memory of Nazism thus served to legitimate imposition of an "antifascist" dictatorship on a country with a fascist past.

Both German democrats and Western victors assumed that liberal democracy was the obvious and indispensable antidote to the Nazi dictatorship and the most important guarantee against a repetition of the crimes of the Nazi era. From Adenauer to Schumacher, the "militant democrats" of the early years passionately believed that however important militarism, anti-Semitism, and aggressive nationalism had been in German history, it was only the destruction of Weimar *democracy* and the establishment of the Nazi *dictatorship* that had made it possible for Hitler to launch World War II and implement the Holocaust. This view of the link between democracy, peace, and human rights was well founded. The choice of democracy in the early postwar years, however, brought with it considerable barriers to clear memory and timely justice in the form of West German voters who had a great deal to lose from an open and early German confrontation with the crimes of the Nazi era. Adenauer and Schumacher offered contrasting visions of how democratization ought to proceed. The former promised voters he would agree to leave the past behind, while the latter clearly believed that democracy demanded a reckoning with the Nazi past. The argument that silence and justice delayed were preconditions for the emergence of democracy per se conflated the CDU's narrow electoral interests with the general interest of democratization. Adenauer "integrated" voters who he feared would constitute a reservoir of support for a postwar antidemocratic right. He thereby built Christian Democratic national electoral majorities, and fostered acceptance of the fragile new democracy among those with a "wide-awake consciousness" of past crimes. In effect, Adenauer struck a bargain with compromised Germans: in exchange for his reticence about the Nazi past, they would agree to accept the new democracy, or at least not try to destroy it.

Restitution and the establishment of warm relations with Israel, combined with few trials for war crimes and a feeble housecleaning of the West German elite were hardly the result of vast Jewish power or the influence of clever West German capitalists. On the contrary, they were the outer limits of what a very conservative West German electorate would accept in the 1950s. In open and free elections, majorities opted for consensus, silence, and putting the past behind instead of the conflict which a policy of memory and justice would have created. As John J. McCloy's experience with the Landsberg decisions made clear, had the United States continued to carry the policies of the Nuremberg era into the 1950s, it would have had to pursue justice in opposition to the wishes of the democratically elected government in Bonn. In the postwar decade, daring more democracy meant attaining less memory and justice.

That said, the establishment of democracy in the West also meant that, in sharp contrast to the dictatorship in the East, the decisions of the early years were not final. The East Germans were able to freeze political memory, with some minor modifications, in the dogmas of the 1950s. In West Germany, political freedom and open debate fostered criticism of the shortcomings of the Adenauer era and a growing knowledge about the Nazi era. When Schumacher lost the election of 1949, public discussion of the Holocaust and the Nazi past, though marginal, did not disappear completely from West German politics. In East Germany the arrest of Merker and the purge of the "cosmopolitans" in 1952–53 had more long lasting implications. Given that the suppression of the Jewish question had been an important chapter in the consolidation of the East German dictatorship, it was fitting that the movement for democracy and political freedom in the mid- and late 1980s led to its reemergence. In April 1990 the first democratically elected parliament in East Germany expressed remorse *both* for the crimes of the Nazi past *and* for the policies of the East German regime. It was a stunning confirmation that an honest effort to face the Nazi past was inseparable from the development of democracy in Germany. Articulation of this message, which Merker and Leo Zuckermann had mistakenly thought could take its place in the East German Communist regime, had to await its collapse.

As we have seen, memory of the Nazi past did not begin in the 1960s. The historic significance of the 1960s was that the relationship between memory and democracy began to change. This was part of the significance of the election of Willy Brandt in 1969 and the Social-Liberal era that extended until 1982 under Helmut Schmidt. For the first time a national electoral majority emerged that was in favor of more public memory and more justice for the Nazi past. Just as Schumacher had been a driving force in bringing the Jewish question to the fore from 1945 to 1952, so Brandt and Schmidt in the era of *Ostpolitik* brought the memory of the Eastern Front in World War II into the West German political consciousness. The Social Democrats were the most vocal critics of the presence in positions of power of compromised elites from the Nazi era and the strongest supporters of extending the statute of limitations on war crimes and crimes against humanity. The New Left, contributed to expanding the public discussion, until its splinter groups degenerated into terrorism, Marxist-Leninist dogmas about fascism, and at times anti-Semitism. The leftist confrontation with the Nazi past in the 1960s had more to do with criticism of capitalism and anti-communism than to grappling with the specifics of the Holocaust. At the same time, in a pattern repeated elsewhere in the Western democracies, the tradition of criticism of communist regimes by "militant democrats" of the left fell into abeyance. Both West German conservatives and the dwindling numbers of Social Democrats who shared Schumacher's willingness to criticize the Communists vigorously made a good point about the double standards of West German liberals and leftists. Those who called for *Vergangenheitsbewältigung* in West Germany far too rarely turned their critical gaze on East German antifascism. Yet the conservative criticism of leftist double standards was weakened by the reluctance of Adenauer and his heirs to confront the Nazi past more sharply in West Germany.

Although the East German Communists praised Thomas Mann as a master of literary realism, they rejected his famous assertion that there were not two Germanys, a good and an evil one, but only one which had placed its virtues in the service of evil. Paul Merker had urged his comrades to reflect critically on their own shortcomings, especially as they concerned anti-Semitism and the memory of the Holocaust. Instead Ulbricht and his colleagues saw themselves and their government as the good and noble Germany opposed to the evil Germany which governed only in Bonn. Communist analysis of the Nazi regime aided in this unburdening effort, for it separated the Nazi dictatorship from the specifics of German history and placed it instead in the context of a general crisis of capitalism. Coming to terms with the "fascist" past thus called for eliminating capitalism and expropriating the Junkers. It could even mean supporting states at war with Israel and rejecting restitution payments for Jewish survivors. A surplus of ideology fostered *Vergangenheitsbewältigung* on the cheap.

Among postwar West Germans—with some important exceptions in the moderate conservative ranks such as Franz Böhm in the 1950s and Richard von Weizsäcker in the 1980s—the political home of the memory of Nazi-era crimes and the Holocaust remained with liberals in the Heussian tradition and Social Democrats in the tradition of Schumacher. As Nahum Goldmann's speech in Bergen-Belsen in November 1952 made apparent, the memory of the destruction of European Jewry transgressed the geography of the Cold War by drawing Western attention to the Nazi attack on "Jewish bolshevism." That is, it drew attention to the causal chain that began in 1933 or with the German invasion of the Soviet Union in June 1941 and ended with the Red Army in Berlin, to the Eastern geography of the war, and to the role that anti-Semitism had played in National Socialist anticommunism. For those Western anticommunist politicians whose Cold War passions rested on memories that often began in the "sellout" at Yalta in 1945, such temporal, geographical, and cultural understandings of the background to the postwar world were unwelcome, to say the least. Memories of the Holocaust invariably included such Eastern coordinates as *Einsatzgruppen,* Auschwitz-Birkenau, and Treblinka—events and places on which West German conservative voters did not wish to dwell. On the contrary, the more important the West German bulwark became for Western containment policy, the greater was the incentive to appease the popular sentiment to say and do as little as possible about the crimes of the Nazi past.

The Holocaust was a tragedy without redemption. It did not fit into any optimistic theory of history or postwar policy of reconstruction, whether it promised the first socialist society in Germany in the East or an "economic miracle" in the West. In both West and East, those who focused only on the bright future saw no place for an evil past. After the purges of the early 1950s had definitively eliminated their own minority view, Communist recollection was a matter of anointing martyrs and heroes, casting past suffering as the prelude to postwar historical redemption, and a call to fight the "fascists" in Bonn. Whereas Adenauer and Heuss looked on 1945 as a time of both defeat and liberation for the Germans, for the Communists it was a pristine Hegelian moment that confirmed the long-standing predictions of Marxist-Leninist dialectics and Soviet power. The contrasts in this regard were defined in the rituals of remembrance in Bergen-Belsen in 1952 and Sachsenhausen in 1961. The photograph of Theodor Heuss and Nahum Goldmann at the Bergen-Belsen memorial ceremonies in 1952 capture essential elements of the distinctively West German national political discourse of shame and remorse about the Nazi era. Heuss's expression is somber. Nahum Goldmann's presence next to Heuss indicates the significance of the memory of mass murder of European Jewry, at least to this *Bundespräsident*, in West German political memory. By comparison, the photo of Walter Ulbricht leading the SED leadership like a phoenix out of the ashes of the Sachsenhausen concentration camp memorial in 1961 captures the distinctively East German approach. Ulbricht is not mourning but is confidently striding toward the future, certain that a history of suffering and martyrdom has ended in redemption and victory.

The repression of the minority Communist tradition of remembrance and solidarity in the early 1950s shaped East German political memory until the regime collapsed in 1989, when East German democrats placed the claims of memory at the top of their political agenda. At the same time, repeated efforts to displace the memory of the Holocaust from the national political memory of the Federal Republic during the 1980s and again during the nationalist euphoria over German unification failed. Over time, memory of the Holocaust assumed an even greater role in West German public discussion. The tradition of *Vergangenheitsbewältigung* inaugurated by Schumacher and Heuss became more significant than it had been during the Adenauer era. Had Schumacher's or Merker's path been chosen during the Nuremberg interregnum or when the two German states were founded in 1949, the 1950s might very well have been a period of honest memory and timely justice.

But neither German elite traditions, popular will, nor international politics favored such an outcome. Instead in both Germanys memory was divided and justice was delayed and too often denied. That said, the Communists did break their promises of wartime solidarity with the Jewish people, while West German democrats argued that any German government after the Holocaust ought to accept the obligations it had left behind. West German memory should have been stronger and justice far more swift and certain, but there was more of both than in the self-described antifascist East German state. While the efforts of the Federal Republic to confront the crimes of the Nazi past in the crucial decade of the 1950s were not adequate, seeds were planted which eventually grew into a broader and more vigorous public memory.

In this case, as in so many others, some of the most interesting and important issues for the historian were first raised by contemporaries. Some of the most perceptive German participants and observers who lived through the war and Holocaust, the Nuremberg interregnum, and the postwar decades understood that whether and how they remembered or forgot the Nazi era and the persecution of the Jews would be of great importance for the nature and prospects of dictatorship and democracy in Germany after Auschwitz. This history of memory, democracy and dictatorship in the occupation era, the era of two Germanys, and the era of a unified Germany has confirmed their judgment. Those political leaders who urged their fellow citizens to look the truth of German history straight in the eye raised issues of general significance for any country emerging from a period of dictatorship, crime, and catastrophe. They left behind an often unpopular, discomforting, demanding, yet precious legacy.

# Notes

# Sources

# Acknowledgments

# Index

# Notes

## Abbreviations

| | |
|---|---|
| AdsD | Archiv der sozialen Demokratie (Social Democratic Party Archives) |
| AICGS/GHI | American Institute for Contemporary German Studies/German Histocal Institute, Washington, D.C. |
| BA/Koblenz | Bundesarchiv, Koblenz, Germany |
| BStU MfSZ | Bundesbeauftragte für die Unterlagen des Staatsicherheitsdienstes der ehemaligen Deutschen Demokratischen Republic, Ministerium für Staatssicherheit Zentralarchiv (Central Archive of the Ministry of State Security, Berlin) |
| GMMA | George Meany Memorial Archives |
| IRR | Investigative Records Repository |
| IVVdN | Internationale Vereinigung des Verfolgten des Naziregimes |
| LBI | Leo Baeck Institute, New York |
| NA | National Archives, Washington, D.C. |
| NL | *Nachlass* |
| NWDR | Nordwestdeutschen Rundfunk |
| RG | Record group |
| SAPMO-BA | Stiftung Archiv der Parteien und Massenorganizationen der DDR im Bundesarchiv (Foundation for the Archive of the GDR's Parties and Mass Organizations in the Bundesarchiv, Berlin) |
| SBAH | Stiftung Bundeskanzler-Adenauer-Haus, Bad Honnef-Rhöndorf, Germany |
| St BKAH | Stiftung Bundeskanzler Konrad Adenauer, Rhöndorf |
| VVN | Vereinigung des Verfolgten des Naziregimes |
| ZK | Zentralkomitee |
| ZPA | Zentral Parteiarchiv (Central Party Archive) |
| ZPKK | Zentralparteikontrollkommission |

# 1. Multiple Restorations and Divided Memory

1. The term "Holocaust" as the designation for the genocide of European Jewry ordered and implemented by the Nazi regime has become unavoidable, in contrast to more cumbersome but also more specific references to the mass murder of European Jewry. Readers should bear in mind that it was not commonly used in German, as in American, public discussions until the 1970s. I use it with a certain reluctance owing to a concern that it unintentionally contributes to lifting events out of a specific historical context. *Vergangenheitsbewältigung* is the German term referring to efforts to come to terms with, face, or master the Nazi past, especially the crimes of that era. *Wiedergutmachung* translated literally means "making good again." I have translated it as "restitution."

Within the Communist and Socialist tradition, "the Jewish question" *(die Judenfrage)* referred to all issues related to the place of Jews in German and European society. It did not necessarily contain the anti-Semitic implications which it always implied when used by German and European anti-Semites, for whom the Jewish people themselves were a "problem" that needed to be "solved" through varieties of persecution. In this work I use the phrase only when doing so helps to convey the language of contemporaries. On "multiple continuities" in German history, see Thomas Nipperdey, *Nachdenken über die deutsche Geschichte* (Munich: Beck, 1986).

2. The literature on representations and narratives of the Holocaust is extensive. See Saul Friedlander, *Memory, History, and the Extermination of the Jews of Europe* (Bloomington: Indiana University Press, 1993); Peter Hayes, ed., *Lessons and Legacies: The Meaning of the Holocaust in a Changing World* (Evanston, Ill.: Northwestern University Press, 1991); Saul Friedlander, ed., *Probing the Limits of Representation: Nazism and the "Final Solution"* (Cambridge, Mass.: Harvard University Press, 1992); Charles Maier, *The Unmasterable Past: History, Holocaust, and German National Identity* (Cambridge, Mass.: Harvard University Press, 1988); Dominick LaCapra, *Representing the Holocaust: History, Theory, Trauma* (Ithaca, N.Y.: Cornell University Press, 1994); and James E. Young, *The Texture of Memory: Holocaust Memorials and Meaning* (New Haven: Yale University Press, 1993). For general historiographical discussions of problems of narrative, see Lionel Gossman, *Between History and Literature* (Cambridge, Mass.: Harvard University Press, 1990); Gertrude Himmelfarb, *On Looking into the Abyss: Untimely Thoughts on Culture and Society* (New York: Knopf, 1994); Michael Geyer and Konrad Jarusch, eds., *Central European History* (special issue), German Histories: Challenges in Theory, Practice, Technique 22, nos. 3–4 (September–December 1989); Jorn Rusen, *Historische Vernunft: Grundzüge einer Historik* (Göttingen: Vandenhoeck and Ruprecht, 1983); idem, *Zeit und Sinn: Strategien Historischen Denkens* (Frankfurt am Main: Fischer Verlag, 1990); and Hayden White, *Metahistory: The Historical Imagination in Nineteenth-Century Europe* (Baltimore: Johns Hopkins University Press, 1973).

3. See Jeffrey Herf, "Multiple Restorations: German Political Traditions and the Interpretation of Nazism, 1945–1946," *Central European History* 26, no. 1 (1993), 21–55, and "Divided Memory, Multiple Restorations: West German Political Reflections on the Nazi Past, 1945–1953," in Stephen Brockman and Frank Trommler, eds., *Revisiting the Zero Hour, 1945: The Emergence of Postwar German Culture* (Washington, D.C.: American Institute for Contemporary German Studies, 1996), pp. 89–102.

4. On the breaks and continuities of German political culture before and after 1945, see Fritz Stern, *Dreams and Delusions: National Socialism in the Drama of the German Past* (New York: Random House, 1987); and George Mosse, *Fallen Soldiers: Reshaping the Memory of the World Wars* (New York: Oxford University Press, 1990). On the persistence of discourse, and belief in the context of political change in particular, see Reinhart Koselleck, *Futures Past: On the Semantics of Historical Time*, trans. Keith Tribe (Cambridge, Mass.: MIT Press, 1985). On social and economic continuities following both world wars, see Charles Maier, "The Two Postwar Eras and the Conditions for Stability in Twentieth-Century Western Europe," *American Historical Review* 86 (1981), 327–352. I first explored the impact of politics on West German memory in 1979 in "The 'Holocaust' Reception in West Germany: Right, Center, and Left," in Anson Rabinbach and Jack Zipes, eds., *Germans and Jews since the Holocaust: The Changing Situation in West Germany* (New York: Holmes and Meier, 1986), originally published in *New German Critique* 20 (1980).

5. In *Life and Fate*, his epic of World War II on the Eastern Front, the Soviet journalist Vasily Grossman recalled the emergence and bitter disappointment of hopes raised during the war that solidarities between Communists and Jews born from shared victimization and shared struggle would continue to shape the postwar world. See Vasily Grossman, *Life and Fate*, trans. Robert Chandler (New York: Harper and Row, 1985). Some of Grossman's wartime reports, including the first eyewitness report on Treblinka, are reprinted in Vasily Grossman, *Années de guerre* (Paris: Éditions Autremont, 1993).

6. See Sigrid Meuschel, *Legitimation und Parteiherrschaft in der DDR* (Frankfurt am Main: Suhrkamp, 1992); essays in Jürgen Kocka, ed., *Historische DDR-Forschung* (Berlin: Akademie Verlag, 1993), esp. Olaf Groehler, "Integration und Ausgrenzung von NS-Opfern," Mario Kessler, "Zwischen Repression und Toleranz: Die SED Politik und die Juden (1949–1967)," and Jürgen Danyel, "Die geteilte Vergangenheit," pp. 105–168; and Mario Kessler, *Die SED und die Juden—zwischen Repression und Toleranz* (Berlin: Akademie Verlag, 1995).

7. Cited in Maier, *The Unmasterable Past*, p. 90. See also Herman Lübbe, "Der Nationalsozialismus im Deutschen Nachkriegsbewusstsein," *Historische Zeitschrift* 236, no. 3 (June 1983), 579–599. On these issues, see also Dennis L. Bark and David R. Gress, *A History of West Germany: From Shadow to Substance, 1945–1964* (Cambridge, Mass.: Basil Blackwell, 1989); Ulrich Brochhagen, *Nach Nürnberg: Vergangenheitsbewältigung und Westintegration in der Ära Adenauer* (Hamburg: Junius Verlag, 1994);

and Thomas Alan Schwartz, *America's Germany: John J. McCloy and the Federal Republic of Germany* (Cambridge, MA: Harvard University Press, 1991).

8. In an important recent work the German historian Norbert Frei concludes that the support in West German society and politics in the early 1950s for rapid amnesty for persons accused of, and in many cases convicted of, war crimes was so broad as to imply an "indirect admission of the entire society's involvement in National Socialism." See Norbert Frei, *Vergangenheitspolitik: Die Anfänge der Bundesrepublik und die NS-Vergangenheit* (Munich: C. H. Beck Verlag, 1996), p. 399. On facing the past, democratization, and integration of compromised persons in Italy after Fascism, see Hans Woller, *Die Abrechnung mit dem Faschismus in Italien, 1943 bis 1948* (Munich: R. Oldenbourg, 1996). On Argentina after its "dirty war" and some comparisons to postwar West Germany, see Mark Osiel, "Ever Again: Law and Collective Memory of Administrative Massacre," *University of Pennsylvania Law Review* 144, no. 2 (December 1995), American readers will recognize parallels between postwar Western Germany and the South after the Civil War. In the Reconstruction South (among white voting southerners) and in postwar West Germany, electoral majorities and their representatives opposed memory of past persecution and justice for its perpetrators. The end of Reconstruction, like the shift from the Nuremberg era to the Cold War, brought more democracy at a price of less justice and self-serving, feeble memory. See Jeffrey Herf, "Multiple Restorations vs. the Solid South: Continuities and Discontinuities in Germany after 1945 and the American South after 1865," in Norbert Finzsch and Jürgen Martschukat, eds., *Different Restorations: Reconstruction and Wiederaufbau in the United States and Germany, 1865, 1945–1989* (Providence: Berghahn Books, 1996), pp. 48–86.

9. See Frank Stern, *Im Anfang war Auschwitz: Antisemitismus und Philosemitismus im deutschen Nachkrieg* (Gerlingen: Bleicher Verlag, 1991).

10. See Jeffrey Herf, "German Communism, the Discourse of 'Antifascist Resistance,' and the Jewish Catastrophe," in Michael Geyer and John Boyer, eds., *Resistance against the Third Reich, 1933–1990* (Chicago: University of Chicago Press, 1994), pp. 257–294.

11. The literature is extensive. On the intellectuals, see Steven Aschheim, *Between Culture and Catastrophe: German and Jewish Confrontations with National Socialism and Other Crises* (New York: New York University Press, 1996); Jeffrey Herf, "Belated Pessimism: Technology and Twentieth-Century German Conservative Intellectuals," in Yaron Ezrahi, Everett Mendelsohn, and Howard Segal, eds., *Technology, Pessimism, and Postmodernism* (Dordrecht: Klewer Academic Publishers, 1994), pp. 115–136; Jerry Z. Muller, *The Other God That Failed: Hans Freyer and the Deradicalization of German Conservatism* (Princeton: Princeton University Press, 1987); Hugo Ott, *Martin Heidegger: A Political Life*, trans. Allan Blunden (New York: Basic Books, 1993); and Anson Rabinbach, *Between Apocalypse and Enlightenment: Central European Thought in the*

*Shadow of Catastrophe* (Berkeley: University of California Press, 1997). Some recent works on film and literature include Brockman and Trommler, *Revisiting the Zero Hour;* Andreas Huyssen, *Twilight Memories: Marking Time in a Culture of Amnesia* (New York: Routledge, 1995); Anton Kaes, *From Hitler to Heimat: The Return of History as Film* (Cambridge, Mass.: Harvard University Press, 1989); Eric Santner, *Stranded Objects: Mourning, Memory, and Film in Postwar Germany* (Ithaca, N.Y.: Cornell University Press, 1990); and Ernestine Schlant and J. Thomas Rimer, *Legacies and Ambiguities: Postwar Fiction and Culture in West Germany and Japan* (Washington, D.C. and Baltimore: Woodrow Wilson Center Press and Johns Hopkins University Press, 1991).

12. See my statement on the issue in Jeffrey Herf, *Reactionary Modernism: Technology, Culture, and Politics in Weimar and the Third Reich* (New York: Cambridge University Press, 1984), and *War by Other Means: Soviet Power, West German Resistance, and the Battle of the Euromissiles* (New York: Free Press, 1991).

13. On the construction of narratives of German history, see Michael Geyer and Konrad Jarusch, "The Future of the German Past: Transatlantic Reflections for the 1990s," *Central European History* (special issue), *German Histories; Challenges in Theory, Practice, Technique* 22, nos. 3–4 (September–December 1989), 229–259.

14. For elaboration of my views on ideas and politics, see Herf, *Reactionary Modernism.* For similar approaches regarding political language and political history, see Keith Michael Baker, "On the Problem of the Ideological Origins of the French Revolution," in Dominick LaCapra and Steven L. Kaplan, eds., *Modern European Intellectual History: Reappraisals and New Perspectives* (Ithaca, N.Y.: Cornell University Press, 1982), pp. 197–219; Karl Dietrich Bracher, *Turning Points in Modern Times: Essays in German and European History,* trans. Thomas Dunlap (Cambridge, Mass.: Harvard University Press, 1995); idem, *The Age of Ideologies: A History of Twentieth-Century Political Thought,* trans. Ewald Osers (London: Weidenfeld and Nicolson, 1984); François Furet, *Interpreting the French Revolution* (New York: Cambridge University Press, 1981); and idem, *Le passé d'une illusion: essaie sur l'idée communiste au XXe siècle* (Paris: Éditions Robert Laffont, 1995).

15. See Alexander and Margarete Mitscherlich, *The Inability to Mourn: Principles of Collective Behavior* (New York: Grove Press, 1975), originally published as *Die Unfähigkeit zu trauern: Grundlagen kollektiven Verhaltens* (Munich: Piper, 1967); and Lawrence Langer, *Holocaust Testimonies: The Ruins of Memory* (New Haven: Yale University Press, 1991).

16. Theodor Adorno, "Was bedeutet: Aufarbeitung der Vergangenheit," in *Theodor Adorno: Gesammelte Schriften,* vol. 10:2 (Frankfurt am Main: Suhrkamp Verlag, 1977), pp. 558.

17. Walter Dirks, "Die restaurative Charakter der Epoche," *Frankfurter Hefte* 5 (1950), 942–954. See also Eugen Kogon, "Die Aussichten der Restauration: Über die

gesellschaftlichen Grundlagen der Zeit," *Frankfurter Hefte* 7 (1952), 166–177, re-printed in his *Die unvollendete Erneuerung: Deutschland in Kräftefeld, 1945–1963: Politische und gesellschaftliche Aufsätze aus zwei Jahrzehnten* (Frankfurt am Main: Europaische Verlagsanstalt 1964), pp. 136–154; and Helmut Schelsky, "Über das Re-staurative in unserer Zeit," *Frankfurter Allgemeine Zeitung,* April 9, 1955. On politics, economics, and society in postwar West Germany, see Harold James, "The Pre-History of the Federal Republic," *Journal of Modern History* 63 (March 1991), 99–115. Charles Maier has focused attention on the ability of established elites to survive the crises of World Wars I and II in "The Two Postwar Eras and the Conditions for Stability in Twentieth-Century Western Europe," *American Historical Review* 86 (1981), 327–352; and see Diethelm Prowe, "The New Nachkriegsgeschichte (1945–49): West Germans in Search of Their Historical Origins," *Central European History* 10 (1977), 312–328, and Alf Luedtke, "'Coming to Terms with the Past': Illusions of Remembering, Ways of Forgetting Nazism in West Germany," *Journal of Modern History* 65 (1993), 542–572.

18. Thomas Nipperdey, "1933 und die Kontinuität der deutschen Geschichte," in *Nachdenken über die deutsche Geschichte,* pp. 186–205.

19. Koselleck, *Futures Past.*

20. See Alexis de Tocqueville, *The Old Regime and the French Revolution,* trans. Stuart Gilbert (New York: Doubleday Anchor, 1955); Max Weber, *The Methodology of the Social Sciences* (New York: Free Press, 1949); and Clifford Geertz, "Ideology as a Cultural System," in *The Interpretation of Cultures* (New York: Basic Books, 1973).

21. On these discontinuities, see Jürgen Kocka, "Zerstörung und Befreiung: Das Jahr 1945 als Wendepunkt deutscher Geschichte," in *Geschichte und Aufklärung* (Göt-tingen: Vandenhoeck and Ruprecht, 1989), pp. 120–139; and Ralf Dahrendorf's classic statement of how Nazism unintentionally brought about changes that pushed the postwar Germanys into modernity in *Society and Democracy in Germany* (Garden City, N.Y.: Doubleday, 1967).

22. Martin Broszat, Klaus Dietmar Henke, and Hans Woller, eds., *Von Stalingrad zur Währungsreform: Zur Sozialgeschichte des Umbruchs in Deutschland,* 3d. ed. (Munich: Oldenbourg, 1990).

23. See Dahrendorf, *Society and Democracy in Germany.*

24. See George Mosse, *Fallen Soldiers: Reshaping the Memory of the World Wars* (New York: Oxford University Press, 1990).

25. Individual ex-Nazi intellectuals were able, however, with a mixture of oppor-tunism, genuine disillusionment, and "deradicalization," to reenter professional intel-lectual life, at times as chastened advocates of liberal democracy. See Muller, *The Other God That Failed.*

26. See Herf, *War by Other Means.*

27. On the dubious prospects for a majority "united front" government in the last

years of Weimar, see Heinrich August Winkler, *Weimar, 1918–1933: Die Geschichte der Ersten Deutschen Demokratie* (Munich: Verlag C. H. Beck, 1993).

## 2. German Communism's Master Narratives of Antifascism

1. François Furet, *Le passé d'une illusion: essai sur l'idée communiste a XXe siecle* (Paris: Éditions Robert Laffont, 1995).

2. The Nazis executed Ernst Thälmann in Buchenwald in 1944. Ulbricht's socialist engagement began before World War I. He participated in a soldiers' council in 1918, was a co-founder of the Communist Party in Leipzig, and was a member of the German Communist Party's Central Committee from 1923 and a member of the Reichstag. Forced into emigration in 1933, he worked in Paris and Prague before going to Moscow in 1938. From 1943 to 1945, he was the leading figure of the Nationale Komitee Freies Deutschland in Moscow. Ulbricht was the director of the Central Committee of the KPD on its return to Berlin in 1945, and (under different titles: chairman, general secretary, first secretary) was the dominant figure of the Socialist Unity Party (SED) from 1946 until he left power in 1971. See "Walter Ulbricht," in Jochen Cerney, ed., *Wer war Wer—DDR: Ein biographisches Lexikon* (Berlin: Ch. Links Verlag, 1992), p. 461; and "Walter Ulbricht," in *Wer ist Wer in der SBZ* ([East] Berlin: Verlag fur Internationale Kulturaustausch, 1958), p. 266. On Ulbricht's loyalty to the Soviets, and on the German Communists in the Soviet Union and in Moscow, see Wolfgang Leonhard, *Die Revolution entlässt ihre Kinder* (Cologne: Kiepenheuer and Witsch, 1955).

3. See Carola Stern, *Walter Ulbricht: Eine Politische Biographie* (Cologne: Kiepenheuer and Witsch, 1963); "Walter Ulbricht," in Cerny, *Wer war Wer*, p. 461; and "Walter Ulbricht," in *Wer ist Wer in der SBZ*, p. 266.

4. See Walter Ulbricht, *Zur Geschichte der Deutschen Arbeiterbewegung: Aus Reden und Aufsätze*, vol. 2, 1933–1946, 2d ed. ([East] Berlin: Dietz Verlag, 1953); Walter Ulbricht, *Zur Geschichte der Neuesten Zeit: Die Niederlage Hitlerdeutschlands und die Schaffung der antifaschistische-demokratischen Ordnung*, 2d ed. ([East] Berlin: Dietz Verlag, 1955); and Institüt für Marxismus–Leninismus beim Zentralkomitee der SED, *Geschichte der Deutschen Arbeiterbewegung*, vol. 4, *Von 1924 bis Januar 1933* ([East] Berlin: Dietz Verlag, 1966).

5. Wilhelm Pieck, *Reden und Aufsätze: Auswahl aus den Jahren 1908–1950*, 2 vols. ([East] Berlin: Dietz Verlag, 1951). See "Wilhelm Pieck," in Cerney, *Wer war Wer*, pp. 349–350; and "Wilhelm Pieck," in *Wer ist Wer in der SBZ*, p. 195.

6. On "social fascism" and the KPD's attacks on the SPD in the last years of the Weimar Republic, see Heinrich August Winkler, *Der Weg in die Katastrophe: Arbeiter und Arbeiterbewegung in der Weimarer Republik, 1930 bis 1933* (Berlin: Verlag J. H. W. Dietz, 1987); and Siegfried Bahne, *Die KPD und das Ende von Weimar: Das Scheitern*

*einer Politik, 1932–1935* (Frankfurt am Main: Campus Verlag, 1976); idem, "Sozial-faschismus in Deutschland: Zur Geschichte eines politischen Begriffs," *International Review of Social History* 10 (1965), 211–245; Franz Borkenau, *World Communism* (Ann Arbor: University of Michigan Press, 1962); Karl Dietrich Bracher, *Die Auflösung der Weimarer Republik*, 5th ed. (Konigstein: Athenaum, 1978); Ossip K. Flechtheim, *Die Kommunistische Partei Deutschland in der Weimarer Republik* (Offenbach: Bollwerk Ver-lag, 1948); idem, *Die KPD in der Weimarer Republik* (Frankfurt am Main: Europaische Verlagsanstalt, 1969); and Albert S. Lindemann, *A History of European Socialism* (New Haven: Yale University Press, 1983), chap. 8. For the official East German narrative, see Walter Ulbricht, *Zur Geschichte der Deutschen Arbeiterbewegung*, vol. 1 ([East] Berlin: Dietz Verlag, 1953); and Institüt fur Marxismus-Leninismus, *Geschichte der Deutschen Arbeiterbewegung.* For Leon Trotsky's contemporaneous criticism of the attacks on "social fascism," see Isaac Deutscher, *The Prophet Outcast: Trotsky, 1929–1940* (New York: Oxford University Press, 1963).

7. In the Reichstag on February 11, 1930, Thälmann said that "fascism rules in Germany." See Ernst Thälmann, "Verhandlungen des Reichstags" (February 11, 1930), reprinted in Ernst Thälmann, *Im Kampf Gegen den Deutschen und den Ameri-kanischen Imperialismus: Drei Reichstagsreden* ([East] Berlin: Dietz Verlag, 1954), pp. 75–98; "Programm/Erklärung zur nationalen und sozialen Befreiung des deut-schen Volkes" (Berlin, August 24, 1930), reprinted in Flechtheim, *Die Kommunistische Partei Deutschland in der Weimarer Republik*, pp. 281–284. See also Ernst Thälmann, *Im Kampf gegen die Faschistische Diktatur: Rede und Schlußwort des Genossen Ernst Thälmann auf der Parteikonferenz der KPD im Oktober 1932* (Berlin: Kommunistischen Partei Deutschland, 1932); and *Ausgewählte Reden und Schriften in zwei Bänden* (Frank-furt am Main: Verlag Marxistische Blätter, 1976). On the Thälmann cult and political symbolism in East Germany, see Maoz Azaryahu, *Von Wilhelmplatz zu Thälmannplatz: Politische Symbole im öffentlichen Leben der DDR* (Gerlingen: Bleicher Verlag, 1991).

8. "Resolution über den Kampf gegen den Faschismus," *Rote Fahne*, June 15, 1930, cited by Winkler, *Der Weg in die Katastrophe*, p. 157.

9. "Wendung der KPD?" *Sozialdemokratische Partei-Korrespondenz*, no. 12 (Decem-ber 1931), 858–860, cited by Winkler, *Der Weg in die Katastrophe*, pp. 444–445.

10. Winkler, *Der Weg in die Katastrophe*, p. 754; see also Barbara Timmermann, "Die Faschismus-Diskussion in der Kommunistischen Internationale (1920–1935)" (Ph.D. diss., University of Cologne, 1977).

11. In October 1932 the KPD Politburo asserted that the "revolutionary surge" in Germany was expressed in the "growing resistance of the proletariat and the working people against fascism and the capitalist offensive." See "Resolution der Parteikonfer-enz der KPD über das 12. Plenum des EKKI und die Aufgaben der KPD" (October 15–17, 1932), reprinted in Flechtheim, *Die Kommunistische Partei Deutschland in der Weimarer Republik*, pp. 285–294.

12. See Wilhelm Pieck, *We Are Fighting for a Soviet Germany* (New York: Workers

Library Publishers, 1934), p. 30. *We Are Fighting for a Soviet Germany* was not republished in Pieck's collected works in the DDR.

13. "Programm/Erklärung zur nationalen und sozialen Befreiung des deutschen Volkes," *Rote Fahne*, August 24, 1930, reprinted in Flechtheim, *Die Kommunistische Partei Deutschland in der Weimarer Republik*, pp. 280–283.

14. On this much-discussed issue, see Hannah Arendt, *The Origins of Totalitarianism* (New York: Harcourt, Brace, 1951); Karl Bracher, *The German Dictatorship* (New York: Praeger, 1970); Lucy Dawidowicz, *The Holocaust and the Historians* (Cambridge, Mass.: Harvard University Press, 1981); and Enzo Traverso, *The Marxists and the Jewish Question: The History of a Debate, 1843–1943* (Atlantic Highland, N.J.: Humanities Press, 1994).

15. See Julius Carlebach, *Karl Marx and the Radical Critique of Judaism* (London: Routledge and Kegan Paul, 1978); and Liah Greenfeld, *Nationalism: Five Paths to Modernity* (Cambridge, Mass.: Harvard University Press, 1992). See also Max Horkheimer and Theodor Adorno, *Dialectic of Enlightenment* (New York: Herder and Herder, 1972).

16. For an early statement of such sentiments, see *Der Jud ist Schuld . . .? Diskussionsbuch über die Judenfrage* (Basel: Zinnen-Verlag, 1932), pp. 272–286. The essay, the only extensive discussion of the Jewish question before 1933, was written by an anonymous member of the party leadership and never widely circulated. See the discussion in Edmund Silberner, *Kommunisten zur Judenfrage: Zur Geschichte von Theorie und Praxis des Kommunismus* (Opladen: Westdeutscher Verlag, 1983), pp. 279–286.

17. Josef Stalin, "Marxismus und nationale Frage," in *Werke*, vol. 2 (Berlin: Dietz, 1950), pp. 266–333.

18. Ibid., p. 272.

19. Ibid., p. 301.

20. See Benjamin Pinkus and Zvi Gitelman, *The Jews of the Soviet Union: The History of a National Minority* (New York: Cambridge University Press, 1988); and Zvi Gitelman, *A Century of Ambivalence: The Jews of Russia and the Soviet Union, 1981 to the Present* (New York: Schocken Books, 1988).

21. On the analysis of fascism in the Comintern, see Timmermann, "Der Faschismus-Diskussion"; and Theo Pirker, *Komintern und Faschismus. Dokumente zur Geschichte und Theorie des Faschismus* (Stuttgart: Deutsche Verlags-Anstalt, 1965). For the official East German history, see Institüt für Marxismus-Leninismus beim Zentralkomitee der SED, *Geschichte der Deutschen Arbeiterbewegung von Januar 1933 bis August 1939*, vol. 10 ([East] Berlin: Dietz Verlag, 1969), p. 108–109.

22. Wilhelm Pieck, "Der Vormarsch des Sozialismus: Bericht, Schlußwort und Resolution zum 1. Punkt der Tagesordnung des Kongresses: Rechenschaftsbericht über die Tätigkeit des Exekutivkomitees der Kommunistischen Internationale," in *VII Weltkongreß der Kommunistischen Internationale, Moskau/Leningrad 1935* (Milan 1967),

p. 40; see also *VII Weltkongreß der Kommunistischen Internationale: Referat: Aus der Diskussion, Schlußwort, Resolution.* (Frankfurt am Main, 1971).

23. Pieck, "Der Vormarsch des Sozialismus," p. 40.

24. Walter Ulbricht, "Der VII. Weltkongreß der Komintern und die Kommunistische Partei Deutschland," *Bolschewik* (Moscow), no. 18 (September 1935), reprinted in *Zur Geschichte der Deutschen Arbeiterbewegung,* 2:71.

25. See Wilhelm Pieck, *Der Neue Weg zum gemeinsamen Kampf für den Sturz der Hitlerdiktatur: Referat uns schlusswort auf der Brusseler Konferenz der Kommunistischen Partei Deutschland (Oktober 1935)* (Strasbourg: Éditions Prométhée, 1935). Though one of the most important speeches of Pieck's political career, it was not reprinted in East Germany until 1972. See Wilhelm Pieck, "Der Neue Weg zum gemeinsamen Kampf für den Sturz der Hitlerdiktatur: Referat uns schlusswort auf der Brusseler Konferenz der Kommunistischen Partei Deutschland, Referat 4, Oktober 1935," in *Gesammelte Reden und Schriften, vol. 5, Februar 1933 bis August 1939* ([East] Berlin: Dietz Verlag, 1972), pp. 167–237. It does not appear in the two-volume collection of his essays and speeches published in 1951, when the spirit of the Popular Front was at odds with the constellation of the early Cold War. See Wilhelm Pieck, *Reden und Aufsätze: Auswahl aus den Jahren 1908–1950,* vol. 1 ([East] Berlin: Dietz Verlag, 1951).

26. Pieck, "Der Neue Weg," p. 183.

27. Ibid., pp. 184–185, 187.

28. Ibid., pp. 198, 199.

29. "Das Program der Kommunistischen Partei Deutschland zum Sturz des Hitlerregimes: Die Brüsseler Parteikonferenz der KPD," in Institüt für Marxismus-Leninismus, *Geschichte der Deutschen Arbeiterbewegung,* 10:112–128.

30. Ibid., p. 233–234.

31. Ibid., p. 235.

32. "Die Berner Konferenz der Kommunistischen Partei Deutschland und das Programm des neuen demokratischen Republik," in Institüt für Marxismus-Leninismus, *Geschichte der Deutschen Arbeiterbewegung,* 10:216–224.

33. Wilhelm Pieck, "Die Gegenwärtigen Lage und die Aufgabe der Partei," in Institüt für Marxismus-Leninismus, *Geschichte der Deutschen Arbeiterbewegung,* 10:217–218. In fact, before 1933 resistance to fascism, and hence anti-imperialism, had often included nationalist attacks, for example, on the Versailles treaty and the Dawes and Young plans; see "Programm/Erklärung zur nationalen und sozialen Befreiung des deutschen Volkes" (August 24, 1930)."

34. "Gegen die Schmach der Judenpogrom! Erklärung des Zentralkomitees der KPD," *Die Rote Fahne: Sonderausgabe gegen Hitlers Judenpogrome,* no. 7 (November 1938), 1. See also Wilhelm Pieck, "Nicht nur Entrüstung, sondern Taten! Gegen die Judenpogrome," in *Reden und Aufsätze, 1908–1950,* 1:326–329.

35. "Gegen die Schmach der Judenpogrome!" p. 1.

36. Ibid.

37. For the official East German version of the Communist response to Nazi persecution, see "Der Kampf zur Sturze der Faschistischen Diktatur und für die Verhinderung des Krieges durch die Schaffung der Aktionseinheit der Arbeiterklasse und aller Antifaschistischen, 1933–1939," in Ulbricht, *Zur Geschichte der Deutschen Arbeiterbeweung*, 2:7–416; and Institut für Marxismus-Leninismus, *Geschichte der Deutschen Arbeiterbewegung*, 10:213–216.

38. Wilhelm Pieck, "Unser Volk gegen die barbarischen Judenpogrome," *Die Rote Fahne: Sonderausgabe gegen Hitlers Judenpogrome*, no. 7 (November 1938), 2. A slightly longer version of the article was published November 24, 1938 in *Rundschau*, the German Communist exile newspaper in Basel. That version was reprinted in Wilhelm Pieck, "Nicht nur Entrüstung, sondern Taten!: Gegen die Judenpogrome," in *Reden und Aufsätze*, 1:327–329.

39. Pieck, "Unser Volk."

40. Ibid.

41. Walter Ulbricht, "Die Pogrome—eine Waffe der faschistischen Kriegspolitik," *Die Rote Fahne*, no. 7 (November 1938), 2. (The article was not reproduced in Ulbricht's *Zur Geschichte der Deutschen Arbeiterbewegung*, vol. 2.) This instrumentalist view of the "function" of anti-Semitism entered into subsequent East German historiography. See Dawidowicz, *The Holocaust and the Historians*.

42. Ulbricht, "Die Pogrome," p. 2.

43. Ibid.

44. The Hitler-Stalin nonaggression pact of August 23, 1939, was another chapter of Communist history which did not find a prominent place in the East German postwar histories of antifascist resistance. On the KPD and the nonaggression pact, see Horst Duhnke, *Die KPD von 1933 bis 1945* (Cologne: Kiepenheuer und Witsch, 1972); and Wayne Thompson, *The Political Odyssey of Herbert Wehner* (Boulder, Colo: Westview, 1993), pp. 72–75. For the KPD Central Committee response to the pact, see "Aus der Erklärung des Zentralkomitees der Kommunistischen Partei Deutschland zum Abschluss des Nichtangriffspaktes zwischen der Sowjetunion und Deutschland," in Ulbricht, *Zur Geschichte der Neuesten Zeit*, pp. 330–333. On German Communists in the Soviet Union who were delivered to the Nazis, see Margarete Buber, *Under Two Dictators* (London: Victor Gollanz, 1949).

45. For Ulbricht's collection of the documents of wartime antifascism, see Ulbricht, *Zur Geschichte der Neuesten Zeit*.

46. Ibid., p. 5.

47. Walter Ulbricht, "Die antifaschistische Opposition in Deutschland," in *Zur Geschichte der Deutschen Arbeiterbewegung*, 2:213–219; originally published in Moscow in *Bolschweik* (January 1939).

48. Walter Ulbricht, "Der Eroberungskrieg des Faschistischen Deutschen Imperialismus und die Zerschlagung der Hitlerarmeen durch die Sowjetarmee," in *Zur Geschichte der Neuesten Zeit*, p. 8.

49. Ibid., p. 9.

50. Ibid., p. 10.

51. Ulbricht, *Zur Geschichte der Neuesten Zeit,* pp. 16–17; see also Walter Ulbricht, "Worin besteht die Wendung in der Kriegslage nach der Niederlage der deutschen Armeen bei Stalingrad?" (Moscow, February 1943), reprinted in *Zur Geschichte der Deutschen Arbeiterbewegung,* 2:302–303. For more perspectives on Stalingrad as the staging point of the German disillusionment with the Nazi regime, see Martin Broszat, Klaus-Dietmar Henke, and Hans Woller, *Von Stalingrad zur Währungsreform: Zur Sozialgeschichte des Umbruchs in Deutschland* (Munich: R. Oldenbourg, 1990).

52. Ulbricht, *Zur Geschichte der Neuesten Zeit,* p. 28–29. On the Jewish and Jewish Communist resistance, see Helmut Eschwege, "Resistance of German Jews against the Nazi Regime," *Leo Baeck Yearbook* 14 (1970), 143–180.

53. Ulbricht, *Zur Geschichte der Neuesten Zeit,* p. 39.

54. See "An die Juden der ganzen Welt," *Freies Deutschland* (Mexico City), June 15, 1942, pp. 1–2, the statement of the "Second Congress of Representatives of the Jewish People" held in Moscow on May 24, 1942. See also Shimon Redlich, *Propaganda and Nationalism in Wartime Russia: The Jewish Antifascist Committee in the USSR, 1941–1948* (Boulder, Colo.: East European Quarterly, 1982).

55. See Pieck, *Reden und Aufsätze,* 1:356–379.

56. Wilhelm Pieck, "Appell zur Einigung und Aktivität für den Sturz Hitler" (German-language Moscow radio, April 8, 1942), in *Wilhelm Pieck: Gesammelte Reden und Schriften, Band 6, 1939 bis Mai 1945* ([East] Berlin: Dietz Verlag, 1979), pp. 90, 92. Pieck's major wartime radio addresses are included in this volume. See also Wilhelm Pieck NL 36/417, SAPMO-BA, ZPA; and Wilhelm Pieck, "Schafft die Kampfeinheit gegen Hitlers Kriegsverbrechen!" (German-language Moscow radio, April 30, 1942), in *Gesammelte Schriften,* 6:93–94.

57. Wilhelm Pieck, "Anklage gegen die Hitlerclique" (German-language Moscow radio, July 26, 1942), in *Gesammelte Schriften,* 6:103–105.

58. Ibid., p. 102.

59. Ibid., pp. 104–105.

60. Wilhelm Pieck, "Wie muß dem Krieg ein Ende gemacht werden?" (German-language Moscow radio, September 1, 1942), in *Gesammelte Reden und Schriften,* 6:106.

61. Wilhelm Pieck, "Gegen die Hitlerbarbarei," (German-language Moscow radio, September 15, 1942), in *Gesammelte Reden und Schriften,* 6:108–112.

62. Ibid., pp. 108–109.

63. Ibid., pp. 109–111.

64. Ibid., p. 111. See also Wilhelm Pieck, "Der Hitlerfaschismus und das deutsche Volk, 1942," in *Gesammelte Reden und Schriften,* 6:120–183.

65. On the NKFD see Nationalkomitee Freies Deutschland, Schulung Deutscher Kriegsgefangener, in Wilhelm Pieck NL 36/582, SAPMO-BA, ZPA. For lectures and

course outlines from the Communist Party school in wartime Moscow, see Walter Ulbricht Papers NL 182/827, SAPMO-BA, ZPA. For Pieck's address to the opening conference, see Wilhelm Pieck, "Es darf kein neues 1918 geben! Wie kann der heraufziehenden Katastrophe Einhalt geboten werden?" (speech at founding conference of Nationalkomitee "Freies Deutschland," July 13, 1943) in *Gesammelte Reden und Schriften,* 6:195–205. See also Herman Weber, *Geschichte der DDR,* (Munich: Deutscher Taschenbuch Verlag, 1985); Bodo Scheurig, *Verrater oder Patrioten: Das Nationalkomitee "Freies Deutschland" und der Bund Deutscher Offiziere in der Sowjetunion, 1943–1945* (Berlin: Propylaen, 1993); idem, *Freies Deutschland. Das Nationalkomitee und der Bund Deutscher Offiziere in der Sowjetunion, 1943–1945* (Cologne: Kiepenheuer and Witsch, 1984); and Bodo Scheurig and Franz von Hammerstein, eds., *Das Nationalkomitee Freies Deutschland: Ein verdrangtes Kapitel des deutschen Widerstands* (Berlin: Evangelisches Bildungswerk Berlin, 1990).

66. "Manifest an die Wehrmacht und an das deutsche Volk," in Ulbricht, *Zur Geschichte der Neuesten Zeit,* pp. 355–361.

67. Ibid., pp. 356–357. At the same congress, Erich Weinert (1890–1953), a writer and Spanish civil war veteran, was chosen president of the NKFD. For his comments on the possibility of national salvation by anti-Nazi revolt, see Erich Weinert, "Protokoll der Gruendungsversammlung," in *Deutsche Wohin? Protokoll der Gruendungsversammlung des National-Komitees Freies Deutschland und des Deutschen Offiziersbundes* (Mexico City: Lateinamerikanisches Komitee der Freien Deutschen, 1944), pp. 15–24; see also "Erich Weinert," in Cerny, *Wer war Wer,* pp. 476–477.

68. Erich Weinert, "Nationalkomitee Freies Deutschland, Anweisungen Nr. 2," in Wilhelm Pieck NL 36/577, SAPMO-BA, ZPA. Pieck, along with Anton Ackermann, another German Communist émigré and future member of the SED Central Committee, and Erik Weinert directed the writing of the NKFD literature and radio broadcasts. For the Moscow Communists' anti-Nazi wartime propaganda, see Wilhelm Pieck NL 36/569 (Frontagitation 1941–1942); NL36/570 (Frontagitation 1942–1943); and NL36/577 (Nationalkomitee Freies Deutschland—Aufrufe und Flugblätter (1941–1942, July 1943–March 1945), SAPMO-BA, ZPA.

69. See Birgit Petrick, *"Freies Deutschland"—die Zeitung des Nationalkomitees "Freies Deutschland" (1943–1945): Ein kommunikationsgeschichtliche Untersuchung* (Munich: K. G. Sauer, 1979).

70. Ibid., p. 268.

71. Ibid., pp. 270, 287.

72. See Lothar Lösche, "Millionen Opfer Klagen An!: Das Todeslager von Auschwitz," *Freies Deutschland,* March 21, 1945, p. 3; "Die Braune Schmach von Blut und Rasse," *Freies Deutschland,* April 11, 1945, p. 3; "Eine Seite aus Hitlers Schuldbuch," *Freies Deutschland,* May 16, 1945, p. 3.

73. "An die Juden der ganzen Welt." The statement was used for fund-raising

efforts abroad. Some of the signers of the statement, such as Solomon Mikhoels and Schachno Epstein, were subsequently executed in the anti-Semitic attacks on Soviet Jews between 1948 and 1952. See Lionel Kochan, *The Jews in the Soviet Union since 1917* (New York: Oxford University Press, 1978); and Arkady Vaksburg, *Stalin's War against the Jews* (New York: Alfred A. Knopf, 1994).

74. "An die Juden der ganzen Welt."

75. See "Einführungskurs, 1942," in Wilhelm Pieck NL 36/582, SAPMO-BA, ZPA. For lectures and course outlines for German prisoners of war, see Wilhelm Pieck NL 36/582, SAPMO-BA, ZPA. For lectures and course outlines of the Communist Party instruction for party cadres in Moscow during the war, see Walter Ulbricht 182/827, SAPMO-BA, ZPA. See also "Nation und Rasse" and "Nation" in "Program für den Kriegs-gefangene, 1942," in Wilhelm Pieck NL 36/582, SAPMO-BA, ZPA; "F. Schneider to Wilhelm Pieck," May 4, 1942, Anton Ackerman NL 109/79, SAPMO-BA, ZPA, p. 11; and "F. Schneider: Die Geschichtslügen des Hitlerfaschismus," Anton Ackerman 109/79, SAPMO-BA, ZPA, pp. 13–20. On twentieth-century German history, see "Program für den Kriegsgefangenenkurs" (1942), Wilhelm Pieck NL 36/582, SAPMO-BA, ZPA, pp. 3–39. On the German Communists in Moscow and the "antifascist schools," see Leonhard, *Die Revolution entlässt ihre Kinder.*

76. "Program für den Kriegsgefangenenkurs," pp. 5–6.

77. "Einführungskurs: Kurs elementarer Begriffe zur Entlarvung der Hauptthesen der faschistischen Ideologie," (1942), Wilhelm Pieck NL, 36/582, SAPMO-BA, ZPA, p. 7.

78. "Lehrplan" (November 1944), Wilhelm Pieck NL 36/582, SAPMO-BA, ZPA, p. 166. Other themes included the wartime alliance between the Soviet Union, England, and the United States; Hitler's war for *Lebensraum;* the industrialization of Germany; essential elements of capitalism; Marx and Engels; the bourgeois revolution of 1848 and the emergence of Prussia; imperialism; the labor movement; 1918; the KPD; Weimar; the consequences of fascism; the Marxist-Leninist theory of the state; the national question; and the role of a "free Germany" in the creation of a future German democracy.

79. "4. Thema: Der Vernichtungsfeldzug der Hitlerfaschisten unter dem Banner der 'Rassentheorie,'" Wilhelm Pieck NL 36/582, SAPMO-BA, ZPA, pp. 170–171.

80. See Franz Neumann, *Behemoth: The Structure and Practice of National Socialism* (New York: Oxford University Press, 1944); David Wyman, *The Abandonment of the Jews; America and the Holocaust* (New York: Pantheon Books, 1984); Martin Gilbert, *Auschwitz and the Allies;* (New York: Holt, Rinehart and Winston, 1981); and Bernard Wasserstein, *Britain and the Jews of Europe* (New York: Oxford University Press, 1979). On the terror against Jewish Communists in 1930s Moscow, see Mario Kessler, "Der Stalinische Terror gegen jüdische Kommunisten 1937/1938," in Hermann Weber and

Dietrich Staritz with Siegfried Bahne and Richard Lorenz, eds., *Kommunisten verfolgen Kommunisten: Stalinistischer Terror und "Säuberungen" in den kommunistischen Parteien Europas seit den dreißiger Jahren* (Berlin: Akademie Verlag, 1993), pp. 87–102.

81. Johannes R. Becher, "Zur Rassentheorie des Deutschen Faschismus," reprinted in *Publizistik*, vol. 2, *1939–1945* (Berlin: Aufbau Verlag, 1978), pp. 384–390.

82. Ibid., p. 386.

83. In 1967 the Czech Communist Party sent a memo of October 27, 1944, from Ernst Kaltenbrunner, then chief of the SD, or German government's Sicherheitsdienst (security service) concerning "Sprachregelung," or language rules for the treatment of the NKFD, to the East German Communists. See "Dr. Kaltenbrunner, 27. Oktober 1944," in Walter Ulbricht NL 182/892, SAPMO-BA, ZPA, p. 279. Kaltenbrunner wrote: "The [*Drahtzieher*] powers behind the scenes of the committee are Jews and Communists who emigrated to the Soviet Union after 1933 . . . [Erich] Weinert, a Communist who has succumbed to the Jews, is the president of the committee. Former General of Artillery [in the Wehrmacht] Walther von Seydlitz has made common cause as president of the committee with him [Weinert] and his Jewish helpers."

84. Wilhelm Pieck, "Berlin von Hitler befreit!" in *Reden und Aufsätze*, pp. 423–426.

85. Ibid., p. 423.

86. Ibid., p. 424.

87. "Besprechung mit Dimitroff" (May 25, 1945), Wilhelm Pieck NL 36/500, SAPMO-BA, ZPA.

88. Norman M. Naimark, *The Russians in Germany: A History of the Soviet Zone of Occupation, 1945–1949* (Cambridge, Mass.: Harvard University Press, 1995), p. 11.

89. See ibid.

90. Zentralkommitee der Kommunistischen Partei Deutschland, "Aufruf der Kommunistischen Partei," *Deutsches Volkszeitung*, June 13, 1945, pp. 1–2; reprinted as "Aufruf der Kommunistischen Partei Deutschland, 11. Juni 1945," in Ulbricht, *Zur Geschichte der Neuesten Zeit*, pp. 370–379. The signers included Wilhelm Pieck, Walter Ulbricht, Franz Dahlem, Anton Ackerman, Gustav Sobottka, Ottomar Geschke, Johannes R. Becher, Edwin Hörnle, Hans Jendretzky, Michel Niederkfrechner, Hermann Matern, Irene Gärtner, Bernhard Koenen, Martha Arendsee, Otto Winzer, and Hans Mahle. See "Anton Ackermann," in *Wer war Wer—DDR*, pp. 9–10; Herman Weber, *Geschichte der DDR*, pp. 47–54; and Leonhard, *Die Revolution entlässt ihre Kinder.*

91. "Aufruf der Kommunistischen Partei Deutschland, 11. Juni 1945," pp. 370–371.

92. Ibid., pp. 371–372.

93. On the interaction of German and Soviet Communists in the occupation, see Naimark, *The Russians in Germany*, pp. 10–12.

94. "Aufruf der Kommunistischen Partei Deutschland, 11. Juni 1945," pp. 371–372.

95. Ibid., pp. 372–373.

96. On this theme, see Sigrid Meuschel, *Legitimation und Parteiherrschaft in der DDR* (Frankfurt am Main: Suhrkamp, 1992), esp. pp. 29–101; also Furet, *Le passé d'une illusion.*

97. "Aufruf der Kommunistischen Partei Deutschland, 11. Juni 1945," p. 373.

98. Ibid., p. 373.

99. Ibid., p. 375.

100. Ibid., pp. 376–377.

101. Ibid., pp. 376–378.

102. Walter Ulbricht, *Die Legende vom "Deutschen Sozialismus"* (Berlin: Dietz Verlag, 1945).

103. "Verlag Neuer Weg, Plan der in Arbeit und in Vorbereitung befindliche Verlagserscheinungen, Stand am 12. Dezember 1945"; "Aufstellung der vom 9. Mai 1945 bis 31. 11 1947 im Verlag Neuer Weg bzw im Verlag JHW Dietz Nachf. GmBH erscheinen Titel," IV 2/9.13/5 Verlag Neuer Weg SAPMO-BA, ZPA.

104. Walter Ulbricht, *Der Faschistische Deutsche Imperialismus (1933–1945) (Die Legende vom "deutschen Sozialismus")*, 4th. ed. (Berlin: Dietz Verlag, 1956). All quotations are from this edition.

105. Ibid., p. 99.

106. Ibid., p. 100.

107. Ibid. p. 101.

108. Ibid., p. 8.

109. Ibid. pp. 105–106.

110. Ibid., pp. 13–30. See also Henry A. Turner, Jr., *German Big Business and the Rise of Hitler* (New York: Oxford University Press, 1985).

111. Ulbricht, *Der Faschistische Deutsche Imperialismus*, p. 21.

112. Ibid., p. 107.

113. Ibid., p. 24. On Himmler, see Richard Breitman, *Heinrich Himmler: The Architect of Genocide* (New York: Knopf, 1991).

114. Ulbricht, *Der Faschistische Deutsche Imperialismus*, p. 109.

115. Walter Ulbricht, "Das Program der antifaschistisch-demokratischen Ordnung: Rede auf der ersten Funktionärkonferenz der KPD Groß-Berlin 25. Juni 1945," in Walter Ulbricht, *Die Entwicklung des deutschen volksdemokratischen Staates, 1945–1948*, 2d ed. ([East] Berlin: Dietz Verlag, 1959), pp. 16–17. Fifty thousand copies had been printed as of the second edition.

116. Ibid., p. 18.

117. Ibid., p. 19.

118. Ibid., pp. 19–20.

119. Ibid., p. 21.

120. Ibid.

121. The expansion of the Stasi was one manifestation of the Communists' distrust

of the Germans. On antifascism and the legitimation of the East German regime, see reports of the German parliament's Enquete Kommission: Deutscher Bundestag 12 Wahlperiode, *Drucksache 12/7820: Bericht der Enquete-Kommission, Aufarbeitung von Geschichte und Folgen der SED-Diktatur in Deutschland* (Bonn: Deutscher Bundestag, 1994); and Meuschel, *Legitimation und Parteiherrschaft in der DDR*, pp. 101–116.

122. Zentralkomitee der Kommunistischen Partei Deutschland, *Vertragsdisposition Nr. 1 Der Sieg des Faschismus in Deutschland und seine Lehren für unseren gegenwärtigen Kampf* ([East] Berlin: Verlag Neuer Weg, 1945); Zentralkomitee der Kommunistischen Partei Deutschland, *Vertragsdisposition Nr. 2: Der Klassencharakter des Faschismus und die Probleme der Einheits- und Volksfront* ([East] Berlin: Berliner Buchdruckerei, 1945); and Zentralkomitee der Kommunistischen Partei Deutschland, *Vertragsdisposition Nr. 3: Die Kriegsschuld Deutschland und die Mitschuld des deutschen Volkes* ([East] Berlin: Berliner Buchdruckerei, 1945).

123. Zentralkomitee der Kommunistischen Partei Deutschland, *Vertragsdisposition Nr. 12: Der Kampf gegen die Naziideologie* ([East] Berlin: Verlag Neuer Weg, 1946), p. 12.

124. Zentralkomiteee der Kommunistischen Partei Deutschland, *Vertragsdisposition Nr. 20: Der zweite Weltkrieg, die Sicherung des Friedens und die Sowjetunion* ([East] Berlin: Verlag Neuer Weg, 1946), p. 7.

125. Ibid., p. 9.

126. Ibid., pp. 10–11.

127. On the persecution of Communists by other Communists, see Herman Weber and Dietrich Staritz, with Siegfried Bahne and Richard Lorenz, eds., *Kommunisten verfolgen Kommunisten: Stalinistischer Terror und Säuberungen in den kommunistischen Parteien Europas seit den dreißiger Jahren* ([East] Berlin: Akademie Verlag, 1993).

## 3. From Periphery to Center

1. On the German emigration from Nazism, see Hans-Albert Walter, *Deutsche Exilliteratur, 1933–1950*, vol. 2, *Europäisches Appeasement und überseeische Asypraxis* (1984); vol. 3, *Internierung, Flucht und Lebensbedingungen im Zweiten Weltkrieg* (1988); vol. 4, *Exilpresse* (1978), all (Stuttgart: Metzlersche Verlagsbuchhandlung).

2. On the German exiles in Mexico, see Fritz Pohle, *Das Mexikanische Exil: Ein Beitrag zur Geschichte der politisch-kulturellen Emigration aus Deutschland (1937–1946)* (Stuttgart: J. B. Metzlersche Verlagsbuchhandlung, 1986); Wolfang Kießling, *Alemania Libre in Mexiko*, vol. 1, *Ein Beitrag zur Geschichte des antifaschistischen Exils (1941–1946)* ([East] Berlin: Akademie Verlag, 1974); Patrik von zur Mühlen, *Fluchtziel Lateinamerika: Die deutsche Emigration, 1933–1945: Politische Aktivitäten und soziokulturelle Integration* (Bonn: Verlag Neue Gesellschaft, 1988), pp. 47–49. See also Herbert

A. Strauss, "Jews in German History: Persecution, Emigration, Acculturation," in *Leo Baeck Institute Yearbook* 28, pt. 2 (1983), 11–26.

3. During the 1930s and early 1940s, about 90,000 persons, 90 percent of them Jews, found refuge from Nazism in Latin America. The largest concentrations of European Jewish refugees were in Argentina (35,000), Brazil (16,000), and Chile (13,00). Pohle, *Das Mexikanische Exil*, pp. 4–5, 76–79. See also Paul Merker, "Uber die 'Bewegung Freies Deutschland' in Latein Amerika," in Heinz Vosske, ed., *Im Kampf bewährt: Erinnerungen deutscher Genossen an den antifaschistischen Widerstand von 1933 bis 1945* ([East] Berlin: Dietz, 1969), pp. 465–526.

4. Kießling, *Alemania Libre in Mexiko*, 1:79, 288.

5. Pohle, *Das Mexikanische Exil*, p. 202.

6. The founders of *Freies Deutschland* in Mexico City were Leo Katz, Otto Katz, Ludwig Renn, Bodo Uhse, Bruno Frei, Rudolf Feistmann, and Theo Balk. Paul Merker, "An die Zentrale Kontrollkommission des ZK. der SED, Berlin: Stellungnahme zur Judenfrage" (June 1, 1956), Paul Merker NL 102/27, SAPMO-BA, ZPA, p. 51. For a bibliography of articles published in the journal and for reference to East German literature, see Volker Riedel, *Freies Deutschland: Mexico, 1941–1946: Bibliographie einer Zeitschrift* ([East] Berlin: Aufbau Verlag, 1975). See also Kießling, *Alemania Libre;* Wolfgang Kießling, ed., *Alemania Libre in Mexiko*, vol. 2, *Texte und Dokumente zur Geschichte des antifaschistischen Exils, 1941–1946* ([East] Berlin: Akademie Verlag, 1974); and Pohle, *Das Mexikanische Exil*. Among the Jewish Communists who arrived in 1940 and 1941 were Anna Seghers, Egon Erwin Kirsch, Erich Jungmann, Otto Katz (alias André Simone), Hans Marum, Alexander Abusch, and Leo Zuckermann. Other members who arrived after the outbreak of World War II and who played an important role in subsequent discussions of the Jewish question were Leo Katz (from Austria) and Rudolf Feistmann. My determination of who was and was not Jewish in the German Communist emigration rests on self-identification as well as identifications by political associates which appear in published and archival materials.

7. Seghers became one of the leading literary figures of postwar East Germany. See Lowell A. Bangerter, *The Bourgeois Proletarian: A Study of Anna Seghers* (Bonn: Bouvier, 1980); Ute Brandes, *Anna Seghers* (Berlin: Colloqium Verlag, 1992); Heinz Neugebauer, *Anna Seghers: Leben und Werk* (Berlin: Das Europäische Buch, 1978); Christine Zell Romero, *Anna Seghers* (Reinbek bei Hamburg: Rowohlt, 1993); Andreas Schrade, *Anna Seghers* (Stuttgart: J. B. Metzler, 1993); and Alexander Stephan, *Anna Seghers im Exil: Essays, Texte, Dokumente* (Bonn: Bouvier, 1993).

8. Alexander Abusch, "Vorwort" to Riedel, *Freies Deutschland: Mexico, 1941–1946*, pp. 7–9. Abusch was born in Cracow. He was a member of the KPD from its founding, and worked full-time as a journalist. From 1935 to 1939 he was editor in chief of *Rote Fahne* in Paris, then was interned in 1939–40 in southern France before escaping to Mexico. See "Alexander Abusch," in Jochen Cerny, ed., *Wer war Wer—DDR* (Berlin:

Ch. Links Verlag, 1992), p. 9; and BStU MfSZ-Archiv, 5079/56 Alexander Abusch, Arbeitsvorgang 2282/53, vol. 1, *Teil* 1, p. 28.

9. Pohle, *Das Mexikanische Exil*, pp. 201–202; and Kießling, *Allemania Libre*, 1:79.

10. Pohle, *Das Mexikanische Exil*, pp. 203–216, 245–274.

11. On relations between the Communists and Menorah, see ibid., pp. 311–315.

12. Merker, "An die Zentrale Kontrollkommission des ZK. der SED," p. 52. Other organizations of Jews from Eastern Europe and from Mexico of a variety of political persuasions—Communist, Socialist, Zionist—also existed.

13. On debates about Zionism among the émigrés, see ibid., p. 53; and Pohle, *Das Mexikanische Exil*, pp. 311–338.

14. This political biography up to the time of Merker's arrival in Mexico draws on Paul Merker, "Fragebogen" (July 24, 1946); "Mein politischer Lebenslauf" (1949); and "Kurz-Biographie" (June 1, 1950), SAPMO-BA, ZPA IV/2/11/V/801 Kaderfragen, pp. 1–2, 4–50, 51–54; and Merker, "Stellungnahme zur Judenfrage."

15. Merker, "Mein politischer Lebenslauf," p. 4.

16. On the Stalinization of the German Communist Party, see Hermann Weber, *Die Wandlung des deutschen Kommunismus: Die Stalinisierung der KPD in der Weimarer Republik* (Frankfurt am Main: Europaische Verlagsanstalt, 1969).

17. Lozovsky was one of the leaders of the Jewish Antifascist Committee during World War II. In 1952 he was among fifteen members of the committee who were arrested, convicted on trumped-up charges of espionage for the United States, and executed. See Arkady Vaksburg, *Stalin against the Jews*, trans. Antonia W. Bouis (New York: Alfred A. Knopf, 1994), esp. chaps. 6 and 8.

18. On Zörgiebel's decision, see Heinrich August Winkler, *Weimar, 1918–1933: Die Geschichte der Ersten Deutschen Demokratie* (Munich: C. H. Beck, 1993), p. 350; Thomas Kurz, *"Blutmai": Sozialdemokraten und Kommunisten in Brennpunkt der Berliner Ereignisse von 1929* (Bonn: Dietz, 1988); and Eve Rosenhaft, *Beating the Fascists? The German Communists and Political Violence, 1929–1933* (Cambridge: Cambridge University Press, 1983). See also Paul Merker, "Der Kampf gegen den Faschismus," *Die Internationale* 13, no. 8/9 (1930), 259–266.

19. Both display his hostility to reformers within the labor movement. See S. Willner, "Building the Revolutionary Trade Union Movement," *The Communist: A Magazine of the Theory and Practice of Marxism-Leninism* 10, no. 11 (December 1931), 995–1005, and "Some Lessons of the Last Miners' Strike," ibid., 11, no. 1 (January 1932), 27–45.

20. The FBI appears not to have learned of Merker's American trip until the 1940s. See "J. Edgar Hoover to Adolf A. Berle, Jr.: Subject: Paul Merker, alias Paul Merker Zeibig, Communist Activities in Mexico" (September 22, 1943), NA RG 319 IRR Paul Merker Box 151, X8590750.

21. Hoover to Berle, pp. 11–12.

22. Franz Dahlem was in the KPD in the 1920s, the Prussian Landtag from 1928 to 1933, and the Reichstag from 1930 to 1932. He was a member, with Merker and Ulbricht, of the KPD Auslandssekretariat in Paris from 1933 to 1937, director of the political commission of International Brigades in Spain from 1937 to 1939, and was interned in France from 1939 to 1942. Dahlem was unable to escape from Vichy internment. In 1942 the Gestapo arrested him and sent him to the Mauthausen concentration camp in Austria, which he survived. See also Chapter 5. For Dahlem's memoirs of the years before World War II in France, see Franz Dahlem, *Am Vorabend des Zweiten Weltkrieges, 1939 bis August 1939: Erinnerungen*, 2 vols. ([East] Berlin: Dietz Verlag, 1977); see also "Franz Dahlem," in Cerny, *Wer war Wer—DDR*, pp. 74–75. Other members of the Auslandssekretariat were Alexander Abusch, Anton Ackermann, Paul Bertz, and Lex Ende.

23. On German exiles in 1930s Paris, see Albrecht Betz, *Exil und Engagement: Deutsche Schriftsteller im Frankreich der Dreissiger Jahre* (Munich: edition text + kritik, 1986), p. 305.

24. Cited in Anton Ackermann, "Betrifft: Antisowjetischen Ausserungen Paul Merker" (August 29, 1950), SAPMO-BA, ZPA ZPKK IV/2/4/117, p. 3. In 1939 Ackermann wrote to KPD Central Committee officials in Moscow (Ulbricht and Pieck) and to Comintern officials (Dimitrov and Gulajew, the director of the cadre office of the Comintern) about Merker's alleged "anti-Soviet statements." In 1950, following the announcement of Merker's contact with the supposed "American agent" Noel Field, Ackermann repeated his denunciation in a memo to the SED's Central Party Control Commission. Hence, as early as 1939, Ulbricht, Pieck, Ackermann, and probably Hermann Matern, who arrived in Moscow in 1941 and was the future head of the Control Commission, had Ackermann's statement to use as evidence of Merker's apparent willingness to criticize Soviet policy. On the impact of the Hitler-Stalin pact on the Communist parties, see Wolfgang Leonhard, *Der Schock des Hitler-Stalin-Paktes in der kommunistischen Weltbewegung* (Freiburg im Breisgau: Herder, 1986).

25. For his comments to Kießling in interviews conducted between 1966 and 1969, see Wolfgang Kießling, *Partner im "Narrenparadies": Der Freundkreis um Noel Field und Paul Merker* (Berlin: Dietz Verlag, 1994), p. 58.

26. On Vernet, see Arthur Koestler, *The Scum of the Earth* (1941; rpt. London: Eland, 1991).

27. Merker, "Mein politischer Lebenslauf," pp. 12–30. On the German exiles in France and the Vichy internment camps in this period, see Hans-Albert Walter's valuable *Deutsche Exilliteratur, 1933–1950, Band 3, Internierung, Flucht und Lebensbedingungen im Zweiten Weltkrieg* (Stuttgart: Metzlersche Verlagsbuchhandlung, 1988). For a detailed account of Merker and German Communists in Vichy France, see Kießling, *Partner im "Narrenparadies,"* pp. 21–158.

28. Paul Merker, *Deutschland—Sein oder Nicht Sein?* vol. 2, *Das Dritte Reich und Sein Ende* (Frankfurt am Main: Materialismus Verlag, 1972), p. 36.

29. Ibid., pp. 36–37.

30. *Merker, "Stellungnahme zur Judenfrage,"* pp. 31–38. Most of this important statement is reprinted in the original German with other documents from the Merker case in Jeffrey Herf, "Dokument 3: An die Zentrale Kontrollkommission des ZK der SED," in "Dokumentation: Antisemitismus in der SED: Geheime Dokumente zum Fall Paul Merker aus SED- und MfS-Archiven," *Vierteljahrshefte für Zeitgeschichte* 42, no. 4 (October 1994), 635–667. See also Chapter 5.

31. Ibid., p. 33.

32. Ibid., p. 34.

33. Ibid.

34. Ibid., pp. 54–55.

35. Paul Merker, "Zweite Front-jetzt!" *Freies Deutschland* 1, no. 10 (August 1942), 6–7, and "Nach drei Jahren," *Freies Deutschland* 1, no. 11 (September 1942), 6–8. Merker's most important essays in *Freies Deutschland* include "Hitlers Antisemitismus und Wir," 1, no. 12 (October 1942), 9–11; "Die Verantwortung der Deutschen und die Nazigruel in der Sowjetunion," 2, no. 1 (November–December 1942), 8–9; "Nationalisierung der deutschen Grossindustrie und Wiedergutmachung," 2, no. 6 (May 1943), 6–8; "Die Aufloesung der Komintern," 2, no. 8 (July 1943), 10–13; "Um die Zukunft Deutschlands: Eine Antwort an Manfred George und Walter Lippmann," 2, no. 11 (October 1943), 6–7; "Brief an einen Freund: Die Bewegung Freies Deutschland und die Zukunft der Juden," 3, no. 5 (April 1944), 5–7; "Die Juden und das neue Deutschland," 4, no. 11 (October 1945), 7–8; "Roosevelts Forderung: "Wir muessen auf dem Wort 'respektabel' bestehen," 3, no. 3 (February 1944), 9–10; "Lord Vansittart, Friedrich Stampfer und die deutsche Untergrundbewegung," 3, no. 7 (June 1944), 7–9; "Deutsche Aussenpolitik in Vergangenheit und in Zukunft," 3, no. 11 (October 1944), 8–10; "Die kommende Frieden und die Freien Deutschen," 3, no. 12 (November 1944), 8–9; "Das Gericht Kommt," 4, no. 1 (December 1944), pp. 5–6; "Demokratische Kraefte in Deutschland? Die Kernfrage nach der militaerischen Niederlage Hitlers: An meinen Bruder in London," 4, no. 6 (May 1945), 6–8; "Die Grundlagen der neuen Demokratie," 4, no. 7 (June 1945), 5–7; "Die Potsdamer Beschluesse," 4, no. 10 (September 1945), 5–7; "Fortschritte und Widersprueche: Die Entwicklung in Deutschland under der Besetzung," 4, no. 12 (November–December 1945), 12–14.

On Merker's writings in Mexico City, see Lisolette Maas, "'Unerschüttert bleibt mein Vertrauen in den guten Kern unseres Volkes': Der Kommunist Paul Merker und die Exil-Diskussion um Deutschlands Schuld, Verantwortung, und Zukunft," in Thomas Koebner, Gert Sautermeister, and Sigrid Schneider-Grube, *Deutschland nach Hitler: Zukunftspläne im Exil und aus der Besatzungszeit, 1939–1949* (Opladen: Westdeutscher Verlag, 1987); Jeffrey Herf, "German Communism, the Discourse of Antifascist Resistance, and the Jewish Catastrophe," in John Boyer and Michael Geyer, eds., *Resistance against the Third Reich* (Chicago: University of Chicago Press, 1994), pp. 257–294; and Pohle, *Das Mexikanische Exil.*

36. Merker, "Die Verantwortung der Deutschen und die Nazigruel in der Sowjetunion," pp. 8–9; idem, "Hitler in der Defensive," *Freies Deutschland* 2, no. 2 (January 1943), 10–12.

37. Paul Merker, "Die Erklaerung von Teheran und die Freien Deutschen," *Freies Deutschland* 3, no. 2 (January 1944), 6–7.

38. Ibid., p. 31.

39. Exekutivkomitee des Lateinamerikanischen Komitees der Freien Deutschen, "Jalta und die Freien Deutschen," *Freies Deutschland* 4, no. 4 (March 1945), 5.

40. Paul Merker, *Deutschland—Sein oder Nicht Sein?* vol. 1, Von Weimar zu Hitler (1944; rpt. Frankfurt am Main: Materialismus Verlag, 1973).

41. Merker, "Hitlers Anti-Semitismus und Wir," pp. 9–11. *Freies Deutschland* had published two previous essays on anti-Semitism. See Leo Katz, "Antisemitismus als Barometer," and Ernst Abusch, "Der gelbe Stern und das deutsche Volk," *Freies Deutschland* 3, no. (January 1942), 13–14, 17–18.

42. Merker, "Hitlers Anti-Semitismus und Wir," p. 9. The German reads: "Wenn alle deutschen Fluesse Tinte und alle deutschen Waeldern Federstiele waeren, so wuerden sie nicht ausreichen, um die unzaehligen Verbrechen zu beschreiben, die der Hitlerfaschismus gegen die juedische Bevoelkerung begangen hat. Wo gibt es heute eine juedische Familie aus Deutschland, die nicht beraubt und nicht auf das tiefste gedemuetigt wurde, von der nicht Angehoerige in Konzentrationslaeger gesperrt, ermordet oder in den unfreiwilliegen Selbsmord getrieben wurden?"

43. Ibid., p. 9.

44. Ibid., p. 10.

45. Ibid.

46. Ibid.

47. Ibid.

48. Ibid.

49. Ibid.

50. Ibid., p. 11.

51. Paul Merker, "Das Echo: Diskussion ueber 'Hitlers Antisemitismus und Wir,'" *Freies Deutschland* 2, no. 4 (March 1943), 33.

52. Ibid. Merker placed the issue of restitution in the context of postwar nationalization of industry in Paul Merker, "Nationalisierung der deutschen Grossindustrie und Wiedergutmachung," *Freies Deutschland* 2, no. 6 (May 1943), 6–8.

53. Merker, "Das Echo," p. 33.

54. Paul Merker, "Um die Zukunft Deutschlands: Eine Antwort an Manfred George and Walter Lippman," *Freies Deutschland* 3, no. 11 (October 1943), 6–7.

55. Ibid., p. 7.

56. Merker, "Demokratische Kraefte in Deutschland?" pp. 6–8.

57. Wilhelm Koenen, "An meinen Bruder in Mexiko," *Freies Deutschland* 4, no. 10 (September 1945), 37–39.

58. Merker, "Demokratische Kraefte in Deutschland?" p. 7.

59. Ibid.

60. Merker, "Brief an einen Freund," and "Die Juden und das neue Deutschland."

61. Merker, "Brief an einen Freund," p. 5.

62. Ibid.

63. Ibid.

64. Ibid., p. 6.

65. Ibid.

66. Ibid.

67. Ibid., pp. 6–7.

68. Merker, "Die Juden und das neue Deutschland," p. 7.

69. Paul Merker, "Der kommende Frieden und die Freien Deutschen," *Freies Deutschland* 3, no. 12 (November 1944), 8.

70. Ibid., p. 9.

71. Vicente Lombardo Toledano, "Zweierlei Deutsche," *Freies Deutschland* 3, no. 4 (March 1944), 6–7. On Merker's contact with the Mexican Communists and the KPD Politburo in Moscow, see Pohle, *Das Mexikanische Exil,* pp. 203–216. Very little of Merker's correspondence with German Communist and leftist émigrés in the United States, Canada, Latin America, and England and the German Communists in Moscow has survived. See "Ubergabebescheinigung" (Berlin, June 13, 1956), BStU MfSZ-Archiv, Untersuchungsvorgang no. 294/52, Paul Merker, vol. 3, no. 192/56, pp. 153–154.

72. Toledano, "Zweierlei Deutsche," pp. 6–7. Merker received birthday wishes from, among others, the Mexican foreign minister Ezequiel Padilla; the Joint Antifascist Refugee Committee of New York and San Francisco; Max Bedacht, listed as "President of the International Workers' Order in USA," actually an official of the American Communist Party; as well as Heinrich Mann, Anna Seghers, Menorah, B'nai B'rith, and the Heinrich Heine Club. See "Ehrung fuer den antifaschistischen Kaempfer Paul Merker," *Freies Deutschland* 3, no. 4 (March 1944), 32–33.

73. Paul Merker, "Paul Merker Antwortrede," *Freies Deutschland* 3, no. 4 (March 1944), 34.

74. Ibid.

75. Merker, *Deutschland—Sein oder Nicht Sein?*

76. For Heinrich Mann's review, see "Paul Merker und sein Buch," *Freies Deutschland* 4, no. 11 (October 1945), 27–29. See also Ernst Bloch to Paul Merker, July 15, 1944, and Thomas Mann to Paul Merker, June 20, 1944, Paul Merker NL 102/31, SAPMO-BA, ZPA, pp. 33, 124. From July 6, 1942, several weeks after his arrival in Mexico, to April 24, 1946, shortly before his departure, Merker and Heinrich Mann exchange fifty-six letters. They are reprinted in Kießling, *Allemania Libre,* 2:353–452. Thomas Mann, in a letter of 1945 to Merker, "fully agreed" with his brother's praise. Thomas Mann's letter appears in Paul Merker to Wilhelm Pieck (November 23, 1945),

SAPMO-BA, ZPA Kaderfragen, IV 2/11/193, and is reprinted in Kießling, *Alemania Libre*, 2:337–338. He wrote: "I was engrossed in the work for days. It is a shattering document, the first deeply argued and historically exact representation of the most frightful and shameful episode in German history . . . I only hope that it reaches Germany soon and will teach the people there who've been hit on the head how it happened to them."

77. The first German reprint edition of the two volumes was published by Materialismus Verlag in Frankfurt am Main in 1972 and 1973. On the West German "fascism discussion" of the 1960s and 1970s, see Anson Rabinbach, "Toward a Marxist Theory of Fascism and National Socialism: A Report on Developments in West Germany," *New German Critique* 3 (Fall 1974), 127–153.

78. It invites comparison with another Marxist analysis of Nazism published by a German left-leaning émigré in 1944, Franz Neumann's *Behemoth*, though Merker devotes more attention to the autonomous dynamic of Nazi racial ideology and to the unfolding Jewish catastrophe. See Franz Neumann, *Behemoth: The Structure and Practice of National Socialism*, 2d ed. (New York: Oxford University Press, 1944).

79. For Merker's discussion of German anti-Semitism, see *Deutschland—Sein oder Nicht Sein?* 2:17–32. He devotes forty pages to the SS alone (pp. 58–96).

80. Merker, *Deutschland—Sein oder Nicht Sein?* 1:14.

81. Ibid., p. 342.

82. Merker, *Deutschland—Sein oder Nicht Sein?* 2:9.

83. Ibid., p. 47.

84. For Otto Katz's writings, see André Simone, "Joseph Stalin," *Freies Deutschland* 2, no. 1 (November–December 1942), 6–7; "Churchill u. Stafford Cripps," *Freies Deutschland* 1, no. 5 (March 1942), pp. 5–6; and "London-Moskau-Washington," *Freies Deutschland* 1, no. 9 (July 1942), pp. 7–8. On Otto Katz see Theodor Draper, "The Man Who Wanted to Hang." *Reporter,* January 6, 1953, pp. 26–30; and Stephen Koch, *Double Lives: Spies and Writers in the Secret Soviet War of Ideas against the West* (New York: Free Press, 1994).

85. On these writings and activities, see Pohle, *Das Mexikanische Exil*, pp. 311–338.

86. See Leo Katz, "Die Juden in der Sowjetunion," *Freies Deutschland* 2, no. 12 (November 1943), p. 18; and "Antisemitismus als Barometer," *Freies Deutschland* 1, no. 3 (January 1942), 13–14.

87. "Auskunftsbericht: Betr.: Dr. Leo Zuckermann" (July 23, 1951), "Personalbogen" (August 1, 1951), and "Dr. Leo Zuckermann, Lebenslauf" (February 13, 1950), BStU MfSZ-Archiv Nr. 147/51 Leo Zuckermann, pp. 6, 13–19.

88. Leo Zuckermann, "Der Rechtsanspruch der deutschen Juden auf Wiedergutmachung," *Freies Deutschland* 3, no. 10 (September 1944), 20–21.

89. Ibid., p. 21.

90. Ibid.

91. Leo Zuckermann, *Tribuna Israelita*, January 15, 1945, p. 7; cited by Pohle, *Das Mexikanische Exil*, pp. 333–334.

92. Alexander Abusch, "Vorwort," in Riedel, *Freies Deutschland: Mexico, 1941–1946*, pp. 5–21.

93. Alexander Abusch, *Der Irrweg einer Nation: Ein Beitrag zum Verständnis deutscher Geschichte* ([East] Berlin: Aufbau Verlag, 1946). It was first published in 1946. By 1951 it had appeared in seven editions and 130,000 copies. An eighth and expanded edition was published in 1960. On Abusch, see also David Pike, *The Politics of Culture in Soviet-Occupied Germany, 1945–1949* (Stanford: Stanford University Press, 1992), p. 161.

94. Alexander Abusch, *Der Irrweg einer Nation: Ein Beitrag zum Verständnis deutscher Geschichte*, 8th ed. ([East] Berlin: Aufbau Verlag, 1960), p. 195.

95. Alexander Abusch, "Hitler, Traum und Wirklichkeit der Bestialität," ibid., chap. 8, pp. 237–244.

96. Ibid., pp. 242–243.

97. Ibid., pp. 198–236.

98. Alexander Abusch, "Die Verantwortung der Deutschen," ibid., chap. 9, pp. 245–264.

99. Ibid., pp. 245–247.

100. Ibid., p. 256.

101. See Merker, "Stellungnahme zur Judenfrage," pp. 63–68.

102. Ibid., p. 67.

103. Ibid., p. 65. See Walter Janka,—*bis zur Verhaftungung: Erinnerungen eines deutschen Verlegers* (Berlin: Aufbau Verlag, 1993), and *Schwierigkeiten mit der Wahrheit* (Reinbek bei Hamburg: Rowohlt Verlag, 1990).

104. The investigations were conducted by the SED's Zentralparteikontrollkommission (Central Party Control Commission), or ZPKK. See Alexander Abusch, "An die ZPKK der SED, z.H. des Gen. Herman Matern" (October 10, 1950), SAPMO-BA, ZPA ZPKK 2/4/111, pp. 25–34; Alexander Abusch, "Erganzungen zu meinen mündlichen Aussagen vom 10.11.1950," SAPMO-BA, ZPA ZPKK IV/2/4/111, pp. 42–51; Leo Katz, "Bericht über Paul Merker und seine Tätigkeit in Mexico: Entstehung der deutschprachigen Gruppe in Mexico," SAPMO-BA, ZPA ZPKK IV/2/4/117, pp. 307–313; and "Dr. Rudolf Neumann and Hilde Neumann an die Z.P.K.K.: Betr. Emigration in Mexiko" (August 30, 1950), SAPMO-BA, ZPA ZPKK IV 2/4/112, pp. 5–6.

105. "James P. Baxter 3d to Colonel Wm. J. Donovan: Memorandum" (September 26, 1941), NA RG 226 OSS Box 06 E 146, Folder 1665.

106. For the Hoover to Donovan memoranda, see "Mexico: Subversive Activity," NA RG 226 OSS Box 326 NM 54, E 17. See, for example, "Nazi Sympathizers in the Mexican Government" (October 31, 1941); "Report on Espionage and Fifth Column

Activities in Mexico" (January 6, 1942); "Pro-Axis and Anti-Axis Forces in Mexico" (May 3, 1942).

107. J. Edgar Hoover to Colonel William J. Donovan (Washington, D.C., January 17, 1942), NA RG 226 OSS Box 42 E16, 9821. The Toledano memorandum listed twenty-two individuals, addresses, and some telephone numbers. It detailed chains of command, modes of operation, and party organization, and reported that "both the Gestapo and the spying apparatus [in Mexico] now act in conjunction with the Japanese diplomats and consuls" (p. 4). Eugene Dennis, the second-ranking figure of the American Communist Party, served as liaison to American intelligence. He may have been "the American Communist official" to whom Hoover referred. On the American Communist party and American intelligence during World War II, see Harvey Klehr and John Haynes, *The Secret World of American Communism* (New Haven: Yale University Press, 1995).

108. "J. Edgar Hoover to Colonel William Donovan: The Nazi Party in Mexico, Articles Published in *El Popular* and Edited by Lombardo Toledano" (February 23, 1942), NA RG 226 OSS E 14, Box 326, Mexico, Subversive Activity. Toledano also came to the attention of the U.S. naval attaché in Mexico City. See "Report of U.S. Naval Attaché, Mexico City, to Intelligence Division, Office of Chief of Naval Operations" (October 24, 1941), NA RG 226 OSS 7127, Microfilm M1499, Roll 22.

109. "Instructions from Moscow to Communist Organizations of Mexico" (July 30, 1941), NA RG 226 OSS Box 06 E146, Folder 1661.

110. Phillip Horton to Mr. Wiley, "German Political Refugees in Mexico" (November 4, 1942), NA OSS Foreign Nationalities Branch Files, 1942–1945, INT-13G-426. Leo Zuckermann also came to the attention of American intelligence. See "H. Gregory Thomas to Captain Henry De Vries: Memorandum" (December 28, 1942), NA RG 226 OSS Box 06, Entry 106, Folder 39, Mexico.

111. Ludwig Renn and André Simone (Otto Katz) wrote directly to George Messersmith, the American ambassador to Mexico, to express their "great pleasure to inform you that an anti-Nazi movement 'Free Germany' has been organized here with the aim to unite all anti-Nazi Germans in Mexico in order to render the greatest possible help to the Allies and to fight Hitler's Fifth Column in this country." Ludwig Renn and André Simone to George Messersmith (Mexico City, March 28, 1942), NA OSS Foreign Nationalities Branch Files, 1942–1945, INT-13G-426.

112. "H. Gregory Thomas to Allen W. Dulles: Office Memorandum" (July 15, 1942), NA RG 226 OSS Box 06, Entry 106, Folder 39. Thomas said that the arrival "was already known to us several weeks ago through Italian, Basque, and Spanish sources."

113. "Navy Department, Office of Naval Intelligence, Washington: Subject, MERKER, Paul" (December 24, 1942), NA RG 319, IRR Paul Merker, Box 151, X 859750.

114. Additional expressions of official American concern about Communist influence include "The German American Emergency Conference and the Freies Deutschland Movement" (February 2, 1943), NA OSS Foreign Nationalities Branch Files, 1942–1945, INT 33GE 7, p. 2; and "The Free Germans and the Allied Information Office" (February 7, 1944), NA OSS Foreign Nationalities Branch Files, INT 13G 984, p. 2.

115. See J. Edgar Hoover to Major General George V. Strong (Washington, D.C., July 3, 1943), NA RG 319 IRR Box 151, Paul Merker X859750.

116. "J. Edgar Hoover to Adolf A. Berle, Jr.: Paul Merker, alias Paul Merker Zeibig, Communist Activities in Mexico" (Washington, D.C., September 22, 1943), NA RG 319 IRR Box 151, Paul Merker X 859750.

117. "J. Edgar Hoover to Adolf A. Berle: Subject Paul Merker" (September 22, 1943), p. 3. On July 3, 1943, Hoover had sent a memo about Merker to Major General George V. Strong, assistant chief of staff at the War Department, which suggests that as late as summer 1943 the FBI had not been aware of Merker's previous presence in the United States. He wrote that the "Department of State as of May 19, 1943, had no record of Merker ever having been in the United States." The FBI did know that in May 1943 Communists in the United States were sending mail to Merker's address in Mexico. "This Bureau is checking to determine whether Merker has entered the United States illegally as a representative of the Communist International." J. Edgar Hoover to George V. Strong (July 3, 1943), NA RG 319 IRR Box 151, Paul Merker X 8590750.

118. Ibid., p. 8.

119. Ibid., p. 4.

120. Ibid., pp. 9–10. The report concludes with a detailed description of Merker's physical characteristics, and lists his religion as "Protestant."

121. "Intelligence Report, Marian E. Porter, Military Attaché, Mexico: Subject, Ludwig RENN" (January 9, 1946), NA RG 319 IRR Box 151, Paul Merker X859750.

122. On the contacts with officials of the World Jewish Congress, see WJC, Folder 232/3, Mexico-WJC Office, Paul Merker to Kate Knopfmacher (May 6, 1944); WJC, H229/13; Kate Knopfmacher to Dr. N [Nahum] Goldmann (February 18, 1943); WJC, Mexico Section, Box H231, Kate Knopfmacher correspondence 1943, American Jewish Archives, Hebrew Union College, Cincinnati.

123. Gerhard Jacoby, "Bericht ueber den ersten Landeskongress der Bewegung 'Freies Deutschland' in Mexiko" (November 4, 1943), WJC, Folder H230/Mexico—Jewish Situation Reports, 1943–1950, American Jewish Archives, Hebrew Union College, Cincinnati.

124. Dr. Kubowitzki to Members of the Executive Committee of the WJC (November 26, 1943), WJC, Folder H230/Mexico—Jewish Situation Reports, 1943–1950, American Jewish Archives, Hebrew Union College, Cincinnati.

## 4. Struggles for Recognition in East Berlin

1. Leo Zuckermann, for example, learned that over twenty-two relatives, including his mother and father, had been murdered in the Holocaust. See "Auskunftsbericht: Betr.: Dr. Leo Zuckermann" (July 23, 1951), "Personalbogen" (August 1, 1951), and "Dr. Leo Zuckermann, Lebenslauf" (February 13, 1950), BStU MfSZ Archiv Einzelvorgang no. 147/51 Leo Zuckermann, pp. 6, 13–19.

2. Gerhard Weinberg, *A World at Arms: A Global History of World War II* (New York: Cambridge University Press, 1994), p. 894.

3. In all of Germany in 1945, not including those in displaced persons camps waiting to go to Israel or other countries, only 21,454 remained of the prewar (1933) population of 600,000 German Jews. See Erica Burgauer, *Zwischen Erinnerung und Verdrängung—Juden in Deutschland nach 1945* (Hamburg: Rowohlt Taschenbuch Verlag, 1993), pp. 356–359.

4. See, for example, "Hitlers 'Hygiene-Institut': Fette, Seifen und Leder aus menschlichen Leichen," *Deutsche Volkszeitung,* July 13, 1945, p. 1; "Die Mitschuld des deutschen Volkes," *Deutsche Volkszeitung,* July 10, 1945, p. 2; "Beschleunigtes Verfahren gegen die Kriegsverbrecher," *Deutsche Volkszeitung,* July 14, 1945, p. 1; "Moloch IG-Farben-Konzern," *Deutsche Volkszeitung,* August 2, 1945, p. 1; "Der Massenmörder von Auschwitz bestätigt Beteiligung an einer Million Morde," *Deutsche Volkszeitung,* August 15, 1945, p. 1; and "Pflicht zur Wiedergutmachung," *Deutsch Volkszeitung,* August 17, 1945, p. 1.

5. "Erste offizielle Tagung des Alliierten Tribunals gegen die Hauptkriegsverbrecher: Anklageschrift veröffentlicht, Die Welt klagt Göring, Krupp, Keitel und Konsorten an," *Deutsche Volkszeitung,* October 19, 1945, pp. 1–2.

6. On Holocaust denial in the United States, see Deborah Lipstadt, *Denying the Holocaust: The Growing Assault on Truth and Memory* (New York: Free Press, 1993); and Pierre Vidal-Naquet, *Assassins of Memory: Essays on the Denial of the Holocaust,* trans. and with a foreword by Jeffrey Mehlman (Minneapolis: University of Minnesota Press, 1992).

7. See especially the opening and closing statements of Robert Jackson, Hartley Shawcross, and Telford Taylor in *The Trial of the Major War Criminals before the International Military Tribunal* (Nuremberg: International Military Tribunal, 1947–1948); Office of United States Counsel for Prosecution of Axis Criminality, *Nazi Conspiracy and Aggression: Opinion and Judgment* (Washington, D.C.: U.S. Government Printing Office, 1947); and Telford Taylor, *The Anatomy of the Nuremberg Trials* (New York: Alfred A. Knopf, 1992).

8. See under "Jews, persecution of," in *The Trial of the Major War Criminals before the International Military Tribunal,* vol. 23, Chronological Index, Subject Index (Nuremberg: International Military Tribunal, 1949), pp. 386–402; and Judith N.

Shklar, *Legalism: Law, Morals, and Political Trials* (Cambridge, Mass.: Harvard University Press, 1964).

9. "Heute vor vier Jahren: Der schwärzeste Tag deutscher Geschichte," *Deutsche Volkszeitung*, June 22, 1945, p. 2. In the week of September 19–25, the paper devoted five articles to Nazi "crimes in the Soviet Union." See "Verbrechen an der Sowjetunion," *Deutsche Volkszeitung*, September 19–25, 1945.

10. "6 Million Juden ermordet: Alle Angeklagten für die bestialischen Pogrome verantwortlich," *Deutsche Volkszeitung*, December 15, 1945, p. 2.

11. Helga A. Welsh, " 'Antifaschistische-demokratische Umwälzung' und politische Säuberung in der sowjetischen Besatzungszone Deutschlands," in Klaus-Dietmar Henke and Hans Woller, eds., *Politische Säuberung in Europa: Die Abrechnung mit Faschismus und Kollaboration nach dem Zweiten Weltkrieg* (Munich: Deutscher Taschenbuch Verlag, 1991), pp. 91–92. On the SMAD and Soviet administration, see Norman M. Naimark, *The Russians in Germany: A History of the Soviet Occupation* (Cambridge, Mass.: Harvard University Press, 1995).

12. Welsh, "Antifaschistische-demokratische Umwälzung," p. 93; see also Karl Wilhelm Fricke, *Politik und Justiz in der DDR: Zur Geschichte der politische Verfolgung, 1945–1968, Bericht und Dokumentation* (Cologne: Verlag Wissenschaft und Politik, 1979).

13. See Norman M. Naimark, "The Camps and Their Victims," in *The Russians in Germany*, pp. 376–378.

14. Welsh, "Antifaschistische-demokratische Umwälzung," pp. 95–96; see also "Denkschrift des Innenministeriums der UdSSR," *Deutschland-Archiv* 23 (1990), 1804.

15. On the Waldheim trials, see Michael Klonovsky and Jan von Flocken, *Stalins Lager in Deutschland: Dokumentation, Zeugenberichte, 1945–1950* (Munich: Deutscher Taschenbuch Verlag, 1993), pp. 205–218. On postwar Soviet justice, see "Strafverfolgung durch deutsche Justizbehörden in der sowjetischen Besatzungszone und dem Sowjetsektor von Berlin," in Deutscher Bundestag, *Zur Verjährung nationalsozialistischer Verbrechen: Dokumentation der parlamentarischen Bewältigung des Problems, 1960–1979, Teil 1* (Bonn: Deutscher Bundestag, Presse- und Informationszentrum, 1980), pp. 103–106; *Die Haltung der beiden deutschen Staaten zu den Nazi-und Kriegsverbrechen* ([East] Berlin: Staatsverlag der Deutschen Demokratischen Republik, 1964) see also *Die Bestrafung des Nazi- und Kriegsverbrecher—Gebot der Menschlichkeit und der Sicherung des Friedens* ([East] Berlin: Kanzlei des Staatrates der Deutschen Demokratischen Republik, 1964).

16. On the Waldheim trials, see "Der Waldheimer Kriegsverbrecherprozesse" and Thomas Mann's critical letter to Ulbricht, "Der Brief Thomas Manns an Walter Ulbricht" (July 1950), in Klonovsky and von Flocken, *Stalins Lager in Deutschland*, pp. 205–218, 219–222.

17. See W. Schubbarth, W. Pschierer, and R. Schmmidt, "Verordneter Antifaschismus und die Folgen: Das Dilemma antifaschistischer Erziehung am Ende der DDR," *Aus Politik und Zeitgeschichte* B9/91, February 22, 1991, p. 4.

18. Welsh, "Antifaschistische-demokratische Umwalzung," pp. 99–100.

19. Franz Dahlem, "Einige Probleme unserer künftigen Arbeit in Deutschland: Rede vor ehemaligen Häftlingen des KZ Mauthausen," in *Ausgewählte Reden und Aufsätze, 1919–1979: Zur Geschichte der Arbeiterbewegung* ([East] Berlin: Dietz Verlag, 1980), pp. 251–269; reprinted from Franz Dahlem, *Weg und Ziel des antifaschistischen Kampfes: Ausgewählte Reden und Aufsätze* ([East] Berlin: VVN Verlag, 1952), pp. 86–105. On Mauthausen, see Gordon J. Horwitz, *In the Shadow of Death: Living outside the Gates of Mauthausen* (New York: Free Press, 1990).

20. Dahlem, "Einige Probleme," pp. 254–255.

21. Ibid., p. 255.

22. Ibid., p. 256.

23. Ibid.

24. Ibid., p. 257.

25. Ibid., p. 258.

26. Ibid.

27. Ibid., pp. 258–259.

28. Franz Dahlem, "Gelöbnis zur Gedächtniskundgebung für die Opfer des Faschismus," *Deutsche Volkszeitung*, September 9, 1945, p. 1. See also "Gedenktag für die Opfer des Faschismus," *Deutsche Volkszeitung*, August 29, 1945, p. 1; and "Heute marschiert Berlin für den Sieg der Menschlichkeit über die nazistische Barbarei," *Deutsche Volkszeitung*, September 9, 1945, p. 1.

29. Dahlem, "Gelöbnis zur Gedächtniskundgebung für die Opfer des Faschismus," p. 1.

30. "Juden sind auch Opfer des Faschismus: Arbeitsprogramm der antifaschistischen Kämpfer," *Deutsche Volkszeitung*, September 26, 1945, p. 1.

31. Ibid. See "Ottomar Geschke," in Jochen Cerny, ed. *Wer war Wer—DDR* (Berlin: Ch. Links Verlag, 1992), pp. 134–135.

32. Johannes R. Becher, "Deutschland Klagt An!" *Aufbau* 1, no. 1 (January 1946), 9–18.

33. Ibid., p. 12.

34. Ibid., p. 17.

35. Walter Ulbricht, "9. November 1918 in Deutschland: Die Große Lehre," *Deutsche Volkszeitung*, November 9, 1945, p. 45; reprinted in Walter Ulbricht, *Die Entwicklung des deutschen volks-demokratischen Staates, 1945–1949* ([East] Berlin: Dietz Verlag, 1959), pp. 44–49. Wilhelm Pieck, "Wortlaut der Rede des Genossen Wilhelm Pieck," *Deutsche Volkszeitung*, November 10, 1945, p. 1.

36. Ulbricht, "9 November 1918 in Deutschland," p. 47.

37. On the political uses of antifascism in the early postwar era and in East Germany, see Sigrid Meuschel, *Legitimation und Parteiherrschaft in der DDR* (Frankfurt am Main: Suhrkamp, 1992); and François Furet, *Le passé d'une illusion: essaie sur l'idée communiste au XXe siècle* (Paris: Éditions Robert Laffont, 1995).

38. See Furet, *Le passé d'une illusion.*

39. Angelika Timm, "Der Streit um Restitution und Wiedergutmachung in der Sowjetischen Besatzungszone Deutschlands," *Babylon: Beiträge zur jüdischen Gegenwart,* nos. 10–11 (1992), 125–138.

40. See Burgauer, *Zwischen Erinnerung und Verdrängung,* pp. 139–143; Robin Ostow, *Judisches Leben in der DDR* (Frankfurt am Main: Jüdischer Athenaum Verlag, 1988); Siegfried Arndt et al., *Juden in der DDR: Geschichte—Probleme—Perspektiven* (Sachsenheim: Burg Verlag, 1988); Angelika Timm, *Has Antisemitism Continued in East Germany after World War II?* (Washington D.C.: AICGS/GHI 1995); and Jerry E. Thompson, "Jews, Zionism and Israel: The Story of the Jews in the German Democratic Republic since 1945 (Ph.D. diss., Washington State University, 1978).

41. On this issue, see Olaf Groehler, "Integration und Ausgrenzung von NS-Opfern: Zur Anerkennungs- und Entschädigungsdebatte in der Sowjetischen Besatzungszone Deutschlands 1945 bis 1949," in Jürgen Kocka, ed., *Historische DDR-Forschung: Aufsätze und Studien* (Berlin: Akademie Verlag, 1993), pp. 105–127. See also Peter Dittmar, "DDR und Israel: Ambivalenz einer nicht Beziehung," *Deutschland Archiv* 10 (July 1977), 736–754; and (August 1977), 848–861.

42. Groehler, "Integration und Ausgrenzung," p. 107–109. The numbers, however, steadily declined. See Burgauer, *Zwischen Erinnerung und Verdrängung.*

43. Alfred Kantorowicz, "Opfer des Faschismus," *Die Weltbühne,* September 1, 1947, pp. 733–735.

44. Ibid., p. 733.

45. Ibid.

46. "Juden sind auch Opfer des Faschismus," *Deutsche Volkszeitung,* September 25, 1945, cited by Groehler, "Integration und Ausgrenzung," p. 109. See Heinrich Grüber, *Erinnerungen aus sieben Jahrzehnten* (Cologne: Kiepenhauer an Witsch, 1968).

47. Groehler, "Integration und Ausgrenzung," p. 109.

48. "Juden sind auch Opfer des Faschismus," p. 1.

49. Ibid.

50. Groehler, "Integration und Ausgrenzung"; see also Constantin Goschler, "Paternalismus und Verweigerung: Die DDR und die Wiedergutmachung für jüdisch Verfolgte des Nationalsozialismus," *Jahrbuch für Antisemitismusforschung* 2 (1993). Raddatz led the VVN (Association of Those Persecuted by the Nazi Regime) until it was dissolved in 1953. He worked in the Committee for German Unity from 1953 to 1960. In 1960 he was arrested and expelled from the SED. In 1962 the East German Supreme Court sentenced him, Heinz Brandt, and Wilhelm Fickenscher to seven and a half

years in prison. He was amnestied in 1964 and worked as a librarian afterwards in Berlin. For his early statement of who was and was not a "victim of fascism," see Carl Raddatz, *Wer ist Opfer des Faschismus?* and Stefan Heymann, *Die politischen Aufgaben der Opfer des Faschismus* (Weimar: Thüringer Volksverlag, 1946).

51. He repeated these arguments in a speech to a meeting of the OdF on February 9–10, 1946, in Berlin. See Carl Raddatz, "Wer ist Opfer des Faschismus."

52. Raddatz, *Wer ist Opfer des Faschismus?* pp. 6–7.

53. Ibid., p. 7. The inclusiveness of this list is evident from the inclusion of participants in the attempted coup of July 20, 1944. As the Cold War crystallized, they fell out of the Communist pantheon while finding an enduring place in the West German canon of memory. See Chapters 7 and 8.

54. Ibid., pp. 10–11.

55. Ibid., p. 14.

56. Heinz Brandt, "Unsere Stellung zu den Opfern der Nürnberger Gesetzgebung," Archiv des IVVdN Akte 27 (October 1945, Leipzig), p. 88; cited by Groehler, "Integration und Ausgrenzung," p. 110. He was also Secretary for Agitation in the Berlin district of the SED from 1945 to 1953. In 1953–54 he lost his position. In 1958 he fled to West Germany, where he worked as an editor with the IG Metall union. He was kidnapped by Stasi agents in 1961 and held in prison until 1964, when he was released. He died on January 11, 1986. See Heinz Brandt, *Ein Traum, der nicht entfuhrbar ist* (Munich: List, 1967).

57. Leo Löwenkopf, Archiv des IVVdN, Akte 27 (October 1945, Leipzig), p. 180; cited by Groehler, "Integration und Ausgrenzung," p. 111. Löwenkopf lived in Dresden from August 1945. He had been a member of the SPD since 1908, and joined the KPD in 1945. In the aftermath of the Noel Field affair, he was arrested in August 1950 and held in prison for three months. He fled to West Germany in January 1953. See Chapter 5.

58. Jenny Matern, Archiv des IVVdN, Akte 27 (October 1945, Leipzig), p. 180; cited by Groehler, "Integration und Ausgrenzung," p. 111.

59. Groehler, "Integration und Ausgrenzung," p. 111.

60. Ibid., p. 112.

61. "Deutsche Zentralverwaltung für Arbeit und Sozialfürsorge in der Sowjetischen Besatzungszone Deutschlands: 18.6.1946," SAPMO-BA, ZPA Sekretariat Lehmann IV 2/2027/29; see also Timm, "Der Streit um Restitution und Wiedergutmachung," p. 127.

62. On restitution in the Western zones, see Constantin Goschler, *Wiedergutmachung: Westdeutschland und die Verfolgten des Nationalsozialismus (1945–1954)* (Munich: R. Oldenbourg Verlag, 1992), pp. 91–148.

63. See Franz Dahlem and Karl R. Raddatz, *Die Aufgaben der VVN: 2 Referate, gehalten auf der Zonendelegiertenkonferenz am 22/23: February 1947 in Berlin* (Berlin: Neues Deutschland Druckerei, 1947), p. 8.

64. Ibid., pp. 25–26.

65. Ibid., pp. 9–10.

66. Ibid., p. 11.

67. Ibid., p. 13.

68. Ibid., p. 16.

69. Helmut Eschwege to Paul Merker (February 2, 1946), SAPMO-BA, ZPA IV 2/2027/29, pp. 3–4. See also Eschwege's memoirs, *Fremd unter Meinesgleichen: Erinnerungungen eines Dresdner Juden* (Berlin: C. H. Links Verlag, 1991).

70. Eschwwege to Merker (February 2, 1946), pp. 3–4.

71. Ibid.

72. "Protokoll 55, Sitzung des Zentralsekretariat, 19.11.1946, Gen. Lehman/Gen. Merker," SAPMO-BA, ZPA Sekretariat Lehmann IV 2/2027/29; and Paul Merker to Kurt Nettball, "Gen. Nettball, Betr.: Bericht über die Lage der jüdischen Bevölkerung" (January 25, 1947), SAPMO-BA, ZPA Sekretariat Lehmann IV 2/2027/30.

73. On Merker's efforts in the Central Secretariat of the SED, see Groehler, "Integration und Ausgrenzung," p. 115.

74. See "Wiedergutmachung gegenüber den Verfolgten des Naziregimes, 1945–1950, "SAPMO-BA, ZPA Sekretariat Lehmann IV/2027/29–33. In February 1947 Merker's aide Kurt Nettball informed him that officials in the Soviet zone had done little to fight anti-Semitism and that the demands of the Jewish survivors for return of their stolen property remained "far from practical realization." See Nettball, "Bericht über die Lage der jüdischen Bevölkerung."

75. Jenny Matern, Deutsche Verwaltung für Arbeit und Sozialfürsorge, "Richtlinien für die Anerkennung und Ausgabe der Ausweise an 'Kämpfer gegen den Faschismus' und an 'Opfer des Faschismus' in der sowjetischen Bestazungzone Deutschlands" (January 14, 1947), SAPMO-BA, ZPA Sekretariat Lehmann IV 2/2027/30. On "fighters" and "victims," see Olaf Gröhler "Aber sie haben nicht gekämpft," *Konkret*, no. 5 (1992), 38–44.

76. Matern, "Richtlinien," pp. 1–3. "Fighters against fascism" were those who had actively fought against the Nazi regime, including those imprisoned, those who escaped arrest, and those who emigrated. The guidelines also included those who had opposed Nazism on religious grounds; members of the revolt of July 20, 1944; veterans of the International Brigades in Spain or other European resistance movements; German soldiers who went over to the Allied forces and whose relatives were murdered as a result; and German citizens imprisoned for more than half a year because of organized activity based on political beliefs or who broke laws regarding listening to Allied radio, hiding persons or things, and destroying weapons. "Victims of fascism" included surviving relatives of those who had been murdered or who had died in concentration camps; Jews; "half-Jews"; Gypsies kept in concentration camps; anyone who "wore the Yellow Star"; Jews who, in order to avoid deportation, had lived illegally, unless they lived in "privileged marriages" and thus were not compelled to live in illegality.

77. Ibid., pp. 3–4.

78. The term "racially persecuted" ("rassische Verfolgte") was often used in documents of the time in place of "Jews" or "Jewish." Even a record of participants in a February 2, 1947, meeting of the Executive Committee of the VVN at the Zentralsekretariat für Arbeit und Sozialfürsorge identifies the two Jewish delegates, Julius Meyer and Leo Löwenkopf, as "rass." (i.e., *rassisch* "racial"). See "Verlage an das Zentralsekretariat: Betr: Enger und erweiterter Vorstand der Vereinigung der Verfolgten des Naziregimes für die sowjetische Besatzungzone," SAPMO-BA, ZPA Sekretariat Lehmann IV 2/2027/30.

79. "Telegram des Genossen Loewenkopf aus Dresden vom 30. Mai 1947," SAPMO-BA, ZPA IV 2/2027/30, p. 87.

80. [Paul] Merker to [Walter] Ulbricht and [Max] Fechner (June 4, 1947), SAPMO-BA, ZPA IV 2/2027/30, p. 88. Fechner (1892–1973) was a member of the SED Central Committee from 1946 to 1953 and minister of justice in the DDR from 1949 to 1953. Following the revolt of June 17, 1953, and his support for reform, he was expelled from the party, fired, arrested, and convicted of "activity hostile to the state." He was released from prison in 1956 and reinstated in the party in 1958. See Cerny, *Wer war Wer-DDR,* p. 108; see also Rudi Beckert and Karl Wilhelm Fricke, *Zur Diskussion/Geschichte aktuell "Auf Weisung des Politburos, Teil II: Der Fall Max Fechner" (Hamburg: Deutschlandfunk, Abteilung/Dokumentation/Ost-West, January 9, 1992).*

81. "Probleme und Grundsätze für die Wiedergutmachung gegenüber Opfern des Faschismus" (August 8, 1947), SAPMO-BA, ZPA Sekretariat Lehmann IV 2/2027/30.

82. Paul Merker and Helmut Lehmann, January 19, 1948, "Vorlage an die Mitglieder des Zentralsekretariats, Betr.: Gesetz über die Betreuung der Verfolgten des Naziregimes und die Vorbereitung für Wiedergutmachung," SAPMO-BA, ZPA Sekretariat Lehmann IV 2/2027/31.

83. Ibid, p. 2.

84. Ibid., p. 3. Advantages extended to employment opportunities, education, housing, clothing, tax reductions, vacations, free health care, and pensions for widows and children of persons murdered or executed for political, racial, or religious reasons.

85. Ibid., p. 5.

86. Ibid., pp. 6–7.

87. Clause 32, ibid., p. 7.

88. Merker's contacts with the leadership of the East German Jewish communities continued. On March 15, 1948, along with Leo Zuckermann and Kurt Nettball, he attended a meeting of representatives of the Jewish communities in the Soviet zone to discuss restitution. See "Betr.: Julius Meyer" (January 16, 1953), and "Sitzung des Landesverbandes der Jüdischen Gemeinden in der Deutschen Demokratischen Republik vom 15.3.1948," SAPMO-BA, ZPA IV 2/4/404 ZPKK, pp. 27, and pp. 46–47.

89. Leo Zuckermann, "Restitution und Wiedergutmachung," *Die Weltbühne* 3 (April 1948), 430–432.

90. Ibid., p. 430.

91. Ibid., p. 431.

92. Ibid., p. 432.

93. Ibid.

94. "Leo Zuckermann to Paul Merker, Berlin, April 30, 1948," SAPMO-BA, ZPA Sekretariat Lehmann IV 2/2027/31.

95. "Paul Merker to Wilhelm Pieck, May 4, 1948," SAPMO-BA, ZPA Sekretariat Lehmann IV2/2027/31.

96. "Abschrift He. 16.6.48, Berger to Gen. Fechner/Ulbricht, May 14, 1948," SAPMO-BA, ZPA Sekretariat Lehmann IV 2/2027/31. Berger was also Jewish and a veteran of the Spanish civil war. Ironically, in the 1950s he served as the defense lawyer for the East German dissident Robert Havemann.

97. Ibid., p. 2. See also "Schäfermayer to Fechner and Ulbricht: Betr.: Wiedergut-machungsgesetz, May 25, 1948," SAPMO-BA, ZPA Sekretariat Lehmann IV 2/2027/31. On a June 4, 1948, meeting in Merker's office about the "party's position on the Jewish question," see "Paul Merker, Betr.: Stellungnahme der Partei zur jüdischen Frage, June 4, 1948," SAPMO-BA, ZPA Sekretariat Lehmann IV 2/2027/31.

98. Leo Zuckermann to Walter Ulbricht, June 16, 1948, "Betrifft: Schreiben der Abt. Justiz von 14.5. und 25.5.48 bezugl. Widergutmachungsgesetz," SAPMO-BA, ZPA Sekretariat Lehmann IV 2/2027/31.

99. Ibid.

100. Ottomar Geschke to Paul Merker, February 18, 1949, SAPMO-BA, ZPA Sekretariat Lehmann IV 2/2027/32.

101. Ibid.

102. On Merker's efforts concerning the restitution law, anti-Semitism in the Soviet zone, and commemoration of the tenth anniversary of "Kristallnacht," see SAPMO-BA, ZPA Sekretariat Lehmann IV 2/2027/31 and IV 2/2027/32.

103. For a report by the SED's Central Party Control Commission regarding a February 1949 meeting between Dr. Karl Linweh, the Israeli consul in Munich, with Walter Bartel, and his invitation to Julius Meyer, Heinz Galinski, and Rabbi Steffan Schwarzchild of Berlin to visit Israel, see "Betr.: Julius Meyer," SAPMO-BA, ZPA ZPKK IV 2/4/404, pp. 26–27; and "Aussprache mit dem Genossen Julius Meier, Präsident der jüdischen Gemeinde am 6.1.53" (January 8, 1953), SAPMO-BA, ZPA ZPKK 2/4/404, pp. 34–35.

104. "Anordnung zur Sicherung der rechtlichen Stellung der anerkannten Verfol-gten des Naziregimes" (October 5, 1949), in *Zentralverwaltung sowie der Deutschen Verwaltungen für Inneres, Justiz und Volksbildung* (Berlin, 1949), p. 765.

105. The East German government made good on threats to withdraw benefits to those who deviated politically. In East Berlin alone, from 1949 to 1953, more than 4,000 of the 15,063 members of the VVN lost their status as victims of fascism as a result of political considerations. See Groehler, "Integration und Ausgrenzung," p. 127.

106. Timm, "Der Streit um Restitution und Wiedergutmachung," p. 137; and "Durchführungsbestimmungen zu der Anordnung zur Sicherung der rechtlichen Stellung der anerkannten Verfolgten des Naziregimes" (February 10, 1950), *Gesetzblatt der Deutschen Demokratischen Republik,* February 18, 1950, p. 77.

107. *Befreiungstag Buchenwald: 9. bis 11. April 1948* (Berlin-Potsdam: VVN Verlag, 1948).

108. Stefan Heymann, "Begrüßungsfeier in der Weimarhalle," in *Befreiungstag Buchenwald,* p. 4. Heymann, a KPD member since 1918–19, had been an inmate in Dachau, Buchenwald, and Auschwitz. From 1945 to 1950 he was director of the Office of Culture and Education in the SED Central Committee, and thereafter held diplomatic and scholarly positions. See "Stefan Heymann," in Untersuchungsausschuß Freiheitlicher Juristen, *SBZ-Biographie,* 3d ed. (Bonn: Bundesministerium für Gesamtdeutsche Fragen, 1964), p. 149.

109. Recent scholarship indicates that about 1.1 million Jews were murdered in Auschwitz, constituting about 90 percent of all those who died there. See Franciszek Piper, "The Number of Victims," and Raul Hilberg, "Auschwitz and the 'Final Solution,'" in Yisrael Gutman and Michael Berenbaum, eds., *Anatomy of the Auschwitz Death Camp* (Washington, D.C., and Bloomington: U.S. Holocaust Memorial Museum and Indiana University Press, 1994), pp. 61–92.

110. Heymann, "Begrüßungsfeier in der Weimarhalle," p. 5.

111. Stefan Heymann, "Entschließung," in *Befreiungstag Buchenwald,* pp. 57–59.

112. "Heinz Galinski, Berlin," in *Befreiungstag Buchenwald,* pp. 39–40. See also Heinz Galinski, "Bedeutung des 12. September für die rassisch Verfolgten," *Berliner VVN Mitteilungen* (Berlin), August 1, 1948, p. 3.

113. "Julius Meyer, Berlin," in *Befreiungstag Buchenwald,* pp. 42–43.

114. "Walter Bartel, Berlin," in *Befreiungstag Buchenwald,* pp. 19–35. See "Walter Bartel," in Cerny, *Wer war Wer—DDR,* p. 24.

115. "Walter Bartel, Berlin," pp. 59–60.

116. "Aussprache mit dem Genossen Julius Meier, Präsident der jüdischen Gemeinde am 6.1.53," p. 34; "Sitzung des Landesverbandes der Jüdischen Gemeinden in der Deutschen Demokratischen Republik vom 15.3.1948" (January 8, 1953), SAPMO-BA, ZPA ZPKK IV 2/4/404, p. 46; and "Betr.: Julius Meyer" (January 16, 1953), pp. 27–28.

117. Paul Merker, "VVN, Liebe Freunde und Kameraden" (n.d.), Paul Merker NL 102/45, SAPMO-BA, ZPA, pp. 6–7.

118. Paul Merker, "Der Krieg in Palästina," Paul Merker NL 102/45, SAPMO-BA, ZPA; see also Paul Merker, "Der neue Staat des jüdischen Volkes entsteht," *Die*

*Weltbühne*, no. 5/6 (1948), 110–116; and Paul Merker, "Der neue Staat des jüdischen Volkes," *Neues Deutschland*, February 24, 1948, p. 2.

119. Merker, "Der Krieg in Palästina," pp. 7–8.

120. Ibid., p. 10.

121. Ibid., p. 12.

122. Ibid., p. 31.

123. Although discussion of the scholarly analysis of anti-Semitism in East Germany is beyond the scope of this study, in this period some works in the Marxist tradition did pay particular attention to anti-Semitism. See Siegbert Kahn, *Antisemitismus und Rassenhetze: Eine Übersicht über Ihre Entwicklung in Deutschland* (Berlin: Dietz Verlag, 1948).

124. Cited in Eschwege, *Fremd unter Meinesgleichen*, p. 63.

125. Eugen Kogon, *The Theory and Practice of Hell*, trans. Heinz Norden (New York: Farrar, Straus and Cudahy, 1950).

126. Ibid., p. 7.

127. Ibid., pp. 319–328.

128. Ibid., p. 319.

129. Ibid., p. 326.

130. Ibid.

131. Eugen Kogon, "Der Politische Untergang des Europäischen Widerstands," *Frankfurter Hefte* 4, no. 5 (May 1949), 405–413.

132. Ibid., p. 408.

133. Ibid., p. 409.

134. See Eugen Kogon, "Politik der Versöhnung," *Frankfurter Hefte* 3, no. 4 (April 1948), 321–322.

135. Stefan Heymann, "Gibt es eine Krise des antifaschistischen Widerstandes?: Eine Antwort an Dr. Kogon," *Die Tat* (Berlin), July 9, 1949, p. 1.

136. Ibid.

137. Leo Zuckermann, "Eine Antwort an die 'Neue Zeitung': Wir werden niemals gegen die Befreier von Maidanek und Auschwitz kämpfen," *Die Tat* (Berlin), June 13, 1949, p. 3. On the Red Army and the camps, see the classic account in Vasily Grossman, *With the Red Army in Poland and Byelorussia*, trans. Helen Altschuler (London: Hutchinson, 1945), and *The Years of War (1941–1945)*, trans. Elizabeth Donnelly and Rose Prokofiev (Moscow: Foreign Languages Publishing House, 1946). See also Vasily Grossman and Ilya Ehrenburg, eds., *The Black Book: The Ruthless Murder of Jews by German-Fascist Invaders throughout the Temporarily Occupied Regions of the Soviet Union and in the Death Camps of Poland during the War of 1941–1945*, trans. John Glad and James S. Levine (New York: Holocaust Publications [distributed by Schocken Books], 1981).

138. Zuckerman, "Eine Antwort an die 'Neue Zeitung,'" p. 3.

139. Ibid.

140. See Arkady Vaksberg, *Stalin against the Jews*, trans. Antonia W. Bouis (New York: Knopf, 1994), pp. 141–182; Lionel Kochan, ed., *The Jews in Soviet Russia since 1917*, 3rd ed. (Oxford: Oxford University Press, 1978); and Shimon Redlich, *Propaganda and Nationlism in Wartime Russia* (Boulder, Colo.: East European Quarterly, 1982), chap. 7, "Postwar Years," pp. 149–170.

141. Paul Merker, "Stalin, der Schmied des Bündnisses zwischen Arbeiterklasse und werktätiger Bauernschaft," Paul Merker NL 102/43, SAPMO-BA, ZPA, p. 256.

142. Paul Merker *Sozialdemokratismus: Stampfer, Schumacher und Andere Gestrige* ([East] Berlin: Dietz Verlag, 1949).

143. Paul Merker, "Was geht im Westen vor?" (February 3, 1950), SAPMO-BA ZPA IV 2/4/117 ZPKK, pp. 232–251.

144. Ibid., p. 236.

145. Ibid., p. 237.

146. Ibid., p. 250.

## 5. Purging "Cosmopolitanism"

1. See Sigrid Meuschel, "Die nationale Frage zwischen Antifaschismus, Sozialismus und Antizionismus," in *Legitimation und Parteiherrschaft in der DDR* (Frankfurt am Main: Suhrkamp, 1992), pp. 101–116. On the Weimar right and the West, see, among much else, Jeffrey Herf, *Reactionary Modernism: Technology, Culture, and Politics in Weimar and the Third Reich* (New York: Cambridge University Press, 1984). On Marxism and anti-Western sentiments in Russia and Germany, see Liah Greenfeld, *Nationalism: Five Paths to Modernity* (Cambridge, Mass.: Harvard University Press, 1992).

2. An early but still valuable work on the Jews, communism, and anti-Semitism after 1945 in Eastern Europe is François Fejto, *Les Juifs et l'antisemitisme dans les pays communistes* (Paris: Librairie Plon, 1960); published in German as *Judentum und Kommunismus in Osteuropa* (Vienna: Europa Verlag, 1967).

3. See Hermann Weber, *Geschichte der DDR*, 3d. ed (Munich: Deutscher Taschenbuch Verlag, 1985), pp. 173–244.

4. Ibid., p. 183.

5. *Dokumente der Sozialistischen Einheitspartei Deutschlands*, vol. 2 ([East] Berlin: Dietz Verlag, 1952), p. 375.

6. Weber, *Geschichte der DDR*, pp. 189–190.

7. On the consolidation of the East German regime, see *Bericht der Enquete-Kommission "Aufarbeitung von Geschichte und Folgen der SED-Diktatur in Deutschland"* (Bonn: Deutscher Bundestag, 1992).

8. "Uberprüfung der Parteimitglieder und kandidaten," in *Protokoll des III. Parteitags der SED*, vol. 2 ([East] Berlin: Dietz Verlag, 1952), p. 250.

9. As George Kennan, who was American ambassador in Moscow in 1952–53, put

it, Stalin viewed the 2.5 million Jews in the Soviet Union and in Eastern Europe as "security risks—potential holes in the iron curtain" and "entering wedges for western, particularly American, efforts to strengthen [East European satellite] resistance to Stalinist domination." George F. Kennan to author, October 31, 1994, Princeton, N.J.

10. Arkady Vaksberg, *Stalin against the Jews*, trans. Antonia W. Bouis (New York: Knopf, 1994), pp. 159–182.

11. Ibid., pp. 184–185, 206.

12. "Die Entlarvung des bürgerlichen Kosmopolitismus," *Neue Zeit* (Moscow), March 16, 1949, p. 4.

13. Walter Ulbricht, *Wer ist der Feind der Deutschen Nation?* (Moscow: Verlaag für Fremdsprachige Literatur, 1943).

14. On postwar politics, see Dennis L. Bark and David R. Gress, *A History of West Germany: From Shadow to Substance, 1945–1963* (London: Basil Blackwell, 1989); and Henry A. Turner, Jr., *The Two Germanies since 1945* (New Haven: Yale University Press, 1987).

15. Walter Ulbricht, "Warum Nationale Front des demokratischen Deutschland? Aus dem Referat auf der Parteiarbeiterkonferenz der SED Groß-Berlin, 17. Mai 1949," in *Zur Geschichte der Deutschen Arbeiterbewegung: Aus Reden und Aufsätzen*, vol. 3, *1946–1950* ([East] Berlin: Dietz Verlag, 1954), pp. 488–509.

16. Ibid., p. 491.

17. Ibid., p. 491.

18. Ibid., pp. 507–508. A 1973 DDR political dictionary defined cosmopolitanism as a "reactionary ideology which imperialism uses as a means to oppress and exploit other nations with the label of integration." *Klein Politisches Wörterbuch* (Berlin: Dietz Verlag, 1973), p. 463.

19. Wilhelm Pieck, "Die Nationale Front: Rede auf der 8. Tagung des Deutschen Volksrats in Berlin am 23. Juli 1949," in Wilhelm Pieck, *Reden und Aufsätze: Auswahl aus den Jahren 1908–1950, Band* 2 ([East] Berlin: Dietz Verlag, 1951), p. 254.

20. Ulbricht, "Warum Nationale Front des demokratischen Deutschland?" p. 491.

21. On the use of antifascist discourse in the Cold War, see Stefan Heymann, "Ein neuer Mythos des XX. Jahrhunderts: Der 'Amerikanismus'—die 'Kultur' des sterbenden Imperialismus," *Einheit* 4, no. 11 (November 1949), 1002–3.

22. See Ernst Hoffmann, "Die Stellung des Marxismus zum bürgerlichen Kosmopolitismus," *Einheit* 4, no. 7 (July 1949), 606–615; "Uber die Bedeutung der ideologischen Offensive in der Sowjetunion," 4, no. 8 (August 1949), 680–687; "Die Bedeutung der ideologischen Offensive in der Sowjetunion für Deutschland," 4, no. 9 (September 1949), 793–799; and "Leninismus und nationale Frage," 4, no. 10 (October 1949), 865–872.

23. See "Hoffmann, Ernst," in Untersuchungsausschuß Freiheitlicher Juristen, *SBZ-Biographie*, 3d ed. (Bonn: Bundesministerium für Gesamtdeutsche Fragen, 1964). pp. 152–153.

24. Hoffmann, "Die Stellung des Marxismus zum bürgerlichen Kosmopolitismus," pp. 606–607.

25. Ibid., p. 609.

26. Ibid., p. 611.

27. Ibid., p. 615.

28. Hoffmann, "Die Bedeutung der ideologischen Offensive in der Sowjetunion für Deutschland," 793–794.

29. The issue of the relationship between the NKVD, later the KGB, and the Stasi is beyond the scope of this work. But see Georg Hermann Hodos, *Schauprozesse. Stalinistische Säuberungen in Osteuropa, 1948–54* (Frankfurt am Main: Campus Verlag, 1988); Norman M. Naimark, *The Russians in Germany: A History of the Soviet Zone of Occupation, 1945–1949* (Cambridge, Mass.: Harvard University Press, 1995); *Bericht der Enquete-Kommission*, pp. 225–227.

30. See Karl Wilhelm Fricke, *Warten auf Gerechtigkeit: Kommunistische Säuberungen und Rehabilitierungen: Bericht und Dokumentation* (Cologne: Verlag Wissenschaft und Politik, 1971), pp. 62–98; Hermann Weber, *Geschichte der DDR* (Munich: Deutscher Taschenbuch Verlag, 1985), pp. 186–245; and Dietrich Staritz, *Die Gründung der DDR* (Munich: DTV, 1984). The purging of the top leadership was handled by the Central Control Commission, while regional control commissions dealt with lower-level and regional organizations.

31. See "Zu den Befugnissen der Parteikontrollkommission," in Fricke, *Warten auf Gerechtigkeit*, pp. 131–133; and "Ausführung zum Beschluß des Parteivorstandes über die Schaffung der Parteikontrollkommission (Beschluß der Parteivorstandes vom 16. September 1948)," in *Dokumente der Sozialistischen Einheitspartei* ([East] Berlin: Dietz Verlag, 1952), 2:97.

32. See "Herman Matern," in *Wer ist Wer in der SBZ: Ein biographisches Handbuch* ([East] Berlin: Berlin-Zehlendorf: Verlag für Internationalen Kulturaustausch, 1958), p. 166; and Fricke, *Warten auf Gerechtigkeit*, p. 66.

33. For a collection of Matern's essays and speeches, see Hermann Matern, *Im Kampf für Frieden, Demokratie und Sozialismus: Ausgewählte Reden und Schriften, Band 1, 1926–1956* ([East] Berlin: Dietz Verlag, 1963).

34. See Karl Wilhelm Fricke, "Das Zusammenwirken von Politbürokratie, Staatssicherheit und Justiz," in *Im Namen des Volkes? Über die Justiz im Staat der SED, Wissenschaftlicher Begleitband* (Leipzig: Forum Verlag, 1994), pp. 167–177. For early reports, see Investigating Committee of Free Jurists, *Injustice the Regime: Documentary Evidence of the Systematic Violation of Legal Rights in the Soviet-Occupied Territory of Germany* (Berlin: Federal Ministry of All German Affairs, 1952), p. 7. See also Untersuchungsausschuss Freiheitlicher Juristen, *Dokumente des Unrechts* (Berlin-Zehlendorf: Bundesministerium für Gesamtdeutsche Fragen, 1952); and *Der Staatssicherheitsdienst: Terror als System* (Berlin-Zehlendorf: Bundesministerium für Gesamtdeutsche Fragen, 1956).

35. On the Merker case, see Jeffrey Herf, "Dokumentation: Antisemitismus in der SED: Geheime Dokumente zum Fall Paul Merker aus SED- und MFS-Archiven," *Vierteljahrshefte für Zeitgeschichte* (Oktober 1994), 1–32; "East German Communists and the Jewish Question: The Case of Paul Merker," *Journal of Contemporary History* 29, 4 (October 1994), 627–662; "Der Geheimprozess," *Die Zeit*, October 7, 1994, pp. 13–16; and "East German Communists and the Jewish Question: The Case of Paul Merker," Fourth Annual Alois Mertes Memorial Lecture, 1994, German Historical Institute: Washington, D.C.; Karl Wilhelm Fricke, *Politik und Justiz in der DDR: Zur Geschichte der politischen Verfolgung, 1945–1968: Bericht und Dokumentation* (Cologne: Verlag Wissenschaft und Politik, 1979); Rudi Beckert and Karl Wilhelm Fricke, "Auf Weisung des Politbüros: Aus den Geheimprozeßakten des Obersten DDR-Gerichts, Teil 3: Der Fall Paul Merker" (Hamburg: Deutschlandfunk, Zur Diskussion/Geschichte Aktuell, January 10, 1992); Hodos, *Schauprozesse;* Wolfgang Kießling, *Paul Merker in den Fangen des Sicherheitsorgane Stalins und Ulbricht* (Berlin: Gesellschaftswissenschaftliches Forum, 1995); "Paul Merker und der 'Sozialismus der dummen Kerls,'" *Neues Deutschland*, December 1, 1992, p. 14; Mario Kessler, *Die SED und die Juden: Zwischen Repression und Toleranz* (Berlin: Akademie Verlag, 1995), pp. 85–99, 153–170; and Meuschel, *Legitimation und Parteiherrschaft*, pp. 101–116.

36. For discussions among German historians concerning the Stasi files, see Klaus Dietmar Henke, ed., *Wann bricht schon mal ein Staat Zusammen! Die Debatte über die Stasi-Akten auf dem 39. Historikertag 1992* (Munich: Deutscher Taschenbuch Verlag, 1993); see also Joachim Gauck, *Die Stasi Akten: Das unheimliche Erbe der DDR* (Hamburg: Rowohlt Taschenbuch, 1992); and Bundesministerium der Justiz, *Im Namen des Volkes?* See also the German parliamentary report with references to supporting analyses, *Bericht der Enquete-Kommission*, especially the sections dealing with the law, justice, and the Ministerium für Staatssicherheit, pp. 86–103, 219–228.

37. The work of former East German historians Helmut Eschwege, Olaf Groehler, Mario Kessler, and Wolfgang Kießling have contributed much to our understanding of this issue. See Helmut Eschwege, *Fremd unter Meinesgleichen Erinnerungen eines Dresdner Juden* (Berlin: Ch. Links Verlag, 1991); Olaf Groehler and Ulrich Herbert, *Zweierlei Bewältigung: Vier Beiträge über den Umgang mit der NS-Vergangenheit in den beiden deutschen Staaten* (Berlin: Ergebnisse, 1992); Olaf Groehler, "Aber sie haben nicht gekämpft!," *Konkret* 5 (May 1992), 38–44; Mario Kessler, "Zwischen Repression und Toleranz: Die SED-Politik und die Juden (1949–1967)," in Jürgen Kocka, ed. *Historische DDR-Forschung* (Berlin: Akademie Verlag, 1993), pp. 149–168; Olaf Groehler and Mario Kessler, *Die SED-Politik, der Antifaschismus und die Juden in der SBZ und der frühen DDR* (Berlin: Gesellschaftswissenschaftliche Forum, 1995); Kießling, *Paul Merker und der 'Sozialismus der dummen Kerls";* and "Paul Merker und die Juden," *antiFA* 5(1990), 10–11; Kessler, *Die SED und die Juden*, pp. 85–99, 153–170.

38. On Noel Field's activities in southern France and Switzerland before and during World War II, see Wolfgang Kießling, *Partner im "Narrenparadies": Der Freundkreis*

*um Noel Field und Paul Merker* (Berlin: Dietz Verlag, 1994); Flora Lewis, *Red Pawn: The Story of Noel Field* (Garden City, N.Y.: Doubleday, 1965); and Maria Schmidt, "The Hiss Dossier," *New Republic,* November 8, 1993, pp. 17–20.

39. Kießling, *Partner im "Narrenparadies,"* pp. 263–75.

40. "Erklärung des Zentralkomitees und der Zentralen Parteikontrollkommission zu den Verbindungen ehemaliger deutscher politischer Emigranten zu dem Leiter des Unitarian Service Committee Noel H. Field," in *Dokumente der Sozialistischen Einheitspartei Deutschlands, Band* 3 (Berlin: Dietz Verlag, 1952), pp. 197–213. For the extensive documentation of the ZPKK preceding the denunciations in the Field affair, see "Inhaltsverzeichnis: Mappe Paul Merker" (September 2, 1950), and "Bericht des Genossen Paul Merker vom 27. Juli 1950," SAPMO-BA, ZPA ZPKK IV/2/4/117.

41. Fricke, *Warten auf Gerechtigkeit,* pp. 81–82. The Stasi arrested Goldhammer on October 23, 1953, on espionage charges, and held him in investigative detention until April 28, 1954, when the East German Supreme Court sentenced him to ten years in prison. BStU MfSZ-Archiv, Untersuchungsvorgang no. 588/53, Bruno Goldhammer, no. 169/54, Gerichtsakte, vol. 2, pp. 4, 121–136. The BStU repaginated documents from the Ministry of State Security Central Archives. Unless indicated otherwise, pagination follows the BStU numbers.

42. "Erklärung des Zentralkomitees und der Zentralen Parteikontrollkommission . . . zu . . . Noel H. Field," in *Dokumente der Sozialistischen Einheitspartei Deutschlands,* vol. 3 p. 205.

43. Ibid., pp. 202, 205 and 212. On August 29, 1950, Anton Ackermann, then a "candidate" for membership in the Politburo and an official in the East German Foreign Ministry, wrote to the ZPKK to repeat the story about Merker's allegedly angry response in Paris in 1939 to the Hitler-Stalin pact. "Anton Ackermann, "Betrifft: Antisowjetische Ausserungen Paul Merkers" (Berlin, August 29, 1950), SAPMO-BA, ZPA ZPKK IV 2/4/117. See also "Anton Ackermann," in Jochen Cerny, ed., *Wer war Wer—DDR* (Berlin: Ch. Links Verlag, 1992), pp. 9–10.

44. See SAPMO-BA, ZPA ZPKK IV 2/4/117.

45. Letters between Merker and his daughters capture the atmosphere of fear and intimidation of this period of the anticosmopolitan purge and espionage hysteria. In a letter to Ruth and Ursula Merker—both then in their mid-twenties—of September 5, 1950, Merker referred to the Field denunciation and his expulsion as "the darkest day of my life and I am very, very worried about you, for you will suffer greatly from it." Paul Merker to Ruth Merker and Ursula Merker (September 5, 1950), SAPMO-BA, ZPA IV 2/4/111 ZPKK. Merker's daughters tried to protect themselves. On September 18, 1950, Ursula Merker wrote to the Central Control Commission that she had first learned of her father's "treasonous actions" with the publication of the Central Committee statement on the Field matter. She viewed the SED's position as "not only correct but also necessary" and supported destroying "this network of class enemies." Precisely because the Central Committee decision "concerns my father," she

grasped the importance of learning the lessons of "greater vigilance" regarding imperialist espionage activities. Ursula Merker, "Erklärung" (September 9, 1950), SAPMO-BA, ZPA IV 2/4/111 ZPKK, pp. 326–327. In November 1950 Ruth Merker, also an SED member, told her "work group" in the Dresden factory in which she worked that she had not known of her father's links to "Anglo-American agents." She too supported the Central Committee, "condemned my father's activity," and drew the lesson that she must study Marxism-Leninism more carefully in order "not to take a path as dangerous as my father." Her statement was to no avail. Her work group concluded that she could no longer remain in the secretariat of the Dresden SED "because she lives with her father. Hence there is a danger that she will be influenced by him and that he will be able to see secret party documents." SED-Betriebsgruppe, Elektrowerk II Dresden, "Entschliessung der SED-Betreibsgruppe des Elektrowerkes II, Dresden" (November 24, 1950), SAPMO-BA, ZPA IV 2/4/111 ZPKK.

46. One scholar has argued that the show trials "were primarily about a Stalinist power struggle rather than anti-Semitism." Paul O'Doherty, "The GDR in the Context of Stalinist Show Trials and Anti-Semitism in Eastern Europe, 1948–1954," *German History* 10, no. 3 (October 1992), 302–318. The trials were about both power and prejudice. The espionage conspiracy theories used to destroy political opponents rested on anti-Semitic stereotypes.

47. Weber, *Geschichte der DDR*, p. 325. An average of 200,000 people a year left in this period. The highest number was 331,390 in the year of the purge and, more important, of the popular rebellion of June 17.

48. See "Ermittlungen über Abusch, Alexander" (September 11, 1952), BStU MfSZ-Archiv no. 5079/56 Alexander Abusch, Arbeitsvorgang 2282/53, pp. 65–68; and "Alexander Abusch," in Cerny, *Wer war Wer—DDR*, p. 9. On the East German Ministry of Culture, see Simone Barck, "Die Dekadenz-Verdikt: Ein kulturpolitisches 'Kampfkonzept,'" in Jürgen Kocka, ed., *Historische DDR-Forschung: Aufsätze und Studien* (Berlin: Akademie Verlag, 1993), pp. 327–344.

49. "Abusch, Alexander: Auszug aus der Bericht der ZPKK" (July 18, 1950), BStU MfSZ-Archiv no. 5079/56 Alexander Abusch Arbeitsvorgang 2282/53, vol. 1, Teil 1, p. 34.

50. Alexander Abusch to Walter Ulbricht (between July 18, 1950, and August 7, 1950), BStU MfSZ-Archiv no. 5079/56 Alexander Abusch Arbeitsvorgang 2282/53, vol. 1, Teil 1, p. 35.

51. On Abusch's testimony, see "Alexander Abusch" (November 10, 1950), pp. 27–34; Alexander Abusch, "Erganzungen zu meine Mündlichen Aussagen vom 10. 11. 1950," pp. 42–45; and "Skizze der innerparteilichen politischen Diskussionen in Mexiko 1942/45," pp. 47–51, all in SAPMO-BA, ZPA ZPKK IV 2/4/111.

52. See "Betr.: Alexander Abusch, Berlin" (December 11, 1950), SAPMO-BA, ZPA ZPKK IV 2/4/111, p. 54.

53. Paul Merker to Alexander Abusch (Luckenwalde, March 19, 1951), BStU

MfSZ-Archiv no. 5079/56 Alexander Abusch Arbeitsvorgang 2282/53, vol. 1, Teil 1, p. 75.

54. Alexander Abusch to Walter Ulbricht (Berlin, April 12, 1951), BStU, MfSZ-Archiv 5079/53 Alexander Abusch, Arbeitsvorgang 2282/53, vol. 1, Teil 1, pp. 76, 78–81. See "Mielke, Erich," in Cerny, *Wer war Wer—DDR*, p. 312.

55. "Verpflichtung" (May 30, 1951), BStU MfSZ-Archiv no. 5079/53 Alexander Abusch, Arbeitsvorgang 2282/53, vol. 1, Teil 1, p. 82.

56. Abusch's code name was "Ernst." His category was "geheimen Informator" (secret informer), or "GI." See "Aktenspiegel" (July 23, 1953), BStU MfSZ-Archiv no. 5079/56 Alexander Abusch, vol. 1, Teil 1, pp. 27–28, 31; "Schlussbericht" (October 26, 1956), BStU MfSZ-Archiv no. 5079/56 Alexander Abusch, vol. 1, Teil 2, p. 224.

57. "Einschätzung des GI 'Ernst'" (Berlin, April 18, 1953), BStU MfSZ-Archiv no. 5079/56 Alexander Abusch, Arbeitsvorgang 2282/53, vol. 1, Teil 1, pp. 2–5.

58. See, for example, Alexander Abusch, "Die innerparteilichen Gruppierungen in Mexiko," in BStU MfSZ-Archiv no. 5079/56 Alexander Abusch, Arbeitsvorgang 2282/53, pp. 46–55.

59. Ibid., p. 3.

60. "Auszug! Betr.: Alexander Abusch, Zuckermann, Simone," BStU MfSZ-Archiv no. 5079/56 Alexander Abusch, Arbeitsvorgang 2282/53, 126.

61. "Einschätzung des GI 'Ernst'" (Berlin, April 18, 1953), pp. 2–5. For Jungmann's extensive testimony, see pp. 101–124.

62. For a list of Abusch's reports to the Stasi, see BStU MfSZ-Archiv no. 5079/56 Alexander Abusch Arbeitsvorgang 2282/53, vol. 1, Teil 2, p. 18.

63. Ibid., p. 5.

64. "Genosse Zuckermann" (November 10, 1950), SAPMO-BA, ZPA ZPKK IV/2/4/112, pp. 418–430. Zuckermann held that position from October 16, 1949, to May 1, 1951. See "Auskunfsbericht: Betr.: Dr. Leo Zuckermann" (July 23, 1951), "Personalbogen" (August 1, 1951), and "Dr. Leo Zuckermann, Lebenslauf" (February 13, 1950), BStU MfSZ-Archiv no. 147/51 Leo Zuckermann, pp. 6, 13–19.

65. "Genosse Zuckermann," p. 424.

66. Ibid., p. 424.

67. Ibid., pp. 425–426.

68. "Leo Zuckermann to Herta Geffke, ZPKK" (November 13, 1950), SAPMO-BA, ZPA ZPKK IV 2/4/112, p. 416.

69. "Leo Zuckermann to Walter Ulbricht" (Berlin, November 27, 1950), SAPMO-BA, ZPA Kaderfragen IV 2/22/V 5248.

70. The original reads: "Deutsche Staatsangehörigkeit (Jude)." See "Aktennotiz: Betr.: Angaben über Zuckermann, Leo" (June 14, 1951), BStU MfSZ-Archiv no. 147/51, p. 5.

71. "Beschluß über Zuckermann, Leo" (June 27, 1951), BStU MfSZ-Archiv Untersuchungsvorgang no. 147/51 Leo Zuckermann, pp. 3–4.

72. "Leo Zuckermann, Abschrift: Lebensbericht" (Berlin, July 18, 1951), SAPMO-BA, ZPA Kaderfragen IV 2/11/V 5248, pp. 27–30.

73. Ibid., pp. 27–30.

74. "Reuscher, Abteilungsleiter, Sicherherstellung von Briefen" (August 5, 1951), BStU MfSZ-Archiv no. 147/51 Leo Zuckermann, p. 10.

75. "Einzelvertrag zwischen Dr. Leo Zuckermann . . . Forst Zinna, DVA und dem Ministerium des Innern der Deutschen Demokratischen Republik" (September 26, 1951), BStU MfSZ-Archiv Untersuchungsvorgang no. 147/51 Leo Zuckermann, pp. 19–23.

76. BStU MfSZ-Archiv no. 147/52 Leo Zuckermann, pp. 33–35.

77. Rudolf Slansky, who was Jewish, was the second most powerful figure in the Czech Communist Party, after Klement Gottwald. On the Slansky trial, see Karel Kaplan, *Report on the Murder of the General Secretary*, trans. Karel Kovanda (Columbus: Ohio State University Press, 1990); idem, *Der politischen Prozesse in der Tschechoslowakei, 1948–1954* (Munich: R. Oldenbourg, 1986); and Jan Osers, "Die Spezifika des Slansky-Prozesses in der CSR im Vergleich mit den übrigen Schauprozessen in Osteuropa," in Hermann Weber et al., eds. *Kommunisten verfolgen Kommunisten: Stalinistische Terror und "Sauberungen" in den kommunistischen Parteien Europas seit den dreißiger Jahren* (Berlin: Akademie Verlag, 1992), pp. 459–469. For the transcript of the trial, see *Rudolf Slansky, Defendant: Transcript of the Slansky Trial* (New York: National Committee for a Free Europe/Radio Free Europe, 1952). See also Fejto, *Les Juifs et l'antisemitisme dans les pays communistes;* Hodos, *Schauprozesse;* Meir Kotik, *The Prague Trial: The First Anti-Zionist Show Trial in the Communist Bloc* (New York: Herzl Press/Cornwell Books, 1987); Eugene Loebl, *Sentenced and Tried: The Stalinist Purges in Czechoslovakia*, trans. Maurice Michael (London: Elek, 1969); and Rudolf Strobinger, *Der Mord am Generalsekretär: Stalins letzter Schauprozess, das Tribunal mit Rudolf Slansky in Prag* (Stuttgart: Burg Verlag, 1983).

78. "Ost-Berlin sucht nach einem Slansky: Emigration im Westen macht verdächtig/ Der Knesseth protestiert," *Frankfurter Allgemeine Zeitung,* December 27, 1953, p. 1.

79. "Verfügung über die Einleitung eines Untersuchungsverfahrens, Merker, Paul" (November 30, 1952), BStU MfSZ-Archiv, Untersuchungsvorgang no. 294/52, Paul Merker, Band 1, no. 192/56, pp. 2–3.

80. Investigating Committee of Free Jurists, *Injustice the Regime*, p. 7.

81. "Festnahmebericht, Bezirksverwaltung Potsdam, Abetilung VIII" (December 3, 1952), BStU MfSZ-Archiv, Untersuchungsvorgang no. 294/52, vol. 1, no. 192/56, pp. 6–8. Although the Stasi files record the date of arrest as December 3, 1953, the *Frankfurter Allgemeine Zeitung* reported the date as November 27, 1953. See "Elf

Todesurteile in Prag, Lebenslängliche Haft für drei weitere Angeklagte/Verzicht auf Revision: Paul Merker verhaftet," *Frankfurter Allgemeine Zeitung,* December 28, 1952, p. 1.

82. The Stasi's last sighting of Zuckermann in East Berlin was on December 13, 1952. "Aktennotiz" (December 20, 1952), "Aktenvermerk" (December 20, 1952), and "Abschluss-Bericht" (April 15, 1953), BStU MfSZ-Archiv no. 147/53 Leo Zuckermann, pp. 37–41. On Zuckermann's flight, see Nathan Margolin, "East German Jews Don't Say Good-Bye; They Silently Vanish to the West," *Look,* March 10, 1953, 73–74.

83. "Lehren aus dem Prozeß gegen das Verschwörerzentrum Slansky," *Dokumente der Sozialistische Einheitspartei, Band* 4 ([East] Berlin: Dietz Verlag, 1954), pp. 199–219. See also Herman Weber, "Schauprozeß-Vorbereitungen in der DDR," in Weber et. al., *Kommunisten verfolgen Kommunisten,* pp. 436–49.

84. "Lehren aus dem Prozeß gegen das Verschwörerzentrum Slansky," p. 202.

85. Ibid.

86. Ibid., p. 203. The accused, true to their Zionist and middle-class deviations, were also denounced for having kept members of the working class out of important party positions while placing their own agents in government offices.

87. Ibid., pp. 203–204.

88. Sigrid Meuschel writes that "in a patriotism with anti-Semitic and anticapitalist features, the SED saw the chance to unite the rightist and leftist critiques of Western capitalist societies and to withdraw its own order from criticism." Meuschel, *Legitimation und Parteiherrschaft in der DDR,* pp. 110–116.

89. "Lehren aus dem Prozeß gegen das Verschwörerzentrum Slansky," p. 205.

90. Ibid., p. 206. I have translated "USA Finanzkapital" as "USA-finance capital" to preserve the awkward, polemical, and hostile tone which it conveys in German no less than it does in English.

91. Ibid., p. 205.

92. Ibid., p. 206.

93. Ibid., p. 207.

94. Ibid.

95. Ibid.

96. "Das Amt Eislers aufgelöst: Auch der Pressechef Albert Norden ohne Funktion," *Frankfurter Allgemeine Zeitung,* December 30, 1952, p. 1.

97. Götz Berger to Hermann Matern (December 31, 1952), SAPMO-BA, ZPA ZPKK IV 2/4/404; and BStU MfSZ-Archiv no. 5079/56 Alexander Abusch, pp. 56–58.

98. Ibid.

99. Ibid., p. 2.

100. Ernst Melsheimer (1897–1960), the future chief state prosecutor who organ-

ized and prosecuted political trials before East Germany's Supreme Court, participated with Berger in some of the restitution debates. As head of the state prosecutor's office, Melsheimer would have had responsibility for the secret trial against Merker in 1955. For a most interesting discussion of Melsheimer's fascinating career in government service in Weimar, Nazi Germany, and East Germany, see Falco Werkentin, "Richter und Ankläger in vier politischen Systemen—die Karriere des Genossen Generalstaatsanwalt Dr. Ernst Melsheimer" (Hamburg: NDR [Norddeutsche Rundfunk], 1993); and "Ernst Melsheimer," in Cerny, *Wer war Wer—DDR*, p. 306.

101. Otto Winzer to Hermann Matern (March 25, 1953) SAPMO-BA, ZPA ZPKK IV 2/4/112, p. 376. See "Otto Winzer," in Cerny, *Wer war Wer—DDR*, p. 490.

102. Leo Zuckermann, "Erkenntnis nicht Mitschuld," SAPMO-BA, ZPA ZPKK IV 2/4/112, pp. 378–380.

103. Ibid. p. 379.

104. Ibid., pp. 379–380.

105. "Aussprache mit dem Genossen Julius Meier, Präsident der jüdischen Gemeinde am 6.1.53," SAPMO-BA, ZPA ZPKK IV 2/4/404, pp. 30–35.

106. Julius Meyer, "Sitzung des Landesverbandes der Jüdischen Gemeinden in der Deutschen Demokratischen Republik vom 15.3.1948" (January 8, 1953), SAPMO-BA, ZPA ZPKK IV 2/4/404, pp. 46–47.

107. Ibid., p. 46.

108. "Betr. Julius Meyer" (January 16, 1953), SAPMO-BA, ZPA ZPKK IV 2/4/404 pp. 26–27.

109. "Four Jewish Leaders in East Zone Flee," *New York Times*, January 16, 1953, p. 3. The date January 13 appears in Walter Sullivan, "Jewish Fugitives Reveal Pressures by East Germans: Eight Leaders Say They Were Asked to Back Slansky Case and Denounce Zionism," *New York Times*, February 8, 1953, pp. 1, 13. See also Groehler, "Integration und Ausgrenzung," p. 109; Margolin, "East German Jews Don't Say Good-Bye," p. 73; Robin Ostow, *Jews in Contemporary East Germany: The Children of Moses in the Land of Marx* (Basingstoke: Macmillan, 1989); and Kessler, "Zwischen Repression und Toleranz: Die SED Politik und die Juden," in Jürgen Kocka, ed., *Historische DDR Forschung* (Berlin: Akadamie Verlag, 1993), p. 153.

110. "Moskau Spricht von einem Komplott der Aertze: Angeblich Anschläge auf hohe Funktionäre: Eine neue antisemitische Welle?" *Frankfurter Allgemeine Zeitung*, January 14, 1953, p. 1; "Stalin stellt prominente Aertze unter Anklage," *Suddeutsche Zeitung*, January 14, 1953, p. 1.

111. "Außenminister Dertinger verhaftet," *Frankfurter Allgemeine Zeitung*, January 17, 1953, p. 1: "Georg Dertinger als Spion vor Gericht?" *Die Welt*, January 17, 1953, p. 1.

112. "Soviet Zone Police Raid Jews' Houses," *New York Times*, January 19, 1953, p. 5. In July 1953, owing to his support for Rudolf Herrnstadt and Wilhelm Zaisser,

Jendretsky was expelled from the Politburo. He later returned to the party's good graces. See "Hans Jendretzky," in Cerny, *Wer war Wer—DDR*, pp. 210–211.

113. "German Reds Hint at Mass Spy Trial," *New York Times*, January 21, 1953, p. 11.

114. See Mario Kessler, "Zwischen Repression und Toleranz: Die SED und die Juden (1949–1967)," in Kocka, *Historische DDR-Forschung*, pp. 149–167.

115. "Moskauer Antizionismus in der DDR: Interview mit geflüchteten Leiter der Jüduschen Gemeinde der Sowjetzone," *Die Neue Zeitung*, January 24, 1953, p. 1.

116. Ibid. This was an interpretation current in American diplomatic circles as well. See "Soviet Purge Laid to Security Fears: Anti-Semitism Viewed as Move to Block Links to Jews Outside Iron Curtain Countries," *New York Times*, January 24, 1953, p. 3.

117. "Moskauer Antizionismus," p. 1.

118. "Jewish Fugitives Reveal Pressures by East Germans," pp. 1, 13.

119. Ibid., p. 13. Meyer had summoned all Jewish community leaders in East Germany to East Berlin, "ostensibly for the drafting of a pro-Communist resolution" which would deny that anti-Semitism existed in Eastern Europe, and denounce the Joint Distribution Committee, Israel, and the Zionist movement. When the leaders arrived, having brought their families with them, they all fled.

120. "CIC Region Zuckermann, Prof. Dr. Leo, Interrogation Report (26 February 1953)," U.S. Army Intelligence and Security Command, Fort Meade, Maryland, Dr. Leo Zuckermann, Case no. 92F-95, pp. 94–98. American intelligence had opened a file on Zuckermann beginning with his arrival in East Berlin in summer 1947. See pp. 121–136.

121. Ibid., p. 94. Zuckermann's information on the GDR left the American counterintelligence officials rather disappointed. "No information could be elicited from SUBJECT on a broad range of topics including "penetration possibilities among Jewish personnel."

122. Alexander Abusch, "Bericht über Wien" (Berlin, December 31, 1952), BStU MfSZ-Archiv no. 5079/56 Alexander Abusch, Arbeitsvorgang 2282/53, Band 1, Teil 2, p. 112.

123. Alexander Abusch, "Meine Fehler in Mexiko und ihre aktuellen Lehren," BStU MfSZ-Archiv no. 5079/56 Alexander Abusch, Arbeitsvorgang 2282/53, Band 1, Teil 2, pp. 75–83.

124. Ibid., p. 76.

125. Ibid., p. 78.

126. Ibid.

127. Ibid., pp. 79–80.

128. Ibid., p. 80.

129. Ibid.

130. Ibid., p. 81.

131. In the lexicon of Communist terms of abuse, "chauvinism" ranks at the upper end of serious ideological and moral sins. A 1967 political dictionary published in the GDR defined chauvinism as a "reactionary bourgeois ideology and policy which aims at the open, direct, and brutal suppression of other peoples, at inflaming national hostility and national hatred, as well as the oppression of one's own nation." See *Kleines Politisches Wörterbuch* ([East] Berlin: Dietz Verlag 1967), p. 113, s.v. "Chauvinismus." To describe the views of Merker and Zuckermann as "Jewish chauvinism" was tantamount to expelling them from the ranks of progressive humanity.

132. Abusch, "Meine Fehler in Mexiko," pp. 81–82.

133. Ibid., p. 82.

134. Ibid., pp. 82–83.

135. Ibid., p. 83.

136. Ibid., p. 84.

137. See, for example, "German Reds Tie Ex-Leader to 'Zionist' Group in Prague," *New York Times*, January 5, 1953, pp. 1, 8.

138. See "Berlin Jews Assail Stand of East Zone," *New York Times*, January 6, 1953, p. 12. Warburg, who had worked as the deputy director of the Overseas Branch of the Office of War Information in Washington and Europe, said, "I have never before heard of any Paul Merker" nor had he had anything to do with restitution issues. "It is interesting, however, that the East German puppet government now considers such actions a crime against the East German state." The anti-Semitism of the Czech trial, and now this purge, he asserted, "eliminates one of the few remaining differences between Hitlerism and Stalinism."

139. "Former High Aide in Soviet Zone Escapes to Avoid a Purge Trial for 'Zionist' Spying," *New York Times*, January 7, 1953, p. 7.

140. "West Berlin Reports Kremlin Has Ordered a Wide-Ranging Purge of Jews in East Germany," *New York Times*, January 8, 1953, p. 9.

141. "East Germans Oust President of Red Party," *New York Times*, January 9, 1953, p. 5.

142. See "Wiedergutmachung als 'Volksverrat': Sozialistische Einheitspartei zieht die 'Lehren' aus dem Prager Slansky-Prozess," and "Schauprozess nach Prager Exempel: SED: Wiedergutmachung heisst Verschiebung des deutschen Volksvermögen," *Allgemeine Wochenzeitung der Juden in Deutschland*, January 9, 1953, p. 1. The *Allgemeine Wochenzeitung* began publication in 1946 in Dusseldorf. It was postwar West Germany's clearest, often lonely, journalistic voice speaking out in favor of restitution, denazification, and keeping alive the uncomfortable and inconvenient memory of the Jewish catastrophe.

143. "Wiedergutmachung als 'Volksverrat,'" p. 1.

144. Ibid.

145. Ibid.

146. Ibid.

147. Ibid.

148. Ibid.

149. H. Torren, "Geheimwaffe des kalten Krieges: Zu den Vorgängen des Eisernen Vorhanges," *Allgemeine Wochenzeitung der Juden in Deutschland,* January 25, 1953, p. 1.

150. Between 1953 and 1955, six to seven thousand prisoners in the GDR were held in "investigative detention" *(Untersuchungshaft).* See Brigitte Oleschinski, "Schlimmer als Schlimm: Strafvollzug in der DDR," in Bundesministerium der Justiz, *Im Namen des Volkes?* p. 257.

151. The Merker file includes letters from Margarete Merker of August 1955 seeking permission to speak to her husband and indicating that she had not spoken to him since his arrest in 1952. See "Margarete Merker an den Genossen Paul Wendel i.H. ZK der Sozialistischen Einheits Partei Deutschlands" (August 27, 1955), and "Margarete Merker an die Präsidialkanzlei des Präsidenten der Deutschen Demokratischen Republik" (August 27, 1955), BStU MfSZ-Archiv, Untersuchungsvorgang no. 294/52, Paul Merker Archiv no. 192/56, pp. 261, 262.

152. BStU MfSZ-Archiv Untersuchungsvorgang no. 294/52, Paul Merker vol. 1–3, no. 192/56, pp. 156–410.

153. Two short documents in Merker's Stasi file suggest that a trial transcript may have existed and was perhaps stolen or destroyed during the collapse of the East German regime in November 1989. The first document reports that "court documents" and "evidence documents" were withdrawn from the file by a member of Hauptabteilung IX/I on November 24, 1989, in the midst of the turmoil of the last days of the East German regime. Another states that "the whereabouts of the protocols of the judicial main proceedings . . . remain unanswered" (p. 182). See "Ubernahmeprotokoll (Berlin, November 24, 1989), and "Vermerk" (November 24, 1989), BStU MfSZ-Archiv, Untersuchungsvorgang no. 294/52, Paul Merker, vol. 3, no. 192/56, pp. 181–182.

154. "Vernehmungsprotokoll des Häftling" (Berlin, December 12, 1952), BStU MfSZ-Archiv, Untersuchungsvorgang no. 294/52, Paul Merker, vol. 1, no. 192/56, pp. 107–108.

155. "Vernehmungsprotokoll des Häftlings" (January 16, 1953), BStU MfSZ-Archiv, Untersuchungsvorgang no. 294/52, Paul Merker, vol. 2, no. 192/56, pp. 52–53.

156. "Vernehmungsprotokoll des Häftlings" (March 3, 1953), BStU MfSZ-Archiv, Untersuchungsvorgang no. 294/52, Paul Merker, vol. 2, no. 192/56, pp. 122–123.

157. "Fristverlängerung" (January 27, 1953; March, 18, 1953; May 26, 1953), BStU MfSZ-Archiv, Untersuchungsvorgang no. 294/52, Paul Merker, vol. 1, no. 192/56, pp. 14–16; "Fristverlängerung" (n.d), BStU MfSZ-Archiv, Untersuchungsvorgang no. 294/52, Paul Merker, Band 1, no. 192/56, p. 17.

158. "Fristverlängerung" (January 15, 1954), BStU MfSZ-Archiv, Untersuchungsvorgang no. 294/52, Paul Merker, Band 1, no. 192/56, pp. 18–19. The last request for an extension, this time for four months, came on May 28, 1954, ibid., p. 20. The requests for extension were approved by the general prosecutor, Ernst Melsheimer.

159. BStU MfSZ-Archiv, Untersuchungsvorgang no. 294/52, Paul Merker, vol. 4, pp. 155–410. For a reconstruction of Merker's "conversations with the cellmate-agent Erwin, the 'partner' in cell 36," see Kießling, *Partner im "Narrenparadies,"* pp. 276–338.

160. Cellmate-agent report (January 12, 1953), BStU MfSZ-Archiv, Untersuchungsvorgang no. 294/52, Paul Merker, vol. 4, pp. 229–234; cellmate-agent report (January 19, 1953), BStU MfSZ-Archiv, Untersuchungsvorgang no. 294/52, Paul Merker, vol. 4, pp. 206–209; and cellmate-agent report (January 15, 1953), BStU MfSZ-Archiv, Untersuchungsvorgang no. 294/56, Paul Merker, vol. 4, p. 218.

161. Cellmate-agent report (January 19, 1953), BStU MfSZ-Archiv, Untersuchungsvorgang no. 294/52, Paul Merker, vol. 4, pp. 207–208. On January 31, 1953, Merker told his cellmate that the Stasi interrogator and "the Russian" were angry because he had "refused to incriminate other persons." They asked him, "Don't you do something for the working class and tell the truth?" Cellmate/agent report (February 2, 1953), BStU MfSZ-Archiv, Untersuchungsvorgang no. 294/52, Paul Merker, vol. 4, p. 156.

162. Cellmate Report of March 11, 1953 concerning interrogation of March 6, 1953, BStU MfSZ-Archiv, Untersuchungsvorgang no. 294/52, Paul Merker, vol. 4, p. 333.

163. Cellmate-agent report (February 4, 1953), BStU MfSZ-Archiv, Untersuchungsvorgang no. 294/52, Paul Merker, vol. 4, pp. 403–406.

164. Cellmate-agent report (February 4, 1953), BStU MfSZ-Archiv, Untersuchungsvorgang no. 294/52, Paul Merker, vol. 4, p. 404. Merker also thought that there were "several other members of the Central Committee who will probably receive treatment no different than mine" (p. 405).

165. Cellmate-agent report (February 4, 1953), BStU MfSZ-Archiv, Untersuchungsvorgang no. 294/52, Paul Merker, vol. 4, p. 406.

166. Paul Merker, "An die Zentrale Kontrollkommission des ZK. der SED, Berlin: 'Stellungnahme zur Judenfrage" (June 1, 1956), Paul Merker NL 102/27, SAPMO-BA ZPA, p. 1.

167. They included Abusch, Franz Dahlem, Johann Schmidt, Erich Jungmann, Wilhelm Koenen, Gerhard Eisler, Anna Seghers, Georg Stibi, Henny Stibi, Budo Uhse, Ludwig Renn, Walter Janka, Hans Marum, Rudolf Neumann, and Maria Weiterer. "Zeugenvorschläge zum Untersuchungsvorgang Paul Merker," BStU MfSZ-Archiv, Untersuchungsvorgang no. 294/52, Paul Merker, vol. 3, no. 192/56, pp. 170–172. See, for example, "Vernehmungsprotokoll des Häftlings" (March 3, 1953), BStU

MfSZ-Archiv, no. 192/56 Paul Merker, vol. 2, pp. 122–123. For testimony against Merker from other leading figures of the SED, see "Vernehmungsprotokoll des Zeugen, Anton Ackermann," (April 25, 1954), BStU MfSZ-Archiv, no. 192/56, Untersuchungsvorgang no. 294/52, Paul Merker, vol. 3, pp. 429–230; "Vernehmungsprotokoll des Zeugen, Wilhelm Koenen" (May 3, 1954), pp. 438–440; "Vernehmungsprotokoll des Zeugen, Alexander Abusch" (June 6, 1954), pp. 447–450; "Vernehmungsprotokoll des Zeugen, Leo Katz" (May 12, 1954), pp. 453–455. For the testimony from German Communists who had been in Mexico City, see the interrogations of Erich Jungmann in 1953 and Alexander Abusch, Erich Jungmann, Johann Schmidt, Claire Quast, Leo Katz, and Henny Stibi in 1954, BStU MfSZ-Archiv, no. 192/56, Paul Merker, vols. 2 and 3.

168. Hermann Matern, "Über die Auswertung des Beschlusses des Zentralkommittees zu den 'Lehren aus den Prozeß gegen das Verschwörerzentrum Slansky" (May 14, 1953), in *Dokumente der Sozialistische Einheitspartei, Band 4* ([East] Berlin: Dietz Verlag, 1954), pp. 394–409; idem, *Über die Durchführung des Beschlusses des ZK der SED "Lehren aus dem Prozess Gegen das Verschwörerzentrum Slansky"* ([East] Berlin: Dietz Verlag, 1953), pp. 3–28. In 1956 Franz Dahlem, unlike Merker, received a full rehabilitation, including readmission to the Central Committee and publication of his essays and memoirs by the government publishing house. See "Franz Dahlem," in Cerny, *Wer war Wer—DDR,* pp. 74–75.

169. For Ackermann's statement, see SAPMO-BA, ZPA IV 2/4/117; cited by Wolfgang Kießling, "Paul Merkers 'Unverständnis für den Hitler-Stalin-Pakt': Gespräche mit dem Sowjetfeind," in Carsten Tessmer, ed., *Jahrbuch für Historische Kommunismusforschung, 1993* (Berlin: Akademie Verlag, 1993), pp. 142–144.

170. Ibid., p. 143.

171. Soon afterwards Ackermann was purged from his position in the Politburo and the Foreign Ministry for supporting Rudolf Hernnstadt and Wilhelm Zaisser's reform proposals in 1953. He was able to retain important cultural positions in the Ministry for Culture thereafter. See "Anton Ackermann," in Cerny, *Wer war Wer—DDR,* pp. 9–10.

172. "Bericht, Anklageschrift gegen Paul Merker" (Berlin, February 14, 1955), BStU MfSZ-Archiv, Untersuchungsvorgang no. 294/52, Paul Merker, vol. 3, no. 192/56, p. 195.

173. See, in particular, Katz, "Bericht über Paul Merker und seine Tätigkeit in Mexico." (March 13, 1953), SAPMO-BA, ZPA ZPKK IV 2/4/117, pp. 307–313; "Dr. Rudolf Neumann and Hilde Neumann an die Z.P.K.K.: Betr. Emigration in Mexiko" (August 30, 1950), SAPMO-BA, ZPA ZPKK IV 2/4/112, pp. 5–6; and the "witness protocols" *(Zeugenprotokoll)* for Alexander Abusch, Leo Katz, Klare Quest, Johann Schmidt, and Henny Stibi, BSTU MfSZ-Archiv, Untersuchungsvorgang no. 294/52, Paul Merker, vol. 3, no. 192/56.

174. Merker, "Stellungnahme zur Judenfrage," p. 65.

175. "Zeugenschaftliche Vernehmung, Jungmann, Erich, Max" (February 18, 1953), BStU MfSZ-Archiv, Untersuchungsvorgang no. 294/52, Paul Merker, vol. 2, no. 192/56, p. 218; and ibid. (February 19, 1953), pp. 223–226. On Jungmann, see "Erich Jungmann," in Untersuchungsausschuss Freiheitlicher Juristen, *SBZ-Biographie* 3d ed. (Bonn: Bundesministerium für Gesamtdeutsche Fragen, 1964), p. 166.

176. Leo Katz, "Bericht über Paul Merker und seine Tätigkeit in Mexico," pp. 307–313.

177. Ibid., p. 311.

178. "Vernehmungsprotokoll, Katz, Leo" (Berlin, May 12, 1954), BStU MfSZ-Archiv, Untersuchungsvorgang no. 294/52, Paul Merker, vol. 3, no. 192/56, p. 71.

179. Interview with Friedrich Katz, January 24, 1994, Chicago.

180. "Vernehmungsprotokoll, Schmidt, Johann" (Berlin, May 4, 1954), BStU MfSZ-Archiv, Untersuchungsvorgang no. 294/52, Paul Merker, vol. 3, no. 192/56, p. 57. The Merker file contains no evidence that the Stasi interrogated Anna Seghers. Her by then well established literary career was not damaged by the purge. Publicly at least, Seghers did not use her prestige and influence to speak out against the purge.

181. Ibid., p. 58.

182. "Aktennotiz: Betr: Genossin Merker" (May 18, 1953), SAPMO-BA, ZPA ZPKK IV 2/4/111, p. 247.

183. "An die Kreisparteikontrollkommission, Luckenwalde, Betr.: Genossin Merker, Luckenwalde" (May 22, 1953), SAPMO-BA, ZPA ZPKK IV 2/4/111.

184. "Begutachtung von Schriften des Merker, Paul" (Berlin, December 13, 1953), BStU MfSZ-Archiv, Untersuchungsvorgang no. 294/52, Paul Merker, vol. 1, no. 192/56, pp. 60–76.

185. Ibid., pp. 62–65.

186. Ibid., p. 64.

187. Ibid., p. 57.

188. Ibid., pp. 67–68.

189. Ibid., p. 68.

190. Ibid., p. 70.

191. Ibid.

192. For the court verdict and other documents, see Jeffrey Herf, "Antisemitismus in der SED: Geheime Dokumente zum Fall Paul Merker aus SED- und MfS-Archiven," *Vierteljahrshefte für Zeitgeschichte*, no. 4 (1994), 635–667. See also Kessler, *Die SED und die Juden*, pp. 153–170.

193. Beckert and Fricke, "Auf Weisung des Politburos," pp. 2–3.

194. "Oberstes Gericht der Deutschen Demokratischen Republik I. Strafsenat I Zst. (I) 1/55: Im Namen des Volkes in der Strafsache gegen den Kellner Paul Merker" (March 29–30, 1955), BStU MfSZ-Archiv, Untersuchungsvorgang no. 294/52, vol. 3, Archiv no. 192/56, pp. 522–536; reprinted as "Dokument I" in Jeffrey Herf, "Antisemitismus in der SED," pp. 643–650.

195. "Oberstes Gericht: Im Namen des Volkes in der Strafsache gegen Paul Merker," p. 6. Hilde Benjamin was the minister of justice in the DDR from 1953 to 1967, and vice president of the Oberste Gericht, in which she presided over many political show trials. For her views on law and politics, see Hilde Benjamin, *Die neuen Aufgaben von Gericht und Staatsanwalt* ([East] Berlin: VEB Deutscher Zentralverlag, 1956), especially pp. 31–33 ("Raising the Educational Impact of Work in the Field of Justice").

196. "Oberstes Gericht: Im Namen des Volkes in der Strafsache gegen Paul Merker," p. 3. The use of the phrase "den Kellner Paul Merker," or "the waiter Paul Merker," refers to Merker's youthful and current occupation.

197. Ibid., p. 4.

198. Ibid., p. 12. On Merker's internment, escape, and efforts to get other German Communists safely out of France, see SAPMO-BA, ZPA ZPKK IV/2/11/V /801 Paul Merker, "Mein politischer Lebenslauf," pp. 12–30.

199. "Oberstes Gericht: Im Names des Volkes iin der Strafsache gegen Paul Merker," p. 13.

200. Ibid., pp. 9–10.

201. Ibid.

202. Ibid., pp. 13–14. The German reads: "Er stütze er sich nicht auf die politische, sondern auf die rassische Emigration . . . emigrierte kapitalistische jüdische Kreise."

203. Beckert and Fricke, "Auf Weisung des Politbüros," p. 26.

204. "Paul Merker to Wilhelm Pieck, April 14, 1956," Paul Merker NL 102/27, SAPMO-BA, ZPA.

205. Ibid., p. 2.

206. Ibid.

207. Ibid., p. 3.

208. See the minutes of the meetings of the Kommission der Zentralkomitee zur Überprüfung von Angelegenheiten von Parteimitgliedern on April 19, April 25, and May 3, 1956, SAPMO-BA, ZPA IV/202/8 Zentralkomitee der SED. The members of the commission were Walter Ulbricht, Hermann Matern, Friedrich Ebert, Karl Schirdewan, Ernst Wollweber, Helmut Lehmann, Hans Kiefert, and Bruno Haid. See also the report of Herta Geffke, the chair of the ZPKK, "Bericht der Gen. Geffke, Protokoll: Über die Sitzung der Kommission der Zentralkomitee zur Überprüfung von Angelgenheiten von Parteimitgliedern" (May 3, 1956), SAPMO-BA, ZPA IV 2/202/8 Zentralkomitee der SED.

209. "Walter Ulbricht to Paul Merker, July 31, 1956," Paul Merker NL 102/27, SAPMO-BA, ZPA, p. 84.

210. "Paul Merker to Walter Ulbricht, August 23, 1956," Paul Merker NL 102/27, SAPMO-BA, ZPA, pp. 85–89.

211. Ibid., p. 91; "Paul Merker to Wilhelm Pieck, August 24, 1956," Paul Merker NL 102/27, SAPMO-BA, ZPA, p. 98.

212. The presiding judge was Walter Ziegler; Richard Krügelstein was the prosecutor. See "Oberstes Gericht der Deutschen Demokratischen Republik 1. Strafsenat 1 Zst (I) 1/55: In der Strafsache gegen Merker, Paul Friedrich" (July 13, 1956), BStU, MfSZ-Archiv Untersuchungsvorgang no. 294/52, Merker, Paul, vol. 3, no. 192/56, p. 206.

213. Ibid., p. 207.

214. The judges argued that Merker's activities in the period 1936–1946 were the subject of judicial condemnation "only" because a "stance hostile to the state" on Merker's part was seen after 1946. If that was no longer supported by the evidence, the "actions of the condemned in the period from 1936 to 1946 lose their judicially significant character" and Merker could no longer be imprisoned on account of them. Ibid., p. 208.

215. Merker, "Stellungnahme zur Judenfrage."

216. Ibid, p. 3. Merker wrote: "The Soviet and the German interrogators repeatedly said that it was completely incomprehensible to them that a non-Jew such as myself would become active on behalf of the Jews unless he was in their pay or being paid by Jewish organizations, all of which, in the opinion of these examiners, were without exception agents of the imperialist powers. Therefore, a non-Jew could be active on behalf of the Jews only as an agent of imperialism. For them, my engagement on behalf of Jewish people, who were going through the most horrible persecution by the Hitler fascists, was by itself sufficient proof that I must be an agent of imperialism and an enemy of the working class. The prosecutor and the [supreme] court agreed."

217. Ibid., p. 16.

218. Ibid., p. 18.

219. He also reminded the members of the ZPKK that the Soviet victory at Stalingrad had "saved the Jews in Palestine living under Zionism from annihilation by Rommel's advancing army." Ibid., p. 19.

220. Ibid., pp. 3–4.

221. "Bericht über die Ergebnisse der Tätigkeit der Kommission des Zentralkomitees zur Überprüfung von Angelgenheiten von Parteimitgliedern" (Berlin, July 12, 1956), SAPMO-BA, ZPA IV/2/202/9, p. 4

222. See "Nachruf des Zentralkomitee für Genossen Paul Merker," and Kurt Seibt, "Trauerfeier für Paul Merker" (May 19, 1969), SAPMO-BA, ZPA IV 2/11V 801. The Merker case does not appear in the East German era historiography of the Communist emigration in Mexico City. See Wolfgang Kießling, *Alemania Libre in Mexiko* ([East] Berlin: Akadamie Verlag, 1974). Memoirs also display gaps in memory. Bruno Frei, *Das Papiersäbel* (Frankfurt am Main: Fischer, 1972), praises the literary and political accomplishments of the German emigration in Mexico, yet says nothing about the persecution of his former comrades in Mexico in postwar Prague and East Berlin. In a chapter on "the anti-Semitic campaign" in the Soviet Union in his short book *Sozialismus und Antisemitismus* (Socialism and Anti-Semitism) (Vienna: Europa Verlag,

1978), Frei refers to the murder of Solomon Mikhoels, the execution of twenty-six Jewish intellectuals in Moscow in 1948, the anticosmopolitan campaign, and the "Doctors' plot" of 1953. But in a chapter dealing with anti-Semitism, Frei does not refer to the events in Prague and East Berlin.

223. Paul Merker, "Über die Bewegung 'Freies Deutschland' in Lateinamerika," in Heinz Voßke, ed., *Im Kampf Bewährt: Erinnerungen deutscher Genossen an den antifaschistischen Widerstand von 1933 bis 1945* ([East] Berlin: Dietz Verlag, 1969), pp. 465–526.

224. On these now familiar themes, see two classic works, George Mosse, *The Crisis of German Ideology* (New York: Schocken Books, 1981); and Fritz Stern, *The Politics of Cultural Despair* (Berkeley: University of California Press, 1961).

225. See Meuschel, *Legitimation und Parteiherrschaft in der DDR*.

# 6. Memory and Policy in East Germany from Ulbricht to Honecker

1. For recent archival material on the events of June 1953, see Armin Mohler and Stefan Wolle, "Die gescheiterte Revolution des Jahres 1953," in *Untergang auf Raten: Unbekannte Kapitel der DDR-Geschichte* (Munich: C. Bertelsmann, 1993), pp. 27–162. See also Henry Ashby Turner, Jr., *The Two Germanies since 1945*, New Haven: Yale University Press, 1987), pp. 116–129; and Hermann Weber, *Geshichte der DDR* (Munich: Deutscher Taschenbuch Verlag, 1985), pp. 232–244.

2. See Rudolf Herrnstadt, *Das Herrnstadt Dokument: Das Politbüro der SED und die Geschichte des 17. Juni 1953*, ed. Nadja Stulz-Herrnstadt (Reinbek bei Hamburg: Rowohlt Verlag, 1990); Helmut Müller-Enbergs, *Der Fall Rudolf Herrnstadt: Tauwetterpolitik vor dem 17. Juni* (Berlin: Ch. Links Verlag, 1991).

3. Herrnstadt then worked as an archivist, Zaisser as a translator. See "Rudolf Herrnstadt," and "Wilhelm Zaisser," in Jochen Cerny, ed., *Wer war Wer—DDR: ein biographisches Lexikon* (Berlin: Ch. Links, 1992), pp. 186–187, and 503–504.

4. Sigrid Meuschel, *Legitimation und Parteiherrschaft in der DDR* (Frankfurt am Main: Suhrkamp, 1992), p. 168.

5. Ibid., pp. 153–154.

6. See Albert Hirschmann, *Exit, Voice, and Loyalty* (Cambridge, Mass.: Harvard University Press, 1970), and *A Propensity to Self-Subversion* (Cambridge, Mass.: Harvard University Press, 1995).

7. "Kundgebung für die Opfer des Faschismus in Berlin vor dem Alten Museuem, Sept. 1950," SAPMO-BA, ZPA Photoarchiv 713/71N.

8. *Referentenmaterial: Zum Internationalen Gedenktag für die Opfer des faschistischen Terrors, 9. September 1951* (Berlin: Zentralvorstand der VVN, 1951). See also Jeffrey

Herf, "German Communism, the Discourse of Antifascism, and the Jewish Catastrophe," in John Boyer and Michael Geyer, eds., *Resistance against the Third Reich: 1933–1990* (Chicago: University of Chicago Press, 1994), pp. 257–294.

9. *Zum Internationalen Gedenktag*, p. 3.

10. Ibid.

11. Ibid., p. 13. On political symbolism in East Germany, including the Thälmann cult, see Maoz Azaryahu, *Von Wilhelmplatz zu Thälmannplatz: Politische Symbole im öffentlichen Leben der DDR* (Gerlingen: Bleicher Verlag, 1991).

12. *Zum Internationalen Gedenktag*, p. 14.

13. *Gedenktag für die Opfer des Faschismus: Referentenmaterial Deutsche Frauen im Widerstandskampf gegen das Naziregime* (Berlin: Generalsekretariat der VVN für die sowjetische Besatzungszone, 1951).

14. See "Internationale Gedenktage für die Opfer des Faschismus in Berlin, 9. Sept. 1951 auf dem August-Bebel Platz, Berlin," SAPMO-BA, ZPA Photoarchiv 1270/79.

15. "Kundgebung für die Opfer des Faschismus in Berlin vor dem Alten Museum, September 1950," SAPMO-BA, ZPA Photoarchiv 1270/79.

16. "Friedenskundgebung der Frauen in Ravensbrück am 13.9.1952," SAPMO-BA, ZPA Photoarchiv 1611/70.

17. "Friedenskundgebung der Frauen in Ravensbrück am 13. Sept. 1952," SAPMO-BA, ZPA Photoarchiv 1269/80N.

18. "Walter Bartel spricht auf dem Ravensbrück-Gedenktag, 1952," SAPMO-BA, ZPA Photoarchiv 1266/79N.

19. Gerhard Weinberg, *A World at Arms: A Global History of World War II* (New York: Cambridge University Press, 1994), p. 894.

20. "Tag der Opfer des Faschismus am 9. Sept. 1951 in Berlin: Kranzniederlegung durch Vertreter der Jüdischen Gemeinde von Berlin," SAPMO-BA, ZPA Photoarchiv 1274/79N.

21. "Eine Delegation ehemalige Widerstandskämpfer im ehemalige KZ Buchenwald. 9. Sept. 1951: Am Ehrenhain Französische Widerstandskämpfer," SAPMO-BA, ZPA Photoarchiv 399/71.

22. Much work remains to be done on the history of memory of World War II, including ideals of manliness and heroism in postwar East Germany and the entire Soviet bloc. For some points of comparison, see Jeffrey Herf, *Reactionary Modernism: Technology, Culture, and Politics in Weimar and the Third Reich* (New York: Cambridge University Press, 1984), and especially George L. Mosse, *Fallen Soldiers: Reshaping the Memory of the World Wars* (New York: Oxford University Press, 1990).

23. *Referentenmaterial, Deutsche Frauen im Widerstandskampf gegen das Naziregime: Gedenktag für die Opfer des Faschismus* ([East] Berlin: Generalsekretariat der VVN für die sowjetische Besatzungszone, 1948).

24. "Friedenskundgebung der Frauen in Ravensbrück am 13. September 1952," SAPMO-BA, ZPA Photoarchiv 1269/80N.

25. "Friedenskundgebung der Frauen in Ravensbrück am 13.9. 1952," SAPMO-BA, ZPA Photoarchiv 1267/79N.

26. "Veranstaltung der VVN zum 14. Jahrestag der Kristallnacht am 9. Nov. 1952 im Haus Vaterland in Berlin," SAPMO-BA, ZPA Photoarchiv 1337/79N.

27. The postwar Ernst Thälmann cult, in its pedagogical-didactic as well as aesthetic and gender connotations, deserves much more extensive analysis in considerations of the meaning of resistance heroism. See Parteivorstand der SED, *Programmhefte für Sozialistische Feierstunden Gedenk- und Erinnerungstage: Ernst Thälmann* ([East] Berlin: Neues Deutschland, 1949); Wilhelm Pieck, "Ernst Thälmann: Das Vorbild der Jungen Friedenskämpfer," and Walter Ulbricht, "Ernst Thälmann," in *Ernst Thälmann: Vorbild der Deutschen Jugend* ([East] Berlin: Volk und Wissen, 1951), pp. 5–12, 13–25; Walter Ulbricht, *Wir Erfüllen Ernst Thälmann Vermächtnis* ([East] Berlin: Dietz Verlag, 1953); and Marx-Engels-Lenin-Stalin Institut beim Zentral Komitee der SED, *Ernst Thälmann: Bilder und Dokumente Aus Seinem Leben* ([East] Berlin: Dietz Verlag, 1955).

28. The Communists did not have a monopoly on the redemptive mode of remembrance. For a critical discussion, see Lawrence L. Langer, *Admitting the Holocaust: Collected Essays* (New York: Oxford University Press, 1995).

29. Liah Greenfeld, *Nationalism: Five Paths to Modernity* (Cambridge, Mass.: Harvard University Press, 1992).

30. Other important figures include Gerhart Eisler, Hermann Axen, and writers such as Anna Seghers, Stefan Heym, Jürgen Kuczynski, Markus Wolf, and Arnold Zweig. Most were in their late fifties or early sixties, and were Communists of long standing who had returned to East Germany from Moscow or Western emigration. See Jerry E. Thompson, "Jews, Zionism, and Israel: The Story of the Jews in the German Democratic Republic since 1945" (Ann Arbor, Mich., 1978), pp. 198–235, though caution should be exercised concerning Thompson's efforts to ascertain who was and who was not of Jewish origin. Wolf was the longtime director of the Ministry for State Security with special focus on foreign intelligence. Axen was a member of the SED Central Committee with great influence on East German foreign policy. See also the memoirs of Jürgen Kuczynski, *"Ein linientrueuer Dissident": Memoiren, 1945–1989* (Berlin: Aufbau Verlag, 1992); and Markus Wolf, *In eigenem Auftrag: Bekenntnisse und Einsichten* (Munich: Schneekluth, 1991).

31. See Alexander Abusch, *Schriften, Band 3, Kulturelle Probleme des sozialistischen Humanismus: Beiträge zur Kulturpolitik, 1946–1961* ([East] Berlin: Aufbau Verlag, 1962).

32. Alexander Abusch, *Stalin und die Schicksalsfragen der Deutschen Nation*, 2d expanded ed. ([East] Berlin: Aufbau Verlag, 1952).

33. Ibid., p. 111.

34. Alexander Abusch, "Das gesellschaftliche Gesetz erkennen," in *Restauration oder Renaissance* ([East] Berlin: Aufbau Verlag, 1954), pp. 9–10.

35. Alexander Abusch, "Geistige Folgen der unvollendsten Revolution," *Aufbau: Kulturpolitische Monatsschrift* 4, no. 4 (1948), 281.

36. Abusch, *Restauration oder Renaissance,* pp. 31–33.

37. Ibid., p. 32–33.

38. Ibid., p. 34. See also Alexander Abusch, "Kunstler und Gesellschaft," ibid., pp. 49–50.

39. Alexander Abusch, "EVG-SS-'Europa,'" ibid., p. 15.

40. Ibid., p. 16.

41. Alexander Abusch, "Das deutsche Kulturministerium und sein Minister," ibid., pp. 47–48.

42. "Präambel der Verordnung ber die Bildung des Ministeriums für Kultur," cited ibid., p. 51.

43. Thompson, "Jews, Zionism, and Israel," p. 200; and "Albert Norden," in Cerny, *Wer war Wer—DDR,* p. 335.

44. See "Albert Norden," in Cerny, *Wer war Wer—DDR,* p. 335.

45. See Michael Lemke, "Kampagnen gegen Bonn: Die Systemkrise der DDR und die West-Propaganda der SED 1960–1963," *Vierteljahrshefte für Zeitgeschichte* 41, no. 2 (April 1993), 153–174. Examples of the offensive against Bonn include Ausschuss für Deutsche Einheit und der Vereinigung Demokratischer Juristen Deutschlands, *Im Namen der Völker, Im Namen der Opfer: Auszüge aus dem Protokoll des Prozesses Gegen Dr. Hans Globke vor dem Obersten Gericht der DDR* ([East] Berlin: 1963); *Der Oberländer Prozess* ([East] Berlin: Auschuss für Deutsche Einheit, 1960).

46. See Gerhart Eisler, Albert Norden, and Albert Schreiner, *The Lesson of Germany: A Guide to Her History* (New York: International Publishers, 1945).

47. Ibid., pp. 209–210.

48. Ibid., p. 213.

49. Ibid., p. 187.

50. Ibid., pp. 218–219.

51. Albert Norden, *Die Nation und Wir: Ausgewählte Aufsätze und Reden, 1933–1964,* 2 vols. ([East] Berlin: Dietz Verlag, 1965).

52. See, for example, Albert Norden, "Eine Schlacht zwischen Faschismus und Anti-Faschismus, 5. Oktober 1933," ibid., 1:32–37; "Der braune Säbel rasselt, April 1935," 1:47–61; "Hitler, der Gendarm des Großkapitals: Was hinter der 'Befreiung der Sudetendeutschen' steckt, 1938," 1:199–219; and "Die Umerziehung hat begonnen, November 1944," 1:281–289.

53. See, for example, Albert Norden, "Deutscher Sozialismus" (April 11, 1933), in *Die Nation und Wir,* 1:27–31; reprinted from "Antifaschistische Front" (Copenhagen), no. 5 (1933).

54. Albert Norden, "Der braune Säbel rasselt," in *Die Nation und wir,* 1:47–60. The literature on the role of anti-Semitism in Hitler's foreign policy is extensive. See Christopher Browning, *The Path to Genocide: Essays on the Launching of the Final*

*Solution* (New York: Cambridge University Press, 1992); Andreas Hillgrüber, *Hitler's Strategie: Politik und Kriegführung, 1940–1941* (Munich: Bernard and Graefe, 1982); idem, "Die 'Endlösung' und das deutsche Ostimperium als Kernstück des rassenideologischen Programms des Nationalsozialismsus," *Vierteljahrshefte für Zeitgeschichte* (April 1972), 133–153; idem, "Die ideologisch-dogmatische Grundlagen der nationalsozialistischen Politik der Ausrottung der Juden in den besetzten Gebieten der Sowjetunion und ihre Durchführung, 1941–1944," *German Studies Review* 2, no. 2 (1979), 263–296; Eberhard Jäckel, *Hitler's World View: A Blueprint for Power,* trans. Herbert Arnold (Middletown, Conn.: Wesleyan University Press, 1972); and Norman Rich, *Hitler's War Aims* (New York: Norton, 1973–74).

55. See in Norden, *Die Nation und Wir,* the following essays: "Aufgaben deutscher Antifaschisten" (September 19, 1945), pp. 296–302; "Die IG-Farben" (August 1, 1946), pp. 321–329; "Hochverrat an der Demokratie" (February 25, 1948), pp. 399–403; "Sechs Jahre nach Potsdam" (July 29, 1951), pp. 507–512; "Die Zukunft gehört Voltaire und nicht Krupp: Aus der Rede auf der 4. Verlegerkonferenz in Leipzig" (December 2, 1954), pp. 577–589; and "Pariser Kriegsverträge oder friedliche Wiedervereinigung Deutschlands: Rede auf der Pressekonferenz des Ausschusses für Deutsche Einheit in Berlin" (January 19, 1955), pp. 590–605.

56. Albert Norden, *Um die Nation: Beiträge zu Deutschlands Lebensfrage* ([East] Berlin: Dietz Verlag, 1952). See also his collected essays in *Die Nation und Wir,* 2d ed. ([East] Berlin: Dietz Verlag, 1964).

57. See Albert Norden, "Verspielte Chance," in *Um die Nation,* pp. 7–23.

58. Albert Norden, "Der zweite westdeutsche Separatstaat," in *Um die Nation,* pp. 117–174.

59. Ibid., p. 119.

60. Ibid., p. 149.

61. Ibid., p. 153.

62. Ibid., p. 157.

63. Ibid., p. 157.

64. Ibid., pp. 160, 163.

65. Ibid., p. 173.

66. On Marxism as a chapter in the history of German nationalism, see Greenfeld, *Nationalism,* pp. 386–395.

67. Albert Norden, "Im Kampf für das Vaterland," in *Um die Nation,* p. 262. For Norden's profiles of West German leaders, notably Adenauer, Schumacher, and the banker Herman Abs, all of whom in his view were "national traitors," see "Nationalverräter im Profil," in *Um die Nation,* pp. 284–384.

68. See Jerry Muller, *The Other God That Failed: Hans Freyer and the Deradicalization of German Conservatism* (Princeton: Princeton University Press, 1987); Jeffrey Herf, *War by Other Means* (New York: Fress Press, 1991); and Jürgen Habermas, "Neoconservative Culture Criticism in the United States and West Germany: An

Intellectual Movement in Two Political Cultures," in Richard J. Bernstein, ed., *Habermas and Modernity* (Cambridge, Mass.: MIT Press, 1985), pp. 79–94.

69. See Albert Norden, "Die Nation und Wir: Ein historische Betrachtung zum 1(5) Jahrestag der DDR, August 1964," in *Die Nation und wir,* 1:9–26. Norden again stressed the continuities between the bourgeoisie under Hitler and in West Germany: "This state was and is actually not at all new. Its rulers see it as a continuation and restoration of the old." The break in German history took place with the creation of the GDR. It was "something unheard of in German history," and was the heir to "democratic movements and efforts to create a unified nation" in German history.

70. Albert Norden, "Kosmopolitismus—die Ideologie der transatlantischen Räuber," in *Um die Nation,* pp. 195–210.

71. Ibid., p. 195.

72. Ibid., p. 197.

73. On right-wing and Nazi "German anticapitalism" and anti-Westernism in Weimar and Nazi Germany, see Herf, *Reactionary Modernism,* pp. 130–152, 152–216.

74. Albert Norden to Arnold Zweig (May 19, 1959), Albert Norden NL 217/14, SAPMO-BA, ZPA, pp. 38–40.

75. Günter Morsch, ed., *Von Erinnerung zum Monument: Die Entstehungsgeschichte der Nationalen Mahn- und Gedenkstätte Sachsenhausen* (Berlin: Stiftung Brandenburgische Gedenkstätten and Edition Hentrich, 1996). For a comparative analysis of Holocaust memorials, see James E. Young, *The Texture of Memory: Holocaust Memorials and Meaning* (New Haven: Yale University Press, 1993). See also Mosse, *Fallen Soldiers.*

76. See Otto Grotewohl NL 90/553, SAPMO-BA, ZPA.

77. Otto Grotewohl, "Mahn- und Gedenkstätte Buchenwald" (January 13, 1958), Otto Grotewohl NL 90/553, SAPMO-BA, ZPA, p. 95.

78. Ibid., p. 96.

79. "Aufruf des Komitees für die Einweihung der Mahn- und Gedenkstätte Buchenwald," Otto Grotewohl NL 90/553, SAPMO-BA, ZPA, p. 46.

80. Ibid.

81. Otto Grotewohl, "Buchenwald Mahnt! Rede zur Weihe der nationalen Mahn- und Gedenkstätte Buchenwald, 14 September 1958," in *Im Kampf um die Einige Deutsche Demokratische Republik: Reden und Aufsätze,* vol. 6, *Auswahl aus den Jahren 1958–1960* ([East] Berlin: Dietz Verlag, 1964), pp. 7–8.

82. Ibid., p. 10.

83. Ibid.

84. Ibid., p. 11.

85. Ibid. See also Otto Grotewohl, "Zur Suezfrage: Erklärung vor ägyptischen Journalisten in Berlin 14. September 1956," in Otto Grotewohl, *Im Kampf um die Einige Deutsche Demokratische Republik: Reden und Aufsätze, Band 4, Auswahl aus den Jahren 1954–1956* ([East] Berlin: Dietz Verlag, 1959), pp. 66–68. Grotewohl expressed

solidarity with the Egyptians in the face of British and French intervention but avoided public attacks on Israel.

86. Grotewohl, "Buchenwald Mahnt!" p. 13.

87. "Walter Ulbricht bei der Einweihung der Gedenkstätte Sachsenhausen: Von der DDR wird stets der Frieden ausstrahlen," *Neues Deutschland,* April 24, 1961, pp. 1, 3.

88. Ibid.

89. Ibid.

90. On early Israeli views about the Holocaust, heroism, resistance, and the European diaspora, see Tom Segev, *The Seventh Million: The Israelis and the Holocuast,* trans. Haim Watzman (New York: Hill and Wang, 1993), pp. 113–186, 421–445.

91. Ulbricht, "Von der DDR wird stets der Frieden ausstrahlen," p. 3.

92. Ibid.

93. See Lemke, "Kampagnen gegen Bonn." On the Waldheim cases, see Deutscher Bundestag, *Zur Verjährung nationalsozialistischer Verbrechen: Dokumentation der parlamentarischen Bewältigung des Problems, 1960–1979, Teil* 1 (Bonn: Deutscher Bundestag, Presse- und Informationszentrum, 1980), pp. 103–106.

94. There was repression of Communists in West Germany. In August 1956 the Federal Republic banned the German Communist Party. Twenty-seven Communists were imprisoned at that time, and by the early 1960s about 200 were in prison. After 1964 the number was under 100. Nevertheless, the dimensions of this regrettable chapter of the Cold War in the Federal Republic do not begin to compare with the numbers of persons imprisoned on political grounds in the GDR. The German historian Falco Werkintin calculates that between 1953 and 1964, the largest number of political prisoners in any given year in West Germany was 171 (1961) and the lowest was 27 (1957) or fewer. The comparable figures for any given year in East Germany were 15,258 just preceeding the amnesty of 1956 and 2,528 in 1964. See Falco Werkentin, "Die Reichweite politischer Justiz in der Ara Ulbricht," in Bundesministerium der Justiz, *Im Namen des Volkes: Über die Justiz im Staat der SED: Wissenschaftlicher Begleitband* (Leipzig: Forum Verlag, 1994), p. 179.

95. On deradicalization, see Muller, *The Other God That Failed.*

96. Lemke, "Kompagnen gegen Bonn," pp. 153–175.

97. Ausschuss fur Deutsche Einheit, *Gestern Hitlers Blutrichter, Heute Bonner Justiz-Elite* ([East] Berlin: Ausschuss fur Deutsche Einheit, 1957).

98. Committee for German Unity, *Hitler's Special Judges—Pillars of the Adenauer Government,* International Press Conference of the Committee for German Unity, October 14, 1957 ([East] Berlin: Committee for German Unity, 1957), p. 1.

99. Committee for German Unity, *We Accuse: Eight Hundred Bloodstained Nazi Judges Uphold the Adenauer Regime* ([East] Berlin: Ausschuss fur Deutsche Einheit, 1959), p. 5.

100. Ibid., pp. 7–8.

101. Albert Norden, "Der Schlüssel zum Geheimnis unserer Siege: Diskussionsrede

auf dem V. Parteitag der Sozialistischen Einheitspartei Deutschlands vom 10. bis. 16. Juli 1958 in Berlin" (July 12, 1958), in *Die Nation und Wir,* 2:104–119.

102. Albert Norden, "Mörder über Westdeutschland: Aus der Rede auf der internationalen Pressekonferenz des Ausschusses für Deutsche Einheit in Berlin" (October 21, 1958), in *Die Nation und Wir,* 2:120–133.

103. Ibid. p. 121.

104. Ibid., p. 128.

105. Ibid., p. 131.

106. See Ausschuss fur Deutsche Einheit, *Der Oberländer Prozess: Gekurztes Protokoll der Verhandlung vor dem Obersten Gericht der Deutschen Demokratischen Republik vom 20.-27. und 29.4.1960* ([East] Berlin: Ausschuss fur Deutsche Einheit, 1960); and *Im Namen der Völker.*

107. Albert Norden, "Aus der Rede auf der internationale Pressekonferenz des Ausschusses für Deutsche Einheit" (February 2, 1960) in *Der Oberlander Prozess,* p. 190.

108. See "Die Anklage," and "Das Urteil," in *Der Oberländer Prozess,* pp. 11–18, 195–233.

109. *Der Oberlander Prozess,* p. 7.

110. Ibid., p. 8.

111. Ibid., p. 162. On Globke, see Klaus Gotto, ed., *Der Staatssekretär Adenauers: Persönlichkeit und politisches Wirken Hans Globkes* (Stuttgart: Klett-Cotta, 1980).

112. Lemke, "Kompagnen gegen Bonn," 168–169.

113. Albert Norden, "Der Eichmann von Bonn" (July 28, 1960), in *Die Nation und Wir,* 2:198–209.

114. Ibid., p. 209.

115. Albert Norden, "Im Namen des Guten Deutschlands," in *Im Namen der Völker,* pp. 9–14.

116. Ibid., p. 10.

117. Ibid., pp. 213–234.

118. Nationalrat der Nationalen Front des Demokratischen Deutschland, Dokumentationzentrum der Staatlichen Archivverwaltung der DDR, *Braunbuch: Kriegs- und Naziverbrecher in der Bundesrepublik: Staat, Wirtschaft, Armee, Verwaltung, Justiz, Wissenschaft* ([East] Berlin: Staatsverlag der Deutschen Demokratischen Republik, 1965). An—undated—English edition, published around the same time, is the edition to which the citations refer. See National Council of the National Front of Democratic Germany, Documentation Center of the State Archives Administration of the German Democratic Republic, *Brown Book: War and Nazi Criminals in West Germany: State, Economy, Administration, Army, Justice, Science* ([East] Berlin: Verlag Zeit im Bild, n.d.). The criticism began in the late 1950s. See Ausschuss für Deutsche Einheit, *Gestern Hitlers Blutrichter.*

119. National Front, *Brown Book,* p. 13.

120. Ibid. These former Nazi officials allegedly included 21 ministers and state secretaries; 100 generals and admirals in the Bundeswehr; 828 high judicial officials, public prosecutors, and judges; 245 leading officials and diplomats in the Foreign Office, the Bonn embassies, and consulates; and 297 high officials of national, state, and local police as well as officials of the Verfassungsschutz, the national police.

121. Untersuchungsausschuss Freiheitlicher Juristen, *Dokumente des Unrechts* (West Berlin: Reiter-Druck, 1952); see also Untersuchungsausschuss Freiheitlicher Juristen, *Der Staats-sicherheitsdienst, Terror als System* (West Berlin–Zehlendorf, 1956).

122. Untersuchungsausschuss Freiheitlicher Juristen, *Ehemalige Nationalsozialisten in Pankows Diensten* (West Berlin–Zehlendorf, 1958). The first edition ran 40 pages. The editions for 1959, 1962, and 1965 grew to 64, 115, and 102 pages, respectively. The 1959 edition was also published in English. See Untersuchungsausschuss Freiheitlicher Juristen, *Ex-Nazis in the German Democratic Republic* (West Berlin–Zehlendorf, 1959). In 1957 the Association of Democratic Jurists in Germany (East Berlin) denounced the Investigating Committee as comprising "fascist and criminal elements." See Vereinigung Demokratischer Juristen Deutschlands, *Faschistische und kriminelle Elemente unter der Maske "freiheitlicher Juristen": Dokumentation uber den leiter und einige Hauptagenten des sogenannten Untersuchungsausschusses Freiheitlicher Juristen in Berlin-Zehlendorf West* ([East] Berlin, 1957).

123. Untersuchungsausschuss Freiheitlicher Juristen, *Ehemalige Nationalsozialisten in Pankows Diensten,* pp. 3–4.

124. Ibid., pp. 4–5.

125. Ibid., p. 6.

126. Ibid., pp. 7–8.

127. Ibid., pp. 8–9.

128. Olaf Kappelt, *Braunbuch DDR: Nazis in der DDR* (Berlin: E. Reichman, 1981), pp. 269–270.

129. Cited in Untersuchungsausschuss Freiheitlicher Juristen, *Ehemalige Nationalsozialisten in Pankows Diensten,* 5th. rev. ed. (West Berlin-Zehlendorf, 1965), p. 4.

130. Ibid., pp. 5, 11, 49.

131. See also Kappelt, *Braunbuch DDR,* pp. 207–208.

132. Untersuchungsausschuss Freiheitlicher Juristen, *Ehemaligen Nationalsozialisten in Pankows Diensten,* pp. 6, 37. Olaf Kappelt reports that an "Internationale Komitee für Information und Soziale Aktion (CIAS)" in Luxembourg had concluded that as a result of his actions in Sachsenhausen, Grossmann "stood under great suspicion of having committed crimes against humanity." Kappelt, *Braunbuch DDR,* pp. 212–213.

133. On Melsheimer, see "Ernst Melsheimer," in Cerny, *Wer war Wer—DDR,* p. 306; "Ernst Melsheimer," in Kappelt, *Braunbuch DDR,* pp. 299–300; and especially Falco Werkentin, "Richter und Ankläger in vier politischen Systemen—die Karriere

des Genossen Generalstaatsanwalt Dr. Ernst Melsheimer," text of radio broadcast for Norddeutsche Rundfunk, January 4, 1993.

134. Werkentin, "Richter und Ankläger," p. 4.

135. "Ernst Melsheimer," in Cerny, *Wer war Wer—DDR*, p. 306; and Werkentin, "Richter und Ankläger," p. 4.

136. "50. Geburtstag von Dr. Melsheimer 1947," SAPMO-BA Bildarchiv 983/670N.

137. He wrote that "if there is to be Anti-Fascism, [it should be aimed] then against all who are Fascists or who make use of fascist methods." The East German propagandists, "who for years have exercised the monopoly of being the constant accuser, should also see that this role does not suit them" because the accusations concerning a Nazi past "can be turned against them too." Simon Wiesenthal, *The Same Language: First for Hitler—Now for Ulbricht: Simon Wiesenthal's Press Conference on September 6, 1968* (Vienna: Deutschland Berichte, 1968), pp. 2, 6.

138. Ibid., p. 14.

139. Ibid.

140. Ibid., p. 13.

141. There is a considerable literature on the relationship between the two Germanys and the conflict in the Middle East. For work that draws on the recently opened SED archives, see Wolfgang Schwanitz, "SED-Naholstpolitik als Chefsache: Die ZK-Abteilung Internationale Verbindungen 1946–1970 sowie die Nachlässe von Otto Grotewohl und Walter Ulbricht," *asien afrika lateinamerika* 21 (1993), 63–90; and "Judenargwohn? Zum Israel-Bild in SED-Akten über arabische Länder (1948–1968)," *Orient* 35, no. 4 (1994), 635–667. See also Erica Burgauer, *Zwischen Erinnerung und Verdrängung—Juden in Deutschland nach 1945* (Reinbek bei Hamburg: Rowohlt, 1993); Inge Deutschkron, *Israel und die Deutschen*, rev. ed. (Cologne: Verlag Wissenschaft und Politik, 1991); Peter Dittmar, "DDR und Israel: Ambivalenz einer Nicht-Beziehung," *Deutschland-Archiv*, pt. 1 (July 1977), 736–754, and pt. 2 (August 1977), 848–861; Lily Gardner Feldman, *The Special Relationship between West Germany and Israel* (Boston: George Allen and Unwin, 1984); and Michael Wolffsohn, *Forty Years of German-Jewish-Israeli Relations*, trans. Douglas Bokovoy (New York: Columbia University Press, 1993).

142. "Agypten: Abschluß eines Abkommens über den Handels- und Zahlungsverkehr mit Agypten," in *Dokumente zur Außenpolitik der Regierung der Deutsche Demokratische Republik*, vol. 1, *1949–1954* ([East] Berlin: Rütten & Loening: 1955), pp. 505–506; hereafter *DARDDR*.

143. See Burgauer, *Zwischen Erinnerung und Verdrängung*, p. 190; Peter Dittmar, "Israel und die Deutschen," pt. 2, *Deutschland Archiv* 10 (August 1977), 850.

144. Peter Dittmar, "DDR und Israel," pt. 1, *Deutschland Archiv* 10 (July 1977), 750–751; see also the documents reprinted in *Dokumente der Außenpolitik der*

*Deutschen Demokratischen Republik,* vols. 5–8 ([East] Berlin: Rutten & Loewing, 1955–1959).

145. Otto Grotewohl to Gamel Abdel Nasser (June 24, 1957), Otto Grotewohl NL 90/497, SAPMO-BA, ZPA, pp. 67–75.

146. Ibid., pp. 70–71.

147. Ibid. See also Grotewohl's letter to Nasser of October 24, 1958, in which he praised the "anti-imperialist liberation struggle of the Arab peoples." Otto Grotewohl to Gamel Abdel Nasser (October 24, 1958), Otto Grotewohl NL 90/497, SAPMO-BA, ZPA, p. 87.

148. Glückwunschtelegramm des Ministerpräsidenten Otto Grotewohl an den Präsidenten der Vereinigten Arabischen Republik, Gamal Abdel Nasser, anläßlich des Nationalfeiertages am 23. Juli 1958," in *DARDDR,* vol. 6, 1958, pp. 481–482.

149. "Erklärung des Ministerpräsident der DDR, Otto Grotewohl über seinen Besuch in der Vereinigten Arabischen Republik," Otto Grotewohl NL 90/491, SAPMO-BA, ZPA, pp. 408–409.

150. Otto Grotewohl, *Neues Deutschland,* November 3, 1956; cited in Deutschkron, *Israel und die Deutschen,* p. 190. He also charged that the Israelis were using West German restitution "to pay for armaments which are used against the Arab peoples." Otto Grotewohl, *Neues Deutschland,* April 4, 1957; cited by Deutschkron, *Israel und die Deutschen,* p. 191; see also Burgauer, *Zwischen Erinnerung und Verdrängung,* pp. 189–190.

151. Gerhard Weiss (Baghdad, October 27, 1958), in *DARDDR, Band* 6, p. 317; see also Dittmar, "DDR und Israel," (pt. 1), p. 751; and Deutsckron, *Israel und die Deutschen,* p. 191. As a German prisoner of war in the Soviet Union, Weiss had attended "antifascist" school while in captivity. See "Gerhard Weiss," in Cerny, *Wer war Wer—DDR,* p. 478.

152. See "Glückwunschtelegramm des Präsidenten Wilhelm Pieck an Gamal Abdel Nasser anläßlich dessen Wahl zum präsidenten der Vereinigten Arabischen Republik am 21. Februar 1958," in *DARDDR, Band* 6, p. 473; Glückwunschtelegramm des Ministerpräsident Otto Grotewohl an den Präsidenten der Vereinigten Arabschen Republik, Gamal Abdel Nasser, anläßlich des Nationalfeiertages am 23. Juli 1958," in *DARDDR,* vol. 6, p. 481.

153. See Deutschkron, *Israel und die Deutschen,* pp. 287–314; and Rolf Vogel, ed., *Der deutsch-israelische Dialog, Teil* 1, *Politik, Band* 1 (Munich: K. G. Sauer, 1987), pp. 253–305.

154. Walter Ulbricht, "Interview der VAR Zeitung 'Al Ahram'" (February 23, 1965), in *DARDDR,* vol. 13 ([East] Berlin: Staatsverlag der Deutschen Demokratischen Republik, 1969), pp. 847–848.

155. Walter Ulbricht (Cairo, February 24, 1965), in *DARDDR,* vol. 13, p. 850.

156. Walter Ulbricht and Gamal Abdel Nasser, "Gemeinsame Erklärung" (Cairo, March 1, 1965), in *DARDDR,* vol. 13, p. 855.

157. "Abkommen zwischen der Regierung der Deutschen Demokratischen Republik und der Regierung der Vereinigten Arabischen Republik über kulturelle und wissenschaftliche Zusammenarbeit vom 1. März 1965," in *DARDDR*, vol. 13, pp. 858–863.

158. Walter Ulbricht, "Rundfunk- und Fernsehinterview . . . mit Gerhart Eisler" (East Berlin, March 7, 1965), in *DARDDR*, vol. 13, pp. 872–873.

159. Ibid., p. 475.

160. Ibid., pp. 875–876.

161. Ibid. p. 876. See "Gerhart Eisler," in Cerny, ed., *Wer war Wer—DDR*, pp. 98–99. Eisler had been in the United States during World War II, then fled congresional anticommunist investigations in 1949 and became a leading figure in the SED and in East German radio and television.

162. Walter Ulbricht, "Kommunique uber die 16. Sitzung des Staatsrates der Deutschen Demokratischen Republik am 12. März 1965," in *DARDDR*, vol. 13, p. 881.

163. Ibid.

164. Lothar Bolz, "Rede des Ministers für Auswärtige Angelegenheiten der DDR" (March 24, 1965), in *DARDDR*, vol. 13, pp. 887–896; see also *Neues Deutschland*, March 25, 1965.

165. Bolz, "Rede des Ministers," pp. 887–896.

166. Ibid., pp. 892–893.

167. "Interview der Kairoer Zeitung 'Akhbar el Yom' mit dem Vorsitzenden des Staatsrates der Deutschen Demokratischen Republik, Walter Ulbricht, über die Beziehungen der DDR zu den arabischen Staaten und die Lösung der deutschen Frage" (August 21, 1965), in *DARDDR*, vol. 13, pp. 909–914; first published in *Neues Deutschland* (East Berlin), August 22, 1965.

168. Ibid., pp. 911–913.

169. Walter Ulbricht, *The Two German States and the Aggression in the Near East* (Dresden: Verlag Zeit im Bild, 1967). See also Walter Ulbricht, "Rede . . . im Leipzig am 15. Juni 1967 zu Fragen der Lage im Nahen Osten und zur westdeutsche Expansionspolitik im Rahmen der USA-Globalstrategie," in *DARDDR*, vol. 15 ([East] Berlin: Staatsverlag der Deutschen Demokratischen Republik, 1971), pp. 515–538; and "Interview mit dem Minister für Auswärtige Angelegenheiten der Deutschen Demokratisiche Republik, Otto Winzer, nach seiner Rückkehr von der Außenministerkonferenz europäischer sozialistischer Staaten in Warschau am 21. Dezember 1967," in *DARDDR*, vol. 15:2 ([East] Berlin: Staatsverlag der Deutschen Demokratischen Republik, 1970), pp. 570–571.

170. "Erklärung eines Sprechers des Ministeriums für Auswärtige Angelegenheiten der Deutschen Demokratischen Republik vom 11. November 1967 zur Reise des früheren westdeutschen Bundeskanzlers Ludwig Erhard nach Israel," in *DARDDR*, vol. 15: 2, p. 566. See also vol. 1 for 1967 for East German statements on the Six Day War. The use of words such as "conspiracy" to describe Western support for Israel may have been on the mind of the historian Walter Laqueur when he observed that

East German's anti-Israel denunciations made Moscow's *Pravda* seem "moderate and statesmanlike." Cited in Dittmar, "DDR und Israel" (pt. 2), p. 850.

171. See Karen Hartewig, "Jüdische Kommunisten in der DDR und ihr Verhältnis zu Israel," in Wolfang Schwanitz, ed., *Jenseits der Legende: Araber, Juden, Deutsche* (Berlin: Dietz, 1994, pp. 130–136; and Helmut Eschwege, *Fremd unter Meinesgleichen: Erinnerungen eines Dresdner Juden* (Berlin: Ch. Links, 1991).

172. Albert Norden to Werner Lamberz (June 9, 1967), in Walter Ulbricht NL 182/1339, SAPMO-BA, ZPA; cited by Hartewig, "Jüdische Kommunisten," pp. 218–219.

173. See Dittmar, "DDR und Israel" (pt. 2), pp. 849–961. One of the leading figures of East German foreign policy in these years was Herman Axen (1916–1992). Axen, who had been interned in Vernet then Buchenwald and Auschwitz, was editor in chief of *Neues Deutschland* (1956–1966), a member of the SED Politiburo from 1970, and from 1966 secretary of the Central Committee responsible for international affairs. See "Herman Axen," in Cerny, *Wer war Wer—DDR*, pp. 19–20. See also Herman Axen, *Starker Sozialismus—sicherer Frieden: Ausgewählte Reden und Aufsätze* ([East] Berlin: Dietz Verlag, 1981); and *Kampf um den Frieden—Schlüsselfrage der Gegenwart: Ausgewählte Reden und Aufsätze* ([East] Berlin: Dietz Verlag, 1986).

174. The many joint communiqués, reports of press conferences in East Berlin and Arab capitals, and official government statements are published in the annual foreign policy documents of the German Democratic Republic *(Dokumente zur Außenpolitik der Deutschen Demokratischen Republik)* for 1971 to the mid-1980s. See also "Erich Honnecker," in Cerny, *Wer war wer—DDR*, pp. 201–202.

175. Peter Florin, "Rede in der Nahostdebatte des Sicherheitsrates der Vereinten Nationen," in *DARDDR, Band* 24, vol. 2, *1976* ([East] Berlin: Staatsverlag der Deutschen Demokratische Republik, 1980), pp. 908–911.

176. See Peter Florin's representative contributions to debate on "the Palestine question" at the United Nations on November 4, 1975, in *DARDDR*, vol. 23:2 ([East] Berlin: Staatsverlag der Deutschen Demokratischen Republik, 1979), pp. 1037–40.

177. "Mitteilung über den Besuch des Mitglieds des Exekutivkomitees und Leiter der Politischen Abteilung der Palästinensischen Befreiungsorganisation (PLO), Farouk al-Kaddoumi, in der Deutschen Demokratischen Republik" (September 9, 1980), and "Mitteilung über das Gespräch zwischen dem Generalsekretär des Zentralkomitees der SED und Vorsitzenden des Staatsrates der DDR, Erich Honecker, und dem Vorsitzenden des Exekutivkomitees der Palästinensischen Befreiungsorganisation (PLO), Yasser Arafat, in Berlin" (December 29, 1980), in *DARDDR*, vol. 28, *Halbband* 1 ([East] Berlin: Staatsverlag der Deutschen Demokratischen Republik, 1980), pp. 525–527, 528–530.

178. See, for example, "Mitteilung über den Empfang einer Militärdelegation der Palästinensischen Befreiungsorganisation (PLO) beim Generalsekretär des Zentralkomitees der SED und Vorsitzenden des Staatrates der DDR, Erich Honecker" (No-

vember 17, 1981), in *DARDDR*, vol. 28:1, pp. 224–225; see also *Neues Deutschland*, November 18, 1981.

179. Harry Ott, "Sondertagung der Vollversammlung der Vereinten Nationen zur Palästinafrage" (September 24, 1982), in *DARDDR*, vol. 30 ([East] Berlin: Staatsverlag der Deutschen Demokratischen Republik, 1985), pp. 514–515; first published in *Neues Deutschland*, September 21, 1982, p. 3.

180. Deutschkron, *Israel und die Deutschen*, pp. 197–198. See *DARDDR*, vols. 14–32 ([East] Berlin: Staatsverlag der Deutschen Demokratischen Republik, 1967–1977).

181. Thomas Mann, "Deutschland und die Deutschen," in *Gesammelte Werke in zwölf Bänden*, vol. 11 (Frankfurt am Main: S. Fischer, 1960), p. 1146.

## 7. Divided Memory in the Western Zones

1. U.S. Department of State, *Documents on Germany, 1944–1985* Department of State Publication no. 9446, (Washington, D.C.: Office of the Historian, Bureau of Public Affairs, 1986), pp. 17–18. On the occupation, see also Dennis L. Bark and David R. Gress, *A History of West Germany*, vol. 1, *From Shadow to Substance, 1945–1963* (Cambridge, Mass.: Basil Blackwell, 1989), pp. 26–29; Wolfgang Benz, ed., *Die Geschichte der Bundesrepublik Deutschland, Band 1, Politik*, rev. and expanded ed. (Frankfurt am Main: Fischer Taschenbuch Verlag, 1989); and Theodor Eschenburg, *Jahre der Besatzung, 1945–1949*, vol. 1 of *Geschichte der Bundesrepublik Deutschland* (Stuttgart: Deutsche Verlags-Anstalt, 1983).

2. U.S. Department of State, *Documents on Germany*, pp. 91–99.

3. Michael H. Kater, *The Nazi Party: A Social Profile of Members and Leaders, 1919–1945* (Cambridge, Mass.: Harvard University Press, 1983), p. 262.

4. The dilemma was one familiar to Americans. In the Reconstruction era following the Civil War, Lincoln's successors opted for a democracy of whites in the South accompanied by segregation in place of fulfillment of the hopes raised by the Civil War for a radical challenge to racist practices. Full equality for blacks in the Reconstruction era was possible only against the will of the racist white majorities in the "solid South." See Jeffrey Herf, "Multiple Restorations vs. the 'Solid South': Continuities and Discontinuities in Germany after 1945 and in the American South after 1865," in Norbert Finzsch, ed., *Different Restorations: Reconstruction and "Wiederaufbau" in Germany and the United States in Comparative Perspective: 1865, 1945, 1990*. (Providence: Berghahn Books, 1996), pp. 48–86. See also John D. Montgomery, *Forced to Be Free: The Artificial Revolution in Germany and Japan* (Chicago: University of Chicago Press, 1957).

5. On disillusionment with Nazism in German society beginning in 1943, see Martin Broszat, Klaus Dietmar Henke, and Hans Woller, eds., *Von Stalingrad bis zur Währungsreform: Zur Sozialgeschichte des Umbruchs in Deutschland*, 3d ed. (Munich: R. Oldenbourg, 1990); and Jerry Z. Muller, *The Other God That Failed: Hans Freyer and*

*the Deradicalization of German Conservatism* (Princeton: Princeton University Press, 1987).

6. Klaus-Dietmar Henke, "Die Trennung vom Nationalsozialismus: Selbstzerstörung, politische Säuberung, 'Entnazifizierung,' Strafverfolgung," in Klaus Dietmar Henke and Hans Woller, eds., *Politische Säuberung in Europa: Die Abrechnung mit Faschismus und Kollaboration nach dem Zweiten Weltkrieg* (Munich: Deutscher Taschenbuch Verlag, 1991), pp. 3, 21–83; and Clemens Vollnhals, *Entnazifizierung: Politische Säuberung und Rehabilitierung in den vier Besatzungszonen, 1945–1949* (Munich: Deutscher Taschenbuch Verlag, 1991).

7. Henke, "Die Trennung vom Nationalsozialismus," p. 54.

8. See Christa Schick, "Die Internierungslager," in Broszat, Henke, and Woller, *Von Stalingrad zur Währungsreform*, pp. 301–326; see also Jörg Friedrich, *Die kalte Amnestie: NS-Täter in der Bunderepublik* (Frankfurt am Main: Fischer, 1984).

9. Henke, "Die Trennung von Nationalsozialismsus," p. 34.

10. Ibid., pp. 41, 51–52. In the American zone, for example, 3,441,800 came under suspicion, three-quarters of whom were amnestied or had their cases closed without an indictment. Of 945,000 cases pursued, only 10 percent led to an oral hearing. Only 1,654 persons. 0.05 percent of the total, were judged to be in "Group I," meaning "major guilt" *(Hauptschuldige)*, and 22,122, or 0.6 percent, were "burdened" *(Belastete);* most of these persons were subsequently reassigned to less incriminating categories.

11. See Lutz Niethammer, *Die Mitläuferfabrik: Entnazifizierung am Beispiel Bayerns* (Berlin: Dietz Verlag, 1982).

12. See Frank Stern, *Im Anfang war Auschwitz: Antisemitismusm und Philosemitismus im deutschen Nachkrieg* (Gerlingen: Bleicher Verlag, 1991), pp. 79–81 and chaps. 1–3, 6, 8 passim.

13. Moses Moskowitz, "The Germans and the Jews: Postwar Report," *Commentary* 1, no. 2 (1946), p. 7; cited ibid., p. 100.

14. See Stern, *Im Anfang war Auschwitz,* pp. 118–124.

15. OMGUS, "Opinion Survey Section, Report no. 49 (March 3, 1947), NA Rg. 260, 5/233–3/5; cited ibid., p. 126.

16. Anna J. Merritt and Richard L. Merritt, *Public Opinion in Occupied Germany: The OMGUS Surveys, 1945–1949* (Urbana: University of Illinois Press, 1970), p. 38. See also Richard L. Merritt, *Democracy Imposed: U.S. Occupation Policy and the German Public, 1945–1949* (New Haven: Yale University Press, 1995).

17. Merritt and Merritt, *Public Opinion,* pp. 32–33, 39.

18. Ibid., p. 40. On anti-Semitism after 1945 in West Germany, see Werner Bergmann and Rainer Erb, eds., *Antisemitismus in der politischen Kultur nach 1945* (Opladen: West deutscher Verlag, 1990); and Frederick Weil, "The Imperfectly Mastered Past: Anti-Semitism in West Germany Since the Holocaust," *New German Critique* 20 (1980), 135–153.

19. Merritt and Merritt, *Public Opinion*, p. 35.

20. In these trials 177 persons were accused; 35 were found innocent, 98 were sentenced to extended prison sentences, and 20 to life in prison. Death sentences were pronounced on 7 doctors who conducted murderous experiments, 3 SS officials who had responsibility for concentration camps, and 14 members of Einsatzgruppen. The Allies carried out 12 of those death sentences. See Jörg Friedrich, "Das Nürnberger Tatschema," in *Die kalte Amnestie*, pp. 51–120; and Henke, "Die Trennung vom Nationalsozialismus," pp. 72–73. See also Frank M. Buscher, *The U.S. War Crimes Trial Program in Germany, 1946 to 1955* (New York: Greenwood Press, 1989); and Telford Taylor, *The Anatomy of the Nuremberg Trials* (New York: Alfred A. Knopf, 1992).

21. See *Trials of War Criminals before the Nuremberg Military Tribunals under Control Council Law No. 10, Nuremberg, October 1946–April 1949*, 15 vols. (Washington, D.C.: U.S. Government Printing Office, 1949–1955).

22. Albrecht Götz, *Bilanz der Verfolgung von NS-Straftaten* (Cologne: Bundesanzeiger, 1986), p. 29.

23. See Michael R. Marrus, *The Nuremberg War Crimes Trial 1945–46: A Documentary History* (Boston: Bedford Books, 1997), pp. 185–216.

24. See Constantine Goschler, *Wiedergutmachung: Westdeutschland und die Verfolgten des Nationalsozialismus (1954–1954)* (Munich: R. Oldenbourg, 1992); and Hans-Dieter Kreikamp, "Zur Entstehung des Entschädigungsgesetzes der amerikanischen Besatzungszone," in Ludolf Herbst and Constantine Goschler, *Wiedergutmachung in der Bundesrepublik Deutschland* (Munich: R. Oldenbourg, 1989), pp. 61–76.

25. Between 1945 and 1950, about 10 million Germans became refugees, and somewhat over 2 million German civilians died. In the Soviet occupation zone, thousands of women were raped by soldiers of the Red Army. An active lobby of "expellees" *(Vertriebene)* kept the memory of these events before the West German public. See Bark and Gress, *A History of West Germany*, 35–39. On rape in the occupation years, see Norman M. Naimark, *The Russians in Germany: A History of the Soviet Zone of Occupation, 1945–1949* (Cambridge, Mass.: Harvard University Press, 1995).

26. See Jeffrey Herf, "Belated Pessimism: Technology and Twentieth-Century German Conservative Intellectuals," in Yaron Ezrahi, Everett Mendelsohn, and Howard Segal, eds. *Technology, Pessimism, and Postmodernism* (Dordrecht: Klewer Academic Publishers, 1994). For criticism of the resort to such reification, see Günter Grass's satire of "the Führerdog attuned to distantiality" in *The Tin Drum*, trans. Ralph Mannheim (New York: Harcourt, Brace and Jovanovich, 1965), pp. 352–353.

27. See statements of Robert Jackson, Hartley Shawcross, and Telford Taylor in *Trial of the Major War Criminals before the International Military Tribunal*, vol. 2 *14 November 1945–30 November 1945* (Washington, D.C.: U.S. Government Printing Office, 1947); *Trial of the Major War Criminals before the International Military Tribunal*, vol. 3 *1 December 1945–14 December 1945* (Washington, D.C.: U.S. Government

Printing Office, 1947); *Trial of the Major War Criminals before the International Military Tribunal*, vol. 19 *19 July 1946–29 July 1946* (Washington, D.C.: U.S. Government Printing Office, 1947), pp. 397–529.

28. Herbert Jäger, *Verbrechen unter totalitärer Herrschaft: Studien zur nationalsozialistischen Gewaltkriminalität* (Frankfurt am Main: Suhrkamp, 1982).

29. Henning Köhler, *Adenauer: Eine politische Biographie* (Frankfurt am Main: Propyläen, 1994), pp. 268–272; and Hans-Peter Schwarz, *Konrad Adenauer: Der Aufstieg, 1876–1952* (Stuttgart: Deutsche Verlagsanstalt, 1986).

30. Köhler, *Adenauer*, pp. 270–271.

31. On Heinemann, see Schwarz, *Konrad Adenauer*, pp. 182–185.

32. See Henning Köhler, "Im Dritten Reich," in *Adenauer*, pp. 273–322; and Schwarz, *Konrad Adenauer*.

33. Kohler, *Adenauer*, pp. 311–312; and Schwarz, *Konrad Adenauer*, pp. 403–411.

34. Köhler, *Adenauer*, pp. 320–321; Schwarz, *Konrad Adenauer*, p. 418.

35. "Konrad Adenauer to Simon J. Vogel" (March 14, 1948), in Hans Peter Mensing, ed., *Adenauer: Briefe, 2: 1947–1949* (Berlin: Siedler Verlag, 1984), p. 187. *Adenauer* never remarried.

36. See Schwarz, *Konrad Adenauer*, pp. 425–616.

37. See my comments on Adenauer and militant democracy in Jeffrey Herf, *War by Other Means: Soviet Power, West German Resistance, and the Battle of the Euromissiles* (New York: Free Press, 1991), pp. 14–26.

38. On the contending voices within the Christian Democratic Union and their views of Nazism, see Maria Mitchell, "Materialism and Secularism: CDU Politicians and National Socialism, 1945–1949," *Journal of Modern History* 67, no. 2 (June 1995), 278–308.

39. Konrad Adenauer, "Ansprache des Oberbürgermeisters Adenauer vor der von der britischen Militärregierung ernannten Kölner Stadtverordneten-Vewrsammlung," in Hans-Peter Schwarz, ed., *Konrad Adenauer: Reden, 1917–1967: Eine Auswahl* (Stuttgart: Deutsche Verlagsanstalt, 1975), pp. 79–81. Adenauer kept his distance from the Christian Democratic Union and did not participate in drafting the CDU's appeal of June 1945. See "Ein Ruf zur Sammlung des deutschen Volkes, Vorläufiger Entwurf zu einem Programm der Christlichen Demokraten Deutschlands, Vorgelegt von den Christlichen Demokraten *Kölns* im June 1945," in Konrad Adenauer Stiftung, ed., *Konrad Adenauer und die CDU der britischen Besatzungszone, 1946–1949* (Bonn: Eichholz Verlag, 1975).

40. Adenauer, *Reden, 1917–1967*, pp. 79–81.

41. Hans-Peter Schwarz, *Konrad Adenauer*, pp. 467–478; and "Entlassung und Ausweisung Adenauers als Oberburgermeister von Köln," in *Adenauer: Briefe, 2: 1945–1947*, pp. 116–118.

42. On the lessons Adenauer drew from German and European history, see Anneli-

ese Poppinga, *Konrad Adenauer: Geschichtsverständnis, Weltanschauung, und politische Praxis* (Stuttgart: Deutsche Verlags-Anstalt, 1975).

43. Konrad Adenauer, "Grundsatzrede des 1. Vorsitzenden der Christlich-Demokratischen Union für die Britische Zone in der Aula der Kölner Universität," in *Reden, 1917–1967*, pp. 82–107.

44. Ibid., p. 84.

45. Ibid., pp. 83–85.

46. Ibid., p. 84.

47. Ibid., p. 85.

48. Ibid.

49. Ibid., p. 86. On the postwar criticism of materialism among CDU politicians in the occupation years, see Mitchell, "Materialism and Secularism."

50. Adenauer, *Reden, 1917–1967*, p. 86.

51. See Herf, "Belated Pessimism," pp. 115–36. In the light of academic debates of recent years, it is often forgotten that the critical examination of the German *Sonderweg* in the postwar years was directed against conservative apologias and early attempts to subsume Nazism within a general crisis of modernity.

52. See Jeffrey Herf, "Center, Periphery, and Dissensus: West German Intellectuals and the Euromissiles," in Liah Greenfeld and Michel Martin, eds., *Center: Ideas and Institutions* (Chicago: University of Chicago Press, 1988), pp. 110–129; and Herf, *War by Other Means*, pp. 14–26.

53. Adenauer, *Reden, 1917–1967*, p. 86.

54. Ibid.

55. Ibid., p. 87.

56. Ibid., p. 88.

57. Ibid., p. 92.

58. On the issues of organizational versus individual guilt as they emerged in prosecutions of the Nuremberg defendants, see Taylor, *Anatomy of the Nuremberg Trials*, esp. chaps. 2, 7, 10, and 18.

59. Adenauer, *Reden, 1917–1967*, p. 93.

60. Ibid., p. 98–99.

61. Ibid., p. 99.

62. Ibid., p. 101.

63. Ibid., p. 102.

64. Ibid., p. 104.

65. Ibid., p. 105.

66. On these themes, see Hans-Peter Schwarz, *Vom Reich zur Bundesrepublik: Deutschland im Widerstreit der außenpolitischen Konzeptionen in den Jahren der Besatzungsherrschaft, 1945–1949*, 2d ed. (Berlin: Luchterhand, 1980); Poppinga, *Konrad Adenauer*, p. 157; and Theodor Adorno, "Was bedeutet: Aufarbeitung der Vergangen-

heit," in *Gesammelte Schriften*, vol. 10:2 (Frankfurt am Main: Suhrkamp Verlag, 1977, pp. 555–572.

67. On "integration" in the Federal Republic, see Thomas Schwartz, *America's Germany: John J. McCloy and the Federal Republic of Germany* (Cambridge, Mass.: Harvard University Press, 1991); Herf, *War by Other Means.*

68. See, for example, Konrad Adenauer, "Rede" (April 7, 1946, Bonn), St BKAH, p. 9. See also "Rundfunkrede Oberbürgermeister a.D. Dr. Konrad Adenauer über das Program der CDU" (March 6, 1946, NWDR), St BKAH.

69. Konrad Adenauer, "Rede" (May 5, 1946, Wuppertal), St BKAH, p. 3.

70. Ibid., p. 17. Adenauer repeated this theme in other speeches. See Konrad Adenauer, "Rede" (June 2, 1946, München-Gladbach), St BKAH, p. 11.

71. Konrad Adenauer, "Rede" (May 12, 1946, Dusseldorf), St BKAH.

72. Ibid., p. 4.

73. Konrad Adenauer, "Rede" (May 13, 1945, Pulheim near Cologne), St BKAH, p. 19.

74. Ibid., p. 19. On POWs, see also Konrad Adenauer, "Rede" (September 29, 1946, Mülheim/Ruhr), St BKAH, p. 9.

75. Ibid., p. 24. Adenauer repeated that not all Germans had been Nazi criminals in Konrad Adenauer, "Rede" (September 3, 1946, Siegeburg), St BKAH, p. 16.

76. Konrad Adenauer, "Rede" (July 24, 1946, Cologne), St BKAH, p. 10.

77. Konrad Adenauer, "Rede" (August 11, 1946, Cologne), St BKAH, p. 12.

78. Ibid., p. 12.

79. Ibid., pp. 12–13.

80. Konrad Adenauer, "Rede" (June 2, 1946, München-Gladbach), St BKAH, p. 19.

81. Konrad Adenauer, "Rede" (July 24, 1946, Cologne), St BKAH, p. 9.

82. Ibid.

83. Konrad Adenauer, "Rede" (April 13, 1947, University of Cologne), St BKAH, pp. 11–12.

84. Konrad Adenaur, "Rede" (August 11, 1946, Cologne), St BKAH, p. 17.

85. On the *Männerkult* following World War I, see the discussion of Ernst Jüenger in Jeffrey Herf, *Reactionary Modernism* (New York: Cambridge University Press, 1984); George Mosse, *Fallen Soldiers* (New York: Oxford University Press, 1990); and Klaus Theweleit, *Männerphantasien*, 2 vols. (Frankfurt am Main: Roter Stern Verlag, 1978–79).

86. Cited by Inge Deutsckron, "Das Verhalten der bundesdeutschen Politiker ist eine Schweinerei gegenüber NS-Opfern," in Dieter Bednarz and Michael Lüders, eds., *Blick zurück ohne Haß: Juden aus Deutschland erinnern sich an Deutschland* (Cologne: Bund-Verlag, 1981), p. 62; see also Stern, *Im Anfang war Auschwitz*, p. 309.

87. Theodor Heuss, *Hitlers Weg: Eine historisch-politische Studie über den National-sozialismus* (Stuttgart: Union Deutsche Verlagsgesellschaft, 1932).

88. Ibid., p. 1.

89. Ibid., p. 31.

90. Ibid., p. 32.

91. Ibid.

92. Ibid., pp. 32–33.

93. Ibid., p. 33.

94. Ibid., p. 38.

95. Ibid., pp. 41–42.

96. Ibid., p. 42.

97. Ibid., pp. 43–44.

98. Ibid., pp. 45–46.

99. Ibid., p. 154.

100. Ibid., p. 156.

101. Theodor Heuss, "Reichstagsrede gegen den Nationalsozialismus," in Ralf Dahrendorf and Martin Vogt, eds., *Theodor Heuss: Politiker und Publizist* (Tübingen: Wunderlich Verlag, 1984), p. 219.

102. Ibid., pp. 225–227.

103. Ibid., p. 230.

104. On Heuss, German liberals, and the collapse of the Weimar Republic, see Jürgen C. Heß, *Theodor Heuss vor 1933: Ein Beitrag zur Geschichte des demokratischen Denkens in Deutschland* (Stuttgart: Klett, 1973); Larry Eugene Jones, *German Liberalism and the Dissolution of the Weimar Party System, 1918–1933* (Chapel Hill: University of North Carolina Press, 1988); and Theodor Heuss, *Die Machtergreifung und das Er-mächtigungsgesetz: Zwei Nachgelassene Kapitel der Erinnerungen, 1905–1933*, ed. Eberhard Pikart (Tübingen: Rainer Wunderlich Verlag, 1967).

105. Theodor Heuss, "Lebenslauf" (August 1945), in *Theodor Heuss: Aufzeichnungen, 1945–1947* (Tübingen: Rainer Wunderlich Verlag 1966), p. 104.

106. Ibid.

107. Theodor Heuss, "Aussage vor dem Untersuchungsausschuß des Würtembergisch-Badischen Landtags über die Abstimmung für das Ermächtigungsgesetz am 23. März 1933," in Dahrendorf and Vogt, *Theodor Heuss: Politiker und Publizist*, pp. 316–321.

108. Heuss, *Die Machtergreifung und das Ermächtigungsgesetz*, p. 23.

109. Ibid., p. 26.

110. For a critical view of Heuss and "philo-Semitism," see Stern, *Im Anfang war Auschwitz*, pp. 248–249.

111. Theodor Heuss, "Das Ende (9–17. Mai 1945)," in *Theodor Heuss: Aufzeich-*

*nungen*, pp. 50–76. On Heuss in the early postwar years, see the valuable essay by Jürgen C. Heß, "'Erste Wege durch die Ruinenfeld': Theodor Heuss und der Neubeginn der liberaler Rhetorik 1945–46," in Jürgen C. Hess, Hartmut Lehmann, and Volker Sellin, eds., *Heidelberg, 1945* (Stuttgart: Franz Steiner Verlag, 1996), pp. 348–386.

112. Ibid., p. 53.

113. Ibid., pp. 65–66.

114. Ibid., p. 73.

115. Theodor Heuss, "Betrachtungen zur Innerpolitischen Lage (30. Mai 1945)," in *Theodor Heuss: Aufzeichnungen*, p. 78.

116. Ibid., pp. 78–79.

117. Ibid. p. 84.

118. Ibid.

119. Ibid., pp. 84–85.

120. Ibid., p. 87.

121. Ibid., p. 88.

122. Theodor Heuss, "In Memoriam: Anspruche im Landestheater Stuttgart, 25. November 1945," in *Theodor Heuss: An und Über Juden* (Düsseldorf: Econ Verlag, 1964), pp. 94–101.

123. Ibid., p. 95.

124. Ibid., pp. 96–97.

125. Ibid., p. 100.

126. Ibid., pp. 100–101.

127. Eberhard Pikart, "Einleitung," in *Theodor Heuss: Aufzeichnungen* pp. 11–31, 374. On Allied occupation policy and the emergence of the press, see Norbert Frei, "Die Presse," in Wolfgang Benz, ed., *Die Geschichte der Bundesrepublik Deutschland, Band 4, Kultur* (Frankfurt am Main: Fischer Taschenbuch Verlag, 1989), pp. 370–417; Theodor Eschenburg, *Jahre der Besatzung', 1945–1949*, vol. 1, *Geschichte der Bundesrepublik Deutschland* (Stuttgart: Deutsche Verlags-Anstalt, 1983); and Harold Hurwitz, *Die Stunde Null der deutschen Presse: Die amerikanische Pressepolitik in Deutschland, 1945–1949* (Cologne: Verlag Wissenschaft und Politik, 1970). Between July 1945 and September 1949, the Western powers licensed 156 new newspapers (62 American, 61 British, 33 French). The license holders *(Lizensträger)* were not permitted to publish "nationalist, pan-German, militarist, fascist or anti-democratic ideas," foster disunity among the Allies, or encourage public antagonism to the occupation.

128. "Der neue Geist: Ein einführendes Wort zu unserem kulturpolitischen Programm," *Rhein-Neckar Zeitung*, September 5, 1945, p. 3.

129. Theodor Heuss, "Politische Erziehung," *Rhein-Neckar Zeitung*, September 17, 1945, pp. 1–2.

130. Theodor Heuss, "Deutsche Presse," *Rhein-Neckar Zeitung*, September 5, 1945, p. 1.

131. Ibid.

132. Theodor Heuss, "Das Ende der deutschen Wehrmacht," *Rhein-Neckar Zeitung,* September 12, 1945, p. 1.

133. Ibid.

134. Ibid., p. 2. On Heuss's important role in the development of a West German military tradition compatible with democracy, see Donald Abenheim, *Reforging the Iron Cross: The Search for Tradition in the West German Armed Forces* (Princeton: Princeton University Press, 1988), pp. 185–193.

135. Theodor Heuss, "Anklageschrift Nürnberg," *Rhein-Neckar Zeitung,* September 24, 1945, p. 1.

136. Ibid.

137. Theodor Heuss, "Kapitulation," *Rhein-Neckar Zeitung,* May 9, 1946, pp. 1–2.

138. Theodor Heuss, "Bindung und Freiheit (6.1.1946)," in *Theodor Heuss: Aufzeichnung,* pp. 164–182.

139. Ibid., p. 172.

140. Ibid., p. 175.

141. Ibid.

142. Theodor Heuss, "Um Deutschlands Zukunft," in *Theodor Heuss: Aufzeichnung,* pp. 184–208.

143. Ibid., p. 192.

144. Ibid., p. 193.

145. Theodor Heuss, "Das deutsche Schicksal und unsere Aufgabe," in Dahrendorf and Vogt, *Theodor Heuss: Politiker und Publizist,* p. 344.

146. Ibid.

147. Theodor Heuss, "Rede im Parlamentarischen Rat über die Grundlagen einer Verfassung," ibid., pp. 349–368.

148. Ibid., p. 351–352.

149. Theodor Heuss, "Vor vier Jahren," *Rhein-Neckar Zeitung,* May 7, 1949, p. 2.

150. Theodor Heuss, "Vor zehn Jahren," *Rhein-Neckar Zeitung,* September 3–4, 1949, p. 2.

151. Ibid.

152. Theodor Heuss, "Rede nach der Wahl zum Bundespräsidenten vor Bundestag, Bundesrat, und Bundesversammlung" (September 12, 1949), in Dahrendorf and Vogt, *Theodor Heuss: Politiker und Publizist,* pp. 378–379.

153. Willy Albrecht, "Einleitung," in *Kurt Schumacher: Reden-Schriften-Korrespondenzen, 1945–1952* (Berlin: J. H. W. Dietz, 1985), pp. 31–34.

154. Cited ibid., pp. 70–71. The text is also reprinted in Kurt Schumacher, *Reden und Schriften: Türmwachter der Demokratie,* vol. 2 (Berlin-Grunewald, 1953), p. 23.

155. Cited by Albrecht, *Kurt Schumacher,* p. xxx. Schumacher here shared the views of Friedrich Stampfer (1874–1957), almost the only member of the SPD leadership who, despite the Communists' denunciations of Social Democrats as "social fascists,"

supported unity with those Communists who recognized the need for common action. On Stampfer and the Social Democratic response to the rise of Nazism, see also Heinrich August Winkler, *Weimar, 1918–1933: Die Geschichte der Ersten Deutschen Demokratie* (Munich: Beck, 1993), pp. 459, 494, 593. See also Friedrich Stampfer, *Erfahrungen und Erkenntnisse* (Cologne: (Verlag für Politik und Wirtschaft, 1957). Stampfer was the editor in chief of the Social Democratic paper *Vorwärts* in Berlin from 1916 to 1933, a member of the Reichstag from 1920 to 1933 and of the SPD Party Executive from 1925 on. He emigrated to Prague, Paris, and then the United States, then returned to Germany in 1948.

156. Kurt Schumacher, "Revolution gegen Hitler"; cited by Albrecht, *Kurt Schumacher,* p. 82; see also Lewis Edinger, *German Exile Politics: The Social Democratic Executive Committee in the Nazi Era* (Berkeley: University of California Press, 1956).

157. Schumacher, "Revolution gegen Hitler," p. 15.

158. Albrecht, *Kurt Schumacher,* p. 84.

159. Ibid., pp. 84–88.

160. Kurt Schumacher, "Wir verzweifeln nicht!" ibid., pp. 203–236.

161. Ibid., p. 204.

162. Ibid., p. 205.

163. Ibid., pp. 205–206.

164. Ibid., p. 206.

165. For Schumacher's comments on Marx, see Kurt Schumacher, "Karl Marx und die Deutschen," in *Kurt Schumacher: Reden und Schriften* (Berlin: Arani Verlag, 1962), pp. 298–300.

166. Schumacher, "Wir verzweifeln nicht!" p. 209.

167. This shortcoming of the political traditions of the nineteenth century was one of the central and most important insights of Hannah Arendt's *Origins of Totalitarianism* (1951; rpt. New York: Harcourt, Brace and Jovanovich, 1973). See also Herf, "Conclusion," in *Reactionary Modernism.*

168. Schumacher, "Wir verzweifeln nicht!" p. 211. See also Henry A. Turner, Jr., *German Big Business and the Rise of Hitler* (New York: Oxford University Press, 1985).

169. Schumacher, "Wir verzweifeln nicht!" pp. 214–215.

170. Ibid., p. 217.

171. Ibid., p. 215.

172. Ibid., p. 217.

173. Ibid.

174. Ibid., p. 218.

175. Ibid., p. 222.

176. Ibid., p. 232.

177. Kurt Schumacher, "Politische Richtlinien für die S.P.D. in ihrem Verhältnis zu den anderen politischen Faktoren," in Albrecht, *Kurt Schumacher,* pp. 256–286.

178. Ibid., p. 258.

179. Ibid., p. 263.

180. Ibid., p. 275.

181. Ibid., p. 277.

182. Ibid., p. 279.

183. Ibid., p. 280.

184. "Stellungnahme Schumacher zur bevorstehenden Zwangsvereinigung von Kommunisten und Sozialdemokraten in der Ostzone," in Albrecht, *Kurt Schumacher,* p. 331.

185. Kurt Schumacher, "9.5.1946: Eröffnung des Parteitages und 'Ehrung der Opfer des Faschismus' durch Schumacher," ibid., p. 386.

186. Ibid.

187. Ibid.

188. Kurt Schumacher, "9.5.1946: Hauptreferat Schumachers: 'Aufgaben und Ziele der deutschen Sozialdemokratie,'" ibid., p. 389.

189. Ibid., p. 394.

190. Ibid., p. 409.

191. Ibid., p. 418.

192. "11.5.1946: Bemerkungen zur allgemeine Aussprache und Schlußworte Schumachers," ibid., pp. 421–422.

193. AdsD NL Kurt Schumacher 40, Kurt Schumacher, "Aus dem Referat von Dr. Kurt Schumacher," (January 11, 1947), p. 3.

194. Ibid.

195. Ibid.

196. Karl Marx, "Dr. Kurt Schumacher über die Frage des jüdischen Neu-Einbaues in Deutschland," *Beilage zum Jüdisches Gemeindeblatt für die britische Zone,* February 17, 1947, pp. 1–2.

197. Ibid., p. 1.

198. Ibid., p. 2.

199. Ibid.

200. Ibid., p. 2.

201. Kurt Schmacher, "29.6.1947: Grundstzreferat Schumachers auf dem Nürnberger Parteitag der SPD: 'Deutschland und Europa,'" in Albrecht, *Kurt Schumacher,* p. 508.

202. Ibid., p. 509.

203. On this issue, see Constantin Goschler, *Wiedergutmachung: Westdeutschland und die Verfolgten des Nationalsozialismus (1954–1954)* (Munich: R. Oldenbourg, 1992); and Shlomo Shafir, "Die SPD und die Wiedergutmachung gegenüber Israel," in Ludolf

Herbst and Constantine Goschler, eds., *Wiedergutmachung in der Bundesrepublik Deutschland* (Munich: R. Oldenbourg Verlag, 1989).

204. Schmacher, "29.6.1947: Grundstzreferat Schumachers auf dem Nürnberger Parteitag der SPD," p. 512.

205. Ibid., pp. 513–514.

206. On the Schumacher trip to the United States, see Albrecht, *Kurt Schumacher,* pp. 547–570; and Shlomo Shafir, "Das Verhältnis Kurt Schumachers zu den Juden und zur Frage der Frage der Wiedergutmachung," in Willy Albrecht, ed., *Kurt Schumacher als deutscher und europäischer Sozialist* (Bonn: Friedrich Ebert Stiftung, 1988), pp. 168–187.

207. The literature is extensive. See Werner Link and Erich Matthias, ed., *Mit dem Gesicht nach Deutschland: Eine Dokumentation über die sozialdemokratische Emigration aus dem Nachlass von Friedrich Stampfer* (Düsseldorf: Droste Verlag, 1968); Joachim Radkau, *Die deutsche Emigration in den USA: Ihr Einfluß auf die amerikanische Europapolitik, 1933–1945* (Düsseldorf: Verlagsgruppe Bertelsmann, 1971); Werner Link, "German Political Refugees in the United States during the Second World War," in Anthony Nicholls and Erich Mathias, eds., *German Democracy and the Triumph of Hitler* (New York: St. Martin's Press, 1971); Anthony Glees, *Exile Politics during the Second World War: The German Social Democrats in Britain* (Oxford: Clarendon Press, 1982); Helmut Gruber, "The German Socialist Executive in Exile, 1933–1939: Democracy as International Contradiction," in Wolfgang Maderthaner and Helmut Gruber, eds., *Chance and Illusion, Labor in Retreat: Studien zur Krise der westeuropäischen Gesellschaft in den dreißiger Jahren* (Vienna: Europaverlag, 1988), pp. 185–225; *Widerstand, Verfolgung und Emigration, 1933–1945* (Bonn: Friedrich Ebert Stiftung, 1967); and volumes of the annual *Exilforschung: Ein Internationales Jahrbuch* (Munich: Edition Text + Kritik), 1982–.

208. On the wartime role of the Jewish Labor Committee and American labor, see Jack Jacobs, *Ein Freund in Not: Das Jüdische Arbeiterkomitee in New York und die Flüchtlinge aus den Deutschsprachigen Ländern, 1933–1945* (Bonn: Friedrich Ebert Stiftung, 1993), pp. 3–4; David Kranzler, "The Role of Relief and Rescue during the Holocaust by the Jewish Labor Committee," in Seymour Maxwell Finger, ed., *American Jewry during the Holocaust* (New York: American Jewish Commission on the Holocaust, 1984); Gail Malmgreen, "Labor and the Holocaust: The Jewish Labor Committee and the Anti-Nazi Struggle," *Labor's Heritage* 3, no. 4 (October 1991), 20–33. On German Social Democrats and the Jewish question after 1945, see the important work of Shlomo Shafir, "Eine ausgestreckte Hand? Frühe amerikanisch-jüdische Kontakte zu deutschen Sozialdemokraten in der Nachkriegszeit," *IWK: Internationale wissenschaftliche Korrespondenz zur Geschichte der deutschen Arbeiterbewegung* 25, 2 (June 1989), 174–187; and *German-American Trade Union Solidarity in the Struggle against Fascism, 1933–1945: How the American Trade Unions Helped Their*

*Persecuted German Colleagues: A Report* (Washington, D.C.: American Federation of Labor and Congress of Industrial Organizations, 1985).

209. Malmgreen, "Labor and the Holocaust," p. 24.

210. Ibid., pp. 28–30. Although they were deeply grateful to the JLC, much of the Social Democratic political leadership decided to stay in London rather than go to New York, since England had an influential Labour Party and was at war with Nazi Germany.

211. Rudolf Katz to Jay Lovestone (Hamburg, December 23, 1946), Jewish Labor Committee Collection, Wagner Archives, Tamiment Institute, New York University, I:E: General Files, Box 15, Folder 32, "Germany—Social Democrats."

212. On Schumacher's New York visit and the "wall of silence" comment, see "German Leader Urges Reparations to Jews," *New York Times*, September 26, 1947, p. 24.

213. See Radkau, *Die deutsche Emigration in den USA;* Link and Matthias, *Mit dem Gesicht nach Deutschland;* Guy Stern, "'Hitler besiegen—das genügt nicht!' Zusammenarbeit zwischen amerikansichen und exilierten Gewerkschaftlern," in Thomas Koebner, Gert Sautermeister, and Sigrid Schneider, eds., *Deutschland Nach Hitler: Zukunftspläne im Exil und aus der Bestazungszeit, 1939–1949* (Opladen: Westdeutscher Verlag, 1987), pp. 151–168.

214. "17.7.1947: Schumacher an Adolph Held (New York): Dank für die Hilfe des Jewish Labor Committee bei der Rettung vom NS-Regime v verfolgter Sozialdemokraten," in Albrecht, *Kurt Schumacher*, pp. 558–559.

215. "7.10.1947: Schumacher an Erich Ollenhauer aus San Francisco: Bericht über die ersten Wochen des USA-Besuches," in Albrecht, *Kurt Schumacher*, p. 560; and "Kundegbung," *Neue Volks-Zeitung* (November 8, 1947), p. 4 AdsD NL Kurt Schumacher Mappe 42.

216. "Schumacher und die jüdischen Arbeiter-Führer," *Aufbau* (October 1947), AdsD NL Kurt Schumacher Mappe 42.

217. "Kundegbung," *Neue Volks-Zeitung*, November 8, 1947, p. 4.

218. Ibid.

219. Kurt Schumacher, "Anfang Okt. 1947: Schumacher in einem Interview mit der New Yorker Wochenzeitung 'Aufbau': Der Antisemitismus in Deutschland," in Albrecht, *Kurt Schumacher*, pp. 988–990.

220. "AFL Stresses Free Labor for World," *Justice: International Ladies Garment Workers Union* (Jersey City, N.J.), November 1, 1947, p. 4.

221. Kurt Schumacher, "14.10.1947: Rede Schumachers auf dem Jahreskongreß der AFL in San Francisco," in Albrecht, *Kurt Schumacher*, p. 562.

222. Ibid., p. 565.

223. Ibid., p. 566.

224. "AFL Stresses Free Labor for World." p. 4.

225. Max Brauer to Adolph Held (Hamburg, December 5, 1946), Jewish Labor Committee Collection, Wagner Archives, Tamiment Institute, New York University, I:E: General Files, Box 15, Folder 32, "Germany–Social Democrats."

226. On the debates over Western integration and neutralism in the occupation years, see Hans-Peter Schwarz, *Vom Reich zur Bundesrepublik: Deutschland im Widerstreit der außenpolitischen Konzeptionen in den Jahren der Besatzungsherrschaft, 1945–1949*, 2d ed. (Berlin: Luchterhand, 1980).

227. See Samuel Gringauz (former chairman of the Council of Liberated Jews in Bavaria), "Our New German Policy and the DP's: Why Immediate Resettlement is Imperative," *Commentary*, no. 5 (1948), 508; cited in Stern, *Im Anfang war Auschwitz*, pp. 145–46.

228. For a recent discussion of the way in which memories of the Nazi war against "Jewish bolshevism" lived on in the Western alliance against the Soviet Union, see Omer Bartov, *Hitler's Army: Soldiers, Nazis, and War in the Third Reich* (New York: Oxford University Press, 1991). The classic statement remains Theodor Adorno's "Was Bedeutet Aufarbeitung der Vergangenheit."

229. See Hans J. Reichhardt, ed., *Ernst Reuter: Artikel, Briefe, Reden*, vol. 2, *1922 bis 1946* (Berlin: Propyläen Verlag and Ullstein Verlag, 1973).

230. For an overview of his political life and views, see Fritz Stern, "Ernst Reuter: The Making of a Democratic Socialist," in *Dreams and Delusions: The Drama of German History* (New York: Random House, 1987), pp. 77–96. See also Hans J. Reichhardt ed., *Ernst Reuter: Schriften, Reden*, vols. 2–4 (Berlin: Propyläen Verlag, 1973–1975).

231. Ernst Reuter, "Referat auf der Funktionärversammlung der Berliner SPD im Admiralspalast am 1.März 1947," in Hans J. Reichhardt, *Ernst Reuter: Artikel, Briefe, Reden*, vol. 3, 1946 bis 1949 (Berlin: Propyläen Verlag and Ullstein Verlag, 1974), p. 122.

232. Ibid., p. 122.

233. Ibid., p. 124.

234. Ibid.

235. Ibid., p. 130.

236. Ibid., p. 132. The sentence comes from Bertolt Brecht's *Three Penny Opera*.

237. Ibid., pp. 138–139.

238. Ernst Reuter, "Aufgaben und Funktion der SPD," Hans J. Reichhardt, *Ernst Reuter: Schriften, Reden*, 3:151–158.

239. Reichhardt, *Ernst Reuter: Schriften, Reden*, 3:152.

240. Ernst Reuter, "Rede auf der Jahreskonferenz der Amerikanischen Bürgermeister in Washington" (March 23, 1949), ibid., 3:669–670.

241. Ibid., 3:674. See also Ernst Reuter, "Ansprache im RIAS zum Beginn der Blockade, 30 Juni 1948," ibid., 3:412–414, where Reuter says that the experience of

the Hitler regime deepened the decisiveness with which the postwar Germans stood up to Soviet pressures.

242. Ernst Reuter, "Rede auf einer Kundgebung vor dem Zehlendorfer Rathaus am 27. Juli 1948," ibid., 3:449.

243. American pollsters had repeatedly asked Germans in the Western zones whether, if forced to choose, they would prefer a Communist or a National Socialist government. In November 1946, 17 percent selected a Nazi regime. In February 1949, after four years of denazification, three years of Cold War, and the Berlin blockade of 1948–49, 43 percent preferred National Socialism, as against 2 percent for communism. Such figures were a devastating commentary on the negative impact of Soviet and SED policies on postwar West German opinion, as well as on the limits of Western denazification policies. Richard and Anna Merritt write that "growing anticommunism got in the way of politics aimed at cultural change," while the Allied occupation became more interested in an anti-Soviet bulwark than in "a clean sweep of the past." In place of a new democratic leadership, the Germans "got a retrenchment of leaders from the discredited Weimar period" along with those clever enough to avoid blatant taint with the Nazi past. See Merritt and Merritt, *Public Opinion in Occupied Germany*, pp. 55–58, 295.

# 8. Atonement, Restitution, and Justice Delayed

1. Konrad Adenauer to Dannie Heinemann, July 6, 1945, St BKAH; Konrad Adenauer to Dannie Heinemann, April 11, 1947, St BKAH, p. 1; Dannie Heinemann to Konrad Adenauer, August 23, 1948, St BKAH.

2. Dannie Heinemann, "Einführungsschreiben" (May 13, 1949), St BKAH, p. 2; "Konrad Adenauer to Dannie Heinemann, June 12, 1949, St BKAH.

3. Konrad Adenauer to Dannie Heinemann, November 15, 1950, St BKAH.

4. Dannie Heinemann to George Messersmith, December 14, 1950, St BKAH.

5. Konrad Adenauer to Dannie Heinemann, November 15, 1950, St BKAH, pp. 2–3.

6. Ibid., p. 4.

7. Dannie Heinemann to John J. McCloy, March 27, 1951, St BKAH. For Heinemann's praise of the West German economic recovery, see Dannie Heinemann to Konrad Adenauer, January 8, 1954, St BKAH.

8. See Henry Ashby Turner, Jr., *The Two Germanies since 1945* (New Haven: Yale University Press, 1987), pp. 54–57. On the founding of both German states, see Christoph Kleßmann, *Die doppelte Staatsgründung: Deutsche Geschichte, 1945–1955*, 4th ed. (Bonn: Schriftenreihe der Bundeszentrale für politische Bildung, 1986).

9. Konrad Adenauer, "20. September 1949: Erste Regierungserklärung von Bundeskanzler Adenauer," in Hans-Peter Schwarz, *Konrad Adenauer: Reden, 1917–1967*

(Stuttgart: Deutsche Verlags-Anstalt, 1975), pp. 153–169; see also *Verhandlungen des Deutsche Bundestag, 5: Sitzung 20 September 1949,* (Bonn: Deutscher Bundestag, 19TK), pp. 22–30.

10. Adenauer, "Erste Regierungserklärung," p. 153.

11. Ibid., p. 163.

12. Ibid.

13. Ibid.

14. Ibid., pp. 163–164.

15. Ibid., p. 169.

16. Kurt Schumacher, "Das Programm der Opposition: Antort Schumachers auf der erste Regierungserklärung Adenauers im Deutschen Bundestag," in Willy Albrecht, ed., *Kurt Schumacher: Reden-Schriften-Korrespondenzen, 1945–1952* (Berlin: J. J .W. Dietz, 1985), pp. 688–713.

17. Schumacher, "Das Programm der Opposition," pp. 696–698.

18. Ibid., p. 699.

19. Ibid., pp. 699–700.

20. Leaders of the Jewish Labor Committee such as Adolph Held and Jacob Pat, as well as American Jewish Committee analysts, viewed Schumacher and the Social Democrats as the firmest supporters of a restitution agreement. See Jacob Pat, "On German Reparations," *JLC Outlook* 1, no. 1 (Summer 1954), 4–5. Pat, the executive secretary of the JLC, wrote that "the German labor movement was the major force making for successful negotiations" between Jewish organizations and Israel on the one hand and the West German government on the other. See also American Jewish Committee, "Information on Democratic and Anti-Democratic Forces in Germany," (August 1949), in "Germany, 1948–1956," Jewish Labor Committee Papers, Robert F. Wagner Archives, New York University.

21. Anna J. Merritt and Richard L. Merritt, *Public Opinion in Semisovereign Germany: The HICOG Surveys, 1949–1955* (Urbana: University of Illinois Press, 1980), pp. 6–10. See also Richard L. Merritt, *Imposing Democracy* (New Haven: Yale University Press, 1995).

22. Merritt and Merritt, *Public Opinion in Semisovereign Germany,* pp. 10–12. In a survey conducted in August 1952, only one West German in eleven (9 percent) thought that the German generals being held as war criminals were guilty, and 63 percent believed them to be not guilty. Those sentiments were concentrated in the more educated and informed sections of the population. See Report no. 153 (September 8, 1953), "Current West German Views on the War Criminals Issue," ibid., pp. 184–185.

23. Karl Marx, "Die Linie des geringsten Widerstands," *Allgemeine Wochenzeitung der Juden in Deutschland,* November 11, 1949, p. 1.

24. Ibid.

25. Ibid.

26. On Western integration and facing the crimes of the Nazi past in the 1950s, see

Ulrich Brochhagen, *Nach Nürnberg: Vergangenheitsbewältigung und Westintegration in der Ära Adenauer* (Hamburg: Junius Verlag, 1994).

27. "Nov. 1950: Interview des Korrespondenten der New Yorker Tageszeitung 'Jewish Daily Forward' mit Schumacher über die Situation der Juden in Deutschland," in Albrecht, *Kurt Schumacher,* pp. 998–1003. The interview was also published in Germany in the *Allgemeine Wochenzeitung der Juden in Deutschland* and the SPD's *Neuer Vorwärts.*

28. Ibid., p. 999.

29. Ibid., p. 1001.

30. Ibid., pp. 1002–3. On Schumacher, the SPD, and restitution, see Shlomo Shafir, "Die SPD und die Wiedergutmachung gegenüber Israel," in Ludolf Herbst and Constantine Goschler, eds., *Wiedergutmachung in der Bundesrepublik Deutschland* (Munich: R. Oldennbourg, 1986).

31. Kurt Schumacher, "30.10.1951: Schumacher an Liebermann Hersch (Genf): Verteidigung seiner Zusammenkunft mit zwei ehemaligen hohen Offizieren der Waffen-SS," in Albrecht, *Kurt Schumacher,* pp. 895–898.

32. Ibid., p. 895.

33. Ibid., p. 896. See David Clay Large, "A Beacon in the German Darkness": The Anti-Nazi Resistance Legacy in West German Politics," in Michael Geyer and John Boyer, eds., *Resistance against the Third Reich,* (Chicago: University of Chicago Press, 1994), pp. 243–256.

34. Albrecht, *Kurt Schumacher,* pp. 897–898. During the Bitburg controversy of 1985, Chancellor Helmut Kohl used Schumacher's arguments to justify the visit of President Reagan to the Bitburg cemetary. But Schumacher was talking about integration into society, not asking an ally to honor the memory of Waffen-SS soldiers. See Chapter 10. For a thorough discussion of the parliamentary debates and political support in favor of amnesty and against sharp West German judicial confrontation with the crimes of the Nazi past, see Norbert Frei, *Vergangenheitspolitik: die Anfänge der Bundesrepublik und die NS-Vergangenheit* (Munich: C. H. Beck, 1996).

35. Dr. H. G. van Dam, "Ein Freund ist von uns gegangen," *Allgemeine Wochenzeitung der Juden in Deutschland,* August 29, 1952, p. 1.

36. Ibid.

37. David Dubinsky to Erich Ollenhauer (August 21, 1952), GMMA, International Affairs Department, Jay Lovestone Files. Expressions of condolence also arrived from Mathew Woll, chairman of the International Relations Committee of the American Federation of Labor, and Jay Lovestone, Executive Secretary at the AFL, who had maintained correspondence with Schumacher since 1947. Lovestone expressed his shock at the loss of a friend who was also a "sterling leader of democracy and free labor in Germany." See Jay Lovestone to Erich Ollenhauer, and Matthew Woll to Erich Ollenhauer (August 21, 1952), GMMA, International Affairs Department, Jay Lovestone Files.

38. In particular, see Goschler, *Wiedergutmachung: Westdeutschland und die Verfolgten des Nationalsozialismus (1945–1954)* (Munich: R. Oldenbourg Verlag, 1992); and Herbst and Goschler, *Wiedergutmachung in der Bundesrepublik Deutschland.* For the major documents, see Rolf Vogel, ed., *Der deutsch-israelische Dialog: Dokumentation eines erregenden Kapitels deutscher Außenpolitik, Teil 1, Politik*, Vols. 1–3 (Munich: K. G. Sauer, 1987); and Bundesminister der Finanzen in cooperation with Walter Schwarz, *Die Wiedergutmachung nationalsozialistischen Unrechts durch die Bundesrepublik Deutschland*, vols. 1–6 (Munich: Beck, 1981–1987).

39. Goschler, *Wiedergutmachung*, pp. 195–196. An organization to gain restitution for those subjected to sterilization and Nazi medical experiments met with limited success. It was not until 1979 that a national organizations representing Gypsies was established.

40. Konrad Adenauer, "Zur Feier des Nationalen Gedenktages des deutschen Volkes," *Verhandlungen des deutschen Bundestages, 1: Wahlperiode (1949), Stenographische Bericht*, Vol. 7, *Sitzung* 133–146, 1951, pp. 3085–86.

41. "Die Note der israelischen Regierung zum 12. März 1951," in Vogel, *Der deutsch-israelische Dialog: Politik*, 1:33–39.

42. Ibid., 1:37–38.

43. Ibid., 1:39.

44. Konrad Adenauer, "Regierungserklärung zur jüdischen Frage und zur Wiedergutmachung," ibid., 1:45–47.

45. Ibid., 1:46–47.

46. Ibid., 1:47.

47. Frank Stern, *Im Anfang war Auschwitz: Antisemitismus und Philosemitismus im deutschen Nachkrieg* (Gerlingen: Bleicher Verlag, 1991), pp. 324–326.

48. Paul Löbe, "Für die Sozialdemokraten sprach der Abgeordnete Paul Löbe," in Vogel, *Der deutsch-israelische Dialog: Politik*, 1:47.

49. Ibid.

50. Ibid.

51. Ibid., 1:47–48. American surveys indicated that restitution for the Jews was less popular than welfare benefits for German widows and orphans. Nevertheless, in 1951, 68 percent of Germans supported the idea and only 21 percent opposed it. A HICOG report of December 5, 1951, found overwhelming support for assistance to "war widows and orhpans" (96 percent), "people who suffered damage through bombing" (93 percent), and "refugees and expellees" (90 percent). Much less overwhelming majorities supported assistance to "relatives of people executed because of participation in the attempt on Hitler's life on July 20, 1944" (73 percent), and "Jews who suffered through the Third Reich and war" (68 percent). While only 1 percent of respondents opposed assistance to war-widows and orphans, 21 percent opposed such assistance to Jews. Cited by Stern, *Im Anfang war Auschwitz*, p. 330; and "German Opinions on Jewish Restitution and Some Associated Issues: Report no. 113 (5 De-

cember 1951)," in Merritt and Merritt, *Public Opinion in Semisovereign Germany*, p. 146.

52. Vogel, *Der deutsch-israelische Dialog: Politik*, 1:202–203.

53. Ibid., 1:205.

54. "German Social Democratic Party Hopes for Reconcilition between Jews and Germans," Jewish Labor Committee Collections, Robert F. Wagner Archives, New York University, "Germany, 1948–1956."

55. Ibid.

56. Kurt Grossman, "Franz Boehm: An Appreciation," *Congress Weekly*, May 23, 1955, LBI, Kurt Grossman Collection, B35/6, Box 33, Folder 11. In appreciation for his efforts, the American Jewish Congress awarded Franz Böhm the Stephen Wise Award in 1954 for his contribution to Jewish welfare.

57. Franz Böhm, "How Can We Overcome Inertia in Restitution Matter" (January 13, 1955), translation in LBI, Kurt Grossman Collection, B35/6, Box 33, Folder 11.

58. Ibid., p. 4.

59. Konrad Adenauer, "6. September 1952: Ansprach vor dem Bundesparteiausschuß der CDU in Bonn (Bundeshaus)," in Schwarz, *Konrad Adenauer: Reden*, pp. 263–280.

60. Ibid., p. 266.

61. Ibid., p. 267.

62. Ibid.

63. Ibid.

64. Michael Wolffsohn, *Eternal Guilt: Forty Jews of German-Jewish Relations*, trans. Douglas Bukovoy (New York: Columbia University Press, 1993), p. 84.

65. Thomas Schwarz, "McCloy and Wiedergutmachung," in *America's Germany: John J. McCloy and the Federal Republic of Germany* (Cambridge, Mass.: Harvard University Press, 1991), pp. 184, 175–184.

66. Michael W. Krekel, *Wiedergutmachung: Das Luxemburger Abkommen vom 10. September 1952* (Bad Honnef-Rhöndorf: SBAH, 1996), p. 40. See also Axel Frohn, ed., *Holocaust and "Shilumim": The Policy of "Wiedergutmachung" in the Early 1950s* (Washington, D.C.: German Historical Institute, 1991); and Wolffsohn, *Eternal Guilt*, p. 84.

67. On the debates over Article 131 see Frei, *Vergangenheitspolitik*, pp. 69–100. See also Stern, *Im Anfang war Auschwitz*, p. 322; Peter Steinbach, *Nationalsozialistische Gewaltverbrechen: Die Diskussion in der deutschen Offentlichkeit nach 1945* (Berlin: Colloquium Verlag, 1981), pp. 38–50.

68. Support for Article 131 came partly from concerns about politicized and embittered former Nazi officials, as well as from a desire to save money: it was far more expensive to be supporting ex-Nazi officials on pensions while also paying a purged, fully denazified civil service. See Jörg Friedrich, *Die kalte Amnestie: NS Täter in der Bundesrepublik* (Frankfurt am Main: Fischer, 1984), pp. 272–281.

69. The discussion that follows draws on Henning Köhler, *Adenauer: Eine politische*

*Biographie* (Berlin: Propyläen, 1994); and Hans-Peter Schwarz, *Adenauer: Der Staatsmann, 1952–1967* (Stuttgart: Deutsche Verlags-Anstalt, 1991).

70. Köhler, *Adenauer*, p. 728.

71. Ibid., pp. 730–731; Schwarz, *Adenauer: Der Staatsmann;* and Horst Osterheld, "Der Staatssekretärs des Bundeskanzleramtes," in Klaus Gotto, ed., *Der Staatssekretär Adenauers* (Stuttgart: Klett-Cotta, 1980), p. 102.

72. "Dr. Adenauers treuester Beamter," *Berliner Allgemeine Wochenzeitung der Juden in Deutschland,* June 8, 1951, p. 1.

73. "Zentralrat der Juden in Deutschland antwortet Dr. Adenauer," *Berliner Allgemeine Wochenzeitung der Juden in Deutschland,* June 8, 1951, p. 1.

74. "Demokratische Reinigung," *Allgemeine Wochenzeitung der Juden in Deutschland,* September 29, 1950, p. 1.

75. Ibid.

76. Brochhagen, *Nach Nürnberg,* pp. 191–192.

77. Ibid., pp. 192–193.

78. Fritz Erler, *Verhandlungen des Deutschen Bundestages 234 Sitzung* (October 22, 1952), pp. 10728–29, 11733.

79. Konrad Adenauer, *Verhandlungen des Deutschen Bundestages 234 Sitzung* (October 22, 1952), pp. 10734–35.

80. On the formation of the Bundeswehr, see Donald Abenheim, *Reforging the Iron Cross: The Search for Tradition in the West German Armed Forces* (Princeton: Princeton University Press, 1988).

81. Konrad Adenauer, *Verhandlungen des Deutschen Bundestages* (April 6, 1951), p. 4983.

82. Cited by Ulrich Brochhagen, *Nach Nürnberg,* p. 198.

83. This apologetic view not only conflicted with the verdicts of the Nuremberg Trials, which many postwar Germans dismissed as victor's justice, but also has been refuted by the authors of the official West German history of World War II. See, in particular, Jürgen Förster, "Das Unternehmen 'Barbarossa' als Eroberungs-und Vernichtungskrieg," in Horst Boog et al., eds., *Der Angriff auf die Sowjetunion,* vol. 4 of *Das Deutsch Reich und der Zweite Weltkrieg* (Stuttgart: Deutsche Verlags-Anstalt, 1983); and Omer Bartov, *Hitler's Army: Soldiers, Nazis, and War in the Third Reich* (New York: Oxford University Press, 1991).

84. Steinbach, *Nationalsozialistische Gewaltverbrechen,* pp. 38–50.

85. Hendrik van Dam, "Neuer Mythos des 20. Jahrhunderts: Kollektive Verantwortungslosigkeit," *Berliner Allgemeine Wochenzeitung der Juden in Deutschland,* April 13, 1951, p. 1.

86. See Schwartz, *America's Germany,* pp. 156–175.

87. McCloy to Adenauer, April 24, 1950, cited ibid., p. 160.

88. Ibid., p. 165.

89. Ibid., pp. 168, 174.

90. Ibid., pp. 170–171.

91. McCloy to Cardinal Frings, March 15, 1951, cited ibid., pp. 171–172.

92. Ibid., p. 172.

93. Ibid., p. 175.

94. Ibid., pp. 156–175; Steinbach, *Nationasozialistische Gewaltverbrechen*, pp. 43–45. For further discussion of the amnesty lobby, see also Frei, *Vergangenheitspolitik*, pp. 133–306; and Ulrich Herbert's important study of Werner Best, a former SS officer and a postwar leader of the amnesty campaigns: *Best: Biographische Studein über Radikalismus, Weltanschauung und Vernunft, 1903–1989* (Bonn: J. H. W. Dietz, 1996).

95. Robert M. Kempner, "Kolloquium über die Bedeutung der Nürenberger Prozesse für die NS-Verbrecherprozesse," in Peter Schneider and Hermann J. Meyer, eds. *Rechtliche und politische Aspekte der NS-Verbrecherprozesse* (Mainz: Druck H. Krach, 1968), p. 14; cited by Steinbach, *Nationalsozialistische Gewaltverbrechen*, p. 44.

96. See Steinbach, *Nationalsozialistische Gewaltverbrechen*, pp. 46–48; and Albrecht Götz, *Bilanz der Verfolgung von NS-Straftaten* (Cologne: Bundesanzeiger, 1986), pp. 117–118.

97. Steinbach, *Nationalsozialistische Gewaltverbrechen*, pp. 48–50. See also Adalbert Rückerl, *NS-Verbrechen vor Gericht: Versuch einer Vergangheitsbewältigung*, 2d ed. (Heidelberg: C. F. Muller 1982).

98. Steinbach, *Nationalsozialistische Gewaltverbrechen*, p. 49.

99. Konrad Adenauer, "20. Oktober 1950: 'Deutschlands Stellung und Aufgabe in der Welt': Rede auf dem 1.Bundesparteitag der CDU in Goslar," in Schwarz, *Konrad Adenauer: Reden*, p. 182.

100. Konrad Adenauer, "8. November 1950: Regierungserklärung vor dem Deutschen Bundestag," ibid., pp. 193–200.

101. Ibid., pp. 184–185.

102. I explored this issues in *War by Other Means: Soviet Power, West German Resistance, and the Battle of the Euromissiles* (New York: Free Press, 1991).

103. Adenauer, "Rede auf dem 1. Bundesparteitag der CDU in Goslar," p. 183; and "14. September 1951: 'Deutschland und der Friede in Europa': Ansprach vor den Nouvelles Equipes Internationales in Bad Ems," in Schwarz, *Konrad Adenauer: Reden*, pp. 224–236.

104. Adenauer, "Rede auf dem 1. Bundesparteitag der CDU in Goslar," p. 183.

105. Ibid, p. 184.

106. Konrad Adenauer, "'Verständigung, Frieden und Freiheit': Ansprache in der Frankfurter Universität," in Schwarz, *Konrad Adenauer: Reden*, pp. 254–259.

107. On Horkheimer in Frankfurt, see Rolf Wiggershaus, *The Frankfurt School*, trans. Michael Robertson (Cambridge, Mass.: MIT Press, 1994), chap. 6.

108. Adenauer, "Ansprache in der Frankfurter Universität," p. 255.

109. Ibid., p. 256.

110. Ibid.

111. Ibid., p. 257.

112. Konrad Adenauer, "14. September 1951: 'Deutschland und der Friede in Europa': Ansprache vor den Nouvelles Équipes Internationales in Bad Ems," in Schwarz, *Konrad Adenauer: Reden,* p. 227.

113. Ernst Reuter, "Rede auf der Gedenkfeier für die Opfer des Nationalsozialismus in der Hinrichtungsstätte Plötzensee am 10. September 1950," in Hans J. Reichhardt, ed., *Ernst Reuter: Schriften, Reden* vol. 4 (Berlin: Propyläen Verlag, 1975) pp. 246–48.

114. Ibid., p. 246.

115. Ibid., p. 247.

116. Ibid., p. 248.

117. On occasion, Reuter also opted in favor of leaving the past behind, as in his insistence on welcoming Werner Krause to Berlin. Krauss was an actor known for his anti-Semtic portrayals during the Nazi years. In response to protests, Reuter said that "past guilt must not forever be dragged forth as the new measure of value." On this episode, see Stern, *Im Anfang war Auschwitz,* p. 320.

118. Ernst Reuter, "RIAS-Ansprache zum 13. Jahrestag der 'Reichskristallknacht' am 9. November 1951," in Reichhardt, *Ernst Reuter: Schriften, Reden,* 4:474–476.

119. Ibid., p. 474.

120. Ibid., p. 475.

121. Ibid.

122. Ibid.

123. Ernst Reuter, "Flucht in die Selbsttäuschung," in Reichhardt, *Ernst Reuter: Schriften, Reden,* 4:634–638.

124. Ibid., 4:636–637.

125. Ibid., pp. 637, 638. On the connection between anti-Americanism, ressentiment, and the forgetting of the Nazi past both on the nationalist right and later on the nationalist left in West Germany, see the West German essayist Wolfgang Pohrt, *Endstation: Uber die Wiedergeburt der Nation* (Berlin: Rotbuch Verlag, 1982), and *Das Jahr danach: Ein Bericht über die Vorkriegszeit* (Berlin: Klaus Bitterman, 1992). On fundamentalism, anti-Americanism, and the new German right of the 1990s, see Richard Herzinger and Hannes Stein, *Endzeit-Propheten oder die Offensive der Antiwestler* (Reinbek bei Hamburg: Rowohlt, 1995).

126. Ernst Reuter, "Ansprache auf der Gedenkfeier des Bezirksamtes Neukölln am 10. Jahrestag der Vernichtung des Warschauer Ghettos am 19. April 1953," in Reichhardt, *Ernst Reuter: Schriften, Reden,* 4:714–721.

127. Ibid., p. 714.

128. Ibid., pp. 714–715.

129. Ibid., p. 715.

130. Ibid.

131. Ibid., p. 716.

132. Ibid., pp. 716–717.

133. Ibid., p. 717.

134. Ibid., p. 718.

135. Ibid., pp. 718–719.

136. Ibid., pp. 719–721.

137. Ibid., p. 721.

138. Goschler, *Wiedergutmachung,* pp. 217–220.

139. Ernst Reuter, "Rede zur Enthüllung des Denkmals für die Opfer des 20. Juli 1944 im Hof des Ehemaligen OKW in der Bendlerstrasse am 20. Juli 1953," in Reichhardt, *Ernst Reuter: Schriften, Reden,* 4:755–759.

140. Ibid., p. 757.

141. Ibid., p. 758.

142. Ibid., p. 758. See also Ernst Reuter, "Rede auf der Trauerkundgebung für die Opfer des 17. Juni vor dem Rathaus Schönberg am 23. Juni 1953," in Reichhardt, *Ernst Reuter: Schriften, Reden,* 4:737–455.

143. Reuter, "Rede zur Enthüllung des Denkmals für die Opfer des 20. Juli 1944," p. 759.

144. See Carlo Schmid, "Wir Deutschen und die Juden," in *Politik als Geistige Aufgabe* (Bern: Scherz, 1973), pp. 282–300.

145. Carlo Schmid, *Deutscher Bundestag, Stenographische Bericht,* vol. 6, 120 *Sitzung* (February 22, 1951), p. 4592; reprinted as "Zur Wiedergutmachung," in Carlo Schmid, *Bundestagsreden* (Bonn: AZ Studio, 1966), p. 52.

146. Schmid, *Bundestagsreden,* p. 52.

147. Ibid., p. 53.

148. Ibid.

149. Ibid., p. 55.

150. Carlo Schmid, *Besinnung: Rede des Vizepräsidenten des Deutschen Bundestages am 6. März 1955 in der Paulskirche zu Frankfurt am Main zur Eröffnung der "Woche der Brüderlichkeit"* (Frankfurt am Main: Gesellschaft für Christlich-Jüdische Zusammenarbeit, 1955), p. 6.

151. Ibid., p. 7.

152. Ibid., p. 8.

153. Ibid.

154. Ibid., p. 9.

155. Ibid., p. 10.

156. Theodor Heuss, "Mut zur Liebe," BA Koblenz NL Theodor Heuss B122 2886.

157. Ibid., p. 4.

158. Ibid., p. 5.

159. Ibid.

160. Ibid., p. 7.

161. Ibid., p. 8.

162. Theodor Heuss, "Akademisches Festrede des Bundespräsidenten Professor Dr. Heuss," BA Koblenz NL Theodor Heuss B122 2886, pp. 1–10.

163. Ibid., p. 11.

164. Ibid., p. 12.

165. Theodor Heuss, "Ansprache von Bundespräsident Dr. Theodor Heuss am 16. Dezember 1949 vor den Studenten der Universität Heidelberg," BA Koblenz NL Theodor Heuss B122 2886.

166. Ibid., p. 11.

167. Theodor Heuss, "Zur Feier des Nationalen Gedenktages des deutschen Volkes," *Verhandlungen des deutschen Bundestages, 1: Wahlperiode (1949), Stenographische Bericht,* vol. 7, *Sitzung* 133–146, *1951,* pp. 3086.

168. For the Heuss-Adorno correspondence, see BA Koblenz NL Theodor Heuss B122 306; see also Heuss-Baeck B122 2083; Theodor Heuss–Martin Buber B122 2056; Theodor Heuss–Alfred Döblin B122 2057; Theodor Heuss–Max Horkheimer B122 2059 and B122 361; Theodor Heuss–Thomas Mann, B122 195; Theodor Heuss–Karl Marx B122 2086.

169. See Theodor Heuss, "Glückwünsche des Herrn Bundespräsidenten an die 'Allgemeine Wochenzeitung der Juden in Deutschland' (Dusseldorf) aus Anlass des jüdischen Neujahrsfestes am 24. September 1949," BA Koblenz NL Theodor Heuss B122 2086.

170. Jacob Blaustein to Theodor Heuss (October 5, 1951), BA Koblenz NL Theodor Heuss B122 2080/026.

171. Theodor Heuss to John J. McCloy, January 16, 1951, BA Koblenz NL Theodor Heuss B122 644, pp. 1–2. For the exchanges between Theodor Heuss and General Handy of February and March 1951 on the Landsberg matter, see also BA Koblenz NL Theodor Heuss B122 644, especially Theodor Heuss to Thomas T. Handy, February 23, 1951.

172. John J. McCloy to Theodor Heuss (January 24, 1951). BA Koblenz NL Theodor Heuss B122 644.

173. Ibid., p. 2.

174. M. S. Henderson, "Speech at Belson, 30th November 1952," BA Koblenz NL Theodor Heuss B122 2082, pp. 1–2.

175. Theodor Heuss, "Diese Scham nimmt uns niemand ab: Der Bundespräsident sprach bei der Weihe des Mahnmals in Bergen-Belsen," *Bulletin des Presse- un Informationsamtes der Bundesregierung,* December 1, 1952, pp. 1655–56. An abridged version appeared as "Das Mahnmal," in Theodor Heuss, *Der Grossen Reden: Der Staatsmann* (Tübingen: Rainer Wunderlich Verlag, 1965), pp. 224–230. See also BA Koblenz NL Theodor Heuss B122 2082.

176. "Belsen Memorial Dedication Ceremony, Invitation List, I: Jewish," BA Koblenz NL Theodor Heuss B122 2082, pp. 1–4. On ceremonies at Dachau, see

Harold Marcuse, "The Politics of Memory: Nazi Crimes and Identity in West Germany, 1945–1990," Occasional Paper, Center for European Studies, Harvard University, 1993.

177. "Entstehungsgeschichte der Gedenkstatte Belsen," BA Koblenz NL Theodor Heuss B122, 2082, pp. 1–2. The Bergen-Belsen ceremonies were exceptional in West Germany in the 1950s. For discussion of opposition at the local level to public discussion and memorial speeches about the Nazi past, see Harold Marcuse, "The Politics of Memory: Nazi Crimes and Identity in West Germany, 1945–1990" Minda de Gunzberg Center for European Studies, Harvard University, 1993.

178. Nahum Goldmann, speech at Bergen-Belsen, November 30, 1952, BA Koblenz NL Theodor Heuss B122 2082, p. 1.

179. Ibid., pp. 1–2.

180. Ibid., p. 3.

181. Ibid., p. 4.

182. Ibid.

183. Ibid., p. 5.

184. Theodor Heuss, "Diese Scham nimmt uns niemand ab!" *Bulletin des Presse-und Informationsamtes der Bundesregierung,* December 2, 1942, pp. 1655–56; "Heuss weiht Mahnmal in Belsen ein: Der Bundespräsident gedenkt der Opfer des ehemaligen Kz," *Frankfurter Rundschau,* December 1, 1952, p. 1.

185. Manfred George to Theodor Heuss December 19, 1952, BA Koblenz NL Theodor Heuss B122 2082.

186. Roger Baldwin to Theodor Heuss, March 23, 1953, BA Koblenz NL Theodor Heuss B122, 2082. Baldwin was the chairman of the International League for the Rights of Man, located in New York.

187. Heuss, "Diese Scham," p. 1655.

188. Ibid.

189. Ibid.

190. Ibid., p. 1656.

191. Ibid.

192. Ibid.

193. Ibid.

194. See Adorno, "Was bedeutet Aufarbeitung der Vergangenheit."

195. Heuss, "Diese Scham," p. 1656.

196. Ibid.

197. Ibid.

198. Ibid. For a recent criticism of efforts to find a redemptive meaning in the Holocaust, see Lawrence L. Langer, *Admitting the Holocaust: Collected Essays* (New York: Oxford University Press, 1995).

199. On the legacy of the resistance in West German politics, see David Clay Lodge,

"'A Beacon in the German Darkness': The Anti-Nazi Resistance Legacy in West German Politics," in Geyer and Boyer, *Resistance against the Third Reich: 1933–1990*, pp. 243–256.

200. Theodor Heuss, "Bundespräsident Theodor Heuss an die Witwe eines der Opfer des 20. Juli" (July 4, 1952), BA Koblenz NL Theodor Heuss B122 2079.

201. Ibid., pp. 3–4.

202. Hans Bott to Max Horkheimer, July 9, 1954; and Max Horkheimer to Hans Bott, July 12, 1954, BA Koblenz NL Theodor Heuss B122 361.

203. Max Horkheimer to Hans Bott, July 12, 1954, pp. 1–2.

204. In 1953 Horkheimer had written that "there are too few people who are able to offer resistance, resistance against the pressure of a situation, resistance against the prejudices of the time, resistance against that which they think is necessary for success, their career and the like." See Theodor W. Adorno, Max Horkheimer, and Eugen Kogon, "Die Menschen und die Terror," in *Max Horkheimer, Gesammelte Schiften*, vol. 13, *Nachgelassene Schriften 1949–1972* (Frankfurt am Main: Fischer Taschenbuch Verlag, 1989), p. 152. Horkheimer had moved quite a distance from his 1939 dictum that "he who does not wish to speak of capitalism should remain silent about capitalism." Max Horkheimer, "Die Juden und Europa," in *Gesammelte Schriften*, vol. 4, *Schriften, 1936–1941* (Frankfurt am Main: Fischer Taschenbuch Verlag, 1991).

205. Marion Gid, "Der jüdische Rektor und seine deutsche Universität," *Allgemeine Wochenzeitung der Juden in Deutschland* 7, no. 7 (July 1952), 3.

206. Theodor Heuss, "Vom Recht zum Widerstand-Dank und Bekenntnis," in Martin Vogt, ed., *Theodor Heuss: Politiker und Publizist* (Tübingen: Wunderlich, 1984), pp. 430–441.

207. Ibid., p. 430.

208. Ibid., p. 432.

209. Ibid., p. 439. One of Heuss's most important practical interventions in the Federal Republic was the fostering of a democratic ethos and independence of judgment within the West German military in place of the previous authoritarian tradition. See the discussion of *Innere Führung* in Donald Abenheim, *Reforging the Iron Cross: The Search for Tradition in the West German Armed Forces* (Princeton: Princeton University Press, 1988), esp. pp. 185–194.

210. Emmi Bonhoeffer to Theodor Heuss, September 12, 1949, BA Koblenz Theodor Heuss NL221 115.

211. Emmi Bonhoeffer to Theodor Heuss, August 25, 1954, BA Koblenz Theodor Heuss NL 221 115.

212. Theodor Heuss, "Der Deutsche Weg—Ruckfall und Fortschritt" (September 29, 1955, Evangelischen Akademie Bad Boll), BA Koblenz Theodor Heuss B122 2890, p. 5.

213. Theodor Heuss, "Bundespräsident Theodor Heuss verabschiedet sich," *Bul-*

*letin der Presse- und Informationsamtes der Bundesregierung,* September 15, 1959, pp. 1693–96; BA Koblenz NL Theodor Heuss 221 21.

214. Ibid., p. 1694.

215. Ibid.

216. Theodor Heuss to Nahum Goldmann, July 27, 1959, BA Koblenz Theodor Heuss B122 2080/026.

217. Heuss's efforts were appreciated in Israel. After leaving office, he was invited to speak at Hebrew University in Jerusalem. See Heuss, "Staat und Volk im Werden: Vortrag an der Hebräischen Universität zu Jerusalem am 8. Mai 1960," BA Koblenz Theodor Heuss NL 221 23. (The speech was actually delivered on May 2, 1960.) Ernst Simon of the faculty of Hebrew University, and a German refugee, expressed the "heartfelt thanks" of the faculty. See "Auszug aus der Ansprache, die Herr Prof. Dr. Ernst Simon anlässlich der Anwesenheit des Altbundespräsidenten Prof. Dr. Heuss in Jerusalem am 2. Mai 1960 gehalten hat," BA Koblenz Theodor Heuss NL 221 23.

218. Heinrich Lübke, "Zwei Bundespräsidenten-zwei Reden: Unsere jüngste Vergangenheit: Mit den Augen von Theodor Heuss und Heinrich Lübke gesehen," *Frankfurter Rundschau,* March 7, 1961, p. 3.

219. Ibid.

220. Ibid.

221. Stern, *Im Anfang war Auschwitz,* p. 337.

## 9. Politics and Memory since the 1960s

1. Peter Steinbach, *Nationalsozialistische Gewaltverbrechen: Die Diskussion in der deutschen Öffentlichkeit nach 1945* (West Berlin: Colloquium Verlag, 1981), p. 74.

2. Ibid., pp. 51–53.

3. Albrecht Götz, *Bilanz der Verfolgung von NS-Straftaten* (Cologn: Bundesanzeiger Verlag, 1986), p. 149; see also Adalbert Rückerl, *Die Strafverfolgung von NS-Verbrechen: 1945–1978* (Heidelberg-Karlsruhe: 1979).

4. Götz, *Bilanz der Verfolgung,* pp. 35–36.

5. Deutscher Bundestag, *Zur Verjährung nationalsozialistischer Verbrechen: Dokumentation der parlamentarischen Bewältigung des Problems, 1960–1979, Teil* 1 (Bonn: Deutscher Bundestag, Presse- und Informationszentrum, 1980), pp. 109–110.

6. Götz, *Bilanz der Verfolgung,* p. 149.

7. Deutscher Bundestag, *Zur Verjährung,* p. 110.

8. Götz, *Bilanz der Verfolgung,* p. 149.

9. On the use of Nazi war crimes charges to convict political opponents, see Michael Klonovsky and Jan von Flocken, *Stalins Lager in Deutschland* (Munich: DTV, 1993).

10. Deutscher Bundestag, *Zur Verjährung,* pp. 103–104.

11. "Antrag der Fraktion der SPD," in Deutscher Bundestag *Zur Verjährung,* pp. 10–13.

12. Götz, *Bilanz der Verfolgung,* p. 143.

13. "Die Debatte im Plenum" (May 24, 1960), in Deutscher Bundestag, *Zur Verjahrung,* pp. 15–47.

14. See *Verhandlungen des deutschen Bundestages 4. Wahlperiode, Stengraphische Bericht,* vol. 58, *Sitzung* 178–186 (March 25, 1965), pp. 8788–90. See also Karl Jaspers, "Für Völkermord gibt es keine Verjährung," reprinted in Karl Jaspers, *Wohin Treibt die Bundesrepublik* (Munich: Piper, 1988), pp. 17–45.

15. Steinbach, *Nationalsozialistische Gewaltverbrechen,* pp. 75–77.

16. Cited in Götz, *Bilanz der Verfolgung,* p. 144.

17. "Benda (CDU/CSU)," in Deutscher Bundestag, *Zur Verjahrung,* p. 163. See also Ernst Benda, *Verjährung und Rechtstaat: Verfassungsprobleme der Verlängerung strafrechtlicher Verjährungsfristen* (Berlin: Colloquium Verlag, 1965).

18. "Benda (CDU/CSU)," pp. 177–185.

19. Ibid., pp. 185–188.

20. Ibid., pp. 193–199.

21. Ibid., pp. 203–214. See also Adolf Arndt, *Politische Reden und Schriften: 1946–1972* (Berlin: Dietz, 1976), and *Gesammelte Juristische Schriften: Ausgewählte Aufsätze und Vorträge* (Munich: C. Beck Verlag, 1976).

22. "Benda (CDU/CSU)," pp. 209–210.

23. Yet when Arndt stressed—to the accompaniment of applause from all parties—that the destruction of European Jewry had "nothing to do" with war crimes, he unduly minimized the connection between the Nazi attack on "Jewish bolshevism" on the Eastern Front and the Holocaust. On these links, see Omer Bartov, *Hitler's Army* (New York: Oxford University Press, 1991); and Jürgen Förster, Manfred Messerschmidt, et al. *Der Angriff auf die Sowjetunion,* vol. 4 of *Das Deutsche Reich und der Zweite Weltkrieg* (Stuttgart: Deutsche Verlags-Anstalt, 1983).

24. "Benda (CDU/CSU)," pp. 211–212. On varieties of German guilt, see Karl Jaspers, *Die Schuldfrage: Von der Politischen Haftung Deutschlands* (1946; rpt. Munich: Piper Verlag, 1987; reprint of 1946 edition).

25. "Benda (CDU/CSU)," p. 214.

26. Ibid., p. 244.

27. Ibid., p. 245.

28. Ibid., pp. 245–246.

29. *Verhandlungen des deutschen Bundestages 4. Wahlperiode,* pp. 8788–90.

30. Horst Ehmke, *Zur Verjährung der nationalsozialistische Verbrechen: Dokumentation der parlamentarischen Bewältigung des Problems, 1960–1979, Teil* 2 (Bonn: Deutscher Bundestag, Presse- und Informationsamt, 1980), pp. 381–390. See also *Verhandlungen*

*des deutschen Bundestages 5. Wahlperiode Stenographische Bericht (1965)*, vol. 70, *Sitzung* 230–247 (June 11, 1969), "Dr. Ehmke," pp. 13053–58.

31. "Bundesgesetzblatt," in *Zur Verjährung,* pp. 436–437; Götz, *Bilanz der Verfolgung,* p. 144.

32. See "Dr. Mertes," in *Verhandlungen des deutschen Bundestages 6. Wahlperiode Stenographische Bericht (1976) Sitzung* 166 (July 3, 1979), pp. 13234–39.

33. Ibid., p. 13238.

34. Ibid., pp. 13238–39.

35. "Frau Dr. Däubler-Gmelin," in *Verhandlungen des deutschen Bundestage 6. Wahlperiode,* pp. 13239–43.

36. Ibid., p. 13239.

37. Ibid., p. 13240–41.

38. "Frau Dr. Hamm-Brucher," ibid., pp. 13282–84.

39. Ibid., p. 13284.

40. Ibid., pp. 13292–94. See also Jeffrey Herf, "The 'Holocaust' Reception in West Germany: Right, Center, and Left," in Anson Rabinbach and Jack Zipes, eds., *Germans and Jews since the Holocaust: The Changing Situation in West Germany* (New York: Holmes and Meier, 1986), p. 226; Steinbach, *Nationalsozialististische Gewaltverbrechen,* pp. 64–67; and *Zur Verjährung der nationalsozialistische Verbrechen: Dokumentation der parlamentarischen Bewältigung des Problems, 1960–1979,* vols. 2,3 (Bonn: Deutscher Bundestag, Presse- und Informationszentrum, 1980).

41. On Erhard, see Dennis L. Bark and David R. Gress, *A History of West Germany,* vol. 1, *From Shadow to Substance, 1945–1963* (Oxford: Basil Blackwell, 1989).

42. See Karl Hohmann, ed., *Ludwig Erhard Gedanken aus fünf Jahrzehnten: Reden und Schriften* (Düsseldorf: Econ Verlag, 1988).

43. Ludwig Erhard, "Trauer und Scham: Ansprache bei der Wiedereinweihung der alten Synagogue zu Worms, 3. Dezember 1961," ibid., pp. 712–716.

44. Ludwig Erhard, "Franz Oppenheimer, dem Lehrer und Freund: Rede zu Oppenheimers 100. Geburtstag in der Freien Universität Berlin, 30. April 1964," ibid., pp. 858–864.

45. Ibid., pp. 863–864.

46. At this time nine Arab states broke diplomatic relations with the Federal Republic. See Inge Deutschkron, *Israel und die Deutschen: das Schwierige Verhältnis* (Cologne: Verlag Wissenschaft und Politik, 1991), pp. 287–223; Lily Gardner Feldman, *The Special Relationship between West Germany and Israel* (Boston: Allen and Unwin, 1984); and Friedrich W. Husemann, "The German-Israeli Relationship: A Critical Chronicle of Three Decades," in Otto R. Romberg and Heiner Lichtenstein, eds., *Thirty Years of Diplomatic Relations between the Federal Republic of Germany and Israel* (Frankfurt am Main: Tribüne Verlag, 1995), pp. 124–135.

47. On the Erhard visit to Israel, see Rolf Vogel, ed., *Der deutsch-israelische Dialog: Dokumentation eines erregenden Kapitels deutscher Aussenpolitik Teil 1, Politik,* vol. 1 (Munich: K. G. Saur, 1987–1990), pp. 382–393.

48. On moral conviction and West German national interest in this matter, see Deutschkron, *Israel und die Deutschen,* and Feldman, *The Special Relationship.*

49. See "Die Aufnahme der diplomatischen Beziehungen zwischen der Bundesrepublik Deutschland und Israel," in Vogel, *Der deutsch-israelische Dialog,* pp. 253–305.

50. See Dennis L. Bark and David R. Gress, *A History of West Germany,* vol. 2, *Democracy and Its Discontents, 1963–1988* (Oxford: Basil Blackwell, 1989), pp. 60–62, 127.

51. See Arnulf Baring, *Die Ära Brandt-Scheel* (Munich: Deutscher Taschenbuch Verlag, 1984).

52. Willy Brandt, *In Exile: Essays, Reflections, Letters, 1933–1947,* trans. R. W. Last (London: Oswald Wolf, 1971).

53. Willy Brandt, *Auf der Zinne der Partei: Parteitagsreden 1960 bis 1983* (Berlin: Verlag J. H. W. Dietz, 1984), pp. 38–39.

54. In the 1950s, in the spirit of a much chastened and guilt-ridden postwar German Protestantism, Heinemann had denounced anti-Semitism and criticized Adenauer for placing Christianity in the service of Cold War anticommunism and West German rearmament. See Gustav Heinemann, "Zum Antisemitismus und zum deutschen Sendungsbewußtsein: Rede im Deutschen Bundestag in der Debatte über antisemitische Vorfälle, 18.2.1960," in *Reden und Schriften, Band 2, Glaubensfreiheit-Bürgerfreiheit, Reden und Aufsätze zu Kirche-Staat-Gesellschaft, 1945–1975* (Frankfurt am Main: Suhrkamp Verlag, 1976), pp. 153–158. For his views while *Bundespräsident,* see Gustav Heinemann, *Reden und Schriften,* vol. 1, *Allen Bürgern verpflichtet: Reden des Bundespräsidenten, 1969–1974* (Frankfurt am Main: Suhrkamp Verlag, 1975).

55. See Willy Brandt, *Friedenspolitik in Europa,* 3d ed. (1968; rpt. Frankfurt am Main: Fischer Verlag, 1971).

56. Ibid., p. 37. See Timothy Garten Ash, *In Europe's Name: Germany and the Divided Continent* (New York: Random House, 1993.

57. I have made this point in Jeffrey Herf, *War by Other Means* (New York: Free Press, 1991), pp. 27–44. For more extensive discussion of *Ostpolitik,* see Ash, *In Europe's Name;* and William Griffith, *The Ostpolitik of the Federal Republic of Germany* (Cambridge, Mass.: MIT Press, 1978). For a West German conservative critique of the political culture of *Ostpolitik,* see Hans-Peter Schwarz *Die gezähmten Deutschen: Von der Machtbessessenheit zur Machtvergessenheit* (Stuttgart: Deutsche Verlags-Anstalt, 1985).

58. Willy Brandt, "Wer rastet, der rostet—Dynamische Politik als deutsche Gemeinschaftsaufgabe: Rede vom 27 Mai 1962," in *Auf der Zinne der Partei,* p. 62.

59. Brandt, *Friedenspolitik in Europa,* p. 148.

60. Ibid., pp. 34–35.

61. For example, see Peter Bender, *Das Ende des ideologischen Zeitalters* (Berlin: Severin and Siedler, 1981), and Herf, *War by Other Means*, pp. 14–44.

62. See Willy Brandt, *Erinnerungen* (Frankfurt am Main: Propyläen, 1989), pp. 213–215.

63. *Ostpolitik*, not the Middle East, was the focus on Brandt's diplomacy. Nevertheless, his sympathies with Israel and its Labor Party were strong. He was the first West German chancellor to visit Israel while in office. See Vogel, *Der deutsch-israelische Dialog*, pp. 349–381, 458–475.

64. I have discussed Schmidt's views in *War by Other Means.*

65. Helmut Schmidt, "Ansprache in Auschwitz-Birkenau" (November 23, 1977), in *Der Kurs Heisst Frieden* (Düsseldorf: Econ Verlag, 1980), pp. 53–54.

66. Ibid., pp. 54–55.

67. Helmut Schmidt, "A Plea for Honesty and Tolerance," in Werner Nachman, Nahum Goldmann, and Helmut Schmidt, *An Exhortation and an Obligation: Speeches Delivered on the Occasion of the Memorial Celebration in Remembrance of 9 November 1938 in the Cologne Synagogue on 9 November 1978* (Bonn: Press- and Information Office of the Federal Republic of Germany, 1979), pp. 21–35.

68. Ibid., p. 21.

69. Ibid., pp. 22–23.

70. On this theme, see Jeffrey Herf, *Reactionary Modernism: Technology, Culture, and Politics in Weimar and the Third Reich* (New York: Cambridge University Press, 1984); and Thomas Mann's *Doctor Faustus.*

71. Schmidt, "A Plea for Honesty and Tolerance," pp. 28–29.

72. The speeches about July 20, 1944, are reprinted in Theodor Heuss, Heinrich Lübke, Gustav W. Heinemann, Walter Scheel, and Karl Karstens, *Gedanken zum 20. Juli 1944*, with introduction by Helmut Kohl and foreword by Karl Dietrich Bracher, 2d ed. (Mainz: Hase and Koehler, 1984). See also David Clay Large, "'A Beacon in the German Darkness': The Anti-Nazi Resistance Legacy in West German Politics," in Michael Geyer and John W. Boyer, eds., *Resistance against the Third Reich, 1933–1990* (Chicago: University of Chicago Press, 1994), pp. 243–256.

73. Heinrich Lübke, "Symbol der Selbstachtung unseres Volkes," in *Gedanken zum 20. Juli 1944*, pp. 51–66.

74. Ibid., p. 58.

75. Gustav W. Heinemann, "Zeugnis des Ringens um Menschenrecht und Menschenwürde," in *Gedanken zum 20. Juli 1944*, pp. 67–79.

76. Walter Scheel, "Das demokratische Geschichtsbild," ibid., pp. 81–98.

77. Karl Carstens, "Mahnung und Verpflichtung des 20. Juli 1944," ibid., pp. 99–110.

78. See Martin W. Kloke, *Israel und die deutsche Linke: Zur Geschichte eines*

*schwierigen Verhältnisses,* 2d ed. (Frankfurt am Main: Haag and Herchen, 1990). See also Micha Brumlik et al., *Der Antisemitismus und die Linke* (Frankfurt am Main: Arnoldshainer Texte, 1991); Dan Diner, *Zivilisationsburch: Denken nach Auschwitz* (Frankfurt am Main: Fischer Taschenbuch Verlag, 1988); Rabinbach and Zipes, *Germans and Jews since the Holocaust;* Karlheinz Schneider and Nikolas Simon, eds., *Solidarität und deutsche Geschichte: Die Linke zwischen Antisemitismus und Israelkritik* (Berlin: Deutsch-Israelischer Arbeitskreis für Frieden im Nahen Osten, 1984), pp. 61–80.

79. On this see Herf, *Reactionary Modernism;* and "Exile and Return," Review of Rolf Wiggershaus, "The Frankfurt School," in *New Republic,* February 27, 1995, pp. 38–41.

80. In 1957 Erich Ollenhauer, Schumacher's successor as chairman of the SPD, became the first West German politician to be invited to Israel by the Israeli government. See Deutschkron, *Israel und die Deutschen,* p. 143.

81. See Kloke, *Israel und die deutsche Linke,* pp. 106–132.

82. For an extensive discussion of these intraleft controversies, see ibid.

83. Ibid., p. 168.

84. Lea Fleischmann, *Die ist nicht mein Land: Eine Judin verläßt die Bundesrepublik* (Hamburg: Hoffmann and Campe, 1980); and Henryk Broder, *Linke Tabus* (Berlin: Bar, 1976); "Antizionismus-Antisemitismus von links?" *Aus Politik und Zeitgeschichte,* June 6, 1976, pp. 31–46.

85. On nationalism and the peace movement, see Wolfgang Pohrt, "Ein Volk, ein Reich, ein Frieden," in *Endstation: Uber die Wiedergeburt der Nation* (West Berlin: Rotbuch Verlag, 1982), pp. 71–77. See also Anton Guha, *Die Nachrüstung: Der Holocaust Europas* (Freiburg im Breisgau: Dreisam Verlag, 1981); and Herf, *War by Other Means.*

86. For a sampling of Kohl's speeches, see Peter Hintze and Gerd Langguth, eds., *Helmut Kohl, Der Kurs der CDU: Reden und Beiträge des Bundesvorsitzenden, 1973–1993* (Stuttgart: Deutsche Verlags-Anstalt, 1993).

87. Helmut Kohl, "Wir kämpfen für Freiheit und Menschenrechte: Rede auf der Großkundgebung der Jungen Union anläßlich der Aktion Menschenrechte in Belsenkirchen am 10. April 1976," ibid., p. 156.

88. Ibid.

89. See Rolf Vogel, ed. *Der deutsch-israelische Dialog: Dokumentation eines erregenden Kapitels deutscher Geschichte Teil 1, Politik,* vol. 2, (Munich: K. G. Saur, 1987–1990), pp. 964–1058.

90. "Die Antwort des Bundeskanzlers" (January 24, 1984), ibid., pp. 970–971.

91. "Regieurngserklärung von Bundeskanzler Helmut Kohl zu seiner Israel-Reise und die Debatte im deutschen Bundestag," ibid., pp. 998–1050.

92. For a chronology of the Bitburg ceremonies, see Geoffrey H. Hartman, *Bitburg*

*in Moral and Political Perspective* (Bloomington: Indiana University Press, 1986), pp. xii–xvi.

93. On coverage of the American protest and the West German response, see *Frankfurter Allgemeine Zeitung*, April 22, 25, and 27, 1985.

94. Helmut Kohl to Ronald Reagan, April 15, 1985, excerpts cited in George Schultz, *Turmoil and Triumph: My Years as Secretary of State* (New York: Charles Scribners's Sons, 1993), pp. 545–546.

95. Ibid., p. 550; and "Kohl besorgt," *Frankfurter Allgemeine Zeitung*, April 25, 1985, p. 2.

96. "Kohl dankt Reagan für die Bereitschaft zu einer Versöhnungsgeste," *Frankfurter Allgemeine Zeitung*, April 26, 1985, p. 1.

97. Helmut Kohl, "Address by Helmut Kohl . . . at the Site of the Former Bergen-Belsen Concentration Camp, April 21, 1985," in Hartman, *Bitburg*, pp. 244–250; and "Kohl: Die Befreiung verhieß nicht allen Freiheit 'Wir haben die Lektion der Geschichte gelernt,'" *Frankfurter Allgemeine Zeitung*, April 22, 1985, p. 1.

98. Hartman, *Bitburg*, p. 244–246.

99. Ibid., p. 247.

100. Ibid., p. 250.

101. This did not prevent Fritz Ulrich Fack, one of the publishers of the flagship of West German conservatism, the *Frankfurter Allgemeine Zeitung*, from blaming "a powerful publicity machinery" in the United States for offering a "distorted picture of ugly Germans" and trying make the president into its "marionette." In this way a "lust for power" was intertwined with "the business interests of the entertainment industry." Fritz Ulrich Fack, "Ein Scherberhaufen," *Frankfurter Allgemeine Zeitung*, April 29, 1985, p. 1.

102. Helmut Kohl, "Address by Chancellor Helmut Kohl to German and American Soldiers and Their Families at Bitburg, May 5, 1985," in Hartman, *Bitburg*, pp. 256–257.

103. Ronald Reagan, "Remarks of President Reagan at Bitburg Air Base, May 5, 1985," ibid., pp. 258–261.

104. Ibid., p. 259. See also "'Wir waren Feinde, wir sind jetzt Freunde,' Kohl und Reagan in Bergen-Belsen und Bitburg," *Frankfurter Allgemeine Zeitung*, May 6, 1985, p. 1.

105. Richard von Weizsäcker, "Speech by Richard von Weizsäcker, President of the Federal Republic of Germany, in the Bundestag during the Ceremony Commemorating the 40th Anniversary of the End of the War in Europe and of National Socialist Tyranny, May 8, 1945," in Hartman, *Bitburg*, pp. 262–273; and Richard von Weizsäcker, "Der 8. Mai 1945: 40 Jahre danach," in Richard von Weizsäcker, *Von Deutschland aus: Reden des Bundespräsidenten* (Munich: Deutscher Taschenbuch Verlag, 1987), pp. 9–36.

106. Richard von Weizsäcker, *Reden und Interviews* (Bonn: Presse- und Information-samt der Bundesregierung, 1988).

107. Weizsäcker, "May 8, 1945," p. 262.

108. Ibid., p. 263.

109. Ibid.

110. Ibid., pp. 263–264. On politics and the memory of the German resistance, see David Clay Large, "'A Beacon in the German Darkness': The Anti-Nazi Resistance Legacy in West German Politics," in Geyer and Boyer, *Resistance against the Third Reich;* and Jeffrey Herf, "German Communism, the Discourse of 'Antifascist Resis-tance,' and the Jewish Catastrophe," in John Boyer and Michael Geyer, eds., *Resistance against the Third Reich, 1933–1990* (Chicago: University of Chicago Press, 1994), pp. 257–294.

111. Weizsäcker, "May 8, 1945," p. 264.

112. Ibid.

113. Ibid.

114. Ibid.

115. Ibid., pp. 264–265.

116. Ibid., p. 265.

117. Ibid.

118. Ibid., pp. 265–266.

119. Ibid., p. 267.

120. Ibid.

121. Ibid., p. 273.

122. Norbert Seitz, "Bemühter Umgang: 50 Jahre 8. Mai—eine deutsche Patholo-gie," *Suddeutsche Zeitung,* April 15, 1995.

123. For a thorough analysis of the *Historikerstreit,* see Charles S. Maier, *The Unmasterable Past* (Cambridge, Mass.: Harvard University Press, 1988). For the docu-ments, see *Forever in the Shadow of Hitler? The Dispute about the Germans' Under-standing of History,* trans. James Knowlton and Truett Cates (Atlantic Highlands, N.J.: Humanities Press, 1993). See also Volker Berghahn, "The Unmastered and Unmas-terable Past," *Journal of Modern History* 63 (September 1991): 546–554; Saul Fried-lander, "Überlegungen zur Historisierung des Nationalsozialismus," in Dan Diner, ed., *Ist der Nationalsozialismus Geschichte? Zur Historisierung und Historikerstreit* (Frankfurt am Main: Fischer Taschenbuch, 1987), pp. 34–50.

124. Richard von Weizsäcker, "Speech by President Richard von Weizsacker at the Opening of the 37th Historians' Congress in Bamburg on 12 October 1988," (Bonn: Bundespräsidialamt Presse), p. 2.

125. "Die Ansprach der Bundeskanzler anlässlich des 50. Jahrestages der Progrom-nacht: Die Menschen von heute sind nicht besser oder mutiger als damals," *Frankfürter Allgemeine Zeitung,* November 10, 1988, p. 5.

126. Ibid.

127. Phillip Jenninger, "Die Opfer wissen was der November 1938 fur sie bedeuten hatte: Die Rede des Bundespräsident im Wortlaut," *Frankfürter Allgemeine Zeitung*, November 11, 1988, p. 6. For the text and commentaries, see Armin Laschet and Heinz Malangre, eds., *Phillip Jenninger: Rede und Reaktion* (Aachen: Rheinischer Merkur, 1989).

128. Jenninger, "Die Opfer," p. 6.

129. Ibid.

130. Ibid.

131. Helmut Eschwege was one of those exceptions. His memoirs, *Erinnerungen eines Dresdner Juden* (Berlin: Ch. Links Verlag, 1991), shed important light on East German Communists and the Jewish question.

132. Michael Wolfsohn, *Eternal Guilt: Forty Years of German-Jewish-Israeli Relations*, trans. Douglas Bokovoy (New York: Columbia University Press, 1993), p. 44.

133. See Meuschel, *Legitimation und Parteiherrschaft*, pp. 273–305.

134. See texts from the GDR opposition collected in Markus Meckel and Martin Gutzeit, *Opposition in der DDR: Zehn Jahre kirchliche Friedensarbeit—kommentierte Quellentexte* (Cologne: Bund Verlag, 1994).

135. Markus Meckel and Martin Gutzeit, "Der 8. Mai 1945—unsere Verantwortung für den Frieden (Februar/April 1985," ibid., pp. 266–273.

136. Ibid., p. 268.

137. Ibid., pp. 271–272.

138. "The East Germans Issue an Apology for Nazis' Crimes," *New York Times*, April 13, 1990, pp. A1, A7.

139. "Volkskammer bekennt Schuld am Holocaust: Erste freigewählte DDR-Regierung im Amt," *Frankfurter Rundschau*, April 14, 1990, pp. 1–2.

140. "Excerpts from East Berlin Statement Apology," *New York Times*, April 13, 1990, p. A7.

141. See "Truth and Healing in Eastern Europe," *New York Times*, April 14, 1990, p. 22; and "East Germany Accepts Burden of Holocaust," *Jerusalem Post*, April 13, 1990, pp. 1, 11. For the text of the Volkskammer declaration, see "Dokumentation: Gemeinsame Erklärung der Volkskammer," *Deutschland Archiv* 23, no. 5 (May 1990): 794–795.

142. Asher Wallfish, "E. German Resolution Needs Fleshing Out," *Jerusalem Post*, April 13, 1990, p. 11; and Yehoshua Trigor, "Germany: Jewry Must Have a Say," *Jerusalem Post*, May 1, 1990, p. 4. On East German diplomacy, see also Wolffsohn, *Eternal Guilt*.

143. See especially Rainer Zitelmann, *Westbindung* (Frankfurt am Main: Ullstein, 1993); and Uwe Backes, Eckhard Jesse, and Rainer Zitelmann, eds., *Die Schatten der Vergangenheit: Impulse zur Historisierung des Nationalsozialismus* (Berlin: Propyläen, 1990). For critical assessments, see Friedbert Pflüger, *Deutschland driftet: Die Konservative Revolution entdeckt ihre Kinder* (Dusseldorf: Econ Verlag, 1994; and Richard

Herzinger and Hannes Stein, *Endzeit-Propheten oder Die Offensive der Antiwestler* (Reinbek bei Hamburg: Rowohlt, 1995).

144. "Präsidentin Dr. Rita Süssmuth," *Verhandlungen des deutschen Bundestages 12. Wahlperiode Stenogrophische Bericht 1990*, vol. 171, *187–200 Sitzung* (November 9, 1993), p. 10181.

145. For criticism by liberal and leftist intellectuals of those who refused to apply the lessons of the appeasement of Hitler in the 1930s to the events in the Persian Gulf, see Wolf Bierman, *Der Sturz des Dädalus* (Cologne: Kiepenhower and Witsch, 1992); Wolfgang Pohrt, *Das Jahre danach: Ein Bericht über die Vorkriegszeit* (Berlin: Tiamat, 1992).

146. "Präsidentin Dr. Rita Süssmuth," pp. 10179–81.

147. Ibid.

148. Ibid., p. 10181.

149. Ibid.

150. "2,700 ehemalige Häftlinge in Ravensbrück und Sachsenhausen," *Frankfurter Allgemeine Zeitung*, April 24, 1995, p. 5.

151. "Bei der Gedenkfeier in Bergen-Belsen Warnung vor Vergessen und Verdrängen," *Frankfurter Allgemeine Zeitung*, April 28, 1995, p. 1.

152. Ibid.

153. "8. Mai 1945—Gegen das Vergessen," *Frankfurter Allgemeine Zeitung*, April 7, 1995, p. 3. See also "Aufruf: 8. Mai 1945 auch Beginn des Vertreibungsterrors, Streit über Bewertung des Kriegsendes, Konservative wollen in München gedenken," *Süddeutsche Zeitung*, April 9, 1995, p. 3. In fact, the plight of postwar Germans expelled from Eastern Europe had been a major theme of West German right-wing politics since 1949. See Bark and Gress, *A History of West Germany*, vol. 2, 2:304–310.

154. "Bubis—Konservative Aufruf zum 8. Mai 'Skandal,'" *Reuter German News Service*, April 8, 1995, p. 2.

155. "8. Mai 1945—Gegen das Vergessen," *Frankfurter Allgemeine Zeitung*, April 27, 1995, p. 3.

156. "Jedem einzelnen Schicksal schulden wir Achtung," *Frankfurter Allgemeine Zeitung*, May 6, 1995, p. 3.

157. Ibid.

158. Stephen Kinzer, "Confronting the Past, Germans Now Don't Flinch," *New York Times*, May 1, 1995, p. 6; see also "Erinnerung kann Wiederholung der Geschichte verhindern," *Frankfurter Allgemeine Zeitung*, April 10, 1995, pp. 1–2.

159. Ashley Seager, "Some German Firms Highlight WWII Slave Labor Use," *Reuter Asia-Pacific Business Report*, May 1, 1995, p. 4.

160. "Gedenken an die Befreiung des Konzentrationslager vor 50 Jahren, Stoiber: Dachau mahnt uns zur Wachsamkeit," *Suddeutsche Zeitung*, May 2, 1995, p. 3.

161. "Katastrophe und Befreiung, Die historische Zäsur des Jahres 1945," *Frankfurter Allgemeine Zeitung*, April 15, 1995, p. 5.

162. "Der Bundespräsident zum Kriegsende vor 50 Jahren: Am 8. Mai wurde ein Tor in die Zukunft aufgestoßen," *Frankfurter Allgemeine Zeitung*, May 9, 1995, p. 6.

163. Ibid.

164. Ibid.

165. "Bubis dringt auf Gedenktag für die NA-Opfer," *Süddeutsche Zeitung*, May 9, 1995, p. 3. On Bubis's trip to Israel with members of the Green Party, see "Davidstern neben Pälästinensertuch. Joschka Fischers Israel-Besuch als grüne Aussenpolitik," *Süddeutsche Zeitung*, May 24, 1995, p. 4.

166. "Auschwitz Anniversary to Be German Remembrance Day," *Agence France Presse*, June 1, 1995.

167. "Speech by Roman Herzog in the German Bundestag in Connection with the Day of Commemoration for the Victims of National Socialism," *Statements and Speeches: German Information Center* 29, no. 1, p. 2.

168. Ibid.

169. Ibid., p. 3.

170. Ibid., p. 5.

# Sources

## Germany

AdsD—Archiv der sozialen Demokratie, Friedrich Ebert Stiftung, Bonn (Social Democratic Party Archives)

    Nachlass (NL) Jakob Altmeier

    NL Kurt Schumacher

BA, Koblenz—Bundesarchiv, Koblenz, Germany

    Nachlass (NL) Theodor Heuss

BStU MfSZ—Bundesbeauftragte für die Unterlagen des Staatsicherheitsdienstes der ehemaligen Deutschen Demokratischen Republik ("Gauck Behörde"), Ministerium für Staatssicherheit Zentralarchiv (Central Archives of the Ministry of State Security, Berlin)

    Files on:

    Alexander Abusch

    Bruno Goldhammer

    Paul Merker

    Leo Zuckermann

SAPMO-BA—Stiftung Archiv der Parteien und Massenorganizationen der DDR im Bundesarchiv (Foundation for the Archive of the GDR's Parties and Mass Organizations in the Bundesarchiv, Berlin)

    ZPA—Zentrales Parteiarchiv (Central Party Archive)

    Nachlass (NL) Alexander Abusch

    NL Anton Ackermann

    NL Franz Dahlem

    NL Lex Ende

    NL Max Fechner

    NL Otto Grotewohl

    NL Herman Matern

    NL Ernst Melsheimer

    NL Paul Merker

    NL Albert Norden

    NL Wilhelm Pieck

NL Walter Ulbricht
Bestand: Sozialistische Einheitspartei Deutschlands, Zentralkomitee (ZK)
Kaderfragen
Zentralparteikontrollkommission (ZPKK)
Dietz Verlag
Sekretariat Lehmann: Abteilung Arbeit und Sozialfursorge
General Sekretariat des Vereinigung des Verfolgten des Naziregimes (VVN)
Politburo J IV 2/202
Protokolle der Sitzungen des Politburos
Verlag Neuer Weg
St BKAH—Stiftung Bundeskanzler Adenauer Haus, Rhöndorf, Germany Nachlass
(NL) Konrad Adenauer

## United States

American Jewish Archives, Hebrew Union College, Jewish Institute of Religion, Cin-
cinnati
Box H231, World Jewish Congress, Mexico Section
Folder H230, Mexico-Jewish Situation Reports, 1943–1950
Folder H227/6, Mexico, Kate Kopfmacher Correspondence, J1-D, 1942
Folders H229/13; H233/1, H232/3, H233/4
LBI—Leo Baeck Institute, New York
Kurt Grossmann Collection
The George Meany Memorial Archives, Silver Spring, Maryland
International Affairs Department, Jay Lovestone Files
NA—National Archives, Washington, D.C.
Record Group (RG) 226—Office of Strategic Services
Boxes 06, 42, 326 (Mexico: Subversive Activity); 327, 329
RG 319 (IRR) Investigative Records Repository File in Military Reference
Paul Merker, X 8590750, Box 151
OSS Foreign Nationalities Branch Files, 1942–1945
United States Army Intelligence and Security Command, Fort Meade, Maryland
Leo Zuckermann, Case no. 92F-95
Robert F. Wagner Labor Archives, Tamiment Institute, New York University
Jewish Labor Committee Collection
I:E: General Files, Box 15, Folder 32 (Germany—Social Democrats.)

## Newspapers and Journals

*Allgemeine Wochenzeitung der Juden in Deutschland,* Dusseldorf, 1945–
*Aufbau: Kulturpolitische Monatschrift* (East Berlin), 1945–1957

*The Communist: A Magazine of the Theory and Practice of Marxism-Leninism* (New York), 1931–1932
*Commentary*, 1946–1953
*Deutsche Volkszeitung* (East Berlin), 1946
*Deutschland Archiv*
*Einheit* (East Berlin), 1946–1950
*Frankfurter Allgemeine Zeitung*, 1950–
*Frankfurter Hefte*, 1946–1952
*Frankfurter Rundschau*, 1945–1995
*Freies Deutschland* (Mexico City), 1942–1945
*Freies Deutschland* (Moscow), 1944–45
*Die Internationale: Eine Zeitschrift der kommunistischen Partei Deutschlands* (Berlin), 1928–1933
*Jerusalem Post*, 1985–
*Jüdische Gemeindeblatt für die Britische Zone*, 1946
*Jüdische Gemeindeblatt für die Nord-Rheinprovinz und Westfalen*, 1946
*New York Times*, 1945–
*Die Neue Volkszeitung* (New York), 1941–1948
*Neue Zeitung* (Munich), 1945–1953
*Neues Deutschland* (East Berlin), 1950–
*Rhein Neckar-Zeitung* (Heidelberg), 1945–1949
*Süddeutsche Zeitung* (Munich), 1945–
*Die Weltbuhne* (East Berlin), 1946–1948
*Die Zeit*, 1950–

## Published Documents

Deutscher Bundestag, Verhandlungen des deutschen Bundestages.
———— Enquete Kommission: Aufarbeitung von Geschichte und Folgen der SED Diktatur in Deutschland
Deutschland-Berichte der Sozialdemokratische Partei (SOPADE)
Dokumente der Aussenpolitik der Deutschen Demokratischen Republik, 1949–1986
Dokumente der Sozialistischen Einheitspartei, vols. I–VI, 1951–1958
Protokoll der Verhandlungen des Ersten Kulturtages der Sozialistischen Einheitspartei Deutschlands, 5. bis 7 Mai 1948

## A Note on East Germany Documents

The archives of the former East German government covering the period up to its end in 1989 became available to researchers between 1989 and 1994. The Central Party Archives of the SED were opened for use in spring 1990. In 1992 the German federal government's Bundesarchiv made the collections—with rare exceptions—accessible to researchers. The Ulbricht, Pieck, and Grotewohl papers offer unprecedented insight into the workings of the East German government. In addition to the papers of individual leading figures in the SED, the Zentralparteikontrollkommission (ZPKK; Central Party Control Commission) files, the Kaderfragen (Cadre Issues) files, and the Politburo files are essential for documenting the internal purges within the SED, including the anticosmopolitan purges. Foreign ministry documents of the former German Democratic Republic are also available, but unlike the collections of the Central Party Archives of the SED, and like the documents of the Federal Republic, they are subject to a thirty-year rule.

The files of the Ministerium für Staatssicherheit ("Stasi") have also become available. Files on individuals who themselves were not "historical figures" are protected by confidentiality guarantees. Files on individuals who were involved in public life are available to researchers through the Abteilung Bildung und Forschung (Office of Education and Research) in the Bundesbeauftragte für die Unterlagen des Staatsicherheitsdienstes der ehemaligen Deutschen Demokratischen Republic (Government Office Responsible for the Documents of the State Security Service of the Former German Democratic Republic) in Berlin, generally known as the "Gauck Behörde" after the name of its director, Wolfgang Gauck. The East German government placed documents of its Oberste Gericht (Supreme Court), in which both public and secret political trials were conducted, in the files of the Ministry of State Security. These documents are now also accessible through the Abteilung Bildung und Forschung.

# Acknowledgments

Many people and institutions made it possible for me to research and write this book. Two grants from the Harry and Lynde Bradley Foundation supported research first at the Minda de Gunzberg Center for European Studies at Harvard University, then at the Paul H. Nitze School of Advanced International Studies (SAIS) of Johns Hopkins University in Washington, D.C. I would like to thank particularly Hillel Fradkin of the foundation for his continued confidence in the project in its early stages. I am also grateful to Stanley Hoffmann at Harvard and Stephen Szabo at SAIS for facilitating the administration of these grants and for their graciousness and interest in the project. A visiting summer fellowship at the Institut für die Wissenschaften vom Menschen in Vienna offered time for further reading, initial archival work in Germany, and conversations with Peter Demetz, Aaron Rhodes, and scholars from Austria and Central Europe; my thanks to Krzysztof Michalski for this opportunity.

The research took an important step forward during a year spent at the German Historical Institute (GHI) in Washington, D.C., with support from a Volkswagen Foundation Research Fellowship. The fellowship was jointly sponsored by the American Institute for Contemporary German Studies (AICGS), also in Washington, D.C. Hartmut Lehmann, then director of the GHI, provided encouragement and thoughtful comments at this early stage of the research. Thanks are also due to Elizabeth Glaser-Schmidt and Lily Gardner Feldman, who administered the Volkswagen program, and to the staff and colleagues at the GHI.

Jürgen Kocka, with support from the Max Planck Gesellschaft, kindly invited me to spend the summer of 1993 working at the Forschungsschwerpunkt für Zeithistorische Studien in Potsdam. There Olaf Groehler, Monika Kaiser, Mario Kessler, and Michael Lemke shared important insights into East German history. In 1993–94 a fellowship from the German Marshall Fund of the United States supported continuing research, as did a Fulbright Award to teach in the Seminar für Wissenschaftliche Politik at the University of Freiburg. My gracious host in Freiburg, Ludger Kuhnhardt, offered stimulating conversations about facing both the Nazi and the Communist past. I am also grateful to my other faculty colleagues, in particular Hugo Ott, as well as to students in my seminar on National Socialism and German political culture, for conversations about memory and politics.

In 1994–95 I wrote the first draft of the manuscript while in residence in the School of Historical Studies at the Institute for Advanced Study in Princeton. I am grateful for support that year from a National Endowment for the Humanities Fellowship.

The Institute offered a perfect blend of community and undisturbed time alone. Peter Paret's encouragement as well as the collegiality and stimulation of Neithard Bulst, Christopher Browning, John Horne, Andrew Lees, and Peter Schäfer helped to make the year a memorable one. Joan Scott and colleagues from the School of Social Science offered spirited and helpful comments on a paper. Albert Hirschman enhanced my understanding of American policy toward the anti-Nazi emigration in Vichy France. George Kennan shared acute insights regarding Stalin and the Jewish question in the Soviet bloc after 1945.

I was extremely fortunate to be working on this book when the archives of the East German government became accessible. We historians are indebted to the citizens of the former East Germany. It was their political struggle for human rights and democracy which made possible the opening of previously closed East German archives. Much important work on this book was also made possible by citizen efforts in 1989 and 1990 to safeguard the files of the Ministry of State Security from destruction or theft. I owe a special debt of gratitude to the staff of the Central Party Archive in Berlin of the former Socialist Unity Party. The assistance of Frau Ruth, Frau Räuber, and Frau Ulbrich was invaluable as I examined the issue of the East German Communists and the Jewish question. I am equally grateful to Klaus-Dietmar Henke, Siegfried Suckot, and Rüdiger Stang of the Abteilung Bildung und Forschung of the Gauck Behörde which oversees the archives of the former Ministry of State Security. They facilitated prompt access to the Stasi files on Alexander Abusch, Paul Merker, and Leo Zuckermann which shed so much light on the anticosmopolitan purges. I appreciate the logistical assistance with these materials offered by Gary Smith of the Einstein Forum in Potsdam.

I also wish to express my gratitude to the staffs of the following archives: Stiftung Konrad Adenauer Haus in Rhondorf; American Jewish Archives, Hebrew Union College, Cincinnati Campus; Leo Baeck Archives in New York; Bundesarchiv in Koblenz; George Meany Memorial Archives, Silver Spring, Maryland; Archives of German Social Democracy in Bonn. Gail Malmgreen guided me to the archives of the Jewish Labor Committee at the Robert F. Wagner Labor Archives in the Tamiment Institute at New York University. In the Military Section of the National Archives, I benefited from the extraordinary knowledge and experience of John Taylor. The prompt response to my requests from the archives of the U.S. Army Intelligence and Security Command at Fort Meade, Maryland, was much appreciated. I am also grateful to James Heinemann for granting access to the correspondence between his father, Dannie Heinemann, and Konrad Adenauer.

A number of senior scholars have shared their scholarly and personal reflections. Robert Tucker recalled the atmosphere of wartime Moscow. Theodore Draper discussed his contact with Otto Katz in wartime Mexico City. Hans-Peter Schwarz shed light on Konrad Adenauer and the Adenauer archives. Daniel Bell offered valuable insights into contacts between German exile Social Democrats and the labor movement and Jewish intellectuals in wartime New York. Friedrich Katz graciously talked to me about the experiences of his father, Leo Katz, in wartime Mexico City. Several younger scholars, especially Richard Herzinger, Jacob Heilbrun, and Elliot Neamann, shared insights regarding recent trends on the German left and right.

I lectured about earlier versions of parts of the work in progress at the Institute for Contemporary German Studies and at Amherst College, the American Historical Association, Columbia University, Cornell University, Emory University, the German Historical Institute, Harvard University, Hampshire College, University of Illinois at Urbana-Champaign, Mount Holyoke College, New York University, the University of Notre Dame, Princeton University, Rutgers University in Camden, and the University of Virginia. In Germany I lectured at the universities of Freiburg and Heidelberg, at Humboldt University in Berlin, at a conference in Potsdam organized by James Hershberg of the Woodrow Wilson Center's Cold War International History Project, and at a conference of the Krefeld Symposium organized by Norbert Finszch. For invitations to speak and/or comments on work in progress, I thank the following colleagues: David Bathrick, Volker Berghahn, Ute Brandes, Detlev Junker, Victoria de Grazia, Konrad Jarusch, Stephen Kotkin, Dominick LaCapra, Catherine LeGouis, Arno Mayer, Allan Megill, Dietrich Orlow, Gerald Siegel, James Wald, and Heinrich August Winkler. I benefited greatly from the questions and discussions that followed all of these presentations.

I am most grateful to the Fraenkel Prize Committee of the Institute of Contemporary History and the Wiener Library in London for awarding the Fraenkel Prize in contemporary history for 1996 to the unpublished manuscript of this work, and to David Cesarini and the staff of the Wiener Library for their gracious hospitality on the occasion of the Fraenkel Prize lecture in December 1996. During the 1996–97 academic year I was fortunate to be able to lecture about the completed but unpublished manuscript in Germany and here in the United States. For their comments and stimulating questions I thank colleagues and students at the universities of Frankfurt-am-main, Bielefeld, Göttingen, Munich, and Freiburg as well as at the Zentrum für Zeithistorische Forschung in Postdam (formerly the Forschungsschwerpunkt für Zeithistorische Studien) and the Institute für Zeitgeschichte in Munich, at Boston University, the University of California–Berkeley, Harvard University, Ohio State University, Ohio University, and Stanford University.

Earlier versions of the work in progress appeared as articles in journals and collected volumes. I thank the editors of these publications for their encouragement and editorial suggestions: Kenneth D. Barkin at *Central European History;* George Mosse and Walter Laqueur at the *Journal of Contemporary History* (Sage Publications, London); Edith Kurzweil and William Phillips at *Partisan Review;* John Boyer and Michael Geyer, editors of *Resistance against the Third Reich;* Stephen Brockmann and Frank Trommler, editors of *Revisiting Zero Hour, 1945;* Manfred Boemeke and Janine Micunek, editors of the text of the Fourth Annual Alois Mertes Memorial Lecture at the German Historical Institute; Hans Woller at the *Vierteljahreshefte für Zeitgeschichte;* and Karl-Heinz Janßen at *Die Zeit.*

The articles in question are the following: "Multiple Restorations vs. the Solid South: Continuities and Discontinuities in Germany after 1945 and the American South after 1865," in Norbert Finzsch and Jürgen Martschukat, eds., *Different Restorations: Reconstruction and Wiederaufbau in the United States and Germany, 1865, 1945–1989* (Providence: Berghahn Books, 1996), pp. 48–86; "Multiple Restorations: German Political Traditions and the Interpretation of Nazism, 1945–1946," *Central European History* 26, no. 1 (1993), 21–55; "German Communism, the Discourse of 'Antifascist Resistance,' and the Jewish Catastrophe," in John Boyer and Michael Geyer, eds., *Resistance against the Third Reich: 1933–1990* (Chicago: University of Chicago Press, 1994), pp. 257–294; "Dokumentation: Antisemitismus in der SED: Geheime Dokumente zum Fall Paul Merker aus SED- und MfS-Archiven," *Vierteljahrshefte für Zeitgeschichte* (Oktober 1994), 1–32; "East German Communists and the Jewish Question: The Case of Paul Merker," *Journal of Contemporary History* 29, 4 (October 1994), 627–662; "Der Geheimprozeß," *Die Zeit,* Dossier section, domestic edition, October 7, 1994, overseas edition, October 14, 1994, pp. 7–8; "East German Communists and the Jewish Question: The Case of Paul Merker," Fourth Annual Alois Mertes Memorial Lecture, 1994 German Historical Institute, Washington, D.C., Occasional Paper no. 11; "The Nazi Past in the Two Germanies," *Partisan Review,* 62, no. 4 (1995), 590–595; "Divided Memory, Multiple Restorations: West German Political Reflections on the Nazi Past, 1945–1953," in Stephen Brockman and Frank Trommler, eds., *Revisiting Zero Hour 1945: The Emergence of Postwar German*

*Culture* (Washington, D.C.: American Institute for Contemporary German Studies, 1996), pp. 89–102.

Several friends and colleagues gave willingly of their time to read and criticize the manuscript. Sigrid Meuschel's important book on East German political culture greatly deepened my understanding of the anticosmopolitan campaign. She nurtured this book with years of friendship and encouragement. Her comments on the chapters dealing with the Communists were much appreciated. I am most grateful for Norman Naimark's detailed comments on the same chapters. I took great pleasure in sharing the excitement of discoveries in the SED archives with him. Katherine Epstein drew on her detailed knowledge of the East German files to offer helpful comments. Harold James read the entire manuscript and offered helpful comments on the West German chapters.

I would also like to thank Aïda Donald at Harvard University Press for her early and enduring support for this project. Two anonymous referees read the entire manuscript for Harvard University Press and offered incisive comments. Elizabeth Suttell expertly guided the text through the press.

My colleagues in the Department of History and the Contemporary History Institute at Ohio University in Athens, Ohio, provided a welcoming, supportive, and stimulating environment in which to prepare the manuscript for publication.

In the preceding decade I have been sustained intellectually and emotionally by a community of scholars working on European and German history. For their support and their valuable remarks on this project, I thank Walter Adamson, Steven Aschheim, Karl Bracher, Richard Breitman, Maurice Friedberg, David Landes, Charles Maier, Jerry Muller, Stephen Schuker, Fritz Stern, and Bernard Wasserstein. That community also includes colleagues in American history (Harvey Klehr, Ronald Radosh, and Thomas A. Schwartz), comparative politics and international relations (Michela Richter, Michael J. Smith and Tony Smith), law (Mark Osiel), and historical sociology (Leah Greenfeld). Heartfelt thanks to Joel Brenner and John Wechter for thirty years of friendship through thick and thin.

Particular thanks are due to the following friends and colleagues. Gerald Feldman's enthusiasm about this work's contribution to German history and his persistent intellectual and practical encouragement are very deeply appreciated. I have been blessed to have George Mosse as teacher and friend, and am grateful for his comments at various stages of the project. Anson Rabinbach shared his acute insights about confronting the Nazi past and the Holocaust in West Germany. Conversations with François Furet about World War II, Communist antifascism, and the Jewish question were very helpful.

I was most fortunate to meet and come to know Thomas Nipperdey. This book builds on some of his arguments regarding the multiple continuities and contingent moments in German history. His death in 1992 deprived us of a great historian, a man of tremendous courage, warmth, and humor, and a German intellectual who thought a great deal about the place of anti-Semitism and the Jews in German history. I deeply regret that he cannot see the results of a project in which he expressed so much interest.

My father, Ernst Herf, was able to flee from Nazi Germany in 1937. He has never forgotten those who were not so lucky. In a sense this book began over forty years ago when he urged me to remember things that too many others would rather forget.

My deepest gratitude goes to my wife, Sonya Michel, and to my daughter, Nadja Michel-Herf. Nadja endured my absences for research with courage and good humor and displayed her bold and independent spirit when she accompanied me to Freiburg in 1994. My debts to Sonya are incalculable. Herself a historian of American women's and social history, she shared my excitement about archival discoveries, especially those related to the Merker case and the anticosmopolitan purges in East Germany. She read and commented on various chapters with the eye of a sympathetic but honest critic. Her engagement in the project has given me enormous pleasure and, I am sure, hastened its completion. I dedicate this book to Sonya, Nadja, and my father with love and gratitude.

# Index

---